Volume Two

The Great Travelers

A COLLECTION OF FIRSTHAND NARRA-
TIVES OF WAYFARERS, WANDERERS AND
EXPLORERS IN ALL PARTS OF THE WORLD
FROM 450 B.C. TO THE PRESENT

Edited, with Introductions, by
MILTON RUGOFF

Simon and Schuster • New York • 1960

ACKNOWLEDGMENTS

Grateful acknowledgment is made for permission to reprint selections from the following works:

The Discovery of the Amazon by J. T. Medina. Used by permission of the American Geographical Society.

Voyages of Samuel de Champlain. Reprinted by permission of Barnes & Noble, Inc.

Travels in Switzerland by Alexandre Dumas. Reprinted by permission of The Chilton Company, Book Division, and Peter Owen, Ltd.

Gold Rush by J. Goldsborough Bruff. Copyright © 1949 by the Columbia University Press. Used by permission of the Columbia University Press.

Black Lamb and Grey Falcon by Rebecca West. Copyright © 1940, 1941 by Rebecca West. Reprinted by permission of The Viking Press, Inc., New York, in the United States and A. D. Peters, London.

Twilight in Italy by D. H. Lawrence. Used by permission of The Viking Press, Inc., and the Estate of the late Mrs. Frieda Lawrence.

Red, Black, Blond and Olive by Edmund Wilson. Copyright © 1956 by Edmund Wilson. Used by permission of the author.

Peter Kalm's Travels in North America. Used by permission of the publisher, Wilson-Erickson, Inc.

Arctic Adventure by Peter Freuchen. Copyright © 1936 by Peter Freuchen. Reprinted by permission of Harold Matson Company, New York.

A Tramp Abroad and *Roughing It*, both by Mark Twain. Reprinted by permission of Harper & Brothers and the Mark Twain Estate.

My Russian Journey by Santha Rama Rau. Copyright © 1959 by Vasanthi Rama Rau Bowers, and copyright © 1958 by The Curtis Publishing Company. Reprinted by permission of Harper & Brothers and Victor Gollancz, Ltd.

Easter in Sicily by Herbert Kubly.

Copyright © 1956 by Herbert Kubly. Reprinted by permission of Simon and Schuster, Inc., and A. M. Heath & Co., Ltd.

Journey to the Far Amazon by Alain Gheerbrant. Copyright © 1954 by Alain Gheerbrant. Reprinted by permission of Simon and Schuster, Inc., and (under the title *The Impossible Adventure*) of Victor Gollancz, Ltd.

My Life with the Eskimo by Vilhjalmur Stefansson. Copyright © 1913, 1941 by Vilhjalmur Stefansson. Reprinted by permission of The Macmillan Company, New York.

One Man's America by Alistair Cooke. Copyright © 1951, 1952 by Alistair Cooke. Reprinted by permission of Alfred A. Knopf, Inc., and (under the title *Letters from America*) of Rupert Hart-Davis, Ltd.

Scott's Last Expedition by R. F. Scott. Copyright 1913, 1941 by Dodd, Mead & Company, Inc. Reprinted by permission of Dodd, Mead & Company, Inc., and John Murray, Ltd.

Coryat's Crudities. Used by permission of Robert Maclehose & Co., Ltd., Glasgow.

The Journal of William Beckford, edited by Boyd Alexander. Copyright © 1954 by Boyd Alexander. Reprinted by permission of The John Day Company, Inc., and Rupert Hart-Davis, Ltd.

Inuk by Roger P. Buliard. Copyright © 1951 by Roger P. Buliard. Reprinted by permission of Farrar, Straus & Cudahy, Inc., and Macmillan & Co., Ltd.

The True History of the Conquest of New Spain (Vol. 2). Used by permission of The Hakluyt Society; passages also appearing in *The Discovery and Conquest of Mexico*, copyright © 1956 by Farrar, Straus and Cudahy, Inc., and used by permission of Farrar, Straus & Cudahy, Inc.

Contents

v

America South

America North

℘olar ℘laces

Illustrations

Volume Two

A Circuit of Europe

Italy: Forks, Fans and Courtesans

THOMAS CORYAT

FROM *Coryat's Crudities*

1608

Possibly the best known of Elizabethan travelers, probably the most loquacious and enthusiastic, and certainly the most whimsical was Thomas Coryat, who signed himself "Peregrine of Odcombe" and declared, "Of all the pleasures in the world, travel is, in my opinion, the sweetest and most delightful."

He made this declaration in Coryat's Crudities, the book he wrote after spending five months (in 1608) on a walking tour through France and northern Italy and then back through Switzerland, Germany and the Netherlands. Coryat's journey was a cultural pilgrimage, with Italy—especially Venice—as its Mecca. He represented the Englishmen who, having made their mark in commerce and empire, felt a need for education and the social graces. Coryat had gone to Oxford, where he shone in Greek and other humane studies, and his trip abroad was to be a finishing touch. Along with his passion for travel went an Elizabethan's exuberance of expression, and the result is a book full of flourishes and superlatives, a pastiche of Latin and Greek quotations, conceits, catalogues of monuments and cathedrals, and fragments of history, not to speak of fanciful "panegyric verses" by Ben Jonson, John Donne and others.

When Coryat got back from his trip, he hung up his shoes in the village church, but in 1612 he was on his way again, and this time he went to Constantinople, Cairo, Jerusalem, the Persian cities of Ecbatana and Isfahan, and finally eastern India, picking up the Persian, Turkish, Arabic and Hindustani tongues on the way. Considering that his Crudities was the

*result of only five months of travel, we can imagine what a magnificent
monster of a book he could have written about this second journey, which
lasted more than five years. But unfortunately he drank too much sack
while suffering from dysentery in India, and died, aged forty, in December
1617.*

FORKS

I observed a custom in all those Italian cities and towns through the
which I passed that is not used in any other country that I saw in
my travels, neither do I think that any other nation of Christendom doth
use it, but only Italy. The Italian and also most strangers that are com-
morant [sojourning] in Italy do always at their meals use a little fork when
they cut their meat. For while with their knife which they hold in one hand
they cut the meat out of the dish, they fasten their fork which they hold in
their other hand upon the same dish, so that whatsoever he be that sitting
in the company of any others at meal should inadvisedly touch the dish of
meat with his fingers from which all at the table do cut, he will give
occasion of offence unto the company, as having transgressed the laws of
good manners, in so much that for his error he shall be at the least browbeaten, if not reprehended in words. This form of feeding I understand
is generally used in all places of Italy, their forks being for the most part
made of iron or steel, and some of silver, but those are used only by gentlemen. The reason of this their curiosity is, because the Italian can not by
any means endure to have his dish touched with fingers, seeing all men's
fingers are not alike clean. Hereupon I myself thought good to imitate the
Italian fashion by this forked cutting of meat, not only while I was in Italy,
but also in Germany, and oftentimes in England since I came home. . . .

FANS AND UMBRELLAS

HERE will I mention a thing that although perhaps it will seem but frivolous to divers readers that have already travelled in Italy . . . The first Italian fans that I saw in Italy did I observe in this space betwixt Pizighiton
and Cremona. But afterwards I observed them common in most places of

Italy where I travelled. These fans both men and women of the country do carry to cool themselves withall in the time of heat, by the often fanning of their faces. Most of them are very elegant and pretty things. For whereas the fan consisteth of a painted piece of paper and a little wooden handle, the paper which is fastened into the top is on both sides most curiously adorned with excellent pictures, either of amorous things tending to dalliance, having some witty Italian verses or fine emblems written under them or of some notable Italian city with a brief description thereof. These fans are of a mean price. For a man may buy one of the fairest of them for so much money as countervaileth our English groat.

Also many of them do carry other fine things of a far greater price, that will cost at the least a ducat, which they commonly call in the Italian tongue umbrellas, that is, things that minister shadow unto them for shelter against the scorching heat of the sun. These are made of leather something answerable to the form of a little canopy, and hooped in the inside with divers little wooden hoops that extend the umbrella in a pretty large compass. They are used especially by horsemen, who carry them in their hands when they ride, fastening the end of the handle upon one of their thighs, and they impart so long a shadow unto them that it keepeth the heat of the sun from the upper parts of their bodies.

> [Characteristic of his reaction to the customs and curiosities of Venice are the following passages on the fashions in dress and the way in which the city's celebrated courtesans practice their ancient profession.]

CLOTHES AND COURTESANS

ALL these gowned men [the knights, or nobility] do wear marvellous little black flat caps of felt, without any brims at all, and very diminutive falling bands, no ruffs at all, which are so shallow that I have seen many of them not above a little inch deep. The colour that they most affect and use for their other apparel, I mean, doublet, hose, and jerkin, is black, a colour of gravity and decency. Besides the form and fashion of their attire is both very ancient, even the same that hath been used these thousand years among them, and also uniform. For all of them use but one and the same form of habit, even the slender doublet made close to the body, without much quilting or bombast, and long hose plain, without those new-fangled curiosities and ridiculous superfluities of panes, plaits, and other light toys used with us English men. Yet they make it of costly stuff, well beseeming gentlemen and eminent persons of their place, as of the best taffetas and satins that Christendom doth yield, which are fairly garnished also with lace of the best sort. In both these things they much differ from us English men. For whereas they have but one colour, we use many more than are in the rainbow, all the most light, garish, and unseemly colours that are in the world. Also for fashion we are much inferior to them. For we wear more phantastical fashions than any nation under the sun, the French only excepted; which hath given occasion both to the Venetian and other Italians to brand the Englishman with a notable mark of levity, by painting him stark naked with a pair of shears in his hand, making his fashion of attire according to the vain invention of his brain-sick head, not to comeliness and decorum.

But to return to these gowned gentlemen: I observed an extraordinary custom amongst them, that when two acquaintances meet and talk together at the walking times of the day, whereof I have before spoken, either in the Duke's Palace, or St. Mark's Place, they give a mutual kiss when they depart from each other, by kissing one another's cheek: a custom that I never saw before, nor heard of, nor read of in any history. Likewise when they meet only and not talk, they give a low congie [obeisance] to each other by very civil and courteous gestures, as by bending of their bodies, and clapping their right hand upon their breasts, without uncovering of their heads, which sometimes they use, but very seldom.

Most of the women when they walk abroad, especially to church, are veiled with long veils, whereof some do reach almost to the ground behind. These veils are either black, or white, or yellowish. The black either wives or widows do wear; the white maids, and so the yellowish also, but they wear more white than yellowish. It is the custom of these maids when they walk in the streets, to cover their faces with their veils, *verecundiae causa* [because of bashfulness], the stuff being so thin and slight that they may easily look through it. For it is made of a pretty slender silk, and very finely curled; so that because she thus hoodwinketh herself, you can very seldom see her face at full when she walketh abroad, though perhaps you earnestly desire only a little glimpse thereof. Now whereas I said before that only maids do wear white veils, and none else, I mean these white silk curled veils, which (as they told me) none do wear but maids. But other white veils wives do much wear, such as are made of holland, whereof the greatest part is handsomely edged with great and very fair bonelace. Almost all the wives, widows and maids do walk abroad with their breasts all naked, and many of them have their backs also naked even almost to the middle, which some do cover with slight linen, as cobweb lawn, or such other thin stuff: a fashion methinks very uncivil and unseemly, especially if the beholder might plainly see them. . . .

There is one thing used of the Venetian women . . . that is not to be observed, I think, amongst any other women in Christendom: which is so common in Venice that no woman whatsoever goeth without it, either in her house or abroad: a thing made of wood and covered with leather of sundry colours, some with white, some red, some yellow. It is called a chapiney, which they wear under their shoes. Many of them are curiously painted; some also I have seen fairly gilt: so uncomely a thing, in my opinion, that it is pity this foolish custom is not clean banished and exterminated out of the city. There are many of these chapineys of a great height, even half a yard high, which maketh many of their women that are very short seem much taller than the tallest women we have in England. Also I have heard that this is observed amongst them, that by how much the nobler a woman is, by so much the higher are her chapineys. All their gentlewomen, and most of their wives and widows that are of any wealth, are assisted and supported either by men or women when they walk abroad, to the end they may not fall. They are borne up most commonly by the left arm, otherwise they might quickly take a fall. For I saw a woman fall a very dangerous fall as she was going down the stairs of one of the little stony bridges with her high chapineys alone by herself; but I did nothing pity her, because she wore such frivolous and, as I may truly term them, ridiculous instruments, which were the occasion of her fall. . . .

All the women of Venice every Saturday in the afternoon do use to anoint their hair with oil or some other drugs, to the end to make it look fair, that is, whitish. For that colour is most affected of the Venetian dames and lasses. And in this manner they do it: first they put on a reed hat without any crown at all, but brims of exceeding breadth and largeness; then they sit in some sun-shining place in a chamber or some other secret room where, having a looking-glass before them, they sophisticate and dye their hair with the aforesaid drugs, and after cast it back round upon the brims of the hat till it be thoroughly dried with the heat of the sun. And last of all they curl it up in curious locks with a frizzling or crisping pin of iron, which we call in Latin *calamistrum*, the top whereof on both sides above their forehead is accuminated in two peaks. That this is true, I know by mine own experience. For it was my chance one day when I was in Venice to stand by an Englishman's wife, who was a Venetian woman born, while she was thus trimming her hair: a favour not afforded to every stranger. . . .

As for the number of Venetian courtesans, it is very great. For it is thought there are of them in the whole city and other adjacent places, as Murano, Malomocco, etc., at the least twenty thousand, whereof many are esteemed so loose that they are said to open their quivers to every arrow. . . . For methinks that the Venetians should be daily afraid lest their winking at such uncleanness should be an occasion to draw down upon them God's curses and vengeance from heaven. But they not fearing any such thing do grant large dispensation and indulgence unto them, and that for these two causes. First, *ad vitanda majora mala* [to avoid greater evils]. For they think that the chastity of their wives would be the sooner assaulted, and so consequently they should be capricornified (which of all the indignities in the world the Venetian cannot patiently endure), were it not for these places of evacuation.

But I marvel how that should be true though these courtesans were utterly rooted out of the city. For the gentlemen do even coop up their wives always within the walls of their houses for fear of these inconveniences, as much as if there were no courtesans at all in the city. So that you shall very seldom see a Venetian gentleman's wife but either at the solemnization of a great marriage, or at the christening of a Jew, or late in the evening rowing in a gondola. The second cause is that the revenues which they pay unto the Senate for their toleration do maintain a dozen of their galleys (as many reported unto me in Venice) and so save them a great charge. . . .

For so infinite are the allurements of these amorous Calypsos that the fame of them hath drawn many to Venice from some of the remotest parts of Christendom to contemplate their beauties and enjoy their pleasing dalliances. And indeed such is the variety of the delicious objects they minister to their lovers that they want nothing tending to delight. For when you come into one of their palaces (as indeed some few of the principalest of them live in very magnificent and portly buildings fit for the entertainment of a great prince), you seem to enter into the Paradise of Venus. For their fairest rooms are most glorious and glittering to behold, the walls round about being adorned with most sumptuous tapestry and gilt leather, such as I have spoken of in my treatise of Padua. Besides you may see the picture of the noble courtesan most exquisitely drawn. As for herself, she comes to thee decked like the queen and goddess of love, in so much that thou wilt think she made a late transmigration from Paphos, Cnidos, or Cythera, the ancient habitations of Dame Venus. For her face is adorned with the quintessence of beauty. In her cheeks thou shalt see the lily and the rose strive for supremacy, and the silver trammels of her hair displayed in that curious manner besides her two frizzled peaks standing up like pretty pyramids that they give thee the true *cos amoris* [whetstone of love]. But if thou hast an exact judgement, thou mayest easily discern the effects of those famous apothecary drugs heretofore used amongst the noble ladies of Rome, even stibium, cerussa, and purpurissum. . . .

> [There follows an elaborate description not only of the courtesan's dress and jewels but also of her skill in playing the lute, in singing and in elegant discourse.]

AND to the end she may minister unto thee the stronger temptations to come to her lure, she will show thee her chamber of recreation, where thou shalt see all manner of pleasing objects, as many fair painted coffers wherewith it is garnished round about, a curious milk-white canopy of needlework, a silk quilt embroidered with gold, and generally all her bedding sweetly perfumed. And amongst other amiable ornaments she will show thee one thing only in her chamber tending to mortification, a matter strange amongst so many *irritamenta malorum* [incitements to evil]: even the picture of Our Lady by her bedside, with Christ in her arms, placed within a crystal glass. But beware . . . that thou enter not into terms of private conversation with her. For then thou shalt find her such a one as Lipsius truly calls her, *callidam et calidam solis filiam*, that is, the crafty and hot daughter of the sun. Moreover I will tell thee this news which is most true, that if thou shouldst wantonly converse with her, and not give her that *salarium iniquitatis* [wages of sin] which thou hast promised her, but perhaps cunningly escape from her company, she will either cause thy throat to be cut by her ruffiano, if he can after catch thee in the city, or procure thee to be arrested (if thou art to be found) and clapped up in the prison, where thou shalt remain till thou hast paid her all thou didst promise her. . . .

THE GLORIES OF VENICE

HAVING now so amply declared unto thee most of the principal things of this thrice-renowned and illustrious city, I will briefly by way of an epitome mention most of the other particulars thereof, and so finally shut up this narration: There are reported to be in Venice and the circumjacent islands two hundred churches in which 143 pairs of organs, 54 monasteries, 26 nunneries, 56 tribunals or places of judgement, 17 hospitals, 6 companies or fraternities, whereof I have before spoken, 165 marble statues of worthy personages, partly equestrial, partly pedestrial, which are erected in sundry places of the city, to the honour of those that either at home have prudently administered the Commonweal, or abroad valiantly fought for the same. Likewise of brass there are 23, whereof one is that of Bartholomew Colleone before mentioned. Also there are 27 public clocks, 10 brazen gates, 114 towers for bells to hang on, 10 brazen horses, 155 wells for the common use of the citizens, 185 most delectable gardens, 10,000 gondolas, 450 bridges partly stony, partly timber, 120 palaces, whereof 100 are very worthy of that name, 174 courts: and the total number of souls living in the city and about the same is thought to be about 500,000, something more or less. . . .

And so at length I finish the treatise of this incomparable city, this most beautiful queen, this untainted virgin, this paradise, this tempe, this rich diadem and most flourishing garland of Christendom: of which the inhabitants may as proudly vaunt as I have read the Persians have done of their Ormus, who say that if the world were a ring, then should Ormus be the gem thereof . . . In like manner I say that had there been an offer made unto me before I took my journey to Venice either that four of the richest manors of Somersetshire (wherein I was born) should be gratis bestowed upon me if I never saw Venice, or none of them if I should see it . . . yet notwithstanding I will ever say while I live that the sight of Venice and her resplendent beauty, antiquities, and monuments hath by many degrees more contented my mind and satisfied my desires than those four Lordships could possibly have done.

Thus much of the glorious city of Venice.

Italy: Glimpses on a Wedding Tour

HESTER LYNCH THRALE PIOZZI

FROM *Observations . . . on a Journey through France, Italy, and Germany*

1784–87

> *Elizabethan travelers generally went to Italy to be tutored in the refinements and amenities, but by the late eighteenth century—when Britain's ascendancy and Italy's decline were an old story—the British attitude was often one of impatience and contempt or that of a rich collector in an old curiosity shop.*
>
> *Such might have been Hester Thrale's attitude had she not visited Italy for the first time as Mrs. Piozzi, the wife of a well-born Italian. Born Hester Lynch Salusbury in 1741 in Wales, she had married a brewer named Thrale. Vivacious, charming, and a writer of sorts, she became the center of a literary circle whose most famous member, Samuel Johnson, virtually lived in her home for sixteen years. When her husband died, she married in 1784 Gabriele Piozzi, a Florentine music master who had been very successful in England. Many of her old friends—Johnson in particular—promptly turned their backs on her, mainly because of Piozzi's profession and despite the fact that the Italian came of a good family.*
>
> *The couple went on a two-years wedding tour of Italy and the continent, and as the wife of an accomplished Italian gentleman she had unusually intimate access to Italian society. She reveals an eighteenth-century British—one might say Johnsonian—view of such matters as the Venetian indulgence in pleasure, Neapolitan indolence, Bolognese religiosity and the growing republican urge toward political independence. But there is a leaven of romanticism and the new sensibility in her admiration of natural*

scenery, the magic of San Marco at night, the grandeur of Vesuvius erupt-
ing. Enhanced by a woman's eye for detail and for fashion, her book is full
of vivid glimpses of the manners and morals, customs and curiosities of
Italy in the 1780s.

[They spend a month in Paris and Lyons and then cross the
Alps to Turin. After a long stay in Milan (where Mrs. Piozzi
describes the social round, including performances at La
Scala) and visits to Genoa and Verona, the couple go on to
Venice.]

VENICE

WHOEVER sees St. Mark's Place lighted up of an evening, adorned with
every excellence of human art and pregnant with pleasure . . . the sea washing its walls, the moonbeams dancing on its subjugated waves, laughter
resounding from the coffee-houses, girls with guitars skipping about, masks
and merrymakers singing as they pass, a barge with a band of music heard
at some distance upon the water . . . whoever is led suddenly, I say, to this
scene of seemingly perennial gaiety will be apt to cry out of Venice, as Eve
says to Adam in Milton:

With thee conversing I forget all time,
All seasons, and their change—all please alike.

A custom which prevails here of wearing little or no rouge, and increasing the native paleness of their skins by scarce lightly wiping the very white
powder from their faces, is a method no French woman of quality would
like to adopt; yet surely the Venetians are not behindhand in the art of
gaining admirers, and they do not, like their painters, depend upon colour-
ing to ensure it.

Nothing can be a greater proof of the little consequence which dress
gives to a woman than the reflection one must make on a Venetian lady's
mode of appearance in her zendalet, without which nobody stirs out of
their house on a morning. It consists of a full black silk petticoat, sloped to
train just a very little on the ground, and flounced with gauze of the same

colour. A skeleton wire upon the head, such as we use to make up hats, throwing loosely over it a large piece of black mode or persian, so as to shade the face like a curtain, the front being trimmed with a very deep black lace or souflet gauze, infinitely becoming. The thin silk that remains to be disposed of they roll back so as to discover the bosom, fasten it with a puff before at the top of the stomacher, and, once more rolling it back from the shape, tie it gracefully behind, and let it hang in two long ends.

The evening ornament is a silk hat, shaped like a man's and of the same colour, with a white or worked lining at most, and sometimes one feather; a great black silk cloak, lined with white, and perhaps a narrow border down before, with a vast, heavy round handkerchief of black lace, which lies over neck and shoulders, and conceals shape and all completely. Here is surely little appearance of art, no craping or frizzing the hair, which is flat at the top and all of one length, hanging in long curls about the back or sides as it happens. No brown powder, and no rouge at all. Thus without variety does a Venetian lady contrive to delight the eye, and without much instruction, too, to charm the ear. . . .

Meantime, nothing conveys to a British observer a stronger notion of loose living and licentious dissoluteness than the sight of one's servants, gondoliers, and other attendants on the scenes and circles of pleasure, where you find them, though never drunk, dead with sleep upon the stairs, or in their boats, or in the open street for that matter, like over-swilled voters at an election in England. One may trample on them if one will, they hardly can be awakened; and their companions who have more life left set the others literally on their feet to make them capable of obeying their master's or lady's call. With all this appearance of levity, however, there is an un-remitted attention to the affairs of state, nor is any senator seen to come late or negligently to council next day, however he may have amused him-self all night.

The sight of the Bucentoro [the Doge's galley] prepared for Gala, and the glories of Venice upon Ascension Day [when the city celebrates its "marriage" with the sea], must now put an end to other observations. We had the honour and comfort of seeing all from a galley belonging to a noble Venetian Bragadin, whose civilities to us were singularly kind as well as extremely polite. His attentions did not cease with the morning show, which we shared in common with numbers of fashionable people that filled his ship and partook of his profuse, elegant refreshments, but he followed us after dinner to the house of our English friends, and took six of us together in a gay bark, adorned with his arms and rowed by eight gondoliers in superb liveries made up for the occasion to match the boat—which was like them white, blue and silver, a flag of the same colours flying from the stern—till we arrived at the Corso (so they call the place of contention where the rowers exert their skill and ingenuity); and numberless oars dashing the waves at once make the only agitation of which the sea seems capable; while ladies, now no longer dressed in black, but ornamented with all their jewels, flowers, etc., display their beauties unveiled upon the water, and, covering the lagoons with gaiety and splendour, bring to one's mind the games in Virgil and the galley of Cleopatra by turns. . . .

We will return to the Bucentoro, which holds two hundred people, and is heavy besides with statues, columns, etc., the top covered with crimson velvet, and the sides enlivened by twenty-one oars on each hand. Musical performers attend in another barge, while foreigners in gilded pajots increase the general show. Meantime, the vessel that contains the doge, etc., carries him slowly out to sea, where, in presence of his senators, he drops a plain gold ring into the water, with these words: *"Desponsamus te mare, in signum veri perpetuique dominii."* [We espouse thee, O sea, in sign of true and perpetual dominion.]

Our weather was favourable, and the people all seemed happy. . . . The praises of Italian weather, though wearisomely frequent among us, seem, however, much confined to this island, for aught I see, who am often tired with hearing their complaints of their own sky now that they are under it —always too cold or too hot, or a sciroc wind [sirocco], or a rainy day, or a hard frost *"che gela fin ai pensieri"* [which freezes even one's fancy] or something to murmur about, while their own great nuisances pass unnoticed—the heaps of dirt and crowds of beggars, who infest the streets and poison the pleasures of society. While ladies are eating ice at a coffee-house door, while decent people are hearing mass at the altar, while strangers are surveying the beauties of the place—no peace, no enjoyment can one obtain for the beggars, numerous beyond credibility, saucy and airy and odd in their manners, and exhibiting such various lamenesses and horrible deformities that I can sometimes hardly believe my eyes, but am willing to be told, what is not very improbable, that many of them come from a great distance to pass the season of Ascension here at Venice. I never, indeed, saw anything so gently endured which it appeared so little difficult to remedy; but though, I hope, it would be hard to find a place where more alms are asked or less are given than in Venice, yet I never saw refusals so pleasantly softened as by the manners of the high Italians towards the low. Ladies in particular are so soft-mouthed, so tender in replying to those who have their lot cast far below them, that one feels one's own harsher disposition corrected by their sweetness. . . .

Here are many theatres, the worst infinitely superior to ours, the best as far below those of Milan [where Mrs. Piozzi had visited La Scala] and Turin; but, then, here are other diversions, and everyone's dependence for pleasure is not placed upon the opera. They have now thrown up a sort of temporary wall of painted canvas, in an oval form, within St. Mark's Place, profusely illuminated round the new-formed walk, which is covered in at top, and adorned with shops round the right-hand side, with pillars to support the canopy, the lamps, etc., on the left hand. This open Ranelagh, so suited to the climate, is exceedingly pleasing. Here is room to sit, to chat, to saunter up and down, from two o'clock in the morning, when the opera ends, till a hot sun sends us all home to rest—for late hours must be complied with at Venice, or you can have no diversion at all, as the earliest casino belonging to your soberest friends has not a candle lighted in it till past midnight. . . .

The perpetual state of warfare maintained by this nation against the Turks has never lessened nor cooled. Their vicinity to Turkey has, however, made them contract some similarity of manners; for what, except being imbued with Turkish notions, can account for the people's rage here, young and old, rich and poor, to pour down such quantities of coffee? I have already had seven cups today, and feel frightened lest we should some of us be killed with so strange an abuse of it. On the opposite shore, across the Adriatic, opium is taken to counteract its effects; but these dear Venetians have no notion of sleep being necessary to their existence, I believe, as some or other of them seem constantly in motion, and there is really no hour of the four-and-twenty in which the town seems perfectly still and quiet.

. . . I am persuaded if one were to live here (which could not be for long, I think), he should forget the use of sleep; for what with the market folks bringing boats from *terra firma* loaded with every produce of nature, neatly arranged in these flat-bottomed conveyances, which begins about three o'clock in a morning and ends about six; the gondoliers rowing home their masters and ladies about that hour, and so on till eight; the common business of the town, which then begins; the state affairs and *pregai*, which often, like our House of Commons, sit late, and detain many gentlemen from the circles of morning amusements—that I find very entertaining, particularly the street orators and mountebanks in Piazza San Marco; the shops and stalls where chickens, ducks, etc., are sold by auction, comically enough, to the highest bidder, a flourishing fellow, with a hammer in his hand, shining in the character of auctioneer; the crowds which fill the courts of judicature when any cause of consequence is to be tried; the clamorous voices, keen observations, poignant sarcasms, and acute contentions of the advocates, who seem more awake, or, in their own phrase, *svelti*, than all the rest: all these things take up so much time that twenty-four hours do not suffice for the business and diversions of Venice, where dinner must be eaten as in other places, though I can scarcely find a minute to spare for it, while such fish waits one's knife and fork as I most certainly did never see before, and as I suppose are not to be seen in any sea but this in such perfection. Fresh sturgeon (*ton*, as they call it) and fresh anchovies, large as herrings, and dressed like sprats in London, incomparable; turbots, like those of Torbay exactly, and plentiful as there, with enormous pipers, are what one principally eats here. The fried liver, without which an Italian can hardly go on from day to day, is so charmingly dressed at Milan that I grew to like it as well as they; but at Venice it is sad stuff, and they call it *fegao*.

Well, the ladies, who hardly dine at all, rise about seven in the evening, when the gentlemen are just got ready to attend them, and sit sipping their chocolate on a chair at the coffee-house door with great tranquillity, chatting over the common topics of the times. Nor do they appear half so shy of each other as the Milanese ladies, who seldom seem to have any pleasure in the soft converse of a female friend. . . .

All literary topics are pleasingly discussed at Quirini's Casino, where everything may be learned from the conversation of the company, as Doctor Johnson said of his literary club, but more agreeably, because women are always half the number of the persons admitted here.

One evening our society was amused by the entrance of a foreign nobleman, exactly what we should in London emphatically call a character— learned, loud and overbearing, though of a carriage that impressed great esteem. I have not often listened to so well-furnished a talker, nor one more capable of giving great information. He had seen the pyramids of Egypt, he told us, had climbed Mount Horeb, and visited Damascus; but possessed the art of detaining our attention more on himself than on the things or places he harangued about . . . He stayed here a very little while among us —is a native of France, a grandee of Spain, a man of uncommon talents, and a traveller. I should be sorry never to meet him more.

[Proceeding south they pass through Bologna, which Mrs. Piozzi finds too solemn and prayerful for her taste, and Florence, which she admires, describing among other things the natural and unaffected behavior of people in society, the bustle of the Piazza del Duomo and an amusing race of riderless horses in a city street. In Rome she finds herself distracted from human beings by objects and is struck by the fact that a city of such wonders should appear in many ways mean and disgusting. Naples, on the other hand, exceeds her expectations.]

NAPLES

ON the tenth day of this month we arrived early at Naples, for I think it was about two o'clock in the morning; and sure the providence of God preserved us, for never was such weather seen by me since I came into the world: thunder, lightning, storm at sea, rain and wind contending for mastery, and combining to extinguish the torches bought to light us the last stage; Vesuvius, vomiting fire, and pouring torrents of red-hot lava down its sides, was the only object visible; and that we saw plainly in the afternoon thirty miles off, where I asked a Franciscan friar if it was the famous volcano. "Yes," replied he, "that's our mountain, which throws up money for us by calling foreigners to see the extraordinary effects of so surprising a phenomenon." The weather was quiet then, and we had no notion of passing such a horrible night; but an hour after dark a storm came on, which was really dreadful to endure, or even look upon. The blue lightning shone round us in a broad expanse from time to time, and sudden darkness followed in an instant; no object then but the fiery river could be seen, till another flash discovered the waves tossing and breaking at a height I never saw before.

Nothing sure was ever more sublime or awful than our entrance into Naples at the dead hour we arrived, when not a whisper was to be heard in the streets, and not a glimpse of light was left to guide us, except the small lamp hung now and then at a high window before a favourite image of the Virgin.

My poor maid had by this time nearly lost her wits with terror, and the French valet, crushed with fatigue and covered with rain and sea-spray, had just life enough left to exclaim: "*Ah madame! il me semble que nous sommes venus ici exprès pour voir la fin du monde!*" [Ah, madam! we must have come here just to see the end of the world!]

The Ville de Londres inn was full, and could not accommodate our family; but calling up the people of the Crocelle, we obtained a noble apartment, the windows of which look full upon the celebrated bay which washes the wall at our door. Caprea [Capri] lies opposite the drawing-room or gallery, which is magnificent; and my bed-chamber commands a complete view of the mountain, which I value more, and which called me the first night twenty times away from sleep and supper, though never so in want of both as at that moment surely. . . .

One need not . . . stare so at the accounts given us in Cook's voyages of tattooed Indians, when Naples will show one the effects of a like operation, very little better executed, on the broad shoulders of numberless lazaroni; he who runs over the Chiaja may read in large characters the gross superstition of the Napolitani, who have no inclination to lose their old classical character for laziness. . . . I wonder, however, whether our people would work much, surrounded by similar circumstances; I fancy not. Englishmen, poor fellows! must either work or starve. These folks want for nothing—a house would be an inconvenience to them; they like to sleep out of doors, and it is plain they have small care for clothing, as many who possess decent habiliments enough—I speak of the lazaroni—throw almost all off till some holiday, or time of gala, and sit by the seaside playing at moro with their fingers.

A Florentine nobleman told me once that he asked one of these fellows to carry his portmanteau for him and offered him a carline—no small sum, certainly, to a Neapolitan, and rather more in proportion than an English shilling—he had not twenty yards to go with it.

"Are you hungry, master?" cries the fellow.

"No," replied Count Manucci; "but what of that?"

"Why, then, no more am I," was the answer, "and it is too hot weather to carry burdens"; so turned about upon the other side, and lay still.

This class of people, amounting to a number that terrifies one but to think on—some say sixty thousand souls—give the city an air of gaiety and cheerfulness that one cannot help honestly rejoicing in. The Strada del Toledo is one continual crowd—nothing can exceed the confusion to a walker; and here are little gigs drawn by one horse which, without any bit in his mouth, but a string tied round his nose, tears along with inconceivable rapidity a small narrow gilt chair, set between two wheels, and no spring to it, nor anything else which can add to the weight. . . .

The truth is, the jolly Neapolitans lead a coarse life, but an unoppressed one. Never, sure, was there in any town a greater show of abundance: no settled market in any given place, I think, but every third shop full of what the French call so properly *ammunition de bouche*, while whole boars, kids, and small calves dangle from a sort of neat scaffolding, all with their skins on, and make a pretty appearance. Poulterers hang up their animals in the feathers, too, not lay them on boards plucked, as at London or Venice.

The Strada del Toledo is at least as long as Oxford Road, and straight as Bond Street—very wide too; the houses all of stone, and at least eight storeys high. Over the shops live people of fashion, I am told, but the persons of particularly high quality have their palaces in other parts of the town, which town at last is not a large one, but full as an egg . . .

My stay has always been much shorter than I wished it in every great town of Italy; but here, where numberless wonders strike the sense without fatiguing it, I do feel double pleasure; and among all the new ideas I have acquired since England lessened to my sight upon the sea, those gained at Naples will be the last to quit me. . . .

[Turning northward, the Piozzis complete the Grand Tour by visiting Switzerland, Germany and Belgium before returning home. Establishing herself on a country estate in England, Mrs. Piozzi remained active in social and literary circles up to her death at the age of eighty.]

France: The Eve of the Revolution

ARTHUR YOUNG

FROM *Travels in France and Italy*

1787–90

Perhaps the most unexpected reason that a traveler ever had for going to France was that of Arthur Young: to observe farm practices. The son of an old Suffolk family, he was supposed to become a merchant but decided to try farming. Although—or perhaps because—he was a failure as a farmer, he became an ardent student of agriculture and husbandry, and eventually an internationally famous writer on those subjects. To gather firsthand information he toured every part of England and Ireland and then made a series of trips to the Continent; out of the latter came his classic Travels in France and Italy.

Part of the book's reputation and indeed its importance arises from the fact that Young made his journeys just before and during the Revolution and, out of his interest in farming, concentrated on the peasantry. Free of the virulence that mars Tobias Smollett's Travels, *but aggressively outspoken, Young's account is—by accident, as it were—an expert report on the conditions that led to the Revolution. He was appalled by the mismanagement and decay he observed and by the contrast between the peasant's poverty and the seigneur's extravagance. But his reaction was not so much that of the radical as of the economist who believes that landlords who manage more wisely can get higher rents.*

The fame of Young's writings, including the 330 articles he contributed to the Annals of Agriculture, *gained him the friendship of many of the great men of his day, so that he wrote with authority of life in*

506

palaces as well as hovels. Unhappy in his marriage, brokenhearted over the death of his youngest daughter and beset by blindness, he suffered in his later years from religious melancholia. He died in 1820.

[On his first trip, starting in May 1787, Young crosses the Channel, passes through Paris and proceeds southward toward the Pyrenees.]

THE INNS

HAVING now crossed the kingdom, and been in many French inns, I shall in general observe that they are on an average better in two respects, and worse in all the rest, than those in England. We have lived better in point of eating and drinking beyond a question than we should have done in going from London to the Highlands of Scotland, at double the expense. But if in England the best of everything is ordered, without any attention to the expense, we should for double the money have lived better than we have done in France; the common cookery of the French gives great advantage. It is true, they roast everything to a chip, if they are not cautioned: but they give such a number and variety of dishes that if you do not like some, there are others to please your palate. The dessert at a French inn has no rival at an English one; nor are the liqueurs to be despised. We sometimes have met with bad wine, but upon the whole, far better than such port as English inns give. Beds are better in France; in England they are good only at good inns; and we have none of that torment, which is so perplexing in England, to have the sheets aired; for we never trouble our heads about them, doubtless on account of the climate. After these two points, all is a blank. You have no parlour to eat in; only a room with two, three, or four beds. Apartments badly fitted up; the walls white-washed; or paper of different sorts in the same room; or tapestry so old as to be a fit nidus for moths and spiders; and the furniture such that an English innkeeper would light his fire with it. For a table, you have everywhere a board laid on cross bars, which are so conveniently contrived as to leave room for your legs only at the end. Oak chairs with rush bottoms, and the back universally a direct perpendicular, that defies all idea of rest after fatigue. Doors give music as well as entrance; the wind whistles through their chinks; and hinges grate discord. Windows admit rain as well as light;

when shut they are not easy to open; and when open not easy to shut. Mops, brooms, and scrubbing-brushes are not in the catalogue of the necessaries of a French inn. Bells there are none; the *fille* must always be bawled for; and when she appears, is neither neat, well dressed, nor handsome. The kitchen is black with smoke; the master commonly the cook, and the less you see of the cooking the more likely you are to have a stomach to your dinner; but this is not peculiar to France. Copper utensils always in great plenty, but not always well tinned. The mistress rarely classes civility or attention to her guests among the requisites of her trade. . . .

BEARS

AMONG the original tenants of this immense range of mountains [the Pyrenees], the first in point of dignity, from the importance of the mischief they do, are the bears. There are both sorts, carnivorous and vegetable-eaters; the latter are more mischievous than their more terrible brethren, coming down in the night and eating the corn, particularly buck-wheat and maize; and they are so nice in choosing the sweetest ears of the latter that they trample and spoil infinitely more than they eat. The carnivorous bears wage war against the cattle and sheep, so that no stock can be left in the fields at night. Flocks must be watched by shepherds, who have fire-arms, and the assistance of many stout and fierce dogs; and cattle are shut up in stables every night of the year. Sometimes, by accident, they wander from their keepers, and if left abroad, they run a considerable risk of being devoured. The bears attack these animals by leaping on their back, force the head to the ground, thrust their paws into the body in the violence of a dreadful hug. There are many hunting days every year for destroying them, several parishes joining for that purpose. Great numbers of men and boys form a cordon, and drive the wood where the bears are known or suspected to be. They are the fattest in winter, when a good one is worth three louis. A bear never ventures to attack a wolf; but several wolves together, when hungry, will attack a bear, and kill and eat him. Wolves are here only in winter. In summer, they are in the very remotest parts of the Pyrenees—the most distant from human habitations; they are here, as everywhere else in France, dreadful to sheep. . . .

[Late in 1787 he returns to Paris.]

PARIS

OCTOBER 25TH.—This great city appears to be in many respects the most ineligible and inconvenient for the residence of a person of small fortune of any that I have seen; and vastly inferior to London. The streets are very narrow, and many of them crowded, nine-tenths dirty, and all without foot-pavements. Walking, which in London is so pleasant and so clean that ladies do it every day, is here a toil and a fatigue to a man and an impossibility to a well-dressed woman. The coaches are numerous, and, what are much worse, there are an infinity of one-horse cabriolets which are driven by young men of fashion and their imitators, alike fools, with such rapidity as to be real nuisances, and render the streets exceedingly dangerous without an incessant caution. I saw a poor child run over and probably killed, and have been myself many times blackened with the mud of the kennels. This beggarly practise of driving a one-horse booby-hutch about the streets of a great capital flows either from poverty or wretched and despicable economy; nor is it possible to speak of it with too much severity. If young noblemen at London were to drive their chaises in streets without foot-ways, as their brethren do at Paris, they would speedily and justly get very well thrashed or rolled in the kennel. This circumstance renders Paris an ineligible residence for persons, particularly families, that cannot afford to keep a coach, a convenience which is as dear as at London. The *fiacres*, hackney-coaches, are much worse than at that city; and chairs there are none, for they would be driven down in the streets. To this circumstance also it is owing that all persons of small or moderate fortune are forced to dress in black, with black stockings; the dusky hue of this in company is not so disagreeable a circumstance as being too great a distinction; too clear a line drawn in company between a man that has a good fortune and another that has not. With the pride, arrogance, and ill-temper of English wealth this could not be borne; but the prevailing good humour of the French eases all such untoward circumstances. Lodgings are not half so good as at London, yet considerably dearer. If you do not hire a whole suite of rooms at a hotel, you must probably mount three, four, or five pairs of stairs, and in general have nothing but a bed-chamber. After the horrid fatigue of the streets, such an elevation is a delectable circumstance. You must search with trouble before you will be lodged in a private family as gentlemen usually are at London, and pay a higher price. Servants' wages are about the same as at that city. It is to be regretted that Paris should have these disadvantages, for in other respects I take it to be a most eligible residence for such as prefer a great city. The society for a man of letters, or who has any scientific pursuit, cannot be exceeded. The intercourse between such men and the great, which, if it is not upon an equal footing, ought never to exist at all, is respectable. Persons of the highest rank pay an attention to science and literature, and emulate the character they confer. I should pity the man who expected, without other advantages of a very different nature, to be well received in a brilliant circle at London because he was a fellow of the Royal Society. But this would not be the case with a member of the Academy of Sciences at Paris; he is sure of a good reception everywhere. . . .

[He makes a second trip to France in the summer of 1788, this time touring Brittany. He describes the Nantes area in the passage below.]

POVERTY AND PRIVILEGE

SEPTEMBER 21ST.—Come to an improvement in the midst of these deserts, four good houses of stone and slate, and a few acres run to wretched grass, which have been tilled, but all savage, and become almost as rough as the rest. I was afterwards informed that this improvement, as it is called, was wrought by Englishmen, at the expense of a gentleman they ruined as well as themselves. I demanded how it had been done? Pare and burn and sow wheat, then rye, and then oats. Thus it is for ever and ever! the same follies, the same blundering, the same ignorance; and then all the fools in the country said, as they do now, that these wastes are good for nothing. To my amazement find the incredible circumstance that they reach within three miles of the great commercial city of Nantes! This is a problem and a lesson to work at, but not at present. Arrive—go to the theatre, new built of fine white stone, and has a magnificent portico front of eight elegant Corinthian pillars, and four others within, to part the portico from a grand vestibule. Within all is gold and painting, and a *coup d'oeil* at entering, that struck me forcibly. It is, I believe, twice as large as Drury Lane, and five times as magnificent. It was Sunday and therefore full. *Mon Dieu!* cried I to myself, do all the wastes, the deserts, the heath, ling, furze, broom, and bog that I have passed for 300 miles lead to this spectacle? What a miracle, that all this splendour and wealth of the cities in France should be so unconnected with the country! There are no gentle transitions from ease to comfort, from comfort to wealth: you pass at once from beggary to profusion—from misery in mud cabins to Mademoiselle St. Huberti, in splendid spectacles at 500 livres a night (£21 17s. 6d.). The country deserted, or if a gentleman in it, you find him in some wretched hole, to save that money which is lavished with profusion in the luxuries of a capital. . . .

> [When he crosses the Channel on his third trip in June 1789, he finds France in revolt. But he continues about his business and is surveying Metz on that memorable July 14 when the Bastille falls; he does not hear the news until he reaches Strasbourg several days later. There he is an eyewitness of mob violence, and a few days later at Lisle he is almost the victim of it.]

REVOLUTION

JULY 21ST [1789].—*Night:* I have been witness to a scene curious to a foreigner but dreadful to Frenchmen that are considerate. Passing through the square of the *hotel de ville*, the mob were breaking the windows with stones, notwithstanding an officer and a detachment of horse was in the square. Perceiving that their numbers not only increased, but that they grew bolder and bolder every moment, I thought it worth staying to see what it would end in, and clambered on to the roof of a row of low stalls opposite the building against which their malice was directed. Here I beheld the whole commodiously. Perceiving that the troops would not attack them, except in words and menaces, they grew more violent, and furiously attempted to beat the doors in pieces with iron crows, placing ladders to the windows. In about a quarter of an hour, which gave time for the assembled magistrates to escape by a back door, they burst all open, and entered like a torrent with a universal shout of the spectators. From that minute a shower of casements, sashes, shutters, chairs, tables, sofas, books, papers, pictures, etc., rained incessantly from all the windows of the house, which is 70 or 80 feet long, and which was then succeeded by tiles, skirting boards, bannisters, frame-work, and every part of the building that force could detach. The troops, both horse and foot, were quiet spectators. They were at first too few to interpose, and, when they became more numerous, the mischief was too far advanced to admit of any other conduct than guarding every avenue around, permitting none to go to the scene of action, but letting every one that pleased retire with his plunder; guards being at the same time placed at the doors of the churches and all public buildings. I was for two hours a spectator at different places of the scene, secure myself from the falling furniture, but near enough to see a fine lad of about fourteen crushed to death by something as he was handing plunder to a woman, I suppose his mother, from the horror that was pictured in her countenance. I remarked several common soldiers, with their white cockades, among the plunderers, and instigating the mob even in sight of the officers of the detachment. There were amongst them people so decently dressed that I regarded them with no small surprise. They destroyed all the public archives; the streets for some way around strewed with papers; this has been a wanton mischief; for it will be the ruin of many families unconnected with the magistrates. . . .

JULY 26TH.— . . . The whole country is in the greatest agitation; at one of the little towns I passed I was questioned for not having a cockade of the *tiers état*. They said it was ordained by the *tiers*, and, if I was not a seigneur, I ought to obey. *But suppose I am a seigneur, what then, my friends?* What then? they replied sternly, why, be hanged; for that most likely is what you deserve. It was plain this was no moment for joking; the boys and girls began to gather, whose assembling has everywhere been the preliminaries of mischief; and if I had not declared myself an Englishman, and ignorant of the ordinance, I had not escaped very well. I immediately bought a cockade, but the hussy pinned it into my hat so loosely that before I got to Lisle it blew into the river and I was again in the same danger. My assertion of being English would not do. I was a seigneur, perhaps in disguise, and without doubt a great rogue. . . .

[The mob surrounds him menacingly but he convinces them that he is English and sympathetic.]

THERE was not a word of this discourse they did not approve of; they seemed to think that I might be an honest fellow, which I confirmed by crying, V*ive le tiers, sans impositions*, when they gave me a bit of a huzza, and I had no more interruption from them. My miserable French was pretty much on a par with their own patois. I got, however, another cockade, which I took care to have so fastened as to lose it no more. . . .

[Having crossed the whole western half of France on his earlier journeys, he then goes into the eastern and south-eastern parts, including the region now known as the Riviera.]

The Riviera

SEPTEMBER 13TH [1789].—Land at St. Maxime, and there hire two mules and a guide to Fréjus. The country the same mountainous and rocky desert of pines and lentiscus; but, towards Fréjus, some arbutus. Very little culture before the plain near Fréjus. I passed today thirty miles, of which five are not cultivated. The whole coast of Provence is nearly the same desert; yet the climate would give, on all these mountains, productions valuable for feeding sheep and cattle; but they are encumbered with shrubs absolutely worthless. . . .

SEPTEMBER 14TH.—Stayed at Fréjus to rest myself, to examine the neighborhood—which, however, contains nothing—and to arrange my journey to Nice. Here are remains of an amphitheatre and aqueduct. On enquiring for a voiture to go post, I found there was no such thing to be had; so I had no resource but mules. I employed the *garçon d'écurie* (for a postmaster thinks himself of too much consequence to take the least trouble), and he reported that I should be well served for 12 livres to Estrelles: this price for ten miles on a miserable mule was a very entertaining idea; I bid him half the money; he assured me he had named the lowest price and left me, certainly thinking me safe in his clutches. I took a walk round the town, to gather some plants that were in blossom, and, meeting a woman with an ass-load of grapes, I asked her employment; and found, by help of an interpreter, that she carried grapes from vineyards for hire. I proposed loading her ass to Estrelles with my baggage and demanded her price—40 *sols*. I will give it. Break of day appointed; and I returned to the inn, at least an economist, saving 10 livres by my walk.

SEPTEMBER 15TH.—Myself, my female, and her ass jogged merrily over the mountains; the only misfortune was, we did not know one word of each other's lingo; I could just discover that she had a husband and three children. I tried to know if he was a good husband, and if she loved him very much; but our language failed in such explanations;—it was no matter; her ass was to do my business and not her tongue. At Estrelles I took post-horses; it is a single house, and no women with asses to be had, or I should have preferred them. It is not easy for me to describe how agreeable a walk of ten or fifteen miles is to a man who walks well, after sitting a thousand in a carriage. Today's journey all through the same bad country, mountain beyond mountain, encumbered with worthless evergreens, and not one mile in twenty cultivated.

The only relief is the gardens at Grasse, where very great exertions are made, but of a singular kind. Roses are a great article for the famous attar, which is commonly supposed all to come from Bengal. They say that 1,500 flowers go to a single drop; 20 flowers sell for 1 *sol*, and an ounce of the attar 400 livres (£17 10s.). Tuberoses, etc., are also cultivated for perfumes in immense quantities, for Paris and London. Rosemary, lavender, bergamot, and oranges are here capital articles of culture. Half Europe is supplied with essences from hence.

Cannes is prettily situated, close on the shore, with the isles of St. Marguerite, where is a detestable state prison, about two miles off, and a distant boundary of the Estrelles mountains, with a bold broken outline. These mountains are barren to excess. At all the villages, since Toulon, at Fréjus, Estrelles, etc., I asked for milk, but no such thing to be had, not even of goats or sheep: the cows are all in the higher mountains; and as to butter, the landlord at Estrelles told me it was a contraband commodity that came from Nice. Good heaven!—what an idea northern people have, like myself, before I knew better, of a fine sun and a delicious climate, as it is called, that gives myrtles, oranges, lemons, pomegranates, jasmines, and aloes in the hedges; yet are such countries, if irrigation be wanted, the veriest deserts in the world. On the most miserable tracts of our heaths and moors you will find butter, milk, and cream; give me that that will feed a cow, and let oranges remain to Provence. The fault, however, is in the people more than the climate; and as the people have never any faults (*till they become the masters*) all is government. . . .

[From the southeastern coast he makes a swing into Italy as far as Florence, returning to France early in 1790. In the passage below he sums up the French approach to life.]

THE ART OF LIVING

JANUARY 18TH [1790].— . . . In the art of living the French have generally been esteemed by the rest of Europe to have made the greatest proficiency, and their manners have been accordingly more imitated and their customs

more adopted than those of any other nation. Of their cookery there is but
one opinion; for every man in Europe that can afford a great table either
keeps a French cook or one instructed in the same manner. That it is far
beyond our own I have no doubt in asserting. We have about half a dozen
real English dishes that exceed anything, in my opinion, to be met with in
France; by English dishes I mean a turbot and lobster sauce—ham and
chicken—turtle—a haunch of venison—a turkey and oysters—and after these
there is an end of an English table. It is an idle prejudice to class roast
beef among them; for there is not better beef in the world than at Paris.
Large handsome pieces were almost constantly on the considerable tables I
have dined at. The variety given by their cooks to the same thing is astonishing; they dress a hundred dishes in a hundred different ways, and most of
them excellent; and all sorts of vegetables have a savouriness and flavour,
from rich sauces, that are absolutely wanted to our greens boiled in water.
The variety is not striking in the comparison of a great table in France with
another in England; but it is manifest in an instant between the tables of a
French and English family of small fortune. The English dinner of a joint
of meat and a pudding, as it is called, or *pot luck*, with a neighbour, is bad
luck in England; the same fortune in France gives, by means of cookery
only, at least four dishes to one among us, and spreads a small table incomparably better. A regular dessert with us is expected at a considerable
table only, or at a moderate one, when a formal entertainment is given;
in France it is as essential to the smallest dinner as to the largest; if it consist only of a bunch of dried grapes, or an apple, it will be as regularly
served as the soup. I have met with persons in England who imagine the
sobriety of a French table carried to such a length that one or two glasses
of wine are all that a man can get at dinner; this is an error; your servant
mixes the wine and water in what proportion you please; and large bowls
of clean glasses are set before the master of the house and some friends
of the family at different parts of the table, for serving the richer and rarer
sorts of wines, which are drunk in this manner freely enough.

The whole nation are scrupulously neat in refusing to drink out of
glasses used by other people. At the house of a carpenter or blacksmith a
tumbler is set to every cover. This results from the common beverage being
wine and water; but if at a large table, as in England, there were porter,
beer, cider, and perry, it would be impossible for three or four tumblers or
goblets to stand by every plate; and equally so for the servants to keep such
a number separate and distinct. In table-linen they are, I think, cleaner and
wiser than the English: that the change may be incessant, it is everywhere
coarse. The idea of dining without a napkin seems ridiculous to a Frenchman, but in England we dine at the tables of people of tolerable fortune

without them. A journeyman carpenter in France has his napkin as regularly as his fork; and at an inn the *fille* always lays a clean one to every cover that is spread in the kitchen for the lowest order of pedestrian travellers. The expense of linen in England is enormous, from its fineness; surely a great change of that which is coarse would be much more rational.

In point of cleanliness I think the merit of the two nations is divided; the French are cleaner in their persons, and the English in their houses; I speak of the mass of the people and not of individuals of considerable fortune. A *bidet* in France is as universally in every apartment as a basin to wash your hands, which is a trait of personal cleanliness I wish more common in England; on the other hand their necessary houses are temples of abomination; and the practise of spitting about a room, which is amongst the highest as well as the lowest ranks, is detestable: I have seen a gentleman spit so near the clothes of a duchess that I have stared at his unconcern. In everything that concerns the stables, the English far exceed the French: horses, grooms, harness, and change of equipage; in the provinces you see cabriolets undoubtedly of the last century; an Englishman, however small his fortune may be, will not be seen in a carriage of the fashion of forty years past; if he cannot have another he will walk on foot. . . .

In dress they have given the *ton* to all Europe for more than a century; but this is not among any but the highest rank an object of such expense as in England, where the mass of mankind wear much better things (to use the language of common conversation) than in France: this struck me more amongst ladies who, on an average of all ranks, do not dress at one half of the expense of English women. Volatility and changeableness are attributed to the French as national characteristics—but in the case of dress with the grossest exaggeration. Fashions change with ten times more rapidity in England, in form, colour, and assemblage; the vicissitudes of every part of dress are fantastic with us: I see little of this in France; and to instance the mode of dressing the gentlemen's hair, while it has been varied five times at London it has remained the same at Paris. . . . In the blended idea I had formed of the French character from reading, I am disappointed from three circumstances which I expected to find predominant. On comparison with the English, I looked for great talkativeness, volatile spirits, and universal politeness. I think, on the contrary, that they are not so talkative as the English, have not equally good spirits, and are not a jot more polite: nor do I speak of certain classes of people but of the general mass. I think them, however, incomparably better tempered. . . .

Elegance and Decay: A Glimpse of Portuguese High Society

WILLIAM BECKFORD

FROM *The Journal of William Beckford in Portugal and Spain* AND *Recollections of the Monasteries of Alcobaça and Batalha*

1787–88 and 1794–95

Those who know of William Beckford's Oriental romance, Vathek, with its hothouse exoticism and its sensual Eastern potentate who sells his soul to the devil, will not be surprised to learn of his strange career and character. A creature of flamboyant gestures and mercurial temper, with a taste for the bizarre, the decadent and the forbidden, Beckford anticipated—and influenced—the Byron who created the image of the doomed youth of wealth and talent driven by some romantic, nameless evil. Although no Byron, Beckford was a sensitive artist with a small but very distinct gift.

Enjoying an immense income from his father's Jamaica plantations, Beckford grew up with a passion for music, art, literature and pretty boys. After his first tour of the Continent he wrote a romantically high-flown account of it called Dreams, Waking Thoughts, and Incidents. Soon after, to break him of an attachment to a young boy, he was hastily married off to the daughter of an earl. But then he was accused of misconduct with a seventeen-year-old youth; the ensuing scandal hounded him so relentlessly that after his wife died he left England in anger and disgust. The fact that his fantasy, Vathek, which he had capriciously written in French, had *been published in translation without acknowledgment of his authorship, added to his bitterness. (Eventually the book was to bring him lasting fame.)*

It was in this mood that in 1787 he betook himself to Portugal and Spain, where, as described in his travel diaries, he spent two years. After a stay in Paris he made a second visit to Portugal, part of which he recorded in his Recollections of an Excursion to the Monasteries of Alcobaça and Batalha.

Returning at last to England, he retired into seclusion on the family estate and devoted all his time and wealth first to building "Fonthill Abbey," a monstrous pseudo-Gothic pile, and then to stocking it with a fabulous collection of rare books, paintings and objets d'art. *Long before his death in 1844 he had become a legendary figure.*

[Leaving England until the scandal over his attachment to a nobleman's son should blow over, Beckford stops in Portugal. There the Queen's favorite, the Marquis of Marialva, is charmed by him and introduces him into the inner sanctums of Portuguese court society. Alternately bored and fascinated by the life of the grandees of the cleric-ridden, decadent royal circles, Beckford stays on for six months, becoming increasingly involved in the cabals of court cliques.]

S UNDAY, 17 JUNE, 1787.—A bright glowing day. I shut all my windows but opened them again for the sake of the Grand Prior who covets every ray of sunshine. He and D. Pedro came early. We had the Penalvas at dinner and the *Conservador* João Teles and were very friendly and comfortable. The young Marquis of Penalva plays upon the forte piano with infinite taste by mere force of genius, for he cannot read a note. The Portuguese fall naturally into plaintive passionate modulations that sink into my heart. Their minuets are at the same time tender and majestic. I cannot hear one without gliding about the room and throwing myself into theatrical attitudes. They seem to affect D. Pedro equally and we danced together till the Marquis was tired of playing to us. The sly old *Conservador* put on his sweetest smiles of admiration and launched forth into the warmest encomiums. I could not help thinking how certain acquaintance of mine in England would laugh could they have seen me and a young boy of the first distinction, educated with more severity than anyone in Portugal, languishing away in a minuet and never taking our eyes off each other. The Marquis' son, a lad of fourteen, who was also of the party, could no longer contain himself, and seizing my hands, pressed them to his lips with a fondness of which you cold-hearted northerners can form no idea. My singing, playing and capering subdues every Portuguese that approaches me, and they cannot help giving way to the most extravagant expression of their feelings. You would have thought the little Penalva bewitched had you seen how he followed me about this evening, smiling in my face and trying to dart his eyes into my very soul. No doubt every circumstance conspired to fascinate and inflame a youthful imagination—an apartment decorated with splendour and elegance; glasses rising from the ground, appearing like the portals of visionary chambers and reflecting light youthful figures swimming; the fragrance of roses, and the delightful music of Haydn, performed by Rumi, Palomino and two others, the first musicians in Lisbon and perhaps in Europe. Gelati, Joaquim de Oliveira, and Polycarpo who was just arrived from the Caldas sang a succession of arias with exquisite feeling. My company did not disperse till after eleven and I have reason to think they went away well satisfied with their entertainment.

30TH JUNE 1787, SATURDAY.— . . . He [the Marquis of Marialva] afterwards proposed accompanying us about half-a-mile to the quinta of Marvila, which belongs to his father. This spot has great picturesque beauties. The trees are old and fantastic, bending over ruined fountains and mutilated statues of heroes in armour, variegated by the lapse of years with innumerable tints of purple, green and yellow. In the center of almost impenetrable thickets of bay and myrtle rise strange pyramids of rockwork surrounded by marble lions that have a magic symbolical appearance. The M[arquis] has feeling enough to respect these uncouth monuments of an age when his ancestors performed so many heroic achievements, and readily promised me never to sacrifice them and the venerable shades in which they are embowered to the pert, gaudy taste of modern Portuguese gardening.

We walked part of the way home by the serene light of the full moon rising from behind the mountains on the opposite shore of the Tagus, at this extremity of the metropolis above nine miles broad. The Marquis exulted in the climate and repeated continually we could expect no such moonlight in England. Lisbon . . . assumed a very different aspect by these soft gleams. The flights of steps, terraces, and chapels, and porticos of several convents and palaces on the brink of the river shone forth like edifices of white marble, whilst the rough cliffs and miserable sheds rising about them were lost in dark shadows. The great square through which we passed was filled with idlers of all sorts and sexes, staring up at the illuminated windows of the Palace in hopes of catching a glimpse of Her Majesty, the Prince, the Infantas, the Confessor, or Maids of Honor, whisking about from one apartment to the other and giving ample scope to amusing conjectures. I am told the Confessor, though somewhat advanced in his career, is far from being insensible to the allurements of beauty, and pursues the young nymphs of the Palace from window to window with juvenile alacrity.

SUNDAY, 8 JULY.—The Marquis and D. Pedro who dined here today accompanied me in the evening to the bull feast. Twelve of these devoted animals were standing with all the dullness and resignation of oxen, in the middle of an open amphitheatre about the size and diameter of Ranelagh, capable of holding two or three thousand people. The poor beasts gave no signs of courage or ferocity, no furious pawings, no tearing up of the ground. I never saw a quieter party in one of the cow yards of Tottenham Court Road. After we had waited a quarter of an hour in our box, there tumbled into the amphitheatre about a dozen hideous Negroes grotesquely dressed in a sort of Indian-Chinese fashion, who after several awkward leaps and vaultings drove the herd of bulls into an enclosure fastened up with painted boards. Then entered a procession of blackamoors in laced jackets, preced-ing the principal combatant and his aide-de-camp mounted on fine managed horses prancing and curvetting. Having paraded round the amphitheatre and saluted the company in the boxes, the door of the enclosure was thrown open and a bull forced out much against his inclination. He stood stock still for a moment or two till the horseman whisking round him, darted his lance into his shoulder. Though stung with pain, he made no violent efforts to defend or revenge himself, and was lanced with lances till he dropped down dead, his joints slackening and his whole frame quivering with agony. Eleven more were slaughtered pretty nearly in the same stupid manner, and though scared with fireworks, pricked with swords, worried by dogs, and provoked by the grinning Negroes, never ventured to attack the horsemen. It requires little courage to attack such patient animals. I was highly disgusted with the spectacle. It set my nerves on edge, and I seemed to feel cuts and slashes the rest of the evening. Gregorio Franchi and Lima came in and I tried to compose myself with music.

SUNDAY, 25 NOVEMBER.— . . . I stayed at home, hearing a rehearsal of Sequidillas, in preparation for a new intermez at the Salitre theatre, till the hour of Mass was over, then getting into the Portuguese chaise, drove headlong to the palace in the Plaça do Commerçio, and hastened to the Marquis of M——'s apartments. All his family were assembled to dine with him.

Had it not been for the thoughts of my approaching departure, I should have felt more comfort and happiness than has fallen to my lot for a long interval. M[arialva], whose attendance upon the Queen may be too justly termed a state of downright slavery, had hardly taken his place at table, before he was called away. The Marchioness, Donna Henriqueta and her little sisters soon retreated to the *Camareira-Mor's* apartments, and I was left alone with Pedro and Duarte. They seized fast hold, each of a hand, and running like greyhounds through long corridors, took me to a balcony which commands one of the greatest thoroughfares in Lisbon.

The evening was delightful, and vast crowds of people moving about, of all degrees and nations, old and young, active and crippled, monks and officers. Shoals of beggars kept pouring in from every quarter to take their stands at the gates of the Palace and watch the Queen's going out; for Her Majesty is a most indulgent mother to these sturdy sons of idleness, and scarcely ever steps into her carriage without distributing considerable alms amongst them. By this misplaced charity, hundreds of stout fellows are taught the management of a crutch instead of a musket, and the art of manufacturing sores, ulcers and scabby pates, in most loathsome perfection. Duarte, who is all life and gaiety, vaulted upon the railing of the balcony, and hung for a moment or two suspended in a manner that would have frightened mothers and nurses into convulsions. The beggars, who had nothing to do till her Majesty should be forthcoming, seemed to be vastly entertained with these feats of agility.

They soon spied me out, and two brawny lubbers, whom an unfortunate combination of small pox and king's-evil had deprived of eyesight, informed no doubt by their comrades of what was going forward, began a curious dialogue with voices still deeper and harsher than those of the Holy Crows: "Heaven prosper his noble Excellency Don Duarte Manoel and Don Pedro and all the Marialvas—sweet dear youths; long may they enjoy the use of their limbs. Is that the charitable Englishman in their sweet company?"— "Yes, my comrade," answered the second blind.—"What!", said the first, "that generous favourite of the most glorious Lord St. Anthony (*O gloriosissimo Senhor Sant-Antonio!*)"—"Yes my comrade."—"Oh that I had but my precious eyes that I might see his heavenly countenance," exclaimed both together.

By the time the duet was thus far advanced, the halt, the maimed, and the scabby, having tied some greasy nightcaps to the end of long poles, poked them up through the very railing, bawling and roaring out, "Charity

charity, for the sake of the Holy One of Lisbon." Never was I looked up to by a more distorted or frightful collection of countenances. I made haste to throw down a plentiful shower of small copper money, or else Duarte would have twitched away both poles and nightcaps, a frolic by no means to be encouraged, as it might have marred our fame for the readiest and most polite attention to every demand in the name of St. Anthony.

Just as the orators were receiving their portion of pence and farthings, a cry of "There's the Queen, there's the Princess!" carried the whole hideous crowd away to another scene of action and left me at full liberty to be amused in my turn with the squirrel-like gambols of my lively companion; he is really a fine enterprising boy, bold, alert and sprightly, quite different from most of his illustrious young relations. . . .

[In 1794, during his second long sojourn in Portugal, Beckford accompanies two of the highest Portuguese churchmen on a visit to the great monasteries at Alcobaça and Batalha. The Infanta in the episode below is the wife of the Prince Regent of Portugal and daughter of Charles III of Spain.]

ENTERTAINING THE INFANTA

14 JUNE, 1794.— . . . The evening was now drawing towards its final close, and the groves, pavillions, and aviaries sinking apace into shadow: a few wandering lights sparkled amongst the more distant thickets—fireflies perhaps, perhaps meteors; but they did not disturb the reveries in which I was wholly absorbed.

"So then," thought I within myself, "the Infanta Donna Carlotta is become the predominant power in these lovely gardens, once so profusely adorned and fondly cherished by the late kind-hearted and saintly king. She is now Princess of Brazil and Princess Regent; and what besides, Heaven preserves me from repeating!"

Reports, I well knew, not greatly to the good fame of this exalted personage, had been flying about, numerous as butterflies; some dark-coloured, like the wings of the death-head moth, and some brilliant and gay, like those of the fritillaria.

This night I began to perceive, from a bustle of preparation already visible in the distance, that a mysterious kind of fête was going forwards; and whatever may have been the leading cause, the effect promised at least to be highly pleasing. Cascades and fountains were in full play; a thousand sportive *jets d'eau* were sprinkling the rich masses of bay and citron, and drawing forth all their odours, as well-taught water is certain to do upon all such occasions. Amongst the thickets, some of which received a tender light from tapers placed low on the ground under frosted glasses, the Infanta's nymph-like attendants, all thinly clad after the example of her royal and nimble self, were glancing to and fro, visible one instant, invisible the next, laughing and talking all the while with very musical silvertoned voices. I fancied now and then I heard gruffer sounds; but perhaps I was mistaken. Be that as it pleases Lucifer, just as I was advancing to explore a dusky labyrinth, out came, all of a sudden, my very dear friend Don Pedro, the young Marquis of Marialva [the son of the Marquis who appears in the record of Beckford's visit of 1787].

"What! at length returned from Alcobaça," said he, lifting me a foot off the ground in a transport of jubilation; "where is my uncle?"

"Safe enough," answered I, perhaps indiscreetly: "he had his audience five or six hours ago, and is gone home snug to his cushions and *calda da galinha*. I am waiting for my turn."

"Which will not come so soon as you imagine," replied Don Pedro, "for the Prince is retired to his mother's apartments, and how long he may be detained there no one can tell. But in the mean while come with me. The Princess, who has learnt you are here, and who has heard that you run like a greyhound, wishes to be convinced herself of the truth of a report she thinks so extraordinary."

"Nothing so easy," said I, taking him by the hand; and we sprang forwards, not to the course immediately, but to an amphitheatre of verdure concealed in the deepest recess of the odoriferous thickets, where, seated in the oriental fashion on a rich velvet carpet spread on the grass, I beheld the Alcina of the place, surrounded by thirty or forty young women, every one far superior in loveliness of feature and fascination of smile to their august mistress.

"How did you leave the fat waddling monks of Alcobaça?" said her royal highness. "I hope you did not run races with them;—but that would indeed have been impossible. There," continued she, "down that avenue, if you like, when I clap my hands together, start; your friend Pedro and two of my donzellas shall run with you—take care you are not beaten."

The avenue allotted for this amusing contest was formed of catalpas and orange trees, and as completely smooth and level as any courser, biped or quadruped, upon whom all the bets in the universe were depending, could possibly desire. The signal given, my youthful friend, all ardour, all agility, and two Indian-looking girls of fourteen or fifteen, the very originals, one would have thought, of those graceful creatures we often see represented in Hindoo paintings, darted forth with amazing swiftness. Although I had given them ten paces in advance, exerting myself in right earnest, I soon left them behind, and reached the goal—a marble statue, rendered faintly visible by lamps gleaming through transparent vases. I thought I heard a murmur of approbation; but it was so kept down, under the terror of disturbing the queen, as to be hardly distinguishable.

"*Muy bien, muy bien,*" said the Princess in her native Castilian, when we returned to the margin of the velvet carpet upon which she was still sitting reclined, and made our profound obeisances. "I see the Englishman can run—report has not deceived me. Now," continued her royal highness, "let me see whether he can dance a bolero; they say he can, and like one of us. If that be true—and I hope it is, for I abhor unsuccessful enterprises —Antonita shall be his partner—and she is by far the best dancer that followed me from Spain."

This command had been no sooner issued, than a low, soft-flowing choir of female voices, without the smallest dissonance, without the slightest break—smooth, well-tuned, and perfectly melodious,—filled my ear with such enchantment, that I glided along in a delirium of romantic delight.

My partner, an Andalusian, as full of fire and animation as the brightest beauties of Cádiz and Seville, though not quite so young as I could have wished her to be, was rattling her castanets at a most intrepid rate, and raising her voice to a higher pitch than was seemly in these regions, when a universal "Hush, hush, hush!" arrested our movements, suspended the harmonious notes of the choir, and announced the arrival of the Marquis of Anjeja.

The Strange Ways of Irishmen and Englishmen

ABU TALEB KHAN

FROM *The Travels of Mirza Abu Taleb Khan*

1799–1803

Westerners, who often behave as though the peoples of the East are merely a curious and backward breed, have in the past escaped a similar reaction from Easterners only because many of the latter were barred from foreign travel by religious or social scruples. Even though Mohammed's example might appear to encourage travel, the friends of Mirza Abu Taleb Khan (both the "Mirza" and the "Khan" were honorary) thought him most imprudent to undertake a journey to so remote a place as England. And he himself would not have been tempted if he hadn't lost his tax collector's post and if a captain in the British Army, returning home, had not proposed to take him along.

Abu Taleb was born in Lucknow, India, where his father—of Persian and Turkish descent—had settled. After long government service, mainly as a revenue officer, he fell out of favor. He proceeded to learn English and sought a post under the British, but he had no success and was becoming despondent when the Scottish captain, a friend of his, offered to pay the expenses of a trip to England. He accepted, and after a wretched voyage by way of Cape Town, where he lingered for many months, he arrived in Ireland late in 1799. Going on to London, he soon became known as "the Persian prince," was received by the King and Queen and was generally lionized. He remained in London for two and a half years;

525

although critical of certain fundamental British values, he was enchanted by Western pleasures and pastimes and might have stayed on if his original plan for teaching Eastern languages had been sufficiently encouraged. He returned home in 1803, going by way of France and Italy and then by boat to Constantinople.

The book that Abu Taleb wrote about his travels is a curious mixture of the trivial and the significant, the superficial and the fairly penetrating. His standards as a Moslem and as an Indian of rather aristocratic tastes sometimes sharpen his perceptions and judgments but at other times distort them. He is naïve or quaint about such matters as ice-skating but sophisticated on such subjects as British materialism or disdain for the foreign. No profound analyst, Abu Taleb was nevertheless refreshingly open-minded in his capacity to see the virtues as well as the defects of a Western way of life.

[Abu Taleb arrived in Cork early in December 1799 and spent about two months in Ireland, chiefly in Dublin.]

WHISKEY DRINKING, SNOW, AND ICE-SKATING

THEIR great national defect, however, is excess in drinking. The rich expend a vast deal in wine; and the common people consume immense quantities of a fiery spirit called whiskey, which is the peculiar manufacture of this country and part of Scotland.

One evening that I dined in a large company, we sat down to table at six o'clock; the master of the house immediately commenced asking us to drink wine and, under various pretenses, replenished our glasses; but perceiving that I was backward in emptying mine, he called for two water glasses and, having filled them with claret, insisted upon my taking one of them. After the tablecloth was removed, he first drank the health of the King, then the Queen, after which he toasted a number of beautiful young ladies with whom I was acquainted, none of which I dared to refuse. Thus the time passed till two o'clock in the morning, and we had been sitting for eight hours; he then called to his servants to bring a fresh supply of wine. Although I was so much intoxicated that I could scarcely walk, on hearing this order I was so frightened that I arose and requested permission to retire. He said he was sorry I should think of going away so soon, that he wished I would stay for supper, after which we might have a bottle or two more by ourselves. I had heard from Englishmen that the Irish, after they get drunk at table, quarrel and kill each other in duels; but I must declare that I never saw them guilty of any rudeness or the smallest impropriety.

About a fortnight after my arrival, there fell a very heavy shower of snow. As I had never before seen anything of the kind, I was much delighted by it. The roofs of the houses and tops of the walls were soon covered with it, and in two or three days the fields and mountains became a white surface as far as the eye could reach. During the time it continued to snow, the cold was not very great; but when it ceased, notwithstanding I had all my doors and windows shut and had three blankets on my bed, I felt the frost pierce through me like an arrow. The fire had scarce any effect on me, for while I warmed one side, I was frozen on the other, and I frequently burned my fingers before I was aware of the heat. At length I discovered that the best remedy was walking, and during the continuation of the frost I walked every day seven or eight miles. I was apprehensive that my health would have suffered from the severity of the climate, but, on the contrary, I had a keen appetite and found myself every day getting stronger and more active.

I recollect that in India, when I wore only a single vest of Dacca muslin, if I walked a mile I was completely tired; but here, when my clothes would have been a heavy load for an ass, I could have run for miles without feeling the smallest fatigue. In India I slept daily seven or eight hours, at different times, without feeling refreshed; but during the two months I remained in Ireland I never slept more than four hours any night, and yet I never felt an inclination to lie down in the daytime.

What I am now about to relate will, I fear, not be credited by my countrymen, but is, nevertheless, an absolute fact. In these countries it frequently happens that the ponds and rivers are frozen over; and the ice being of sufficient strength to bear a great weight, numbers of people assemble thereon and amuse themselves in *skating*. For this purpose it is requisite to be provided with a kind of wooden shoes, having pieces of iron fixed to the soles. At first this appears a very difficult operation, and many get severe falls; but after some months' practice, they can slide along the ice with the rapidity of a horse on a fine road and turn in all directions quicker than the best-trained charger. I have seen them engrave the name of a lady on the ice with the heel of their skate. In England and Ireland this art is practiced only for amusement; but in Holland, I have been informed, the women will carry a basket of eggs or butter in this manner twenty miles to market and return home to dinner.

[He goes on to London late in January 1800 and is at once faced with a number of curious social adjustments.]

QUESTIONABLE NEIGHBORS AND AN INTRODUCTION TO A ROUT

A FEW days after I was settled in my new lodgings, some of my friends called, to remonstrate with me on having taken up my abode in a street one half of the houses of which were inhabited by courtesans. They assured me that no ladies, or even gentlemen of character, would visit me in such a place; however, as I found my house very comfortable, and the situation was in many respects very convenient, I determined to remain where I was. My friends had the condescension and goodness to overlook this indiscretion; and not only was I visited there by the first characters in London, but even ladies of rank, who had never in their lives before passed through this street, used to call in their carriages at my door and either send up their compliments or leave their names written on cards. . . .

I one day received an invitation card from a lady, on which was written only "Mrs. ——— at home on ——— evening." At first I thought it meant an assignation; but, on consulting one of my friends, I was informed that the lady gave a *rout* that night; and that a rout meant an assemblage of people, without any particular object; that the mistress of the house had seldom time to say more to any of her guests than to inquire after their health; but that the servants supplied them with tea, coffee, ice, etc., after which they had liberty to depart and make room for others. I frequently afterward attended these routs, to some of which three or four hundred persons came during the course of the night.

[At one point he summarizes what he considers the chief vices and virtues of the English, including among the former some sharp comments on their waste of time, lack of chastity and prejudice in favor of their own customs.]

SOME ENGLISH VICES

THE sixth defect of the English is their throwing away their time in sleeping, eating and dressing: for, besides the necessary ablutions, they every morning shave, and dress their hair; then, to accommodate themselves to the fashion, they put on twenty-five different articles of dress; all this, except shaving, is repeated before dinner, and the whole of these clothes are again to be taken off at night, so that not less than two complete hours can be allowed on this account. One hour is expended at breakfast, three hours at dinner, and the three following hours are devoted to tea and the company of the ladies. Nine hours are given up to sleep: so that there remain just six hours out of the twenty-four, for visiting and business. If they are reproached with this waste of time, they reply, "How is it to be avoided?" I answer them thus: "Curtail the number of your garments; render your dress simple; wear your beards; and give up less of your time to eating, drinking, and sleeping." ...

The tenth vice of this nation is want of chastity; for under this head I not only include the reprehensible conduct of young women running away with their lovers, and others cohabiting with a man before marriage, but the great degree of licentiousness practiced by numbers of both sexes in London, evinced by the multiplicity of public houses and bagnios in every part of the town. I was credibly informed that in the single parish of Marylebone there reside sixty thousand courtesans; besides which, there is scarcely a street in the metropolis where they are not to be found. The conduct of these women is rendered still more blamable by their hiring lodgings in or frequenting streets which, from their names, ought only to be the abode of virtue and religion—for instance, Providence Street, Modest Court, St. James's Street, St. Martin's Lane and St. Paul's Churchyard. ...

Their twelfth defect is a contempt for the customs of other nations, and the preference they give to their own, although theirs, in fact, may be much inferior. I had a striking instance of this prejudice in the conduct of my fellow passengers on board ship: some of these, who were otherwise respectable characters, ridiculed the idea of my wearing trousers and a nightdress when I went to bed and contended that they slept much more at their ease by going to bed nearly naked. I replied that I slept very comfortably, that mine was certainly the most decent mode and that in the event of any sudden accident happening I could run on deck instantly and, if requisite, jump into the boat in a minute, while they must either lose some time in dressing, or come out of their cabins in a very immodest manner. In answer to this, they said such sudden accidents seldom occurred, but that, if it did happen, they would not hesitate to come on deck in their shirts only. This I give merely as a specimen of their obstinacy and prejudice in favor of their own customs.

FIRES AND FIREMEN

THE number of fires which happen in London are a very serious evil, especially as most of them originate from the quantity of wood used in the construction of houses. It has been before mentioned that the houses of this city are seldom lower than four stories, and join each other; all the floors, stairs, doors and roof are of wood; nay, many have great part of the walls supported by timbers, and some have the apartments lined with painted wainscot. In every room there is a fireplace; so that if, by the carelessness or malevolence of a servant, one of these houses is set on fire, it quickly communicates to the others and, before it can be extinguished, burns down half a street.

I should be guilty of an act of injustice were I not to give the English credit for their invention and adroitness in extinguishing fires. They have machines which, being placed upon wheels and drawn by horses, can be conveyed to any part of the town in a very short time. These machines are worked by a mechanical power and will throw up water fifty yards high; and as there are pipes of running water under every street, the situation of which is perfectly known to certain persons, a hole is in a few minutes dug in the pavement, and a plug being drawn from one of the pipes, the water rushes forth and supplies the engine, which may then be worked for twenty-four hours, or longer if necessary.

To each of these machines a number of people are attached and are paid by the parish. These persons are called *firemen*; they are remarkable for their courage and their honesty: they have been known to enter a house all in flames and bring thence many valuable articles, which they have delivered to the proprietor.

The only complaint I have against this system is that a considerable sum of money must be paid to the first engine that arrives, a smaller to the second, and so on; thus, if fifty machines should come to extinguish a fire, and all their efforts prove ineffectual, the sufferer, who is already ruined by the destruction of his property, is obliged to pay a large sum to the firemen, which doubles his loss and adds to the anguish of his mind. . . .

Their Uncomfortable Beds

THE beds, and mode of sleeping, in England, are by no means to my taste. They have, in general, two or three beds, laid one over the other; and the upper one being composed of feathers, a person is immediately swallowed up in them and finds the greatest difficulty in turning from one side to the other. In the very depth of winter this is bearable; but as the weather becomes warmer, it causes pains in the back and a general relaxation of the frame. Above them, they spread a sheet two blankets and a quilt, all of which are closely tucked under the bedding on three sides, leaving an entrance for the person to creep in next the pillows, which always reminded me of a bear climbing into the hole of a large tree. The bed being broad, and the clothes stretched out, they do not close about the neck and for a long time do not afford any warmth; and if a person turns about incautiously, the four coverings separate and either fall off the bed or cause so much trouble that sleep is completely banished. All my other Indian customs I laid aside without difficulty, but sleeping in the English mode cost me much trouble. Our quilts, stuffed with cotton and lined with muslin, are so light and adhere so closely to the body that they are infinitely more comfortable and warmer than blankets; and although it may be objected that to sleep the whole season with the same quilt next the body is an uncleanly custom, I reply that *we* always sleep in a night dress, which prevents the quilt's touching the skin; whereas the English go to bed nearly naked and use the same sheets for a fortnight together. It also frequently happens that a person, in traveling, is put into a bed with damp sheets, the moisture of which is quickly absorbed into the body and infallibly brings on cold, surfeits or a deadly fever.

London: Plum Pudding and Pugilists

LOUIS SIMOND

FROM *Journal of a Tour and Residence in Great Britain*

1810–11

As a reporter of English life, few foreign visitors have been as well equipped as Louis Simond. He was born in France but lived for more than twenty years in the United States, wrote English fluently, and traveled throughout Great Britain for two years with no other purpose than to see what he could see. The fact that he had an English wife, moreover, helped to open many doors.

Simond ranges widely, analyzing everything from cooking to political economy. His discussions of English politics, as the Napoleonic upheaval neared its climax, are especially interesting, and his comments on the paintings and sculpture in many public and private collections make his book an informed review of English taste in art. With his background in American institutions as well as French culture, he is a sound and discriminating guide.

Simond returned to the United States in 1811, but spent the years from 1817 through 1819 sojourning in various parts of Switzerland, Italy and Sicily. Encouraged by the reception of his book on England, he published a journal of his travels in Switzerland together with a history of the country, and, shortly before his death in 1831, a record of his stay in Italy and Sicily.

[Landing at Falmouth, Simond and his wife went up to London by way of Exeter, Bristol and Bath. He describes London and its life, including the way its inhabitants eat and the homes they live in.]

BIG DINNERS AND PRIVATE HOUSES

MARCH 5, 1810.— ... An English dinner is very different from a French one; less so, however, than formerly—the art of cookery being in fact now half French. England was always under great obligations to its neighbors in that respect; and most of the culinary terms are French, as well as those of tactics. It is singular, that the same animal which, when living, has an English name, has a French one when slaughtered. A sheep becomes mutton; an ox, beef; and a hog, pork. I overheard, the other day, an old Frenchman, who has lived thirty years among the English, tell one of his children who happened to have dirty hands, to go and wash them, adding, by way of reproof, "Go, you are a little *pork*." Such misapplications of words shock like discords in music, or ill-assorted colors, the more as they come nearer without being right, and are extremely ludicrous.

The master and mistress of the house sit at each end of the table— narrower and longer than the French tables—the mistress at the upper end; and the places near her are the places of honor. There are commonly two courses and a dessert. I shall venture to give a sketch of a moderate dinner for ten or twelve persons. Although contemporary readers may laugh, I flatter myself it may prove interesting in future ages ...

FIRST COURSE

Oyster Sauce	Fowls	Vegetables
Fish	Soup	Roasted or
Spinage	Bacon	Boiled Beef
		Vegetables

SECOND COURSE

Creams	Pastry	Cauliflowers
Ragoût à la	Cream	Game
Françoise	Macaroni	Pastry
Celery		

DESSERT

Walnuts	Oranges	Raisins and
Apples	Cakes	Almonds
		Pears

The soup is always a *consommé*, succulent, and high-seasoned. Vegetables, on the contrary, are exhibited in all the simplicity of nature, like hay to horses, only a little boiled instead of dried. Such a dinner as I have described is now perhaps a little antiquated. Among people of fashion the master and mistress generally abandon the ends of the table—which indeed has often no end, being round; there are more made-dishes, or French ragouts; they are served in succession, hot and hot, and vegetables do not appear quite in *naturalibus*. Good old English families have frequently no soup at all, and the dishes are only roast and boiled.

> *Selons leurs goûts, leurs moeurs, et leurs besoins,*
> *Un gros* rost beef *que beurre assaisonne,*
> *Des* plum-puddings, *des vins de la Garonne.*

This plum-pudding, celebrated by Voltaire, is quite a national dish, and my French readers will thank me for the receipt of it, which they will find in a note.* The German mineralogists have given the name of *pudding-stein* to a ponderous and hard stone, composed of fragments bound together by a common cement. I do not know whether the pudding is derived from the stone, or the stone from the pudding, and either might be considered as a reflection; but to my taste plum-pudding is excellent.

The wine generally drunk is Port—high in color, rough, and strong—Madeira, and Sherry; Bourdeaux wine, usually called here Claret, Burgundy, Champagne, and other French wines, are luxuries: few of these wines come to England without some heightening of brandy. People generally taste of fewer dishes here than at Paris, each dining generally on one or two. You are not pressed to eat or drink. The ordinary beverage during the dinner is small-beer, porter rarely, and sparkling ale, which is served in high shaped glasses like Champagne glasses; water, acidulated by the carbonic gas, is frequently used: few drink wine and water mixed. The

---

*Plum-pudding is a mass of paste, formed of equal quantities of crumb of bread, of firm fat from the kidneys of beef, of dried raisins properly stoned, and of *corinths*, a little dry fruit which comes from the Mediterranean. A small quantity of milk is also added; and, to improve the whole, a little citron comfit, spices, and brandy. All this, well mixed, is tied in a piece of linen cloth, and boiled for five or six hours in a pot full of water, but suspended so as not to touch the bottom, which might burn it. The longer it is boiled the better; and this precious faculty of not losing any thing from waiting, has made it be named emphatically Hunter's Pudding—*Pudding de Chasseur.* The cloth is taken from it before serving. The pudding forms a large ball, which is cut into slices, upon which each pours a sauce composed of butter, sugar, and wine.

crystal vessels, called decanters, in which wine is brought on table, are remarkably beautiful. Formerly it was the invariable custom to drink everybody's health round the table; and although less general now, it is by no means entirely abolished. It was done in this way: One of the guests challenged another, male or female; this being accepted by a slight inclination of the head, they filled respectively, each watching the motions of his adversary, then raised their glasses, bowing to each other, and in this attitude, looking round the table, they had to name every one of the company successively. This ceremony finished, the two champions eyed each other gravely, and carrying their glasses to their lips, quaffed their wine simultaneously. As one challenger did not wait for another, and each guest matched himself without minding his neighbors, the consequence was, circular glances, calls of names, and mutual bows, forming a running-fire round the table, crossing in every direction. It was then the invariable custom to introduce guests to each other by name, and it was quite necessary to recollect these names, in order to drink their healths at table. This custom of introducing is losing ground every day; and in fact the height of fashion is, to banish everything like *gêne* and ceremony. This is certainly very well; but some people go a little farther; and, under pretence of ease, every appearance of mutual goodwill is excluded. Voltaire has said somewhere, "*Qui n'est que juste est dur.*" I would add, *Qui n'est que franc est brutal.* True politeness, I presume, is merely benevolence in small things; which costs so little, and requires so few sacrifices, that it is not worth while to dispense with it. When politeness promises no more, it is consistent with perfect sincerity. The manners of those who have that sort of politeness resemble each other in all countries, while the arbitrary politeness of fashion is more local. Fashionable people in England are very apt to be insolent, in France probably impertinent.

Soon after dinner the ladies retire, the mistress of the house rising first, while the men remain standing. Left alone, they resume their seats, evidently more at ease, and the conversation talks a different turn, less reserved, and either graver or more licentious:

> Le dîner fait, on digère, on raisonne,
> On conte, on rit, on médit du prochain.

Politics are a subject of such general interest in England, both for men and women, that it engrosses the conversation before as much as after the retreat of the ladies; the latter, indeed, are still more violent and extravagant than the men, whenever they meddle at all with politics, and the men out of Parliament, I think, more than those in Parliament. Women, however, do not speak much in numerous and mixed company.

The political topics most usually agitated relate to the measures of administration; and the ministers are infallibly blamed or praised for the same things, and for every thing, as the person who speaks happens to belong to one or the other party....

There are some customs here not quite consistent with that scrupulous delicacy on which the English pique themselves. Towards the end of dinner, and before the ladies retire, bowls of colored glass full of water are placed before each person. All (women as well as men) stoop over it, sucking up some of the water, and returning it, and, with a spitting and washing sort of noise, quite charming—the operation frequently assisted by a finger elegantly thrust into the mouth! This done, and the hands dipped also, the napkins, and sometimes the tablecloths, are used to wipe hand and mouth. This, however, is nothing to what I am going to relate. Drinking much and long leads to unavoidable consequences. Will it be credited, that, in a corner of the very dining-room, there is a certain convenient piece of furniture, to be used by anybody who wants it. The operation is performed very deliberately and undisguisedly, as a matter of course, and occasions no interruption of the conversation. I once took the liberty to ask why this convenient article was not placed out of the room, in some adjoining closet; and was answered, that in former times, when good fellowship was more strictly enforced than in these degenerate days, it had been found that men of weak heads or stomachs took advantage of the opportunity to make their escape shamefully, before they were quite drunk; and that it was to guard against such an enormity, that this nice expedient had been invented. I have seen the article in question regularly provided in houses where there was no man, that is, no master of the house; the mistress, therefore, must be understood to have given the necessary orders to her servants—a supposition rather alarming for the delicacy of an English lady. Yet I find these very people up in arms against some uncleanly practises of the French; for instance, spitting on the floor, the carpet, etc. etc., or spreading in full view a snuff-taking handkerchief, with an innocence of nastiness quite inconceivable. To take a lump of sugar with their fingers, is another offence the French are apt to give, but of a lesser dye. Dr. Johnson was once exposed to an abomination of the latter sort during his tour in France, and the astonishment and wrath of the Doctor are faithfully recorded somewhere.

It may be a matter of curiosity in France to know how the people of London are lodged. Each family occupy a whole house, unless very poor. There are advantages and disadvantages attending this custom. Among the first, the being more independent of the noise, the dirt, the contagious disorders, or the danger of your neighbor's fires, and having a more complete home. On the other hand, an apartment all on one floor, even of a few rooms only, looks much better, and is more convenient. These narrow houses, three or four stories high—one for eating, one for sleeping, a third for company, a fourth under ground for the kitchen, a fifth perhaps at top for the servants—and the agility, the ease, the quickness with which the individuals of the family run up and down, and perch on the different stories, give the idea of a cage with its sticks and birds. The plan of these houses is very simple, two rooms on each story; one in the front with two or three windows looking on the street, the other on a yard behind, often very small; the stairs generally taken out of the breadth of the back room. The ground-floor is usually elevated a few feet above the level of the street, and separated from it by an area, a sort of ditch, a few feet wide, generally from three to eight, and six or eight feet deep, inclosed by an iron railing; the windows of the kitchen are in this area. A bridge of stone or brick leads to the door of the house. The front of these houses is about twenty or twenty-five feet wide; they certainly have rather a paltry appearance—but you cannot pass the threshold without being struck with the look of order and neatness of the interior. Instead of the abominable filth of the common entrance and common stairs of a French house, here you step from the very street on a neat floor-cloth or carpet, the wall painted or papered, a lamp in its glass bell hanging from the ceiling, and every apartment in the same style:—all is neat, compact, and independent, or, as it is best expressed here, snug and comfortable—a familiar expression, rather vulgar perhaps, from the thing itself being so common.

On the foot pavement before each house is a round hole, fifteen or eighteen inches in diameter, covered with an iron grate; through that hole the coal-cellar is filled without endangering the neatness of the house. The streets have all common sewers, which drain the filth of every house. The drains preclude that awkward process by which necessaries are emptied at Paris, poisoning the air of whole streets, during the night, with effluvia, hurtful and sometimes fatal to the inhabitants. Rich houses have what are called water-closets; a cistern in the upper story, filled with rain-water, communicates by a pipe and cock to a vessel of earthenware, which it washes.

[After a visit to Wales and the Liverpool area, he makes an extended tour of Scotland. Returning to London, he describes some popular pastimes, including the novel one of watching men fight with their fists.]

THE BOXING MATCH

MAY 22, 1811.—The expected meeting between Molineux, the black from America, and a Lancashire pugilist (Rimmer) took place yesterday. These sorts of combats being peculiar to the country, I wished to be present at one of them, and repaired early to the field (Molesey Hurst, near Hampton Court, fifteen miles from London) with Mr. S., who had the goodness to accompany me. We found an immense ring already formed —a sort of Scythian entrenchment of carts and waggons, arranged side by side in double and treble rows, without horses. This is a contrivance of the country people, who speculate on the curiosity of the Londoners, and let their elevated vehicles to the amateurs of the fist. We made our bargain, and mounted a cart, whence we had a full view of the immense crowd already assembled inside the ring of carts, in the centre of which we could see a smaller ring, perhaps 40 feet across, surrounded with stakes, and a rope.

About half after twelve o'clock, Rimmer appeared in the ring, a tall, good-looking young man, with a high color. The black arrived soon after, mounted on the box of a barouche and four, with some young men of fashion; he was muffled up in great-coats, and seemed a clumsy-looking fellow. Here began a scene quite unexpected to me, the clearing of the ring. All the boxers in town, professional and amateurs, charged the mob at once, which giving way in confusion, formed a sort of irregular circle outside the rope-ring, but not large enough. With sticks and whips applied, *sans cérémonie*, these champions of the fist pressed back the compact mass. I expected every moment a general engagement;—nothing of the kind: the mob shrunk from the flogging, but without resentment. 'Tis true the blows appeared to be directed mostly over the heads of the first ranks, and fell on those five or six deep; the weapons being mostly coachmen's or carters' long whips. These rear ranks, assailed by an invisible hand, had no recourse but a retreat, and made way for those in front; the latter, squatting down on the turf, formed, at last, a sort of barrier over which the crowd could see. The combatants soon stripped; the black exhibiting the arms, breast, and shoulders of Hercules, with the "head, scarce more extensive than the sinewy neck"; his legs also extremely muscular, and not much of the Negro make. The Lancashire man, taller, and broader, but not so deep,* square, and muscular, appeared undaunted, and had lost none of

---

*Pugilists consider the depth of the chest as a surer indication of strength than the breadth.

his color. They shook hands and stood on their defence, shy to begin for some minutes. I could not tell who gave the first blow, so quickly was it returned. The Lancashire man fell and fell again. One of the rounds he closed with the black, threw him, and fell over himself. Twice more, I think, he attempted to wrestle, with various success, but was often knocked down. His left eye appeared closed, and he was all stained with blood; I could not well distinguish where it came from. The blood was not so visible on the skin of the black, but I observed that he was much more out of breath than his adversary.

> C'est un plaisir de les voir se baisser
> Se relever, reculer, avancer
> Parer, sauter, se ménager des feintes,
> Et se porter les plus vives atteintes.

At every round, which is generally terminated by a fall, the seconds raise their friend, wipe the blood, bathing his temples with a sponge dipped in vinegar and water. The champion who did not fall sits in the meantime on the bended knee of one of his seconds, leaning upon him, to take as much rest as he can, and is refreshed also by sponging. The battle had lasted half an hour—about twenty rounds—the Lancashire-man always thrown; when all at once the barrier was broken, an irruption of the mob took place, and soon became general, rushing towards the centre, and overwhelming the ring and its occupants. I lost sight of the combatants. Whips and sticks were lifted up in vain—there was not even room to strike. All was clamor, and struggle, and confusion, for twenty minutes. At last we saw the ropes and stakes taken away, as if any further battle was out of the question, or an adjournment intended to some other spot. Unwilling to lose their sport, the mob seemed to give way a little, and had no sooner made an opening, than a desperate charge drove them back to their former situation, where squatting again, order was restored, and the combatants stood. The white man seemed still able and stout, but fell like an ox under the club of the butcher at the first round, at the second, and so on, from bad to worse, rising each time with more difficulty. It became a shocking sight. Victory was out of the question, and had been so almost from the beginning. His better wind might have afforded him a chance—he had lost it by the interruption. The black was now fresh— he pressed his exhausted adversary, retreating before him. At last a knockdown blow laid him prostrate near the ring of spectators (for the rope-ring was gone). In vain his seconds, exerting themselves about him, raised him from the ground; his head hung on his breast, he could not stand, he appeared *hors de combat;* and the prescribed time to face his adversary having expired (two or three minutes), victory was declared on the other side. Hats flew, cries rent the air; the black, meantime, grinning over his fallen adversary in Homeric triumph! The mob rushed in from all parts; and we rushed out, not wishing to see any more, and, finding our vehicle, drove back to London.

This was not deemed a good battle. Young Rimmer over-rated his own strength, and has received a good lesson for his temerity. The black will not meet with many pugilists equal to him in point of muscle, but he wants wind and coolness; he puts himself in a passion, and will be beat by the professors, if he dares try them. A pleasing reflection softened the brutality of this sight; it was the impartiality with which the populace observed the *loi du combat,* and saw one of their own people thus mauled and bruised by a foreigner and a Negro, suffering him to enjoy his triumph unmolested; for the interruption had been a mere ebullition of curiosity and enthusiastic admiration for the art—not ill will or unfair interference. When I call this collection of people populace, I do not mean that they were all low people; there were no ragged coats in sight, and half the mob were gentlemen.

The English Aristocracy: A Rake's Report

PRINCE HERMANN PÜCKLER-MUSKAU

FROM A Tour of England, Ireland, and France

1826–28

Dandy, rover and bankrupt German nobleman, a daredevil in youth and a roué in old age, successful author of many books, spendthrift who lavished a fortune on his parks and gardens, libertine who amidst a stream of mistresses remained devoted to one woman for almost forty years, Prince Pückler-Muskau was baroque of the baroque, a fantastic even among eccentrics.

But we are especially interested in him because among his books of travel is one that gives us a narrow but intimate view of the frivolities and pastimes of the idle rich in England's Age of Elegance. The curious purpose that brought the forty-one-year-old but still dashing and attractive Prince to England in 1826 was to find another heiress (he had run through the fortune of his first wife, Lucie, Countess of Pappenheim, and she had agreed to divorce him) who would enable him to continue to indulge his expensive tastes—especially for making his estate at Muskau into the most beautiful of parks. For two years he attended the routs, balls, fetes and concerts that were the routine of the haut monde. He failed to carry off an heiress, but the acute and occasionally brilliant letters he wrote to his Lucie—he had divorced her in name but not in spirit—became a book that set agog fashionable circles all over Europe.

Back in Germany, the Prince tired of his estate at Muskau, and set out for Africa in 1834. Accompanied by what soon amounted to a harem as well as a menagerie, he stayed in Algiers and Tunis for a time, went on to Greece and then proceeded in a kind of triumphal procession through Egypt to Khartoum. After archaeologizing in Jerusalem, Beyrouth (where he visited the equally eccentric Lady Hester Stanhope in her bizarre domain) and Syria, he returned to Germany in 1839. Thereafter he confined his travels to Europe, but continued to indulge in park building and extravagant amours until his death in 1871 at the age of eighty-six.

[Returning from England to Muskau in 1828 without a bride, Pückler assembled the letters he had written to Lucie, gallantly pruning away all references to the various women he had courted or rejected, and published them anonymously in book form. In England they were translated by Sarah Austin, who edited Pückler prudishly but later fell violently in love with him. But enough remains of his experiences in the stately country homes, at the exclusive clubs, the races, the opera, the musical soirees and other gathering places to afford a fascinatingly intimate glimpse of England's upper crust in the days of George IV.]

The Manners of the Elegant

THE peculiarity of English manners may be much better observed here, at the first *abord*, than in the great world, which is everywhere more or less alike, whereas the same individuals of whom it is in part composed show themselves here with much less restraint. In the first place, the stranger must admire the refinement of convenience with which Englishmen sit: it must be confessed that a man who is ignorant of the ingenious English chairs, of every form and adapted to every degree of fatigue, indisposition or constitutional peculiarity, really loses a large share of earthly enjoyment. It is a positive pleasure even to see an Englishman sit, or rather lie, in one of these couchlike chairs by the fireside. A contrivance like a reading desk attached to the arm, and furnished with a candlestick, is so placed before him that with the slightest touch he can bring it nearer or farther, push it to the right or the left, at pleasure. A curious machine, several of which stand around the large fireplace, receives one or both of his feet; and the hat on his head completes this enchanting picture of superlative comfort.

This latter circumstance is the most difficult of imitation to a man brought up in the old school. Though he can never refrain from a provincial sort of shudder when he enters the brilliantly lighted saloon of the club, where dukes, ambassadors and lords, elegantly dressed, are sitting at the card tables, yet if he wishes to be "fashionable" he must keep on his hat, advance to a party at whist, nod to one or two of his acquaintances, then, carelessly taking up a newspaper, sink down on a sofa and, not till after some time, *nonchalamment* throw down his hat (which perhaps has all the while been a horrid annoyance to him); or, if he stays but a few minutes, not take it off at all.

The practice of half lying instead of sitting; sometimes of lying at full length on the carpet at the feet of ladies; of crossing one leg over the other in such a manner as to hold the foot in the hand; of putting the hands in the armholes of the waistcoat, and so on, are all things which have obtained in the best company and the most exclusive circles; it is therefore very possible that the keeping on the hat may arrive at the same honor. In this case it will doubtless find its way into Paris society, which, after being formerly aped by all Europe, now disdains not to ape the English— sometimes grotesquely enough—and, as is usual in such cases, often outdoes its original.

On the other hand, the English take it very ill of foreigners if they reprove a waiter who makes them wait, or brings one thing instead of another, or if they give their commands in a loud or lordly tone of voice; though the English themselves often do this in their own country, and much in ours, and though the dining room of the club is in fact only a more elegant sort of restauration [restaurant], where every man must pay his reckoning after he has dined. It is regarded not only as improper, but as unpleasant and offensive, if anyone reads during dinner. It is not the fashion in England; and, as I have this bad habit in a supreme degree, I have sometimes remarked satirical signs of displeasure on the countenances of a few Islanders of the old school, who shook their heads as they passed me. One must be on one's guard, generally, to do things as little as possible unlike the English, and yet not to try to imitate them servilely in everything, for no race of men can be more intolerant. Most of them see with reluctance the introduction of any foreigner into their more private societies, and all regard it as a distinguished favor and obligation conferred on us.

But of all offenses against English manners which a man can commit, the three following are the greatest: to put his knife to his mouth instead of his fork; to take up sugar or asparagus with his fingers; or, above all, to spit anywhere in a room. These are certainly laudable prohibitions, and well-bred people of all countries avoid such practices—though even on these points manners alter greatly, for Marshal Richelieu detected an adventurer who passed himself off for a man of rank, by the single circumstance of his taking up olives with his fork and not with his fingers. The ridiculous thing is the amazing importance which is attached to them. The last-named crime is so pedantically proscribed in England that you might seek through all London in vain to find such a piece of furniture as a spitting box. A Dutchman who was very uncomfortable for the want of one declared with great indignation that an Englishman's only spitting box was his stomach. These things are, I repeat, more than trivial, but the most important rules of behavior in foreign countries almost always regard trivialities. Had I, for example, to give a few universal rules to a young traveler, I should seriously counsel him thus: In Naples, treat the people brutally; in Rome, be natural; in Austria, don't talk politics; in France, give yourself no airs; in Germany, a great many; and in England, don't spit. With these rules, the young man would get on very well. What one must justly admire is the well-adapted arrangement of everything belonging to the economy of life and of all public establishments in England, as well as the systematic rigor with which what has once been determined on is unalterably followed up. In Germany, all good institutions soon fall asleep, and new brooms alone sweep clean; here it is quite otherwise. On the other hand, everything is not required of the same person, but exactly so much, and no more, as falls within his department. The treatment of servants is as excellent as their performance of their duties. Each has his prescribed field of activity, in which, however, the strictest and most punctual execution of orders is required of him, and in any case of neglect the master knows whom he has to call to account. At the same time, the servants enjoy a reasonable freedom and have certain portions of time allotted to them, which their master carefully respects. The whole treatment of the serving classes is much more decorous and combined with more *égards* than with us; but then they are so entirely excluded from all familiarity, and such profound respect is expected from them, that they appear to be considered rather as machines than as beings of the same order. This, and their high wages, are no doubt the causes that the servants really possess more external dignity than any other class in England, relatively to their station. . . .

At the Theater

THE most striking thing to a foreigner in English theaters is the unheard-of coarseness and brutality of the audiences. The consequence of this is that the higher and more civilized classes go only to the Italian opera, and very rarely visit their national theater. Whether this be unfavorable or otherwise to the stage, I leave others to determine.

English freedom here degenerates into the rudest license, and it is not uncommon in the midst of the most affecting part of a tragedy, or the most charming cadenza of a singer, to hear some coarse expression shouted from the galleries in stentor voice. This is followed, according to the taste of the bystanders, either by loud laughter and approbation, or by the castigation and expulsion of the offender.

Whichever turn the thing takes, you can hear no more of what is passing on the stage, where actors and singers, according to ancient usage, do not suffer themselves to be interrupted by such occurrences, but declaim or warble away, *comme si rien n'était.* And such things happen not once, but sometimes twenty times, in the course of a performance, and amuse many of the audience more than that does. It is also no rarity for someone to throw the fragments of his *goûter,* which do not always consist of orange peels alone, without the smallest ceremony on the heads of the people in the pit, or to scale them with singular dexterity into the boxes; while others hang their coats and waistcoats over the railing of the gallery, and sit in shirt sleeves; in short, all that could be devised for the better excitement of a phlegmatic *Harmonie* society of the workmen in Berlin, under the renowned Wisotsky, is to be found in the national theater of Britain.

Another cause for the absence of respectable families is the resort of hundreds of those unhappy women with whom London swarms. They are to be seen of every degree, from the lady who spends a splendid income, and has her own box, to the wretched beings who wander houseless in the streets. Between the acts they fill the large and handsome foyers and exhibit their boundless effrontery in the most revolting manner.

It is most strange that in no country on earth is this afflicting and humiliating spectacle so openly exhibited as in the religious and decorous England. The evil goes to such an extent, that in the theaters it is often difficult to keep off these repulsive beings, especially when they are drunk, which is not seldom the case. They beg in the most shameless manner, and a pretty, elegantly dressed girl does not disdain to take a shilling or a sixpence, which she instantly spends in a glass of rum, like the meanest beggar. And these are the scenes, I repeat, which are exhibited in the national theater of England, where the highest dramatic talent of the country should be developed; where immortal artists like Garrick, Mrs. Siddons, Miss O'Neil, have enraptured the public by their genius, and where such actors as Kean, Kemble and Young still adorn the stage. . . .

TAILORS AND FISHMONGERS

EVERYTHING here is in colossal dimensions, even the workshop of my tailor, which is like a manufactory. You go to ask about the fate of a coat you have ordered; you find yourself surrounded by hundreds of bales of cloth, and as many workmen; a secretary appears with great formality and politely asks the day on which it was ordered. As soon as you have told him, he makes a sign for two folios to be brought, in which he pores for a short time. "Sir," is at last the answer, "tomorrow at twenty minutes past eleven the *frac* will be so far advanced that you can try it on in the dressing room." There are several of these rooms, decorated with large looking glasses and *Psychés*, continually occupied by fitters, where the wealthy tailor in person makes a dozen alterations without ever betraying the least impatience or ill humor.

As soon as justice was done to the *frac*, I continued my walk, and came to a butcher's shop, where not only are the most beautiful garlands, pyramids, and other fanciful forms constructed of raw meat, and elegant vessels filled with ice give out the most delightful coolness, but a playbill hangs behind every leg of mutton, and the favorite newspapers lie on the polished tables.

A few houses farther on, a dealer in sea monsters competes with him and sits, like King Fish in the fairy tale, between the marble and the fountain. He would, however, find it difficult to rival his celebrated colleague Crockford, who understands how to catch something better than common fish.

This person is a man of genius, who has raised himself from the estate of a poor fishmonger to that of the scourge, and at the same time the favorite, of the rich and fashionable world. He is a gambler, who has won millions and with them has built a gaming palace on the plan of the salons at Paris, but with a truly Asiatic splendor almost surpassing that of royalty.

Everything is in the now revived taste of the time of Louis the Fourteenth; decorated with tasteless excrescences, excess of gilding, confused mixture of stucco painting, etc.—a turn of fashion very consistent in a country where the nobility grows more and more like that of the time of Louis the Fourteenth.

Crockford's cook is the celebrated Ude, practically and theoretically the best in Europe. The table and attendance are in the highest perfection, combined with *un jeu d'enfer*, at which twenty thousand pounds and more has often been lost in one evening, by one man. The company forms a club; admission is very difficult to obtain; and although games of hazard are illegal in England, most of the ministers are members, and the Duke of Wellington, the Premier, is one of the managers of this gaming club. . . .

"EXCLUSIVES" AND DANDIES

A LONDON Exclusive of the present day is in truth nothing more than a bad, flat, dull impression of a roué of the Regency and a courtier of Louis the Fifteenth: both have in common selfishness, levity, boundless vanity and an utter want of heart; both think they can set themselves above everything by means of contempt, derision and insolence; both creep in the dust before one idol alone—the Frenchman of the last age before his King, the Englishman of this before any acknowledged ruler in the empire of fashion. But what a contrast if we look further! In France, the absence of all morality and honesty was at least in some degree atoned for by the most refined courtesy; the poverty of soul, by wit and agreeableness; the impertinence of considering themselves as something better than other people rendered bearable by finished elegance and politeness of manners; and egotistical vanity in some measure justified, or at least excused, by the brilliancy of an imposing court, a high-bred air and address, and the perfect art of polished intercourse, winning *aisance*, and a conversation captivating by its wit and lightness. What of all this has the English "dandy" to offer?

His highest triumph is to appear with the most wooden manners, as little polished as will suffice to avoid castigation; nay, to contrive even his civilities so that they are as near as may be to affronts—this indeed is the style of deportment which confers upon him the greatest celebrity. Instead of a noble, high-bred ease, to have the courage to offend against every restraint of decorum; to invert the relation in which our sex stands to women, so that they appear the attacking, and he the passive or defensive party; to treat his best friends, if they cease to have the stamp and authority of fashion, as if he did not know them—"to cut them," as the technical phrase goes; to delight in the ineffably *fade* jargon, and the affectation of his "set"; and always to know what is "the thing"—these are pretty nearly the accomplishments which form a young "lion" of the world of fashion. If he has, moreover, a remarkably pretty mistress, and if it has also happened to him to induce some foolish woman to sacrifice herself on the altar of fashion and to desert husband and children for him, his reputation reaches its highest nimbus. If, added to this, he spends a great deal of money, if he is young, and if his name is in the *Peerage*, he can hardly fail to play a transient part; at any rate, he possesses in full measure all the ingredients that go to make a Richelieu of our days.

That his conversation consists only of the most trivial local jests and scandal, which he whispers into the ear of a woman in a large party, without deigning to remark that there is anybody in the room but himself and the happy object of his delicate attentions; that with men he can talk only of gambling or of sporting; that, except a few fashionable phrases which the shallowest head can the most easily retain, he is deplorably ignorant; that his awkward *tournure* does not go beyond the nonchalance of a plowboy who stretches himself at his length on the alehouse settle; and that his grace is very like that of a bear which has been taught to dance—all this does not rob his crown of a single jewel.

Worse still is it that, notwithstanding the high-bred rudeness of his exterior, the moral condition of his inward man must, to be fashionable, stand far lower. That cheating is prevalent in the various kinds of play which are here the order of the day, and that when long successfully practiced it gives a sort of *relief*, is notorious: but it is still more striking that no attempt is made to conceal that *crasse* selfishness which lies at the bottom of such transactions—nay, that it is openly avowed as the only rational principle of action, and "good nature" is laughed at and despised as the *comble* of vulgarity. This is the case in no other country; in all others, people are ashamed of such modes of thinking, even if they are wretched enough to hold them. "We are a selfish people," said a favorite leader of fashion, "I confess; and I do believe that what in other countries is called *amor patriae* is amongst us nothing but a huge conglomeration of love of ourselves. *But I am glad of it; I like selfishness;* there's good sense in it." And he added, not satirically, but quite in earnest, "Good nature is quite *mauvais ton* in London; and really it is a bad style to take up, and will never do."

Musketeer in the Alps

ALEXANDRE DUMAS

FROM *Travels in Switzerland*

1832

In the number of his travel books, as in his writing in
general, his bodily girth, sexual appetite, vanity and enthusiasm, Alexandre
Dumas père was gargantuan. He recorded his journeys in at least twenty
volumes—exuberant narratives, punctuated by dramatic scenes and
adorned, one suspects, with fictional flourishes.

First there was the tour of Switzerland in 1832, when, after a bout with
the plague, he was advised to go abroad for his health. Then came trips to
Italy and the Sinai Desert later in the 1830s. At the height of his fame, in
1846, the French Minister of Education suggested that he visit and, by
writing about it, popularize Algeria—to which was added a journey across
Spain and a voyage through the Mediterranean on a warship. In 1858, following in the footsteps of Dumas fils, he visited Russia and the Caucasus.
At this point he published a collection of his Impressions de Voyage in
seven volumes, but his travels were hardly over: after setting out in his own
schooner from Marseilles in 1860, he quixotically joined Garibaldi's campaign against Sicily and Naples, which led to his living in Naples for four
years. As he grew older he spent more and more time abroad, and in one
year, 1866, we find him first in Italy and then later traveling in Germany,
Austria and Hungary.

Dumas was at once a child of nature and a force of nature. Naïve,
romantic, infinitely inventive, he brought to his travels—and his accounts
of them—an immense gusto, a sense of the comic, a boyish boastfulness, a
nose for the dramatic, not to say the sensational, and a tendency to convert
every incident into an adventure.

Although only thirty years old, he was already a popular playwright and fast becoming the talk of Paris when he made that first journey to Switzerland—ostensibly for his health but possibly to escape arrest for his republican sympathies. Travels in Switzerland *is a lighthearted, buoyant account of adventures among glaciers, guides, inns and icy streams, including the tallish story of the bear that was served as steak and then revealed to have dined on a hunter just before.*

[In the following, setting out for a climb in the Bernese Oberland, he sums up the exhilaration of travel and then describes a few typical experiences.]

So here I was once more in the role of climber, hunter, artist and writer, my album in my pocket, my gun on my shoulder, my stick in my hand. Surely, to travel is to live in all the meaning of the word; is to forget the past and future in the present; is to breathe the free air, feel the joy of living, to become an integral part of creation. . . .

The next morning, at eight o'clock, we set out, determined to carry out the most testing climb we had yet made: we meant to sleep in the highest habitation in Europe, that is to say, at 8,120 feet above sea level—569 feet higher than the St. Bernard hospice, the limit of the snow line. The Faulhorn is, if not the highest, at any rate one of the highest mountains of the chain which separates the valleys of Thun, Interlaken and Brienz from those of Grindelwald and Rosenlaui. Only a year or two back an innkeeper, speculating on the curiosity of travelers, had established on the plateau that lies below the summit a small inn, usable only in the summer months. With the advent of October he removes the doors and shutters, to save remaking them, and abandons his house to the winter storms, which play havoc with it until not a post is left standing.

Our host took the charitable precaution of warning us that, animal life being scarce in the upper regions, the innkeeper, forced to obtain his provisions from Grindelwald and Rosenlaui, got a week's supply in each Monday—a fact which, while perfectly satisfactory for midweek travelers, was anything but satisfactory for those who, like ourselves, happened to arrive on a Sunday. He therefore invited us, in our own interests—or so he told us—to return to him for a good bed and meal. But we replied that we had made up our minds, if we did come back that day, to make for Rosenlaui, and thus save a day's journey. Upon hearing which all his solicitude for our welfare gave way to the completest indifference, even to the point of refusing point blank to sell me a cold chicken which I had counted on making my comrade en route. We set off, therefore, somewhat uneasy about our gastronomical future. My only hope rested in my rifle; but everyone is aware, in Switzerland, of the precariousness of such a hope. Game, normally rare, is still harder to come by near the frequented routes. I therefore wandered off the track as much as I could, beating every possible bush in the hope of game.

I had regained the path, feeling very chastened after five or six unsuccessful attempts to run to earth the elusive marmots which I could hear uttering their sharp cries all round, when all at once a bird flew up from under my feet. I was taken unawares, with the result that the creature was a good fifty yards off when I fired. In spite of the distance, I saw clearly that I had hit it; my guide shouted to me that it was wounded. The bird continued its flight, and I ran after it. Only a hunter can appreciate the obstacles one takes in one's stride when in close pursuit of one's quarry. The reader is already aware that I am no intrepid mountaineer; but on this occasion, indifferent to danger, and seeing nothing but the unknown bird, I rushed along the side of a mountain with a slope like a rooftop, leaped over bushes and boulders, bringing in the train of my furious course a perfect avalanche of stones. It fell to earth at last on the other side of a torrent, which, in the heat of the chase, I took at a leap, and in another moment my future roast was clutched in my triumphant hand. It turned out to be a magnificent fat pullet.

I now had to retrace my way, which proved to be a good half mile and more, and, in colder blood, far from simple. First came the torrent. I approached it and became aware of the fact that it must have been some fourteen or fifteen feet across, a respectable distance which made me pause. Twice I took my run, and twice I stopped short on the brink; the laughter of my guide came to my ears. I recalled Payot, at whom I had laughed in similar circumstances, and I decided to copy his example and to look for a narrower place higher up; but after a quarter of an hour's climb I discovered that the stream took a turn in the opposite direction from that I wanted to take. Observing that a hill conveniently hid me from my guide, I picked up a sturdy pine branch and sounded the depth of the stream with it; then, convinced of its being only two or three feet, I plunged in and reached the other side wet through as far as my mid-regions. I was still only halfway through my troubles: there remained the mountainside to climb.

As I began the operation, the form of my guide appeared at the top. I called to him to bring me my stick. It would have been kinder, perhaps, if I had asked him to throw it; but quite apart from the fact that it might not have reached me, I was not sorry to get my own back for a certain burst of laughter which still sounded in my ears, and which the chilliness of the sousing I had given myself did not help me to forget. Willer hurried down to me with all the customary good-natured willingness that characterizes these fellows, and helped me along so energetically that after some three quarters of an hour I retraced the ground it had taken me ten minutes to cover earlier.

We climbed steadily, and soon we began to meet with patches of snow which had defied the summer warmth; a cold wind blew from the passes. In normal circumstances I should have paid little attention, but the bath I had recently taken made me acutely conscious of them. On reaching a little lake some seven thousand feet up, I shivered gently; by the time we attained the summit of the Faulhorn I was shivering very decidedly. Consequently, instead of looking at the view I had come to see, I flung myself into the hut and demanded a fire. Mine host asked me how much wood I wanted.

"Oh, *pardieu!* a good bundle. I am too frozen to go in for small quantities."

He found and weighed a fair-sized bundle.

"Thirty francs," he said.

This seemed somewhat unreasonable to a man brought up in the middle of a forest.

"You see," my host explained in answer to my grimace, "we have to pay a man to bring the wood here on his back, and that makes the price of things a bit high, since we have to use wood for cooking . . ."

The significance of the last part of his explanation was not lost on me, boding as it did no good for my pocket; but since I had my pullet, I counted on my meal costing me no more than the thirty francs' worth of wood I had bought in order to warm myself. I took about a third of the bundle with me to my room, rammed the ten francs' worth into the stove and, taking a dry change of clothing out of my bag, I began a toilet appropriate to the situation.

[After watching a mountain storm he retires for the night.]

SCARCELY had I put my head on the pillow when a fearful racket began in the room above. Apparently the electric fluid in the atmosphere had affected our guides and inclined them for an evening's revelry. About a dozen of them had got together in the loft which formed the first story of the hut; and since it was separated from the ground-floor room given over to travelers by a mere inch of pine wood which constituted the ceiling, I could hear every syllable of conversation, which might have proved as interesting as it was evidently gay had it not been in German. The noise of glasses being clinked continually, of empty bottles rolling across the floor, the introduction of two or three more companions of a different sex, the complete absence of lights banned on account of the possibility of fire, became at last more than I could bear, to such an extent that, seizing my steel-tipped stick which was close to hand, I rapped vigorously with it on the ceiling. The din instantly ceased; voices were lowered. But evidently this was only to plot a campaign of resistance, for after a few seconds a loud laugh announced plainly enough what they thought of my injunction. I gave a second rap with my stick, accompanying it with the worst oath known to me in the Teutonic repertoire. Their reply was not long in coming. One of them took a chair, gave the same number of knocks that I had given and, not to be outdone, replied in French with the most trenchant indecency I had ever heard. It was open rebellion. For a moment or two I was dumfounded; then I began to search about for ways and means of turning the tables on the rebels. My silence was taken as a sign of defeat, and the roars of laughter and the infernal din recommenced worse than ever.

Suddenly it came into my mind that the flue of my stove came out in a corner of the loft above. This recollection was like a flash of light; another, less modest, might have called it an inspiration of genius. I sprang from my bed, hurried into the kitchen, gathered all the hay I could lay my hands on, carried it back to my fortress, which I proceeded to barricade firmly, and set about my preparations of vengeance. These consisted, as the reader will have already guessed, in damping the hay to ensure its giving off the maximum fumigation; then, this done, I stuffed the stove to bursting point with the hay and proceeded to set it alight, after which operation I regained my bed and awaited results.

Several minutes passed; then one of the guides coughed, a second sneezed, and a third, after sniffing violently, declared there was a smell of something burning. At this everyone stood up. Now was the time to press home my advantage. I rushed to the stove, rammed in a fresh charge of ammunition and, closing the door, stood by with my arms crossed like an artilleryman guarding his gun. The result exceeded all my expectations. Coughings and sneezings gave way to shouts of rage and imprecations of despair: I had smoked them out like foxes! Five minutes later a truce-bearer knocked at my window; it was my turn to lay down terms, which I did like a veritable hero of old. Like Alexander, I pardoned the family of Darius on the clear understanding that they made no more noise, while I, on my part, made no more smoke. The treaty was scrupulously observed by both parties, and I settled myself yet once again in my bed in the hopes of falling asleep. Again I was to be thwarted, this time by the guides' dogs, which, after giving vent to plaintive cries, ended by howling uninterruptedly. I began to think that they must be in league with their masters to damn me. In a state of fury I seized my stick and made for the kennels with the intention of chastising the inhabitants, whatever their breed.

But scarcely had I gained the outside door when Willer caught me by the arm and made a sign to me to be quiet. I obeyed and stood listening intently, wondering what I should hear. Soon a cry came faintly from a far distance.

"Someone in distress," said one of the guides, who by this time had assembled in order to listen. "Light the torches, loose the dogs, and off!"

Few speeches can have had such an immediate effect. Everyone hurried to his post, some to the kitchen for rum, others to the loft for lanterns and torches, others again to the kennels to unfasten the dogs; then, all together with one voice, they sent out into the night a mighty shout to let the lost travelers know that help was on the way.

I took a torch along with the others, not because I presumed to believe that I could be of any help, but because I wanted to take part in a drama which was new to me. Unfortunately for me, we had traversed a bare quarter of a mile or so when I found myself crawling along paths practicable only to guides, and I soon perceived that if I persisted in going farther in my quest for others, others would have to begin searching for me, which in the circumstances would obviously have been a stupid waste of valuable time. I therefore took the less heroic but more prudent part of sitting on a rock and following with my eyes the wandering lights which darted about in the distance below me like will-o'-the-wisps on a marsh. For half an hour they danced crazily in all directions, disappearing into ravines, reappearing on summits, their gyrations accompanied by cries of men, the barking of dogs and pistol shots, all combining to give the spectacle a wild and weird nature.

At last the lights converged onto one spot; then, moving with a certain order, they came nearer and nearer my rock. Soon I was able to distinguish a fairly numerous troop of men, women and children, mules, horses and dogs, all talking, neighing, barking at once in different languages, so that it resembled a Noah's ark left high and dry in the Tower of Babel. I tagged myself onto the caravan and arrived with it at the inn. Sorted out, the medley was seen to be composed of ten Americans, a German and an

Englishman, all in the worst possible state, the American party having been discovered in the lake, the German in the snow and the Englishman suspended from a branch of a tree immediately above a precipice of three thousand feet.

The remainder of the night passed in the utmost tranquillity.

> [The next morning the entire party—a Frenchwoman, an American and his family, an Englishman and six guides—set out to visit the Rosenlaui glacier. They get caught in a thunderstorm.]

. . . WE decided to make a dash for the inn, where we eventually arrived, looking like running gutters. As Willer had sent on our luggage to Meiringen, we found ourselves without so much as a spare pocket handkerchief among us; not only so, but we found the storm had made the road to Meiringen impracticable. We did the only possible thing, which was to have our beds warmed and to stay in them until our clothes were dry. We dined, horizontally, like Roman emperors, then settled down for sleep.

In the deepest part of my slumbers the maid entered my room carrying a torch.

"What is it?" I grumbled like a man interrupted in one of his dearest labors.

"Nothing, sir, only you must get up."

"What on earth for?"

"It's the storm, sir. The stream has carried away the bridge, and the house may go at any time—"

"What! The house? This house?"

"Yes, sir. It happened once before, not to this one, but another."

"Quick, then! Where are my clothes?"

"You will only just have time to put them on."

"Bring me them, then."

Getting dressed, I swear to you, was never in all my life done so quickly. Half in and half out of my blouse, I tore down the staircase, deaf to the cries of the girl, and spying the kitchen door at the bottom, I opened it and rushed in.

"Good Lord!" I cried, stopping short.

I was up to my knees in water.

"Sir, sir!" cried the maid.

Still I took no notice, and seeing another door I made a dash for it.

"Sir, you will be swept away by the stream if you go out there!"

I let go the handle, and jumping on top of the ovens, I tried the window.

"Sir, there's a torrent just outside the window!"

"How the devil am I to get out, then? It would have been better to stay in bed; at least I should have had a boat."

"Sir, you can get out through the first-floor window."

"Why on earth didn't you tell me so at first, girl?"

"I've been trying to tell you for the last ten minutes, but you've been running all over the place without listening to me."

"That's true. It's my fault. Show me, then."

We went back up to the first floor, where she pointed out to me a plank of which the near end rested on the window sill and the far one on the mountainside. This was altogether too much like the famous bridge of Mohammed for a good Christian to try to cross it without certain reservations.

"Tell me, my dear," I said to the maid, "is there no other way out?"

"Why? Does it worry you? Your friend the Englishman ran across it."

"Did he, now? That was very clever of him. And what about the ladies? Did they go across too?"

"Oh, no. The guides carried them."

"And where are the guides?"

"Up in the mountain, cutting down trees to dam the torrent."

There was no way of getting out of it. I put on the best face I could, and went; only instead of making the journey on foot I made it astride. Anyone seeing me from below would undoubtedly have taken me for a sorcerer on his way to the witches' Sabbath astride a broomstick. Arrived safely at my destination, and once more in possession of my five wits, momentarily dissipated by this unusual mode of transport, I walked toward the place where I could see the gleam of torches. Never shall I forget the strange and magnificent sight that presented itself to my eyes. The waterfall, which on our arrival we had admired for its slender grace, had become a raging torrent; originally gentle and silver-laced with foam, now it rushed along, discolored and muddy, bringing down with it rocks which it propelled like pebbles, trees which it snapped like drumsticks. All this time our guides, stripped to the waist and armed with axes, were furiously cutting down trees which grew along the bank and controlling their fall so that they formed a dam. Four or five, ready to act as relays, held torches whose vacillating light lit the scene. But soon all available hands were needed; those holding torches seized their axes and looked around for suitable places to put their lights. Seeing their difficulty and the urgency of the situation, I took a torch from one of them, and running up to a fir which dominated the scene, I laid the torch against its resinous branches. Ten minutes later the tree was blazing from foot to tip, a huge candelabrum in keeping with the scene.

Soon cries of "Enough!" were raised. All axes stayed poised, all eyes were directed to the torrent: it was vanquished.

We returned to the inn, fairly certain now of an undisturbed night; nevertheless, two guides stayed on guard, and we took advantage of their precaution to sleep without batting an eyelid until eight o'clock the next morning.

From a Bullfight in Madrid to the Fair at Nizhni Novgorod

THÉOPHILE GAUTIER

FROM *Travels in Spain* AND *Travels in Russia*

1840 and 1858–60

Born in 1811, Théophile Gautier came to maturity in the hey-
day of French Romanticism and was powerfully drawn to the exotic, primitive and mysteriously remote. Like Hugo and his circle he was fascinated
by far-off places and strange peoples, but unlike them he was himself soon
visiting Spain and Italy, and eventually Greece, Constantinople, Algeria
and Russia.

Attracted to Romanticism from the very first, the youthful Gautier was
a conspicuous figure—with a great head of dark hair and a crimson doublet
—at that stormy first night when Hugo's Hernani flouted the classical tradition. And all his life he was to remain the flamboyant Bohemian, the passionate spokesman of the cult of "Art for art's sake." He began as a painter
but under the influence of Hugo soon turned to writing. In the course of
a long and prolific career he produced a small body of verse, countless plays
and novels (of which Mademoiselle de Maupin remains the best known)
and a vast quantity of drama and art criticism.

But it is as a feuilletonist and a writer on travel that his gifts are seen to
best advantage. With a painter's sense of color, a poet's mastery of images,
and a dramatist's feeling for incident, he is a caster of spells, magically
evoking distant scenes and filling them with bold detail and pulsating life.
Unabashedly approaching each place as an artist, a worshiper of the

form and color of the visible world, he ignores questions of politics, philosophy, economics and morals, and pours out a brilliant sensory record in a rich and glittering style. "Our duty," he once declared, "is to visit the planet that God has given us for our habitation and to bring out its infinite beauties in works as perfect as possible."

[Gautier went to Spain in 1840 and made of its cities— Burgos, Madrid, Toledo, Granada, Cordova, Seville, Cádiz— an exultant series of personal discoveries. Characteristic of his dazzling descriptions is that of a *corrida* (reprinted below) in Madrid. Later he returned to the same theme with an extraordinary account of a performance by the celebrated matador Montés.]

BULLFIGHT IN MADRID

THE circus . . . contains twelve thousand spectators, all comfortably seated and seeing easily; an indispensable matter in a spectacle intended purely for the eyes. The vast place is always full, and those who cannot procure *sombra* seats (shady seats) would rather cook alive on the benches in the burning sun than miss a fight. It is the proper thing for people who wish to be considered in good society to have their box at the bullfight, just as in Paris one has a box at the Italian opera.

When I issued from the corridor to take my seat, I felt dazzled and giddy. Torrents of light poured down upon the circus, for the sun is a superior light-giver which has the advantage of not shedding oil, and it will be long before gas itself will replace it. A vast rumor rose, like a mist of noise, above the arena; on the sunny side fluttered and sparkled thousands of fans, and little round parasols with reed handles. They looked like swarms of birds in changing colors, trying to take flight. There was not a single empty seat. I can assure you that to see twelve thousand spectators in a theater so vast that God alone can paint the ceiling of it with the splendid blue which he draws from the urn of eternity is in itself a wonderful spectacle.

The mounted national guards, very well horsed and very well dressed, were riding around the arena, preceded by two alguazils wearing hats and plumes of the time of Henry IV, black doublet and cloak and knee boots. They drove away a few obstinate *aficionados* and belated dogs. The arena having been cleared, the two alguazils went to fetch the *toreros,* composed of the picadors, the *chulos,* the *banderilleros* and the *espada,* who is the chief actor in the drama. These entered to the sound of trumpets. The picadors ride blindfolded horses, for the sight of the bull might frighten the steeds and cause them to swerve dangerously. . . .

The picadors, escorted by the *chulos,* proceed to the box of the *ayunta-miento,* where they perform a salute, and whence are thrown to them the keys of the *toril.* These keys are picked up and handed to the alguazil, who bears them to the official of the ring and gallops off as hard as he can, amid the yells and shouts of the crowd; for alguazils and all representatives of justice are no more popular in Spain than are the police and city guard with us. Meanwhile the two picadors take their stand on the left of the gates of the *toril,* which is opposite the Queen's box, the entrance of the bull being one of the most interesting points in the performance. They are posted close to each other, backed up against the *tablas,* firmly seated in their saddles, lance in rest and ready to receive bravely the fierce animal. The *chulos* and *banderilleros* stand at a distance or scatter about the arena.

All these preparations, which are longer in description than in reality, excite curiosity to the highest degree. All eyes are anxiously fixed upon the fatal gate, and of the twelve thousand glances there is not one turned in any other direction. The handsomest woman upon earth could not obtain the alms of a look at that moment.

I confess that for my part I felt my heart clutched, as it were, by an invisible hand, my temples throbbed, and cold and hot sweat broke out over me; the emotion I then felt was one of the fiercest I have ever experienced.

A shrill blare of trumpets was heard, the two red halves of the door were thrown open noisily, and the bull dashed into the arena, welcomed by a tremendous cheer. It was a superb animal, almost black, shining, with a huge dewlap, square head, sharp polished crescentlike horns, a restless tail, clean-limbed and bearing between the two shoulders a bunch of ribbons of the colors of its *ganaderia,* held to the skin by sharp points. It stopped for a second, breathed heavily two or three times, dazzled by the daylight and astonished by the tumult; then, catching sight of the first picador, it charged him furiously. The picador thus attacked was Sevilla. I cannot resist the pleasure of describing that famous Sevilla, who is really the ideal picador. Imagine a man about thirty years of age, handsome, highbred-looking, and as robust as Hercules, brown as a mulatto, with superb eyes and a face recalling that which Titian gave to his Caesars. The expression of jovial and disdainful serenity which marks his features and his attitude has really something heroic about it. On that day he wore an orange jacket embroidered and trimmed with silver, which has remained imprinted on my mind with ineffaceable accuracy. He lowered the point of his lance, steadied himself and bore the shock of the bull so admirably that the furious brute staggered past him bearing away a wound which before long rayed its black skin with red streaks. It stopped, hesitating, for a few moments, then charged with increased fury the second picador, posted a little farther along.

Antonio Rodríguez drove in a great lance thrust which opened a second wound close to the first, for the shoulder alone must be struck; but the bull charged upon him with lowered head and plunged his whole horn into the horse's belly. The *chulos* hastened up, fluttering their capes, and the stupid animal, attracted and distracted by this new bait, pursued them at full speed; but the *chulos*, setting foot upon the ledge we have mentioned, sprang lightly over the fence, leaving the animal greatly disconcerted at seeing no one.

The thrust of the horn had ripped open the horse's belly so that the entrails were running out and falling almost to the ground. I thought the picador would withdraw to take another horse. Not in the least. He touched the animal's ear to see if the blow was mortal. The horse was merely ripped up; the wound, though hideous to behold, might be healed. The intestines were pushed back into the belly, two or three stitches taken, and the poor brute served for another charge. He spurred it and galloped off to take his place farther away.

The bull began to perceive that he had not much to gain except lance thrusts in the direction of the picadors, and felt a desire to go back to the pasturage grounds. Instead of charging without hesitation, he started, after a short rush, to return to his *querencia* with imperturbable obstinacy. The *querencia* is the technical name for any corner of the arena which the bull chooses for a refuge and to which it always returns after the *cogida*, as its attack is called, and after the *suerte*, or *torero*'s attack, which is called *diestro*.

A cloud of *chulos* flashed before its eyes their capes of brilliant colors; one of them carried his insolence so far as to place his rolled-up mantle on the bull's head. The maddened animal got rid, as well as it could, of this unpleasant ornament and tossed the harmless piece of stuff, which it trampled with rage when it fell to the ground. Profiting by this renewed burst of wrath, a *chulo* began to tease it and to draw it toward the picadors.

Finding itself opposite its enemies, the bull hesitated, then making up its mind, charged Sevilla so fiercely that the horse rolled over, for Sevilla's arm is a bronze buttress which nothing can bend. Sevilla fell under the horse, which is the best way to fall, for the man is thus protected from being gored, and the body of the horse serves as a shield. The *chulos* intervened and the horse was got off with a ripped thigh; Sevilla was picked up, and he got back into the saddle with perfect coolness. The steed of Antonio Rodríguez, the other picador, was less fortunate. It was gored so fiercely in the chest that the horn went right in and disappeared completely in the wound. While the bull was trying to disengage its head, caught in the body of the horse, Antonio clutched with his hands the top of the fence, which he leaped with the help of the *chulos*, for the picadors, when thrown, weighed down by the metal linings of their boots, can move scarcely more easily than the knights of old, boxed up in their armor.

The poor horse, left to itself, could but stagger across the arena as if it were intoxicated, stumbling over its own entrails, torrents of black blood flowed from its wound and marked irregular zigzags upon the sand which betrayed the unevenness of its gait. Finally it fell near the *tablas*. It raised its head two or three times, its blue eye already glazed, turning up its lips white with foam, which showed its bare teeth; its tail faintly beat the ground, its hind legs were convulsively drawn up and struck out in a last kick, as if it had tried to break with its hard hoof the thick skull of death. Its agony was scarcely over when the *muchachos* on duty, seeing the bull busy elsewhere, hastened to take off the saddle and bridle. The dead horse remained stripped, lying on its side, its brown silhouette showing against the sand. It was so thin, so flattened out, that it might have been cut out of black paper. I had already noticed at Montfaucon the strangely fantastic forms which death gives to horses. Its head, so noble, so cleanly shaped, modeled and molded by the terrible finger of nothingness, seems to have been the dwelling of human thought; the mane which flows out, the tail which is spread out, have something picturesque and poetic about them. A dead horse is a corpse; every other animal from which life has departed is nothing but a dead brute.

I have spoken at length of the death of this horse because it gave me the most painful sensation which I felt at the bullfight. It was not the only victim, however; fourteen other horses were slain; one bull alone killed five of them.

The picador returned with a fresh mount, and there were several charges more or less fortunate, but the bull was beginning to tire and its fury to abate. The *banderilleros* arrived with their papered arrows, and soon the bull's neck was adorned with a collar of cut paper which the very efforts that he made to get rid of it drove in more firmly. A small *banderillero* called Majarón drove in the darts with great skill and boldness, and sometimes even he performed a cross-caper before withdrawing. Needless to say, he was loudly applauded. When the bull had in him seven or eight *banderillas*, the irons of which tore his head and the paper of which rattled in his ears, he began to gallop here and there and to bellow horridly. His black muzzle was wet with foam, and in his rage he dealt such a fierce blow with his horns to one of the doors that he threw it from the hinges. The carpenters, who were watching his movements, immediately replaced the door. A *chulo* drew him in another direction, but was pursued so fiercely that he scarcely had time to leap the fence. The maddened and exasperated bull made a prodigious effort and leaped the fence. All those who were in the passage sprang with marvelous speed into the arena, and the bull re-entered by another gate, driven off with sticks and hats by the spectators in the lowest row of benches.

The picadors withdrew, leaving the field to Juan Pastor, the *espada*, who proceeded to pay his respects to the *ayuntamiento* and asked leave to slay the bull. The permission being granted, he threw away his montera, by way of showing that he was going to stake his all, and walked up deliberately to the bull, concealing his sword in the red folds of the muleta.

The *espada* waved rapidly the scarlet stuff, which the bull blindly charged. A slight movement of the body sufficed to avoid the rush of the fierce animal, which soon charged again, striking fiercely at the light stuff, which it pushed aside without being able to pierce it. A favorable opportunity presenting itself, the *espada* took up his position exactly opposite the bull, waving his muleta in his left hand and holding his sword horizontally, the point on a level with the animal's horns. It is difficult to render in words the anguished curiosity, the frenzied tensions excited by this situation, which is worth all the dramas Shakespeare ever wrote. In a few seconds more, one of the two actors will be dead. Which shall it be, the man or the bull? There they are alone, facing each other; the man has no defensive armor, he is dressed as if for a ball, in pumps and silk stockings, a pin could pierce his satin jacket; all he has is a bit of stuff and a frail sword. All the material advantages in this duel are on the side of the bull. He has terrible horns, sharp as poniards, immense impetus, the rage of a brute unconscious of danger; but the man has his sword and his courage, and twelve thousand glances fixed upon him; beautiful women will applaud him presently with their white hands.

The muleta was pulled aside, uncovering the matador's chest; the bull's horns were within an inch of it. I believed him lost. A silvery gleam flashed, swift as thought, between the two crescents, and the bull fell on his knees uttering a bellow of pain, with the sword hilt between his shoulders, like St. Hubert's stag which bore a crucifix between his antlers, as he is represented in Albrecht Dürer's marvelous engraving.

A whirlwind of applause swept over the amphitheater; the nobility on the *palcos*, the middle classes on the *gradas cubiertas*, the *manolos* and *manolas* on the *tendido*, shouted and yelled, with true southern ardor and excitement, "*Bueno! Bueno! Viva el Barbero! Viva!*"

The blow just dealt by the *espada* is, as a matter of fact, very highly thought of and is called *estocada a vuela pies*. The bull dies without losing a drop of blood, which is the highest point of the art, and, falling on his knees, seems to acknowledge his adversary's superiority. The dilettanti say that this stroke was invented by Joaquín Rodríguez, a famous *torero* of the last century.

When the bull is not slain at one blow, there springs over the fence a mysterious being dressed in black, who has heretofore taken no part in the fight. It is the *cachetero*. He advances furtively, watches the last convulsions of the animal, notices whether it may still pick itself up, which does happen sometimes, and treacherously strikes it from behind with a cylindrical poniard ending in a lancet, which cuts the spinal cord and destroys life with the rapidity of lightning. The correct place is behind the head, a few inches from the parting of the horns.

The military band played at the death of the bull; one of the gates was opened, and four mules magnificently harnessed, all plumes, balls and woolen tufts and little red-and-yellow flags—the Spanish colors—galloped into the arena. They were destined to remove the bodies, to which they are made fast by a rope and a hook. The horses were first dragged out, and then the bull. These four mules, with their dazzling and sonorous equipment, dragging over the sand at mad speed all those bodies which but now had galloped so well themselves, had a strange, wild aspect which helped to diminish the gloom of their functions. The attendant came up with a basketful of earth and scattered it over the pools of blood, in which the *toreros* might slip; the picadors resumed their places by the gate, the orchestra played a few bars, and another bull dashed into the arena; for there are no intervals to this spectacle, nothing stops it, not even the death of a *torero*. . . .

[Gautier was to return again and again to Spain. But he also made journeys to North Africa and Italy (where Venice so enchanted him that he devoted almost his entire book on

Italy to it), to Constantinople and to Russia. Returning to Russia for a second time to cover the coronation of Alexander II in 1860, he made a long journey on the Volga, and it is from this part of his *Travels in Russia* that the following is taken. Nizhni Novgorod is today known as Gorki.]

THE FAIR AT NIZHNI NOVGOROD

I HASTENED to descend to the fair grounds, situated at the foot of the city, on a sort of beach formed by the confluence of the Oka and the Volga. No guide was necessary to find the place, for everybody was going in that direction.

At the foot of the hill my attention was attracted by a small chapel; on the upper steps were bowing, with a mechanical movement of salutation, resembling that of wooden birds which mechanically raise and drop their heads, frightfully squalid beggars, regular human rags, which the funereal ragpicker had doubtlessly refused, through disgust, to pick up and cast into his basket; a few nuns wearing a tall hood of black velvet and a narrow, close-fitting serge dress, who shook before me an alms box in which rattled the kopecks of the previous givers (these nuns are to be found wherever the congregating of the public leads them to hope for a successful quest). Five or six old women, who would have made Panzoust's Sybil appear young and pretty, completed the picture. A great number of small lighted tapers made the silver-gilt plates of the iconostas, which was further lighted by lamps, blaze in the interior like a mass of goldsmith work. I found it difficult to make my way into the small building, which was crowded with the faithful who were making the sign of the cross as hard as they could, and swinging like dervishes. A thread of water, no doubt possessing some miraculous property, that dropped into a stone shell placed against the wall like a holy-water vessel, struck me as being the special object of devotion in the place.

Public droshkies and telegas were flying along, making deep ruts in the mud and driving foot passengers to the edge of the road. Sometimes a more elegant droshky came along, bearing two ladies showily dressed, with widespread crinolines, rouged and painted like idols, smiling to show their teeth and casting to right and left that courtesan glance which is the net with which they catch the unwary. The Nizhni Novgorod fair draws these birds of prey from all the evil places in Russia and from even farther away; whole cargoes of them come by steamer, and a special quarter is reserved for them. The ogre of lust must have its prey of more or less fresh flesh. By one of those contrasts due to chance, that admirable worker of antithesis, the swift droshky often shaved a peaceful cart drawn by a little hairy horse bowing its head under its painted *duga*, and drawing a whole patriarchal group: the grandfather, the father, and the mother carrying a baby.

On that day—though the others were no doubt good also—the whiskey monopoly must have taken in a large amount of cash; a great number of drunkards were staggering along the boardwalks, or splashing about in the muddy road; some, still more drunk and incapable of walking alone, got along with two friends that served as crutches. The faces of some were livid and those of others bloodshot and apoplectic-looking, according to their temperament or their degree of intoxication. One young fellow, overwhelmed by too frequent libations of vodka, had rolled from the sidewalk on to the sloping beach, through the piles of wood, bales and heaps of filth; he fell, he got up, he fell again, laughing idiotically and uttering inarticulate cries like a *teriaki* or a *haschachin* under the influence of the drug. His hands full of earth, his face soiled with mud, his clothes torn and stained, he crawled on all fours, sometimes managing to reach the top of the quay, at other times again tumbling down into the river up to his waist, without noting the coldness of the water or being aware of the danger of drowning, which is the most disagreeable of all deaths for a drunkard. . . .

The bridge over the Oka was a bridge of boats on which were laid beams and boardwalks. The crowd filled it from one side to the other, and in the center the carriages dashed along at a speed which nothing moderates in Russia and which does not involve accidents, thanks to the extreme skill of the drivers, who are, besides, helped by the docility of the foot passengers in drawing aside. The sound was as if the car of Capanea were passing over the brazen bridge. Both sides of the river disappeared under the immense multitude of boats and the inextricable maze of rigging. Perched on the high saddles of their little horses, the Cossacks charged with the police of the fair and, known from afar by their long lances as they came, rode gravely among the droshkies, telegas, vehicles of all sorts and foot passengers of both sexes. But there was not a human sound; anywhere else such a vast multitude would have given forth a mighty murmur, a tumultuous clatter like that of the sea; a vapor of noise would have floated above that prodigious congregation of individuals. But crowds composed of Russian elements are always silent.

At the end of the bridge hung signs of acrobats and paintings of freaks, colored in the most barbaric manner—boa constrictors, bearded women, giants, dwarfs, strong men and three-headed calves—which to me had an exotic and peculiar character, thanks to the gigantic inscriptions in Russian letters. Small stalls for the sale of the usual cheap trifles and small wares, of holy images, ridiculously low-priced, of cakes, green apples, sour milk, beer, kvass, rose to right and left of the planked causeway; at the back of them stuck out the ends of the joists, which had not been sawed off, so that they looked like baskets the ribs of which have not yet been filled in by the basketmaker.

The boot dealers' stall, with their shoes, boots and felt socks, attracted my attention as being peculiar to the country. There were the daintiest women's shoes of white felt, adorned with red or blue stitching, not unlike the shoes called *sorties-de-bal* which dancing girls put on over their thin satin shoes to go to the carriage which awaits them—Cinderella alone could have put her foot into them.

The fair at Nizhni Novgorod is a city in itself. The long streets cut each other at right angles and end in squares with a fountain in the center. The wooden houses that border them are composed of a ground floor, containing a shop and a storeroom, and an overhanging story supported by posts, in which the dealer and his clerks sleep; this overhanging story and the posts upon which it rests form in front of the stalls a show place and a continuous covered gallery; the bales which are unloaded in front may, in case of rain, be put under shelter there, and the passers-by, safe from the carriages, talk over what they want or satisfy their curiosity without running any greater risk than that of being elbowed.

The streets sometimes end in the plain. A most curious thing it is to see outside the fairgrounds the camps of carts, with the half-wild horses unharnessed and fastened to the sideboards, the drivers sleeping on a bit of coarse stuff or fur. Unfortunately the costumes are more ragged than picturesque, although they do not lack a certain amount of characteristic savageness. There are no bright colors, save here and there a pink shirt; ochre, sienna, Cassel earth and bitumen would suffice to paint these things; something, however, can be made out of the smock frocks, the tulupes, the bands crossed around the legs, the esparto shoes, the yellow-bearded faces, and the little thin horses whose bright eyes shine upon you through the long hair of their wild manes. . . .

An enormous business is done [at the fair]—sales of ten thousand cases of tea, for instance, which remain on the river, or five or six vessels laden with grain worth several millions, or else a quantity of furs to be delivered at such a price, which are not shown. The great movement of business is therefore, so to speak, invisible. Teahouses furnished with a fountain for ablutions and intended for the Mussulmans, serve as a meeting place and stock exchange to the contracting parties. Jets of vapor hiss from the samovar; muzhiks, wearing red or white shirts, move around with trays in their hands; long-bearded merchants in blue caftans, seated opposite Asiatics wearing black Astrakhan lambskin caps, drain their saucerfuls of the hot infusion with a small piece of sugar between their teeth, with as much indifference as if immense interests were not being discussed in these apparently idle conversations. In spite of the diversity of races and dialects, Russian is the only language spoken in business transactions, and over and above the confused murmur of talk floats, perceptible even to the stranger, the sacred word *rubl' serebrom* (silver ruble).

The various faces in the crowd excited my curiosity more than the sight of the shops. The Tartars, with prominent cheekbones, wrinkled eyes, concave noses such as we imagine the moon's profile to have, thick lips, yellow complexion turning grayish, and close-shaved temples, were to be met with in great numbers, with their little *piqué* chintz caps placed on top of the skull, their brown caftans and their metal-plated belts. The Persians were easily known by their long oval faces, their great arched noses, their brilliant eyes, thick black beards and noble Oriental physiognomy; one could not have helped noticing them even though attention had not been drawn to them by their conical lambskin caps, their striped silk gowns and their cashmere sashes. A few Armenians in tattered tunics with hanging sleeves; wasp-waisted Circassians wearing a sort of low buckskin cap, stood out in the crowd; but what I was eagerly looking for, especially when I reached the particular quarter where tea is sold, was the Chinese. For a moment I thought my wish would be fulfilled, as I saw the shops with upcurved roofs, fretted trellises, with smiling figures on the acroteria, which might justify the fancy that one had been transported by the touch of a wand into a city of the Celestial Empire. But on the threshold of the shops and behind the counters I could see none but kindly Russian faces; there was not a single plaited pigtail, not a single face with oblique eyes and eyebrows in the shape of circumflexes, not a single hat in the form of a stew-pan cover, not a single blue or violet silk gown; there were no Chinese at all. . . .

Having finished dinner, I went back to the fair, still expecting to find something new. A feeling akin to that which keeps people at the Opéra balls in spite of the heat, the dust and the fatigue, prevented my returning to the hotel. After having traversed a few lanes I reached a square on which arose on one hand a church and on the other a mosque. The church was surmounted by a cross, the mosque by a crescent; the two symbols shone peacefully in the air of evening, gilded by an impartial or indifferent ray of the sun, which is about one and the same thing. The two forms of worship seem to live like good neighbors, for religious tolerance is widely practiced in Russia, which counts even idolators among its subjects—the Parsees, who worship fire.

The door of the Orthodox church was open and evening prayer was being said in it. It was not easy to enter, for the compact multitude filled the building as completely as liquid fills a vase. Yet by using my elbows I managed to make my way in. The interior of the church looked like a golden furnace: forests of candles and constellations of chandeliers made the gilding of the iconostas flame again as the metallic reflections mingled with the rays of light in sudden flashes and dazzling phosphorescence. This mass of light formed in the upper part of the cupola a dense red mist into which ascended the glorious chants of the Greek liturgy sung by the popes and repeated in a low voice by the congregation. The bowings called for by the ritual made the whole of that assembly of believers bend and rise at the prescribed moment with a regularity comparable to that of a well-executed military maneuver.

After a few moments I went out, for I already felt the perspiration streaming over my body as if I were in a vapor bath. I should much have liked to visit the mosque also, but it was not Allah's hour.

What was I to do with the remainder of my evening? A droshky passing by, I hailed it, and without asking me where I wanted to go the driver started his horse at a gallop: that is quite the way the *izvozchiks* do; they rarely inquire whither they are to take their fare. A *"Na leva"* or *"Na prava"* tells them at need which way to go. My driver, after having traversed the bridge that leads to Nikita's, began to gallop across the country along rudimentary roads marked only by horrid ruts; I let him go on, for I took it for granted he would drive me somewhere, and indeed the intelligent fellow had bethought himself that a gentleman of my kidney could not have intended to go anywhere at that hour of the evening but to the quarter reserved to the tea, music and pleasure houses.

Night was falling. We traversed with terrific velocity rough ground with many pools of water, in a penumbra through which partially built houses showed like skeletons. At last lights began to pierce the darkness with red points; bursts of music reached my ears, telling of orchestras. We had got to the place. From the house, with open doors and wretched windows, issued the drone of balaleikas mingled with guttural cries; strange silhouettes showed against the windows; on the narrow plank platform staggered intoxicated shadows and showed extravagant toilettes, alternately lost in darkness and brilliantly lighted....

In the squares, at the crossings of streets, the waters, owing to the flat-

ness of the ground, collected and formed deep quagmires in which the
wheels of carriages, stirring up the most noisome stenches, sank up to the
axles. Caring little to be upset in such a quagmire, amid a block of half-
submerged droshkies, I ordered my driver to turn around and to take me
back to the Smyrnof Hotel. By his amazed glance I understood he looked
upon me as an individual of not much account, and as an absurdly rigorous
person; but he obeyed and I wound up my evening by walking round the
kremlin [the old citadel of this city]. . . .

RIGHT, a Venetian courtesan displaying her stilt-like *cioppini*. Bettmann Archive. BELOW, gay Venetian canal scene about 1610. Note the huge musical instrument in the gondola at left bottom and the tipplers around a table in the boat at center bottom. Bettmann Archive. [See pages 489-496.]

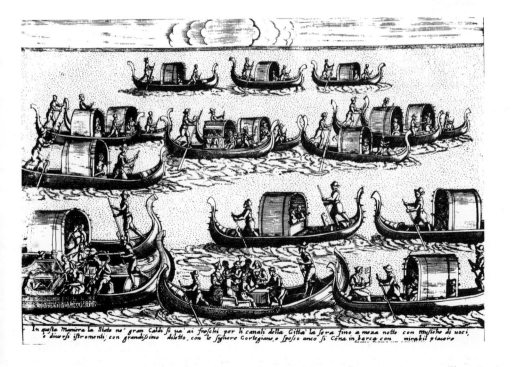

In questa Maniera la State ne' gran Caldi si ua ai freschi per li canali della Citta la sera fino a meza notte con musiche di uoci, e diuersi istromenti, con grandissimo diletto, con le signore Cortegiane, e spesso anco si Cena in barca con mirabil piacere

ABOVE, Hester Lynch Thrale Piozzi and her Italian husband, about six years after their wedding tour of Italy. Drawn by George Dance; courtesy of the National Portrait Gallery, London. BELOW, an early view of Vesuvius erupting, as described by Mrs. Piozzi. [*See pages 497-505.*]

ABOVE, scene on the Grand Canal showing at right the Bucentaur, or Doge's Galley, and other vessels celebrating the marriage of Venice with the sea. BELOW, the Piazza San Marco. Both are mid-eighteenth-century engravings by Antonio Canaletto. [See pages 497-505.]

ABOVE, the fashion in Paris hats in 1784. BELOW, a view of a section of Paris on the eve of the Revolution, showing the famous church of Le Temple. [See pages 506-516.]

ABOVE, an English boxing match such as that described by Louis Simond, about 1815. [See pages 532-540.] BELOW, London high life: a ball at Almack's about 1820. [See pages 541-548.]

ABOVE, Prince Pückler-Muskau, German noble and dandy, during his visit to London in 1827. BELOW, an English theater, the Royal New Haymarket, at the time of the Prince's visit. Bettmann Archive. [*See pages 541-548.*]

ABOVE, Théophile Gautier as he looked at about the time he visited Nizhni-Novgorod. Etching from a photograph by Nadar. RIGHT, entertainment booths at the fair at Nizhni-Novgorod as they appeared in the late 1860s. [*See pages 558-570.*]

Two aquatints by Francisco Goya showing feats of the Spanish bullfight ring in the early nineteenth century. The above shows the *salto de la garrocha* as performed in Madrid. Courtesy of The Metropolitan Museum of Art, Rogers Fund, 1921. [*See pages* 558-570.]

Men and women in a Finnish steam bath. The clouds of vapor are created by pouring water on heated stones, and the bathers are massaged with switches. Bettmann Archive. [See pages 612-618.]

ABOVE and RIGHT, the Austrian saloon (note the mugs of beer) and the Russian café at the Paris World's Fair of 1879. BELOW, a turtle being beheaded in the kitchens of a Paris restaurant. [See pages 628-639.]

Changing styles in mountain-climbing costume. ABOVE LEFT, French lithograph of an early nineteenth-century climber with fur knapsack. [See pages 549-557.] ABOVE RIGHT, French woman Alpinist of about 1900. BELOW, photograph of tourists on the Mer de Glace at Chamonix in the 1880s. [See pages 619-627.] All pictures from Bettmann Archive.

Photograph showing the costume worn by women of Mostar, in Herzgovina, as seen by Rebecca West during her visit to Yugoslovia. By permission of Macmillan & Co. Ltd. [See pages 619-627.]

Photograph by Herbert Kubly of part of the Easter procession at Trapani in Sicily. [See pages 668-677.]

Roman Carnival and Other Scenes

CHARLES DICKENS

FROM *Pictures from Italy*

1844–45

As a writer on travel, Charles Dickens is best known for his American Notes *(see pages 844–52) with its often critical and sometimes harsh views of the American scene. Because it is a controversial work, it has overshadowed* Pictures from Italy, *his only other book of travel, despite the fact that the latter contains a few descriptions of Italian life that are among the best of their kind.*

Dickens was only thirty-two years old but already famous for The Pickwick Papers, Oliver Twist *and other novels when he went south. He approached Italy in a genial mood and with none of the grievances that had marred his American visit. Taking his family along, he spent a year touring areas from Venice to Naples but passing most of his time in Genoa and Rome. Although, like Mark Twain, he could not resist any satiric thrust that might puncture some hypocrisy or absurdity, he is for the most part sympathetic and responsive. Thus he generally takes his mood from the place and time, writing of Venice as though it were a dream and of Pompeii with a poignant sense of a city transfixed forever in a moment.*

In the first excerpt below he catches the wild gaiety of a Roman carnival, his prose rising, like the occasion itself, to a dazzling crescendo of color and sound; in the second he evokes some of the scenes that make up the inexhaustible variety of Rome.

THE CARNIVAL

THE Corso is a street a mile long; a street of shops, and palaces, and private houses, sometimes opening into a broad piazza. There are verandahs and balconies, of all shapes and sizes, to almost every house—not on one storey alone, but often to one room or another on every storey—put there in general with so little order or regularity, that if, year after year, and season after season, it had rained balconies, hailed balconies, snowed balconies, blown balconies, they could scarcely have come into existence in a more disorderly manner.

This is the great fountain-head and focus of the Carnival. But all the streets in which the Carnival is held, being vigilantly kept by dragoons, it is necessary for carriages, in the first instance, to pass, in line, down another thoroughfare, and so come into the Corso at the end remote from the Piazza del Popolo; which is one of its terminations. Accordingly, we fell into the string of coaches, and, for some time, jogged on quietly enough; now crawling on at a very slow walk; now trotting half-a-dozen yards; now backing fifty; and now stopping altogether: as the pressure in front obliged us . . .

Some quarter of an hour of this sort of progress, brought us to the Corso; and anything so gay, so bright, and lively as the whole scene there, it would be difficult to imagine. From all the innumerable balconies: from the remotest and highest, no less than from the lowest and nearest: hangings of bright red, bright green, bright blue, white and gold, were fluttering in the brilliant sunlight. From windows, and from parapets, and tops of houses, streamers of the richest colours, and draperies of the gaudiest and most sparkling hues, were floating out upon the street. The buildings seemed to have been literally turned inside out, and to have all their gaiety towards the high-way. Shop-fronts were taken down, and the windows filled with company, like boxes at a shining theatre; doors were carried off their hinges, and long tapestried groves, hung with garlands of flowers and evergreens, displayed within; builders' scaffoldings were gorgeous temples, radiant in silver, gold, and crimson; and in every nook and corner, from the pavement to the chimney-tops, where women's eyes could glisten, there they danced, and laughed, and sparkled, like the light in water. Every sort of bewitching madness of dress was there. Little preposterous scarlet jackets; quaint old stomachers, more wicked than the smartest bodices; Polish pelisses, strained and tight as ripe gooseberries; tiny Greek caps, all awry, and clinging to the dark hair, Heaven knows how; every wild, quaint, bold, shy, pettish, madcap fancy had its illustration in a dress; and every fancy was as dead forgotten by its owner, in the tumult of merriment, as if the three old aqueducts that still remain entire had brought Lethe into Rome, upon their sturdy arches, that morning.

The carriages were now three abreast; in broader places four; often stationary for a long time together; always one close mass of variegated brightness; showing, the whole street-full, through the storm of flowers, like flowers of a larger growth themselves. In some, the horses were richly caparisoned in magnificent trappings; in others they were decked from head to tail, with flowing ribbons. Some were driven by coachmen with enormous double faces: one face leering at the horses: the other cocking its extraordinary eyes into the carriage: and both rattling again, under the hail of sugar-plums. Other drivers were attired as women, wearing long ringlets and no bonnets, and looking more ridiculous in any real difficulty with the horses (of which, in such a concourse, there were a great many) than tongue can tell, or pen describe. Instead of sitting *in* the carriages, upon the seats, the handsome Roman women, to see and to be seen the better, sit in the heads of the barouches, at this time of general license, with their feet upon the cushions—and oh the flowing skirts and dainty waists, the blessed shapes and laughing faces, the free, good-humoured, gallant figures that they make! There were great vans, too, full of handsome girls—thirty or more together, perhaps—and the broad-sides that were poured into, and poured out of, these fairy fire-ships, splashed the air with flowers and bonbons for ten minutes at a time. Carriages, delayed long in one place, would begin a deliberate engagement with other carriages, or with people at the lower windows; and the spectators at some upper balcony or window, joining in the fray, and attacking both parties, would empty down great bags of confetti, that descended like a cloud, and in an instant made them white as millers. Still, carriages on carriages, dresses on dresses, colours on colours, crowds upon crowds, without end. Men and boys clinging to the wheels of coaches, and holding on behind, and following in their wake, and diving in among the horses' feet to pick up scattered flowers to sell again; maskers on foot (the drollest, generally) in fantastic exaggerations of court-dresses, surveying the throng through enormous eye-glasses, and always transported with an ecstasy of love, on the discovery of any particularly old lady at a window; long strings of Policinelli, laying about them with blown bladders at the ends of sticks; a waggon-full of madmen, screaming and tearing to the life; a coach-full of grave Mamelukes, with their horse-tail standard set up in the midst; a party of gipsy-women engaged in terrific conflict with a ship-full of sailors; a man-monkey on a pole, surrounded by strange animals with pigs' faces, and lions' tails, carried under their arms, or worn gracefully over their shoulders; carriages on carriages, dresses on dresses, colours on colours, crowds upon crowds, without end. Not many actual characters sustained, or represented, perhaps, considering the number dressed, but the main pleasure of the scene consisting in its perfect good temper; in its bright, and infinite, and flashing variety; and in its entire abandonment to the mad humour of the time—an abandonment so perfect, so contagious, so irresistible, that the steadiest foreigner fights up to his middle in flowers and sugar-plums, like the wildest Roman of them all, and thinks of nothing else till half-past four o'clock, when he is suddenly reminded (to his great regret) that this is not the whole business of his existence, by hearing the trumpets sound, and seeing the dragoons begin to clear the street.

How it ever *is* cleared for the race that takes place at five, or how the horses ever go through the race, without going over the people, is more than I can say. But the carriages get out into the by-streets, or up into the Piazza del Popolo, and some people sit in temporary galleries in the latter place, and tens of thousands line the Corso on both sides, when the horses are brought out into the Piazza—to the foot of that same column which, for centuries, looked down upon the games and chariot-races in the Circus Maximus.

At a given signal they are started off. Down the live lane, the whole length of the Corso, they fly like the wind: riderless, as all the world knows: with shining ornaments upon their backs, and twisted in their plaited manes: and with heavy little balls stuck full of spikes, dangling at their sides, to goad them on. The jingling of these trappings, and the rattling of their hoofs upon the hard stones; the dash and fury of their speed along the echoing street; nay, the very cannon that are fired—these noises are nothing to the roaring of the multitude: their shouts: the clapping of their hands. But it is soon over—almost instantaneously. More cannon shake the town. The horses have plunged into the carpets put across the street to stop them; the goal is reached; the prizes are won (they are given, in part, by the poor Jews, as a compromise for not running foot-races themselves); and there is an end to that day's sport.

But if the scene be bright, and gay, and crowded, on the last day but one, it attains, on the concluding day, to such a height of glittering colour, swarming life, and frolicsome uproar, that the bare recollection of it makes me giddy at this moment. The same diversions, greatly heightened and intensified in the ardour with which they are pursued, go on until the same hour. The race is repeated; the cannon are fired; the shouting and clapping of hands are renewed; the cannon are fired again; the race is over; and the prizes are won. But the carriages: ankle-deep with sugar-plums within, and so be-flowered and dusty without, as to be hardly recognizable for the same vehicles that they were, three hours ago: instead of scampering off in all directions, throng into the Corso, where they are soon wedged together in a scarcely moving mass. For the diversion of the *moccoletti*, the last gay madness of the Carnival, is now at hand; and sellers of little tapers like what are called Christmas candles in England, are shouting lustily on every side, *"Moccoli, moccoli! Ecco moccoli!"*— a new item in the tumult, quite abolishing that other item of *"Ecco fiori! Ecco fior-r-r!"* which has been making itself audible over all the rest, at intervals, the whole day through.

As the bright hangings and dresses are all fading into one dull, heavy, uniform colour in the decline of the day, lights begin flashing, here and there: in the windows, on the house-tops, in the balconies, in the carriages, in the hands of the foot-passengers: little by little: gradually, gradually: more and more: until the whole long street is one great glare and blaze of fire. Then, everybody present has but one engrossing object: that is, to extinguish other people's candles, and to keep his own alight; and everybody: man, woman, or child, gentleman or lady, prince or peasant, native or foreigner: yells and screams, and roars incessantly, as a taunt to the subdued, *"Senza moccolo, senza moccolo!"* (Without a light! Without a light!) until nothing is heard but a gigantic chorus of those two words, mingled with peals of laughter.

The spectacle, at this time, is one of the most extraordinary that can be imagined. Carriages coming slowly by, with everybody standing on the seats or on the box, holding up their lights at arms' length, for greater safety; some in paper shades; some with a bunch of undefended little tapers, kindled altogether; some with blazing torches; some with feeble little candles; men on foot, creeping along, among the wheels, watching their opportunity, to make a spring at some particular light, and dash it out; other people climbing up into carriages, to get hold of them by main force; others, chasing some unlucky wanderer, round and round his own coach, to blow out the light he has begged or stolen somewhere, before he can ascend to his own company, and enable them to light their extinguished tapers; others, with their hats off, at a carriage-door, humbly beseeching some kind-hearted lady to oblige them with a light for a cigar, and when she is in the fulness of doubt whether to comply or no, blowing out the candle she is guarding so tenderly with her little hand; other people at the windows, fishing for candles with lines and hooks, or letting down long willow-wands with handkerchiefs at the end, and flapping them out, dexterously, when the bearer is at the height of his triumph; others, biding their time in corners, with immense extinguishers like halberds, and suddenly coming down upon glorious torches; others, gathered round one coach, and sticking to it; others, raining oranges and nosegays at an obdurate little lantern, or regularly storming a pyramid of men, holding up one man among them, who carries one feeble little wick above his head, with which he defies them all! *Senza moccolo! Senza moccolo!* Beautiful women, standing up in coaches, pointing in derision at extinguished lights, and clapping their hands, as they pass on, crying, "*Senza moccolo! Senza moccolo!*"; low balconies full of lovely faces and gay dresses, struggling with assailants in the streets; some repressing them as they climb up, some bending down, some leaning over, some shrinking back—delicate arms and bosoms—graceful figures—glowing lights, fluttering dresses, *Senza moccolo, senza moccolo, senza moc-co-lo-o-o-o!*—when in the wildest enthusiasm of the cry, and fullest ecstasy of the sport, the Ave Maria rings from the church steeples, and the Carnival is over in an instant—put out like a taper, with a breath!

Roman Scenes

ONE day we walked out, a little party of three, to Albano, fourteen miles distant; possessed by a great desire to go there by the ancient Appian Way, long since ruined and overgrown. We started at half-past seven in the morning, and within an hour or so were out upon the open Campagna. For twelve miles we went climbing on, over an unbroken succession of mounds, and heaps, and hills, of ruin. Tombs and temples, overthrown and prostrate; small fragments of columns, friezes, pediments; great blocks of granite and marble; mouldering arches, grass-grown and decayed; ruin enough to build a spacious city from; lay strewn about us. Sometimes, loose walls, built up from these fragments by the shepherds, came across our path; sometimes, a ditch between two mounds of broken stones, obstructed our progress; sometimes, the fragments themselves, rolling from beneath our feet, made it a toilsome matter to advance; but it was always ruin. Now, we tracked a piece of the old road, above the ground; now traced it, underneath a grassy covering, as if that were its grave; but all the way was ruin. In the distance, ruined aqueducts went stalking on their giant course along the plain; and every breath of wind that swept towards us, stirred early flowers and grasses, springing up, spontaneously, on miles of ruin. The unseen larks above us, who alone disturbed the awful silence, had their nests in ruin; and the fierce herdsmen, clad in sheep-skins, who now and then scowled out upon us from their sleeping nooks, were housed in ruin. . . .

To come again on Rome, by moonlight, after such an expedition, is a fitting close to such a day. The narrow streets, devoid of foot-ways, and choked, in every obscure corner, by heaps of dunghill-rubbish, contrast so strongly, in their cramped dimensions, and their filth, and darkness, with the broad square before some haughty church: in the center of which, a hieroglyphic-covered obelisk, brought from Egypt in the days of the Emperors, looks strangely on the foreign scene about it; or perhaps an ancient pillar, with its honoured statue overthrown, supports a Christian saint: Marcus Aurelius giving place to Paul, and Trajan to St. Peter. Then, there are the ponderous buildings reared from the spoliation of the Coliseum, shutting out the moon, like mountains: while here and there, are broken arches and rent walls, through which it gushes freely, as the life comes pouring from a wound. The little town of miserable houses, walled, and shut in by barred gates, is the quarter where the Jews are locked up nightly, when the clock strikes eight—a miserable place, densely populated, and reeking with bad odours, but where the people are indus-trious and money-getting. In the day-time, as you make your way along the narrow streets, you see them all at work: upon the pavement, oftener than in their dark and frowsy shops: furbishing old clothes, and driving bargains.

Crossing from these patches of thick darkness, out into the moon once more, the fountain of Trevi, welling from a hundred jets, and rolling over mimic rocks, is silvery to the eye and ear. In the narrow little throat of street, beyond, a booth, dressed out with flaring lamps, and boughs of trees, attracts a group of sulky Romans round its smoky coppers of hot broth, and cauliflower stew; its trays of fried fish, and its flasks of wine. As you rattle round the sharply-twisting corner, a lumbering sound is heard. The coachman stops abruptly, and uncovers, as a van comes slowly by, preceded by a man who bears a large cross; by a torch-bearer; and a priest: the latter chaunting as he goes. It is the Dead Cart, with the bodies of the poor, on their way to burial in the Sacred Field outside the walls, where they will be thrown into the pit that will be covered with a stone tonight, and sealed up for a year. . . .

From one part of the city, looking out beyond the walls, a squat and stunted pyramid (the burial-place of Caius Cestius) makes an opaque triangle in the moonlight. But, to an English traveller, it serves to mark the grave of Shelley too, whose ashes lie beneath a little garden near it. Nearer still, almost within its shadow, lie the bones of Keats, "whose name is writ in water," that shines brightly in the landscape of a calm Italian night.

Men and Manners in Wild Wales

GEORGE BORROW

FROM *Wild Wales*

1854

Combining *extraordinary gifts, passionate prejudices and immense zest, George Borrow cut a unique figure on the mid-Victorian scene. The son of a recruiting officer whose family went along on his travels, Borrow early in life displayed the gift of tongues and had soon acquired a score of languages, learning Welsh, for example, by reading twice through a Welsh version of* Paradise Lost. *He also developed an affinity for gypsies that led to an astonishing understanding of their lingo and their life.*

After spending a few years in a solicitor's office and in literary hack work he took to the open road and wandered through southern Europe as well as England. At the age of thirty he was commissioned by the British Bible Society to translate the New Testament into Manchu—and characteristically walked the 112 miles to London for his first interview with the society. Completing the translation after two years in Russia, Borrow was sent by the society on an even stranger mission in 1835—that of circulating the Bible in Catholic Spain. He described the five years devoted to this task in The Bible in Spain *(1842), which, despite its repetitiousness and Borrow's towering vanity as a linguist, made him famous. Later he added to the legend with two romanticized autobiographies,* Lavengro *and* The Romany Rye.

In 1842 he married a widow and settled on her estate in Suffolk, but occasionally he took to the road again. On one of these tours, in 1854, he spent almost four months in Wales, following every byway that took his fancy and covering almost 250 miles. The book that resulted, Wild Wales, *gives unforgettable glimpses of Borrow as an outspoken foe of affectation, railroads and Catholicism and a lover of walking, good ale, wild countryside, the memory of great poets and, above all, talk with people. Borrow sometimes let his prejudices—and love of the dramatic—get the better of him, but the result, as in the passages below, often makes wonderfully good reading.*

[Starting from Chester, Borrow walks to Llangollen and, leaving his wife and stepdaughter there, tramps up and back across the countryside. The following incident occurs when he goes in search of the birthplace of the poet Huw Morris.]

For the Sake of a Poet

At the entrance of this valley and just before you reach the Pandy, which it nearly overhangs, is an enormous crag. After I had looked at the place for some time with considerable interest we proceeded towards the south, and in about twenty minutes reached a neat kind of house, on our right hand, which John Jones told me stood on the ground of Huw Morris. Telling me to wait, he went to the house, and asked some questions. After a little time I followed him and found him discoursing at the door with a stout dame about fifty-five years of age, and a stout buxom damsel of about seventeen, very short of stature.

"This is the gentleman," said he, "who wishes to see anything there may be here connected with Huw Morris."

The old dame made me a curtsey and said in very distinct Welsh, "We have some things in the house which belonged to him, and we will show them to the gentleman willingly."

"We first of all wish to see his chair," said John Jones.

"The chair is in a wall in what is called the *hen ffordd* (old road)," said the old gentlewoman; "it is cut out of the stone wall, you will have maybe some difficulty in getting to it, but the girl shall show it to you." The girl now motioned to us to follow her, and conducted us across the road to some stone steps, over a wall to a place which looked like a plantation.

"This was the old road," said Jones; "but the place has been enclosed. The new road is above us on our right hand beyond the wall."

We were in a maze of tangled shrubs, the boughs of which, very wet from the rain which was still falling, struck our faces, as we attempted to make our way between them; the girl led the way, bare-headed and bare-armed, and soon brought us to the wall, the boundary of the new road. Along this she went with considerable difficulty, owing to the tangled shrubs, and the nature of the ground, which was very precipitous, shelving down to the other side of the enclosure. In a little time we were wet to the skin, and covered with the dirt of birds, which they had left whilst roosting in the trees; on went the girl, sometimes creeping, and trying to keep herself from falling by holding against the young trees; once or twice she fell, and we after her, for there was no path, and the ground, as I have said before, very shelvy; still as she went her eyes were directed towards the wall, which was not always very easy to be seen, for thorns, tall nettles and shrubs were growing up against it. Here and there she stopped, and said something, which I could not always make out, for her Welsh was anything but clear; at length I heard her say that she was afraid we had passed the chair, and indeed presently we came to a place where the enclosure terminated in a sharp corner.

"Let us go back," said I; "we must have passed it."

I now went first, breaking down with my weight the shrubs nearest to the wall.

"Is not this the place?" said I, pointing to a kind of hollow in the wall, which looked something like the shape of a chair.

"Hardly," said the girl, "for there should be a slab, on the back, with letters, but there's neither slab nor letters here."

The girl now again went forward, and we retraced our way, doing the best we could to discover the chair, but all to no purpose; no chair was to be found. We had now been, as I imagined, half an hour in the enclosure, and had nearly got back to the place from which we had set out, when we suddenly heard the voice of the old lady exclaiming, "What are ye doing there, the chair is on the other side of the field; wait a bit, and I will come and show it you"; getting over the stone stile, which led into the wilderness, she came to us, and we now went along the wall at the lower end; we had quite as much difficulty here, as on the other side, and in some places more, for the nettles were higher, the shrubs more tangled, and the thorns more terrible. The ground, however, was rather more level. I pitied the poor girl who led the way and whose fat naked arms were both stung and torn. She at last stopped amidst a huge grove of nettles, doing the best she could to shelter her arms from the stinging leaves.

"I never was in such a wilderness in my life," said I to John Jones; "is it possible that the chair of the mighty Huw is in a place like this? which seems never to have been trodden by human foot. Well does the Scripture say *'Dim prophwyd yw yn cael barch yn ei dir ei hunan.'*"

This last sentence tickled the fancy of my worthy friend, the Calvinistic-Methodist; he laughed aloud and repeated it over and over again to the females with amplifications.

"Is the chair really here," said I, "or has it been destroyed? if such a thing has been done it is a disgrace to Wales."

"The chair is really here," said the old lady, "and though Huw Morris was no prophet, we love and reverence everything belonging to him. Get on, Llances, the chair can't be far off"; the girl moved on, and presently the old lady exclaimed, "There's the chair, *Diolch i Duw!*"

I was the last of the file, but I now rushed past John Jones, who was before me, and next to the old lady, and sure enough there was the chair, in the wall, of him who was called in his day, and still is called by the mountaineers of Wales, though his body has been below the earth in the quiet church-yard one hundred and forty years, Eos Ceiriog, the Nightingale of Ceiriog, the sweet caroller Huw Morus, the enthusiastic partisan of Charles, and the Church of England, and the never-tiring lampooner of Oliver and the Independents, there it was, a kind of hollow in the stone wall, in the *hen ffordd*, fronting to the west, just above the gorge at the bottom of which murmurs the brook Ceiriog, there it was, something like a half barrel chair in a garden, a mouldering stone slab forming the seat, and a large slate stone the back, on which were cut these letters—

H. M. B.

signifying Huw Morus Bard.

"Sit down in the chair, Gwr Boneddig," said John Jones, "you have taken trouble enough to get to it."

"Do, gentlemen," said the old lady; "but first let me wipe it with my apron, for it is very wet and dirty."

"Let it be," said I; then taking off my hat I stood uncovered before the chair, and said in the best Welsh I could command, "Shade of Huw Morus, supposing your shade haunts the place which you loved so well when alive —a Saxon, one of the seed of the Coiling Serpent, has come to this place to pay that respect to true genius, the Dawn Duw, which he is every ready to pay. He read the songs of the Nightingale of Ceiriog in the most distant part of Lleogr, when he was a brown-haired boy, and now that he is a grey-haired man he is come to say in this place that they frequently made his eyes overflow with tears of rapture."

I then sat down in the chair, and commenced repeating verses of Huw

Morris. All which I did in the presence of the stout old lady, the short, buxom and bare-armed damsel, and of John Jones the Calvinistic weaver of Llangollen, all of whom listened patiently and approvingly, though the rain was pouring down upon them, and the branches of the trees and the tops of the tall nettles, agitated by the gusts from the mountain hollows, were beating in their faces, for enthusiasm is never scoffed at by the noble, simple-minded, genuine Welsh, whatever treatment it may receive from the coarse-hearted, sensual, selfish Saxon. . . .

> [Borrow and his friend Jones enter a nearby hostelry and meet two young men, one of whom, somewhat drunken, declares he will be called up if the war against Russia in the Crimea doesn't soon come to an end.]

I MADE no other answer than by taking my glass and drinking.

His companion now looking at our habiliments which were in rather a dripping condition, asked John Jones if we had come from far.

"We have been to Pont y Meibion," said Jones, "to see the chair of Huw Morris," adding that the Gwr Boneddig was a great admirer of the songs of the Eos Ceiriog.

He had no sooner said these words than the intoxicated militiaman started up, and striking the table with his fist said: "I am a poor stone-cutter—this a rainy day and I have come here to pass it in the best way I can. I am somewhat drunk, but though I am a poor stone-mason, a private in the militia, and not so sober as I should be, I can repeat more of the songs of the Eos than any man alive, however great a gentleman, however sober—more than Sir Watkin, more than Colonel Biddulph himself."

He then began to repeat what appeared to be poetry, for I could distinguish the rhymes occasionally, though owing to his broken utterance it was impossible for me to make out the sense of the words. Feeling a great desire to know what verses of Huw Morris the intoxicated youth would repeat I took out my pocket-book and requested Jones, who was much better acquainted with Welsh pronunciation, under any circumstances, than myself, to endeavour to write down from the mouth of the young fellow any verses uppermost in his mind. Jones took the pocket-book and pencil and went to the window, followed by the young man scarcely able to support himself. Here a curious scene took place, the drinker hiccuping up verses, and Jones dotting them down, in the best manner he could, though he had evidently great difficulty to distinguish what was said to him. At last, me-thought, the young man said, "There they are, the verses of the Nightingale, on his death-bed."

I took the book and read aloud the following lines beautifully descriptive of the eagerness of a Christian soul to leave its perishing tabernacle, and get to Paradise and its Creator:

> *Myn'd i'r wyl ar redeg,*
> *I'r byd a beryi chwaneg,*
> *I Beradwys, y ber wiw deg,*
> *Yn Enw Duw yn union deg.*

"Do you understand those verses?" said the man on the settle, a dark swarthy fellow with an oblique kind of vision, and dressed in a pepper-and-salt coat.

"I will translate them," said I; and forthwith put them into English— first into prose and then into rhyme, the rhymed version running thus:

> Now to my rest I hurry away,
> To the world which lasts for ever and aye,
> To Paradise, the beautiful place,
> Trusting alone in the Lord of Grace.

"Well," said he of the pepper-and-salt, "if that isn't capital I don't know what is."

A scene in a public-house, yes! but in a Welsh public-house. Only think of a Suffolk toper repeating the death-bed verses of a poet; surely there is a considerable difference between the Celt and the Saxon.

[As Borrow walks on the pier at Holyhead in northwest Wales a group of Irish reapers mistake him for an Irish priest.]

"Father" Borrow Bestows a Blessing on Some Irishmen

THE day was as hot as the preceding one. I walked slowly towards the west, and presently found myself upon a pier, or breakwater, at the mouth of the harbour. A large steamer lay at a little distance within the pier. There were fishing boats on both sides, the greater number on the outer side, which lies towards the hill of Holy Head. On the shady side of the breakwater under the wall were two or three dozen of Irish reapers; some were lying asleep, others in parties of two or three were seated with their backs against the wall, and were talking Irish; these last all appeared to be well-made middle-sized young fellows, with rather a ruffianly look; they stared at me as I passed. The whole party had shillelahs either in their hands or by their sides. I went to the extremity of the pier, where was a little lighthouse, and then turned back. As I again drew near the Irish, I heard a hubbub and observed a great commotion amongst them. All, whether those whom I had seen sitting, or those whom I had seen reclining, had got or were getting on their legs. As I passed them they were all standing up, and their eyes were fixed upon me with a strange kind of expression, partly of wonder, me-thought, partly of respect. "Yes, 'tis he, sure enough," I heard one whisper. On I went, and at about thirty yards from the last I stopped, turned round and leaned against the wall. All the Irish were looking at me—presently they formed into knots and began to discourse very eagerly in Irish, though in an undertone. At length I observed a fellow going from one knot to the other, exchanging a few words with each. After he had held communication with all he nodded his head, and came towards me with a quick step, the rest stood silent and motionless with their eyes turned in the direction in which I was, and in which he was advancing. He stopped within a yard of me and took off his hat. He was an athletic fellow of about twenty-eight, dressed in brown frieze. His features were swarthy, and his eyes black; in every lineament of his countenance was a jumble of savagery and roguishness. I never saw a more genuine wild Irish face—there he stood looking at me full in the face, his hat in one hand and his shillelah in the other.

"Well, what do you want?" said I, after we had stared at each other about half a minute.

"Sure, I'm just come on the part of the boys and myself to beg a bit of a favour of your reverence."

"Reverence," said I, "what do you mean by styling me reverence?"

"Och sure, why because to be styled your reverence is the right of your reverence."

"Pray what do you take me for?"

"Och sure, we knows your reverence very well."

"Well, who am I?"

"Och, why Father Toban to be sure."

"And who knows me to be Father Toban?"

"Och, a boy here knows your reverence to be Father Toban."

"Where is that boy?"

"Here he stands, your reverence."

"Are you that boy?"

"I am, your reverence."

"And you told the rest that I was Father Toban?"

"I did, your reverence."

"And you know me to be Father Toban?"

"I do, your reverence."

"How do you know me to be Father Toban?"

"Och, why because many's the good time that I have heard your reverence, Father Toban, say mass."

"And what is it you want me to do?"

"Why, see here, your reverence, we are going to embark in the dirty steamer yonder for ould Ireland, which starts as soon as the tide serves, and we want your reverence to bless us before we goes."

"You want me to bless you?"

"We do, your reverence, we want you to spit out a little bit of a blessing upon us before we goes on board."

"And what good would my blessing do you?"

"All kinds of good, your reverence; it would prevent the dirty steamer from catching fire, your reverence, or from going down, your reverence, or from running against the blackguard Hill of Howth in the mist, provided there should be one."

"And suppose I were to tell you that I am not Father Toban."

"Och, your reverence will never think of doing that."

"Would you believe me if I did?"

"We would not, your reverence."

"If I were to swear that I am not Father Toban?"

"We would not, your reverence."

"On the evangiles?"

"We would not, your reverence."

"On the Cross?"

"We would not, your reverence."

"And suppose I were to refuse to give you a blessing?"

"Och, your reverence will never refuse to bless the poor boys."

"But suppose I were to refuse?"

"Why in such a case, which bye the bye is altogether impossible, we should just make bould to give your reverence a good big bating."

"You would break my head?"

"We would, your reverence."

"Kill me?"

"We would, your reverence."

"You would really put me to death?"

"We would not, your reverence."

"And what's the difference between killing and putting to death?"

"Och, sure there's all the difference in the world. Killing manes only a good big bating, such as every Irishman is used to, and which your reverence would get over long before matins, whereas putting your reverence to death would prevent your reverence from saying mass for ever and a day."

"And you are determined on having a blessing?"

"We are, your reverence."

"By hook or by crook?"

"By crook or by hook, your reverence."

"Before I bless you, will you answer me a question or two?"

"I will, your reverence."

"Are you not a set of great big blackguards?"

"We are, your reverence."

"Without one good quality."

"We are, your reverence."

"Would it not be quite right to saddle and bridle you all, and ride you violently down Holyhead or the Giant's Causeway into the waters, causing you to perish there, like the herd of swine of old?"

"It would, your reverence."

"And knowing and confessing all this you have the cheek to come and ask me for a blessing?"

"We have, your reverence."

"Well, how shall I give the blessing?"

"Och, sure your reverence knows very well how to give it."

"Shall I give it in Irish?"

"Och, no, your reverence—a blessing in Irish is no blessing at all."

"In English?"

"Och, murder, no, your reverence, God preserve us all from an English blessing."

"In Latin?"

"Yes, sure, your reverence; in what else should you bless us but in holy Latin?"

"Well, then, prepare yourselves."

"We will, your reverence—stay one moment whilst I whisper to the boys that your reverence is about to bestow your blessing upon us."

Then turning to the rest who all this time had kept their eyes fixed intently upon us, he bellowed with the voice of a bull:

"Down on your marrow bones, ye sinners, for his reverence Toban is about to bless us all in holy Latin."

He then flung himself on his knees on the pier, and all his countrymen, baring their heads, followed his example—yes, there knelt thirty bareheaded Eirionaich on the pier of Caer Gybi beneath the broiling sun. I gave them the best Latin blessing I could remember, out of two or three which I had got by memory out of an old Popish book of devotion, which I bought in my boyhood at a stall. Then turning to the deputy I said, "Well, now are you satisfied?"

"Sure, I have a right to be satisfied, your reverence; and so have we all— sure we can now all go on board the dirty steamer, without fear of fire or water, or the blackguard Hill of Howth either."

"Then get up, and tell the rest to get up, and please to know and let the rest know, that I do not choose to receive further trouble, either by word or look, from any of ye, as long as I remain here."

"Your reverence shall be obeyed in all things," said the fellow, getting up. Then walking away to his companions he cried, "Get up, boys, and plase to know that his reverence Toban is not to be farther troubled by being looked at or spoken to by any one of us, as long as he remains upon this dirty pier."

"Divil a bit farther trouble shall he have from us!" exclaimed many a voice, as the rest of the party arose from their knees.

In half a minute they disposed themselves in much the same manner as that in which they were, when I first saw them—some flung themselves again to sleep under the wall, some seated themselves with their backs against it and laughed and chatted, but without taking any notice of me; those who sat and chatted took, or appeared to take, as little notice as those who lay and slept of his reverence Father Toban.

[On the way to Festiniog to see the stone on which Rhys Goch, a celebrated bard, sat, he falls in with another walker.]

DIALOGUE WITH A CRUSTY COUNTRYMAN

STROLLING along in this manner I was overtaken by an old fellow with a stick in his hand, walking very briskly. He had a crusty and rather conceited look. I spoke to him in Welsh, and he answered in English, saying that I need not trouble myself by speaking Welsh, as he had plenty of English, and of the very best. We were from first to last at cross purposes. I asked him about Rhys Goch and his chair. He told me that he knew nothing of either, and began to talk of Her Majesty's ministers and the fine sights of London. I asked him the name of a stream which, descending a gorge on our right, ran down the side of the valley, to join the river at its bottom. He told me that he did not know and asked me the name of the Queen's eldest daughter. I told him I did not know, and remarked that it was very odd that he could not tell me the name of a stream in his own vale. He replied that it was not a bit more odd than that I could not tell him the name of the eldest daughter of the Queen of England; I told him that when I was in Wales I wanted to talk about Welsh matters, and he told me that when he was with English he wanted to talk about English matters. I returned to the subject of Rhys Goch and his chair, and he returned to the subject of Her Majesty's ministers, and the fine folks of London. I told him that I cared not a straw about Her Majesty's ministers and the fine folks of London, and he replied that he cared not a straw for Rhys Goch, his chair or old women's stories of any kind.

Regularly incensed against the old fellow I told him he was a bad Welshman, and he retorted by saying I was a bad Englishman. I said he appeared to know next to nothing. He retorted by saying that I knew less than nothing, and almost inarticulate with passion added that he scorned to walk in such illiterate company, and suiting the action to the word sprang up a steep and rocky footpath on the right, probably a short cut to his domicile, and was out of sight in a twinkling. We were both wrong: I most so. He was crusty and conceited, but I ought to have humoured him and then I might have got out of him anything he knew, always supposing that he knew anything.

[He returns to Llangollen and then takes a long journey to the southernmost parts of Wales and thence eastward to Chepstow and home.]

The Schoolroom, the Iron Mills and the Slums

HIPPOLYTE TAINE

FROM *Notes on England*

1859–71

Taine was already the most influential critic of art and litera-
ture in France when he revealed himself in his Notes on England *as also*
one of the most penetrating and sensitive observers of the social scene.
Coming of age after the first great advance in science and technology, he
sought to apply the scientific approach to society and its institutions. The
result was a determinist view of life, in which every man was a "creature
of circumstance" who could be classified according to three criteria: race,
milieu and moment. Disturbed by his unorthodoxy, the authorities, in-
cluding the Académie Française, held up appointments and honors. But
Taine's brilliance and erudition were too great to be denied and he was
advanced to a professorship at the École des Beaux-Arts. Later he began
to devote all his time to writing, producing a score of books on such
diverse subjects as philosophy, the art of Flanders, Greece and Italy, the
origin of French institutions, and English literature.

In preparing some of these he traveled widely; among the by-products
of his journeys were several books of travel, including A Tour through the
Pyrenees *(1855) and* Notes on England *(1872). The former, based on a trip*
to the watering places of the Pyrenees, is a mixture of poetic descriptions
of landscape with local history and legend. Notes on England *is an incom-*

parably richer book. Its graphic descriptions, the maturity and vigor of its judgments, and its shrewd comparisons between the English way and the French make it one of the most illuminating reports on Victorian life.

Lacking the novelist's power, Taine is weakest in characterizing individuals; his strength is in interpreting an institution or in capturing a quality or a scene: the gin drinking of workingmen; harlots following their trade; slums (see the excerpts below); the fagging system in the schools (see below); Epsom Downs on Derby Day; the turreted and gabled mansions of the rich; the decorous church service; zealots preaching in Hyde Park; the tidy cottage and the decent inn; the National Gallery, stiff with moral epics and conscientious landscapes. In these we see how clearly he was the contemporary of Balzac and the forerunner of Zola.

CODE OF THE SCHOOLBOY

ALONG with other unpleasant effects, the ruder instincts are developed. An Eton master states that "play takes the first place, books the second." The child makes it his glory, like Tom Brown, to be a good athlete; he spends three, four or five hours daily in rough and violent exercises. At hares and hounds they flounder for hours in plowed fields and in muddy meadows, stumble in the mud, lose their shoes, pick themselves up as well as they can. At football the sides throw themselves upon each other; the child underneath bears the weight of the entire mass, arms and legs are dislocated, collarbones broken. At cricket the great heavy ball is thrown with such force that the unskilful wicket keeper, if struck by it, is knocked down. Nearly all the games habitually yield bruises; pride is taken in not minding them; and by a natural consequence, there is no more hesitation in inflicting than in submitting to them. The child becomes a fighter, a boxer; the author of *Tom Brown* says, "To fight with fists is the natural and English way for English boys to settle their quarrels." All the men I have met did so when at school, and this is still common. This kind of duel has its rules, its appointed place, its audience, its seconds. Each combatant has two seconds who sponge his face and put forward their knee for a seat during the rounds; these encounters are renewed, and sometimes prolonged for half an hour. The idea is to go on fighting as long as one can see clearly and stand upright; after the fight there are black eyes, swollen and livid cheeks, and sometimes a thumb put out of joint or a lip cut open.

Unfortunately the school's own practice tends in the same direction; in addition to fines, being kept from play and confined, the birch cane is used. In certain schools it is enough for a boy to appear three times on the blacklist for him to have to prepare for a flogging. This morning four were flogged at Harrow (fourteen strokes, not drawing blood). In all the schools it is the headmaster who carries out this amiable office; there is hardly a headmaster in France who would accept, at such a price, a salary of £6,000. In principle all are liable to the birch, even the bigger boys; yet scarcely any but the younger and smaller ones are subjected to it. A strange thing is that it is not unpopular. Fifty years ago at Charterhouse the boys, hearing that it was proposed to substitute a fine for it, rebelled, crying, "Down with fines! Hurrah for the rod!" and on the morrow they renewed acquaintance with the beloved birch. The teachers with whom I have discussed it consider that this chastisement is not humiliating and that it develops special courage in the child. According to them the strokes are a natural form of repression; it is enough that opinion does not regard them as shameful, and that the sufferer does not feel himself insulted. Under the headmaster, the big boys entrusted with maintaining discipline have the right to inflict the same punishment. For this purpose they carry a cane in certain schools, and use it.

Here a shocking institution must be brought up; this is "fagging," the obligation of the little boys to be the servants of the bigger ones. It has been modified and softened, at Harrow, at Rugby, and in some other establishments. But in itself it still continues to be bad; for it is a school of brutality, and pushes the English child in the direction to which he already inclines, toward all those excesses to which the energetic, violent, tyrannical and harsh temperament tends. A lady whom we know—who is, it is true, of foreign extraction—could not bring herself to subject her son to fagging and has put him in a Parisian school. According to official inquiries the small boys are valets and slaves. Each big boy has several, who are bound to run errands for him, sweep his room, clean his candlesticks, toast his bread and his cheese, call him at an appointed time, help him at his games, frequently for two or three hours daily, to run after his ball, to be at his command during all his waking hours, and to endure his caprices. . . .

"I state as a simple fact," said one witness, "that from the first of January to the thirty-first of December, the young scholar has not a single moment that is not open to interruption. At half past three in the morning, two of the younger, chosen in succession, rise to light the fire, boil the water, call up those of the big boys who have ordered this to be done. Frequently the senior, awakened at four o'clock, does not get up till half past seven and must therefore be called every half hour. This task falls to each of the small boys two or three times weekly."

Add to this all the things that must be done during the evening: "The seniors are very fond of tea, they must have it three times in the course of the evening, without mentioning coffee. Every two minutes the kettles must be filled for them." One of the witnesses relates that on Saturday night, which is a holiday at Westminster, his son arrived home from school so thoroughly exhausted for want of sleep that he had no other desire than to go to bed.

In order to maintain such a strict and minute obedience the big boys use terror. "Slapping a boy's ears and kicking him are considered merely pranks and are not counted as punishment. . . . The first degree of real punishment is a systematic boxing of the ears; the offender must keep his hands at his sides and hold his head forward to receive a dozen slaps, right and left. On other occasions he places the palm of his hand on a table, and the back of his hand is then beaten with the blade of a paper knife till sometimes a gash is inflicted. Caning comes next, then two kinds of 'tanning.' The boy is beaten on the fleshy part of the leg with a racket bat, which breaks the skin and draws blood. He places his foot on a sink the height of a table, and the executioner, taking a run of two or three paces, kicks the exposed part." The reporter declares, "I have heard of two or three cases in which the boys were so cruelly bruised that they were unable for a long time to join in the games and other exercises." Tom Brown was tossed in a blanket and thrown up with such force that he struck the ceiling. One day, having refused to sell his lottery tickets to the big boys, he was seized, held up before a blazing fire and roasted till he was ready to faint. This actually occurred, the novel being but a record of authentic incidents. Other equally revolting examples can be found in the lives of Cowper, Lord Byron and Sir Robert Peel. Doubtless the instances just cited are the darkest, and, as the English are persevering in matters of reform, the picture is becoming brighter. Yet, even supposing that reforms are being carried out, the impression one gets is still unpleasant; for, on the whole, a school conducted in this style is a sort of primitive society where force reigns almost uncontrolled—the more so because it is considered a point of honor among the oppressed not to denounce their oppressors. The master interferes as little as possible; he is not, as among us, the perpetual representative of humanity and justice; very seldom and in very few schools is an appeal made to him or to the authorities. The weak are left to themselves and can but suffer and be patient. . . .

MANCHESTER: FOG AND SOOT

WE now enter the coal and iron country; on every side are the marks of industrial life: the cinder heaps form mountains; the earth is pitted with excavations; tall furnaces belch flames. We are nearing Manchester. In the bronzed sky at sunset a strangely shaped cloud hangs over the plain; under this motionless covering bristle hundreds of chimneys, as tall as obelisks; next a huge, black mass is distinguishable; then endless rows of buildings, and we enter the Babel made of bricks.

Walked through the city. Seen close at hand, it is even more dismal. Air and earth appear charged with fog and soot. Factories with blackened bricks, naked fronts, windows without shutters, resembling huge, tawdry penitentiaries, succeed each other in rows. A vast bazaar for the sale of low-priced goods, a workhouse to accommodate four hundred thousand persons, a prison for convicts condemned to penal servitude—such are the ideas brought to mind by the spectacle. One of the buildings is a rectangle of six stories in each of which there are forty windows; there, lit by gas, amid the deafening noise of looms, thousands of working people, boxed in, classified, tied down, mechanically drive their machines every day from morning to night. Can any form of existence be more opposed to man's natural instincts?

About six o'clock a bustling, noisy crowd pours from the mills into the streets. Men, women and children flock along in the open air; their clothes are filthy; many of the children are barefooted, the faces of all are pinched and gloomy; several halt at the gin palaces; the others scatter and hasten toward their hovels. We follow them. What wretched streets! Through a half-open window may be seen a miserable room on the ground floor, sometimes below the level of the damp pavement; at the threshold a group of pale, flabby and untidy children breathe the air of the street, only less foul than that of the room. A strip of carpet can be seen, and clothes hung up to dry. We continue our walk in the direction of the suburbs; there, in a more open space, rows of small cheap houses have been erected as a speculation. The blackish street is paved with iron slag; the rows of low red-tiled roofs stand out against the prevailing gray of the sky; yet each family dwells apart, and the fog it breathes is not too impure. These are the select, the fortunate few. And this is summer, the finest time of the year! We wonder what sort of life they lead in winter, when the fog bathes, chokes and engulfs the whole world; and we become conscious of how heavily man is oppressed by this pitiless climate and this industrial system.

THE SLUMS OF LIVERPOOL

LIVERPOOL, like Manchester, is a giant; the shops and warehouses are on a huge scale; the streets are vast, and the houses which line them are, like those of London, overladen with arcades, pillars and pilasters, the effect produced being one of crowding and clutter. The inhabitants number five hundred thousand and the port is the busiest after that of London.

Along the docks the cotton warehouses form a kind of cyclopian, endless and monotonous rampart; a great part of all the cotton in the world is housed here. But the docks themselves overshadow everything else. The Mersey, as large as an arm of the sea, stretches toward the west, carrying vessels on their way out and on their way back. For a distance of six miles along its bank these vessels pass through canals into basins lined with stone, resembling watery streets and squares endlessly multiplied and ramified. Here they are repaired or discharge their cargoes. In winter their closely packed masts look like a forest, extending as far as the eye can reach, and filling the entire horizon to the north. Yet these docks, however spacious and numerous, do not suffice for the multitude of ships; these are crowded in rows and masses at the entrances, awaiting their turn to pass. At Birkenhead, on the opposite bank, new docks are being built for them.

I believe this spectacle is one of the grandest in the world. Some of the vessels are 3,500 and others 4,000 tons burden. One steamer here is upwards of three hundred feet in length. Another vessel, the *Great Britain*, is about to carry 1,200 emigrants to Australia. Descending the drydocks to the keels of the ships, one sees that the hulls are from forty to fifty feet in height. The swelling and copper-sheathed sides have the graceful curves of a sea bird resting upon the waves.

The view from Birkenhead commands the harbor and the vast reaches of the river; the surface is slightly agitated and gleams with a yellow light under a faint haze. Steamboats ascend and descend the river, cross and recross it, with stiff mechanical movements, like black crabs. Sailing ships, heeling over lightly, skim along like beautiful swans. The *George*, a man-of-war of eighty-six guns, arrives in lordly style, all the others making way for her. On the far side the endless rows of masts and rigging line the sky, and behind them masses the huge city. . . .

It is now six o'clock, and we turn back through the poorer quarter of the city. What a sight! In the vicinity of Leeds Street there are fifteen or twenty streets across which are stretched cords covered with rags and bed linen hung up to dry. Bands of children swarm on every flight of stairs, with five or six clustered on each step, the eldest carrying the smallest. Their faces are pale, their light hair is disheveled, their clothes are in tatters, they have neither shoes nor stockings, and they are all incredibly dirty, their faces and hands apparently encrusted with dust and soot. Perhaps two hundred children romp and wallow in a single street. On coming closer one sees a mother and a grown daughter, both wearing little more than chemises, crouching in a dim passageway. What interiors! One glimpses a little piece of worn oilcloth, and perhaps a shell or a plaster ornament or two; in one corner sits a doddering grandmother; the wife is busy mending wretched rags of clothing; the children push each other about. The smell is like that of an old-clothes shop. The ground floor of nearly every dwelling is a damp flagstone basement. Can you imagine what life must be like in these cellars during the winter?

Some of the younger children are still fresh and rosy-cheeked, but their large blue eyes are painful to behold; their blood will deteriorate; as they grow older they will waste away, the flesh becoming pasty and pallid. Many of them are scrofulous, their faces marked with small sores covered with a kind of plaster. As we proceed the crowd becomes more dense. Youths sit or half crouch at the side of the pavement, playing with soiled cards. Bearded old hags come out of gin shops; they stagger; their glazed stares and besotted smiles are indescribable: it is as if their features had been eaten away by vitriol. The rags they wear, once the fashionable dresses of fine ladies, are falling to pieces, revealing patches of filthy skin.

One is shocked to note that these streets are built in a regular style and seem to be new. Probably this is a quarter modernized and made more airy by a beneficent municipality; this, then, is evidently the best that can be done for the poor. A uniform row of buildings and pavements borders both sides of the way, enclosing within their rigid mathematical lines this teeming heap of horrors and human wretchedness. The air is close and oppressive, the light wan and dim; there is not a color or a shape on which the eye can rest with pleasure; Rembrandt's beggars were far better off in their picturesque holes. And I have not yet seen the Irish quarter! The Irish abound here; it is said there are a hundred thousand of them; and their quarter is the lowest circle of hell. . . .

Living on the Grand Canal

WILLIAM DEAN HOWELLS

FROM *Venetian Life*

1861–65

Like his great contemporaries, Mark Twain and Henry James, William Dean Howells published books of travel almost from the very beginning of his literary career. Because he had written a biography of Lincoln when the latter was nominated for the Presidency, he was appointed consul in Venice in 1861 (he was only twenty-four), and he spent four years there. Out of this experience came Venetian Life (1866) and, a year later, Italian Journeys. These are the work of a young man, full of infectious enthusiasm and a charming sense of humor. During the next half century, in the intervals between some forty novels, thirty comedies and many other books, Howells wrote of travels in Tuscany, England, French Switzerland and, as late as 1912, Spain. But although he never lost the capacity to be interested in new faces and strange places and to write about them ingratiatingly, he never came to know anyone as well as he knew the Venetians.

Howells was later to gain a reputation as a pioneer of realism, but it was realism only in that it dealt faithfully with the commonplace, the daily round of middle-class life. This quality is already evident in Venetian Life, along with the novelist's eye for scene and character and the playwright's ear for dialogue. From the very beginning he was a fine craftsman, master of a deft and felicitous style. But there are also defects: a condescending treatment of Italians as charming but irresponsible, the preference for poverty that is "picturesque" and a contempt for the ghetto Jew because the ghetto is squalid. A gifted writer and the courageous sponsor of some of the harshest naturalists of the next generation, Howells still never quite overcame the limitations of nineteenth-century Anglo-Saxon gentility.

[When Howells arrived in Venice the city had been under occupation by Austria since the fall of the Venetian Republic in 1849 and its traditional gaiety had been dimmed for more than a decade. But the city itself was unchanged. Living in rooms of old palaces on the Grand Canal and wandering its byways constantly, Howells came to know Venice with unusual intimacy. In the excerpts that follow he describes some of its characteristic types and the tenor of its life.]

FLATTERERS, QUARRELERS AND MERCHANTS

THAT exuberance of manner which one notes, the first thing, in his intercourse with Venetians characterizes all classes, but is most excessive and relishing in the poor. There is a vast deal of ceremony with every order, and one hardly knows what to do with the numbers of compliments it is necessary to respond to. A Venetian does not come to see you, he comes to revere you; he not only asks if you be well when he meets you, but he bids you remain well at parting, and desires you to salute for him all common friends; he reverences you at leave-taking; he will sometimes consent to incommode you with a visit; he will relieve you of the disturbance when he rises to go. All spontaneous wishes which must, with us, take original forms, for lack of the complimentary phrase, are formally expressed by him: good appetite to you, when you go to dinner; much enjoyment, when you go to the theatre; a pleasant walk, if you meet in promenade. He is your servant at meeting and parting; he begs to be commanded when he has misunderstood you. But courtesy takes its highest flights, as I hinted, from the poorest company. Acquaintances of this sort, when not on the *Ciò ciappa* footing, or that of the familiar thee and thou, always address each other in *Lei* (lordship), or *Elo*, as the Venetians have it; and their compliment-making at encounter and separation is endless: I salute you! Remain well! Master! Mistress! (*Patron! Patrona!*) being repeated as long as the polite persons are within hearing.

One day, as we passed through the crowded Merceria, an old Venetian friend of mine, who trod upon the dress of a young person before us, called out, "*Scusate, bella giovane!*" (Pardon, beautiful girl!) She was not so fair nor so young as I have seen women; but she half turned her face with a forgiving smile, and seemed pleased with the accident that had won her the amiable apology. The waiter of the *caffè* frequented by the people says to the ladies for whom he places seats, "Take this place, beautiful blonde," or "Sit here, lovely brunette," as it happens.

A Venetian who enters or leaves any place of public resort touches his hat to the company, and one day at the restaurant some ladies, who had been dining there, said, "*Complimenti!*" on going out, with a grace that went near to make the beefsteak tender. It is this uncostly gentleness of bearing which gives a winning impression of the whole people, whatever selfishness or real discourtesy lie beneath it. At home it sometimes seems that we are in such haste to live and be done with it, we have no time to be polite. Or is popular politeness merely a vice of servile peoples? And is it altogether better to be rude? I wish it were not. If you are lost in his city (and you are pretty sure to be lost there, continually), a Venetian will go with you wherever you wish. And he will do this amiable little service out of what one may say old civilization has established in place of good-ness of heart, but which is perhaps not so different from it.

You hear people in the streets bless each other in the most dramatic fashion. I once caught these parting words between an old man and a young girl:

GIOVANETTA: Revered sir! (*Patron riverito!*)

VECCHIO: (With that peculiar backward wave and beneficent wag of the hand, only possible to Italians.) Blessed child! (*Benedetta!*)

It was in a crowd, but no one turned round at the utterance of terms which Anglo-Saxons would scarcely use in their most emotional moments. The old gentleman who sells boxes for the theatre in the Old Procuratie always gave me his benediction when I took a box.

There is equal exuberance of invective, and I have heard many fine maledictions on the Venetian streets, but I recollect none more elaborate than that of a gondolier who, after listening peacefully to a quarrel between two other boatmen, suddenly took part against one of them, and saluted him with "Ah! baptized son of a dog! And if I had been present at thy baptism, I would have dashed thy brains out against the baptismal font!"

All the theatrical forms of passion were visible in a scene I witnessed in a little street near San Samuele, where I found the neighborhood assembled at doors and windows in honor of a wordy battle between two poor women. One of these had been forced in-doors by her prudent husband, and the other upbraided her across the marital barrier. The assailant was washing, and twenty times she left her tub to revile the besieged, who thrust her long arms over those of her husband, and turned each reproach back upon her who uttered it, thus:

ASSAILANT: Beast!

BESIEGED: Thou!

A: Fool!

B: Thou!

A: Liar!

B: Thou!

E via in seguito! At last the assailant, beating her breast with both hands, and tempestuously swaying her person back and forth, wreaked her scorn in one wild outburst of vituperation, and returned finally to her tub, wisely saying, on the purple verge of asphyxiation, "O, *non discorro più con gente.*"

I returned half an hour later, and she was laughing and playing sweetly with her babe.

It suits the passionate nature of the Italians to have incredible ado about buying and selling, and a day's shopping is a sort of campaign, from which the shopper returns plundered and discomfited, or laden with the spoil of vanquished shopmen.

The embattled commercial transaction is conducted in this wise:

The shopper enters, and prices a given article. The shopman names a sum of which only the fervid imagination of the South could conceive as corresponding to the value of the goods.

The purchaser instantly starts back with a wail of horror and indignation, and the shopman throws himself forward over the counter with a protest that, far from being dear, the article is ruinously cheap at the price stated, though they may nevertheless agree for something less.

What, then, is the very most ultimate price?

Properly, the very most ultimate price is so much. (Say, the smallest trifle under the price first asked.)

The purchaser moves toward the door. He comes back, and offers one third of the very most ultimate price.

The shopman, with a gentle desperation, declares that the thing cost him as much. He cannot really take the offer. He regrets, but he cannot. That the gentleman would say something more! So much, for example. That he regard the stuff, its quality, fashion, beauty.

The gentleman laughs him to scorn. Ah, heigh! and, coming forward, he picks up the article and reviles it. Out of the mode, old, fragile, ugly of its kind.

The shopman defends his wares. There is not such quantity and quality elsewhere in Venice. But if the gentleman will give even so much (still something preposterous), he may have it, though truly its sale for that money is utter ruin.

The shopper walks straight to the door. The shopman calls him back from the threshold, or sends his boy to call him back from the street.

Let him accommodate himself—which is to say, take the thing at his own price.

He takes it.

The shopman says cheerfully, "*Servo suo!*"

The purchaser responds, "*Bon dì! Patron!*" (Good day! my Master!)

Thus, as I said, every bargain is a battle, and every purchase a triumph or a defeat. The whole thing is understood; the opposing forces know perfectly well all that is to be done beforehand, and retire after the contest, like the captured knights in Morgante Maggiore, "calm as oil," however furious and deadly their struggle may have appeared to strangers. . . .

Your Venetian is *simpatico*, if he is anything. He is always ready to feel and to express the deepest concern, and I rather think he likes to have his sensibilities appealed to, as a pleasant and healthful exercise for them. His sympathy begins at home, and he generously pities himself as the victim of a combination of misfortunes which leave him citizen of a country without liberty, without commerce, without money, without hope. He next pities his fellow-citizens, who are as desperately situated as himself. Then he pities the degradation, corruption, and despair into which the city has fallen. And I think his compassion is the most hopeless thing in his character. That alone is touched; that alone is moved; and when its impulse ceases he and everything about him remain just as before.

With the poor, this sensibility is amusingly mischievous. They never speak of one of their own class without adding some such ejaculation as "Poor fellow!" or, "Poor little creature!" They pity all wretchedness, no matter from what cause, and the greatest rogue has their compassion when under a cloud. It is all but impossible to punish thieves in Venice, where they are very bold and numerous; for the police are too much occupied with political surveillance to give due attention to mere cutpurses and housebreakers, and even when they make an arrest people can hardly be got to bear witness against their unhappy prisoner. *Povareto anca lu!* There is no work and no money: people must do something; so they steal. *Ci vuol pazienza!* Bear witness against an ill-fated fellow-sufferer? God forbid! Stop a thief? I think a burglar might run from Rialto to San Marco, and not one compassionate soul in the Merceria would do aught to arrest him—*povareto!* Thieves came to the house of a friend of mine at noonday, when his servant was out. They tied their boat to his landing, entered his house, filled their boat with plunder from it, and rowed out into the canal. The neighbors on the floor above saw them, and cried, "Thieves! thieves!" It was in the most frequented part of the Grand Canal, where scores of boats passed and repassed; but no one molested the thieves, and these *povareti* escaped with their booty.

One night, in a little street through which we passed to our ferry, there came a wild rush before us, of a woman screaming for help, and pursued by her husband with a knife in his hand; their children, shrieking piteously, came after them. The street was crowded with people and soldiers, but no one put out his hand; and the man presently overtook his wife and stabbed her in the back. We only knew of the rush, but what it all meant we could not tell till we saw the woman bleeding from the stab, which, happily, was slight. Inquiry of the bystanders developed the facts, but, singularly enough, scarcely a word of pity. It was entirely a family affair, it seemed: the man, poor little fellow, had a mistress, and his wife had maddened him with reproaches. *Come si fa?* He had to stab her. The woman's case was not one that appealed to popular compassion, and the only words of pity for her which I heard were expressed by the wife of a fruiterer, whom her husband angrily silenced.

IN A PALACE ON THE GRAND CANAL

AND here I am reminded of another pleasure of modern dwellers in Venetian palaces, which could hardly have been indulged by the patricians of old, and which is hardly imaginable by people of this day, whose front doors open upon dry land: I mean to say the privilege of sea-bathing from one's own threshold. From the beginning of June till far into September all the canals of Venice are populated by the amphibious boys, who clamor about in the brine, or poise themselves for a leap from the tops of bridges, or show their fine, statuesque figures, bronzed by the ardent sun, against the façades of empty palaces, where they hover among the marble sculptures, and meditate a headlong plunge. It is only the Venetian ladies, in fact, who do not share this healthful amusement. Fathers of families, like so many plump, domestic drakes, lead forth their aquatic broods, teaching the little ones to swim by the aid of various floats, and delighting in the gambols of the larger ducklings. When the tide comes in fresh and strong from the sea the water in the Grand Canal is pure and refreshing; and at these times it is a singular pleasure to leap from one's door-step into the swift current, and spend a half-hour, very informally, among one's neighbors there. The Venetian bathing-dress is a mere sketch of the pantaloons of ordinary life; and when I used to stand upon our balcony, and see some bearded head ducking me a polite salutation from a pair of broad, brown shoulders that showed above the water, I was not always able to recognize my acquaintance, deprived of his factitious identity of clothes. But I always knew a certain stately consul-general by a vast expanse of baldness upon the top of his head; and it must be owned, I think, that this form of social assembly was, with all its disadvantages, a novel and vivacious spectacle. The Venetian ladies, when they bathed, went to the Lido, or else to the bath-houses in front of the Ducal Palace, where they saturated themselves a good part of the day, and drank coffee, and, possibly, gossiped.

I think that our balconies at Palazzo Giustiniani were even better places to see the life of the Grand Canal from than the balcony of Casa Falier, which we had just left. Here at least we had a greater stretch of the Canal, looking, as we could, up either side of its angle. Here, too, we had more gondola stations in sight, and as we were nearer the Rialto, there was more picturesque passing of the market-boats. But if we saw more of this life, we did not see it in greater variety, for I think we had already exhausted this. There was a movement all night long. If I woke at three or four o'clock, and offered myself the novel spectacle of the Canal at that hour, I saw the heavy-laden barges go by to the Rialto, with now and then also a good-sized coasting schooner making lazily for the lagoons, with its ruddy fire already kindled for cooking the morning's meal, and looking very enviably cosey. After our own breakfast we began to watch for the gondolas of the tourists of different nations, whom we came to distinguish at a glance. Then the boats of the various artisans went by, the carpenter's, the mason's, the plasterer's, with those that sold fuel, and vegetables, and fruit, and fish, to any household that arrested them. From noon till three or four o'clock the Canal was comparatively deserted; but before twilight it was thronged again by people riding out in their open gondolas to take the air after the day's fervor. After nightfall they ceased, till only at long intervals a solitary lamp, stealing over the dark surface, gave token of the movement of some gondola bent upon an errand that could not fail to seem mysterious or fail to be matter of fact. We never wearied of this oft-repeated variety, nor of our balcony in any way; and when the moon shone in through the lovely arched window and sketched its exquisite outline on the floor, we were as happy as moonshine could make us. . . .

We enjoyed our whole year in Palazzo Giustiniani, though some of the days were too long and some too short, as everywhere. From heat we hardly suffered at all, so perfectly did the vast and lofty rooms answer to the purpose of their builders in this respect. A current of sea air drew through to the painter's garden by day, and by night there was scarcely a mosquito of the myriads that infested some parts of Venice. In winter it was not so well. Then we shuffled about in wadded gowns and boots lined with sheep-skin— the woolly side in, as in the song. The passage of the *sala* was something to be dreaded, and we shivered as fleetly through it as we could, and were all the colder for the deceitful warmth of the colors which the sun cast upon the stone floor from the window opening on the court.

I do not remember any one event of our life more exciting than that attempted burglary of which I have spoken. In a city where the police gave their best attention to political offenders, there were naturally a great many rogues, and the Venetian rogues, if not distinguished for the more heroic crimes, were very skilful in what I may call the *genre* branch of robbing rooms through open windows, and committing all kinds of safe domestic depredations. It was judged best to acquaint Justice (as they call law in Latin countries) with the attempt upon our property, and I found her officers housed in a small room of the Doge's palace, clerkly men in velvet skull-caps, driving loath quills over the rough official paper of those regions. After an exchange of diplomatic courtesies, the commissary took my statement of the affair down in writing, pertinent to which were my father's name, place, and business, with a full and satisfactory personal history of myself down to the period of the attempted burglary. This, I said, occurred one morning about daylight, when I saw the head of the burglar peering above the window-sill, and the hand of the burglar extended to prey upon my wardrobe.

"Excuse me, Signor Console," interrupted the commissary, "how could you see him?"

"Why, there was nothing in the world to prevent me. The window was open."

"The window was open!" gasped the commissary. "Do you mean that you sleep with your windows open?"

"Most certainly!"

"Pardon!" said the commissary, suspiciously. "Do *all* Americans sleep with their windows open?"

"I may venture to say that they all do, in summer," I answered; "at least, it's the general custom."

Such a thing as this indulgence in fresh air seemed altogether foreign to the commissary's experience; and but for my official dignity, I am sure that I should have been effectually browbeaten by him. As it was, he threw himself back in his arm-chair and stared at me fixedly for some moments. Then he recovered himself with another *"Perdoni!"* and, turning to his clerk, said, "Write down that, *according to the American custom,* they were sleeping with their windows open." But I know that the commissary, for all his politeness, considered this habit a relic of the times when we Americans all abode in wigwams; and I suppose it paralyzed his energies in the effort to bring the burglars to justice, for I have never heard anything of them from that day to this.

The truth is, it was a very uneventful year; and I am the better satisfied with it as an average Venetian year on that account. We sometimes varied the pensive monotony by a short visit to the cities of the mainland; but we always came back to it willingly, and I think we unconsciously abhorred any interruption of it. The days, as they followed each other, were wonderfully alike, in every respect. For eight months of summer they were alike in their clear-skied, sweet-breathed loveliness; in the autumn, there where the melancholy of the falling leaf could not spread its contagion to the sculptured foliage of Gothic art, the days were alike in their sentiment of tranquil oblivion and resignation, which was as autumnal as any aspect of woods or fields could have been; in the winter they were alike in their dreariness and discomfort. As I remember, we spent by far the greater part of our time in going to the Piazza, and we were devoted Florianisti, as the Italians call those that lounge habitually at the Caffè Florian. We went every evening to the Piazza, as a matter of course; if the morning was long, we went to the Piazza; if we did not know what to do with the afternoon, we went to the Piazza; if we had friends with us, we went to the Piazza; if we were alone, we went to the Piazza; and there was no mood or circumstances in which it did not seem a natural and fitting thing to go to the Piazza. There were all the prettiest shops; there were all the finest *caffès;* there was the incomparable Church of St. Mark; there was the whole world of Venice.

Venice: The Color and the Sound

HENRY JAMES

FROM *Portraits of Places*

1869–82

Before the time of Henry James many American writers and artists had gone to Europe in search of something America lacked—a usable past, cultural roots, an aesthetic heritage. But to no other did the Old World become so challenging a theme, so rich in significance. By means of it, James was to project a series of images—the rawness of America, the innocence of Americans, the sense of Europe's past and the meaning of tradition, to name only a few—that would influence American writers both in their work and in their lives.

As a traveler, James was unique in his time, for he concerned himself almost entirely with the spirit of a place that resulted from its traditions and its history. (Later, such writers as Loti and Hearn and Gissing might occasionally resemble him in this.) That is why he was rarely interested in the contemporary inhabitants, why most American places had little meaning for him, and why those that did, such as Newport and Boston, stirred only a form of nostalgia in him.

James was a truly inveterate traveler. He was taken to Europe in the very year of his birth, 1843, for a two-year stay, later spent the years from 1855 to 1859 abroad with his parents and, after being educated in America, moved to Europe in 1869 and lived there—eventually becoming a British citizen—until his death in 1916. He was a passionate traveler as well as a constant one, and his first visit to Rome, or any of his visits to Venice (see below), was a tremendous emotional and intellectual experience. His many collections of travel sketches were only one evidence of his interest; much

*more significant was the fact that he not only used Europe as the setting
of many of his greatest stories but used the European idea as a motive of
narrative and characters. The travel sketches were indeed only raw material that would later feed the fires of his creative imagination.*

*These sketches are, nonetheless, pure James: analytical and discrimi-
nating, beating the gold of every impression into the finest leaf. Faced by
the need to choose from among the hundreds of his travel essays, the
anthologist can say only that the impressions of Venice reprinted below
are of a city which affected James more deeply than most, and that they
display the exquisite sensibility that is his inimitable mark.*

*An early but characteristic reaction to America is represented on pages
887–91 in the America North section.*

[The long essay from which the following passages are taken
originally appeared in *The Century Magazine* for November
1882 and was one of five that he wrote on Venice in the
course of his career.]

VENICE

IT is a great pleasure to write the word; but I am not sure there is not a
certain impudence in pretending to add anything to it. Venice has been
painted and described many thousands of times, and of all the cities of
the world it is the easiest to visit without going there. Open the first book
and you will find a rhapsody about it; step into the first picture-dealer's
and you will find three or four high-colored "views" of it. There is nothing
more to be said about it. Every one has been there, and every one has
brought back a collection of photographs. There is as little mystery about
the Grand Canal as about our local thoroughfare; and the name of St.
Mark is as familiar as the postman's ring. It is not forbidden, however,
to speak of familiar things, and I believe that, for the true Venice-lover,
Venice is always in order. There is nothing new to be said about it certainly, but the old is better than any novelty. It would be a sad day,
indeed, when there should be something new to say. I write these lines
with the full consciousness of having no information whatever to offer.
I do not pretend to enlighten the reader; I pretend only to give a fillip

to his memory; and I hold any writer sufficiently justified who is himself in love with his topic.

. . . If we were asked what is the leading color at Venice we should say pink, and yet, after all, we cannot remember that this elegant tint occurs very often. It is a faint, shimmering, airy, watery pink; the bright sea-light seems to flush with it, and the pale whitish-green of lagoon and canal to drink it in. There is, indeed, in Venice a great deal of very evident brickwork, which is never fresh or loud in color, but always burnt out, as it were, always exquisitely mild.

There are certain little mental pictures that rise before the sentimental tourist at the simple mention, written or spoken, of the places he has loved. When I hear, when I see, the magical name I have written above these pages, it is not of the great Square that I think, with its strange basilica and its high arcades, nor of the wide mouth of the Grand Canal, with the stately steps and the well-poised dome of the Salute; it is not of the low lagoon, nor the sweet Piazzetta, nor the dark chambers of St. Mark's. I simply see a narrow canal in the heart of the city—a patch of green water and a surface of pink wall. The gondola moves slowly; it gives a great, smooth swerve, passes under a bridge, and the gondolier's cry, carried over the quiet water, makes a kind of splash in the stillness. A girl is passing over the little bridge, which has an arch like a camel's back, with an old shawl on her head, which makes her look charming; you see her against the sky as you float beneath. The pink of the old wall seems to fill the whole place; it sinks even into the opaque water. Behind the wall is a garden, out of which the long arm of a white June rose—the roses of Venice are splendid—has flung itself by way of spontaneous ornament. On the other side of this small water-way is a great shabby façade of Gothic windows and balconies—balconies on which dirty clothes are hung and under which a cavernous-looking doorway opens from a low flight of slimy watersteps. It is very hot and still, the canal has a queer smell, and the whole place is enchanting.

. . . After the middle of May the whole place was in a glow. The sea took on a thousand shades, but they were only infinite variations of blue, and those rosy walls I just spoke of began to flush in the thick sunshine. Every patch of color, every yard of weather-stained stucco, every glimpse of nestling garden or daub of sky above a *calle*, began to shine a sparkle— began, as the painters say, to "compose." The lagoon was streaked with odd currents, which played across it like huge smooth finger-marks. The gondolas multiplied and spotted it all over; every gondola and gondolier looking, at a distance, precisely like every other.

There is something strange and fascinating in this mysterious impersonality of the gondola. It has an identity when you are in it, but, thanks to their all being of the same size, shape and color, and of the same deportment and gait, it has none, or as little as possible, as you see it pass before you. From my windows on the Riva there was always the same silhouette—the long, black, slender skiff, lifting its head and throwing it back a little, moving yet seeming not to move, with the grotesquely-graceful figure on the poop. This figure inclines, as may be, more to the graceful or to the grotesque—standing in the "second position" of the dancing-master, but indulging, from the waist upward, in a freedom of movement which that functionary would deprecate. One may say, as a general thing, that there is something rather awkward in the movement of even the most graceful gondolier, and something graceful in the movement of the most awkward. In the graceful men of course the grace predominates, and nothing can be finer than the large firm way in which, from their point of vantage, they throw themselves over their tremendous oar. It has the boldness of a plunging bird, and the regularity of a pendulum. Sometimes, as you see this movement in profile, in a gondola that passes you—see, as you recline on your own low cushions, the arching body of the gondolier lifted up against the sky—it has a kind of nobleness which suggests an image on a Greek frieze. The gondolier at Venice is your very good friend—if you choose him happily—and on the quality of the personage depends a good deal that of your impressions. He is a part of your daily life, your double, your shadow, your complement. Most people, I think, either like their gondolier or hate him; and if they like him, like him very much. In this case they take an interest in him after his departure; wish him to be sure of employment, speak of him as the gem of gondoliers, and tell their friends to be certain to "secure" him. There is usually no difficulty in securing him; there is nothing elusive or reluctant about a gondolier. They are, for the most part, excellent fellows, and the sentimental tourist must always have a kindness for them. More than the rest of the population, of course, they are the children of Venice; they are associated with its idiosyncrasy, with its essence, with its silence, with its melancholy.

When I say they are associated with its silence, I should immediately add that they are associated also with its sound. Among themselves they are an extraordinarily talkative company. They chatter at the *traghetti*, where they always have some sharp point under discussion; they bawl across the canals; they bespeak your commands as you approach; they defy each other from afar. If you happen to have a *traghetto* under your window, you are well aware that they are a vocal race. I should go even farther than I went just now, and say that the voice of the gondolier is, in fact, the sound of Venice. There is scarcely any other, and that, indeed, is part of the interest of the place. There is no noise there save distinctly human noise; no rumbling, no vague uproar, no rattle of wheels and hoofs. It is all articulate, personal sound. One may say, indeed, that Venice is, emphatically, the city of conversation; people talk all over the place, because there is nothing to interfere with their being heard. Among the populace it is a kind of family party. The still water carries the voice, and good Venetians exchange confidences at a distance of half a mile. It saves a world of trouble, and they don't like trouble. Their delightful garrulous language helps them to make Venetian life a long *conversazione*. This language, with its soft elisions, its odd transpositions, its kindly contempt for consonants and other disagreeables, has in it something peculiarly human and accommodating. If your gondolier had no other merit, he would have the merit that he speaks Venetian. . . .

May in Venice is better than April, but June is best of all. Then the days are hot, but not too hot, and the nights are more beautiful than the days. Then Venice is rosier than ever in the morning and more golden than ever as the day descends. It seems to expand and evaporate, to multiply all its reflections and iridescences. Then the life of its people and the strangeness of its constitution become a perpetual comedy, or at least a perpetual drama. Then the gondola is your sole habitation, and you spend days between sea and sky. You go to the Lido, though the Lido has been spoiled. When I was first in Venice, in 1869, it was a very natural place, and there was only a rough lane across the little island from the landing-place to the beach. There was a bathing-place in those days, and a restaurant, which was very bad, but where, in the warm evenings, your dinner did not much matter as you sat letting it cool upon the wooden terrace that stretched out into the sea. Today the Lido is a part of united Italy, and has been made the victim of villainous improvements. A little cockney village has sprung up on its rural bosom, and a third-rate boulevard leads from Santa Elisabetta to the Adriatic. There are bitumen walls and gas-lamps, lodging-houses, shops, and a *teatro diurno*. The bathing-establishment is bigger than before, and the restaurant as well; but it is a compensation, perhaps, that the cuisine is no better. Such as it is, however, you will not scorn occasionally to partake of it on the breezy platform under which bathers dart and splash, and which looks out to where the fishing-boats, with sails of orange and crimson, wander along the darkening horizon. The beach at the Lido is still lonely and beautiful, and you can easily walk away from the cockney village. The return to Venice in the sunset is classical and indispensable, and those who, at that glowing hour, have floated toward the towers that rise out of the lagoon, will not easily part with the impression. But you indulge in larger excursions—you go to Burano and Torcello, to Malamocco and Chioggia. Torcello, like the Lido, has been improved; the deeply interesting little cathedral of the eighth century, which stood there on the edge of the sea, as touching in its ruin, with its grassy threshold and its primitive mosaics, as the bleached bones of a human skeleton washed ashore by the tide, has now been restored and made cheerful, and the charm of the place, its strange and suggestive desolation, has well-nigh departed.

It will still serve you as a pretext, however, for a day on the lagoon, especially as you will disembark at Burano and admire the wonderful fisher-folk, whose good looks—and bad manners, I am sorry to say—can scarcely be exaggerated. Burano is celebrated for the beauty of its women and the rapacity of its children, and it is a fact that though some of the ladies are rather bold about it, every one of them shows you a handsome face. The children assail you for coppers, and, in their desire to be satisfied, pursue your gondola into the sea. Chioggia is a larger Burano, and you carry away from either place a half-sad, half-cynical, but altogether pictorial impression; the impression of bright-colored hovels, of bathing in stagnant canals, of young girls with faces of a delicate shape and a susceptible expression, with splendid heads of hair and complexions smeared with powder, faded yellow shawls that hang like old Greek draperies, and little wooden shoes that click as they go up and down the steps of the convex bridges; of brown-cheeked matrons with lustrous tresses and high tempers, massive throats encased with gold beads, and eyes that meet your own with a certain traditional defiance. The men throughout the islands of Venice are almost as handsome as the women; I have never seen so many good-looking fellows. At Burano and Chioggia they sit mending their nets, or lounge at the street corners, where conversation is always high-pitched, or clamor to you to take a boat; and everywhere they decorate the scene with their splendid color—cheeks and throats as richly brown as the sails of their fishing-smacks—their sea-faded tatters which are always a "costume"—their soft Venetian jargon, and the gallantry with which they wear their hats—an article that nowhere sits so well as on a mass of dense Venetian curls. If you are happy, you will find yourself, after a June day in Venice (about ten o'clock), on a balcony that overhangs the Grand Canal, with your elbows on the broad ledge, a cigarette in your teeth, and a little good company beside you.

Scandinavia: Smörgåsbord and Communal Steam Baths

PAUL DU CHAILLU

FROM *The Land of the Midnight Sun*

1871–78

As described in the introduction to Paul Du Chaillu's African travels (page 290), in 1871 suddenly he turned his attention from the equatorial latitudes of Africa to the near-arctic latitudes of northern Europe. For the greater part of the next seven years he crossed and crisscrossed the Scandinavian peninsula from southern Sweden to northernmost Lapland, everywhere living with the people on the most familiar terms. The characteristically intimate episodes described below are taken from that voluminous and enthusiastic record of his experiences, The Land of the Midnight Sun.

SMÖRGÅSBORD

DINNER in Sweden is invariably preceded by a *smörgås*, a series of strange dishes eaten as a relish.

I was led to a little table, called *smörgåsbord*, around which we all clustered, and upon which I saw a display of smoked reindeer meat, cut into small thin slices; smoked salmon with poached eggs; fresh, raw, sliced salmon, called *graflax*, upon which salt had been put about an hour before; hard-boiled eggs; caviare; fried sausage; a sort of anchovy, caught on the western coast; raw salted Norwegian herring, exceedingly fat, cut into small pieces; *sillsallat*, made of pickled herring, small pieces of boiled meat, potatoes, eggs, red beets and raw onions, and seasoned with pepper, vinegar, and olive-oil; smoked goose-breast; cucumbers; soft brown and white bread, cut into small slices; *knäckebrod*, a sort of flat, hard bread, made of coarse rye flour, and flavored with anise-seed; *siktadt* bread, very thin, and made of the finest bolted flour; butter; *gammal ost*, the strongest old cheese one can taste, and *kummin ost*, a cheese seasoned with cara-way; three crystal decanters, containing different kinds of *bränvin* (spirits); *renadt*, made from rye or potatoes; *pomerans*, made from renadt, with the addition of oil of bitter orange, and somewhat sweet; and *finkelbränvin*, or unpurified spirit. Around the decanters were ranged tiny glasses, and the gentlemen of the party drank one or the other of these potations as an appetizer; the dishes and the spirits were alike strange to me. Every-thing was tastefully arranged upon a snowy cloth—the plates, knives, forks, and napkins being placed as at a collation; but when, as the guest, I was invited to help myself first, I was at a loss how to begin; the meal was eaten standing. Observing my predicament, the hostess came kindly to my rescue, and helped herself first—taking a piece of bread and spreading butter upon it, and then selecting tidbits with a fork. I kept up a conver-sation with the host, but observed the proceedings warily all the time, in order to know what to do next; knives and forks were used in common. I began with bread, butter, and reindeer meat, which were good; and seeing that everyone was enjoying the graflax, I resolved to try it; but the slice was hardly in my mouth before I wished I had not made the experi-ment. It was too late; I had to eat it; there was no possibility of escape. My stomach was ready to give way; but the only thing to be done was to swallow what I had taken; a small glass of renadt, drunk immediately afterwards, saved me. I did not repeat the experiment of eating graflax that day, nor for many days thereafter. The smoked salmon was an im-provement upon the graflax, but that was bad enough; the sillsallat, which is considered a great delicacy when the herrings are fat, I found to be palatable; and sundry other dishes I liked very much, the smoked goose-breast being particularly delicate; but I shall never forget my first impres-sions of the raw salmon. Afterwards I became very fond of sillsallat, and, in fact, of everything that was put upon a smörgåsbord, with the exception of graflax, which I can now eat, but have serious doubts whether I shall ever be able to enjoy. . . .

AROUND A LAPLAND TENT

THERE was not the slightest appearance of shyness in these people; we were welcomed at once; the coffee-kettle was put over the fire; coffee, already roasted, was ground, boiled, and clarified with a piece of dry fish-skin, and served to me in a queer-shaped little silver cup, which I admired very much; it was a family heirloom, said to be about a hundred years old. The shape of the spoon was very graceful. This also was a family relic, and a great deal older than the cup; it was not clean, reindeer milk having dried upon it, and I was much amused at the way the girl washed it. As there was no water at hand, she passed her little red tongue over it several times until it was quite clean and smooth; and then, as if it had been a matter of course, filled it with milk from a bowl, stirred up the coffee, and handed me the cup. I did not altogether admire this way of cleaning spoons. Happily, her teeth were exquisitely white, and her lips as red as a cherry; and, although I have seen many Laplanders since, I think she was the prettiest one I ever met.

The coffee was excellent. I had hardly finished a second cup when a Laplander came in, followed by several dogs; he had just arrived with two hundred and seventy-three reindeer, which were around the tent, but the approach had been so quiet that we did not hear him. Some of the animals were eating the moss, using their forefeet to detach it, while others were lying down; the males were of large size, with spreading horns, the females much smaller. Not one showed any inclination to move off, the whole herd being as still as the cows which come to the farm-yard to be milked; the bulls were quiet, though several were butting one another; I was told that their horns often become so entangled that the animals cannot be separated, and have to be killed.

I watched the milking with great interest. The women knew every animal around the tent, and if one had been missing they would have been able to designate it at once. Those which were to be milked were approached carefully, and a lasso was thrown gently over the horns, and knotted over the muzzle, to prevent the deer from running away; but they made no effort to escape. Sometimes one would hold the deer while another was milking; but the animals were so gentle that they required no coercion. The process was peculiar: the woman held in one hand a wooden scoop, frequently pressing hard with the other, for the thick fluid seemed to come with difficulty; it was poured from the scoop into a keg-like vessel closed by a sliding cover, and so contrived that it could be carried on the back of an animal. Skin bladders were also filled, to be used by the Lapps who were to remain the whole day with the herds. I was surprised at the small yield—some not giving enough to fill a small coffee-cup; but it was very thick and rich—so much so, that water had to be added before drinking; it is exceedingly nourishing, and has a strong flavor, not unlike that of goat's milk. The milk of the reindeer forms a very important item in the food of the Lapps, and possesses an amount of nutrition far greater than that of the cow or the ass; strange to say, the butter made from it is so bad that one might almost fancy that he was eating tallow; accordingly, the Lapps make very little butter, but cheese is produced in large quantities.

In the making of cheese, the milk is first heated, and the scum rising to the top is put in a wooden bowl, while the greater part is then placed in an empty bladder, which is afterwards hung up for its contents to dry; this dried scum, which they call *kappa* (cream) is considered a great dainty, and is always given to distinguished guests. Then rennet is added to the milk. The cheese is pressed by hand, and is packed in round wooden boxes, or put in forms made of plaited spruce roots; after it is dried it is hung up in the smoke in the *kåta*; it is white inside, and tastes of the milk, a great deal of which is kept for winter use. . . .

[Du Chaillu describes the following quaint custom in a chapter on the innocent simplicity of the people of northern Scandinavia.]

BATHING *en Famille*

MY usual experience ran thus: I express the wish to take a warm bath, and at once the preparation begins. The cow-house undergoes a complete transformation; the great iron pot, encased in solid masonry in a corner, used to cook food for the cattle, is thoroughly cleansed and filled with water; when this has become heated the fire is extinguished; everything has been thoroughly swept, and new straw is spread around for me to step upon, so I shall not soil my feet: I am just in the kettle when a stout girl of twenty summers, more or less, jumps in, dress and all, saying, "Paulus, I have come to help you." The words are hardly spoken before she begins to rub me with soap in a most forcible manner, and then to switch me with birch-twigs! The only thing to be done is to consider myself her little brother, and I submit in the meekest possible manner. I have been subjected to the same treatment, minus the switching, in Stockholm and other places, but by women old enough to be my grand-mother.

One of the most characteristic institutions of the country is the *sauna* (bath-house), called *badstuga* in Swedish. It is a small log-house, built very tight, with no windows, having a single aperture above to let the smoke out; in the centre is an oven-like structure built of loose stones, under which a fire is kept burning till they are very hot; then the fire is extinguished, and the women clean the place thoroughly of ashes and soot, the smoke-hole having been in the meantime closed. A large vessel filled with water is placed within; a number of slender twigs, generally of young birch-trees, are put into it, to be used as switches. The bath-house stands by itself, and at some distance from the other buildings, for safety in case it should take fire. Every Saturday evening, summer and winter, all over that northern country smoke is seen issuing from these structures. It is the invariable custom for all the household, on that day, to take a bath, for the work of the week is ended and the beginning of Sunday has come. After washing, all put on clean linen and their best clothes.

The stranger, the passing inhabitant of the cities, does not bathe with the people, for they are shy: he may have his bath, but all alone. It was only when they had come to regard me as one of themselves that I was allowed to accompany them; then the neighbors, old and young, would often come to bathe and keep company with Paulus. I remember well my first bath *en famille*. One Saturday afternoon a couple of young fellows, friends of mine, as the girls were giving the last touches in cleaning the badstuga, shouted, "Paulus, take a bath with us today!" "Yes, do," ex-claimed the rest of the company, among whom were the father and mother of the large family. The weather was piercing cold, the ground covered with snow, and I was glad that the bathing-place was within a stone's throw of the dwelling. From my window I noticed several maidens wending their way with rapid steps towards it, in a costume that reminded me of Africa, minus the color. I did not wonder at their speed, for the thermometer stood below zero. Soon three rather elderly women took the same route from a neighboring farm, but the two oldest were clothed with old skirts around their waists; other young women followed, and all were quickly lost to sight behind the door, which they at once shut. They must be about to hold a sort of levee in the bath, thought I. Several aged men then made their appearance, followed in quick succession by younger ones, and children of all sizes; none had on any clothing whatever, and they also joined the throng inside.

When I saw the field clear, I thought it was time to make a rush for the building. I emerged from my room at a running pace, for I was dressed as scantily as those who had preceded me. I hastily pushed the door open, and was welcomed by the voices of all the company as I closed it behind me. The heat was so intense that I could hardly breathe, and I begged them not to raise any more steam for awhile; the sudden transition from twenty degrees below zero to such an atmosphere overpowered me. As my eyes became accustomed to the darkness of the place, by the dim light which came through the cracks of the door I began to recognize the faces of my friends. There were more people than usual, for all the neighbors had come to have a bath with Paulus. At first I seated myself on one of the lower benches built around, after awhile getting on the other above. More water was poured on the hot stones, and such a volume of steam arose that I could not endure it, so I jumped down again, and reclined in a half seated posture in order to breathe more freely. In a short time I was in a most profuse perspiration; again and again steam was raised by pouring water on the stones, till at last the hot air and steam became extremely oppressive.

Now and then we poured water on each other, which caused a delightful sensation of relief; then with boughs every one's back and loins were switched till they smarted severely. "Let me give you a switching, Paulus," a fair-haired damsel or a young fellow would say; "and after you get yours I want you to give me one." This operation is beneficial, as it quickens the circulation of the blood in the skin. In about half an hour the people began to depart, first submitting to a final flagellation, after which cold water was poured upon the body; then all went home as naked as they came. As I emerged from the hut the sensation was delightful, the breathing of the cold air imparting fresh vigor and exhilarating my spirits; I rolled myself in the snow, as did some others, and afterwards ran as fast as I could to the farm-house. In some places the men and women, as if by agreement, do not return together, and the old women wear something around their loins as they go to or come from the bath. I have gone out of the bath-house with the mercury at thirty-two degrees below zero. It is not dangerous to walk a short distance, as long as the perspiration is not suddenly and entirely checked.

On returning one does not dress at once, for he must get cool gradually and check the dripping perspiration. I had hardly been fifteen minutes in my room, when suddenly the door opened (the people here, as is the case in most parts of Sweden, never knock at the door) and the wife, who had dressed herself, came in, and was not in the least abashed at my appearance; she talked with me as if I were in my morning-gown. The door opened again, and a grown daughter entered, and then another. I began to fear that all the neighbors were coming, as if to a reception. Though they did not seem in the least troubled, I was; I seated myself on a chair, however, and for a short time we carried on a rambling conversation; they then left, and I dressed myself and went into the stuga, or family room. At first I could hardly keep my countenance, for the sight was extremely ludicrous. There was a crowd of visitors, neighbors of different ages, and among them three old fellows—a grandfather, father, and an uncle—who were sitting upon one of the benches with legs crossed, minus a particle of clothing, shaving themselves without a looking-glass. Nobody seemed to mind them, for the women were knitting, weaving, and chatting. This was certainly a scene primitive enough. When the men had finished shaving, clean shirts were brought, and they then dressed themselves while seated. The men usually shave once a week, oftener when courting, and always after the bath, for the beard then becomes soft.

The Fine Art of Seeing an Alpine Sunrise

MARK TWAIN

FROM A *Tramp Abroad*

1878

*Ever on the move, young Samuel Clemens—Mark Twain—
was in succession (as described in the introduction to* Roughing It *on
pages 880–81) a journeyman printer, a Mississippi pilot, a Nevada pros-
pector and a newspaperman in California. His first success as a writer
came in 1866 with the publication of the letters he wrote during a trip
to the Sandwich Islands. They in turn brought him a commission for a
similar series on a Mediterranean cruise in which he toured France, Italy,
Greece, Constantinople, the Holy Land and Egypt; and it was this that
yielded the travel book that made him famous,* The Innocents Abroad
(1869).

*The Innocents Abroad also established his formula in travel writing:
passages of straightforward information or history—or sometimes the
consciously elevated prose of a "set piece"—punctuated by irreverent
opinions or outrageous tall tales.*

*Although there had been Americans before Twain who found Europe's
wonders exaggerated, faded or even fake, the usual attitude was that of a
pilgrim at a shrine or a countryman in the big city. Twain was a little of
both, capable of writing a panegyric on the gardens of Versailles or Athens
in the moonlight but invariably interrupting even the most solemn-seeming
passages with absurd digressions or tall tales, and giving as much space to*

619

mocking those who admired art hypocritically or worshiped church relics blindly.

A few years later he added another dimension to his reputation with the publication of The Adventures of Tom Sawyer. *But in 1880 he returned to travel writing with* A Tramp Abroad, *this time concentrating on Germany and Switzerland but serving up the same wildly whimsical melange of local history, legend, satire and farcical incident. The comic exuberance had, however, begun to flag, and the third of his travel books,* Following the Equator (1897), *based on a round-the-world lecture tour which he undertook at the age of sixty to pay off debts, has the earmarks of a work written out of habit rather than inspiration.*

[In A *Tramp Abroad* Twain first describes a tour of Germany, including Heidelberg with its dueling societies, the Black Forest, and a trip down the Neckar River on a log raft; then he goes on to Switzerland, bringing back from the Alps such reports as the one below, with its resemblances to those which Dumas (see pages 549–57) had made fifty years before.]

T HE Rigi-Kulm is an imposing Alpine mass, six thousand feet high, which stands by itself, and commands a mighty prospect of blue lakes, green valleys, and snowy mountains—a compact and magnificent picture three hundred miles in circumference. The ascent is made by rail, or horseback, or on foot, as one may prefer. I and my agent panoplied ourselves in walking-costume, one bright morning, and started down the lake on the steamboat; we got ashore at the village of Wäggis, three-quarters of an hour distant from Lucerne. This village is at the foot of the mountain.

We were soon tramping leisurely up the leafy mule-path, and then the talk began to flow, as usual. It was twelve o'clock noon, and a breezy, cloudless day; the ascent was gradual, and the glimpses, from under the curtaining boughs, of blue water, and tiny sailboats, and beetling cliffs, were as charming as glimpses of dreamland. All the circumstances were perfect—and the anticipations, too, for we should soon be enjoying, for the first time, that wonderful spectacle, an Alpine sunrise—the object of our journey. There was (apparently) no real need to hurry, for the guidebook made the walking-distance from Wäggis to the summit only three hours and a quarter. . . . When we had walked half an hour, we were fairly into the swing and humor of the undertaking, so we cleared for action; that is to say, we got a boy whom we met to carry our alpenstocks and satchels and overcoats and things for us; that left us free for business. I suppose we must have stopped oftener to stretch out on the grass in the shade and take a bit of a smoke than this boy was used to, for presently he asked if it had been our idea to hire him by the job, or by the year? We told him he could move along if he was in a hurry. He said he wasn't in such a very particular hurry, but he wanted to get to the top while he was young. We told him to clear out, then, and leave the things at the uppermost hotel and say we should be along presently. He said he would secure us a hotel if he could, but if they were all full he would ask them to build another one and hurry up and get the paint and plaster dry against we arrived. Still gently chaffing us, he pushed ahead, up the trail, and soon disappeared. By six o'clock we were pretty high up in the air, and the view of lake and mountains had greatly grown in breadth and interest. We halted awhile at a little public house, where we had bread and cheese and a quart or two of fresh milk, out on the porch, with the big panorama all before us—and then moved on again.

Ten minutes afterward we met a hot, red-faced man plunging down the mountain, with mighty strides, swinging his alpenstock ahead of him, and taking a grip on the ground with its iron point to support these big strides. He stopped, fanned himself with his hat, swabbed the perspiration from his face and neck with a red handkerchief, panted a moment or two, and asked how far it was to Wäggis. I said three hours. He looked surprised, and said:

"Why, it seems as if I could toss a biscuit into the lake from here, it's so close by. Is that an inn, there?"

I said it was.

"Well," said he, "I can't stand another three hours, I've had enough for today; I'll take a bed there."

I asked: "Are we nearly to the top?"

"Nearly to the *top!* Why, bless your soul, you haven't really started yet."

I said we would put up at the inn, too. So we turned back and ordered a hot supper, and had quite a jolly evening of it with this Englishman.

The German landlady gave us neat rooms and nice beds, and when I and my agent turned in, it was with the resolution to be up early and make the utmost of our first Alpine sunrise. But of course we were dead tired, and slept like policemen; so when we awoke in the morning and ran to the window it was already too late, because it was half past eleven. It was a sharp disappointment. . . .

We got under way about the turn of ncon, and pulled out for the summit again, with a fresh and vigorous step. . . .

Presently we came upon half a dozen sheep nibbling grass in the spray of a stream of clear water that sprang from a rock wall a hundred feet high, and all at once our ears were startled with a melodious "Lul . . . l . . . l . . . lul-lul-*la*hee-o-o-o!" pealing joyously from a near but invisible source, and recognized that we were hearing for the first time the famous Alpine *jodel* in its own native wilds. And we recognized, also, that it was that sort of quaint commingling of barytone and falsetto which at home we call "Tyrolese warbling."

The jodeling (pronounced yodling—emphasis on the *o*) continued, and was very pleasant and inspiriting to hear. Now the jodeler appeared— a shepherd boy of sixteen—and in our gladness and gratitude we gave him a franc to jodel some more. So he jodeled and we listened. We moved on, presently, and he generously jodeled us out of sight. After about fifteen minutes we came across another shepherd boy who was jodeling, and gave him half a franc to keep it up. He also jodeled us out of sight. After that, we found a jodeler every ten minutes; we gave the first one eight cents, the second one six cents, the third one four, the fourth one a penny, contributed nothing to Nos. 5, 6, and 7, and during the remainder of the day hired the rest of the jodelers, at a franc apiece, not to jodel any more. . . .

At ten minutes past six we reached the Kaltbad station, where there is a spacious hotel with great verandas which command a majestic expanse of lake and mountain scenery. We were pretty well fagged out, now, but as we did not wish to miss the Alpine sunrise, we got through with our dinner as quickly as possible and hurried off to bed. It was unspeakably comfortable to stretch our weary limbs between the cool, damp sheets. And how we did sleep!—for there is no opiate like Alpine pedestrianism.

In the morning we both awoke and leaped out of bed at the same instant and ran and stripped aside the window-curtains; but we suffered a bitter disappointment again: it was already half past three in the afternoon.

We dressed sullenly and in ill spirits, each accusing the other of oversleeping. Harris said if we had brought the courier along, as we ought to have done, we should not have missed these sunrises. I said he knew very well that one of us would have had to sit up and wake the courier;

and I added that we were having trouble enough to take care of ourselves, on this climb, without having to take care of a courier besides.

During breakfast our spirits came up a little, since we found by the guide-book that in the hotels on the summit the tourist is not left to trust to luck for his sunrise, but is roused betimes by a man who goes through the halls with a great Alpine horn, blowing blasts that would raise the dead. . . .

[It is after 4 P.M. before they get started again.]

WE climbed, and climbed; and we kept on climbing; we reached about forty summits, but there was always another one just ahead. It came on to rain, and it rained in dead earnest. We were soaked through and it was bitter cold. Next a smoky fog of clouds covered the whole region densely, and we took to the railway-ties to keep from getting lost. Sometimes we slopped along in a narrow path on the left-hand side of the track, but by and by when the fog blew aside a little and we saw that we were treading the rampart of a precipice and that our left elbows were projecting over a perfectly boundless and bottomless vacancy, we gasped, and jumped for the ties again.

The night shut down, dark and drizzly and cold. About eight in the evening the fog lifted and showed us a well-worn path which led up a very steep rise to the left. We took it, and as soon as we had got far enough from the railway to render the finding it again an impossibility, the fog shut down on us once more.

We were in a bleak, unsheltered place, now, and had to trudge right along, in order to keep warm, though we rather expected to go over a precipice, sooner or later. About nine o'clock we made an important discovery —that we were not in any path. We groped around a while on our hands and knees, but could not find it; so we sat down in the mud and the wet scant grass to wait. . . .

At some time or other the fog thinned a little; we did not know when, for we were facing the empty universe and the thinness could not show; but at last Harris happened to look around, and there stood a huge, dim, spectral hotel where the precipice had been. One could faintly discern the windows and chimneys, and a dull blur of lights. Our first emotion was deep, unutterable gratitude, our next was a foolish rage, born of the suspicion that possibly the hotel had been visible three-quarters of an hour while we sat there in those cold puddles quarreling.

Yes, it was the Rigi-Kulm hotel—the one that occupies the extreme summit, and whose remote little sparkle of lights we had often seen glinting high aloft among the stars from our balcony away down yonder in Lucerne. The crusty portier and the crusty clerks gave us the surly reception which their kind deal in in prosperous times, but by mollifying them with an extra display of obsequiousness and servility we finally got them to show us to the room which our boy had engaged for us.

We got into some dry clothing, and while our supper was preparing we loafed forsakenly through a couple of vast cavernous drawing-rooms, one of which had a stove in it. This stove was in a corner, and densely walled around with people. We could not get near the fire, so we moved at large in the arctic spaces, among a multitude of people who sat silent, smileless, forlorn, and shivering—thinking what fools they were to come, perhaps. There were some Americans and some Germans, but one could see that the great majority were English. . . .

Supper warmed us, and we went immediately to bed—but first, as Mr. Baedeker requests all tourists to call his attention to any errors which they may find in his guide-books, I dropped him a line to inform him that when he said the foot journey from Wäggis to the summit was only three hours and a quarter, he missed it by just about three days. I had previously informed him of his mistake about the distance from Allerheiligen to Oppenau, and had also informed the Ordnance Department of the German government of the same error in the imperial maps. I will add, here, that I never got any answer to these letters, or any thanks from either of these sources; and, what is still more discourteous, these corrections have not been made, either in the maps or the guide-books. But I will write again when I get time, for my letters may have miscarried.

We curled up in the clammy beds, and went to sleep without rocking. We were so sodden with fatigue that we never stirred nor turned over till the blooming blasts of the Alpine horn aroused us. It may well be imagined that we did not lose any time. We snatched on a few odds and ends of clothing, cocooned ourselves in the proper red blankets, and plunged along the halls and out into the whistling wind bareheaded. We saw a tall wooden scaffolding on the very peak of the summit, a hundred yards away, and made for it. We rushed up the stairs to the top of this scaffolding, and stood there, above the vast outlying world, with hair flying and ruddy blankets waving and cracking in the fierce breeze.

"Fifteen minutes too late, at last!" said Harris, in a vexed voice. "The sun is clear above the horizon."

"No matter," I said, "it is a most magnificent spectacle, and we will see it do the rest of its rising, anyway."

In a moment we were deeply absorbed in the marvel before us, and dead to everything else. The great cloud-barred disk of the sun stood just above a limitless expanse of tossing white-caps—so to speak—a billowy chaos of massy mountain domes and peaks draped in imperishable snow, and flooded with an opaline glory of changing and dissolving splendors, while through rifts in a black cloud-bank above the sun, radiating lances of diamond dust shot to the zenith. The cloven valleys of the lower world swam in a tinted mist which veiled the ruggedness of their crags and ribs and ragged forests, and turned all the forbidding region into a soft and rich and sensuous paradise.

We could not speak. We could hardly breathe. We could only gaze in drunken ecstasy and drink it in.

Presently Harris exclaimed: "Why—'nation, it's going *down!*"

Perfectly true. We had missed the morning hornblow, and slept all day. This was stupefying.

Harris said: "Look here, the sun isn't the spectacle—it's us, stacked up here on top of this gallows, in these idiotic blankets, and two hundred and fifty well-dressed men and women down here gawking up at us and not caring a straw whether the sun rises or sets, as long as they've got such a ridiculous spectacle as this to set down in their memorandum-books. They seem to be laughing their ribs loose, and there's one girl there that appears to be going all to pieces. I never saw such a man as you before. I think you are the very last possibility in the way of an ass."

"What have *I* done?" I answered, with heat.

"What have you done? You've got up at half past seven o'clock in the evening to see the sun rise, that's what you've done."

"And have you done any better, I'd like to know? I always used to get up with the lark, till I came under the petrifying influence of your turgid intellect." . . .

And so the customary quarrel went on. When the sun was fairly down, we slipped back to the hotel in the charitable gloaming, and went to bed again. We had encountered the horn-blower on the way, and he had tried to collect compensation, not only for announcing the sunset, which we did see, but for the sunrise, which we had totally missed; but we said no, we only took our solar rations on the "European plan"—pay for what you get. He promised to make us hear his horn in the morning, if we were alive.

He kept his word. We heard his horn and instantly got up. It was dark and cold and wretched. As I fumbled around for the matches, knocking things down with my quaking hands, I wished the sun would rise in the middle of the day, when it was warm and bright and cheerful, and one wasn't sleepy. We proceeded to dress by the gloom of a couple of sickly candles, but we could hardly button anything, our hands shook so. I thought of how many happy people there were in Europe, Asia, and America, and everywhere, who were sleeping peacefully in their beds, and did not have to get up and see the Rigi sunrise—people who did not appreciate their advantage, as like as not, but would get up in the morning wanting more boons of Providence.

While thinking these thoughts I yawned, in a rather ample way, and my upper teeth got hitched on a nail over the door, and while I was mounting a chair to free myself, Harris drew the window-curtain, and said: "Oh, this is luck! We sha'n't have to go out at all—yonder are the mountains, in full view."

That was glad news, indeed. It made us cheerful right away. One could see the grand Alpine masses dimly outlined against the black firmament, and one or two faint stars blinking through rifts in the night. Fully clothed, and wrapped in blankets, we huddled ourselves up, by the window, with lighted pipes, and fell into chat, while we waited in exceeding comfort to see how an Alpine sunrise was going to look by candlelight. By and by a delicate, spiritual sort of effulgence spread itself by imperceptible degrees over the loftiest altitudes of the snowy wastes—but there the effort seemed to stop.

I said, presently: "There is a hitch about this sunrise somewhere. It doesn't seem to go. What do you reckon is the matter with it?"

"I don't know. It appears to hang fire somewhere. I never saw a sunrise act like that before. Can it be that the hotel is playing anything on us?"

"Of course not. The hotel merely has a property interest in the sun, it has nothing to do with the management of it. It is a precarious kind of property, too; a succession of total eclipses would probably ruin this tavern. Now what can be the matter with this sunrise?"

Harris jumped up and said: "I've got it! I know what's the matter with it! We've been looking at the place where the sun *set* last night!"

"It is perfectly true! Why couldn't you have thought of that sooner? Now we've lost another one! And all through your blundering. It was exactly like you to light a pipe and sit down to wait for the sun to rise in the west."

"It was exactly like me to find out the mistake, too. You never would have found it out. I find out all the mistakes."

"You make them all, too, else your most valuable faculty would be wasted on you. But don't stop to quarrel now—maybe we are not too late yet."

But we were. The sun was well up when we got to the exhibition-ground. . . .

I believed we could walk down to Wäggis or Vitznau in a day, but I knew we could go down by rail in about an hour, so I chose the latter method. I wanted to see what it was like, anyway. The train came along about the middle of the afternoon, and an odd thing it was. The locomotive-boiler stood on end, and it and the whole locomotive were tilted sharply backward. There were two passenger-cars, roofed, but wide open all around. These cars were not tilted back, but the seats were; this enables the passenger to sit level while going down a steep incline. . . .

We got front seats, and while the train moved along about fifty yards on level ground, I was not the least frightened; but now it started abruptly down-stairs, and I caught my breath. And I, like my neighbors, unconsciously held back all I could, and threw my weight to the rear, but, of course, that did no particular good. I had slidden down the balusters when I was a boy, and thought nothing of it, but to slide down the balusters in a railway-train is a thing to make one's flesh creep. . . .

By the time one reaches Kaltbad, he has acquired confidence in the railway, and he now ceases to try to ease the locomotive by holding back. . . . There is nothing to interrupt the view or the breeze; it is like inspecting the world on the wing. However—to be exact—there is one place where the serenity lapses for a while; this is while one is crossing the Schnurrtobel Bridge, a frail structure which swings its gossamer frame down through the dizzy air, over a gorge, like a vagrant spider-strand.

One has no difficulty in remembering his sins while the train is creeping down this bridge; and he repents of them, too; though he sees, when he gets to Vitznau, that he need not have done it, the bridge was perfectly safe.

So ends the eventful trip which we made to the Rigi-Kulm to see an Alpine sunrise.

Dining in Paris: An Englishman's Report

GEORGE AUGUSTUS SALA

FROM *Paris Herself Again*

1878-79

When in 1856 young George Augustus Sala persuaded Charles Dickens, then editor of Household Words, *to send him to Russia to do a series of articles, he became one of the first of the breed we now call foreign correspondents. Thereafter for more than forty years Sala went off at intervals to report on life in America, Algeria, Italy, Germany, Spain, France, Constantinople, Hawaii, Australia and a host of other places. Besides a vast mass of magazine and newspaper correspondence, these journeys yielded a stream of travel books marked by a style that was generally exuberant and sometimes gaudy. Obviously influenced by Dickens' technique of characterizing by exaggeration, Sala went a step further and relied heavily on caricature. Naturally discursive—and apparently paid by the installment—he tended to enlarge on every theme until he had exhausted it, and sometimes the reader too. In such books as* Journey Due North (Russia in 1856) *and* America Revisited (he had been in the United States during the Civil War and went back again in 1879-80) *this tendency produced much high-colored froth, but in* Paris Herself Again, *written of a country where he had gone to school as a boy and visited a score of times, it led to some very penetrating and amusing pictures of French life and manners in the 1870s.*

[The immediate reason for Sala's trip to France in 1878 was
to report on the latest Universal Exhibition in Paris, which
also marked France's recovery from defeat at the hands of
the Prussians in 1870. So *Paris Herself Again* is a critical survey both of the exhibits at the fair and of the state of things
in the City of Light. Having recalled the great Paris restaurants he had known as a youth in the 1850s, he describes in
the passages below what visitors to the fair could expect in
the city's dining places and markets.]

THE Café Anglais still, to my thinking, maintains its place as the very
best for dining purposes in Paris. You will dine well if you order any one of
the dishes specified in the bill of fare; but you will dine much better (if
you know enough about French cookery to dismiss the *carte du jour* entirely from consideration) by ordering a dinner altogether "out of your own
head." . . . A very modest little dinner at the Café Anglais for two people
of long experience, but moderate appetites and limited means, consisted of
a dozen of Marennes oysters, of goodly size and delicious flavour; *no fish*
(I hold fish to be a surplusage when you have had more than three oysters);
a *Crécy* soup; a *perdrix aux choux*—a tiny partridge braised with cabbage,
carrots, and small sausages; some *gruyère* cheese, a *salade à la romaine*, and
a bottle of the excellent Bordeaux wine called Pontet Canet. The partridge
and cabbage cost ten francs, and the dish was dear at the price; but the
Pontet Canet, which cost eight francs, was worth the money, and more,
for it was so much purple velvet to the palate; and it had a flavour which
reminded you at once of the odour of violets and the taste of raspberries.
This dinner—stay, it included a *demi-tasse* of coffee and an undeniably
authentic Havana cigar, the last an almost unattainable luxury in Paris—
cost twenty-eight francs and some centimes: with the waiter's fee, thirty
francs; say twelve shillings a head. Now there is good *vin ordinaire* to be
had at the Café Anglais for three francs—I am not quite sure that it is not
two francs fifty—a bottle, and the average price of an *entrée* is three francs
and a half; thus you may set down our oysters, our *perdrix aux choux*, and
our Pontet Canet as so much reckless extravagance; but please to remember that a Frenchman, or even an Englishman, who had set his heart on
having "a regular tip-top French dinner," even if he had suppressed the

preliminary bivalves, would have thought his repast incomplete without a dish of fish, a *rôti*—say a *Chateaubriand* or an *entrecôte à la Bordelaise*; a sweet—say a *parfait au café* or a *soufflé de chocolat*; and some fruit.

The Frenchman would assuredly have taken a tiny glass of *fine champagne* cognac, chartreuse, or some other liqueur, with his *demi-tasse*; and the Englishman would, in all probability, have wound up with at least half a bottle of Pommery Sec or Heidsieck's Dry Monopole. As for the French, it is with the extremest rarity that, save at Carnival time, or at a *repas de noces*, they ever touch champagne, which is often alluded to contemptuously, as "*le vin des cocottes*," and more frequently "*le vin des Allemands*." They are content to make it in order to sell it to the foreigner. Thus such a complete dinner as that which I have specified, at the Café Anglais, would cost at least twenty-five francs a head. . . .

The drawbacks to this very admirable house are, normally, in the smallness of the rooms, the low ceilings of which render them in summer nearly as hot as the *piombi* of Venice; and, abnormally, in the tremendous crowds of visitors brought by the Exhibition, and the clatter and *tapage* made by some of the foreign guests, whose nationality I will not particularise, at whose guttural gabble the English simply stare with stupefied amazement, while the few French gentlemen whom the guttural gabblers have not driven away sit silent in corners glowering with rage at the Invaders. They are as objectionable in peace as in war. This is especially the case on Sundays, when a Frenchman, having in all likelihood been to the races, is very fond of enjoying a good dinner. Unless he be one of a party, or has secured a *cabinet particulier* in advance, he will have considerable difficulty in making headway against this alien cohort, who—men, women, and children—come six or eight strong, and virtually monopolise the public rooms. They are all gifted with enormous appetites, and they have an unquenchable thirst for champagne; so that I imagine that the Parisian *restaurateurs* console themselves for the nuisance inflicted upon them by these turbulent (and upon occasion insolent) customers by making out the very biggest bills imaginable against them. . . .

[He then goes on to discuss dining in what he calls a "forty-sous restaurant."]

. . . ONE of the direst characteristics of the one-and-eightpenny repast is its being the caricature, the parody, the grotesque but effete phantom of a good dinner. . . . Thus in the number of its component parts the banquet provided by Gargottier *aîné* or Boustifaille *jeune* corresponds to the lord-liest dinner that you could order at Bignon's or Durand's. For your forty sous you shall have *hors d'oeuvres*, a *potage*, fish, an *entrée*, a roast, a vege-table, a sweet, salad, cheese, and dessert. But there the resemblance to the good dinner comes to an end. You are in a Shadowy Land, where "all things wear an aspect not their own." Somehow a fishy flavour gets into the bruised peach or the sleepy pear of the dessert; and it *must* have been *fromage de Brie* that you tasted just now in the chocolate cream. My own opinion is that it is "the gravy that does it"; and that the foundation of that gravy is something beyond mortal ken. The fish induces you to think that there are finny denizens of the deep as yet undiscovered by Mr. Frank Buckland; and as for the meat, well, what was it that the wicked Count Cenci gave his daughters to eat?—"the fevered flesh of buffaloes," or some such unholy viands? I have partaken of many strange meals, but there is a *je ne sais quoi* about some of the dishes at the cheap Paris restaurants altogether beyond my powers of definition or analysis. . . .

I have hinted that I tried the "Dîner Burnand." It was, not excepting a "Court" night at the hall of one of our civic companies, the most wire-drawn dinner to which I ever sat down; and yet there were no speeches, no glees, no songs. There was a little money-taker's box on the landing of the staircase leading from the Galérie de Valois to the saloons of the "Dîner Burnand," and an elegantly-attired lady gave me, in exchange for my five francs, a large octagonal metal ticket with "Un Dîner" stamped upon it. That was enough to make you uncomfortable to begin with. Who likes to be badged and ticketed, and to be sent a-wandering through strange rooms with "Good for One Dinner" branded, so to speak, on his back?

The Administration, having got hold of your money, has no further personal interest in you. You are an incumbrance; and the Administration may be looking on peevishly while you are consuming your five francs' worth of victuals. "You just gnaw it out," said an American friend to me. . . .

The oldest waiters in Paris had seemingly been "laid on" to attend on the guests at the "Dîner Burnand." But that these ancient servitors pos-sessed, to all appearance, the proper complement of arms and legs, they might have been so many *vieux grognards* from the Hôtel des Invalides, in civilian garb, with their moustaches shaved off, and their medals stowed away in their trousers-pockets. I was waited upon by a *vieux de la vieille*, a veteran of the first line, who might—so old did he look—have been at Marengo when the historic *poulet* was first fried in oil, owing to Napoleon's cook being for the moment short of butter. Marengo! He looked old enough to have been the inventor of that Sauce Robert, the oldest of all known sauces for pork-chops, and which Mr. Dallas has ascertained to be a sauce of English origin, and to have been known to the *gourmets* of Chaucer's time. I hasten to admit that this patriarch waited upon us with much zeal and assiduity, and was particularly anxious to explain to us the extent of our rights and privileges in the matter of dinner. "You are entitled to yet another *hors d'oeuvre*," he gently remarked, when I contented myself with a single sardine; "be not afraid; you may have butter and olives, radishes or sausage." He was quite scandalised when one of the ladies of our party declined the ice which he proferred her. "*Pas de glace!*" he exclaimed; "*mais vous avez droit à une glace.*" Similarly he exhibited signs of the deepest dejection when we refused to have anything to do with the salad, which was as soft and clammy as cold boiled turnip-tops, and was dressed apparently with asafoetida and verjuice; and he was affected almost to tears when, unable to endure the lengthiness of the Dîner Burnand any longer, we rose to depart without partaking of any dessert. "*Vous partez,*" he murmured; "yet there remains a choice of four fruits. You are entitled to a peach or a pear, an apple or a grape. There are even figs." ...

The uproar prevailing in the Paris restaurants just now—always in consequence of the Exhibition—has become positively appalling. The *vacarme* of one house is only equalled by the *Charivari* of the next; and you have simply a choice, so to speak, between marrow-bones and cleavers on the Boulevard des Capucines and frying-pans and tongs on the Boulevard des Italiens.

As regards breakfast, you have, it is true, a chance of relief. Take a victoria and hie straight away to the Champs Élysées, and there you will be able to lunch peacefully and well. Laurent's, for example, in the Avenue Marigny, is, in the morning, a beautifully quiet house. ... Abutting on the façade of Laurent's there is quite a Bower of Bliss, open on two sides to the garden, and on a third to the interior of the restaurant; and in this arbour you may regale yourself with an absence of noise and confusion eminently soothing to nerves that have been shattered by that brabbling brawling Paris beyond the Place de la Concorde yonder.

We were served in the Bower of Bliss by an admirably civil and intelligent waiter, whose only fault was that, knowing a little English, he was slightly too anxious to increase his knowledge of that tongue by propounding questions after the manner of the beneficent but somewhat irritating Ollendorff. As an atonement for this trifling fault, he caused to be brewed for us a pot of the very best tea that I have tasted since I have been in Paris. How is it that the French people cannot make tea? ... The herb has always been looked upon as an exotic, and it remains one. Not one French working man or working woman in a thousand has ever, I apprehend, so much as tasted tea, which, indeed, is looked upon by the poor as a kind of *tisane* or diet drink, to be taken only during sickness.

We came away from the quiet breakfast at Laurent's enchanted with the beauty of the garden, the quietude of the Bower of Bliss, the succulence of the fare, and the moderate charge which was made for it. It was quite a model bill in the way of cheapness. Only seventy-five centimes for a pear. "You come, evening, dine," quoth the Ollendorffian waiter as with many smiles he swept up his *pourboire*. "You come, evening, dinner in the garden. In the garden you dine under the trees green. Over the green trees of the garden during the dinner of evening comes the illumination of the gas. Now I give you the hat and the umbrella. Have you his umbrella?" (Lesson XIV.) "François, where is the umbrella of the English gentleman? Stay, I have the Cashmere shawl" (it was only a Paisley one) "of the English lady." (Lesson XV.) "Good-bye; you come dine." Good-bye, Ollendorff. We made haste to get away, fearing lest in his ardour for linguistic improvement he should become still more Ollendorffian . . .

So we strolled through the pretty garden, and by the murmuring fountain, and out into the always merry but tranquil Elysian Fields. Pleasant fields, lightly haunted by the apparitions of little children. There were many little manikins and toddlekins and *bébés* in the flesh gambolling under the trees that day. The sun shone very brightly. There were goat-chaises, and even goat *chars-à-bancs*, about. The "Théâtre de Guignol" had attracted a large audience of small folks; the sweetstuffs stalls were doing a prosperous trade; and there were distant symptoms of a hare and tabor and of a dancing dog. But everything was quiet and subdued. The Champs Élysées are bordered by some of the handsomest private houses in Paris; and on week-days, by some curious tacit agreement among the classes, so it would seem, the place is the playground of the rich. On Sundays the mob comes, and the Champs Élysées roar. This afternoon the children, with their *bonnes*, had things all to themselves, and the showmen were as polite and affable as Mr. Cremer junior's young men, who go out conjuring to juvenile parties. I was quite surprised at the elegant attire and aristocratic mien of the little *demoiselles* of from eight, who patronised the wooden steeds of the merry-go-rounds. Silk stockings, embroidered slippers with high heels, *gants Jouvin* with three buttons, laced skirts, plumed and flowered hats of the newest mode, were common among these small ladies of fashion. There were a few *bourgeois* children in pinafores and blue-linen trousers; but they kept themselves aloof shrinkingly, and refrained from engaging hobby-horses when the cavalcade was a patrician one. I noticed one leader of fashion, aged about nine, who had a scent-bottle and a fan. She managed her fiery steed, notwithstanding those trifling encumbrances, with so much skill and dexterity; she pointed her small lance with so much adroitness when she passed the pendant circles—for a French merry-go-round includes the game of skill of "running at the ring"; she indulged in so many charming *minauderies*; she gave herself, in a word—the little minx! —so many airs, that I fancied she must be cousin-german to the tiny aristocrat of seven, who, when asked to hold one handle of a skipping-rope in the Parc Monceaux, replied, with a toss of her head, "I only play with children who are dressed in velvet." The skipping-rope party were dressed in cotton. I was glad, however, to see when this superb young damsel descended from her charger that her stirrup was held by a muffin-faced boy in knickerbockers. They were velvet knickerbockers, mind you; and the edging to his cuffs and collars was of Brussels lace. I was still more glad to see La Princesse Toto and M. le Marquis de Petit Salé go off amicably to the nearest sweetstuff-stall to partake of barley-sugar; but I was pained subsequently to observe both of them engaged in a very fierce up-and-down fight over a pennyworth of gingerbread. The way in which M. le Marquis pummelled the Princess said little for the gallantry of juvenile Frenchmen; and the manner in which her Highness tugged at the hay-coloured ringlets of the muffin-faced Marquis was, to say the least, unlady-like. Perhaps children are pretty much the same all the world over. *Qu'en dites vous?*

[Sala devotes the next chapter to the new Central Market.]

.... THE Halles Centrales form an Exposition Universelle of victuals. It is Grandgousier's larder. It is the Tom Tiddler's Ground of things eatable. It is the grandest "Grub Street" in Europe. Take and roll into one New Smithfield, Farringdon, Covent Garden, Billingsgate, Leadenhall, and the Borough; throw in the New Cut, Lambeth Marsh, and High Street, Camden Town, on a Saturday night, and the proportions of the Halles Centrales would not yet be reached. . . .

The picturesque is not altogether absent from the Halles Centrales, all modern though they be. Entering the market from the Place St. Eustache, I found myself in the midst of a very wilderness of pumpkins, which the small *cultivateurs* from the villages around Paris are permitted to sell in the open air from break of day to nine A.M. After that hour the "pumpkineers" are rigidly moved on by the police. They are ridiculously cheap, a very fine pumpkin being obtainable for a franc, and seem to be used exclusively for soup-making among the *petite bourgeoisie* and by the working classes. I have never yet met with *potage de potiron* in the bill of fare of any restaurant: nor do the French cooks appear to have any idea of pumpkin in the form of custard or of a pie. Among the pumpkin dealers and their customers circulated numbers of itinerant soup-sellers—the soup being "*à l'oignon*," a racy, toothsome, and nourishing pottage, but too inelegant to find a place in the menus of the Café Anglais or the Maison Dorée. Beyond the *soupe à l'oignon*, and a slice of bread now and then, with, perhaps, an occasional visit to a neighbouring *marchand de vins*, the market people did not seem to require any refreshment. They had all had their morning coffee at six A.M., and about eleven they would breakfast seriously. Every Frenchman breakfasts seriously when he has any money. It is a ceremony which must be gone through *ab ovo usque ad malum*— from the omelette to the apple or the pear or the grapes of the dessert. The poorest cabman has his two *plats* and his dessert. The consumption of fruit is thus much larger than it is with us; and the same, in degree, may be said of vegetables. A Frenchman does not hold himself as in duty bound to eat at least a pound of potatoes every day. We do. But no day passes without the Frenchman partaking at one meal, and generally at two, of pulse or green vegetables in his soup, as a *plat* or as salad. When we eat salad we generally eschew the mild and wholesome oil, and drench our green meat with bad vinegar, to the ruin of the flavour of the salad and the injury of the coats of our stomachs. The variety of salad alone sold in the Halles Centrales is simply amazing. Of tomatoes, likewise, there is a splendid display. We are beginning at home slowly to recognise the culinary virtue of the "love apple," with its salutary subacid properties. Mr. Serjeant Buzfuz has made "chops and tomato sauce" immortal; but within recent years English people have found out that tomatoes are very good and very wholesome, fried, stewed, baked, stuffed, and *au gratin*. Tomato soup is one of the finest of *purées*; and raw tomatoes sliced, with oil and vinegar, *à l'Américaine*, is a most succulent breakfast dish. In France every dish *à la Portugaise* is garnished with tomatoes, and "Portuguese" eggs are as delicious as "Portuguese" fowl and "Portuguese" cutlets; but the Parisian cooks have a bad habit of mingling shredded onion with tomato salad. The tomato has a distinct and independent flavour of its own, which needs neither enhancement nor diminution. What would you think of asparagus and onions? I question, even, whether mint with green peas be not a barbarism. Among the vegetables in the Halles Centrales not usually found in

England, save, perhaps, in the Central Avenue of Covent Garden, where you can obtain everything that grows if you can afford to pay the price asked for it, I note "*aubergines*"—the American name for which is, I believe, "egg plant," but the English appellation of which has escaped me; I saw it the other day in an Anglo–French dictionary, but it was not a familiar name, and it fled from my mind—the black radish, as big as a large carrot, very pungent, and very good eating with bread and cheese; "*salsifis*" and "*cardons.*"

As for "strange meats," I observed with admiration in the game department a huge wild-boar, fresh killed, and which the dealer told me had been shot in the Ardennes. The last wild boar I met in a continental market was in that behind the Pantheon at Rome. He came from the Pontine marshes, but he was only a poor little fellow compared with the formidable *aper* in the Halles. Venison, too, was abundant. It is expensive; but the French are very fond of it. In London venison, with the exception of the haunch, is cheaper than butcher's meat. I have seen neck of venison offered at sixpence-halfpenny a pound. The common people won't eat it. We are a wonderful people. Frogs by the score, frogs by the hundred, already skinned and trussed and spitted, were plentiful in the Halles. I ate some once at a dinner in London of the Acclimatisation Society. They were *en fricassé* with a white sauce; but so far as flavour went they presented no definite purport or signification to my palate. An obliging French friend, a confirmed frog-eater, tells me that the diminutive creature who once a-wooing went, contrary to the advice of his mamma, with his Roley-Poley, Gammon, and Spinach, and who was an immediate factor in the discovery of galvanism, is truly delicious fried, with parsley. My friend brought three dozen this morning for the family breakfast. He told the dealer that he would send his chef to fetch them by and by, jokingly telling her not to eat them all in the meantime. "Y *a pas de danger*," quoth Madame la Grenouillière. "*Jamais de la vie je ne mangerais de cette volaille-là. Peuh! une pourriture, allez!*" So you see that the prejudice against frog-eating is not confined to England. Snail-soup, however, I have heard of as recommended by English physicians for consumptive patients; but in France the *colimaçon*, or rather the *escargot*, is habitually eaten, stewed, with a stuffing of *fines herbes*. . . . And yet we eat periwinkles. I am glad to know that we do not eat squirrels; and I was heartily sorry to see a brace of those beautiful and harmless little nutcrackers exposed for sale this morning in the game department. Well, we eat "the merry brown hare" and the inoffensive, albeit idiotic, rabbit. As for the thousands of quails and larks to be found in this part of the Halles, and which are brought, they tell me, from North

Africa, it would be better, perhaps, to say nothing of a sentimental nature. Those small fowl are such *very* nice eating.

But touching that "Jewellery" department in the Halles Centrales of which I spoke. My conductor, the most obliging of Frenchmen, amicably insisted that the "*Section de la Bijouterie*" should be the very last visited in our survey of the Great Central Market of Paris. "*C'est très drôle à voir,*" quoth he. . . .

Here is the "jewellery" at last. We pass between a double line of stalls heaped high with the most astonishing array of cooked food that I have ever set eyes upon. Fish, flesh, fowl, vegetables, fruit, pastry, confectionery, and cheese are all represented here, ready cooked, but cold, and arranged, not on plates or dishes, but on quarter-sheets of old newspapers. Imagine one pile, consisting of the leg of a partridge, the remnants of an omelette, the tail of a fried sole, two ribs of a jugged hare, a spoonful of haricot beans, a scrap of *filet*, a cut pear, a handful of salad, a slice of tomato, and a dab of jelly. It is the microcosm of a good dinner, abating the soup. The pile constitutes a *portion*, and is to be bought for five sous, or twopence-halfpenny. There are *portions* as low as two sous; indeed the scale of prices is most elastic in ascending and descending. There are piles here to suit all pockets. Are your funds at a very low ebb, indeed? On that scrap of a back number of the *Figaro* you will find a hard-boiled egg, the gizzard of a fowl, two pickled gherkins, and a macaroon. A breakfast for a Prince, if his Highness be impecunious. Are you somewhat in cash? Behold outspread on a trenchant leading article from the *République Française,* a whole veal chop, a golden store of cold fried potatoes, an artichoke, *à la barigoule,* a sumptuous piece of Roquefort, some *barbe de capucin* salad, and the remains of a *Charlotte russe.* A luncheon for a King, if his Majesty's civil list be a restricted one. But there are loftier luxuries to be had. Behold an entire fowl. See at least the moiety of a *Chateaubriand aux champignons.* Yonder are the magnificent relics of a *demie-selle de pré salé,* the remains of a sole *à la Normande,* the ruins of a *buisson d'écrevisses,* half-a-dozen smelts, the backbone of a pheasant, and, upon my word, some truffles; yes, positively, truffles. It is true that they are mingled with bits of cheese and beetroot, with a dash of *meringue à la rème,* and a suspicion of *sauce Robert.* All this is gathered together on a front page of the *Pays.* . . .

And yet it is precisely from establishments of the kind just named [Café Riche and the Maison Dorée] that the heterogeneous *portions* come. . . . The cheap eating-houses have few "leavings" to dispose of. Their guests are generally too hungry to leave anything on their plates; and, if aught, indeed, remains, it is devoured by the scullions and *gâte-*

sauces, or is manipulated by the *chef*, who should be an adept in the "*art d'accommoder les restes*." The fragments which form the "jewellery" of the Halles Centrales are brought down in big baskets, between seven and eight every morning, by the *garçons* of the great Boulevard restaurants, or by the *larbins* from the hotels of the Ministers and the foreign Ambassadors. If there have been overnight a dinner at the Ministry of the Interior or at the Baratarian Embassy, the show of "jewellery" in the morning will be superb. Whole turkeys and capons, all but entire hams and *hures de sanglier* scarcely impinged upon, *pièces montées*, the majestic vestiges of a *poulet à la Marengo* or a *saumon à la Chambord*, will decorate the deal boards of the stalls in the Halles. Out of the fashionable season the supply comes principally from the leading restaurants, where the "leavings" are the perquisites of the *garçons*. Whether the proprietors levy any tolls on the proceeds accruing from the sale of this astonishing *omnium gatherum*, this *macédoine*, this *pot-pourri*, this salmagundi, this *galimatias* of edible odds and ends, I do not know; but, so far as my inquiries have extended, I incline to the belief that the fragments become the property of the *garçons*, in frank-almoign, and go to swell the aggregate sum in the *tronc* or money-box vase on the restaurant counter into which all the fees received by the waiters are cast, to be divided at the end of every month in equitably proportionate shares among all the servants of the establishment—from the lofty *premier garçon*, who will be a *maître d'hotel* soon, and who may become a patron some of these days, to the lowliest *marmiton* in the regions below.

The "jewellery" is not sold by auction. The sales are always "*à l'amiable*"; and there are some dealers who have yearly contracts for the "leavings" of a particular restaurant. So soon as the merchandise has been received at the Halles the dealers—nearly always women—proceed to arrange it for sale; and this arrangement is, to all intents and purposes, an art. The *marchande de bijouterie* has a twofold object in view. First, she wishes to make a very little seem like a great deal; and, next, she is desirous to make the *portions* look as attractive to the eye as possible. Some *marchandes*, fortunate enough to possess the sentiment of artistic beauty, make up their own *portions*; others engage the services of a *metteur en oeuvre* or a *donneur de coup d'oeil*—the great jewellers of the Rue de la Paix can only do as much—to give the *portions* the requisite infusion of the picturesque in the way of composition and colour. These *metteurs en oeuvre* are a kind of professors of culinary peripatetics, flitting from stall to stall, and giving here and there a dash of green, in the shape of some spinach or a *chou de Bruxelles*, or a touch of red in the way of a carrot or a tomato, to a *portion* the hues of which seem too monotonous in tone. . . .

The purchasers are the Quiet Poor, the people who are ashamed to beg, and who, but for the merciful cheapness of these toothsome scraps, would not taste meat from month's end to month's end. To watch the decent but wretchedly-clad people, men, women, and children, critically examining this "jewellery" for the indigent—jewellery to be worn inside instead of outside the stomach—to watch them slowly passing from stall to stall and turning over the coppers in their hands before they made their final choice; to watch them at last going off with their newspaper-enwrapped parcels, and with just a gleam of tranquil satisfaction in their wan pinched faces, was more than curious, more than interesting. It was inexpressibly pathetic.

To the Magnetic South: A Flight from Switzerland

D. H. LAWRENCE

FROM *Twilight in Italy*

1912–13

From the age of twenty-three, when he left the English min-ing town of his birth, D. H. Lawrence was to spend his life moving from one country to another in search of a home. A mere list of the successive places in which he lived is staggering even in this rootless age: Germany, Austria, Italy, England, Italy, Capri, Sicily, Austria, Ceylon, Australia, New Mexico, Mexico, England, France, Germany, New Mexico, Mexico, Eng-land, Italy, Capri, Italy, England, Austria, Germany, Switzerland, France, Majorca, Italy, Germany. And he traveled not as a tourist or a Bohemian vagabond but as a man seeking to make a home for himself and his wife. Perhaps because he sought a resting place for the inner as well as the outer self, he probed each place—and each people—for its essence. Henry James, too, had sought the spirit of place, but Lawrence's quest was passionate to the point of desperation, whereas James's was intellectual and urbane. Where James is of the drawing room, Lawrence is of the hills and woods.

His earliest book of travel essays, Twilight in Italy, was written shortly after his elopement with Frieda von Richtofen in 1912 and describes a journey south through Bavaria, the Tyrol and Switzerland into Italy. In it he brings into play all the many instruments at his command: the animal sensitivity to the natural world, the uncanny insights into character, the gift for mimicry and the rage at what he considered to be the life-chilling, blood-denying forces in modern life.

Later he interrupted the stream of his novels, poetry and criticism with other impressions of travel: Sea and Sardinia, *the journal of a week-long boat journey in 1921 from Sicily to Sardinia;* Mornings in Mexico (1927), *a series of wonderfully atmospheric portraits and incidents drawn from a sojourn in Mexico; and* Etruscan Places (1932), *an interpretation of the Etruscan spirit based on ruins and tomb-paintings in central Italy.*

[Of the ten essays—or collections of impressions—in *Twilight in Italy,* seven are actually about Italy, focusing on the Lago di Garda area, where the Lawrences spent several months late in 1912 and early in 1913. The opening one, however, is on the Austrian Tyrol, and the last two are on Switzerland. It is from the closing piece, describing a journey Lawrence took from Zurich south to Italy, that the following passages come.]

W HEN one walks, one must travel west or south. If one turns northwards or eastwards it is like walking down a cul-de-sac, to the blind end.

So it has been since the Crusaders came home satiated, and the Renaissance saw the western sky as an archway into the future. So it is still. We must go westwards and southwards.

It is a sad and gloomy thing to travel even from Italy into France. But it is a joyful thing to walk south to Italy, south and west. It is so. And there is a certain exaltation in the thought of going west, even to Cornwall, to Ireland. It is as if the magnetic poles were south-west and north-east, for our spirits, with the south-west, under the sunset, as the positive pole. So whilst I walk through Switzerland, though it is a valley of gloom and depression, a light seems to flash out under every footstep, with the joy of progression.

It was Sunday morning when I left the valley where the Italians lived. I went quickly over the stream, heading for Lucerne. It was a good thing to be out of doors, with one's pack on one's back, climbing uphill. But the trees were thick by the roadside; I was not yet free. It was Sunday morning, very still.

In two hours I was at the top of the hill, looking out over the intervening valley at the long lake of Zurich, spread there beyond with its girdle of low hills, like a relief-map. I could not bear to look at it, it was so small and unreal. I had a feeling as if it were false, a large relief-map that I was looking down upon, and which I wanted to smash. It seemed to intervene between me and some reality. I could not believe that that was the real world. It was a figment, a fabrication, like a dull landscape painted on a wall, to hide the real landscape.

So I went on, over to the other side of the hill, and I looked out again. Again there were the smoky-looking hills and the lake like a piece of looking-glass. But the hills were higher: that big one was the Rigi. I set off down the hill.

There was fat agricultural land and several villages. And church was over. The church-goers were all coming home: men in black broadcloth and old chimney-pot silk hats, carrying their umbrellas; women in ugly dresses, carrying books and umbrellas. The streets were dotted with these black-clothed men and stiff women, all reduced to a Sunday nullity. I hated it. It reminded me of that which I knew in my boyhood, that stiff, null "propriety" which used to come over us, like a sort of deliberate and self-inflicted cramp, on Sunday. I hated these elders in black broadcloth, with their neutral faces, going home piously to their Sunday dinners. I hated the feeling of these villages, comfortable, well-to-do, clean, and proper. . . .

But climbing gradually higher, mile after mile, always between the shadows of the high mountains, I was glad I did not live in the Alps. The villages on the slopes, the people there, seemed as if they *must* gradually, bit by bit, slide down and tumble to the water-course, and be rolled on away, away to the sea. Straggling, haphazard little villages ledged on the slope, high up, beside their wet, green, hanging meadows, with pine trees behind and the valley bottom far below, and rocks right above, on both sides, seemed like little temporary squattings of outcast people. It seemed impossible that they should persist there, with great shadows wielded over them, like a menace, and gleams of brief sunshine, like a window. There was a sense of momentariness and expectation. It seemed as though some dramatic upheaval must take place, the mountains fall down into their own shadows. The valley beds were like deep graves, the sides of the mountains like the collapsing walls of a grave. The very mountain-tops above, bright with transcendent snow, seemed like death, eternal death.

There, it seemed, in the glamorous snow, was the source of death, which fell down in great waves of shadow and rock, rushing to the level earth. And all the people of the mountains, on the slopes, in the valleys, seemed to live upon this great, rushing wave of death, of breaking-down, of destruction.

The very pure source of breaking-down, decomposition, the very quick of cold death, is the snowy mountain-peak above. There, eternally, goes on the white foregathering of the crystals, out of the deathly cold of the heavens; this is the static nucleus where death meets life in its elementality. And thence, from their white, radiant nucleus of death in life, flows the great flux downwards, towards life and warmth. And we below, we cannot think of the flux upwards, that flows from the needle-point of snow to the unutterable cold and death.

The people under the mountains, they seem to live in the flux of death, the last, strange, overshadowed units of life. Big shadows wave over them, there is the eternal noise of water falling icily downwards from the source of death overhead.

And the people under the shadows, dwelling in the tang of snow and the noise of icy water, seem dark, almost sordid, brutal. There is no flowering or coming to flower, only this persistence, in the ice-touched air, of reproductive life.

But it is difficult to get a sense of a native population. Everywhere are the hotels and the foreigners, the parasitism. Yet there is, unseen, this overshadowed, overhung, sordid mountain population, ledged on the slopes and in the crevices. In the wider valleys there is still a sense of cowering among the people. But they catch a new tone from their contact with the foreigners. And in the towns are nothing but tradespeople. . . .

At the bottom was a little town with a factory or quarry, or a foundry, some place with long, smoking chimneys; which made me feel quite at home among the mountains.

It is the hideous rawness of the world of men, the horrible, desolating harshness of the advance of the industrial world upon the world of nature, that is so painful. It looks as though the industrial spread of mankind were a sort of dry disintegration advancing and advancing, a process of dry disintegration. If only we could learn to take thought for the whole world instead of for merely tiny bits of it.

I went through the little hideous, crude factory-settlement in the high valley, where the eternal snows gleamed, past the enormous advertisements for chocolate and hotels, up the last steep slope of the pass to where the tunnel begins. Göschenen, the village at the mouth of the tunnel, is all railway sidings and haphazard villas for tourists, postcards, and touts and weedy carriages; disorder and sterile chaos, high up. How should any one stay there! . . .

So I came, in the early darkness, to the little village with the broken castle that stands for ever frozen at the point where the track parts, one way continuing along the ridge to the Furka Pass, the other swerving over the hill to the left, over the Gotthard.

In this village I must stay. I saw a woman looking hastily, furtively from a doorway. I knew she was looking for visitors. I went on up the hilly street. There were only a few wooden houses and a gaily lighted wooden inn, where men were laughing, and strangers, men, standing talking loudly in the doorway.

It was very difficult to go to a house this night. I did not want to approach any of them. I turned back to the house of the peering woman. She had looked hen-like and anxious. She would be glad of a visitor to help her pay her rent.

It was a clean, pleasant wooden house, made to keep out the cold. That seemed its one function: to defend the inmates from the cold. It was furnished like a hut, just tables and chairs and bare wooden walls. One felt very close and secure in the room, as in a hut, shut away from the other world.

The hen-like woman came.

"Can I have a bed," I said, "for the night?"

"*Abendessen, ja!*" she replied. "Will you have soup and boiled beef and vegetables?"

I said I would, so I sat down to wait, in the utter silence. I could scarcely hear the ice-stream, the silence seemed frozen, the house empty. The woman seemed to be flitting aimlessly, scurriedly, in reflex against the silence. One could almost touch the stillness as one could touch the walls, or the stove, or the table with white American oilcloth.

Suddenly she appeared again.

"What will you drink?"

She watched my face anxiously, and her voice was pathetic, slightly pleading in its quickness.

"Wine or beer?" she said.

I would not trust the coldness of beer.

"A half of red wine," I said.

I knew she was going to keep me an indefinite time.

She appeared with the wine and bread.

"Would you like omelette after the beef?" she asked. "Omelette with cognac—I can make it *very* good."

I knew I should be spending too much, but I said yes. After all, why should I not eat, after the long walk?

So she left me again, whilst I sat in the utter isolation and stillness, eating bread and drinking the wine, which was good. And I listened for any sound: only the faint noise of the stream. And I wondered, Why am I here, on this ridge of the Alps, in the lamp-lit, wooden, close-shut room, alone? Why am I here?

Yet somehow I was glad, I was happy even: such splendid silence and coldness and clean isolation. It was something eternal, unbroachable: I was free, in this heavy, ice-cold air, this upper world, alone. London, far away below, beyond, England, Germany, France—they were all so unreal in the night. It was a sort of grief that this continent all beneath was so unreal, false, non-existent in its activity. Out of the silence one looked down on it, and it seemed to have lost all importance, all significance. It was so big, yet it had no significance. The kingdoms of the world had no significance: what could one do but wander about?

The woman came with my soup. I asked her, did not many people come in the summer. But she was scared away, she did not answer, she went like a leaf in the wind. However, the soup was good and plentiful.

She was a long time before she came with the next course. Then she put the tray on the table, and looking at me, then looking away, shrinking, she said:

"You must excuse me if I don't answer you—I don't hear well—I am rather deaf."

I looked at her, and I winced also. She shrank in such simple pain from the fact of her defect. I wondered if she were bullied because of it, or only afraid lest visitors would dislike it.

She put the dishes in order, set me my plate, quickly, nervously, and was gone again, like a scared chicken. Being tired, I wanted to weep over her, the nervous, timid hen, so frightened by her own deafness. The house was silent of her, empty. It was perhaps her deafness which created this empty soundlessness. . . .

So I went to bed, in the silent, wooden house. I had a small bedroom, clean and wooden and very cold. Outside, the stream was rushing. I covered myself with a great depth of feather-bed, and looked at the stars, and the shadowy upper world, and went to sleep.

In the morning I washed in the ice-cold water, and was glad to set out. An icy mist was over the noisy stream, there were a few meagre, shredded pine trees. I had breakfast and paid my bill: it was seven francs—more than I could afford; but that did not matter, once I was out in the air. . . .

Then I saw another figure striding along, a youth with knee-breeches and Alpine hat and braces over his shirt, walking manfully, his coat slung in his rucksack behind. I laughed, and waited. He came my way.

"Are you going over the Gotthard?" I said.

"Yes," he replied. "Are you also?"

"Yes," I said. "We will go together."

So we set off, climbing a track up the heathy rocks.

He was a pale, freckled town youth from Basel, seventeen years old. He was a clerk in a baggage-transport firm—Gondrand Frères, I believe. He had a week's holiday, in which time he was going to make a big circular walk, something like the Englishman's. But he was accustomed to this mountain walking: he belonged to a *Sportverein*. Manfully he marched in his thick hob-nailed boots, earnestly he scrambled up the rocks.

We were in the crest of the pass. Broad snow-patched slopes came down from the pure sky; the defile was full of stones, all bare stones, enormous ones as big as a house, and small ones, pebbles. Through these the road wound in silence, through this upper, transcendent desolation, wherein was only the sound of the stream. Sky and snow-patched slopes, then the stony, rocky bed of the defile, full of morning sunshine: this was all. We were crossing in silence from the northern world to the southern.

But he, Emil, was going to take the train back, through the tunnel, in the evening, to resume his circular walk at Göschenen.

I, however, was going on, over the ridge of the world, from the north into the south. So I was glad.

We climbed up the gradual incline for a long time. The slopes above became lower, they began to recede. The sky was very near, we were walking under the sky.

Then the defile widened out, there was an open place before us, the very top of the pass. Also there were low barracks, and soldiers. We heard firing. Standing still, we saw on the slopes of snow, under the radiant blue heaven, tiny puffs of smoke, then some small black figures crossing the snow patch, then another rattle of rifle-fire, rattling dry and unnatural in the upper, skyey air, between the rocks.

"*Das ist schön*," said my companion, in his simple admiration.

"*Hübsch*," I said.

"But that would be splendid, to be firing up there, manoeuvring up in the snow."

And he began to tell me how hard a soldier's life was, how hard the soldier was drilled.

"You don't look forward to it?" I said.

"Oh yes, I do. I want to be a soldier, I want to serve my time."

"Why?" I said.

"For the exercise, the life, the drilling. One becomes strong."

"Do all the Swiss want to serve their time in the army?" I asked.

"Yes—they all want to. It is good for every man, and it keeps us all together. Besides, it is only for a year. For a year it is very good. The Germans have three years—that is too long, that is bad."

I told him how the soldiers in Bavaria hated the military service.

"Yes," he said, "that is true of Germans. The system is different. Ours is much better; in Switzerland a man enjoys his time as a soldier. I want to go." . . .

The descent on the south side is much more precipitous and wonderful than the ascent from the north. On the south, the rocks are craggy and stupendous; the little river falls headlong down; it is not a stream, it is one broken, panting cascade far away in the gulley below, in the darkness.

But on the slopes the sun pours in, the road winds down with its tail in its mouth, always in endless loops returning on itself. The mules that travel upwards seem to be treading in a mill.

Emil took the narrow tracks, and, like the water, we cascaded down, leaping from level to level, leaping, running, leaping, descending head-long, only resting now and again when we came down on to another level of the high-road.

Having begun, we could not help ourselves, we were like two stones bouncing down. Emil was highly elated. He waved his thin, bare, white arms as he leapt, his chest grew pink with the exercise. Now he felt he was doing something that became a member of his *Sportverein*. Down he went, jumping, running, britching.

It was wonderful on this south side, so sunny, with feathery trees and deep black shadows. It reminded me of Goethe, of the romantic period:

Kennst du das Land, wo die Citronen blühen?

So we went tumbling down into the south, very swiftly, along with the tumbling stream. But it was very tiring. We went at a great pace down the gulley, between the sheer rocks. Trees grew in the ledges high over our heads, trees grew down below. And ever we descended.

Till gradually the gulley opened, then opened into a wide valley-head, and we saw Airolo away below us, the railway emerging from its hole, the whole valley like a cornucopia full of sunshine. . . .

It is strange how different the sun-dried, ancient, southern slopes of the world are, from the northern slopes. It is as if the god Pan really had his home among these sun-bleached stones and tough, sun-dark trees. And one knows it all in one's blood, it is pure, sun-dried memory. So I was content, coming down into Airolo.

We found the streets were Italian, the houses sunny outside and dark within, like Italy, there were laurels in the road. Poor Emil was a foreigner all at once. He rolled down his shirt-sleeves and fastened his shirt-neck, put on his coat and collar, and became a foreigner in his soul, pale and strange.

I saw a shop with vegetables and grapes, a real Italian shop, a dark cave.

"*Quanto costa l'uva?*" were my first words in the south.

"*Sessanta al chilo,*" said the girl.

And it was as pleasant as a drink of wine, the Italian.

So Emil and I ate the sweet black grapes as we went to the station....

When I got out at my station I felt for the first time ill at ease. Why was I getting out at this wayside place, onto the great, raw high-road? I did not know. But I set off walking. It was nearly tea-time.

Nothing in the world is more ghastly than these Italian roads, new, mechanical, belonging to a machine life. The old roads are wonderful, skilfully aiming their way. But these new great roads are desolating, more desolating than all the ruins in the world.

I walked on and on, down the Ticino valley, towards Bellinzona. The valley was perhaps beautiful: I don't know. I can only remember the road. It was broad and new, and it ran very often beside the railway. It ran also by quarries and by occasional factories, also through villages. And the quality of its sordidness is something that does not bear thinking of, a quality that has entered Italian life now, if it was not there before.

Here and there, where there were quarries or industries, great lodging-houses stood naked by the road, great, grey, desolate places; and squalid children were playing round the steps, and dirty men slouched in. Everything seemed under a weight.

Down the road of the Ticino valley I felt again my terror of this new world which is coming into being on top of us. One always feels it in the suburb, on the edge of a town, where the land is being broken under the advance of houses. But this is nothing, in England, to the terror one feels on the new Italian roads, where these great blind cubes of dwellings rise stark from the destroyed earth, swarming with a sort of verminous life, really verminous, purely destructive....

I was no longer happy in Switzerland, not even when I was eating great blackberries and looking down at the Lago Maggiore, at Locarno, lying by the lake; the terror of the callous, disintegrating process was too strong in me....

Leningrad and a Hospital in Odessa

EDMUND WILSON

FROM *Red, Black, Blond and Olive*

1935

From time to time, political factors have hindered or restricted travelers in certain countries, and such places as Tibet and Mecca
have always been difficult to visit. But rarely has there been such an effort
to control or influence visitors as in Soviet Russia during the past forty
years. The result has been few unprejudiced reports, and even fewer that
go beyond politics, economics and questions of ideology. Of that few, one
of the most interesting is by Edmund Wilson, who visited the U.S.S.R.
for five months in 1935.

Wilson's journal was originally published in 1936, when he was already
a leading literary and social critic in the United States. Despite his pro-
Communist feelings at that time, he retained a remarkable amount of the
objectivity and sheer respect for fact that has always distinguished his
writing. Although he turned sharply against the Soviet Union soon after
his visit, he reissued the journal in 1956 (in Black, Red, Blond and Olive)
with notes indicating that he thought many of its observations still valid.

A loan of Soviet rubles from author's royalties earned by his friend
John Dos Passos, plus a temporary relaxation of travel restrictions, enabled
Wilson to move about without official interpreters or surveillance. He
went to Leningrad and then, after a stay in Moscow, visited Gorki, Kiev
and Odessa. In Odessa he came down with scarlet fever and spent six
weeks in the hospital. Like much of his journal of the trip, his report on
this experience is entirely informal and, in its intimacy and sharp focus,
seems far more revealing than broad generalizations.

649

Wilson's other travels include a visit to Europe in 1908 as a boy of thirteen, and a year and a half in France during World War I. At the end of World War II he returned to Europe again for The New Yorker, *and wrote the series of post-war reports that later appeared in* Europe without Baedeker: Sketches among the Ruins of Italy, Greece and England. *His latest book of travel,* Red, Black, Blond and Olive, *covers sojourns in New Mexico among the Zuñi Indians in 1947, Haiti in 1949 and Israel in 1954.*

[Leaving depression-ridden America in May 1935, Wilson went to London and from there took a Russian boat to Leningrad.]

IMPRESSIONS OF LENINGRAD

THE first impression of Leningrad is absolutely dreamlike and dazing.

If one has never seen a really backward country, if one knows only the western European countries, one can form no real idea beforehand of what Russia and the Russians are like; and outside the Soviet Union, one can have had no experience of socialism. It is probably impossible for an American—it was impossible for me, at any rate—to imagine Russia correctly. Before one goes there, one is likely to feel, as I had done with the young engineers [whom he had met on the boat from London], the affinities between Russians and Americans; and if one is an advocate of socialism and a reader of *U.S.S.R. in Construction,* one is likely to have a vision of the Soviet Union as simply the United States plus one's ideal of socialism.

Actually, the Soviet Union is not like that at all. My own first impression of Leningrad was of something completely unfamiliar. It is impossible to realize till one gets there what a shock it is to find a city where there are not, as there are in other countries, well-dressed people on the principal streets. All the people on all the streets seem to be dressed about the same, and they are all very badly dressed—or rather, they are dressed drably. The men are bareheaded or wear caps; the women very rarely wear colors, and the soles of their footwear are invariably flat, shoes or sneakers or slippers. They are not noisy like the crowds in America, and to an American this makes them seem unreal. They move quietly and, compared to Americans, slowly; and the background of old St. Petersburg sets them off in a peculiar fashion. These dingy and mute and monotonous hordes inhabit a town of wide boulevards that were designed as the thoroughfares of an empire, and of enormous public buildings and palaces that give an illusion of going on for miles. (Leningrad is, I suppose, the only city in Europe which does not look small when one comes to it after living in American cities. Though there is nothing like the high buildings of New York, it has inordinate horizontal extension.) From these mansions, the nobility have vanished; and—what is unimaginable to an American—in the offices and the shops there is no more business class. And past the shabby palaces, along the straight interminable streets, the crowds move like slow floods of water—not straining, not anxious like our people, not pitted against an alien environment, but as if the whole city belonged to them, as if they could make use of its facilities and feel at ease in any part of it.

> [He goes by train to Moscow, where he stays in an American correspondent's apartment and visits theaters, collectives, cafés, bathing places and, of course, homes. He then continues eastward to Gorki (formerly Nizhni Novgorod) and down the Volga to Ulyanovsk and Stalingrad; thence south to Rostov-on-the-Don; and from there westward to Kiev and Odessa. Arriving in Odessa with scarlet fever, he is sent to the local hospital.]

HOSPITAL IN ODESSA

I SPENT six weeks in that Odessa hospital. I recovered very quickly from my original attack; but had to stay on account of the quarantine; then, just as I seemed to be cured and they were going to let me out, I had a relapse and had to spend another week.

The life was pretty monotonous: it was a little like living in a monastery. At the end of a few days, they moved me out of the doctor's room into a ward with other patients; and my world was contracted to that ward, the corridor and the operating room, which they let me use at night for a study. I would read Marx and Engels during the daytime and

Gibbon in the evening. An old Jewish doctor who knew some English brought me a volume of Sir Alfred Lyall's poems and a small book of selections from *Little Women*, edited for German readers. The only thing to be seen out the window was the Bacteriological Institute across the street, and one of the events of my stay was when it was repainted.

Yet it was interesting to watch day by day, from inside, the working of a Soviet institution, and I got in some ways a much clearer idea of the processes and relations of Russian life than I had been able to do in Moscow.

The hospital itself was old and dirty. It had been built about 1795—one of the oldest public buildings in Odessa—and it seemed to have remained practically untouched. Those high-ceilinged, high-windowed rooms had been harboring contagious diseases since years before the exile of Pushkin, when he had come to live in Odessa, almost ever since the days when the town had been only a Turkish fort. Odessa, which has very few factories and little value now as a port, has been neglected in the Soviet programs. There is, I understand, one fine new hospital, but efforts on the part of the Odessans to get a new contagious hospital have so far been unsuccessful; and what I saw was a bit of old Russia with very few of the cobwebs knocked off. I was subjected, for example, to treatments which I had supposed were entirely obsolete: at one time they "cupped" me daily with a set of twenty heavy brass cups which must have been a part of the original equipment, and they dosed me continually with valerian, an old-fashioned bitter drug, of which, according to the modern pharmacopoeia, the effects are "largely psychic."

There was evidently a scarlatina epidemic: the cases were coming in by the dozen—women, children and men. At one time there were three hundred cases, out of a city of half a million. One woman died while I was there. They would allow them to accumulate in the corridor, in their lazy Russian fashion putting off as long as possible the necessity of opening another room, which would involve the displacement of furniture. Everybody, as far as I could see, got exactly the same care and the same food, and everybody was treated with kindness. The *besprizórnye*, little homeless tramps, and the children of Communist officials were put to bed just as they came, and all the rooms were crowded—though the little waifs, to be sure, had nobody to bring them toys, fruit and books, as the children of well-to-do parents did.

It was a public service, of course, and nobody paid a kopek. I was not even allowed to pay for telegrams or cables: they told me that there was money set aside for such things. The food, although greasy like all Russian

food and tiresome like all hospital diet—I got terribly fed up with potatoes—was good of its kind, and there was plenty of it: the vegetables and
fruit of the Ukraine. Only the milk did not seem to me what it ought to
be, and they did not have any real coffee.

The hospital, as I have said, was terribly dirty. I never realized how
extremely low the Russian standard of cleanliness had been till I saw the
conditions which were tolerated in one of the places where sanitation
was most necessary but where the new broom had not yet swept clean.
The washbasin in our room, for example, though it did have running
water, was used for face-washing, dish-washing, gargling and emptying
urine; and I once saw one of the older doctors spit into it without bothering to turn on the faucet. The toilet had no seat and no way of fastening
the door, and, though the hospital people tried to keep it in order, the
patients, as is usual in Russia, generally left it in a mess. The glass panes
in the door could not have been cleaned up since at least 1915, for that
was the earliest date which had been scratched in the paint, or whatever
it was, with which they were partly coated. When you went to take a
bath, you were likely to find garbage in the bathroom (just as in Chekhov's
story of a provincial hospital, *Ward Number Six*, the potatoes are kept in
the bathtub). I never understood why they put it there, unless they used
it for fuel for the stove that heated the water. The flies were frightful,
and nothing was done in the way of screening the windows, except for a
single piece of netting nailed over one of the windows in the doctor's
room, which did not, of course, prevent the flies from entering through
the other window. Nor was anything done to prevent them from breeding
in the long grass outside, which was allowed to grow rank with weeds.

Periodically there was a bug crisis. The only thing they knew to do
about them was to apply the torch to the iron bedsteads, and I never
could convince them that bugs also lived in the cracks of the wood.
Finally one day, however, a fastidious woman doctor, who always smelled
of lavender water, discovered some *klópy* on the old horsehair chair in
which I used to read every day, and insisted that action be taken. The
sensible thing to do would have been to burn the chair, but it is hard for
them to take summary measures in Russia. At first they would go only
so far as to peel off the strips of ribbon that were tacked along the back
and arms, and then when, a few days later, the doctor was still able to
show bugs walking in and out of the cracks, they took to spraying it with
something or other.

The nurses were almost entirely untrained. They were generally middle-
aged women, with children and no husbands, who had been forced to

earn their livings. They would make wrong entries on the temperature charts (I was once given a rise for the following day) and lose the papers out of the dossiers for the cases. One nurse smoked continual cigarettes and made the patients cough. One, whose husband had left her, frankly disliked the whole thing and paid as little attention to it as possible. One got sick at the operations. The ward, to be sure, was understaffed: ten nurses to a hundred patients; and they had to do all the things which in our hospitals are done by orderlies. Visiting mothers and grandmothers were permitted to sleep in the ward and take care of their own children. The nurses had no control over the little boys, who kept climbing in and out of bed, went to sleep at any hour they pleased and engaged in hilarious roughhousing when they were running high temperatures. The way of handling the hospital nightgowns was typical of nurses and patients alike: I used to wonder at first why so many of the nightgowns had the strings about the neck left tied but one of them always torn off. Then I noticed that when they removed them, they would never go to the trouble of untying the knot, but simply rip them apart. What the nurses did best was amuse the children, reading to them, telling them stories and acting out little plays. They had for themselves, the nurses, two principal sources of diversion: a shabby geranium plant, which they would water from time to time but which never flowered; and an old volume of Lermontov's *A Hero of Our Time*, which they would read in moments of leisure, each one, apparently, taking it up where the last one had left off. . . .

The Head Nurse was quite a different matter. She was a much more energetic and positive person, and she was also much bulkier and taller. She looked a little like the Ugly Duchess, but her expression of haughtiness or indignation would melt into tenderness or humor when the slightest appeal was made to her. She had that ready humanity of Russians which, when character backs the generous impulse, may take such heroic forms; and she worked exceedingly hard, wrestling with the hospital arrangements, seeing to it that the nurses gave the treatments on time and did not lose the records, banging the hands of the neophytes when they tried to fool with the surgical instruments, and, in the moments when she had nothing else to do, reading to the children herself. One day she showed me her Communist card and told me that she had formerly done more active work, but that her heart was bad and that they had put her here where the work was not so exhausting.

In the hospital, as I gradually came to find out who were and who were not Communists, I got a much clearer notion than I had had before of the relations between the Communists and their followers, on the one hand, and the rest of the Russian community, on the other. The Communists, it was plain to me in Odessa, were the people who took all the responsibility. And though I had sometimes resented in Moscow the constraining and intimidating effect which their presence had on other Russians, I was grateful to them when I got into the hospital, because they seemed to be the only people who were sensible, efficient and up-to-date. If you really wanted to get anything done, you had to go to a Communist about it. I came to sympathize with their constant trials in making the other Russians get things done.

[On being released from the hospital he went by rail to the Polish border and then westward across Europe. About France he made only a single comment: "*Rigor mortis* has set in in Paris." That was October 1935.]

Bosnian Jews, a Magician as Bishop, and a Woman Who Questioned Her Fate

REBECCA WEST

FROM *Black Lamb and Grey Falcon*

1937

Rebecca West was already well known as a novelist and even better known for having made an art out of reporting on contemporary life when she went to Yugoslavia in 1936. She was so profoundly attracted by its peoples, its landscape, and its past that she returned twice again and then spent three years writing Black Lamb and Grey Falcon, *one of the most remarkable books of travel of this or any other time.*

In the spring of 1937 and again in 1938 the author together with her husband, Henry Maxwell Andrews, a London banker, crossed and re-crossed Croatia, Dalmatia, Herzegovina, Bosnia, Serbia, Macedonia, Old Serbia and Montenegro. Accompanied by Constantine, a distinguished Serbian poet (and occasionally by his German wife, Gerda, who despised the South Slavs they admired and was increasingly unfriendly to the English visitors), they stayed in scores of homes, as well as hotels and monasteries, and talked to people everywhere.

Back in England, writing her book in that hour of supreme crisis when the Nazis seemed about to engulf Europe, Rebecca West found among the South Slavs—who had so valiantly resisted the Turks in the fourteenth century and were to defy the Axis powers in the twentieth—a series of

*object lessons that took her twelve hundred wonderfully articulate pages
to explore. She pours out social analysis, history, narrative and characterization in prodigal quantities, carrying off the mixture through sheer passion
and eloquence, by richness of characterization, and by interpretations as
unexpected and dazzling as fireworks. Her style ranges from lyric appreciation to savage denunciation; the excerpts below, concentrating on
character studies, illustrate only a few of the book's many facets.*

*Since her first visit to Spain, which she made as a young girl before
World War I, and a trip to America in 1923, Rebecca West has lectured,
toured or lived for brief periods in nearly every part of Europe and the
United States. She also visited the Middle East in 1937 and South Africa
in 1959–60.*

[Miss West and her husband go first to Zagreb and are witness to the political dissension that rends intellectual circles
there. They then go to Fiume and down the Dalmatian
coast, stopping at Split, lovely Korčula and other towns. They
pass through Mostar (in Herzegovina) and, entering Bosnia,
stop in Sarajevo, where Miss West dwells on the significance
of the Archduke's assassination in 1914. Outside Sarajevo
they visit a Jewish family.]

A BOSNIAN JEWISH HOME

WE had been invited to luncheon with the father and mother of the
lovely Jewess in Sarajevo whom we called the Bulbul [the Persian word
for nightingale], and we found their home in an apartment house looking
over the blossoming trench of the valley from the main road, under a hill
crowned with a fortress built by the old Bosnian kings. We found it, and
breathed in our nostrils the odour of another civilization. Our appearance
there caused cries of regret. The father stood in the shadow of the doorway, a handsome man in his late fifties, whose likeness I had seen often
enough in the Persian miniatures, gazelle-eyed and full-bodied. In the
delicious voice of the Sephardim, honey-sweet but not cloying, he told
us that he was ashamed to let us in, for we would find nothing worthy
of us. He had thought we meant to call at his factory, which was a couple
of miles outside the town, so he had ordered a real meal, a meal appro-

priate to us, to be cooked there, and he had left an explanation that he could not be with us, as his wife had broken her ankle and till she was well he would eat all his meals with her. He bowed with shame that he should have blundered so. But a voice, lovely as his own but a woman's, cried from the darkened room beyond and bade him bring the strangers in. It was at once maternal, warm with the desire to do what could be done to comfort our foreignness, and childlike, breathless with a desire to handle the new toy.

She lay on a sofa, fluttering up against the downward pull of her injury, as hurt birds do; and she was astonishing in the force of her beauty. She was at least in her late forties, and she was not one of those prodigies unmarked by time, but she was as beautiful, to judge by her effect on the beholder, as the Bulbul. That could not really be so, of course. As a general rule Horace must be right, for reasons connected with the fatty deposits under the skin and the working of the ductless glands, when he writes, "O *matre pulchra filia pulchrior.*" Yet in this case he would have been wrong. He should have ignored his metre and written of "*mater pulchrior pulcherrimae filiae,*" for there was the more beautiful mother of the most beautiful daughter. The Bulbul was the most perfect example conceivable of the shining Jewish type, but so long as one looked on this woman she seemed lovelier than all other women. Her age was unimportant because it did not mean to her what it means to most Western women: she had never been frustrated, she had always been rewarded for her beautiful body and her beautiful conduct by beautiful gratitude.

My husband and I sat down beside her, smiling as at an unexpected present; and she apologized to us for the poor meal she would have to improvise, and cried over our heads directions to her cook in a voice that floated rather than carried, and then settled to ask us questions which were by Western standards personal, which were extremely sensible if she wished to be able to like us quickly before we left her house. In a painted cage a canary suddenly raised fine-drawn but frantic cheers for the universe, and they checked it with gentle laughter that could not have hurt its feelings. The canary, it seemed, her husband had brought home to divert her while she must lie on the sofa. The room was littered with gifts he had fetched her for that purpose: a carved flute, a piece of brocade, an eighteenth-century book of Italian travel with coloured illustrations, an amber box—a trifle, I should say, for each day she had been kept in the house. Their household rocked gently on a tide of giving and receiving.

They watched us sadly while we ate, uttering coos of regret for the meal that was really worthy of us, waiting uneaten in the factory. But we were not discontented. We were given home-made spaghetti, those eggs called "Spanish eggs" which are boiled for three days in oil and come out greaseless and silky to the palate, lamb chops from small ethereal lambs who probably had wings, sheep's cheese, pure white and delicately sharp, peaches and quinces foundered in syrup that kept all their summer flavour, and raki, the colourless brandy loved by Slavs. As we ate we told them of our meetings with their daughter in Sarajevo, and they stretched like cats in pride and pleasure, owning that all we said of her was true, and reciting some of her accomplishments that they thought we might not have had the chance to observe. Nothing could have been less like the uneasy smile, the depreciating mumble, which is evoked in an Englishman by praise of his family.

But this was a long way from England. Constantine went on to tell the gossip he had picked up in Sarajevo, and the more ambassadorial gossip he had brought from Belgrade, and while they rewarded his perfect story-telling by perfect listening, I looked about the room. It was certainly provincial; anything that had reached the room from Vienna, Berlin, Paris, or London had taken so long to get there and had been so much modified by the thought of the alien taste for which it was destined that it would be antiquated and bizarre. But built into this room, and inherent in every word and gesture of its owners, was a tradition more limited in its scope than the traditions of Vienna, Berlin, Paris, or London, but within its limits just as ancient and sure and competent. Whatever event these people met they could outface; the witness to that was their deep serenity. They would meet it with a formula compounded of Islam and Judaism. Their whole beings breathed the love of pleasure which is the inspiration of Sarajevo, which was perhaps the great contribution the Turks had to make to culture. But it was stabilized, its object was made other than running water, by the Jewish care for the continuity of the race. It was a fusion that would infuriate the Western moralist, who not only believes but prefers that one should not be able to eat one's cake and have it. I went later to comb my hair and wash my hands in these people's bathroom. A printed frieze of naked nymphs dancing in a forest ran from wall to wall, and several pictures bared the breasts and thighs of obsoletely creamy beauties. Naïvely it was revealed that these people thought of the bath as the uncovering of nakedness, and of nakedness as an instrument of infinite delight. It was the seraglio spirit in its purity; and it was made chaste as snow by the consideration that these people would have offered this flesh of which they so perfectly understood the potentialities to burn like tallow in flame if thereby they might save their dearer flesh, their child.

So one can have it, as the vulgar say, both ways. Indeed one can have a great deal more than one has supposed one could, if only one lives, as these people did, in a constant and loyal state of preference for the agreeable over the disagreeable. It might be thought that nothing could be easier, but that is not the case. We in the West find it almost impossible, and are caught unawares when we meet it in practice. That was brought home to me by this woman's tender gesture of farewell. First she took all the lilacs from a vase beside her sofa and gave them to me, but then felt this was not a sufficient civility. She made me lay down the flowers, and took a scent-bottle from her table and sprinkled my hands with the scent, gently rubbing it into my skin. It was the most gracious farewell imaginable, and the Western world in which I was born would not have approved.

[The husband takes them for a walk and they stop at a café.]

THERE we sat and drank black coffee and ate Turkish delight on tooth-picks, while a gentle wind stirred the flowering trees that met above the table, and set the grasses waving round a prostrate pillar which had fallen by one of the pashas' tombs. There strolled up and sat down some of those mysterious impoverished and dignified Moslems who seem to have no visible means of support, but some quite effective invisible means. They watched us without embarrassment; we were unembarrassed; and the men talked of country pastimes. Here, the Bulbul's father said, was real game for shooting in winter.

There is deep snow here in winter-time, it seems; and the beasts come down from the heights and loiter hungrily on the outskirts of the town. A friend of his had sauntered a few yards out of his garden, his gun loaded with pellets. He paused to look at a black bush that had miraculously escaped the snow. It stood up and was a bear, a lurch away. His friend raised his gun and shot. The pellets found the bear's brain through the eye, he staggered, charged blindly, and fell dead. He himself had been driving down to his factory one November afternoon when he saw a pack of wolves rushing down the mountain on a herd of goats. He stopped his car and watched. They came straight down like the water we had seen rushing down by the dam. They leaped on the goats and ate what they wanted. He had heard the goats' bones cracking, as loud, he said, as gunshots. When the wolves had eaten their fill they rushed up the mountain again, dragging what was left of the goats. It took only five minutes, he thought, from the time he first saw them till they passed out of sight.

He pointed up to the mountains. "It is only in winter you see them," he said, "but all the same they are up there, waiting for us and the goats." We looked in wonder at the heights that professed the stark innocence of stone, that was honeycombed with the stumbling weighty hostility of bears, the incorporated rapacity of wolves. And as we lowered our eyes we saw that we were ourselves being regarded with as much wonder by other eyes, which also were speculating what the sterile order of our appearance might conceal. A gaunt peasant woman with hair light and straight and stiff as hay and a mouth wide as a door had stopped in the roadway at the sight of us. She was so grand, so acidulated, so utterly at a disadvantage before almost anyone in the civilized world, and so utterly unaware of being at a disadvantage at all, that I made Constantine ask her to let herself be photographed. She whinnied with delight, and arranged herself before the camera with her chin forward, her arms crossed, her weight on her heels, acting a man's pride; I think nothing in her life had ever suggested to her that there is a woman's kind of pride.

She was poor. Dear God, she was poor. She was poor as the people in Rab [a town they had visited, on the Dalmatian coast]. Her sleeveless white serge coat, her linen blouse, the coarse kerchief she had twisted round her head, were stained with age. The wool of the embroidery on her coat was broken so that here and there the pattern was a mere fuzz. Garments of this sort have a long life. To be in this state they must have been worn by more than one generation. She had probably never had new clothes in all her days. This was not the most important aspect of her.

There were others which were triumphant. It could be seen that she was a wit, a stoic, a heroine. But for all that it was painful to look at her, because she was deformed by the slavery of her ancestors as she might have been by rheumatism. The deep pits round her eyes and behind her nostrils, the bluish grooves running down her neck, spoke of an accumulated deprivation, an amassed poverty, handed down like her ruined clothes from those who were called rayas, the ransomed ones, the Christian serfs who had to buy the right to live. To some in Bosnia the East gave, from some it took away.

[Moving on into Serbia, they stay in the Belgrade area. From there they turn southward and cross the plains of Kossovo to Skoplje. Farther south they visit a bishop at Ohrid, near the Albanian border.]

MAGICIAN AS BISHOP

. . . WE got out and stood on a ledge; below us a long untended garden ran down to some houses that were mere lath and plaster, and above us, beside a house which had lost its whole façade and had grimly replaced it with a sheet of rusted iron, was the mouth of an alley that rose to a plot of waste ground. A few steps up this alley was a doorway, and Dragutin [their driver] said, "Go in there and you will find the Bishop, the church is having its feast." I went in and found an unkempt garden before a small and battered church, full of people who were all looking at the loggia in front of it. There was Bishop Nikolai at the head of a table laid for a meal, where some priests and a nun, a man in uniform, and several men and women in ordinary clothes were sitting, all with their faces turned towards him. I was surprised that the feast of a church should be a real feast, where there was eating and drinking.

Bishop Nikolai stood up and welcomed us, and I knew that he was not at all glad to see us. I was aware that he did not like Constantine and that he was not sure of me, that he thought I might turn and rend any situation at which he permitted me to be present by some Western treachery. I did not greatly care what he thought of me, for I was too greatly interested in him, and any personal relations between us could not aid my interest, for I could get everything out of him that I could ever get by watching him. He struck me now, as when I had seen him for the first time in the previous year, as the most remarkable human being I have ever met, not because he was wise or good, for I have still no idea to what degree he is either, but because he was the supreme magician. He had command over the means of making magic, in his great personal beauty, which was of the lion's kind, and in the thundering murmur of his voice, which by its double quality, grand and yet guttural, suggests that he could speak to gods and men and beasts. He had full knowledge of what comfort men seek in magic, and how they long to learn that defeat is not defeat and that love is serviceable. He had a warm knowledge of how magic can prove this up to the hilt. He had a cold knowledge, which he would not share with any living thing, of the limited avail of magic, and how its victories cannot be won on the material battlefield where man longs to see them. He was so apt for magic that had it not existed he could have invented it. He saw all earth as its expression. When he greeted our undesired party, when he turned to command order in the mob of peasants and children and beggars that filled the garden and looked over the walls from outside, there was a blindish and blocked look in his eyes, as if he asked himself, "Of what incantation is this the end? What is the rite we are now performing? Is this white magic or black?"

He bade us take seats at the table, and I looked round and saw some people whom I had met at Ochrid on the first visit. There was the Abbot of the Monastery of Sveti Naum, which lies at the other end of the lake: an old man with a face infinitely fastidious, yet wholly without peevishness, a Macedonian who was a priest under the Turks and lived all his youth and manhood under the threat of sudden death and yet remained uninfected by the idea of violence; and there was a red-haired priest who sings marvellously, like a bull with a golden roar, and laughs like a bull with a golden nature, and who is much in request in Ochrid for christenings and weddings. Others were new: among them a schoolmistress who had been a Serbian pioneer here long before the Balkan wars, a jolly old soul; an immense officer of the gendarmerie, a Montenegrin, like all Montenegrins sealed in the perfection of his virility, as doubtless the Homeric heroes were; a functionary who was in charge of the Works Department of Ochrid, a dark and active man, one of those enigmatic beings who fill such posts, facing the modern world with a peasant strength and a peasant reticence, so that the stranger cannot grasp the way of it.

We all began to eat. The crowd in the garden bought rolls from pedlars, and ice-cream cones from a barrow that was standing under the church steps. We at the table had cold lamb, hard-boiled eggs, sheep's cheese, cold fried fish, unleavened bread and young garlic, which is like a richer and larger spring onion. The Bishop said to my husband, with hatred of Western Europe's hatred of the Balkans in his voice, "This is something you English do not eat, but we are an Eastern people, and all Eastern peoples must have it." He gave me a hard-boiled egg and took one himself, and made me strike his at the same time that he struck mine. "The one that cracks the other's egg shall be the master," he said.

It was to amuse the people and to give himself a moment's liberty not to think, for he was heavy with fatigue. Ever since Easter he had been going from church to church, carrying on the sorcery of these long services, and offering himself as a target for the trust of the people. He had to go on to some other church, and soon he let the crowd see that he must before long dismiss them.

They grieved at it, they gobbled up their rolls and ice-cream cones or threw them on the ground and crushed forward to the table. Bishop Nikolai stood up and cried, "Christ is risen!" and they answered, "Indeed He is risen!" Three times he spoke and they answered, and then they stretched out their hands and he gave them eggs from a great bowl in front of him. This was pure magic. They cried out as if it were talismans and not eggs that they asked for; and the Bishop gave out the eggs with an air of generosity that was purely impersonal, as if he were the conduit for a force greater than himself. When there were no more eggs in the bowl the people wailed as if there were to be no more children born into the world, and when more eggs were found elsewhere on the table the exultation was as if there were to be no more death. There was a group of little boys standing by the Bishop, who wailed and cheered with the passion of their elders, but had to wait until the last, since they were children. To these Gerda now began to distribute eggs from a bowl that was near her. . . .

[In usurping, as it were, the Bishop's magic role, Gerda shocks the company. Her husband, Constantine, starts making a speech, but no one listens and the anger of the Bishop is not assuaged.]

HE [the Bishop] surged out of his chair and, looming about the small Constantine, bade the children give three cheers for him. But when they had finished Constantine went on speaking. The Bishop filled his glass, pouring the wine so wildly that the cloth round it was purpled, and stretched out his huge arm over the table, in front of Constantine's flushed and shining face, and drank a toast to the company. Even then Constantine still went on speaking, so utterly fixed was he in his double intention, which every moment disclosed a more dreadful beauty, to uphold Gerda in her attack on the world, and to uphold her in her contempt for him. The Bishop beat down his glass on the table, said his farewells with a stateliness that was the calm at the heart of a storm, thrust back his chair so that it fell into the hands of the children behind him, and strode out of the garden, the crowd shuffling after him. Soon there was nothing to be seen but the trodden grass. We were left standing at the table, the other guests looking at us curiously.

[On the way back to Skoplje, they witness the sacrifice of a black lamb, which becomes the symbol in these pages of the horrid belief that God blesses only in return for bloody cruelty. Miss West comes upon her second major symbol, the gray falcon, standing for the acceptance of self-annihilation, when she crosses the plains of Kossovo, where the Turks won their historic victory over the Serbs in 1389. From there the party drives by car into the mountains of Montenegro.]

THE WOMAN WHO QUESTIONED HER FATE

. . . UP and up we drove until we had to stop, to cool the engine. We none of us regretted it, for there were many gentians on the banks beside the road, and below us the woods lay like bonfires of green flame on the mild rolling turf, and further the distant infinity of mountains was blue as wild hyacinths. We sat there so long that a woman who had passed on a lower curve of the road overtook us, halted in her trudging, came up to the car, and laid her arm along the frame of the open window, looking round at us all. Her face had once been perfect but was no longer so, and was the better for it. "Good morning," she said to Constantine, "who are you?" "I am Constantine," he said. "I am from Shabats and I am a poet." "And who are you?" she asked my husband and me. "They are English," said Constantine. "A very fine people," she said. "Why do you think that?" said Constantine. "Because they are great fighters, and they love nature," she said. "How do you know they are like that?" asked Constantine. She lifted her arm from the window, took a ball of fine white wool and knitting-needles from her other hand, and set to work again, as if sensing from his question an indication that the conversation might not be of the first order and she might as well get on with her material duties. "Oh, everybody knows that," she answered absently. "And you," said Constantine, "who are you? Are you a native of this place?" "No," she said, "I live here now, but I was born by Durmitor." Durmitor is the great snow mountain, with a black lake at its foot, on the northern side of Montenegro. "Who brought you here?" asked Constantine.

She laughed a little, lifted her ball of wool to her mouth, sucked the thin thread between her lips, and stood rocking herself, her eyebrows arching in misery. "It is a long story. I am sixty now," she said. "Before the war I was married over there, by Durmitor. I had a husband whom I liked very much, and I had two children, a son and a daughter. In 1914 my husband was killed by the Austrians. Not in battle. They took him out of our house and shot him. My son went off and was a soldier and was killed, and my daughter and I were sent to a camp. There she died. In the camp it was terrible, many people died. At the end of the war I came out and I was alone. So I married a man twenty years older than myself. I did not like him as I liked my first husband, but he was very kind to me, and I had two children of his. But they both died, as was natural, for he was too old, and I was too old, and also I was weak from the camp. And now my husband is eighty, and he has lost his wits, and he is not kind to me any more. He is angry with everybody; he sits in his house and rages, and I cannot do anything right for him. So I have nothing." "Are you poor?" asked Constantine. "Not at all," she said. "My husband's son by his first wife is a judge in Old Serbia, and he sends me three hundred dinars a month to hire a man to work our land, so we want nothing. Oh, that is all right, but the rest is so wrong." "Oh, sister, sister," said Constantine, "this is very hard." "Yes, it's hard," she said. "And can we do nothing for you," asked Constantine, "for we feel very friendly towards you? Can we not give you a lift to where you are going?" "That you cannot do, though you mean so kindly," she said, "for I am not going anywhere. I am walking about to try to understand why all this has happened. If I had to live, why should my life have been like this? If I walk about up here where it is very high and grand it seems to me I am nearer to understanding it." She put the ball of wool to her forehead and rubbed it backwards and forwards, while her eyes filled with painful speculation. "Good-bye," she said, with distracted courtesy, as she moved away, "good-bye."

This woman was of no importance. It is doubtful whether, walk as she would on these heights, she would arrive at any conclusion that was of value even to herself. She was, however, the answer to my doubts. She took her destiny not as the beasts take it, nor as the plants and trees; she not only suffered it, she examined it. As the sword swept down on her through the darkness she threw out her hand and caught the blade as it fell, not caring if she cut her fingers so long as she could question its substance, where it had been forged, and who was the wielder. She wanted to understand the secret which Gerda denied, the mystery of process. I knew that art and science were the instruments of this desire, and this was their sole justification, though in the Western world where I lived I had seen art debauched to ornament and science prostituted to the multiplication of gadgets. I knew that they were descended from man's primitive necessities, that the cave man who had to hunt the aurochs drew him on the rock-face that he might better understand the aurochs and have fuller fortune in hunting and was the ancestor of all artists, that the nomad who had to watch the length of shadows to know when he should move his herd to the summer pasture was the ancestor of all scientists. But I did not know these things thoroughly with my bowels as well as my mind. I knew them now, when I saw the desire for understanding move this woman. It might have been far otherwise with her, for she had been confined by her people's past and present to a kind of destiny that might have stunned its victims into an inability to examine it. Nevertheless she desired neither peace nor gold, but simply knowledge of what her life might mean. The instrument used by the hunter and the nomad was not too blunt to turn to finer uses; it was not dismayed by complexity and it could regard the more stupendous aurochs that range within the mind and measure the diffuse shadows cast by history. And what was more, the human will did not forget its appetite for using it.

Trapani: The Mystery of Easter

HERBERT KUBLY

FROM *Easter in Sicily*

1954

Two qualities distinguish Herbert Kubly's books of travel, American in Italy *and* Easter in Sicily: *his interest in individuals, which helps him quickly to become the confidant of those he meets, and his ability to shape his material into what are virtually short stories or scenes from plays. His background may help to explain this: although he is a fifth-generation American, his ancestors—and those of his neighbors in his native town in Wisconsin—came from one small Swiss town; he has been a newspaper reporter in Pittsburgh and New York; and he is the author of several plays.*

In 1951, when he was an associate professor of speech at the University of Illinois, Kubly was granted a Fulbright Fellowship that enabled him to spend fourteen months studying the theater in Italy and Sicily. It was this experience that resulted in American in Italy *and, after other journeys to Sicily, in* Easter in Sicily. *These are above all books about people, with* American in Italy *ranging from an industrialist's son in Turin to abandoned street boys in Naples. The scope of* Easter in Sicily *is narrower, concerned as it is with men who dream only of going to America or of the next amatory adventure. But at times, as in the following description of the Good Friday procession in Trapani which lasts without interruption for twenty-two hours, the book achieves an extraordinary narrative intensity and an unforgettable vision of a passionate, half-pagan expression of Christian faith.*

668

[Traveling mostly by bus, Kubly explores Palermo, Syracuse, Enna, Tyndari, Taormina and other places, tracing not only such ancient legends as those of Demeter and Persephone but also such stories as that of Salvatore Giuliano, a young bandit-hero murdered in 1950.

Having described Easter celebrations in Taormina and in Piana degli Albanesi, Kubly climaxes his book with the following account of Good Friday in Trapani.]

T RAPANI is a noisy seaport beneath Aphrodite's rampart of Erice. It was dry and dusty. An African wind turned the Dutch windmills peculiar to this part of Sicily, and white sails wafted like butterflies on the bright sea. Disastrously bombed during the war, Trapani is only now rising from its ruins with a frenzy of building. . . .

[Gerardo, a young man who has an American fiancée, undertakes to guide him.]

THE next day Gerardo came early to indoctrinate me in the procession of mysteries.

"The clergy have little to do with it," he said. "It is organized by the *ceti*, or trade guilds, which began the *processione* in the sixteenth century. Each guild presents one event from the Passion of Christ and the life of Mary. In the beginning the scenes were enacted by living men as they are still done today in Marsala. A feud developed in Marsala several years ago between the Christ and one of the Roman soldiers taking Him to the Crucifixion. The Christ was angry because the Roman soldier pulled the rope too tightly. After several stops in wineshops, the Christ drew a knife from his robe and threatened to stab the Roman soldier. The *carabinieri* had to calm the Christ before the procession could continue."

Since the seventeenth century the Trapani guilds, like those at Caltanissetta, parade realistic statue groups built of wood and sculptured in *cartapista*, a combination of glue and papier-mâché which gives the figures a hard, stonelike finish. . . .

The procession ends with the weeping Madonna searching interminably for her son. Because the search must take her over every street of the city, the long hide-and-seek continues without interruption for more than twenty hours. "Does she find him at the end or doesn't she?" I asked.

"That is the everlasting mystery," said Gerardo. "Every year people argue the same problem. Some say she does; some say she doesn't. No one is sure."

We went to the Church of the Collegio in the heart of the town. At the door a guard was fighting back the crowds to keep them from entering. With a word from Gerardo we were permitted to pass. Inside, flowers were piled everywhere. Orange marigolds, white lilies, roses and carnations, fruit blossoms, iris, tulips, paradise flowers—all lay in stacks like hay. The workers of Trapani were weaving them into blankets, canopies, and every manner of arrangement with which to decorate their statue groups. Gerardo told me it was traditional to award prizes to the guilds for the most beautiful floral decorations as well as for the liveliest dancing of the groups through the street.

The statues were dramatic, the faces filled with anguish or cruelty. Except for the figures of Christ, which were fair in coloring, they were of a dark, African and Moorish cast. The Roman soldiers were men of pomp, glistening with silver and feathers like Paladins in the puppet plays. There was a profusion of silver. Swords were of silver, the column of the flagellation was silver and so was the cross. Each group was supplied with scores of candles, some thick enough to require four wicks. In addition, the groups were wired for electricity, with huge storage batteries hidden in the iron scaffolding underneath. A workman said each group weighed up to eight hundred kilos and took twelve men to carry it.

Burning wax had fouled the air in the church and the heavy odor of flowers was nauseating. We pressed through the crowded streets to the sea front. The day was sunny but windy and cold. Great waves beat against the quay and on the esplanade the tall palms crackled as if they were laden with icicles. The multicolored clusters of balloons threatened to lift the vendors into the heavens. We followed the sea to Gerardo's home, the Villa Nespoli. From the street we entered through a heavily bolted gate set in a solid stone wall. We walked through shaded rooms with mosaicked floors of eighteenth-century fishing scenes, into a cloistered garden of tropical lushness. On one side colonnades opened on the sea. There at a table set under a hibiscus tree, Gerardo and I were served a pleasant lunch of fish and veal and an assortment of vegetables and greens. For desert we picked the fruits of medlar trees in the garden. We were alone; Gerardo's parents had gone to their house in the country for the day. With a touch of snobbishness, Gerardo said, "The *processione* does not greatly interest people of culture. Only the poor care deeply about it."

. . . The procession had begun at two and it was now four. Walking down the Via Fardella we heard its trumpets in the distance, and then we saw it swaying toward us through the dusty afternoon like a caravan in the desert. Leading it were forty figures in bright scarlet robes, their white hoods slit at the eyes. They carried flaming torches. The sight of the procession struck a terror such as only masked unknown figures can. It reminded me of the Ku Klux Klan cross-burnings of my Wisconsin childhood. These hooded men were members of a *confraternita*, a secret society harking back to medieval times. No procession ever moved so slowly or in such curious spurts. The men carrying groups bolted with them for a hundred feet or so and then stopped to rest. Each group of carriers was directed by a captain with a *ciaccola*, a castanetlike wooden clacker with which he controlled their movements. A set of auxiliary carriers in each group rattled coin boxes and begged money from the public. To a generous donor the carriers turned and bowed their statues.

Each group was preceded by a band of twenty-four or more instruments, the largest belonging to the *muratori* (stonemasons), who, in the fever of Trapani building, had become the most prosperous guild in town. Their great bass drum, riding on the back of a small boy, had printed on it in large letters, JAZZ. Bands blared a variety of melodies, including funeral marches from Puccini, Toselli, and Lombardi, and pieces entitled "Weeping Virgin," "The War Dead," "To the Memory of a Valorous Major," "The Gravediggers," and a popular one played by several bands, "Povero Fiore," or "Poor Flower," in honor of the suffering Virgin. All the bands played in the same slow waltz tempo.

Behind each band marched a black-robed guard of some twenty men. The guards were captained by two standard-bearers, a man and a small boy, both of whom danced in slow motion on the alternate beat, two steps front and one step back.

The combined effect of all this was one of excruciating melancholy. Still there was a counterpoint of gaiety and high spirits among the guild carriers. They were for the most part impious younger men who were still full of animal spirits. They were dressed alike in blue denim coveralls and hats with pompoms; many wore the felt and gum shoes worn throughout southern Italy, where leather is expensive. During rests they leaned on their statues and puffed on cigarettes, or reached underneath the statues for a straw-covered bottle of wine which they passed among themselves. Like the dice-throwing soldiers at the foot of the cross, or the impish Serpotta cherubs in the Palermo oratories, they made a merry game of the Crucifixion.

Especially was this true of their dancing. It had a rocking, jungle sensuousness that was like slow-motion jitter-bugging. Gerardo said the movement was a Sicilian hop known as *anmacata,* which was carefully rehearsed for the occasion. The result was a most unseemly jigging of the tragic Crucifixion figures riding on the men's shoulders. As time passed I even became accustomed to the Christ bouncing in His glass coffin. But I never failed to be startled by the *Ecce Homo* Christ, hands bound before Him, naked except for a breechcloth and the crown of thorns. The body, bent in anguish, seemed, each time I saw it, to be bowing to a lady, inviting her to the waltz.

The climax was the appearance of the weeping Madonna, a priestess symbolizing all mother-sorrow. Except for her sacred heart pierced by a dagger and a white handkerchief, she was undecorated. She rode above the crowd like a stark, black-robed Hecuba. But a handkerchief, of silk lace lovingly embroidered with the initial M and delicately hung from a little finger, gave her the air of a character in a Victorian melodrama.

She was followed by the sorrowing veiled women of the town, who had medallions of the Virgin pinned to their breasts. Many were old and barefoot, with feet caked by dust. Some wore black stockings worn through at the toes. "These are the penitents," Gerardo said. "To walk barefoot is to be humble. If they have strength to endure the night they will walk to the end." Some of the women carried children, and most of the grandmothers clutched the hand of a grandchild, who trotted alongside. At the end of it all came the colorful, lighthearted auxiliary procession, the balloon vendors fighting in the wind for possession of their wares, the *noci* and *caramelle* carts decorated with bunting and pennants, and behind them a contingent of excited and happy children.

Though we did not see the procession again for eight hours, we never stopped hearing it. Most of the early evening it was crawling through the residential streets of the town. A timetable had been made public, and people were ready and waiting wherever it went. At midnight we climbed to the roof of a movie theater managed by one of Gerardo's friends. The new theater was set in a field of bombed rubble and jagged ruins which stood out in bold relief in the bright moonlight. The bands were amplified by the damp night air so that even streets and buildings seemed to be moaning. We caught glimpses of the candlelit procession winding in and out of the narrow little streets and once or twice we saw four or five fragments of it at a time, like the body of a snake coiling in and out the stones. About half an hour past midnight it advanced on to our street.

The torches and thousands of candles had made little impression in the sunlight of the afternoon. Now, in the wild and eerie night, with the city lights turned out, the character of the spectacle was completely changed. The flickering lights sent wild shadows leaping up and down the narrow canyons of the streets. People hung from balconies and windows, in intimate contact with the procession below. The red robes of the *confraternita* glowed like coals; their leader was carrying a cross. It was awesome and frightening.

By now the carriers of the statues had lost their buoyancy. They rested more frequently, almost every fifty feet, and leaned heavily on their burdens when they set them down. Advancing, they laid their arms on each other's shoulders and moved as a unit, rocking the statues gently as if they were putting them to sleep. And they danced. "It is necessary to dance to keep the blood going," said Gerardo. A small boy standard-bearer marching with his father staggered sleepily out of line. His father prodded him back into step with a candle. The black canopies covering the scaffolding underneath the statues were streaked with wax. So was the clothing of the carriers. Said Gerardo, "Wax is difficult to remove from clothing, so the people wear it proudly through the year to show they participated in the procession."

Seen from above, the statue faces appeared human and emotionally overwrought. In the deposition group the wind flapped a beautiful lace shawl around the dead Jesus, and the carriers extinguished some candles to keep it from going up in flames. I could see Jesus in His coffin wearing a watch and chain; the white lilies trembled about the corpse like ghosts. The carriers of the weeping Madonna had put on red robes and white turbans. Waltzing by us into an area of rubble and ruin, the Madonna might have been Persephone entering hell. Mourning women and barefoot grandmothers stumbled silently behind her, while the money-gatherers clanked their cans and harvested a shower of coins and notes from roofs and windows.

I had a question which had been bothering me throughout the night. "Whose festa is Easter?" I asked. "Mary's or Jesus'?"

Gerardo didn't hesitate. "It is a festa for both," he said. "But of course it is her son who was crucified and is resurrected."

There it was. *Her son* was crucified, not *Jesus*. The emotions being aroused were not sympathy for His agonies but sympathy for the suffering of bereaved motherhood.

"It was very inconsiderate of Jesus to get Himself crucified and bring such anguish on His mother," Gerardo said. "At least many people think so. They will say to you He was a little *pazzo* [crazy]. One who could work miracles could easily have saved Himself. However," Gerardo added with deep piety, "that is not the way I think."

Since it was now three o'clock, Gerardo said good night and I went to my hotel. But the bands wailed on and sleep was impossible. So I put my clothes back on and followed the sounds. The procession was moving along Via Torrearsa toward the Piazza Marina. I ran down a parallel street to meet it head on. People were leaning wearily against buildings; frightened cats leaped in the direction of the harbor. I cut back to the Via Torrearsa and found myself in the fishermen's quarter. At the far ends of a street I saw two large electric signs: PAX and INRI. The occasion had flushed out all the variables of humanity. Hunchbacks and cripples huddled next to mothers with nursing babies. A befurred infant or two jigged to the approaching music. Other children slept on the pavement like corpses. Women in chenille robes and children rolled in blankets looked down from the roofs.

The procession was staggering at a snail's pace now, taking long, silent rests. A boy ran to the rescue of the barbers with several liters of wine. The fishermen entered a tavern to get their own; they drank so long and deeply they held up the procession. Other groups followed their example, and the ropemakers' standard-bearer leaned his cross against a barrel. The wineshops had become the Stations of the Cross.

Some of the bands were stumbling silently along and there was less music. The saltworkers drank from bottles as they moved. One of the fruit growers fell to the pavement; his friends hoisted him up. Women dropped hard-boiled eggs into carriers' gullets like birds feeding nestlings. The silver teeth of the men flashed in the candle glow; their black hair was matted with candle wax. The tiny standard-bearer who had slept four hours earlier was back in waltz step with his father. Little girls wore pink and blue sweaters over their white angels' dresses to keep warm, and the exhausted, barefoot grandmothers leaned on the Madonna to keep from falling. Behind the peanut carts, which were lit up with colored electric bulbs, a brass band was trying to catch up. The musicians had stopped too long in the wineshop and were playing somewhat livelier than usual.

I walked through the town, past movie houses which stayed open all night, noisy cafés, and wineshops. Cafés featured great bowls of hard-boiled eggs, which the people were eating in quantity. Men sang songs. Business was good.

Over the sea dawn was breaking. On the quay fish nets were piled high. Cats, confused by the night-long excitement, still scurried about. Two young men bargained with a prostitute. I could hear the strains of "Poor Flower" echoing over the town and a church clock striking six.

An hour later Gerardo arrived at my hotel refreshed by sleep and a bath. My room had a balcony over the Corso Vittorio Emanuele, the street of the Church of the Collegio, where the procession would end. "The *processione* is finished when the Madonna enters those doors," Gerardo said. "There is always suspense whether or not she will enter by ten-thirty so that the celebration of Easter can begin at noon. Almost every year she is late. Today she is already an hour behind schedule."

The town glittered and the music blew loud against the deep and steady drums. The street below was choked with people, for the population, spread over the city in the night, was now concentrated outside the Collegio Church for the climax of the mysteries. The procession approached from the upper end of the street. The carriers were stumbling only short distances, for the pavements, now coated with candle drippings, were as slippery and perilous as ice. During the long rests the men collapsed on the stones or leaned prostrate on their poles. Their faces were as anguished and tortured as those of the statues they carried. The candles which had brought such brilliance to the night, in the sunlight gave only thin spirals of smoke. Ragged children skidded excitedly over the pavements, harvesting wax which hung like stalactites from the statues; it would be salvaged to light the nights of the poor.

So slowly did the procession move that the final thousand feet took four hours. Each guild spent a quarter of an hour carrying its group into the church. Exhausted though they were, the men were reluctant to relinquish their burden. As they approached the church they seemed to tap new wells of energy, like athletes entering the final heat. The bands, all playing different tunes, shook the city like Joshua's trumpets, and a frightened dog, caught in the frenzy, broke through the crowd with a yelp of terror and disappeared. The money-gatherers rattled their cans and brought down a blizzard of currency.

For the carriers it was the last opportunity to compete for the prizes. As each group approached the church steps the men went into an ecstasy of dance. The praying Jesus of Gethsemane, the bloody Jesus of the flagellation, Jesus on the cross, and Jesus dead in His casket—all swayed and bowed, protesting their return to darkness with a final orgy of waltz.

Through the hours of waiting the standard-bearers continued their own curious footwork. Carrying the stonemasons' flag was a golden-haired youth of twenty whose black bow tie and long black gloves had become spotted with wax. Without moving from the spot where he stood, he solemnly kept on dancing, one step front, one step to the side, and a third step back, never smiling, always watching his knee as he crooked it and his slippered toe tip as he pointed. With his eyes fixed lovingly on himself he seemed to be waltzing on a cloud. He reminded me of the narcissistic John the Baptist of the Agrigento museum.

People were anxiously consulting their watches; it was ten-thirty and the Madonna was not even approaching. Finally they saw her coming, the black figure bobbing over a sea of humanity. The blood-colored robes of her guard were clotted with wax and grime. The red-faced, swollen-eyed penitents who plodded behind her waved to friends like victorious athletes. Their number was small, and one who was young nursed an infant. The Madonna's candles flickered low, her lilies were encrusted with wax. A woman tore one off for a souvenir and then throngs of screaming women crushed forward to strip the flowers away. One woman fainted from the excitement. A screeching ambulance plowed through the human ocean like a ship.

For almost an hour the Madonna waited. At a given moment all the bands joined together with "Poor Flower" in lively Viennese tempo, one playing in a higher pitch and a full measure behind, providing an echo of the melody. The avalanche of sound was the signal that the Madonna was at the end of her search. Her carriers were ready on the steps.

"This is her moment of indecision," Gerardo said. "She does not know whether to enter it or not. She has searched for twenty-one hours and she is tired. If she knew her son were inside she would go, but she is not sure and she knows once she is inside she cannot come back out."

There could be no doubt in anyone's mind that she would enter as she had for the past three hundred years. But rationality had no part in this. I felt myself being caught up in the inexplicable and overwhelming suspense. Gerardo's brow was beaded with sweat, and I felt moisture on my own.

For several agonizing minutes the Madonna jigged and swayed outside the door. As she hesitated the music grew softer and softer until the drums were counting my heartbeats. She began a long to-and-fro movement, starting for the door and withdrawing, reaching closer each time. Below me the people were silent and breathless. It was like watching a human sacrifice. The Madonna swayed toward her fate, to a rhythm that was unabashedly erotic. The music finally faded away, like a wisp of smoke from one of the dying candles.

The world stopped. With a sudden, terrible thrust the Mother of God plunged into darkness. Persephone was swallowed by the underworld.

"*Ecco!*" Cries of relief everywhere. "She's in. It's done. *Così sia!*" As the church doors closed the bands struck up such a thunderous fortissimo of "Poor Flower" that the world could have waltzed to it.

In Gerardo's eyes there were tears.

"Did she find Him?" I asked.

He shrugged. "As you will," he said. "To some she finds Him and her entrance is a triumph; to others it is a defeat, like the closing of the door to a tomb. It is a procession of mystery. You may believe what you will."

The twenty-two-hour ordeal was over. The crowd melted away so quickly that it seemed an hallucination.

"In Sicily Jesus rises from the tomb at noon on Saturday," Gerardo said. "The celebration of Easter begins in a half hour." In a tone of voice that was decidedly carping, he added, "The Madonna was an hour late."

Young Love in Moscow

SANTHA RAMA RAU

FROM *My Russian Journey*

1957

Daughter of a distinguished Brahman family—her father was a diplomat and her mother a leader of social movements—Santha Rama Rau has had an unusual orientation to both East and West. After eight years of education in England, she returned to India for a while, and in Home to India *she describes how she then began to realize that she was Indian and Asian. Later she attended college in the United States and made that country her home.*

Then, in 1947, she visited Japan and from there set out across southeast Asia. Along with an American woman journalist and Faubion Bowers, an American authority on the dance and the drama of the East, whom she later married, she went by truck as far west as the lamasery at Kumbum, where Fathers Huc and Gabet had stopped a hundred years before. They then traveled widely in Indochina, Siam and Indonesia. In the book that resulted from this trip, East of Home, *and especially in such a section as the one on Bali, she gives us a sense of the rich color and texture of the East as well as its relaxed approach to living.*

Another book, View to the Southeast, *followed a year-long journey in 1955 through the Philippines and all of southeast Asia again. In the autumn of 1957, taking advantage of the relaxation of restrictions against foreigners, they went to the Soviet Union with their five-year-old son and his nurse, a beautiful Negress—a quartet that understandably attracted much attention and, because of the Indian element, was made especially welcome. They visited Leningrad, Tashkent and Samarkand but spent*

678

most of their three-month stay in Moscow. Avoiding model collectives and such, Santha Rama Rau tried instead (aided by her husband's serviceable command of the language) to get to know as many Russians as intimately as possible. Though her book may therefore lack a broad base and statistical backing, it abounds in such revealing glimpses of life in Moscow as the one recorded in the extract below.

[While they are sitting at a table in the Gorki Park of Culture and Rest, Boris, a language student at the University, introduces himself and eventually becomes their best friend in Moscow.]

Bɪᴛ by bit we learned a good deal about Boris, that he was considered a very good student and received a relatively large government stipend because of his high grades, that he was a serious worker in his Young Communist League group, that he was ambitious, that, unlike Sasha, he was not particularly interested in sights and monuments and visual art, but preferred reading and had devoured any novel in English that he could find. But he was reticent about his home life, and it was only after a rather unexpected conversation one day in the park that we began to know more of how he lived, the moment, really, that we began to be friends.

It was a pleasantly mild, sunny afternoon at the moment just before evening when the sun is slanting low between the trees. We were all sitting at our usual place and looking around at the other people making the most of the short season. Autumn is, in any case, a sentimental time of year, and as we watched the couples strolling along the paths or sitting on the park benches under the yellowing leaves of the trees, eating ice cream, smiling, talking to each other in low voices, I asked Boris, "Tell me, have you equivalents in Russian for a saying like 'All the world loves a lover,' or 'All's fair in love and war,' or 'It's love that makes the world go round'?"

Boris thought for a moment. "Sometimes we say, 'Love is not a potato, do not throw it out the window.' Ah, yes, and—this is very difficult of translation—'Love is so-so,' " he thumped his head with his fist in exasperation, " 'so cruel-and-stubborn, you can even fall in love with a mountain goat.' "

"Those don't sound very romantic," I said.

Boris looked astonished. With a characteristic gesture he pushed his blond hair back from his forehead, which only made it messier, and said very seriously, "But we are the most romantic people in the world! We—especially students—think of it all the time. Often it interferes with our study—"

"Are there many college romances?"

"Of course, many."

"With girls that you meet in class?"

"In class, or at a *vecherinka*" (any evening party, sometimes given by schools or clubs or the Young Communist League), "or, if he has a job in the vacation, then in the office can also be. But really, it is time for the boy to fall in love—he is in love even before he speaks to the girl."

"And then he makes a date with her?"

"So quick? No. He sees her at an evening party, in school, in the office. He is too shy to dance with her. His friend urges him, but he says, 'No, no! Never with no one!' " (Boris never grasped the principle of the double negative—in Russian it is a perfectly reasonable construction.) "He will perhaps be braver on the phone, but still so shy that he is rude—abrupt?—and she is very annoyed. 'Who is this boy? He is very uncultured.' " Boris made a face of extreme scorn. "At last he has the courage to ask her to the cinema. He is certain she will not come. He waits in front of the cinema watching every person getting off at the bus stop. Perhaps she has decided to come by métro? He runs to the corner to watch the métro entrance. He runs back to find her waiting in the lobby. Will she forgive him for not reaching there first? He is so proud to buy her ticket, he thinks that even the woman in the *kassa*—what is *kassa*?"

"Box office."

"So. Box office. Even the box-office woman notices him with his girl." Boris sat back in his chair looking vaguely at the golden leaves above us. "After this he *knows* he is in love. He cannot concentrate. He walks about the streets in a dream. He sees the flower seller on the corner. He stops to stare at the flowers—the raindrops are still on them—they look so fresh, they remind him of his girl, and he buys some for her."

Boris' words immediately brought to mind the scene I had often noticed on Moscow streets, of an elderly Russian woman in her knitted shawl and shabby jacket from a man's suit worn over a black dress, sitting on a folding stool, hip-deep in flowers. Stiff bunches of chrysanthemums and snapdragons stuck into tall tin cans all around her on the sidewalk. She always caused a small eddy in the stream of pedestrians hurrying back from work in the early evening—she used to make me stop too whenever I passed her.

I liked the sudden sight of the massed reds and yellows and purples against the sober coloring of Moscow's streets and, besides, she seemed to me such an odd reminder of pre-Revolutionary life in Russia—the bright flowers and the dingy clothes—in my mind I had peopled the street corners of old Russian novels with women like her.

"At last the day comes," Boris was saying, "when the girl invites him to meet her parents. Terrible! He has too many feet. He falls over the furniture. He does not dare to pick up his tea glass for fear it spills. When he has gone, her parents say, 'How can you go out with such a clumsy boy, an educated girl like you? Whatever else, we have always had good manners in this house.' Then she goes to meet his parents and is so shy that she cannot talk. Afterwards they say, 'She may be a sweet girl, but evidently she is too dull even to speak.' The young people decide that their parents do not understand them. They are old-fashioned and have forgotten what it is to be in love. From then on they meet in public places."

As you live in Moscow you learn that there are a number of popular rendezvous places—the steps of the Bolshoi or the porch of the Lenin Museum right next to Red Square—but the favorite one, the equivalent of under-the-clock-at-the-Biltmore, is the statue of Pushkin. There are always flowers on its pedestal or its steps, and always a few impatient young men pacing about nearby, glancing up occasionally at the sad, dark face with its curly hair and long sideburns, then looking quickly back at each girl that crosses the square. If a young man has brought flowers for his girl, she will certainly pull one out of the bunch and throw it to join the others on the steps before she turns away and takes her escort's arm.

"And then what do they do?" I asked Boris. "Since they can't go home, I mean."

"In any case they cannot go home," he said casually. And I realized a bit guiltily that I should have known that privacy must be one of the biggest problems that young couples have to cope with. Conditions at home are almost always, in Boris' phrase, "somewhat crowded." On the whole, you are lucky if your family has an apartment to itself and does not share at least the kitchen or the bath with other families. Even then it is very unlikely that such an apartment would have a separate living room. If a married couple has a grown son they are usually entitled to an extra room for him; often there is only a flimsy partition between the two rooms, or simply a curtained glass door. If they have two sons, of course the boys share the second room. And then (again if they are fortunate and the kitchen is large enough) the kitchen becomes the dining room as well, and one of the bedrooms doubles as a living room. In these circumstances it is quite understandable that romantic exchanges are impossible at home. Besides, private automobiles are extremely rare, so access to the family car is no solution.

"So they just walk about the streets together?" I asked Boris.

"Or the parks," he said. "Everything else costs money."

Apparently, if they can't afford the theater or a movie, they wander about the city. Often they can be seen standing close together against the first chill of the late evening, in plazas and some of the wide sidewalks listening to the recorded music pouring from outdoor loud-speakers, perhaps the clear brilliance of Oistrakh's violin mixing strangely with the sound of traffic. Russians seem to enjoy listening to music in the open air—even in cold weather—and for the young people street concerts have the added advantage of costing nothing.

Somewhere in this conversation I began to realize that Boris was telling us about himself, and I listened carefully, picturing him in the middle of a romance, while he told us how young Russians love to take long walks along the Moscow River, under the walls of the Kremlin, sometimes crossing one of the big bridges to the island in the middle of the river, pausing on the bridge to watch the water and the boats go by. Often they sit by the river and read poetry aloud to each other. "To a girl at one time I read *Eugene Onegin* by Pushkin. She was very moved. She determined to learn it all by heart."

"But it's immensely long."

"Of course. Nearly as a novel. The boys and girls are always very serious," Boris assured us. It was easy to believe, for frivolity is, in any case, strikingly absent in Russian life.

"Also," Boris continued, "they have long conversations. They criticize each other. He says, 'You should study harder. It is as important for a girl to be intellectual as a man.' She says, 'You have no sense of money. You spend too much on me—on everything—you must save.' "

In extreme cases, if being in love is clearly interfering with a student's work, if he is spending too much time on romance and his grades are getting low, then a friend—or sometimes even his girl—can report him to the local head of the Young Communist League, who will reprimand him, and this can well mean a black mark on his record.

"That doesn't sound very nice," I said carefully. "What business is it of his?"

"It is a good thing," Boris said with emphasis. "A Komsomol leader must know that the members of his group are reliable and serious."

"I see. Well, how do they prove that? By getting married?"

"Perhaps. If they are really in love. They decide to get married." This time when they meet each other's parents things are very different. "They show their maturity. Now they have confidence." Now the young man will not only pick up his girl from her apartment whenever they have a date, and drop her home every evening (instead of leaving her at the street corner), he will also be expected to spend a short while with her parents before they go out and will often come to meals at her home. He will, in fact, behave like a fiancé rather than a beau, even though he will not give her an engagement ring or make any formal declaration of their intention to marry.

The wedding is a simple, unromantic signing of forms at the marriage registration office. Usually there is no fuss beforehand and possibly only a celebration party for a few friends that evening. The parents, even if they disapprove of the match, have to take an accepting attitude. They can express their displeasure, of course, but can do very little about enforcing their wishes. A father cannot, for instance, cut his daughter off without a penny. If she is a student she is, in any case, receiving a government stipend to cover both her tuition and her living expenses. If she is a very good student she may receive as much as 800 rubles ($80) a month, though the stipend varies according to her grades and capabilities. This amount, combined with her husband's allowance, will give them enough to live on.

"But sometimes," Boris said consideringly, "they are not really in love. They do not get married." During the time of their courtship perhaps another man has come along, and "the girl realizes that the other was only a friend, or because he was the first she had no judgment," and mistook a passing fancy for love. They break each other's hearts, they are miserable. They talk together for hours about how they can't bear to hurt each other. "Then the girl marries the second man. At least," Boris finished abruptly, "that is how it was with me."

"Cheer up, Boris," I said. "There are other girls, and one day you'll be glad you didn't marry the first."

"But I *am* married," Boris replied.

"Oh." I paused to work out the situation. "So you were the second man?"

He smiled. "To *her* I was the second man."

He appeared to feel that this rather cryptic remark needed no explanation, so rather timidly I asked, "But to some other girl you were the first?"

"Ah," he said, "that is the difficulty."

Certainly, I thought, he had been describing his own romance, but had it been with a girl who had jilted him and caused him to marry his wife on the rebound? Or had he met someone since his marriage who made him wish he *hadn't* been the second man to his wife? It was some time before we learned the answers.

[They later meet Boris' wife, a severe young woman whom he no longer loves but dares not divorce, because she has given him no reason to do so and it will therefore be held against him. Then they meet the girl he now loves, an attractive young actress. When they leave Moscow there is still no solution in sight for Boris.]

America South

A Landfall in the Bahamas

CHRISTOPHER COLUMBUS

FROM *Journal of the First Voyage of Columbus*

1492–93

> *Christopher Columbus was certainly not the only man of his time who believed that the rich Indies lay across the seas to the west, but he pursued his conviction with a determination and courage that literally knew no bounds.*
>
> *Probably the most familiar story in the annals of discovery is that of the captain from Genoa spending years seeking royal support, winning it at last from Ferdinand and Isabella of Spain, and setting out with eighty-eight men in three tiny vessels on August 3, 1492. He reached land on October 12, 1492, in what is today known as the Bahamas, and then sailed on to touch at many other islands, including Cuba and Haiti, before returning to Spain in triumph. During the next ten years he made other expeditions through the West Indies and along the coast of South America, but his shortcomings as a colonial administrator, together with his failure to find either Cathay or the gold and spices he had promised, gradually undermined him. After suffering incredible hardships on his fourth voyage, he abandoned his efforts and returned to Spain.*
>
> *The extracts that follow are from his journal as preserved in an abridged form in the* History of the Indies *of Bartolomé de Las Casas, a missionary who devoted his life to the Indians of the Spanish colonies in the early sixteenth century.*

[After two months at sea the little fleet, favored for the most part by the trade winds, approaches land. To allay the increasing anxiety of his men, the Admiral often does not reveal to them the full number of leagues covered each day.]

S UNDAY, 7TH OF OCTOBER [1492].—The west course was continued; for two hours they went at the rate of 12 miles an hour, and afterward 8 miles an hour. They made good 23 leagues, counting 18 for the people. This day, at sunrise, the caravel *Niña*, which went ahead, being the best sailer, and pushed forward as much as possible to sight the land first, so as to enjoy the reward which the Sovereigns had promised to whoever should see it first, hoisted a flag at the masthead and fired a gun, as a signal that she had sighted land, for such was the Admiral's order. He had also ordered that, at sunrise and sunset, all the ships should join him; because those two times are most proper for seeing the greatest distance, the haze clearing away. No land was seen during the afternoon, as reported by the caravel *Niña*, and they passed a great number of birds flying from N. to S.W. This gave rise to the belief that the birds were either going to sleep on land or were flying from the winter which might be supposed to be near in the land whence they were coming. The Admiral was aware that most of the islands held by the Portuguese were discovered by the flight of birds. For this reason he resolved to give up the west course, and to shape a course W.S.W. for the two following days. He began the new course one hour before sunset. They made good, during the night, about 5 leagues, and 23 in the day, altogether 28 leagues.

MONDAY, 8TH OF OCTOBER.—The course was W.S.W., and 11½ or 12 leagues were made good in the day and night; and at times it appears that they went at the rate of 15 miles an hour during the night (if the handwriting is not deceptive). The sea was like the river at Seville. "Thanks be to God," says the Admiral, "the air is very soft like the April at Seville; and it is a pleasure to be here, so balmy are the breezes." The weed seemed to be very fresh. There were many land birds, and they took one that was flying to the S.W. Terns, ducks, and a booby were also seen.

TUESDAY, 9TH OF OCTOBER.—The course was S.W., and they made 5 leagues. The wind then changed, and the Admiral steered W. by N. 4 leagues. Altogether, in day and night, they made 11 leagues by day and 20½ leagues by night; counted as 17 leagues altogether. Throughout the night birds were heard passing.

WEDNESDAY, 10TH OF OCTOBER.—The course was W.S.W., and they went at the rate of 10 miles an hour, occasionally 12 miles, and sometimes 7. During the day and night they made 59 leagues, counted as no more than 44. Here the people could endure no longer. They complained of the length of the voyage. But the Admiral cheered them up in the best way he could, giving them good hopes of the advantages they might gain from it. He added that, however much they might complain, he had to go to the Indies, and that he would go on until he found them, with the help of our Lord.

THURSDAY, 11TH OF OCTOBER.—The course was W.S.W., and there was more sea than there had been during the whole of the voyage. They saw sandpipers, and a green reed near the ship. Those of the caravel *Pinta* saw a cane and a pole, and they took up another small pole which appeared to have been worked with iron; also another bit of cane, a land plant, and a small board. The crew of the caravel *Niña* also saw signs of land, and a small branch covered with berries. Everyone breathed afresh and rejoiced at these signs. The run until sunset was 26 leagues.

After sunset the Admiral returned to his original west course, and they went along at the rate of 12 miles an hour. Up to two hours after midnight they had gone 90 miles, equal to 22½ leagues. As the caravel *Pinta* was a better sailer, and went ahead of the Admiral, she found the land, and made the signals ordered by the Admiral. The land was first seen by a sailor named Rodrigo de Triana. But the Admiral, at ten in the previous night, being on the castle of the poop, saw a light, though it was so uncertain that he could not affirm it was land. He called Pedro Gutiérrez, a gentleman of the King's bedchamber, and said that there seemed to be a light, and that he should look at it. He did so, and saw it. The Admiral said the same to Rodrigo Sanchez of Segovia, whom the King and Queen had sent with the fleet as inspector, but he could see nothing, because he was not in a place whence anything could be seen. After the Admiral had spoken he saw the light once or twice, and it was like a wax candle rising and falling. It seemed to few to be an indication of land; but the Admiral made certain that land was close. When they said the *Salve*, which all the sailors were accustomed to sing in their way, the Admiral asked and admonished the men to keep a good lookout on the forecastle, and to watch well for land, and to him who should first cry out that he saw land he would give a silk doublet, besides the other rewards promised by the Sovereigns, which were 10,000 maravedis to him who should first see it. At two hours after midnight the land was sighted at a distance of two leagues. They shortened sail, and lay by under the mainsail without the bonnets. The vessels were hove to, waiting for daylight; and on Friday they arrived at a small island of the Lucayos, called, in the language of the

Indians, Guanahani. Presently they saw naked people. The Admiral went on shore in the armed boat, and Martin Alonso Pinzon, and Vicente Yañez, his brother, who was captain of the *Niña*. The Admiral took the royal standard, and the captains went with two banners of the green cross, which the Admiral took in all the ships as a sign, with an F and a Y and a crown over each letter, one on one side of the cross and the other on the other. Having landed, they saw trees very green, and much water, and fruits of diverse kinds. The Admiral called to the two captains, and to the others who leaped on shore, and to Rodrigo Escovedo, secretary of the whole fleet, and to Rodrigo Sanchez of Segovia, and said that they should bear faithful testimony that he, in presence of all, had taken, as he now took, possession of the said island for the King and for the Queen, his Lords, making the declarations that are required, as is more largely set forth in the testimonies which were then made in writing.

Presently many inhabitants of the island assembled. What follows is in the actual words of the Admiral in his book of the first navigation and discovery of the Indies. "I," he says, "that we might form great friendship, for I knew that they were a people who could be more easily freed and converted to our holy faith by love than by force, gave to some of them red caps, and glass beads to put round their necks, and many other things of little value, which gave them great pleasure, and made them so much our friends that it was a marvel to see. They afterward came to the ship's boats where we were, swimming and bringing us parrots, cotton threads in skeins, darts, and many other things; and we exchanged them for other things that we gave them, such as glass beads and small bells. In fine, they took all, and gave what they had with good will. It appeared to me to be a race of people very poor in everything. They go as naked as when their mothers bore them, and so do the women, although I did not see more than one young girl. All I saw were youths, none more than thirty years of age. They are very well made, with very handsome bodies, and very good countenances. Their hair is short and coarse, almost like the hairs of a horse's tail. They wear the hairs brought down to the eyebrows, except a few locks behind, which they wear long and never cut. They paint themselves black, and they are the color of the Canarians, neither black nor white. Some paint themselves white, others red, and others of what color they find. Some paint their faces, others the whole body, some only round the eyes, others only on the nose. They neither carry nor know anything of arms, for I showed them swords, and they took them by the blade and cut themselves through ignorance. They have no iron, their darts being wands without iron, some of them having a fish's tooth at the end, and others being pointed in various ways. They are all of fair stature and size, with good faces, and well made. I saw some with marks of wounds on their bodies, and I made signs to ask what it was, and they gave me to understand that people from other adjacent islands came with the intention of seizing them, and that they defended themselves. I believed, and still believe, that they come here from the mainland to take them prisoners. They should be good servants and intelligent, for I observed that they quickly took in what was said to them, and I believe that they would easily be made Christians, as it appeared to me that they had no religion. I, our Lord being pleased, will take hence, at the time of my departure, six natives for your Highnesses, that they may learn to speak. I saw no beast of any kind except parrots, on this island." The above is in the words of the Admiral.

SATURDAY, 13TH OF OCTOBER.—"As soon as dawn broke many of these people came to the beach, all youths, as I have said, and all of good stature, a very handsome people. Their hair is not curly, but loose and coarse, like horse hair. In all the forehead is broad, more so than in any other people I have hitherto seen. Their eyes are very beautiful and not small, and themselves far from black, but the color of the Canarians. Nor should anything else be expected, as this island is in a line east and west from the island of Hierro in the Canaries. Their legs are very straight, all in one line, and no belly, but very well formed. They came to the ship in small canoes, made out of the trunks of a tree like a long boat, and all of one piece, and wonderfully worked, considering the country. They are large, some of them holding forty to forty-five men, others smaller, and some only large enough to hold one man. They are propelled with a paddle like a baker's shovel, and go at a marvelous rate. If the canoe capsizes they all promptly begin to swim, and to bail it out with calabashes that they take with them. They brought skeins of cotton thread, parrots, darts, and other small things which it would be tedious to recount, and they give all in exchange for anything that may be given to them. I was attentive, and took trouble to ascertain if there was gold. I saw that some of them had a small piece fastened in a hole they have in the nose, and by signs I was able to make out that to the south, or going from the island to the south, there was a king who had great cups full, and who possessed a great quantity. I tried to get them to go there, but afterward I saw that they had no inclination. I resolved to wait until tomorrow in the afternoon and then to depart, shaping a course to the S.W., for, according to what many of them told me, there was land to the S., to the S.W., and N.W., and that the natives from the N.W. often came to attack them, and went on to the S.W. in search of gold and precious stones.

"This island is rather large and very flat, with bright green trees, much water, and a very large lake in the center, without any mountain, and the whole land so green that it is a pleasure to look on it. The people are very docile, and for the longing to possess our things, and not having anything to give in return, they take what they can get, and presently swim away. Still, they give away all they have got, for whatever may be given to them, down to broken bits of crockery and glass. I saw one give sixteen skeins of cotton for three ceotis [coins] of Portugal, equal to one blanca of Spain, the skeins being as much as an arroba of cotton thread. I shall keep it, and shall allow no one to take it, preserving it all for your Highnesses, for it may be obtained in abundance. It is grown in this island, though the short time did not admit of my ascertaining this for a certainty. Here also is found the gold they wear fastened in their noses. But, in order not to lose time, I intend to go and see if I can find the island of Cipango [Japan]. Now, as it is night, all the natives have gone on shore with their canoes."

SUNDAY, 14TH OF OCTOBER.—"At dawn I ordered the ship's boat and the boats of the caravels to be got ready, and I went along the coast of the island to the N.N.E., to see the other side, which was on the other side to the east, and also to see the villages. Presently I saw two or three, and the people all came to the shore, calling out and giving thanks to God. Some of them brought us water, others came with food, and when they saw that I did not want to land, they got into the sea, and came swimming to us. We understood that they asked us if we had come from heaven. One old man came into the boat, and others cried out, in loud voices, to all the men and women, to come and see the men who had come from heaven, and to bring them to eat and drink. . . . I examined all that port, and afterward I returned to the ship and made sail. I saw so many islands that I hardly knew how to determine to which I should go first. Those natives I had with me said, by signs, that there were so many that they could not be numbered, and they gave the names of more than a hundred. At last I looked out for the largest, and resolved to shape a course for it, and so I did. It will be distant five leagues from this of San Salvador, and the others some more, some less. All are very flat, and all are inhabited. The natives make war on each other, although these are very simple-minded and handsomely formed people."

[Still believing he is somewhere in the East and searching with unflagging optimism for gold and spices, the Admiral sails along the coasts of Cuba, Haiti and other islands in the vicinity. Constantly the *Journal* describes in glowing terms the natural wealth—both real and rumored—of the land, and the innocence and gentleness (in later voyages their cannibalism was to disenchant Columbus) of the natives. The following episode on the north coast of Haiti is characteristic of the many exchanges with natives recorded in the *Journal*.]

WEDNESDAY, 12TH OF DECEMBER.—The Admiral did not leave the port today, for the same reason: a contrary wind. He set up a great cross on the west side of the entrance, on a very picturesque height, "in sign," he says, "that your Highnesses hold this land for your own, but chiefly as a sign of our Lord Jesus Christ." This being done, three sailors strolled into the woods to see the trees and bushes. Suddenly they came upon a crowd of people, all naked like the rest. They called to them, and went toward them, but they ran away. At last they caught a woman; for I had ordered that some should be caught, that they might be treated well, and made to lose their fear. This would be a useful event, for it could scarcely be otherwise, considering the beauty of the country. So they took the woman, who was very young and beautiful, to the ship, where she talked to the Indians on board; for they all speak the same language. The Admiral caused her to be dressed, and gave her glass beads, hawks' bells, and brass ornaments; then he sent her back to the shore very courteously, according to his custom. He sent three of the crew with her, and three of the Indians he had on board, that might open communications with her people. The sailors in the boat, who took her on shore, told the Admiral that she did not want to leave the ship, but would rather remain with the other women he had seized at the port of Mares, in the island of Juana or Cuba. The Indians who went to put the woman on shore said the natives came in a canoe, which is their caravel, in which they navigate from one place to another; but when they came to the entrance of the harbor, and saw the ships, they turned back, left the canoe, and took the road to the village. The woman pointed out the position of the village. She had a piece of gold in her nose, which showed that there was gold in that island.

THURSDAY, 13TH OF DECEMBER.—The three men who had been sent by the Admiral with the woman returned at three o'clock in the morning, not having gone with her to the village, because the distance appeared to be long, or because they were afraid. They said that next day many people would come to the ships, as they would have been reassured by the news brought them by the woman. The Admiral, with the desire of ascertaining whether there were any profitable commodities in that land, being so beautiful and fertile, and of having some speech with the people, and being desirous of serving the Sovereigns, determined to send again to the village, trusting in the news brought by the woman that the Christians were good people. For this service he selected nine men well armed, and suited for such an enterprise, with whom an Indian went from those who were on board. They reached the village, which is 4½ leagues to the S.E., and found that it was situated in a very large and open valley. As soon as the inhabitants saw the Christians coming they all fled inland, leaving all their goods behind them. The village consisted of a thousand houses, with over three thousand inhabitants. The Indian whom the Christians had brought with them ran after the fugitives, saying that they should have no fear, for the Christians did not come from Cariba, but were from heaven, and that they gave many beautiful things to all the people they met. They were so impressed with what he said, that upwards of two thousand came close up to the Christians, putting their hands on their heads, which was a sign of great reverence and friendship, and they were all trembling until they were reassured. The Christians related that, as soon as the natives had cast off their fear, they all went to the houses, and each one brought what he had to eat, consisting of yams, which are roots like large radishes, which they sow and cultivate in all their lands, and is their staple food. They make bread of it, and roast it. The yam has the smell of a chestnut, and anyone would think he was eating chestnuts. They gave their guests bread and fish, and all they had. As the Indians who came in the ship had understood that the Admiral wanted to have some parrots, one of those who accompanied the Spaniards mentioned this, and the natives brought out parrots, and gave them as many as they wanted, without asking anything for them. The natives asked the Spaniards not to go that night, and that they would give them many other things that they had in the mountains. While all these people were with the Spaniards, a great multitude was seen to come, with the husband of the woman whom the Admiral had honored and sent away. They wore hair over their shoulders, and came to give thanks to the Christians for the honor the Admiral had done them, and for the gifts. The Christians reported to the Admiral that this was a handsomer and finer people than any that had hitherto been met with. But the Admiral says that he does not see how they can be a finer people than the others, giving to understand that all those he had found in the other islands were very well conditioned. As regards beauty, the Christians said there was no comparison, both men and women, and that their skins were whiter than the others. They saw two girls whose skins were as white as any that could be seen in Spain. They also said, with regard to the beauty of the country they saw, that the best land in Castille could not be compared with it. The Admiral also, comparing the lands they had seen before with these, said that there was no comparison between them, nor did the plain of Cordova come near them, the difference being as great as between night and day. They said that all these lands were cultivated, and that a very wide and large river passed through the center of the valley, and could irrigate all the fields. All the trees were green and full of fruit, and the plants tall and covered with flowers. The roads were broad and good. The climate was like April in Castille; the nightingale and other birds sang as they do in Spain during that month, and it was the most pleasant place in the world. Some birds sing sweetly at night. The crickets and frogs are heard a good deal. The fish are like those of Spain. They saw much aloe and mastick, and cotton fields. Gold was not found, and it is not wonderful that it should not have been found in so short a time.

> [After visits to other islands and the loss of the *Santa Maria*, he turns homeward. The two vessels survive weeks of hurricanes and arrive back in Palos on March 15, 1493.]

Conquistador

BERNAL DÍAZ DEL CASTILLO

FROM *The True History of the Conquest of New Spain*

1517–21

As author of the most stirring chronicle of the conquest of New Spain, Bernal Díaz contributed inestimably to the legend of the conquistadors as the most passionate seekers of fortune, the boldest adventurers in history. Born in Castilian Spain about 1492, he was in Cuba by the time he was twenty-two and in 1518 joined an expedition sailing for Mexico under Hernando Cortés. Serving throughout as a foot soldier, but evidently as one of the most trusted in the corps, he is said to have fought in no less than 119 battles and skirmishes. Dissatisfied with his share of the spoils, he went on other expeditions, but finally accepted a grant in Guatemala and died there, a respected magistrate, at the age of ninety-two.

It was in Guatemala almost fifty years after the events that, provoked by the accounts of historians who had never even been out of Spain, he set down his richly detailed recollections. No classic stylist or scholar, Bernal Díaz wrote plainly and even at times naïvely, but always with spirit and feeling, of the frenzy of combat, the hunger and thirst, the triumphs and spoils that were the lot of the handful of Spaniards that destroyed the Aztec power.

From memories that time seems to have made only more intense, he conjures up a score of unforgettable images: Cortés, dynamic, insatiable, astute; the splendor of the Aztec capital with lovely gardens all around and bloody sacrificial altars at its heart; the indomitable Indians, led by the noble, curiously gentle Montezuma, and the agonizing siege of the city.

As underlying themes are the gold the Spaniards dreamed of, as contrasted with the suffering they actually endured, their crusading in the name of Christ, as against their pride in men slaughtered, and finally the fantasy of the Indians—their belief that the coming of these white men had been prophesied by the gods.

[The expedition under Cortés lands on the mainland and after several skirmishes is joined by a few native chieftains who are hostile to Montezuma. They found a settlement at Vera Cruz and later start inland from Cempoala toward Mexico City, marching across mountains, swamps and sandy stretches and battling the Tlaxcalans and Cholulans. As they approach Mexico, Montezuma comes out to greet them.]

The Great Montezuma

EARLY next day we left Iztapalapa with a large escort of those great caciques whom I have already mentioned. We proceeded along the causeway, which is here eight paces in width and runs so straight to the city of Mexico that it does not seem to me to turn either much or little, but, broad as it is, it was so crowded with people that there was hardly room for them all, some of them going to and others returning from Mexico, besides those who had come out to see us, so that we were hardly able to pass by the crowds of them that came; and the towers and *cúes* were full of people as well as the canoes from all parts of the lake. It was not to be wondered at, for they had never before seen horses or men such as we are.

Gazing on such wonderful sights, we did not know what to say, or whether what appeared before us was real, for on one side, on the land, there were great cities, and in the lake ever so many more, and the lake itself was crowded with canoes, and in the causeway were many bridges at intervals, and in front of us stood the great city of Mexico, and we—we did not even number four hundred soldiers! and we well remembered the words and warnings given us by the people of Huexotzingo and Tlaxcala, and the many other warnings that had been given that we should beware of entering Mexico, where they would kill us, as soon as they had us inside.

Let the curious readers consider whether there is not much to ponder over in this that I am writing. What men have there been in the world who have known such daring? But let us get on, and march along the causeway. When we arrived where another small causeway branches off (leading to Coyoacán, which is another city) where there were some buildings like towers, which are their oratories, many more chieftains and caciques approached clad in very rich mantles, the brilliant liveries of one chieftain differing from those of another, and the causeways were crowded with them. The great Montezuma had sent these great caciques in advance to receive us, and when they came before Cortés they bade us welcome in their language, and as a sign of peace they touched their hands against the ground and kissed the ground with the hand.

There we halted for a good while, and Cacamatzin, the Lord of Texcoco, and the Lord of Iztapalapa and the Lord of Tacuba and the Lord of Coyoacán went on in advance to meet the great Montezuma, who was approaching in a rich litter accompanied by other great lords and caciques, who owned vassals. When we arrived near to Mexico, where there were some other small towers, the great Montezuma got down from his litter, and those great caciques supported him with their arms beneath a marvelously rich canopy of green-colored feathers with much gold and silver embroidery and with pearls and chalchuites suspended from a sort of bordering, which was wonderful to look at. The great Montezuma was richly attired according to his usage, and he was shod with sandals, the soles were of gold and the upper part adorned with precious stones. The four chieftains who supported his arms were also richly clothed according to their usage, in garments which were apparently held ready for them on the road to enable them to accompany their prince, for they did not appear in such attire when they came to receive us. Besides these four chieftains, there were four other great caciques who supported the canopy over their heads, and many other lords who walked before the great Montezuma, sweeping the ground where he would tread and spreading cloths on it, so that he should not tread on the earth. Not one of these chieftains dared even to think of looking him in the face, but kept their eyes lowered with great reverence, except those four relations, his nephews, who supported him with their arms.

When Cortés was told that the great Montezuma was approaching, and he saw him coming, he dismounted from his horse, and when he was near Montezuma, they simultaneously paid great reverence to one another. Montezuma bade him welcome and our Cortés replied through Doña Marina [the native princess, given to Cortés by a chieftain, who lived with him and was invaluable in his relations with the Indians], wishing him very good health. And it seems to me that Cortés, through Doña Marina, offered him his right hand, and Montezuma did not wish to take it, but he did

ABOVE, an engraving made about 1500 and said to be the earliest portrayal of natives of the New World. It shows natives of the northern coast of South America decked out in feathers, with precious stones on their chests; others of their kind are being roasted over fires. [See pages 687-695.] BELOW, Montezuma, Emperor of Mexico, greeting the conquistador Cortés. Bettmann Archive. [See pages 696-706.]

Quitlauhtique

Xonacatla.

ABOVE, contemporary drawings showing Cortés receiving gifts from the inhabitants of Tlaxcala, and Spaniards in battle against the Indians. BELOW, drawing of a human sacrifice on an Aztec altar. [See pages 696-706.]

ABOVE, Francisco Pizarro, conqueror of Peru. [See pages 707-716.]

BELOW, The Amazons, as depicted in a sixteenth-century engraving. [See pages 717-723.]

Two early-eighteenth-century drawings of the city of Mexico as it appeared during Spanish rule. The one above shows the city when it was still surrounded by water and called Tenochtitlán. Of the various sections of the city, that in which the court and nobility were to be found was called Mexico. [See pages 724-734.]

The City of Mexico.

ABOVE, South American Indians hunting wild horses with bolas. BELOW, ladies of Lima at home. Bettmann Archive. [See pages 735-745.]

Mid-nineteenth-century Mexico City types such as those whose street cries are described by Frances Calderón de la Barca. ABOVE LEFT, the night watchman; ABOVE RIGHT, the peddler; BELOW LEFT, water carrier; BELOW RIGHT, the baker. All courtesy of The Metropolitan Museum of Art, Whittelsey Fund, 1946. [See pages 752-759.]

ABOVE LEFT, a Jivaran woman of the Amazon jungle carrying a monkey. ABOVE RIGHT, a miner of the Cerro de Pasco region of central Peru as seen in an engraving of the 1850s. BELOW, a sketch by an artist (who is in the cupola of the boat) of an Indian village on the shore of the upper Amazon. [See pages 760-766.]

An Oyana boy about to undergo torture from stinging ants during a puberty ceremony.
Photograph by Dominique Darbois. [See pages 767-776.]

give his hand to Cortés and then Cortés brought out a necklace which he had ready at hand, made of glass stones, which I have already said are called margaritas, which have within them many patterns of diverse colors; these were strung on a cord of gold and with musk so that it should have a sweet scent, and he placed it round the neck of the great Montezuma and when he had so placed it he was going to embrace him, and those great princes who accompanied Montezuma held back Cortés by the arm so that he should not embrace him, for they considered it an indignity.

Then Cortés through the mouth of Doña Marina told him that now his heart rejoiced at having seen such a great prince, and that he took it as a great honor that he had come in person to meet him and had frequently shown him such favor.

Then Montezuma spoke other words of politeness to him, and told two of his nephews who supported his arms, the Lord of Texcoco and the Lord of Coyoacán, to go with us and show us to our quarters, and Montezuma with his other two relations, the Lord of Cuitlahuac and the Lord of Tacuba, who accompanied him, returned to the city, and all those grand companies of caciques and chieftains who had come with him returned to his train. As they turned back after their Prince we stood watching them and observed how they all marched with their eyes fixed on the ground without looking at him, keeping close to the wall, following him with great reverence. Thus space was made for us to enter the streets of Mexico, without being so much crowded. But who could now count the multitude of men and women and boys who were in the streets and on the *azoteas* [rooftops], and in canoes on the canals, who had come out to see us. It was indeed wonderful, and, now that I am writing about it, it all comes before my eyes as though it had happened but yesterday....

The great Montezuma was about forty years old, of good height and well proportioned, slender and spare of flesh, not very swarthy, but of the natural color and shade of an Indian. He did not wear his hair long, but so as just to cover his ears, his scanty black beard was well shaped and thin. His face was somewhat long, but cheerful, and he had good eyes and showed in his appearance and manner both tenderness and, when necessary, gravity. He was very neat and clean and bathed once every day in the afternoon. He had many women as mistresses, daughters of chieftains, and he had two great *cacicas* as his legitimate wives. He was free from unnatural offenses. The clothes that he wore one day, he did not put on again until four days later....

For each meal, over thirty different dishes were prepared by his cooks according to their ways and usage, and they placed small pottery braziers beneath the dishes so that they should not get cold. They prepared more than three hundred plates of the food that Montezuma was going to eat, and more than a thousand for the guard. . . .

I have heard it said that they were wont to cook for him the flesh of young boys, but as he had such a variety of dishes, made of so many things, we could not succeed in seeing if they were of human flesh or of other things, for they daily cooked fowls, turkeys, pheasants, native partridges, quail, tame and wild ducks, venison, wild boar, reed birds, pigeons, hares and rabbits, and many sorts of birds and other things which are bred in this country, and they are so numerous that I cannot finish naming them in a hurry; so we had no insight into it, but I know for certain that after our captain censured the sacrifice of human beings, and the eating of their flesh, he ordered that such food should not be prepared for him thenceforth.

Let us cease speaking of this and return to the way things were served to him at mealtime. It was in this way: If it was cold they made up a large fire of live coals of a firewood made from the bark of trees which did not give off any smoke, and the scent of the bark from which the fire was made was very fragrant, and so that it should not give off more heat than he required, they placed in front of it a sort of screen adorned with figures of idols worked in gold. He was seated on a low stool, soft and richly worked, and the table, which was also low, was made in the same style as the seats, and on it they placed the tablecloths of white cloth and some rather long napkins of the same material. Four very beautiful cleanly women brought water for his hands in a sort of deep basin which they call *xicales* [gourds], and they held others like plates below to catch the water, and they brought him towels. And two other women brought him tortilla bread, and as soon as he began to eat they placed before him a sort of wooden screen painted over with gold, so that no one should watch him eating. Then the four women stood aside, and four great chieftains who were old men came and stood beside them, and with these Montezuma now and then conversed, and asked them questions, and as a great favor he would give to each of these elders a dish of what to him tasted best. . . .

Let us leave this and proceed to the aviary, and I am forced to abstain from enumerating every kind of bird that was there and its peculiarity, for there was everything from the royal eagle and other smaller eagles, and many other birds of great size, down to tiny birds of many-colored plumage, also the birds from which they take the rich plumage which they use in their green featherwork. The birds which have these feathers are about the size of the magpies in Spain, they are called in this country *quetzales*, and there are other birds which have feathers of five colors—green, red, white, yellow and blue; I don't remember what they are called; then there were parrots of many different colors, and there are so many of them that I forget their names, not to mention the beautifully marked ducks and other larger ones like them. . . .

Let us go on and speak of the skilled workmen Montezuma employed in every craft that was practiced among them. We will begin with lapidaries and workers in gold and silver and all the hollow work, which even the great goldsmiths in Spain were forced to admire, and of these there were a great number of the best in a town named Atzcapotzalco, a league from Mexico. Then for working precious stones and chalchuites, which are like emeralds, there were other great artists. Let us go on to the great craftsmen in featherwork, and painters and sculptors who were most refined . . . to the Indian women who did the weaving and the washing, who made such an immense quantity of fine fabrics with wonderful featherwork designs . . .

Let us go on and tell about the great number of dancers kept by the great Montezuma for his amusement, and others who used stilts on their feet, and others who flew when they danced up in the air, and others like Merry Andrews, and I may say that there was a district full of these people who had no other occupation. Let us go on and speak of the workmen that he had as stone cutters, masons and carpenters, all of whom attended to the work of his houses; I say that he had as many as he wished. We must not forget the gardens of flowers and sweet-scented trees, and the many kinds that there were of them, and the arrangement of them and the walks, and the ponds and tanks of fresh water where the water entered at one end and flowed out of the other; and the baths which he had there, and the variety of small birds that nested in the branches, and the medicinal and useful herbs that were in the gardens. It was a wonder to see, and to take care of it there were many gardeners. Everything was made in masonry and well cemented, baths and walks and closets, and apartments like summerhouses where they danced and sang. There was as much to be seen in these gardens as there was everywhere else, and we could not tire of witnessing his great power.

IDOLS AND SACRIFICIAL ALTARS

THEN our Cortés said to Montezuma through the interpreter Doña Marina: "Your Highness is indeed a very great prince and worthy of even greater things. We are rejoiced to see your cities, and as we are here in your temple, what I now beg as a favor is that you will show us your gods and *teules*." Montezuma replied that he must first speak with his high priests, and when he had spoken to them he said that we might enter into a small tower and apartment, a sort of hall, where there were two altars, with very richly carved boardings on the top of the roof. On each altar were two figures, like giants with very tall bodies and very fat, and the first which stood on the right hand they said was the figure of Huichilobos, their god of war; it had a very broad face and monstrous and terrible eyes, and the whole of his body was covered with precious stones, and gold and pearls, and with seed pearls stuck on with a paste that they make in this country. . . .

There were some braziers with incense which they call copal, and in them they were burning the hearts of the three Indians whom they had sacrificed that day, and they had made the sacrifice with smoke and copal. All the walls of the oratory were so splashed and encrusted with blood that they were black, the floor was the same and the whole place stank vilely. . . .

They had an exceedingly large drum there, and when they beat it the sound of it was so dismal and like, so to say, an instrument of the infernal regions, that one could hear it a distance of two leagues, and they said that the skins it was covered with were those of great snakes. In that small place there were many diabolical things to be seen, bugles and trumpets and knives, and many hearts of Indians that they had burned in fumigating their idols, and everything was so clotted with blood, and there was so much of it, that I curse the whole of it, and as it stank like a slaughterhouse we hastened to clear out of such a bad stench and worse sight. Our Captain said to Montezuma through our interpreter, half laughing: "Señor Montezuma, I do not understand how such a great prince and wise man as you are has not come to the conclusion, in your mind, that these idols of yours are not gods, but evil things that are called devils, and so that you may know it and all your priests may see it clearly, do me the favor to approve of my placing a cross here on the top of this tower, and that in one part of these oratories where your Huichilobos and Tezcatepuca stand we may divide off a space where we can set up an image of Our Lady (an image which Montezuma had already seen) and you will see by the fear in which these idols hold it that they are deceiving you."

Montezuma replied half angrily (and the two priests who were with him showed great annoyance), and said: "Señor Malinche, if I had known that you would have said such defamatory things I would not have shown you my gods, we consider them to be very good, for they give us health and rains and good seed times and seasons and as many victories as we desire, and we are obliged to worship them and make sacrifices, and I pray you not to say another word to their dishonor."

When our Captain heard that and noted the angry looks he did not refer again to the subject, but said with a cheerful manner: "It is time for your Excellency and for us to return"; and Montezuma replied that it was well, but that he had to pray and offer certain sacrifices on account of the great *tatacul*, that is to say sin, which he had committed in allowing us to ascend his great *cu*, and being the cause of our being permitted to see his gods, and of our dishonoring them by speaking evil of them, so that before he left he must pray and worship.

Then Cortés said: "I ask your pardon if it be so"; and then we went down the steps, and as they numbered one hundred and fourteen, and as some of our soldiers were suffering from tumors and abscesses, their legs were tired by the descent.

THE SEIZING OF MONTEZUMA

WHEN Cortés entered, after having made his usual salutations, he said to him through our interpreters: "Señor Montezuma, I am very much astonished that you, who are such a valiant prince, after having declared that you are our friend, should order your captains, whom you have stationed on the coast near to Tuxpan, to take arms against my Spaniards, and that they should dare to rob the towns which are in the keeping and under the protection of our King and master and to demand of them Indian men and women for sacrifice, and should kill a Spaniard, one of my brothers, and a horse." (He did not wish to speak of the captain nor of the six soldiers who died as soon as they arrived at Villa Rica, for Montezuma did not know about it, nor did the Indian captains who had attacked them), and Cortés went on to say: "Being such a friend of yours I ordered my captains to do all that was possible to help and serve you, and you have done exactly the contrary to us. Also in the affair at Cholula your captains and a large force of warriors had received your own commands to kill us. I forgave it at the time out of my great regard for you, but now again your vassals and captains have become insolent, and hold secret consultations stating that you wish us to be killed. I do not wish to begin a war on this account nor to destroy this city, I am willing to forgive it all, if silently and without raising any disturbance you will come with us to our quarters, where you will be as well served and attended to as though you were in your own house, but if you cry out or make any disturbance you will immediately be killed by these my captains, whom I brought solely for this purpose."

When Montezuma heard this he was terrified and dumfounded, and replied that he had never ordered his people to take arms against us, and that he would at once send to summon his captains so that the truth should be known, and he would chastise them, and at that very moment he took from his arm and wrist the sign and seal of Huichilobos, which was only done when he gave an important and weighty command which was to be carried out at once. With regard to being taken prisoner and leaving his palace against his will, he said that he was not the person to whom such an order could be given, and that he would not go. Cortés replied to him with very good arguments and Montezuma answered him with even better, showing that he ought not to leave his house. In this way more than half an hour was spent over talk, and when Juan Velásques de Léon and the other captains saw that they were wasting time over it and could not longer await the moment when they should remove him from his house and hold him a prisoner, they spoke to Cortés somewhat angrily and said: "What is the good of your making so many words, let us either take him prisoner, or stab him, tell him once more that if he cries out or makes an uproar we will kill him, for it is better at once to save our lives or to lose them"; and as Juan Velásques said this with a loud and rather terrifying voice, for such was his way of speaking, Montezuma, who saw that our captains were angered, asked Doña Marina what they were saying in such loud tones. As Doña Marina was very clever, she said: "Señor Montezuma, what I counsel you, is to go at once to their quarters without any disturbance at all, for I know that they will pay you much honor as a great prince such as you are, otherwise you will remain here a dead man, but in their quarters you will learn the truth."

Then Montezuma said to Cortés: "Señor Malinche, if this is what you desire, I have a son and two legitimate daughters, take them as hostages, and do not put this affront on me, what will my chieftains say if they see me taken off as a prisoner?" Cortés replied to him that he must come with them himself and there was no alternative. At the end of much more discussion that took place, Montezuma said that he would go willingly, and then Cortés and our captains bestowed many caresses on him and told him that they begged him not to be annoyed, and to tell his captains and the men of his guard that he was going of his own free will, because he had spoken to his idol Huichilobos and the priests who attended him, and that it was beneficial for his health and the safety of his life that he should be with us. His rich litter in which he was used to go out with all the captains who accompanied him was promptly brought, and he went to our quarters, where we placed guards and watchmen over him.

All the attentions and amusements which it was possible for him to have, both Cortés and all of us did our best to afford him, and he was not put under any personal restraint, and soon all the principal Mexican chieftains and his nephews came to talk with him, and to learn the reason of his seizure, and whether he wished them to attack us. Montezuma answered them, that he was delighted to be here some days with us of his own free will and not by force . . .

There, where he remained, he had his service and his women and his baths in which he bathed himself, and twenty great chiefs always stayed in his company holding their ancient offices, as well as his councilors and captains, and he stayed there a prisoner without showing any anger at all, and ambassadors from distant lands came there with their suits, and brought him his tribute, and he carried on his important business. . . .

[Hearing that another expedition has arrived on the coast to take him prisoner and return him to Cuba, Cortés marches there and defeats it. He then learns that Montezuma has revolted; when he approaches the capital the squadrons of Mexicans attack and a fierce battle ensues.]

Death of Montezuma

Let us go back to our story. It was decided to sue for peace so that we could leave Mexico, and as soon as it was dawn many more squadrons of Mexicans arrived and very effectually surrounded our quarters on all sides, and if they had discharged many stones and arrows before, they came much thicker and with louder howls and whistles on this day, and other squadrons endeavored to force an entrance in other parts, and cannon and muskets availed nothing, although we did them damage enough.

When Cortés saw all this, he decided that the great Montezuma should speak to them from the roof and tell them that the war must cease, and that we wished to leave his city. When they went to give this message from Cortés to the great Montezuma, it is reported that he said with great grief: "What more does Malinche want from me? I neither wish to live nor to listen to him, to such a pass has my fate brought me because of him." And he did not wish to come, and it is even reported that he said he neither wished to see nor hear him, nor listen to his false words, promises or lies. Then the Padre de la Merced and Cristóbal de Olid went and spoke to him with much reverence and in very affectionate terms, and Montezuma said: "I believe that I shall not obtain any result toward ending this war, for they have already raised up another lord and have made up their minds not to let you leave this place alive, therefore I believe that all of you will have to die."

Let us return to the attack they made on us. Montezuma was placed by a battlement of the roof with many of us soldiers guarding him, and he began to speak to his people with very affectionate expressions telling them to desist from the war, and that we would leave Mexico. Many of the Mexican chieftains and captains knew him well and at once ordered their people to be silent and not to discharge darts, stones or arrows, and four of them reached a spot where Montezuma could speak to them, and they to him, and with tears they said to him: "Oh! Señor, and our great Lord, how all your misfortune and injury and that of your children and relations afflicts us; we make known to you that we have already raised one of your kinsmen to be our Lord"; and there he stated his name, that he was called Cuitlahuac, the Lord of Ixtapalapa, and moreover they said that the war must be carried through, and that they had vowed to their idols not to relax it until we were all dead . . .

They had hardly finished this speech when suddenly such a shower of stones and darts were discharged that (our men who were shielding him having neglected for a moment their duty, because they saw how the attack ceased while he spoke to them) he was hit by three stones, one on the head, another on the arm and another on the leg, and although they begged him to have the wounds dressed and to take food, and spoke kind words to him about it, he would not. Indeed, when we least expected it, they came to say that he was dead. Cortés wept for him, and all of us captains and soldiers, and there was no man among us who knew him and was intimate with him, who did not bemoan him as though he were our father, and it is not to be wondered at, considering how good he was. It was stated that he had reigned for seventeen years and that he was the best king there had ever been in Mexico, and that he had conquered in person, in three wars which he had carried on in the countries he had subjugated.

[Cortés retreats to the coast, fighting desperately all the way. But tens of thousands of Tlaxcalan and other Indians join him there and he returns to lay siege to the city. After reverses and much fighting along causeways and canals, the Spaniards enter the devastated city on August 13, 1521.]

Capture of an Inca King

FRANCISCO PIZARRO

FROM *Narrative of the Conquest of Peru, by his secretary, Francisco de Xeres*

1530–34

No sooner had the curtain fallen on the conquest of Mexico than an amazingly similar drama began thousands of miles away in the flourishing empire of the Incas. There the protagonists were again a relentless conquistador and a native emperor moving like a bewitched victim through the rites of sacrifice.

After serving with Balboa and other captains, Francisco Pizarro established himself in Panama. He then made a few attempts, for the most part disastrous, to reach the empire of Birú, which was rumored to be somewhere to the south. Finally, having gone to Spain and secured royal approval, he sailed from Panama in 1531 with fewer than two hundred foot soldiers, horsemen and crossbowmen. Landing on the coast of Ecuador, he stormed Tumbes, crossed the Andes and made his way—stopping occasionally to torture caciques or take loot—to Cajamarca. There the Inca overlord Atahualpa awaited him passively, influenced perhaps by the Incas' belief that godlike white men would one day come to them. What happened when they met is described in the excerpt below.

The account from which it is taken was written by Francisco de Xeres, who accompanied Pizarro as both soldier and secretary. This explains the passages that paint Pizarro as a Christian hero and the Inca lord as a cruel barbarian.

. . . O<small>N</small> reaching the entrance to Caxamalca [Cajamarca], they [the Spaniards] saw the camp of Atahualpa at a distance of a league, in the skirts of the mountains. The Governor [Pizarro] arrived at this town of Caxamalca on Friday, the fifteenth of November, 1532, at the hour of vespers. In the middle of the town there is a great open space, surrounded by walls and houses. The Governor occupied this position, and sent a messenger to Atahualpa to announce his arrival and arrange a meeting, and that he might show him where to lodge . . . .

After examining the town it was found that there was no better position in the neighborhood. This town, the principal place in the valley, is situated on the skirts of a mountain, with a league of open plain in front of it. Two rivers flow through the valley, which is level, well peopled, and surrounded by mountains. The town had two thousand inhabitants. At its entrance there were two bridges, because two rivers flow past. The plaza is larger than any in Spain, surrounded by a wall, and entered by two doorways which open upon the streets of the town. The houses are more than two hundred paces in length, and very well built, being surrounded by strong walls three times the height of a man. The roofs are covered with straw and wood, and rest on the walls. The interiors are divided into eight rooms, much better built than any we had seen before. Their walls are of very well cut stones, and each lodging is surrounded by a masonry wall with doorways and in an open court has a fountain of water conveyed from a distance by pipes for the supply of the house. In front of the plaza, toward the open country, a stone fortress is connected with it by a staircase leading from the square to the fort. Toward the open country there is another small door, with a narrow staircase, all within the outer wall of the plaza. Above the town, on the mountainside, where the houses commence, there is another fort, the greater part of which is hewn out of the rock. This is larger than the other, and surrounded by three walls, rising spirally. They are of a strength such as had not before been seen among the Indians. Between the mountain and the great open space there is another smaller court, entirely surrounded by buildings, in which there were many women for the service of Atahualpa.

As one enters this city there is a house built in a court surrounded by walls, and in the court there is a grove of trees planted by hand. They say that this is the House of the Sun, for in each village they build their mosques to the sun. There are many other mosques in this town, and they hold them in veneration throughout the land. When they enter them, they take off their shoes at the doors. The people of all the villages we came to after ascending the mountains are superior to those we left behind. Those of the mountains are clean and more intelligent, and the women are very modest. The women wear over their clothes highly ornamented girdles fastened round the middle. Over the gown they wear a mantle which reaches from the head to halfway down the legs and is like the mantilla of Spain. The men dress in shirts without sleeves and in outer mantles. They all weave wool and cotton in their houses, and make their cloth and men's shoes of wool and cotton.

The Governor was a long time in the plaza with his men, waiting for Atahualpa either to come or to assign him a lodging. As it was getting late, he sent a captain with twenty horse to speak with Atahualpa and to say that he should come and confer with the Governor. The captain had orders to preserve peace, and to pick no quarrel even if his men were provoked, but to do his best to obtain a hearing and return with the reply. . . .

The captain . . . left his men on this side the river, that the Indians might not be excited, and he did not go by the bridge, fearing for his horse, but crossed by the water, taking an interpreter with him. He passed through a squadron of infantry, and came to the lodging of Atahualpa, where there were four hundred Indians in an open space, who appeared to be a bodyguard. The tyrant was at the door of his lodging, sitting on a low stool, with many Indians before him, and women at his feet, who almost surrounded him. He wore across his forehead a woolen fringe, which looked like silk, of a crimson color, and it was fastened to his head by cords so as to come down to his eyes, which made him look much graver than he really is. His eyes were cast on the ground, and he did not look in any other direction.

When the captain came before him, he said, through the interpreter, that he was a captain sent by the Governor to express the great desire he [the Governor] had to see him, and that if Atahualpa would come the Governor would greatly rejoice; and the captain added other arguments. Atahualpa gave no answer, nor did he even raise his eyes to look at the captain. But a chief replied to what the captain had said. At this juncture another captain [Hernando Pizarro?] came to where the first captain had left his men and asked what had become of him; they answered that he had gone to speak with the Cacique.

Leaving his people, this captain crossed the river, and, approaching near to where Atahualpa was seated, he said: "This is a brother of the Governor who comes to see you."

Then Atahualpa raised his eyes and said: "Malçabilica, the cacique that I have on the river of Turicara sent to say that you ill-treat the caciques and put them in chains, and he sent me a collar of iron, and they say that he killed three Christians and a horse. But I intend to go tomorrow to see the Governor, and to be a friend of the Christians, because they are good."

Hernando Pizarro answered: "Malçabilica is a scoundrel, and neither he nor all the Indians of that river together could kill a single Christian. How could they kill either a Christian or a horse, seeing that they are mere chickens? The Governor and the Christians do not ill-treat the caciques unless they are hostile, and those who are friendly are treated very well. . . ."

Atahualpa said: "A cacique refuses to obey me. If my troops go with yours, will you make war upon him?" Hernando Pizarro replied, "On account of one cacique, it is not necessary that you should send any of your Indians, though you have so large a force. Ten Christians on horseback will suffice to destroy him."

Atahualpa laughed, and said that they should drink. The captains excused themselves from drinking the Indian liquor by saying that they were fasting; but they were importuned by him, and accepted. Presently women came with vases of gold containing *chicha* of maize. When Atahualpa saw them he raised his eyes to them, and without saying a word they went back quickly, and returned with other larger vases of gold, and from these he gave them to drink. Afterward they took their leave, expecting Atahualpa to come and see the Governor on the following morning. . . .

[Atahualpa sends a messenger to say that he will bring his men unarmed into the town. Pizarro agrees, and the Indians stream out of their camp all morning long.]

PRESENTLY the Governor ordered all the Spaniards to arm themselves secretly in their lodgings, and to keep the horses saddled and bridled, and under the orders of three captains; but none were to show themselves in the open space. Men were stationed in the streets leading to the open space, and, taking twenty men with him, the Governor went to his lodging. These had the duty of seizing the person of Atahualpa, if he should come cautiously with so large a force as was coming; but the Governor ordered that he should be taken alive. The sentries were to be on the alert, and, if they saw that the enemy intended treachery, they were to give the signal; and all were to sally out of the lodgings, with the cavalry mounted, when they heard the cry of "Santiago!" ...

[Pizarro sends for Atahualpa.]

As soon as the messenger came before Atahualpa, he made an obeisance to him, and made signs that he should come to where the Governor waited. Presently he and his troops began to move, and the Spaniard returned and reported that they were coming, and that the men in front carried arms concealed under their clothes, which were strong tunics of cotton, beneath which were stones and bags and slings; all which made it appear that they had a treacherous design. Soon the van of the enemy began to enter the open space. First came a squadron of Indians dressed in a livery of different colors, like a chessboard. They advanced, removing the straws from the ground and sweeping the road. Next came three squadrons in different dresses, dancing and singing. Then came a number of men with armor, large metal plates, and crowns of gold and silver. Among them was Atahualpa in a litter lined with plumes of macaws' feathers of many colors and adorned with plates of gold and silver. Many Indians carried it on their shoulders on high ...

On reaching the center of the open space, Atahualpa remained in his litter on high, and the others with him, while his troops did not cease to enter. A captain then came to the front and, ascending the fortress near the open space, where the artillery was posted, raised his lance twice, as for a signal. Seeing this, the Governor asked the Father Friar Vicente if he wished to go and speak to Atahualpa, with an interpreter. He replied that he did wish it, and he advanced, with a cross in one hand and the Bible in the other, and going amongst the troops up to the place where Atahualpa was, thus addressed him: "I am a priest of God, and I teach Christians the things of God, and in like manner I come to teach you. What I teach is that which God says to us in this Book. Therefore, on the part of God and of the Christians, I beseech you to be their friend, for such is God's will, and it will be for your good. Go and speak to the Governor, who waits for you."

Atahualpa asked for the Book, that he might look at it, and the priest gave it to him closed. Atahualpa did not know how to open it, and the priest was extending his arm to do so, when Atahualpa, in great anger, gave him a blow on the arm, not wishing that it should be opened. Then he opened it himself, and, without any astonishment at the letters and paper, as had been shown by other Indians, he threw it away from him five or six paces, and, to the words which the monk had spoken to him through the interpreter, he answered with much scorn, saying: "I know well how you have behaved on the road, how you have treated my chiefs, and taken the cloth from my storehouses." The monk replied: "The Christians have not done this, but some Indians took the cloth without the knowledge of the Governor, and he ordered it to be restored." Atahualpa said: "I will not leave this place until they bring it all to me." The monk returned with this reply to the Governor.

Atahualpa stood up on the top of the litter, addressing his troops and ordering them to be prepared. The monk told the Governor what had passed between him and Atahualpa, and that he had thrown the Scriptures to the ground. Then the Governor put on a jacket of cotton, took his sword and dagger, and, with the Spaniards who were with him, entered amongst the Indians most valiantly; and, with only four men who were able to follow him, he came to the litter where Atahualpa was, and fearlessly seized him by the arm, crying out, "*Santiago!*" Then the guns were fired off, the trumpets were sounded, and the troops, both horse and foot, sallied forth. On seeing the horses charge, many of the Indians who were in the open space fled, and such was the force with which they ran that they broke down part of the wall surrounding it, and many fell over each other. The horsemen rode them down, killing and wounding, and following in pursuit. The infantry made so good an assault upon those that remained that in a short time most of them were put to the sword. The Governor still held Atahualpa by the arm, not being able to pull him out of the litter because he was raised so high. Then the Spaniards made such a slaughter amongst those who carried the litter that they fell to the ground, and, if the Governor had not protected Atahualpa, that proud man would there have paid for all the cruelties he had committed. The Governor, in protecting Atahualpa, received a slight wound in the hand. During the whole time no Indian raised his arms against a Spaniard.

So great was the terror of the Indians at seeing the Governor force his way through them, at hearing the fire of the artillery, and beholding the charging of horses, a thing never before heard of, that they thought more of flying to save their lives than of fighting. All those who bore the litter of Atahualpa appeared to be principal chiefs. They were all killed, as well as those who were carried in the other litters and hammocks. . . .

The Governor went to his lodging, with his prisoner, Atahualpa, despoiled of his robes, which the Spaniards had torn off in pulling him out of the litter. It was a very wonderful thing to see so great a lord taken prisoner in so short a time, who came in such power. The Governor presently ordered native clothes to be brought, and when Atahualpa was dressed, he made him sit near him, and soothed his rage and agitation at finding himself so quickly fallen from his high estate. Among many other things, the Governor said to him: "Do not take it as an insult that you have been defeated and taken prisoner, for with the Christians who come with me, though so few in number, I have conquered greater kingdoms than yours, and have defeated other more powerful lords than you, imposing upon them the dominion of the Emperor, whose vassal I am, and who is King of Spain and of the universal world. We come to conquer this land by his command, that all may come to a knowledge of God, and of His Holy Catholic Faith . . ."

. . . Atahualpa feared that the Spaniards would kill him, so he told the Governor that he would give his captors a great quantity of gold and silver. The Governor asked him: "How much can you give, and in what time?" Atahualpa said: "I will give gold enough to fill a room twenty-two feet long and seventeen wide, up to a white line which is halfway up the wall." The height would be that of a man's stature and a half. He said that, up to that mark, he would fill the room with different kinds of golden vessels, such as jars, pots, vases, besides lumps and other pieces. As for silver, he said he would fill the whole chamber with it twice over. He undertook to do this in two months. The Governor told him to send off messengers with this object, and that, when it was accomplished, he need have no fear. . . .

After some days some of the people of Atahualpa arrived. There was a brother of his, who came from Cuzco, and sisters and wives. The brother brought many vases, jars, and pots of gold, and much silver, and he said that more was on the road; but that, as the journey is so long, the Indians who bring the treasure become tired, and cannot all come so quickly, so that every day more gold and silver will arrive of that which now remains behind. Thus on some days twenty thousand, on others thirty thousand, on others fifty thousand or sixty thousand pesos of gold arrived, in vases, great pots weighing two or three arrobas, and other vessels. The Governor ordered it all to be put in the house where Atahualpa had his guards, until he had accomplished what he had promised.

[After receiving the huge ransom from Atahualpa, Pizarro charges the Inca with conspiring against him.]

. . . I WILL now say something of the place that was subject to the Cuzco and now belongs to Atahualpa. They say that it contained two houses made of gold, and that the straws with which it was roofed were all made of gold. With the gold that was brought from Cuzco, there were some straws made of solid gold, with their spikes, just as they would grow in the fields. If I was to recount all the different varieties in the shape of the pieces of gold my story would never end. There was a stool of gold [the throne of the Incas, which Pizarro himself took] that weighed eight arrobas. There were great fountains with their pipes, through which water flowed into a reservoir on the same fountains, where there were birds of different kinds, and men drawing water from the fountain, all made of gold. It was also ascertained from Atahualpa and Chilicuchima, and many others, that in Xauxa Atahualpa had sheep and shepherds tending them, all made of gold; and the sheep and shepherds were large, and of the size that they are met with in this land.

Now I must mention a thing which should not be forgotten. A chief, who was Lord of Caxamalca, appeared before the Governor and said to him through the interpreters: "I would have you to know that, after Atahualpa was taken prisoner, he sent to Quito, his native land, and to all the other provinces, with orders to collect troops to march against you and your followers, and to kill you all; and all these troops are coming under the command of a great captain called Lluminabi. This army is now very near to this place. It will come at night and attack the camp . . ."

The Governor then spoke to Atahualpa, saying: "What treason is this that you have prepared for me? For me who have treated you with honor, like a brother, and have trusted in your words!" Then he told him all the information he had received. Atahualpa answered, saying: "Are you laughing at me? You are always making jokes when you speak to me. What am I and all my people that we should trouble such valiant men as you are? Do not talk such nonsense to me." He said all this without betraying a sign of anxiety; but he laughed the better to conceal his evil design, and practiced many other arts such as would suggest themselves to a quick-witted man. After he was a prisoner, the Spaniards who heard him were astounded to find so much wisdom in a barbarian. . . .

Then the Governor, with the concurrence of the officers of his Majesty, and of the captains and persons of experience, sentenced Atahualpa to death. His sentence was that, for the treason he had committed, he should die by burning, unless he became a Christian . . .

They brought out Atahualpa to execution; and, when he came into the square, he said he would become a Christian. The Governor was informed, and ordered him to be baptized. The ceremony was performed by the very reverend Father Friar Vicente de Valverde. The Governor then ordered that he should not be burned, but that he should be fastened to a pole in the open space and strangled. This was done, and the body was left until the morning of the next day, when the monks, and the Governor with the other Spaniards, conveyed it into the church, where it was interred with much solemnity, and with all the honors that could be shown it. Such was the end of this man, who had been so cruel. He died with great fortitude, and without showing any feeling . . .

THE PLUNDER

. . . THE Governor gave some sheep and Indians to the Spaniards who had obtained leave to go home, to carry their gold and silver and clothes to the town of San Miguel. On the road some of them lost gold and silver to the amount of more than 25,000 castellanos, because the sheep ran away with the gold and silver, and some of the Indians also fled. On this journey they suffered much hunger and thirst, and many hardships from a want of people to carry their loads. From the city of Cuzco to the port the distance is nearly two hundred leagues. At last they embarked and went to Panama, and thence to Nombre de Dios, where they again embarked, and our Lord conducted them to Seville, at which port four ships have arrived . . .

In the year 1534, on the ninth of January, the second ship arrived, named the *Santa Maria de Campo*, with the Captain Hernando Pizarro on board, brother of Francisco Pizarro, the Governor and Captain-General of New Castille. In this ship there came, for his Majesty, 153,000 pesos of gold and 5,048 marcs of silver. Besides this, several passengers and private persons brought 310,000 pesos of gold and 13,500 marcs of silver. This treasure came in bars and planks, and in pieces of gold and silver enclosed in large boxes.

In addition to all this, the ship brought, for his Majesty, thirty-eight vases of gold and forty-eight of silver, among which there was an eagle of silver. In its body were fitted two vases and two large pots, one of gold and the other of silver, each of which was capable of containing a cow cut into pieces. There were also two sacks of gold, each capable of holding two fanegas of wheat; an idol of gold, the size of a child four years old; and two small drums. The other vases were of gold and silver, each one capable of holding two arrobas and more. In the same ship passengers brought home forty-four vases of silver and four of gold. . . .

One of the last two ships that arrived, in which Francisco Rodriguez was master, belonged to Francisco de Xeres [he had received his shares of the loot as both horseman and secretary], a native of the town of Seville, who wrote this narrative by order of the Governor Francisco Pizarro, being in the province of New Castille, in the city of Caxamalca, as Secretary to the Governor. PRAISE TO GOD.

[Going on to conquer Cuzco, Pizarro was made *adelantado* and master of a vast territory. But such was the ferocity with which he subdued the people and the duplicity he practiced in his relations with his chief partner in conquest, Diego de Almagro, that rebellion and internal dissension followed, culminating in his assassination in 1541.]

The Amazon Women

FRANCISCO DE ORELLANA

FROM *Account by Friar Gaspar de Carvajal of the Voyage down the River That Captain Francisco de Orellana Discovered*

1541–42

From the very first, the dream that lured men to the New World was gold and spices. No sooner, therefore, did Francisco Pizarro conquer Peru than his half brother Gonzalo, appointed Governor of Quito, set out to the east to find El Dorado, the Golden One, and La Canela, the Land of Cinnamon. Gonzalo started with 220 Spaniards, four thousand conquered Indians, two thousand live hogs and one thousand dogs. But in seven months of marching through wilderness and over icy mountains, the Indians perished, the hogs and dogs were eaten, and the survivors faced starvation.

Meanwhile, the expedition had been joined by Francisco de Orellana, who had fought under Francisco Pizarro, founded Santiago de Guayaquil and become its Captain General. Gonzalo made him Lieutenant General of the expedition, and when the crisis came it was he who volunteered to take fifty or sixty men down the Napo (a major tributary of the Amazon) in search of food. The Orellana party embarked on Christmas Day, 1541. After about nine days, finding themselves far down the river and without food, they decided to keep going instead of turning back. Whether this was an act of treachery or necessity, it resulted in the discovery of the Amazon, the first crossing of South America and one of the boldest journeys on record. As related by a Dominican friar in the party, Gaspar de Carvajal, it is a chronicle of more than 2,500 miles of perilous travel in frail crafts on a violent waterway, of great hardships, and assault by natives, including

717

—so Carvajal declares—those fierce women of legend, the Amazons. After almost nine months on the river they reached the Atlantic and made port in September 1542 at Cubagua.

But such was the fever gripping Orellana that after returning to Spain he soon set about organizing an expedition to explore the great river further. Frustrated by lack of support, he finally started out in 1545 in a few utterly unseaworthy and ill-equipped ships, crossed the Atlantic under frightful conditions, sailed into the Amazon and after untold suffering perished in December 1546.

[After much privation and countless skirmishes with native tribes they approach the land of the Amazons.]

In this manner we were proceeding on our way, searching for a peaceful spot to celebrate and to gladden the feast of the blessed Saint John the Baptist, herald of Christ, when God willed that, on rounding a bend which the river made, we should see on the shore ahead many villages, and very large ones, which shone white. Here we came suddenly upon the excellent land and dominion of the Amazons. These said villages had been forewarned and knew of our coming, in consequence whereof they [i.e., the inhabitants] came out on the water to meet us, in no friendly mood. When they had come close to the Captain, he would have liked to induce them to accept peace, and so he began to speak to them and call them, but they laughed, and mocked us and came up close to us and told us to keep on going and added that down below they were waiting for us, and that there they were to seize us all and take us to the Amazons. The Captain, angered at the arrogance of the Indians, gave orders to shoot at them with the crossbows and arquebuses, so that they might reflect and become aware that we had wherewith to assail them. In this way damage was inflicted on them and they turned about toward the village to give the news of what they had seen. As for us, we did not fail to proceed and to draw close to the villages, and before we were within half a league of putting in, there were along the edge of the water, at intervals, many squadrons of Indians, and, in proportion as we kept on going ahead, they gradually came together and drew close to their living quarters.

There was in the center of this village a very great horde of fighters, formed in a good squadron, and the Captain gave the order to have the brigantines beached right there where these men were, in order to go look for food. And so it came about that, as we began to come in close to land, the Indians started to defend their village and to shoot arrows at us, and as the fighters were in great numbers it seemed as if it rained arrows. But our harquebusiers and crossbowmen were not idle, because they did nothing but shoot, and although they killed many, they [i.e., the Indians] did not become aware of this, for in spite of the damage that was being done to them they kept it up, some fighting and others dancing. And here we all came very close to perishing, because as there were so many arrows our companions had all they could do to protect themselves from them, without being able to row, in consequence whereof they did so much damage to us that before we could jump out on land they had wounded five of us, of whom I was one, for they hit me in one side with an arrow, which went in as far as the hollow region. If it had not been for the thickness of my clothes, that would have been the end of me. . . . More than an hour was taken up by this fight, for the Indians did not lose spirit, rather it seemed as if it was being doubled in them, although they saw many of their own number killed, and they passed over them [i.e., their bodies] and they merely kept retreating and coming back again.

I want it to be known what the reason was why these Indians defended themselves in this manner. It must be explained that they are the subjects of, and tributaries to, the Amazons, and, our coming having been made known to them, they went to them to ask help, and there came as many as ten or twelve of them, for we ourselves saw these women, who were there fighting in front of all the Indian men as women captains. These latter fought so courageously that the Indian men did not dare to turn their backs, and anyone who did turn his back they killed with clubs right there before us, and this is the reason why the Indians kept up their defense for so long. These women are very white and tall, and have hair very long and braided and wound about the head, and they are very robust and go about naked, but with their privy parts covered, with their bows and arrows in their hands, doing as much fighting as ten Indian men. And indeed there was one woman among these who shot an arrow a span deep into one of the brigantines, and others less deep, so that our brigantines looked like porcupines.

> [In a skirmish at this time Friar Carvajal loses an eye. Later Orellana interrogates a captured Indian concerning the Amazons. This interview, with its seeming corroboration of the legend of Amazon women, caused Carvajal's whole account to be dismissed as riddled with lies, but the story remains one of the most famous of all traveler's tales.]

. . . THE Captain asked him what women those were who had come to help them and fight against us. The Indian said that they were certain women who resided in the interior of the country, a seven-day journey from the shore, and it was because this overlord Couynco was subject to them that they had come to watch over the shore. The Captain asked him if these women were married; the Indian said they were not. The Captain asked him about how they lived; the Indian replied that, as he had already said, they were off in the interior of the land and that he had been there many times and had seen their customs and mode of living, for as their vassal he was in the habit of going there to carry the tribute whenever the overlord sent him. The Captain asked if these women were numerous; the Indian said that they were, and that he knew by name seventy villages, and named them before those of us who were there present, and that he had been in several of them.

The Captain asked him if the houses in these villages were built of straw; the Indian said they were not, but out of stone and with regular doors, and that from one village to another went roads closed off on one side and on the other and with guards stationed at intervals among them so that no one might enter without paying duties. The Captain asked if these women bore children; the Indian answered that they did. The Captain asked him how, not being married, and there being no man residing among them, they became pregnant; he said that these Indian women consorted with Indian men at times, and, when that desire came over them, they assembled a great horde of warriors and went off to make war on a very great overlord whose residence is not far from that of these women, and by force they brought them to their own country and kept them with them for the time that suited their caprice, and after they found themselves pregnant they sent them back to their country without doing them any harm. Afterward, when the time came for them to have children, if they gave birth to male children, they killed them and sent them to their fathers, and, if female children, they raised them with great solemnity and instructed them in the arts of war.

He said furthermore that among all these women there was one ruling mistress who subjected and held under her hand and jurisdiction all the rest, which mistress went by the name of Coñori. He said that there was in their possession a very great wealth of gold and silver and that in the case of all the mistresses of rank and distinction their eating utensils were nothing but gold or silver, while the other women, belonging to the plebeian class, used a service of wooden vessels, except what was brought in contact with fire, which was of clay. He said that in the capital and principal city in which the ruling mistress resided there were five very large buildings which were places of worship and houses dedicated to the Sun, which they called *caranain*, and inside, from half a man's height above the ground up, these buildings were lined with heavy wooden ceilings covered with paint of various colors, and that in these buildings they had many gold and silver idols in the form of women, and many vessels of gold and of silver for the service of the Sun. These women were dressed in clothing of very fine wool, because in this land there are many sheep of the same sort as those of Peru. Their dress consisted of blankets girded about them from the breasts down, in some cases merely thrown over the shoulders and in others clasped together in front, like a cloak, by means of a pair of cords. They wore their hair reaching down to the ground at their feet, and upon their heads were placed crowns of gold, as wide as two fingers, and their individual colors.

He said in addition that in this land, as we understood him, there were camels that carried them [i.e., the inhabitants] on their backs, and he said that there were other animals, which we did not succeed in understanding about, which were as big as horses and which had hair as long as the spread of the thumb and forefinger, measured from tip to tip, and cloven hoofs, and that people kept them tied up; and that of these there were few. He said that there were in this land two salt-water lakes, from which the women obtained salt. He related that they had a rule to the effect that when the sun went down no male Indian was to remain in all of these cities, but that any such must depart and go to his country. He said in addition that many Indian provinces bordering on them were held in subjection by them and made to pay tribute and to serve them, while other provinces there were with which they carried on war, in particular with the one which we have mentioned, and that they brought the men of this province there to have relations with them. These were said to be of very great stature and white and numerous, and he claimed that all that he had told here he had seen many times as a man who went back and forth every day. All that this Indian told us and more besides had been told to us six leagues from Quito, because concerning these women there were a great many reports, and in order to see them many Indian men came down the river one thousand four hundred leagues . . .

[They push desperately on, trying to steer clear of inhabited areas.]

ONCE again, while we were in the midst of this suffering, Our Lord manifested the special care which He was exercising over us sinners, for He saw fit to provide in this time of shortage of food as in all other instances I have quoted. It happened as follows: One day toward evening there was seen coming down the river a dead tapir, the size of a mule, and when the Captain saw it he ordered certain companions to go after it for him and to take a canoe to bring it in. They did bring it, and it was divided up among all the companions in such a way that for each one there turned out to be enough to eat for five or six days, which was no small help, but on the contrary a great one, for all. This tapir had been dead for only a short time, because it was still warm, and it had no wound whatsoever on it.

. . . We went on in our journey, continually passing by settled country, where we secured a certain amount of food, although only a small amount, because the Indians had carried it off, but we found a few roots which they call *inanes*, for, if we had not found these, we should all have perished from hunger. Thus we came out of there very short of supplies. In all these villages the Indians met us without weapons, because they are a very docile people, and they gave us to understand by signs that they had seen Christians before. These Indians are at the mouth of the river through which we came out, where we took on water, each one a jarful, and some half an almud of roasted maize and others less, and others supplied themselves with roots, and in this manner we got ready to navigate by sea wherever fortune might guide us and cast us, because we had no pilot, nor compass, nor navigator's chart of any sort, and we did not even know in what direction or toward what point we ought to head. . . . Thus it was that with great toil we got out of the Mouths of the Dragon (for so this may be called for us), because we came very close to staying inside there forever. We got out of this prison; we proceeded onward for two days along the coast, at the end of which, without knowing where we were nor whither we were going nor what was to become of us, we made port on the island of Cubagua and in the city of Nueva Cádiz, where we found our company and the small brigantine, which had arrived two days before, because they arrived on the ninth of September and we arrived on the eleventh of the month with the large brigantine, on board which was our Captain. So great was the joy which we felt, the ones at the sight of the others, that I shall not be able to express it, because they considered us to be lost and we so considered them. . . .

From this island the Captain decided to go and give an account to His Majesty of this new and great discovery and of this river, which we hold to be the Marañón . . .

I, Brother Gaspar de Carvajal, the least of the friars of the order of our brother and friar, Father Saint Dominic, have chosen to take upon myself this little task and recount the progress and outcome of our journey and navigation, not only in order to tell about it and make known the truth in the whole matter, but also in order to remove the temptation from many persons who may wish to relate this peregrination of ours or publish just the opposite of what we have experienced and seen; and what I have written and related is the truth throughout. And because profuseness engenders distaste, so I have related sketchily and summarily all that has happened to Captain Francisco de Orellana and to the hidalgos of his company and to us companions of his who went off with him from the expeditionary corps of Gonzalo Pizarro, brother of Don Francisco Pizarro, the Marquis, and Governor of Peru. God be praised. Amen.

English Freebooters and Spanish Terror

MILES PHILIPS

FROM *The Voyage of Miles Philips*

1567–82

Among the chronicles of freebooters in Hakluyt's great collection of English voyages, one of the most remarkable is that of Miles Philips. A seaman, he joined an expedition under Hawkins and Drake in 1567; after raiding for Negro slaves on the African coast, the fleet sailed to America. At Vera Cruz three of the ships were sunk by a Spanish flotilla but there was not enough room on the two remaining vessels for all survivors, and many were put ashore. Philips was one of them. What happened to him in the years he spent as prisoner and servitor in New Spain makes a tale of overwhelming hardship and misfortune. But he finally escaped, managed to get aboard a Spanish fleet going home, and reached England at last in 1582—sixteen years after leaving it.

In the passage that follows, Philips has just described the defeat of the English ships at Vera Cruz and goes on to tell how some of the survivors were put ashore. The account in Hakluyt is apparently in Philips' own words.

AFTER that, the Viceroy, Don Martin Henriques, contrary to his faith and promise, most cruelly dealt with our General Master Hawkins at S. John de Ullua [Vera Cruz], where most of his men were slain and drowned by Spaniards, and all his ships sunk and burnt, saving the *Minion,* and the *Judith,* which was a small bark of fifty tons, wherein was Captain Master Francis Drake. The same night the said bark lost us, we being in great necessity and enforced to remove with the *Minion* two bow-shot from the Spanish fleet, where we anchored all that night. The next morning we weighed anchor and recovered an island a mile from the Spaniards, where a storm took us with a north wind, in which we were greatly distressed, having but two cables and two anchors left. The morrow after, the storm being ceased and the weather fair, we weighed and set sail. Being many men in number and with but small store of victuals, we were in despair and fear that we should perish through famine, so that some were in mind to yield themselves to the mercy of the Spaniards, and some to the savages or infidels. Wandering thus in these unknown seas, hunger constrained us to eat hides, cats and dogs, mice, rats, parrots and monkeys. To be short, our hunger was so great that we thought savory and sweet whatever we could get to eat.

On the eighth of October we came to land again, in the bottom of the Bay of Mexico, where we hoped to have found some inhabitants that we might have some relief of victuals and a place to repair our ship, which was so greatly bruised that we were scarce able with our weary arms to keep forth the water. Being thus oppressed with famine on the one side and danger of drowning on the other, not knowing where to find relief, we began to be in wonderful despair, and we were of many minds, amongst whom there were a great many that did desire our General to set them on land, making their choice rather to submit to the mercy of the savages or infidels than to hazard themselves at sea. To which request our General did very willingly agree, considering with himself that it was necessary for him to lessen his number, both for the safety of himself and the rest. Thereupon being resolved to set half his people ashore, it was a world to see how suddenly men's minds altered; for they that a little before desired to be set on land were now of another mind, and requested rather to stay. Our General was therefore forced for the more content of all men's minds to take this order: First he made choice of such persons as were needful to stay. That being done, of those which were willing to go he appointed such as he thought might be best spared, promising us that the next year he would either come himself or else send to fetch us home. Here again it would have caused any stony heart to have relented to hear the pitiful moan that many did make, and how loath they were to depart. The weather was then somewhat stormy and tempestuous, and therefore we were to pass with great danger, yet there was no remedy, but we that were appointed to go away must of necessity do so.

Those that went in the first boat were set safely on shore; but with those that went in the second boat, of which I myself was one, the seas wrought so high that we could not attain the shore. Therefore we were constrained through the cruel dealing of John Hampton, Captain of the *Minion*, and John Sanders, boatswain of the *Jesus*, and Thomas Pollard, his mate, to leap out of the boat into the main sea, more than a mile from shore, and so shift for ourselves, and either sink or swim. And of those that were, as it were, thrown out and compelled to leap into the sea, two were drowned.

In the evening of the same day, it being Monday, the eighth of October, 1568, when we came to shore, we found fresh water, whereof some of our men drank so much that they had almost cast themselves away, for we could scarce get life out of them for two or three hours after. Others were so cruelly swollen, what with drinking salt water and eating the fruit we found on land, having a stone in it much like an almond (which fruit is called capule) that they were all in very ill case, so that we were all of us feeble, faint and weak.

The next morning we thought it best to travel along the seacoast to seek out some place of habitation, whether of Christians or savages we were indifferent, so that we might have wherewithal to sustain our hungry bodies. And so we departed from a hill where we had rested all night, not having a dry thread about us, for those that were not wet from being thrown into the sea were thoroughly wet with rain, for it rained cruelly all night. As we came into the plain, we were greatly troubled to pass grass and weeds that grew there higher than any man. On the left hand we had the sea and upon the right hand great woods, so that we must needs pass through marshes on our way westward; and going thus, we were suddenly assaulted by Indians, a war-like kind of people, which are like cannibals, although they do not feed upon man's flesh.

These people are called Chichimici, and they wear their hair long, even down to their knees. They also colour their faces green, yellow, red and blue, which makes them very ugly and terrible to behold. These people make war against the Spaniards, by whom they have been often very cruelly handled, for with the Spaniards there is no mercy. Perceiving us at our first coming on land, they supposed us to have been their enemies, the bordering Spaniards, and their fore-runners having descried how many we were, and how feeble and weak, without armour or weapons, they suddenly raised a terrible cry and came running fiercely upon us, shooting arrows as thick as hail, unto whose mercy we were constrained to yield, not having any kind of armour or weapon saving one caliver and two rusty old swords.

When they perceived that we sought only mercy at their hands, and were not their enemies the Spaniards, they had compassion on us, and came and caused us all to sit down. And when they had a while surveyed and taken a perfect view of us, they came to all those that had any coloured clothes amongst us, and those they did strip stark naked and took their clothes away, but those that were apparelled in black they did not meddle with. And so they went their ways, and left us without doing us any further hurt; only in the first brunt they killed eight of our men. At our departure, perceiving how weak we were, they pointed which way we should go to come to a town of the Spaniards, which as we afterwards perceived was not past ten leagues from there, using these words: *Tampice, Tampice, Christiano, Tampice Christiano,* which is as much (we think) as to say in English: At Tampice you shall find the Christians.

They use no other weapons but bows and arrows, and their arm is so good that they very seldom miss anything they shoot at. Shortly after they had left us stripped, we thought it best to divide ourselves into two companies, half of us going under the leading of one Anthony Godard (who is yet alive and dwells at this instant in the town of Plymouth), whom we chose to be captain over us. And those which went under his leading, of which number I, Miles Philips, was one, travelled that way westward which the Indians had pointed us to go.

> [Harried by Indians and facing starvation, they are after a time captured by Spaniards and marched toward the city of Mexico.]

THE next morning, we departed thence on our journey towards Mexico, and so travelled till we came within two leagues of it, where the Spaniards had built a very fair church, called Our Lady's church, in which there is an image of Our Lady, of silver and gilt, as high and as large as a tall woman. In this church, and before this image, there are as many lamps of silver as days in the year, which upon high days are all lighted. Whenever any Spaniards pass this church, although they be on horseback, they alight and come into it and kneel before the image and pray to Our Lady to defend them from all evil . . . which image they call in the Spanish tongue, Nuestra Senora de Guadalupe. At this place there are certain cold baths, springing up as though the water did seethe [boil], the water whereof is somewhat brackish in taste but very good for any that have any sore or wound. And every year upon Our Lady Day the people repair thither to offer and to pray before the image in that church, and they say that Our Lady of Guadalupe doth work miracles. Around this church there is no town of Spaniards but only Indians dwelling in houses of their own country building.

Here we met a great number of Spaniards on horseback, who came from Mexico to see us, both gentlemen and men of occupations, and they came as people to see a wonder. We were called upon to march on; and so about four of the clock in the afternoon we entered the city of Mexico by the way or street called La Calle Santa Catherina. And we stayed not till we came to the house or palace of the Viceroy, Don Martin Henriques, which stands in the midst of the city hard by the market-place, called La Plaça del Marquese. . . . After our coming, many of the company that came with me from Panuco died within fourteen days. Soon after, we were taken from that place and put into Our Lady's hospital, in which we were courteously used, and visited oftentimes by virtuous gentlemen and gentlewomen of the city, who brought us divers things to comfort us withal, such as suckets [sweets] and marmalades, and would also give us many things, and that very liberally. In this hospital we remained for the space of six months, until we were all whole and sound of body, and then we were appointed by the Viceroy to be carried unto the town of Tescuco, which is eight leagues south-west from Mexico. In this town there are certain houses of correction and punishment for ill people called Obraches (like Bridewell in London) into which Indians are sold as slaves, some for ten years and some for twelve. It was no small grief unto us when we understood that we should be carried thither and be used as slaves. We had rather be put to death; howbeit, there was no remedy, so we were carried to the prison of Tescuco, where we were not put to any labour, but were very straitly kept and almost famished. Yet by the good providence of our merciful God we happened there to meet with one Robert Sweeting, who was the son of an Englishman born of a Spanish woman.

This man could speak very good English and by his means we were helped very much with victuals from the Indians, such as mutton, hens and bread. If we had not been so relieved, we had surely perished; and yet all the provision we had gotten that way was but slender. Continuing thus straitly kept in prison there for the space of two months, we agreed at length amongst ourselves to break forth from prison, come of it what would, for we were minded rather to suffer death than to live longer in that miserable state.

Having escaped from prison, we knew not what way to fly for safety.

The night was dark and it rained terribly, and not having any guide, we went we knew not whither. In the morning, at the appearing of the day, we perceived ourselves to be come hard by the city of Mexico, which is twenty-four English miles from Tescuco. The day being come we were espied by the Spaniards, and pursued, and taken, and brought before the Viceroy and head justices, who threatened to hang us for breaking from the king's prison.

[They are made to serve various wealthy masters.]

THE gentlemen that took us for their servants or slaves did new apparel us throughout. We abode with them, doing such service as they appointed us unto, which was for the most part to attend upon them at the table, be their chamberlains and wait upon them when they went abroad. In that country no Spaniards will serve one another, but they are all attended and served by Indians, and by Negroes that are their slaves during their life. In this sort we remained and served in the city of Mexico and thereabouts for the space of a year and somewhat longer. Afterwards many of us were appointed by our masters to go to sundry of their mines where we had to serve as overseers of the Negroes and Indians that laboured there. In these mines many of us did profit and gain greatly; for we were allowed three hundred pesos a man for a year, which is threescore pound sterling, and besides that the Indians and Negroes under our charge, upon our well using and entreating them, would at times, as upon Saturdays when they had left work, labour for us, and blow as much silver as would be worth three marks or thereabouts, which, being worth 19½ pesos of their money, is worth 4 li. 10s. of our money. Sundry weeks we did gain so much by this means besides our wages that many of us became very rich, and were worth three thousand or four thousand pesos, for we lived and gained thus in those mines some three or four years. . . .

THE INQUISITION

Now, after six years were fully expired since our first coming into the Indies . . . in the year of our Lord 1574 the Inquisition began to be established, very much against the minds of many of the Spaniards themselves;

for never until this time since their first conquering and planting in the Indies were they subject to that bloody and cruel Inquisition. The chief Inquisitor was named Don Pedro Moya de Contreres, and John de Bovilla was his companion, and John Sanches the Fischall, and Pedro de los Rios the Secretary. They being settled in a very fair house near the White Friars, considering with themselves that they must make a beginning of that most detestable Inquisition here in Mexico, to the terror of the whole country, thought it best to call us that were Englishmen first in question, and so much the more because they had perfect knowledge and intelligence that many of us were very rich, and therefore were a very good booty and prey. So that now our sorrows began afresh, for we were sought out, and proclamation was made that, on pain of losing goods and excommunication, no man should hide or keep secret any Englishmen or any part of their goods. By this means we were all soon apprehended and all our goods seized and taken for the Inquisitors' use. And so from all parts of the country we were sent as prisoners to the city of Mexico and there committed to sundry dark dungeons, where we could not see but by candle-light, and were never more than two together in one place.

Thus we remained close imprisoned for a year and a half, and others for some less time, for they came to prison as they were apprehended. At the beginning we were often called before the Inquisitors alone and severely examined of our faith, and commanded to say the Paternoster, the Ave Maria, and the Creed in Latin, which, God knows, a great number of us could not say in other than the English tongue. Having the said Robert Sweeting who was our friend at Tescuco always present as an interpreter, he made report that in our own speech we could say them perfectly, although not word for word as they were in Latin. Then did they demand upon oath what we did believe of the sacrament and whether there did remain any bread or wine after the words of consecration, yea or no, and whether we did not believe that the host of bread which the priest did hold up over his head, and the wine that was in the chalice, were the very true and perfect body and blood of our Saviour Christ, yea or no. To which, if we answered not yea, then was there no way but death. Then they would demand of us what opinions we had held or had been taught contrary to the same while we were in England. To which we, for the safety of our lives, were constrained to say that we never did believe nor had been taught otherwise than as we had said. . . .

Yet all this would not serve; for still from time to time we were called upon to confess, and about three months before they proceeded to their judgement, we were all racked; and some forced to utter against themselves that which afterwards cost them their lives. And thus having gotten from our own mouths matter sufficient for them to proceed in judgement against us, they caused a large scaffold to be made in the midst of the market-place right against the head church. And fourteen or fifteen days before the day of their judgement; with the sound of a trumpet and the noise of attabilies (which are a kind of drum), they did assemble the people in all parts of the city, and then solemnly proclaimed that whosoever would upon such a day repair to the market-place should hear the sentence of the holy Inquisition against the English heretics, Lutherans, and also see the same put in execution. This being done, and the time approaching for this cruel judgement, they came the night before to the prison where we were, with certain officers of that holy hellish house, bringing with them certain fools' coats called in their language San Benitos, made of yellow cotton, with red crosses upon them, both before and behind. They were so busied in putting the coats about us and bringing us out into a large yard and placing and pointing us in what order we should go to the scaffold or place of judgement upon the morrow that they did not suffer us to sleep all that night. The next morning there was given to every one of us for our breakfast a cup of wine and a slice of bread fried in honey, and so about eight of the clock we set forth from the prison, every man alone in his yellow coat, and a rope about his neck, and a great green wax candle in his hand unlighted, having a Spaniard appointed to go upon either side of every one of us. And so marching in this order towards the scaffold in the market-place, a bow-shot distance or thereabouts, we found a great assembly of people all the way, and such a throng that certain of the Inquisitors' officers on horseback were constrained to make way. Coming to the scaffold, we went up by a pair of stairs and found seats prepared for us. Presently the Inquisitors came up another pair of stairs, and the Viceroy and all the Chief Justices with them. Then came up a great number of friars, White, Black and Grey. Then a solemn *Oyes* was made, and silence commanded, and presently their severe and cruel judgement began.

The first man that was called was one Roger, Chief Armourer of the *Jesus*, and he had judgement to have 300 stripes on horseback, and after condemned to the galleys as a slave for ten years. After him were called John Gray, John Browne, John Rider, John Moone, James Collier, and one Thomas Browne: these were adjudged to have 200 stripes on horseback and after to be committed to the galleys for the space of eight years. . . . Then were severally called 53 men, and every man had his judgement, some to have 200 stripes on horseback, and some 100, and condemned to the galleys, some for six years, some for eight and some for ten.

And then I Miles Philips was called, and was adjudged to serve in a monastery for five years, without any stripes, and to wear a fool's coat, or San Benito, during all that time.

Then were called John Story, Richard Williams, David Alexander, Robert Cooke, Paul Horsewell and Thomas Hull: the six were condemned to serve in monasteries . . . Which being done, and it now drawing towards night, George Rively, Peter Momfrie, and Cornelius the Irishman, were called and had their judgement to be burnt to ashes, and so were presently sent away to the place of execution in the market-place but a little from the scaffold, where they were quickly burnt and consumed.

And as for us that had received our judgement, being 68 in number, we were carried back that night to prison again. And the next day in the morning, being Good Friday, the year of our Lord 1575, we were all brought into a court of the Inquisitor's palace, where we found a horse in readiness for every one of our men which were condemned to have stripes and to be committed to the galley, which were in number 60. They being enforced to mount up on horseback naked from the middle upwards, were carried to be showed as a spectacle throughout the chief streets of the city, and had stripes most cruelly laid upon their naked bodies with long whips by sundry men appointed to be the executioners thereof. And before our men there went a couple of criers that cried: *Behold these English dogs, Lutherans, enemies to God!* and all the way as they went there were some Inquisitors themselves, and familiars of that rakehell order, that cried to the executioners, *Strike! Lay on those English heretics, Lutherans, God's enemies!* And so this horrible spectacle being showed round about the city, they returned to the Inquisitor's house, with their backs all gory and swollen with great bumps, and were then taken from their horses and carried again to prison, where they remained until they were sent to Spain to the galleys, there to receive the rest of their martyrdom. And I and the six others with me who were condemned among the rest to serve an apprenticeship in the monastery, were sent to certain religious houses appointed for the purpose. . . .

I and William Lowe were sent to the Black Friars, where I was appointed to be an overseer of Indian workmen, who were building a new church. Amongst the Indians I learned their language or Mexican tongue very perfectly, and had great familiarity with many of them, whom I found to be a courteous and loving kind of people, ingenious, and of great understanding. They hate and abhor the Spaniards with all their hearts.

The Spaniards have used such horrible cruelties against them and do still keep them in such subjection and servitude that they and the Negroes daily lie in wait to practise their deliverance out of that thralldom and bondage that the Spaniards keep them in. William Lowe was appointed to serve the cook in the kitchen, Richard Williams and David Alexander were appointed to the Grey Friars, and John Story and Robert Cooke to the White Friars. The Secretary took Paul Horsewell to be his servant. Thomas Hull was sent to a monastery of priests, where he afterwards died. Thus we served out the years that we were condemned for, with the use of our fools' coats. We must needs confess that the friars did use us very courteously, for every one of us had his chamber with bedding and diet, and all things clean and neat. Yea, many of the Spaniards and friars themselves do utterly abhor that cruel Inquisition, and would bewail our miseries and comfort us the best they could, although they stood in such fear of that devilish Inquisition that they dared not let the left hand know what the right did.

Now, after the time was expired for which we were condemned to serve in those religious houses, we were brought again before the chief Inquisitor, and had all our fools' coats pulled off and hanged up in the head church, called Ecclesia Major and every man's name and judgement written thereupon, with this addition, *A heretic Lutheran reconciled*. And all the coats of those condemned to the galleys were also hanged there, with their names and judgements, and underneath each coat, *Heretic Lutheran reconciled*. And also the coats and names of the three that were burnt, whereupon were written, *An obstinate heretic Lutheran burnt*. Then we were suffered to go up and down the country and to place ourselves as we could, and yet were not so free but that we very well knew that there was good espial always attending us and all our actions, so that we dared not once speak or look awry. David Alexander and Robert Cooke returned to serve the Inquisitor, who shortly after married them both to two of his Negro women. Richard Williams married a rich widow of Biscay with 4,000 pesos. Paul Horsewell is married to a mestizo, as they name those whose fathers were Spaniards and whose mothers Indians, and this woman is said to be the daughter of one that came in with Hernando Cortes the Conqueror, and had with her in marriage 4,000 pesos and a fair house. John Story is married to a Negro woman; and William Lowe had leave to go into Spain where he is now married.

For mine own part I could never thoroughly settle myself to marry in that country, although many fair offers were made unto me by such as were of great ability and wealth, but I could have no liking to live in a place where I must everywhere see and know such horrible idolatry and dared not once speak against it. And therefore I had always a longing for this my native country. To return and serve again in the mines where I might have gathered great riches and wealth, I very well saw that at one time or another I should fall again into the danger of that devilish Inquisition, and so be stripped of all, with loss of life also. Therefore I made my choice to learn to weave grosgrains and taffetas, and so, compounding with a silkweaver, I bound myself for three years to serve him, and gave him 150 pesos to teach me the science; otherwise he would not have taught me under seven years apprenticeship. And by this means I lived the more quiet, and free from suspicion. . . .

So I remained at my science the full time, and learned the art, at the end whereof there came news to Mexico that certain Englishmen had landed with a great power at the port of Acapulco, upon the south sea. . . .

[Philips attempts without success to join the English fleet reported off Acapulco. Then he reaches Vera Cruz, is caught, escapes, and flees to a port in Guatemala. Passing himself off as a Spaniard, he boards a ship bound for Spain and eventually reaches England again.]

Ladies of Lima, Vicuñas and Coca Chewers

JOHANN JAKOB VON TSCHUDI

FROM *Travels in Peru*

1838–42

Some of the most fascinating descriptions of any South American area were written by a Swiss naturalist and diplomat, Johann Jakob von Tschudi. After studying under the great scientist, Louis Agassiz, he set out on his first journey to South America, described in Travels in Peru, when he was scarcely twenty years old. He made several stops on the way up the west coast of South America, and in the course of a five-year stay in Peru he took a degree in medicine to support himself. During that time he traveled energetically, crossing the Cordilleras, visiting the Cerro de Pasco mining region and venturing into mountain areas where no European had preceded him.

In 1857 he went to South America a second time and, impatient to reach the Pacific, crossed the continent from Buenos Aires to Chile in midwinter. Later he recorded his observations in a five-volume work called Reisen durch Süd-amerika (Travels through South America). These travels led to his appointment as ambassador to Brazil (1860–62) and a diplomatic career that culminated in his becoming minister plenipotentiary to Austria from 1866 to 1883. But even in Vienna he pursued his interest in ancient Peruvian civilization and languages, publishing several books on Inca and pre-Inca antiquities.

Tschudi's judgments of the Spanish-Indian-Negro culture of Peru are

735

sometimes colored by a mid-nineteenth-century view of behavior, but he is always a thoroughly informed and interesting reporter on native customs as well as rare birds, exotic beasts and curious plants.

THE LADIES OF PERU

F<small>AR</small> superior to the men, both physically and intellectually, are the women of Lima. Nature has lavishly endowed them with many of her choicest gifts. In figure they are usually slender and rather tall, and they are especially remarkable for small, elegantly formed feet. Their fair faces, from which the glowing breath of the tropics banishes every trace of bloom, are animated by large, bright, dark eyes. Their features are pleasing—the nose being well formed, though in general not small—the mouth invariably adorned with two rows of brilliant white teeth, and their long black hair, arranged in plaits, falls gracefully over the bosom and shoulders. Add to all this a captivating grace of manner and deportment, joined to an exceeding degree of gentleness and amiability, and it will be readily admitted that the Limeña is a noble specimen of female loveliness.

At home, especially in the summer season, the ladies of Lima dress lightly and even negligently. For visiting, or going to the theaters, they adopt the French fashion. When walking in the streets, attending church, joining religious processions, &c., they appear in a very singular costume, peculiar to Lima, and consisting of two garments called the saya and the manto. Of the saya there are two kinds. The one called the *saya ajustada* was formerly in general use, but is now seldom seen. It consists of a petticoat, or skirt of thick stiff silk, pleated at top and bottom, in small fluted folds, drawn very close together at the waist and widening toward the ankles, beneath which the saya does not descend. It is tight to the form, the outline of which it perfectly displays, and its closeness to the limbs naturally impedes rapid movement. When wearing the *saya ajustada*, the ladies find it no very easy task to kneel down at the church, and at the termination of every genuflexion they are obliged to twist and twirl about for a considerable time before they can again stand on their feet.

The other description of saya is called the *saya culeça*, or the *saya desplegada*. It is pleated close at the waist, and from thence downward it stands out like a hooped petticoat. This sort of saya is made by first being pleated both at top and bottom like the *saya ajustada;* but afterward the lower pleats are undone to form the *saya desplegada.* The saya is always made of some dark-colored silk, black, green, blue, or cinnamon color.

The manto is a veil of thick black silk fastened by a band at the back of the waist, where it joins the saya. From thence it is brought over the shoulders and head, and drawn over the face so closely that only a small triangular space, sufficient for one eye to peep through, is left uncovered. A rich shawl thrown over the shoulders conceals the whole of the under-garment, except the sleeves. One of the small, neatly gloved hands confines the folds of the manto, while the other holds a richly embroidered pocket handkerchief. . . .

A *tapada* indulges in a vast deal of freedom when in the streets, and scruples not to make satirical observations on anybody or anything that strikes her as strange or ludicrous. The veil, or manto, is sacred, and should a man attempt to remove it by force, he would run the risk of being severely handled by the populace.

In intrigues of gallantry the *saya y manto* play a conspicuous part. A lady has been known to arrange an assignation with a gentleman in the street, while her husband, standing at the distance of a few yards and conversing with a friend on some matter of business, has little suspected that the *tapada* whose graceful figure he admired was his own faithful better half. It frequently happens that Doña Mariquita obliges Doña Merceditas, or Doña Panchita, with the loan of her saya, for the purpose of hoodwinking the Argus eyes of a jealous husband—the lady being well convinced that her kind friends will render her the like service in similar circumstances. Sometimes a lady may be seen in an old tattered saya, such as scarcely the poorest female might be expected to wear; but the costly shawl, the worked pocket handkerchief, the silk stockings and satin shoes betray the rank of the *tapada* and plainly denote that she has sallied forth on an adventure. It is difficult, nay, almost impossible, to recognize a lady thus muffled up. The one eye alone visible is, as may be supposed, a very uncertain token of identity, and the figure and walk may be easily disguised. . . .

Most foreigners who marry Limeñas stipulate that from the time of betrothal their wives shall no longer wear the *saya y manto.* The condition is agreed to; but how far it is faithfully observed the husbands best know. Many, no doubt, lull themselves in the confidence of their wishes being implicitly obeyed; but female ingenuity readily devises opportunities for deception. The women of Lima never willingly renounce the *saya y manto,* for it is inseparably associated with customs to which they are, heart and soul, devoted.

If we follow the Limeña (the white Creole [that is, born in the New World], be it understood) into the retirement of domestic life, we find that she is an affectionate mother, but not a very clever housekeeper. Every lady has at her command a great many more domestics than are necessary; some are servants, but most of them slaves. The establishment usually consists of a cook, a nursemaid, one or two housemaids, a needle-woman, several men servants, and a little Negro or Indian whose chief business is to carry a carpet behind his mistress when she goes to church. These servants all do as they please, and the lady of the house concerns herself very little about the indolence which her want of vigilance encourages. She rises at a late hour, and having dressed herself and decorated her hair with sprigs of jasmine and orange blossom, she takes her breakfast. That meal being ended, she goes out to make visits. During the sultry hours of midday she reposes, either by swinging in a hammock or reclining on a sofa, and meanwhile smokes a cigar. After dinner she again makes visits, and the evening is spent in the theater, on the plaza, or on the bridge. Some few ladies employ themselves in needlework, in which they are often most accomplished adepts; they especially excel in embroidery and fancy work; but they never pursue these employments before company.

The ladies of Lima are passionately fond of music. Most of them play the pianoforte or the guitar, and also sing; but for want of good instruction neither their playing nor their singing is above mediocrity. Smoking is pretty general among females, at least those of mature age; but they indulge in this practice only in their own apartments. Of late years the custom of smoking has been on the decline in Lima, in proportion as it has been increased on the continent of the Old World. Though snuff-taking is prohibited in the convents, yet the nuns practice it to a great extent. They use an exceedingly fine kind of red snuff, which has the effect of closing the breathing passage through the nostrils, and of producing a peculiar nasal tone of voice.

With the ladies of Lima, vanity and the love of dress appear to have reached their climax. To this passion for personal adornment they sacrifice everything. Formerly, when none but *real* pearls and diamonds were worn, many a lady was known to have ruined her husband by the purchase of those costly articles; now, however, thanks to French mock jewelry, they are enabled to bedeck themselves in glittering ornaments at trivial expense. Another of their passions is a fondness for perfumes. They are continually besprinkling themselves with *eau de Cologne, esprit de Lavande, agua rica,* or *mistura.* The latter is a fragrant yellow-colored water, prepared from gillyflower, jasmine and flor de mistela (*Talinum umbellatum*). They perfume their apartments daily with *sahumerios* (pastiles). When the lady of the house wishes to show particular attention to her visitors, she offers them perfumed water, dropping it into the bosoms of the ladies and on the pocket handkerchiefs of the gentlemen. Considering their free use of perfumes, it is not surprising that the fair Limeñas should be constantly complaining of headache, vertigo and other nervous ailments, or, to use their own phrase, *los nervios.*

Above all things the Limeñas pride themselves in the excessive smallness of their feet. Whether walking, standing, sitting, swinging in the hammock or reclining on the sofa, the grand object invariably is to display to advantage the tiny foot. To praise her virtue, her intelligence, her wit, or even her beauty, would be less complimentary to a Limeña than to admire the elegance of her feet. All possible care is taken to preserve the small form of the foot, and the Lima ladies avoid everything that may tend to spread or enlarge it. Their shoes are usually made of embroidered velvet or satin, or of very fine kid, and are so exceedingly small that they cannot be drawn on and off without difficulty. It is usual to have two new pairs every week, and the expense of a lady's shoes not unfrequently amounts to two hundred dollars per annum. A large foot is a thing held in horror by the Limeñas: they call it *una pataza inglesa* (an English paw). I once heard some Lima ladies extolling in high terms the beauty of a fair European; but all their praises ended with the words "*Pero que pie, valgame Dios! parece una lancha.*" (But what a foot, good Heaven! It is like a great boat.) Yet the feet of the lady alluded to would not, in Europe, have been thought by any means large.

Gourmanderie is one of the evil habits of the female inhabitants of Lima. Between meals they are continually eating sweetmeats and a variety of things. At one moment they order *tamal* (a preparation of finely bruised maize mixed with morsels of pork and rolled in maize leaves) served up, next *omitas* (sweet cakes made of maize and raisins), then *pan de chancay* (a sweet sort of bread) and biscuits, then *masamorita morada* (a syrup made from the pulp of fruit), or *frijoles coladas* (preserved peas with syrup), &c.; and yet dinner is partaken with as hearty an appetite as though none of these interludes had been introduced. Can it be matter of surprise that the good ladies are constantly complaining of indigestion and *mal de estomago?*

In the interior of the houses cleanliness does not extend beyond those apartments which are open to visitors, namely, the *sala* and the *cuadro*. The other rooms of the house frequently bear more resemblance to a stable than a human habitation, and their condition reflects little credit on the domestic habits of the female inmates. But even this is typical of the national character—a great outward show and little inward worth....

On attaining a certain age, the Limeñas totally alter their habits of life. When their beauty fades, and they cease to be the objects of compliment and flattery, or when weary of an idle, luxurious and, in too many instances, a not very virtuous life, they betake themselves to piety, and become *beatas* [literally, bigots]. The Limeña who thus renounces the vanities of the world attends church two or three times every day, confesses at least once every week, retires during Lent to a house of penitence; fasts, prays, and receives the visits of her confessor, to whom she sends presents of sweetmeats—and should the holy man, as is usually the case, prefer riding to walking, she shows her piety by giving him the use of her *calesa* to convey him from place to place.

The women of Lima are gifted by nature with extraordinary natural talent, though unfortunately it is rarely cultivated. They possess shrewd and penetrating intelligence, clear judgment, and in general very just views on the ordinary affairs of life. Like the women of the southern provinces of Spain, they are remarkable for quickness and smartness of repartee, and in a wordy contest a Limeña is sure to come off triumphant. They have a great deal of decision of character, and a degree of courage which does not usually fall to the lot of the female sex. In these respects they are infinitely superior to the timid, spiritless men. In the various political revolutions of the country, the women have often taken an active, and, in some instances, a more decided part than the men....

Vicuña Hunt

THE vicuña is a more beautiful animal than any of those just described. Its size is between that of the llama and the alpaca. It measures from the sole of the foot to the top of the head four feet one inch, and two and a half feet to the shoulders. The neck is longer and more slender than in either of the other relative species; and from them the vicuña is also distinguished by the superior fineness of its short, curly wool. The crown of the head, the upper part of the neck, the back, and thighs, are of a peculiar reddish-yellow hue, called by the people of the country *color de vicuña*. The lower part of the neck, and the inner parts of the limbs, are of a bright ocher color, and the breast and lower part of the body are white.

During the rainy season the vicuña inhabits the ridges of the Cordillera, where some scanty vegetation is to be found. It never ventures up to the naked rocky summits, for its hoofs, being accustomed only to turfy ground, are very soft and tender. It lives in herds consisting of from six to fifteen females and one male, who is the protector and leader of the herd. While the females are quietly grazing, the male stands at the distance of some paces apart, and carefully keeps guard over them. At the approach of danger he gives a signal, consisting of a sort of whistling sound and a quick movement of the foot. Immediately the herd draws closely together, each animal anxiously stretching out its head in the direction of the threatening danger. They then take to flight, first moving leisurely and cautiously, and then quickening their pace to the utmost degree of speed; while the male vicuña who covers the retreat frequently halts, to observe the movement of the enemy. The females, with singular fidelity and affection, reward the watchful care of their protector. If he is wounded or killed, they gather round him in a circle, uttering their shrill tones of lamentation, and they will suffer themselves to be captured or killed, rather than desert him by pursuing their flight. The neigh of the vicuña, like that of the other animals of its class, resembles a short, sharp whistle. But when the shrill sound vibrates through the pure *puna* air, the practiced ear can readily distinguish the cry of the vicuña from that of the other animals of the same family.

The Indians seldom employ firearms in hunting the vicuñas. They catch them by what they term the *chacu*. In this curious hunt, one man at least belonging to each family in the *puna* villages takes a part, and women accompany the train, to officiate as cooks to the hunters. The whole company, frequently amounting to seventy or eighty individuals, proceeds to the *altos* (the most secluded parts of the *puna*), which are the haunts of the vicuñas. They take with them stakes, and a great quantity of rope and cord. A spacious open plain is selected, and the stakes are driven into the ground in a circle, at intervals of from twelve to fifteen feet apart, and are connected together by ropes fastened to them at the height of two or two and a half feet from the ground. The circular space within the stakes is about half a league in circumference, and an opening of about two hundred paces in width is left for entrance. On the ropes by which the stakes are fastened together the women hang pieces of colored rags, which flutter about in the wind. The *chacu* being fully prepared, the men, some of whom are mounted on horseback, range about within a circuit of several miles, driving before them all the herds of vicuñas they meet with, and forcing them into the *chacu*. When a sufficient number of vicuñas is collected, the entrance is closed. The timid animals do not attempt to leap over the ropes, being frightened by the fluttering rags suspended from them, and, when thus secured, the Indians easily kill them by the bolas. These bolas consist of three balls, composed either of lead or stone; two of them heavy, and the third rather lighter. They are fastened to long, elastic strings, made of twisted sinews of the vicuña, and the opposite ends of the strings are all tied together. The Indian holds the lightest of the three balls in his hand and swings the two others in a wide circle above his head; then, taking his aim at the distance of about fifteen or twenty paces, he lets go the hand ball, upon which all the three balls whirl in a circle, and twine round the object aimed at. The aim is usually taken at the hind legs of the animals, and, the cords twisting round them, they become firmly bound. It requires great skill and long practice to throw the bolas dexterously, especially when on horseback; a novice in the art incurs the risk of dangerously hurting either himself or his horse, by not giving the balls the proper swing, or by letting go the hand ball too soon. . . .

[In describing the mountain Indians Tschudi records with remarkable scientific accuracy the effect on them of their addiction to the leaves of the coca plant. The drug cocaine, which comes from the same shrub, was not isolated until 1860.]

The Coca Chewers

The Indians masticate the coca. Each individual carries a leather pouch, called the *huallqui*, or the *chuspa*, and a small flask gourd, called the *ishcupuru*. The pouch contains a supply of coca leaves, and the gourd is filled with pulverized unslaked lime. Usually four times, but never less than three times a day, the Indian suspends his labor, for the purpose of masticating coca. This operation (which is termed *chacchar* or *acullicar*) is performed in the following manner: Some of the coca leaves, the stalks having been carefully picked off, are masticated until they form a small ball, or, as it is called, an *acullico*. A thin slip of damp wood is then thrust into the *ishcupuru,* or gourd, and when drawn out some portion of the powdered lime adheres to it. The *acullico,* or ball of masticated coca leaves, is, while still lying in the mouth, punctured with this slip of wood, until the lime mixing with it gives it a proper relish, and the abundant flow of saliva thus excited is partly expectorated and partly swallowed. When the ball ceases to emit juice, it is thrown away, and a new one is formed by the mastication of a fresh mouthful of coca leaves. In Cerro de Pasco, and in places still farther south, the Indians use, instead of unslaked lime, a preparation of the pungent ashes of the quinua (*Chenopodium quina,* L.). This preparation is called *llucta* or *llipta.* In using it a piece is broken off and masticated along with the *acullico.* In some of the Montaña regions the *llucta* is made from the ashes of the musa root. The application of the unslaked lime demands some precaution, for if it comes in direct contact with the lips and gums it causes a very painful burning. During a fatiguing ride across the level heights, where, owing to the cold wind, I experienced a difficulty of respiration, my *arriero* recommended me to chew coca, assuring me that I would experience great relief from so doing. He lent me his *huallqui,* but owing to my awkward manner of using it, I cauterized my lips so severely that I did not venture on a second experiment.

The flavor of coca is not unpleasant. It is slightly bitter, aromatic, and similar to the worst kind of green tea. When mixed with the ashes of the musa root it is somewhat piquant, and more pleasant to European palates than it is without that addition. The smell of the fresh dried leaves in a mass is almost overpowering; but this smell entirely goes when they are packed in the sacks. All who masticate coca have a very bad breath, pale lips and gums, greenish and stumpy teeth, and an ugly black mark at the angles of the mouth. An inveterate *coquero,* or coca chewer, is known at the first glance. His unsteady gait, his yellow-colored skin, his dim and sunken eyes encircled by a purple ring, his quivering lips and his general apathy, all bear evidence of the baneful effects of the coca juice when taken in excess. All the mountain Indians are addicted more or less to the practice of masticating coca. Each man consumes, on the average, between an ounce and an ounce and a half per day, and on festival days about double that quantity. The owners of mines and plantations allow their laborers to suspend their work three times a day for the *chacchar,* which usually occupies upwards of a quarter of an hour; and after that they smoke a paper cigar, which they allege crowns the zest of the coca mastication. He who indulges for a time in the use of coca finds it difficult, indeed almost impossible, to relinquish it. This fact I saw exemplified in the cases of several persons of high respectability in Lima, who are in the

habit of retiring daily to a private apartment for the purpose of masticating coca. They could not do this openly because among the refined
class of Peruvians the *chacchar* is looked upon as a low and vulgar practice,
befitting only to the laboring Indians. Yet Europeans occasionally allow
themselves to fall into this habit; and I knew two in Lima, the one an
Italian and the other a Biscayan, who were confirmed *coqueros* in the
strictest sense of the word. In Cerro de Pasco there are societies having
even Englishmen for their members, which meet on certain evenings for
the *chacchar*. In these places, instead of lime or ashes, sugar is served
along with the coca leaves. A member of one of these clubs informed me
that on the few first trials the sugar was found very agreeable, but that
afterward the palate required some more pungent ingredient.

The operation of the coca is similar to that of narcotics administered
in small doses. Its effects may be compared to those produced by the
thorn apple rather than to those arising from opium. I have already
noticed the consequences resulting from drinking the decoction of the
datura. In the inveterate *coquero* similar symptoms are observable, but
in a mitigated degree. I may mention one circumstance attending the
use of coca, which appears hitherto to have escaped notice: it is, that
after the mastication of a great quantity of coca the eye seems unable to
bear light, and there is a marked distension of the pupil. I have also
observed this peculiarity of the eye in one who had drunk a strong extract
of the infusion of coca leaves. In the effects consequent on the use of
opium and coca there is this distinction, that coca, when taken even in
the utmost excess, never causes a total alienation of the mental powers or
induces sleep; but, like opium, it excites the sensibility of the brain, and
the repeated excitement occasioned by its intemperate use after a series
of years wears out mental vigor and activity.

It is a well-known fact, confirmed by long observation and experience,
that the Indians who regularly masticate coca require but little food, and,
nevertheless, go through excessive labor with apparent ease. They, therefore, ascribe the most extraordinary qualities to the coca, and even believe
that it might be made entirely a substitute for food. Setting aside all
extravagant and visionary notions on the subject, I am clearly of opinion
that the moderate use of coca is not merely innoxious, but that it may
even be very conducive to health. In support of this conclusion, I may
refer to the numerous examples of longevity among Indians who, almost
from the age of boyhood, have been in the habit of masticating coca
three times a day, and who in the course of their lives have consumed no
less than two thousand seven hundred pounds, yet, nevertheless, enjoy
perfect health. The food of the Indians consists almost exclusively of

vegetable substances, especially roasted maize and barley converted into flour by crushing, which they eat without the admixture of any other substance. The continued use of this farinaceous food occasions severe obstructions, which the well-known aperient qualities of the coca counteract, and many serious diseases are thereby prevented. That the coca is in the highest degree nutritious is a fact beyond dispute. The incredible fatigues endured by the Peruvian infantry, with very spare diet, but with the regular use of coca; the laborious toil of the Indian miner, kept up, under similar circumstances, throughout a long series of years; certainly afford sufficient ground for attributing to the coca leaves, not a quality of mere temporary stimulus, but a powerful nutritive principle. Of the great power of the Indians in enduring fatigue with no other sustenance than coca, I may here mention an example. A Chola of Huari, named Hatun Huamang, was employed by me in very laborious digging. During the whole time he was in my service, viz., five days and nights, he never tasted any food, and took only two hours' sleep nightly. But at intervals of two and a half or three hours, he regularly masticated about half an ounce of coca leaves, and he kept an *acullico* continually in his mouth. I was constantly beside him, and therefore I had the opportunity of closely observing him. The work for which I engaged him being finished, he accompanied me on a two days' journey of twenty-three leagues across the level heights. Though on foot, he kept up with the pace of my mule, and halted only for the *chacchar*. On leaving me, he declared that he would willingly engage himself again for the same amount of work, and that he would go through it without food if I would but allow him a sufficient supply of coca. The village priest assured me that this man was sixty-two years of age, and that he had never known him to be ill in his life.

The Indians maintain that coca is the best preventive of that difficulty of respiration felt in the rapid ascents of the Cordillera and the *puna*. Of this fact I was fully convinced by my own personal experience. I speak here, not of the mastication of the leaves, but of their decoction taken as a beverage. When I was in the *puna*, at the height of fourteen thousand feet above the level of the sea, I drank, always before going out to hunt, a strong infusion of coca leaves. I could then during the whole day climb the heights and follow the swift-footed wild animals without experiencing any greater difficulty of breathing than I should have felt in similar rapid movement on the coast. Moreover, I did not suffer from the symptoms of cerebral excitement or uneasiness which other travelers have observed.

Journey to a Mayan Ruin

JOHN LLOYD STEPHENS

FROM *Incidents of Travel in Central America, Chiapas, and Yucatan*

1839–40

Encouraged by the great success of the two books he had written on his travels first in Egypt and the Holy Land (see the excerpt on pages 182–91 in the section on the Levant) and then in Turkey and Russia, a young New York attorney, John Lloyd Stephens, set out for Central America in 1839 on a combined diplomatic and archaeological expedition. Although he did not succeed in his diplomatic mission (mainly because he could not find a duly constituted Central American government), he returned with the material for a two-volume work, Incidents of Travel in Central America, Chiapas, and Yucatan, *that was to prove a great success. Accompanied by an artist friend, Frederick Catherwood, who made superb sketches of the ruins, he went to Belize in British Honduras and then south to the remains of Copán. Continuing inland, the pair visited Guatemala City, and on reaching the Pacific they sailed south to Costa Rica. On the long mule journey back they passed through Nicaragua, Salvador, Guatemala, and Chiapas, where they explored the ruins of Palenque and even undertook to purchase them. They had traveled two thousand miles and uncovered some of the most important sites of Mayan civilization.*

They returned to New York from Yucatán in July 1840. But before leaving Mexico they had glimpsed extraordinary ruins in Yucatán and by October 1841 they were on their way south again. During the following winter and spring they visited no less than forty-four ruined cities, includ-

ing Uxmal and Chichén Itzá, most of them utterly forgotten and over-
grown by tropical vegetation. The resulting book, Incidents of Travel in
Yucatan, *is a mine of Mayan archaeology (magnificently rendered by*
Catherwood) studded with vignettes of Yucatán society.

An urbane, rather high-minded young man, Stephens was not so much
an explorer as an ardent traveler with a keen interest in archaeology and
a talent for vivid reporting. Although Central America had known the
white man and Christianity from the time of the conquistadors and had
old and highly civilized cities as well as wildernesses, much of it was still
extremely primitive. In the passage below Stephens describes the unique
conveyance in which he approached Palenque, a main site of Mayan ruins.

Early the next morning the sugar party started, and at five minutes
before seven we followed with silla and men; altogether our party had
swelled to twenty Indians.

The country through which we were now travelling was as wild as
before the Spanish conquest, and without a habitation until we reached
Palenque. The road was through a forest so overgrown with brush and
underwood as to be impenetrable; the branches were trimmed barely high
enough to admit a man's travelling under them on foot, so that on the
backs of our mules we were constantly obliged to bend our bodies and
even to dismount. In some places, for a great distance around, the woods
seemed killed by the heat; the foliage was withered and the leaves dry
and crisp, as if burned by the sun. In addition, a tornado had swept the
country, of which no mention had been made in the San Pedro papers.

We met three Indians carrying clubs in their hands; they were naked
except for a small piece of cotton cloth wound around the loins and
passed between the legs. One of them, young, tall, and of admirable
symmetry of form, looked the free-born gentleman of the woods. Shortly
afterwards, we passed a stream where naked Indians were setting rude
nets for fish—wild and primitive as in the first ages of savage life.

At twenty minutes past ten we commenced ascending the mountain.
It was very hot, and I can give no idea of the toil of ascending these
mountains. Our mules could barely clamber up with their saddles only.
We disencumbered ourselves of sword, spurs, and all useless trappings;
in fact, we came down to shirt and pantaloons, and as near the condition
of the Indians as we could. Our procession would have been a spectacle
on Broadway: first were four Indians, each with a rough oxhide box,

secured by an iron chain and large padlock, on his back; then Juan, with only a hat and pair of thin cotton drawers, driving two spare mules and carrying a double-barrelled gun over his naked shoulders; then ourselves, each one either driving before him or leading his own mule; then an Indian carrying the silla, with relief carriers and several boys bearing small bags of provisions, the Indians of the silla being much surprised at our not using their services, according to contract and the price paid. Though toiling excessively, we felt a sense of degradation at being carried on a man's shoulders. At that time I was in the worst condition of the three, and the night before had gone to bed at San Pedro without supper, which for any of us was a sure evidence of being in a bad way.

We had brought the silla with us merely as a measure of precaution, without much expectation of being obliged to use it; but at a steep pitch, which made my head almost burst to think of climbing, I resorted to it for the first time. It was a large, clumsy arm-chair, put together with wooden pins and bark strings. The Indian who was to carry me was, like all the others, small and not more than five feet seven; he was very thin but symmetrically formed. A bark strap was tied to the arms of the chair and, sitting down, he placed his back against the back of the chair, adjusting the length of the strings and smoothing the bark across his forehead with a little cushion to relieve the pressure. An Indian on each side lifted it up, and the carrier rose on his feet, stood still a moment, threw me up once or twice to adjust me on his shoulders, and set off with one man on each side. It was a great relief, but I could feel every movement, even to the heaving of his chest. The ascent was one of the steepest on the whole road. In a few minutes he stopped and sent forth a sound, usual with Indian carriers, between a whistle and a blow; it was a sound which was always painful to my ears, but which I had never before felt to be quite so disagreeable. My face was turned backwards; I could not see where he was going but observed that the Indian on the left fell back.

Not to increase the labour of carrying me, I sat as still as possible; but in a few minutes, looking over my shoulder, I saw that we were approaching the edge of a precipice more than a thousand feet deep. Here I became very anxious to dismount; but I could not speak intelligibly, and the Indians could or would not understand my signs. My carrier moved along carefully: he put his left foot out to feel whether the stone on which he put it down was steady and secure before he brought up the other; by degrees and after a particularly careful movement, he brought both feet up to within half a step of the edge of the precipice, where he stopped and gave a fearful whistle and blow. I rose and fell with every breath, feeling his body trembling under me and his knees seeming to give way. The precipice was awful, and the slightest irregular movement on my part might bring us both down together. I would have given him a release in full for the rest of the journey to be off his back; but he started again, and with the same care ascended several steps, so close to the edge that even on the back of a mule it would have been very uncomfortable. My fear lest he should break down or stumble was excessive.

To my extreme relief, the path finally turned away; but I had hardly congratulated myself upon my escape before he descended a few steps. This was much worse than ascending; if he fell, nothing could keep me from going over his head; but I remained till he put me down of his own accord. The poor fellow was wet with perspiration and trembled in every limb. Another stood ready to take me up, but I had had enough. Pawling tried it, but only for a short time. It was bad enough to see an Indian toiling with a dead weight on his back; but to feel him trembling under one's own body, hear his hard breathing, see the sweat rolling down him, and feel the insecurity of the position, made this a mode of travelling which nothing but constitutional laziness and insensibility could endure. Walking, or rather climbing, stopping very often to rest, and riding when it was at all practicable, we reached a thatched shed, where we wished to stop for the night, but there was no water.

We could not understand how far it was to Nopa, our intended stopping-place, which we supposed to be on the top of the mountain. To every question the Indians answered *una legua*. Thinking it could not be much higher, we continued. For an hour more we had a very steep ascent, and then commenced a terrible descent. At this time the sun had disappeared; dark clouds overhung the woods and thunder rolled heavily on the top of the mountain. As we descended a heavy wind swept through the forest; the air was filled with dry leaves, branches were snapped and broken, trees bent, and there was every appearance of a violent tornado. To hurry down on foot was out of the question, we were so tired that it was impossible. But, afraid of being caught on the mountain by a hurricane and deluge of rain, we spurred down as fast as we could go. It was a continued descent, without any relief, stony, and very steep. Very often the mules stopped, afraid to go on; and in one place the two empty mules bolted into the thick woods rather than proceed. Fortunately for the reader, this is our last mountain, and I can end honestly with a climax: it was the worst mountain I ever encountered in that or any other country, and, under our apprehension of the storm, I will venture to say that no travellers ever descended in less time. At a quarter before five we reached the plain. The mountain was hidden by clouds, and the storm was now raging above us. We crossed a river, and continuing along it through a thick forest, reached the rancho of Nopa.

It was situated in a circular clearing about one hundred feet in diameter, near the river, with the forest around so thick with brush and underwood that the mules could not penetrate it, and with no opening but for the passage of the road through it. The rancho was merely a pitched roof covered with palm leaves and supported by four trunks of trees. All around were heaps of snail shells; the ground of the rancho was several inches deep with ashes, the remains of fires for cooking them. We had hardly congratulated ourselves upon our arrival at such a beautiful spot before we suffered such an onslaught of mosquitoes as we had not before experienced in the country. We made a fire, and with appetites sharpened by a hard day's work, sat down on the grass to dispose of a San Pedro fowl; but we were obliged to get up and, while one hand was occupied with eatables, use the other to brush off the venomous insects. We soon saw that we had bad prospects for the night; we lighted fires all around the rancho and smoked inordinately. We were in no hurry to lie down, and sat till a late hour, consoling ourselves with the reflection that, but for the mosquitoes, our satisfaction would be beyond all bounds. The dark border of the clearing was lighted up by fireflies of extraordinary size and brilliancy; they darted among the trees, not flashing and disappearing, but carrying a steady light; they seemed like shooting stars except that their course was serpentine. In different places there were two that remained stationary; emitting a pale but beautiful light, they seemed like rival belles holding levees. The fiery orbs darted from one to the other; and when one, more daring than the rest, approached too near, the coquette withdrew her light and the flutterer went off. One, however, carried all before her, and at one time we counted seven hovering around her.

At length we prepared for sleep. Hammocks would leave us exposed on every side to the merciless attacks of the mosquitoes, and we spread our mats on the ground. We did not undress. Pawling, with a great deal of trouble, rigged his sheets into a mosquito net, but it was so hot that he could not breathe under them, and he roamed about or was in the river nearly all night. The Indians, who had occupied themselves in catching snails and cooking them for supper, then lay down to sleep on the banks of the river. But at midnight, with sharp thunder and lightning, the rain broke in a deluge and they all came under the shed, lying there perfectly naked, and mechanically and without seeming to disturb themselves, slapping their bodies with their hands. The incessant hum and bite of the insects kept us in a constant state of wakefulness and irritation. Our bodies we could protect, but with a covering over the face the heat was insufferable. Before daylight I walked to the river, which was broad and shallow, and stretched myself out on the gravelly bottom, where the water was barely deep enough to run over my body. It was the first comfortable moment I had had. My heated body came cooled, and I lay till daylight. When I rose to dress they came upon me with appetites whetted by a spirit of vengeance. Our day's work had been tremendously hard, but the night's was worse.

The morning air, however, was refreshing, and as day dawned our tormentors disappeared. Mr. Catherwood had suffered least, but in his restlessness he had lost from his finger a precious emerald ring which he had worn for many years and prized for associations. We remained some time looking for it, but at length mounted and made our last start for Palenque. The road was level, but the woods were still as thick as on the mountain. At a quarter before eleven we reached a path which led to the ruins, or somewhere else. We had abandoned the intention of going directly to the ruins, for, besides being in a shattered condition, we could not communicate with our Indians, and probably they did not know where the ruins were. At length we came out upon an open plain and looked back at the range we had crossed, running off to Petén and the country of unbaptized Indians.

Street Cries, Nuns and Gamblers

FRANCES CALDERÓN DE LA BARCA

FROM *Life in Mexico*

1839–42

As a child in Edinburgh in the early 1800s, Frances Inglis could not have dreamed that she would one day move in the highest social circles of the United States, Mexico and Spain, and end her days as a marquesa in the royal palace in Madrid.

Life began to change for her when financial difficulties caused the Inglis family to move to Normandy and then, after the death of the father, to the United States. In Boston, talented, lively, Frances attracted the attention of such men as Prescott and Lowell and eventually married a distinguished Spanish diplomat, Don Angel Calderón de la Barca. She accompanied him when he became ambassador to the new republic in Mexico, minister to Washington, and finally Minister of State in his homeland.

Everywhere Madame Calderón took the greatest interest in life around her. In Mexico, she set down her impressions in the series of richly detailed and spirited letters that make up her Life in Mexico. These letters present animated glimpses of that country in the years after it had thrown off the Spanish yoke but while social life was still marked by the glitter and ostentation of the old viceregal days.

Later, Madame Calderón found herself in Madrid during the popular uprising of 1854, which forced the Calderóns to flee Spain for a time. She wrote another book, Attaché in Madrid; or, Sketches of the Court of Isabella II, but much of it is only a glamorous view of the royal family and the *nobility. Her devotion was well rewarded, for she continued high in royal favor even after the death of her husband in 1861 and for the remainder of her life.*

STREET CRIES AND TORTILLAS

THERE are an extraordinary number of street-cries in Mexico, which begin at dawn and continue till night, performed by hundreds of discordant voices, impossible to understand at first; but Señor —— has been giving me an explanation of them, until I begin to have some distinct idea of their meaning. At dawn you are awakened by the shrill and desponding cry of the Carbonero, the coalmen, "Carbon, Señor?" which, as he pronounces it, sounds like "Carbosiu?" Then the grease-man takes up the song, "Mantequilla! lard! lard! at one real and a half." "Salt beef! good salt beef!" ("Cecina buena!") interrupts the butcher in a hoarse voice. "Hay cebo-o-o-o-o-o?" This is the prolonged and melancholy note of the woman who buys kitchen-stuff, and stops before the door. Then passes by the *cambista*, a sort of Indian she-trader or exchanger, who sings out, "Tejocotes por venas de chile?" a small fruit which she proposes exchanging for hot peppers. No harm in that.

A kind of ambulating peddler drowns the shrill treble of the Indian cry. He calls aloud upon the public to buy needles, pins, thimbles, shirt-buttons, tape, cotton-balls, small mirrors, etc. He enters the house, and is quickly surrounded by the women, young and old, offering him the tenth part of what he asks, and which, after much haggling, he accepts. Behind him stands the Indian with his tempting baskets of fruit, of which he calls out all the names, till the cook or housekeeper can resist no longer, and putting her head over the balustrade, calls him up with his bananas, and oranges, and granaditas, etc.

A sharp note of interrogation is heard, indicating something that is hot, and must be snapped up quickly before it cools. "Gorditas de horna caliente?" "Little fat cakes from the oven, hot?" This is in a female key, sharp and shrill. Follows the mat-seller. "Who wants mats from Puebla? mats of five yards?" These are the most matinal cries.

At midday the beggars begin to be particularly importunate, and their cries, and prayers, and long recitations, form a running accompaniment to the other noises. Then above all rises the cry of "Honey-cakes!" "Cheese and honey?" "Requeson and good honey." (*Requeson* being a sort of hard curd, sold in cheeses.) Then comes the dulce-men, the sellers of sweetmeats, of meringues, which are very good, and of all sorts of candy. "Caramelos de esperma! bocadillo de coco!" Then the lottery-men, the messengers of Fortune, with their shouts of "The last ticket yet unsold, for half a real!" a tempting announcement to the lazy beggar, who finds it easier to gamble than to work, and who may have that sum hid about his rags.

Towards evening rises the cry of "Tortillas de cuajada?" "Curd-cakes?" or, "Do you take nuts?" succeeded by the night-cry of "Chestnuts hot and roasted!" and by the affectionate vendors of ducks: "Ducks, oh my soul, hot ducks!" "Maize-cakes," etc., etc. As the night wears away, the voices die off, to resume next morning in fresh vigour.

Tortillas, which are the common food of the people, and which are merely maize cakes mixed with a little lime, and of the form and size of what we call *scones*, I find rather good when very hot and fresh-baked, but insipid by themselves. They have been in use all through this country since the earliest ages of its history, without any change in the manner of baking them, excepting that, for the noble Mexicans in former days, they used to be kneaded with various medicinal plants, supposed to render them more wholesome. They are considered particularly palatable with *chile*, to endure which, in the quantities in which it is eaten here, it seems to me necessary to have a throat lined with tin.

[On visiting the convent of Santa Teresa, Madame Calderón was "horror-struck" at the self-imposed penance of the nuns; nevertheless, she later became a Catholic and after her husband died in Spain she retired for a time to a convent there.]

SELF-TORTURE OF THE NUNS OF THE SANTA TERESA

THE Santa Teresa, however, has few ornaments. It is not nearly so large as the *Encarnación*, and admits but twenty-one nuns. At present there are, besides these, but three novices. Its very atmosphere seems holy, and its scrupulous and excessive cleanness makes all profane dwellings appear dirty by comparison. We were accompanied by a bishop, Señor Madrid, the same who assisted at the archbishop's consecration—a good-looking man, young and tall, and very splendidly dressed. His robes were of purple satin, covered with fine point-lace, with a large cross of diamonds and amethysts. He also wore a cloak of very fine purple cloth lined with crimson velvet, crimson stockings, and an immense amethyst ring.

When he came in we found that the nuns had permission to put up their veils, rarely allowed in this order in the presence of strangers. They have a small garden and fountain, plenty of flowers, and some fruit, but all is on a smaller scale, and sadder than in the convent of the Incarnation. The refectory is a large room, with a long narrow table running all round it—a plain deal table, with wooden benches; before the place of each nun, an earthen bowl, an earthen cup with an apple in it, a wooden plate and a wooden spoon; at the top of the table a grinning skull, to remind them that even these indulgences they shall not long enjoy.

In one corner of the room is a reading-desk, a sort of elevated pulpit, where one reads aloud from some holy book, whilst the others discuss their simple fare. They showed us a crown of thorns, which, on certain days, is worn by one of their number, by way of penance. It is made of iron, so that the nails entering inwards, run into the head, and make it bleed. While she wears this on her head, a sort of wooden bit is put into her mouth, and she lies prostrate on her face till dinner is ended; and while in this condition her food is given her, of which she eats as much as she can, which probably is none.

We visited the different cells, and were horror-struck at the self-inflicted tortures. Each bed consists of a wooden plank raised in the middle, and on days of penitence crossed by wooden bars. The pillow is wooden, with a cross lying on it, which they hold in their hands when they lie down. The nun lies on this penitential couch, embracing the cross, and her feet hanging out, as the bed is made too short for her upon principle. Round her waist she occasionally wears a band with iron points turning inwards; on her breast a cross with nails, of which the points enter the flesh, of the truth of which I had melancholy ocular demonstration. Then, after having scourged herself with a whip covered with iron nails, she lies down for a few hours on the wooden bars, and rises at four o'clock. All these instruments of discipline, which each nun keeps in a little box beside her bed, look as if their fitting place would be in the dungeons of the Inquisition. They made me try their *bed and board*, which I told them would give me a very decided taste for early rising.

Yet they all seem as cheerful as possible, though it must be confessed that many of them look pale and unhealthy. It is said, that when they are

strong enough to stand this mode of life, they live very long; but it frequently happens that girls who come into this convent are obliged to
leave it from sickness, long before the expiration of their novitiate. I met
with the girl whom I had seen take the veil, and cannot say that she looked
either well or cheerful, though she assured me that "of course, in doing
the will of God," she was both. There was not much beauty amongst them
generally, though one or two had remains of great loveliness. My friend,
the Madre A——, is handsomer on a closer view than I had supposed her,
and seems an especial favourite with old and young. But there was one
whose face must have been strikingly beautiful. She was as pale as marble,
and though still young, seemed in very delicate health; but her eyes and
eyebrows as black as jet, the eyes so large and soft, the eyebrows two pen-
cilled arches; and her smiles so resigned and sweet, would have made her
the loveliest model imaginable for a Madonna.

Again, as in the Incarnation, they had taken the trouble to prepare an
elegant supper for us. The bishop took his place in an antique velvet chair,
the Señora —— —— and I were placed on each side of him. The room
was very well lighted, and there was as great profusion of custards, jellies,
and ices, as if we had been supping at the most profane *café*. The nuns did
not sit down, but walked about, pressing us to eat, the bishop now and then
giving them cakes, with permission to eat them, which they received laughing. They have the most humble and caressing manners, and really appear
to be the most amiable and excellent women in the world. They seem to
make no ostentation of virtue, but to be seriously impressed with the conviction that they have chosen the true road to salvation; nor are there in
them any visible symptoms of that spiritual pride from which few devotees
are exempt.

After supper a small harp was brought in, which had been sent for by
the bishop's permission. It was terribly out of tune, with half the strings
broke; but we were determined to grudge no trouble in putting it in order,
and giving these poor recluses what they considered so great a gratification.
We got it into some sort of condition at last, and when they heard it
played, they were vehement in their expressions of delight. The Señora
——, who has a charming voice, afterwards sang to them, the bishop being
very indulgent, and permitting us to select whatever songs we chose, so
that when rather a profane canticle, "The Virgin of the Pillar" (La Virgen
del Pilar), was sung, he very kindly turned a deaf ear to it, and seemed
busily engaged in conversation with an old madre, till it was all over.

We were really sorry to leave them; particularly as it is next to impossible that we shall ever see them again; and it seemed as if in a few hours

a friendship had been formed between us and these recluses, whose sensations are so few, they must be the more lasting. The thoughts of these poor women cost me a sad and sleepless night. They have sent me some wax figures, dressed in the costumes of the different orders, beginning with their own. They wear the coarsest and hardest stuff next their skin, in itself a perpetual penance.

THE GAMBLERS AT SAN AGUSTÍN

On the third night of the fête, C[alderón] and I having left the ball-room, about ten o'clock, walked out in the direction of the copper-tables which filled the middle of the square, and were covered with awnings. It is a sight that, once seen, can never be forgotten. Nothing but the pencil of Hogarth, or the pen of Boz, could do justice to the various groups there assembled. It was a gambling *fête champêtre*, conducted on the most liberal scale.

On each table were great mountains of copper, with an occasional sprinkling of silver. There was a profusion of evergreens, small tin lamps dripping with oil, and sloping tallow candles shedding grease upon the board. Little ragged boys, acting as waiters, were busily engaged in handing round pulque and chia in cracked tumblers. There was, moreover, an agreeable tinkling produced from several guitars, and even the bankers condescended to amuse their guests with soothing strains. The general dress of the company consisted of a single blanket, gracefully disposed in folds about the person, so as to show various glimpses of a bronze skin. To this some added a pair of Mexican pantaloons, and some a shirt of a doubtful colour. There were many with large hats, most of which had crowns or parts of crowns, but all affording free entrance to the fresh air. Generally speaking, however, the head was uncovered, or covered only with its native thatching of long, bushy, tangled black hair.

This might be out of compliment to the ladies, of whom there were several, and who ought in politeness to have been mentioned first. Nothing could be simpler than their costume, consisting of a very dirty and extremely torn chemise, with short sleeves, a shorter petticoat, and a pair of shoes, generally of dirty satin; also a reboso, and the long hair hanging down as Eve's golden locks may have done in Paradise. "They call this place a Paradise," a Spanish soldier wrote to his father; "and so I think it is, it is so full of *Adams*."

There was neither fighting, nor swearing, nor high words. I doubt whether there be as much decorum at Crockford's; indeed, they were scrupulously polite to each other. At one table, the banker was an enormously fat gentleman, one half of whose head was bound up with a dirty white handkerchief, over which a torn piece of hat was stuck, very much to one side. He had a most roguish eye, and a smile of inviting benignity on his dirty countenance. In one hand he held and tingled a guitar, while he most ingeniously swept in the copper with the other. By his side sat two wretched-looking women, with long matted hair, their elbows on the table, and their great eyes fixed upon the game with an expression of the most intense anxiety. At another, the *banker* was a pretty little Indian woman, rather clean, comparatively speaking, and who appeared to be doing business smartly. A man stood near her, leaning against one of the poles that supported the awning, who attracted all our attention. He was enveloped in a torn blanket, his head uncovered, and his feet bare, and was glaring upon the table with his great dark, haggard-looking eyes, his brown face livid, and his expression bordering on despair. It needed no one to tell us that on the table was his last stake. What will such a man do but go upon the road?

I have heard it mentioned as a strong circumstance in favour of the Mexican character, that there is neither noise nor disturbance in these reunions; none of that uproar and violence that there would be in an English mob, for example. The fact is certain, but the inference is doubtful. These people are degraded, and accustomed to endure. They are gentle and cunning, and their passions are not easily roused, at least to open display; but once awakened, it is neither to uproar that these passions will be excited, nor by fair fight that they will be assuaged. In England, a boxing-match decides a dispute amongst the lower orders; in Mexico, a knife; and a broken head is easier mended than a cut throat....

While "high life below stairs" is thus enacting, and these people are courting fortune in the fresh air, the gentlemanly gamblers are seated before the green cloth-covered tables, with the gravity befitting so many cabinet councils; but without their mystery, for doors and windows are thrown open, and both ladies and gentlemen may pass in and out, and look on at the game, if they please. The heaps of ounces look tempting, and make it appear a true El Dorado. Nor is there any lack of creature-comforts to refresh the flagging spirits. There are supper-spread tables, covered with savoury meats to appease their hunger, and with generous wines to gladden their hearts; and the gentlemen who surrounded that board seemed to be playing, instead of Monte, an excellent knife and fork.

You must not suppose that those who hold gaming-tables are the less considered on that account; on the contrary, as the banks generally win, they are amongst the richest, and, consequently, the most respected men in Mexico. These bankers are frequently Spaniards, who have found gambling the readiest stepping-stone to fortune. Señor ——— explained to me one plan of those who hold the banks, a sort of *hedging*, by which it is next to impossible that they can lose. For example, one of these gentlemen proposes to his friends to take a share in a *vaca*, each contributing a few ounces. Having collected several hundred ounces, they go to play at *his bank*. If they win, he receives his share, of course; and if they lose his bank wins the whole. It is proceeding upon the principle of "Heads I win, tails you lose."

At the tables, few words are spoken. The heaps of gold change masters; but the masters do not change countenance. I saw but one person who looked a little out of humour, and he was a foreigner. The rich man adds to his store, and the poor man becomes a beggar. He is ruined, but "makes no sign."

The ladies who have collected ounces and made purses, send their friends and admirers to the tables to try their luck for them; and in some of the inferior houses, the Señoras of a lower class occasionally try their fortune for themselves. I saw one of these, who had probably lost, by no means "taking it coolly." She looked like an over-charged thunder-cloud; but whether she broke forth in anger or in tears, thunder or rain, we did not stay to see. . . .

We returned to San Antonio by the brightest possible moonlight, and in perfect safety, it being on the highroad to Mexico, and therefore guarded by soldiers. We heard the next morning, that a nephew of General ———'s, who had ventured upon going by a cross-road to his house, at Mizcuaque, has been attacked and robbed of his winnings, besides being severely wounded. This being the natural consequence, the *morale* to the story can excite no surprise. The robbers who, in hopes of plunder, flocked down at the time of the fête, like sopilotes seeking carrion, hide themselves among the barren rocks of the *Pedregal*, and render all cross-roads insecure, except with a very strong escort.

Down the Amazon

WILLIAM LEWIS HERNDON

FROM *Exploration of the Valley of the Amazon*

1851–52

Back in the days when the United States armed forces had a somewhat broader conception of their role, a young naval officer was ordered to investigate the potentialities for commerce and colonization of the great Amazon River valley. The official report that he wrote about his mission has a flavor and perceptiveness that are definitely above and beyond the call of duty.

Lieutenant William Herndon set out from Lima in May 1851 on orders from the United States Navy. He crossed the Andes by mule and made his way down a Peruvian tributary, the Huallaga, and then down the Amazon itself to Para on the Atlantic coast. Traveling by native canoe, he covered some four thousand miles in ten months. His modest but expert account mingles vignettes of native life with observations on the wildlife, terrain and natural resources of the uncharted valley of the Amazon. It aroused much interest at the time, even inspiring Mark Twain to consider seeking his fortune in South America—and probably influencing him in his own account of life on the Mississippi.

[Setting out from Lima with several mules and muleteers, Lieutenant Herndon crosses the Cordillera and passes through the Cerro de Pasco mining region. After 335 miles and two and a half months he reaches the Huallaga and starts down it by canoe.]

BLOWGUNS AND JUNGLE MONKEYS

I saw here, for the first time, the blow-gun of the Indians, called, by the Spaniards, *cerbatana;* by the Portuguese of the river, *gravatana* (a corruption, I imagine, of the former, as I find no such Portuguese word); and by the Indians, *pucuna.* It is made of any long, straight piece of wood, generally of a species of palm called chonta—a heavy, elastic wood, of which bows, clubs, and spears are also made. The pole or staff, about eight feet in length, and two inches diameter near the mouth end (tapering down to half an inch at the extremity), is divided longitudinally; a canal is hollowed out along the centre of each part, which is well smoothed and polished by rubbing with fine sand and wood. The two parts are then brought together; nicely woolded [wrapped together] with twine; and the whole covered with wax, mixed with some resin of the forest, to make it hard. A couple of boar's teeth are fitted on each side of the mouth end, and one of the curved front teeth of a small animal resembling a cross between a squirrel and a hare, is placed on top for a sight. The arrow is made of any light wood, generally the wild cane, or the middle fibre of a species of palm-leaf, which is about a foot in length, and of the thickness of an ordinary lucifer match. The end of the arrow, which is placed next to the mouth, is wrapped with a light, delicate sort of wild cotton, which grows in a pod upon a large tree and is called *huimba;* and the other end, very sharply pointed, is dipped in a vegetable poison prepared from the juice of the creeper called *bejuco de ambihuasca,* mixed with *aji,* or strong red pepper, *barbasco, sarnango,* and whatever substances the Indians know to be deleterious. The marksman, when using his pucuna, instead of stretching out the left hand along the body of the tube, places it to his mouth by grasping it, with both hands together, close to the mouth-piece, in such a manner that it requires considerable strength in the arms to hold it out at all, much less steadily. If a practised marksman, he will kill a small bird at thirty or forty paces. In an experiment that I saw, the Indian held the pucuna horizontally, and the arrow blown from it stuck in the ground at thirty-eight paces. Commonly the Indian has quite an affection for his gun, and many superstitious notions about it. I could not persuade one to shoot a very pretty black and yellow bird for me because it was a carrion bird; and the Indian said that it would deteriorate and make useless all the poison in his gourd. Neither will he discharge his pucuna at a snake, for fear of the gun being made crooked like the reptile; and a fowling-piece or rifle that has once been discharged at an alligator is considered entirely worthless. A round gourd, with a hole in it for the huimba, and a joint of the *caña brava* as a quiver, completes the hunting apparatus.

AUGUST 3.—Went to church. The congregation—men, women, and children—numbered about fifty; the service was conducted by the governor, assisted by the alcalde. A little naked, bow-legged Indian child, of two or three years, and Ijurra's pointer puppy, which he had brought all the way from Lima on his saddle-bow, worried the congregation with their tricks and gambols; but altogether they were attentive to their prayers, and devout. I enjoyed exceedingly the public worship of God with these rude children of the forest; and, although they probably understood little of what they were about, I thought I could see its humanizing and fraternizing effect upon all.

At night we had a ball at the governor's house. The alcalde, who was a trump, produced his fiddle; another had a rude sort of guitar, or banjo; and under the excitement of his music, and the aguadiente of the governor, who had had his cane ground in anticipation of our arrival, we danced till eleven o'clock. The custom of the dance requires that a gentleman should choose a lady and dance with her, in the middle of the floor, till she gives over (the company around clapping their hands in time to the music, and cheering the dancers with *vivas* at any particular display of agility or spirit in the dance). He then presents his partner with a glass of grog, leads her to a seat, and chooses another. When he tires there is a general drink, and the lady has the choice. The *Señor Commandante* was in considerable request; and a fat old lady, who would not dance with anybody else, nearly killed me. The governor discharged our guns several times, and let off some rockets that we had brought from Huanuco; and I doubt if Tingo Maria had ever witnessed such a brilliant affair before.

AUGUST 4.—I waked up with pain in the legs and headache from dancing, and found our men and canoes ready for embarkation. After breakfast the governor and his wife (though I grievously fear that there had been no intervention of the priest in the matter of the union), together with several of our partners of the previous night, accompanied us to the port. After loading the canoes the governor made a short address to the canoemen, telling them that we "were no common persons; that they were to have a special care of us: to be very obedient, &c., and that he would put up daily prayers for their safe return"; whereupon, after a glass all round, from a bottle brought down specially by our hostess, and a hearty embrace of the governor, his lady, and my fat friend of the night before, we embarked and shoved off; the boatmen blowing their horns as we drifted rapidly down with the current of the river, and the party on shore waving their hats and shouting their adieus.

We had two canoes; the largest about forty feet long, by two and a half broad; hollowed out from a single log, and manned each by five men and a boy. They are conducted by a *puntero,* or bowman, who looks out for rocks or sunken trees ahead; a *popero,* or steersman, who stands on a little platform at the stern of the boat and guides her motions; and the *bogas* or rowers, who stand up to paddle, having one foot in the bottom of the boat and the other on the gunwale. When the river was smooth and free from obstructions, we drifted with the current; the men sitting on the trunks and boxes, chatting and laughing with each other; but, as we approached a mal-paso, their serious looks, and the firm position in which each one planted himself at his post, showed that work was to be done. I felt a little nervous at first; but when we had fairly entered the pass, the rapid gesture of the puntero, indicating the channel, the elegant and graceful position of the popero, giving the boat a broad sheer with the sweep of his long paddle, the desperate exertions of the bogas, the railroad rush of the canoe, and the wild, triumphant, screaming laugh of the Indians, as we shot past the danger, made a scene that was much too exciting to admit of any other emotion than that of admiration.

. . . It is almost impossible to estimate the distance travelled with any degree of accuracy. The force of the current is very variable, and the Indians very irregular in their manner of rowing—sometimes paddling half an hour with great vigour, and then suffering the boat to drift with the tide. Averaging the current at three and a half miles the hour, and the rowing at one and a half, with nine hours of actual travel, we have forty-five miles for a day's journey at this season. I have estimated the number of travelling hours at nine, for we get off generally at 5 A.M. and stop at 5 P.M. We spend two hours for breakfast, in the middle of the day, and another hour is lost at the shallows of the river, or stopping to get a shot at an animal or bird. . . .

These Indians have very keen senses, and see and hear things that are inaudible and invisible to us. Our canoe-men this morning commenced paddling with great vigour. I asked the cause, and they said that they heard monkeys ahead. I think we must have paddled a mile before I heard the sound they spoke of. When we came up to them, we found a gang of large red monkeys in some tall trees on the river-side, making a noise like the grunting of a herd of enraged hogs. We landed, and in a few minutes I found myself beating my way through the thick undergrowth, and hunting monkeys with as much excitement as I had ever hunted squirrels when a boy. I had no balls with me, and my No. 3 shot only served to sting them from their elevated position in the tops of the trees, and bring them within reach of the pucunas of the Indians. They got two and I one, after firing about a dozen shots into him. I never saw animals so tenacious of life; this one was, as the Indians expressed it, *bathed in shot* (*bañado en municion*). These monkeys were about the size of a common terrier-dog, and were clad with a long, soft, maroon-coloured hair; they are called *cotomonos*, from a large goitre (coto) under the jaw. This is an apparatus of thin bone in the wind-pipe, by means of which they make their peculiar noise. The male, called *curaca* (which is also the appellation of the chief of a tribe of Indians), has a long red beard. They are called *guariba* in Brazil, where they are said to be black as well as red; and I believe they are of the species commonly called *howling monkeys*.

It is scarcely worth while to say that the Indians use parts of this animal for the cure of diseases, for I know no substance that could possibly be used as a remedial agent that they do not use for that purpose. The mother carries the young upon her back until it is able to go alone. If the dam dies, the sire takes charge. There are vast numbers in all the course of the river, and no day passes to the traveller that they are not heard or seen.

When I arrived at the beach with my game, I found that the Indians had made a fire and were roasting theirs. They did not take the trouble to skin and clean the animal, but simply put him in the fire, and, when well scorched, took him off and cut pieces from the fleshy parts with a knife; if these were not sufficiently well done, they roasted them further on little stakes stuck up before the fire. I tried to eat a piece, but it was so tough that my teeth would make no impression upon it. The one I killed was *enceinte*; the foetus about double the size of a wharf-rat. I wished to preserve it, but it was too large for any bottles I had; whereupon the Indians roasted and ate it without ceremony.

[They arrive at the port of Sion.]

A Native Dance and the Lost Soul
That Became a Bird

THE town appears to have been once in a better condition than it is now. There are remains of a garden attached to the convent, and also of instruments of husbandry and manufacture—such as rude mortars, hollowed out from the trunk of a tree, for beating (with pestles) the husk from rice, and a press for putting into shape the crude wax gathered from the hollow trees by the Indians, used by the friars "lang syne"—all now seem going to decay. The people are lazy and indifferent. They cultivate plantains sufficient to give them to eat, and yuccas enough to make masato to get drunk on; and this seems all they need. Most of their time is spent in sleeping, drinking, and dancing. Yesterday they were dancing all day, having a feast preparatory to going to work to clear ground, and make a chacra for our "Lady of something," which the priest, in his recent visit, had commanded (the produce of this chacra is doubtless for the benefit of the church or its ministers); and I have no doubt that the Indians will have another feast when the job is done.

The dance was a simple affair so far as figure was concerned—the women whirling round in the centre, and the men (who were also the musicians) trotting around them in a circle. The music was made by rude drums, and fifes of reed, and it was quite amusing to see the alcalde, a large, painted, grave-looking Indian, trotting round like a dog on a tread mill, with a penny whistle at his mouth. I am told that they will dance in this way as long as there is drink, if it reach to a month. I myself have heard their music—the last thing at night as I was going to bed, and the first thing in the morning as I was getting up—for days at a time. The tune never changes, and seems to be the same everywhere in the Montaña. It is a monotonous tapping of the drum, very like our naval *beat to quarters*. . . .

AUGUST 16.—Lovely morning. On stepping out of the house my attention was attracted by a spider's web covering the whole of a large lemon tree nearly. The tree was oval and well shaped; and the web was thrown over it in the most artistic manner, and with the finest effect. Broad flat cords were stretched out, like the cords of a tent, from its circumference to the neighbouring bushes; and it looked as if some genius of the lamp, at the command of its master, had exhausted taste and skill to cover with this delicate drapery the rich-looking fruit beneath. I think the web would have measured full ten yards in diameter. . . .

After we had retired to our mats beneath the shed for the night, I asked the governor if he knew a bird called *El alma perdida*. He did not know it by that name, and requested a description. I whistled an imitation of its notes; whereupon, an old crone, stretched on a mat near us, commenced, with animated tones and gestures, a story in the Inca language, which, translated, ran somehow thus:

An Indian and his wife went out from the village to work their chacra, carrying their infant with them. The woman went to the spring to get water, leaving the man in charge of the child, with many cautions to take good care of it. When she arrived at the spring she found it dried up, and went further to look for another. The husband, alarmed at her long absence, left the child and went in search. When they returned the child was gone; and to their repeated cries, as they wandered through the woods in search, they could get no response save the wailing cry of this little bird, heard for the first time, whose notes their anxious and excited imagination "syllabled" with *pa-pa*, *ma-ma* (the present Quichua name of the bird). I suppose the Spaniards heard this story, and, with that religious poetic turn of thought which seems peculiar to this people, called the bird "The lost soul."

The circumstances under which the story was told—the beautiful still, starlight night—the deep, dark forest around—the faint-red glimmering of the fire, flickering upon the old woman's grey hair and earnest face as she poured forth the guttural tones of the language of a people now passed away—gave it a sufficiently romantic interest to an imaginative man. The old woman was a small romance in herself. I had looked at her with interest as she cooked our supper. She wore a costume that is sometimes, though not often, seen in this country. The body, or upper part of the dress, which was black, consisted of two parts—one coming up from the waist behind and covering the back, the other in front, covering the breast; the two tied together over each shoulder with strings, leaving her lank sides and long skinny arms perfectly bare.

[After travelling seven hundred miles on tributaries of the Amazon, they enter the main trunk of the great river, cross Brazil and in April 1852 reach the river's estuary and the Atlantic.]

Trial by Pain

ALAIN GHEERBRANT

FROM *Journey to the Far Amazon*

1948–50

Alain Gheerbrant was a poet and editor of a Paris magazine when his interest in primitive peoples took him to South America in 1948. After a year of preparation, he set out from Bogotá with three young companions, reached the Orinoco and followed it to its source, crossed the unexplored Sierra Parima Mountains and then sailed down the Amazon into Brazil. During their fourteen strenuous months of journeying the group lived with the poor and backward Piaroa Indians, traveled with the civilized—and civil—Maquiritares, and visited the fierce, Stone-Age Guaharibos. They made films and recordings of the Piaroans, only to lose them all when their boat overturned on the last lap of their journey.

Gheerbrant's approach to the natives is marked by a passionate desire to know their true feelings, and he writes about them not only with scrupulous fairness but with an almost mystic sympathy. In his book he describes the barbarous manhood tests of the Piaroans (see below), the way he cast a spell over them with Mozart recordings, and how he heard the ancient chant in which a Maquiritare chieftain transmits to his people the sum of the tribe's knowledge and secrets.

Not long after his return to France from the Orinoco area he made a trip to the Belgian Congo which he has described in Congo, noir et blanc (1955).

[Gheerbrant and his companions have recorded the celebrations of the Piaroa Indians during the month leading up to the manhood initiation ceremonies. The final preparations now begin.]

THE two old men crouched on the ground beside us, bending over an aluminum cooking pot such as all the stores in the Orinoco area sell to the Indians. Mario and the other men who now surrounded us looked alternately at the two old men and at the three children who stood there close together, their eyes fixed on the hands of the old chief.

Lukewarm water steamed gently in the pot and big black insects were swimming around in it.

"Twenty-fours," I murmured.

They were not the usual ants to be met with along the banks of the Orinoco, but an exceptional variety, black ants about an inch and a half in length, the biggest and most dangerous species to be found anywhere in the Amazonian forests. They have developed an enormous pair of hard, powerful pincers like surgical clamps, and in the tail there is a sting like that of a bee. This sting is used to paralyze their victims before they are devoured. The mestizos of the Orinoco declared that to be stung by such an ant meant a twenty-four-hour bout of fever, hence the name "twenty-fours."

With the precision of a watchmaker using his tweezers, the sorcerer and his assistant picked the ants out of the water one by one, holding them in the middle between finger and thumb. Now and again they were bitten, however, and the pincers bit into the flesh, closing tightly like a clasp. Without turning a hair the men would then seize the insect with the other hand and quickly remove it. The pincers were embedded so firmly in the flesh that when an ant was removed in this fashion its head came away and was left adhering to the finger. One by one the ants were fixed by the thorax in the interstices of a square piece of wickerwork about the size of a man's palm. The strips were then drawn together round the ants in such a fashion that their heads with their waving pincers protruded on one side of the wickerwork and their tails with the stings protruded on the other. Fastened in rows like this the ants gradually formed a living, wriggling square in the center of the wickerwork mat.

Mario raised his voice and began to talk in Piaroa to the three children, who were fascinated by the strange operation the sorcerer and his assistant were carrying out. Two of the children were Mario's sons, neither of them much older than perhaps twelve. The third boy might have been thirteen or even fourteen years old. Mario delivered a long lecture to them in a bantering tone. All the other men listened to what he said, nodding their heads and laughing heartily with him at the important passages, while all the time they kept their eyes fixed on the three boys.

"What are you saying to them?" I asked Mario.

"I'm telling them that the ants are for them and that it hurts. They say they are men now and there's no longer any need for them to live with the women. They can go into the little hut and see who it is that puts on the masks. They will play the trumpets and the flutes and get to know all the musical instruments. Then don't you think that they ought also to get hurt badly, just once, very badly, in front of everyone else? They must bear it like men. Without that they will never really grow up to be men, and there will be nothing to prove that they won't go off and tell the women what they've seen. So they are going to be stung by the ants, and in that way we can be quite sure that they will say nothing of what they see."

"When is the ceremony going to take place?"

"When the moon is dead. The day after tomorrow, the day of the great feast, the day we drink all the juice prepared by the women. You will see it. It will take place in the great hut when the sun is there."

He pointed to the center of the sky.

"After the drinking," he added.

Night approached. The sorcerer and his assistant went off toward the tribal hut, and the men around us dispersed. A moment or so later the first notes of the flutes sounded from the edge of the lagoon and their melody rose softly to the village. One star after the other began to appear in the sky. The moon came out, touching the silhouette of a tall and bosky tree. It was now no more than a small horizontal crescent, a brilliant milky yellow, somewhat the color of the cassava brew which was already fermenting in the canoes and awaiting the hour of the final ceremony. The trumpets began to sound from the other side of the village, something like swine grunting in the night, responding to the sound of the flutes and blindly punctuating their melody.

We had gone back to our hut and we lay in our hammocks discussing the work to be done tomorrow and the day after if we were to miss nothing of what was going on. At last we had grasped the significance of the celebrations. The harvest festival was in reality an initiatory rite for the induction of the adolescents of the tribe into man's estate. All that we had seen during the greater part of a month, and everything that we had filmed and recorded, represented the propitiatory ceremonies carried out before the great day itself. To film the initiation of the children, which was to take place in the tribal hut, would not be easy. We should not be able to take repeat shots as we had done with the ceremony of the masks. In this case we should have to work throughout a ceremony whose various phases were unknown to us, reacting speedily according to the circumstances as they arose, quickly moving our camera, the battery of accumulators and our portable arc light. We should also have to persuade the sorcerer to let us place our apparatus as close to the scene as possible.

[The morning of the ritual finally arrives.]

AT seven o'clock in the morning the masked priests uncovered the two canoes of fermented cassava juice and the old sorcerer gave the order for the drinking to begin. A large space had been cleared around the two canoes. In the center of the tribal hut a small stool had been set up. It was carved out of one piece of some dark wood and it represented the ritual seat from which the spiritual leader of the tribe officiated at the ceremony. The old man sat down on the stool. An old woman came forward and took the first calabash of liquid from the larger of the two canoes and brought it to him. A man was crouching on the ground before him. The old man slowly raised the calabash and made three circles with it round his head and across his chest and then three circles over the head of the man before him, to whom he then handed the calabash. The man drank the contents straight off and rose. A woman took the empty calabash from him and handed him a full one. In the meantime a second man had advanced toward the old sorcerer to receive his first calabash. Then came a third and a fourth, and so on and on until all the men had come forward. They were followed by all the women and their children.

The old sorcerer sat there stripped to the waist, performing his office impassively, repeating the same ritual gestures to each member of the tribe who came forward. When the last calabash of liquid had been handed over he still did not move from his seat. Lighting one of his large cigarettes rolled in banana leaf, he began to smoke quietly. All around him and out in the square, which could be seen through the wide open door, the cassava-juice orgy began.

He was the only one who did not drink. He was the one who watched, the one who knew, the one who led his people through the ceremonies of the sacred day as he led them every night with his prayers and his invocation of the spirits.

The orgy gradually increased in vehemence, as though in accordance with the slow movement of the sun as it rose higher and higher in the sky. Most of the tribe had now moved out into the square. Some of them drank standing up, others sitting or even lying down. Attentive women handed round brimming calabashes of cassava juice and saw to their replenishment as soon as they were empty, going swiftly backward and forward from the square to the two big canoes in the tribal hut. Each calabash held about a quart of liquid, and before long the stomachs of the drinkers could hold no more, and after each calabash they had to vomit before they could drink the succeeding one. They simply bent their heads forward to vomit, and then they bent them back to drink. Gradually the ground all around them turned into a shallow lake of yellowish liquid in which they stood or sat. While we were filming this scene Mario did not move from our side. Women whose hair was decorated with strips of liana and glistening from the amount of vegetable oil applied to it came up to us smiling and offered us calabashes, their fingers half in the liquid. They had stuck gaily colored feathers in their hair and their shining faces were painted with complicated patterns. We could not always refuse to drink, and before long our stomachs began to swell too. Jean began to have difficulty in managing his camera at all. In the end we vomited too, and as we did so a great shout of delight went up from the Indians. We went on with our filming.

We noticed that Mario was following our example and drinking as little as he could. However, the Piaroan drinking ritual was strict and there were no heel taps. He had to drink with the others, but our presence embarrassed him. He was unwilling to behave like a real Indian in front of us. He was afraid of what we might think of him. When we took a close-up of a man who was vomiting in great streams his face became severe and he looked anxiously at us. We took care not to laugh or to show disgust at the spectacle, and we began to take the side of the Indians against him, applauding those who drank and vomited most, particularly his own brother and his wife, who were leaning against the wall of the tribal hut and drinking calabash after calabash. We explained to him that the only reason that we did not do the same was because of our work: we had to keep reasonably sober if we were to operate our apparatus right to the end of the ceremony.

The old sorcerer went by. He walked slowly and his face was grave. He looked round at the men, the women and the children, and watched to see that each one did his duty. Gradually the level of the liquid in the two canoes began to sink. Many hundreds of quarts had already been scooped out to flow into the stomachs of the Indians and then be vomited out again. Naturally, we were wondering what reason there could be for such deliberate and forced excess. Why did all these people have to swallow such enormous quantities of the cassava juice? I used the word orgy, and yet I could not help feeling that it was not an orgy in the sense in which we understood the word. Among all these men and women there was no one who was really drunk. Indeed, how could anyone get drunk on liquid which could hardly have contained more than three degrees of alcohol? No, there must be some other explanation.

All these Indians were preparing themselves for the coming test. They were preparing themselves for the one object toward which the ceremonies we had been privileged to witness since the beginning of the ritual month all converged. During the night all the men of the tribe had followed the example of the old sorcerer and taken niopo, and at dawn their spirits had not entirely returned to their bodies. Indeed, it was necessary that this should be so and that the men should not be in a normal state. The desired *other* state was attained both physically and mentally by progressive relaxation, during which the whole organism gradually approached a state of total surrender. After about two hundred gallons of liquid had passed rapidly through their bodies they would have attained the necessary freedom of soul.

No doubt there was a profounder and more complex significance to the ritual but I feel that was as much as I managed to grasp, and what I have tried to convey here approximates the truth. It is enough for me to recall the concentrated, almost ecstatic, faces of those men and women, who were, so to speak, taken possession of, ravished, by the vast quantities of liquid they took into themselves and then vomited out, to know that something of the sort was true.

They had gone beyond their ordinary, everyday world and were feeling their way forward into the unknown spaces of their tribal destiny under the guidance of the tranquil old sorcerer who was in charge of their souls. And part of his task was to guide the boys safely through the initiatory rites to the great culmination which would make them into men.

I looked around for the young neophytes, and after a while I saw them. They were sprawled on the ground quite incapable of taking any further part in the proceedings on their own initiative. Their relatives were around them, attending to them zealously and pouring calabash after calabash of liquid into their open mouths. They had to drink more than anyone else, and soon the cassava juice was being pumped out of their mouths almost as it was poured in.

Gradually the scene grew calmer. One after the other the drinkers returned to the tribal hut as the old sorcerer gave the signal to stop drinking. It was just midday and there were no shadows on the ground. The puddles of yellowish liquid steamed in the sun. Then the sound of maracas came from the tribal hut and the five masked priests appeared again. They gathered round the three boys who were soon to be men and took them by the arms, leading them, half carrying them toward the hut. The boys dragged along the ground between the long fringes of the costumes of the tiger priests. The priests made their way across the village square, dancing backward and forward slowly, and then they went into the hut. Men crowded forward to meet them and took the boys from their arms. Across their backs the boys each carried a package done up with liana. The package contained the hammock which an Indian always takes with him on a journey. These hammocks were now unfolded and slung to the nearest posts in the hut, and the masked priests picked up the boys and laid them in them. Then they left the hut. The old sorcerer had sat down on his stool again to the right of the canoes, which were now almost empty. To his side, on the floor, were various accessories: two flat pieces of wickerwork, long cigarettes of green tobacco rolled in banana leaf, and a calabash of cassava juice. The five masked priests reappeared. On the forehead of each one, in place of the usual painted design, was a rectangular piece of wickerwork containing two hundred imprisoned and wriggling ants, black and shining. Facing the old sorcerer, they danced from one foot to the other while their acolytes detached the five pieces of wickerwork containing the ants from their headdress and placed them at the feet of the sorcerer. Then the tiger priests retreated a couple of paces and began to pant louder and louder. This was the original chant of the tribe, the chant of the tigers who had brought the first infant Piaroas to the earth in their claws.

One of the boys got out of his hammock and went toward the old sorcerer with a firm and assured step and sat down facing the old man on a second stool which had been placed there. He looked into the old man's face, and leaning forward he placed his hands on the old man's knees. The ceremony of initiation was about to begin.

The old man picked up one of the squares of wickerwork with the ants. The masked priests no longer chanted. In the absolute silence which now prevailed one could hear the wild clicking movements of the legs and pincers of the ants. But apparently the insects were still not sufficiently excited to sting at once and all together as the ritual required, so the old sorcerer dipped the wickerwork square into the calabash of liquid at his side. Then taking a lighted cigarette he gently blew the smoke over the ants. The blue fumes filtered through the wickerwork and rose up to the roof of the hut. The wild excitement of the ants caused the sound of their struggles to increase in volume like the crackling of a fire as it flares up. Holding the square in his hands, the old man described three circles with it as he had done earlier with the first calabash of liquid. Leaning forward, he described another three circles round the head of the seated boy. Up to then the old man had held the square so that the heads of the ants were facing the boy. Now he turned it round. Several men stepped forward and seized the boy by the wrists and the head, and the old man then placed the square on the boy's chest. This time two hundred abdomens of the giant ants touched the boy's flesh and two hundred stings penetrated simultaneously, injecting their venom. The boy's body suddenly contracted, but he forced it back. A large hand closed over his mouth firmly to prevent him from crying out.

Slowly the old man moved the wickerwork square over the most sensitive parts of the boy's body. He performed the operation with great care and a minimum of movement. It went on for two, three, four minutes, and then finally the ants were passed in a last slow, caressing movement over the cheeks and forehead of the boy. The men released their grip. The boy's body straightened. He still sat there with his hands on the old man's knees without moving. In the eyes of all he was now a man. His eyelids opened slowly and a somnambulistic look filtered between the lashes. A woman came forward and bathed his chest, his arms and his back with a little of the liquid which she scooped out of the calabash with the palm of her hand. The old man had taken up his cigarette again and now he puffed great clouds of bluish smoke over the body of the tortured boy.

Until then the lad's eyes had been half closed; now they opened wide. He looked around slowly, as though astonished. He seemed to have returned from another world, or to have entered a world which was completely new to him. He stood up, walked back to his hammock and lay down. From all parts of the great hut now wreathed in smoke rose a long, shrill cry. It was a shout of triumph from a community which now had another man in its ranks.

The second boy came forward and took his place in front of the old sorcerer. Behind him the masked priests performed their dance and panted the chant of the tigers to the rhythm of their maracas. The lad suffered the torture of the initiation in his turn, and then the third boy took his place.

If this Indian ritual is hard for the boys, it is no less hard for the adults. It demands that those who watch must also suffer, and therefore after the last of the three boys had gone through the initiatory ritual, all the men came forward one by one, and then all the women, to sit before the old sorcerer and submit to the imposition of the wickerwork and ant screens, though the squares used for the women were not so large. When Mario's turn came the old man took particular care to see that his ordeal should be greater than that of the others because he was the chief. In the middle of it Mario fainted. Four men sprang forward at once to raise him up again. Imperturbably the old sorcerer continued to pass the ants over the flesh of Mario's inert body. We knew that on our account Mario had not drunk so much as the others and now he had not the same resistance to the torture. He had to suffer his ordeal to the very end.

Then came the turn of the women. They came forward arrogantly and defiantly to sit before the sorcerer. Instead of putting their hands on his knees they put them behind their heads, their elbows raised high and spread wide to lift their naked breasts proudly and present them in the most favorable position. While the ant screens were being applied to them they affected a complete indifference to the pain. They even seemed to be very proud to be the center of attention. Not a muscle of their faces twitched and they had no need of any assistance. They did not even wink an eyelid, but continued to chat in high-pitched tones with their friends during the whole ordeal, and not once did their voices break. One would have said that they felt nothing at all. When it was over they walked back to their hammocks with a firm tread and then collapsed into a coma.

I rose, covered with sweat and dust, for I had spent the whole ceremony lying flat on the ground holding the battery of accumulators, while Pierre lit up the various phases of the torture with our lamp and Jean took reel after reel of film. The old sorcerer had forbidden us to film the torture of the women, but we had been able to record all the details of the initiatory rites suffered by the three boys and the subsequent ordeal of the men. . . .

[That night they hear a girl screaming. The following morning they question the chief, Mario, about it.]

HE then explained that the cries we had heard in the night had really been those of a young girl. In her dreams she had suffered the tortures of the stinging all over again.

"If the full celebrations had taken place, as they do on the Sipapo, you would have heard still more," he added.

"What!" exclaimed Pierre. "The celebrations weren't complete, then?"

"No," he replied, "the old man didn't want to, because of you. There should have been twice as much to drink, for one thing. And then in the morning, after the ordeal of the ants, the children would have been whipped in the village square while the masked priests moved around them in a circle in the dance of the whales. They dance round and round, and the palm leaves are pushed back from their faces. It is then usually that the children see for the first time who it is beneath the masks. Everybody gets whipped, and everyone drinks twice as much. But, you see, after that our men go mad for four or five days, and if they had turned on you and killed you we should have had trouble with the white men. That was why the old man didn't want to have the full celebrations."

We passed the rest of the day filming one or two scenes we needed to join up our previous material, and the next morning the time came for us to leave. Our things were loaded on board our canoe and we pushed off.

America North

Visit to a Virgin Coast

PHILIP AMADAS and
ARTHUR BARLOW

FROM *The First Voyage Made to the Coast of Virginia*

1584

Plunging into England's belated efforts to gain a foothold in the New World, Sir Walter Raleigh sent an expedition to the coast of America in 1584. Little is known of the two captains of the expedition, Philip Amadas and Arthur Barlow, but according to Barlow's account their voyage by way of the West Indies was one of the few uneventful ones of the period and their experiences on reaching the coast of what is now North Carolina were most agreeable. In fact modern historians feel that they probably suppressed some of the less rosy aspects of their reception by the Indians in order not to discourage prospective colonists. At any rate, Barlow's brief but glowing report to Raleigh led Queen Elizabeth to give the name Virginia to the land (not to be confused with modern Virginia) and paved the way for Raleigh in 1587 to send out the settlers who were to establish the ill-fated colony on Roanoke Island.

The description below is taken from Barlow's report to Raleigh.

THE 27th day of April in the year of our redemption, 1584, we departed the west of England with two barks well furnished with men and victuals, having received our last and perfect directions by your letters, confirming the former instructions and commandments delivered by yourself at our leaving the river Thames. And I think it a matter both

779

unnecessary, for the manifest discovery of the country as also for tedious-
ness' sake, to remember unto you the diurnal of our course, sailing
thither and returning: only I have presumed to present unto you this
brief discourse, by which you may judge how profitable this land is
likely to succeed . . .

The second of July we found shoal water, where we smelled so sweet
and so strong a smell, as if we had been in the midst of some delicate
garden abounding with all kind of odoriferous flowers, by which we were
assured that the land could not be far distant: and keeping good watch,
and bearing but slack sail, the fourth of the same month we arrived upon
the coast, which we supposed to be a continent and firm land, and we
sailed along the same 120 English miles before we could find any entrance
or river issuing into the sea. The first that appeared unto us we entered,
though not without some difficulty, and cast anchor about three harquebus-
shot within the haven's mouth, on the left hand of the same: and after
thanks given to God for our safe arrival thither we manned our boats
and went to view the land next adjoining, and to take possession of the
same, in the right of the Queen's most excellent Majesty, as rightful
Queen, and Princess of the same, and after delivered the same over to
your use, according to Her Majesty's grant, and letters patents, under
Her Highness' great seal. Which being performed, according to the ceremonies used in such enterprises, we viewed the land about us, being,
whereas we first landed, very sandy and low towards the water's side, but
so full of grapes, as the very beating and surge of the sea overflowed them
of which we found such plenty, as well there as in all places else, both
on the sand and on the green soil on the hills as in the plains, as well
on every little shrub, as also climbing towards the tops of high cedars,
that I think in all the world the like abundance is not to be found. . . .

We passed from the seaside towards the tops of those hills next
adjoining, being but of mean height, and from thence we beheld the sea
on both sides to the north and to the south, finding no end any of both
ways. This land lay stretching itself to the west, which after we found
to be but an island twenty miles long and not above six miles broad.
Under the bank or hill whereon we stood, we beheld the valleys replenished
with goodly cedar trees, and having discharged our harquebus-shot, such
a flock of cranes (the most part white) arose under us, with such a cry
redoubled by many echoes, as if an army of men had shouted all together.

This island had many goodly woods full of deer, conies, hares, and
fowl, even in the midst of summer in incredible abundance. The woods
are not such as you find in Bohemia, Moscovia, or Hercynia, barren and

fruitless, but the highest and reddest cedars of the world, far bettering the cedars of the Azores, of the Indies, or Lybanus, pines, cypress, sassafras, the lentisk, or the tree that beareth the mastic, the tree that beareth the rine of black cinnamon, which Master Winter brought from the Straights of Magellan, and many other of excellent smell and quality. We remained by the side of this island two whole days before we saw any people of the country. The third day we espied one small boat rowing towards us having in it three persons: this boat came to the island side, four harquebus-shot from our ships, and there two of the people remaining, the third came along the shoreside towards us, and we being then all within board, he walked up and down upon the point of the land next unto us. Then the Master and the Pilot of the Admiral, Simon Ferdinando, and Captain Philip Amadas, myself, and others rowed to the land, whose coming this fellow attended, never making any show of fear or doubt. And after he had spoken of many things not understood by us, we brought him with his own good liking aboard the ships, and gave him a shirt, a hat and some other things, and made him taste of our wine and our meat, which he liked very well: and after having viewed both barks, he departed, and went to his own boat again, which he had left in a little cove or creek adjoining. As soon as he was two bow-shot into the water he fell to fishing and in less than half an hour he had laden his boat as deep as it could swim, with which he came again to the point of the land and there he divided his fish into two parts, pointing one part to the ship and the other to the pinnace: which, after he had (as much as he might) requited the former benefits received, departed out of our sight.

The next day there came unto us divers boats, and in one of them the King's brother, accompanied with forty or fifty men, very handsome and goodly people, and in their behaviour as mannerly and civil as any of Europe. His name was Granganimo, and the King is called Wingina, the country Wingandacoa, and now by Her Majesty Virginia. The manner of his coming was in this sort: he left his boats, altogether as the first man did, a little from the ships by the shore, and came along to the place over against the ships, followed with forty men. When he came to the place, his servants spread a long mat upon the ground on which he sat down, and at the other end of the mat four others of his company did the like. The rest of his men stood round about him, somewhat afar off. When we came to the shore to him with our weapons, he never moved from his place, nor any of the other four, nor never mistrusted any harm to be offered from us, but sitting still he beckoned us to come and sit by him, which we performed: and being set he made all signs of joy and welcome, striking on his head and his breast, and afterwards on ours, to show we were all one, smiling and making show the best he could of all love and familiarity. After he had made a long speech unto us, we presented him with divers things, which he received very joyfully and thankfully. None of the company durst speak one word all the time: only the four which were at the other end spake one in the others' ears very softly.

The King is greatly obeyed, and his brothers and children reverenced: the King himself in person was at our being there sore wounded in a fight which he had with the king of the next country, and was shot in two places through the body, and once clean through the thigh, but yet he recovered: by reason whereof, and for that he lay at the chief town of the country, being six days' journey off, we saw him not at all.

After we had presented this his brother with such things as we thought he liked, we likewise gave somewhat to the other that sat with him on the mat: but presently he arose and took all from them and put it into his own basket, making signs and tokens that all things ought to be delivered unto him, and the rest were but his servants and followers. A day or two after this, we fell to trading with them, exchanging some things that we had, for chamois, buff, and deer skins. When we showed him all our packet of merchandise, of all things that he saw, a bright tin dish most pleased him, which he presently took up and clapped it before his breast, and after made a hole in the brim thereof and hung it about his neck, making signs that it would defend him against his enemies' arrows: for these people maintain a deadly and terrible war with the people and king adjoining.

We exchanged our tin dish for twenty skins, worth twenty crowns, or twenty nobles: and a copper kettle for fifty skins worth fifty crowns. They offered us good exchange for our hatchets and axes, and for knives, and would have given anything for swords: but we would not part with any. After two or three days the King's brother came aboard the ships, and drank wine, and ate of our meat and of our bread, and liked exceedingly thereof: and after a few days overpassed, he brought his wife with him to the ships, his daughter and two or three children. His wife was very well favoured, of mean stature, and very bashful. She had on her back a long cloak of leather, with the fur side next to her body, and before her a piece of the same: about her forehead she had a band of white coral, and so had her husband many times: in her ears she had bracelets of pearls hanging down to her middle (whereof we delivered your worship a little bracelet), and those were of the bigness of good peas. The rest of her women of the better sort had pendants of copper hanging in either ear, and some of the children of the King's brother and other noblemen have five or six in either ear. He himself had upon his head a broad plate of gold, or copper, for being unpolished we knew not what metal it should be, neither would he by any means suffer us to take it off his head, but feeling it, it would bow very easily. His apparel was as his wives'; only the women wear their hair long on both sides, and the men but on one. They are of colour yellowish, and their hair black for the most part, and yet we saw children that had very fine auburn and chestnut-coloured hair.

. . . Their boats are made of one tree, either of pine or of pitch trees: a wood not commonly known to our people, nor found growing in England. They have no edge-tools to make them withal: if they have any they are very few, and those it seems they had twenty years since, which, as those two men declared, was out of a wreck which happened upon their coast of some Christian ship, being beaten that way by some storm and outrageous weather, whereof none of the people were saved, but only the ship, or some part of her being cast upon the sand, out of whose sides they drew the nails and the spikes, and with those they made their best instruments. The manner of making their boats is thus: they burn down some great tree, or take such as are wind-fallen, and putting gum and rosin upon one side thereof, they set fire into it, and when it hath burnt it hollow, they cut out the coal with their shells, and ever where they would burn it deeper or wider they lay on gums, which burn away the timber, and by this means they fashion very fine boats, and such as will transport twenty men. Their oars are like scoops, and many times they set with long poles, as the depth serveth.

The King's brother had great liking of our armour, a sword, and divers other things which we had: and offered to lay a great box of pearls in gage for them: but we refused it for this time, because we would not make them know that we esteemed thereof, until we had understood in which places of the country the pearls grew: which now Your Worship doth very well understand.

He was very just of his promise: for many times we delivered him merchandise upon his word, but ever he came within the day and performed his promise. He sent us every day a brace or two of fat bucks, conies, hares, fish the best of the world. He sent us divers kinds of fruits, melons, walnuts, cucumbers, gourds, peas, and divers roots, and fruits very excellent good, and of their country corn, which is very white, fair and well tasted, and groweth three times in five months: in May they sow, in July they reap, in June they sow, in August they reap, in July they sow, in September they reap: only they cast the corn into the ground, breaking a little of the soft turf with a wooden mattock, or pickaxe: ourselves proved the soil, and put some of our peas in the ground, and in ten days they were fourteen inches high. They have also beans very fair of divers colours and wonderful plenty: some growing naturally and some in their gardens, and so have they both wheat and oats.

The soil is the most plentiful, sweet, fruitful and wholesome of all the world. There are above fourteen several sweet-smelling timber trees, and the most part of their underwoods are bays and such like. They have those oaks that we have, but far greater and better. After they had been divers times aboard our ships, myself with seven more went twenty mile into the river that runneth toward the city of Skicoak, which river they call Occam: and the evening following we came to an island which they call Roanoak, distant from the harbour by which we entered, seven leagues: and at the north end thereof was a village of nine houses built of cedar and fortified round about with sharp trees to keep out their enemies, and the entrance into it made like a turnpike very artificially. When we came towards it, standing near unto the water's side, the wife of Granganimo the King's brother came running out to meet us very cheerfully and friendly, her husband not then in the village; some of her people she commanded to draw our boat on shore for the beating of the billows: others she appointed to carry us on their backs to the dry ground, and others to bring our oars into the house for fear of stealing. When we were come into the outer room, having five rooms in her house, she caused us to sit down by a great fire, and after took off our clothes and washed them, and dried them again. Some of the women plucked off our stockings and washed them, some washed our feet in warm water, and she herself took great pains to see all things ordered in the best manner she could, making great haste to dress some meat for us to eat.

After we had thus dried ourselves, she brought us into the inner room, where she set on the board standing along the house some wheat like fermenty, sodden venison, and roasted, fish sodden, boiled, and roasted, melons raw, and sodden, roots of divers kinds, and divers fruits. Their drink is commonly water, but while the grape lasteth they drink wine, and for want of casks to keep it, all the year after they drink water, but it is sodden with ginger in it, and black cinnamon, and sometimes sassafras, and divers other wholesome and medicinable herbs and trees. We were entertained with all love and kindness, and with as much bounty (after their manner) as they could possibly devise. We found the people most gentle, loving, and faithful, void of all guile and treason, and such as live after the manner of the golden age. The people only care how to defend themselves from the cold of their short winter, and to feed themselves with such meat as the soil affordeth. Their meat is very well sodden and they make broth very sweet and savoury. Their vessels are earthen pots, very large, white and sweet, their dishes are wooden platters of sweet timber. Within the place where they feed was their lodging, and within that their Idol, which they worship, of whom they speak incredible things. While we were at meat, there came in at the gates two or three men with their bows and arrows from hunting, whom when we espied, we began to look one towards another and offered to reach our weapons: but as soon as she espied our mistrust, she was very much moved and caused some of her men to run out and take away their bows and arrows and break them, and withal beat the poor fellows out of the gate again. When we departed in the evening and would not tarry all night, she was very sorry, and gave us into our boat our supper half dressed, pots and all, and brought us to our boatside, in which we lay all night, removing the same a pretty distance from the shore. She perceiving our jealousy, was much grieved, and sent divers men and thirty women to sit all night on the bankside by us, and sent us into our boats five mats to cover us from the rain, using very many words to entreat us to rest in their houses: but because we were few men, and if we had miscarried, the voyage had been in very great danger, we durst not adventure anything, though there was no cause of doubt: for a more kind and loving people there can not be found in the world, as far as we have hitherto had trial.

Life among the Hurons

SAMUEL DE CHAMPLAIN

FROM *Voyages of Samuel de Champlain*

1604–18

Compared to the savagery of a Pizarro or a Cortés, the attitude of the Frenchman Samuel de Champlain toward natives seems reasonable and humane. Despite the violence almost inseparable from exploration and settlement in a wilderness world, his dealings with the Indians were characterized by conscience and a sense of responsibility.

Long in love with the sea, he made his first major voyage as captain of a vessel going to the West Indies. After two years in the Spanish colonies of the Caribbean and Mexico he returned to France in 1601 and published a very able report on his observations. He then decided to explore the lands to the north that the Spanish did not dominate, which Jacques Cartier had opened up in the 1530s. Going back across the Atlantic, he reconnoitered the St. Lawrence region and came home with a cargo of furs and an account of the land and its natives. In 1604 he returned to North America and for several years tried to get a colony started on Nova Scotia, meanwhile exploring the coast as far south as Cape Cod.

Finally, in 1608, he established at Quebec the first permanent French settlement in America. It was about this time that he discovered Lake Champlain and helped a war party of Hurons defeat the Iroquois, thereby, it is said, earning for France the enduring enmity of the Iroquois. After establishing a trading post at Quebec, he explored the Lake Huron area until he was wounded during another engagement between Hurons and Iroquois. For most of his remaining years he worked to strengthen the Quebec settlement, winning the respect of colonists, his countrymen in France, and Hurons alike.

786

[Accompanying a party of Hurons, Champlain discovers the lake that bears his name and helps the Hurons in a battle with the Iroquois.]

LAKE CHAMPLAIN AND THE BATTLE WITH THE IROQUOIS

THE next day we entered the lake, which is of great extent, say eighty or a hundred leagues long, where I saw four fine islands, ten, twelve, and fifteen leagues long, which were formerly inhabited by the savages, like the River of the Iroquois; but they have been abandoned since the wars of the savages with one another prevail. There are also many rivers falling into the lake, bordered by many fine trees of the same kinds as those we have in France, with many vines finer than any I have seen in any other place; also many chestnut trees on the border of this lake, which I had not seen before. There is also a great abundance of fish, of many varieties; among others, one called by the savages of the country *chaousarou* [the garpike], which varies in length, the largest being, as the people told me, eight or ten feet long. I saw some five feet long, which were as large as my thigh; the head being as big as my two fists, with a snout two feet and a half long, and a double row of very sharp and dangerous teeth. . . .

Continuing our course over this lake on the western side, I noticed, while observing the country, some very high mountains on the eastern side, on the top of which there was snow. I made inquiry of the savages whether these localities were inhabited, when they told me that the Iroquois dwelt there, and that there were beautiful valleys in these places, with plains productive in grain, such as I had eaten in this country, together with many kinds of fruit without limit. They said also that the lake extended near mountains, some twenty-five leagues distant from us, as I judge. I saw, on the south, other mountains, no less than the first, but without any snow [the Adirondacks]. The savages told me that these mountains were thickly settled, and that it was there we were to find their enemies; but that it was necessary to pass a fall in order to go there (which I afterward saw), when we should enter another lake [Lake George], nine or ten leagues long. After reaching the end of the lake, we should have to go, they said, two leagues by land, and pass through a river [the Hudson] flowing into the sea on the Norumbegue coast . . .

Now, as we began to approach within two or three days' journey of the abode of their enemies, we advanced only at night, resting during the day. But they did not fail to practice constantly their accustomed superstitions, in order to ascertain what was to be the result of their undertaking; and they often asked me if I had had a dream, and seen their enemies, to which I replied in the negative. Yet I did not cease to encourage them, and inspire in them hope. . . .

When it was evening, we embarked in our canoes to continue our course; and, as we advanced very quietly and without making any noise, we met on the twenty-ninth of the month the Iroquois, about ten o'clock at evening, at the extremity of a cape which extends into the lake on the western bank. They had come to fight. We both began to utter loud cries, all getting their arms in readiness. We withdrew out on the water, and the Iroquois went on shore, where they drew up all their canoes close to each other and began to fell trees with poor axes, which they acquire in war sometimes, using also others of stone. Thus they barricaded themselves very well.

Our forces also passed the entire night, their canoes being drawn up close to each other, and fastened to poles, so that they might not get separated, and that they might be all in readiness to fight, if occasion required. We were out upon the water, within arrow range of their barricades. When they were armed and in array, they dispatched two canoes by themselves to the enemy to inquire if they wished to fight, to which the latter replied that they wanted nothing else; but they said that, at present, there was not much light, and that it would be necessary to wait for daylight, so as to be able to recognize each other; and that, as soon as the sun rose, they would offer us battle. This was agreed to by our side. Meanwhile, the entire night was spent in dancing and singing, on both sides, with endless insults and other talk; as, how little courage we had, how feeble a resistance we should make against their arms, and that, when day came, we should realize it to our ruin. Ours also were not slow in retorting, telling them they would see such execution of arms as never before, together with an abundance of such talk as is not unusual in the siege of a town. After this singing, dancing, and bandying words on both sides to the fill, when day came, my companions and myself continued under cover, for fear that the enemy would see us. We arranged our arms in the best manner possible, being, however, separated, each in one of the canoes of the savage Montagnais. After arming ourselves with light armor, we each took a arquebus, and went on shore. I saw the enemy go out of their barricade, nearly two hundred in number, stout and rugged in appearance. They came at a slow pace toward us, with a dignity and assurance which greatly amused me, having three chiefs at their head. Our men also advanced in the same order, telling me that those who had three large plumes were the chiefs, and that they had only these three, and that they could be distinguished by these plumes, which were much larger than those of their companions, and that I should do what I could to kill them. I promised to do all in my power, and said that I was very sorry they could not understand me, so that I might give order and shape to their mode of attacking their enemies, and then we should, without doubt, defeat them all; but that this could not now be obviated, and that I should be very glad to show them my courage and good will when we should engage in the fight.

As soon as we had landed, they began to run for some two hundred paces toward their enemies, who stood firmly, not having as yet noticed my companions, who went into the woods with some savages. Our men began to call me with loud cries; and, in order to give me a passageway, they opened in two parts and put me at their head, where I marched some twenty paces in advance of the rest, until I was within about thirty paces of the enemy, who at once noticed me and, halting, gazed at me, as I did also at them. When I saw them making a move to fire at us, I rested my musket against my cheek, and aimed directly at one of the three chiefs. With the same shot, two fell to the ground; and one of their men was so wounded that he died some time after. I had loaded my musket with four balls. When our side saw this shot so favorable for them, they began to raise such loud cries that one could not have heard it thunder. Meanwhile, the arrows flew on both sides. The Iroquois were greatly astonished that two men had been so quickly killed, although they were equipped with armor woven from cotton thread, and with wood which was proof against their arrows. This caused great alarm among them. As I was loading again, one of my companions fired a shot from the woods, which astonished them anew to such a degree that, seeing their chiefs dead, they lost courage and took flight, abandoning their camp and fort, and fleeing into the woods, whither I pursued them, killing still more of them. Our savages also killed several of them, and took ten or twelve prisoners. The remainder escaped with the wounded. Fifteen or sixteen were wounded on our side with arrow shots; but they were soon healed.

After gaining the victory, our men amused themselves by taking a great quantity of Indian corn and some meal from their enemies, also their armor, which they had left behind that they might run better. After feasting sumptuously, dancing and singing, we returned three hours after, with the prisoners. The spot where this attack took place is in latitude 43 degrees and some minutes, and the lake has been named Lake Champlain.

After going some eight leagues, toward evening they took one of the prisoners, to whom they made a harangue, enumerating the cruelties which he and his men had already practiced toward them without any mercy, and that, in like manner, he ought to make up his mind to receive as much. They commanded him to sing, if he had courage, which he did; but it was a very sad song.

Meanwhile, our men kindled a fire; and, when it was well burning, they each took a brand, and burned this poor creature gradually, so as to make him suffer greater torment. Sometimes they stopped, and threw water on his back. Then they tore out his nails, and applied fire to the extremities of his fingers and private member. Afterward, they flayed the top of his head, and had a kind of gum poured all hot upon it; then they pierced his arms near the wrists, and, drawing up the sinews with sticks, they tore them out by force; but, seeing that they could not get them, they cut them. This poor wretch uttered terrible cries, and it excited my pity to see him treated in this manner, and yet showing such firmness that one would have said, at times, that he suffered hardly any pain at all. I remonstrated with them, saying that we practiced no such cruelties, but killed them at once; and that, if they wished me to fire a musket shot at him, I should be willing to do so. They refused, saying that he would not in that case suffer any pain. I went away from them pained to see such cruelties as they practiced upon his body. When they saw that I was displeased, they called me, and told me to fire a musket shot at him. This I did without his seeing it, and thus put an end, by a single shot, to all the torments he would have suffered, rather than see him tyrannized over. After his death, they were not yet satisfied, but opened him, and threw his entrails into the lake. Then they cut off his head, arms, and legs, which they scattered in different directions; keeping the scalp, which they had flayed off, as they had done in the case of all the rest whom they had killed in the contest. They were guilty also of another monstrosity in taking his heart, cutting it into several pieces, and giving it to a brother of his to eat, as also to others of his companions, who were prisoners; they took it into their mouths, but would not swallow it. Some Algonquin savages, who were guarding them, made some of them spit it out, when they threw it into the water. This is the manner in which these people behave toward those whom they capture in war, for whom it would be better to die fighting, or to kill themselves on the spur of the moment, as many do, rather than fall into the hands of their enemies. After this execution, we set out on our return with the rest of the prisoners, who kept singing as they went along, with no better hopes for the future than he had had who was so wretchedly treated. . . .

[The following is taken from a summation in Champlain's last book, *Voyages and Discoveries in New France from 1615 to 1618*, of all that he had learned of the Hurons.]

THE WAYS OF THE HURONS

THE country of the nation of the Attigouantans is in latitude 44° 30′, and extends two hundred and thirty leagues in length westerly, and ten in breadth. It contains eighteen villages, six of which are enclosed and fortified by palisades of wood in triple rows, bound together, on the top of which are galleries, which they provide with stones and water, the former to hurl upon their enemies and the latter to extinguish the fire which their enemies may set to the palisades. The country is pleasant, most of it cleared up. It has the shape of Brittany and is similarly situated, being almost surrounded by the Mer Douce [Lake Huron]. They assume that these eighteen villages are inhabited by two thousand warriors, not including the common mass, which amounts to perhaps thirty thousand souls.

Their cabins are in the shape of tunnels or arbors and are covered with the bark of trees. They are from twenty-five to thirty fathoms long, more or less, and six wide, having a passageway through the middle from ten to twelve feet wide, which extends from one end to the other. On the two sides there is a kind of bench, four feet high, where they sleep in summer, in order to avoid the annoyance of the fleas, of which there were great numbers. In winter they sleep on the ground on mats near the fire, so as to be warmer than they would be on the platform. They lay up a stock of dry wood, with which they fill their cabins, to burn in winter. At the extremity of the cabins there is a space, where they preserve their Indian corn, which they put into great casks made of the bark of trees and placed in the middle of their encampment. They have pieces of wood suspended, on which they put their clothes, provisions and other things, for fear of the mice, of which there are great numbers. In one of these cabins there may be twelve fires, and twenty-four families. It smokes excessively, from which it follows that many receive serious injury to the eyes, so that they lose their sight toward the close of life. There is no window nor any opening, except that in the upper part of their cabins for the smoke to escape. . . .

Their life is a miserable one in comparison with our own; but they are happy among themselves, not having experienced anything better, and not imagining that anything more excellent is to be found. Their principal articles of food are Indian corn and Brazilian beans, which they prepare in various ways. By braying in a wooden mortar they reduce the corn to meal. They remove the bran by means of fans made of the bark of trees. From this meal they make bread, using also beans which they first boil, as they do the Indian corn for soup, so that they may be more easily crushed. Then they mix all together, sometimes adding blueberries or dry raspberries, and sometimes pieces of deer's fat, though not often, as this is scarce with them. After steeping the whole in lukewarm water, they make bread in the form of bannocks or pies, which they bake in the ashes. After they are baked they wash them, and from these they often make others by wrapping them in corn leaves, which they fasten to them, and then putting them in boiling water.

But this is not their most common kind. They make another, which they call *migan*, which is as follows: They take the pounded Indian corn, without removing the bran, and put two or three handfuls of it in an earthen pot full of water. This they boil, stirring it from time to time, that it may not burn or adhere to the pot. Then they put into the pot a small quantity of fish, fresh or dry, according to the season, to give a flavor to the *migan*, as they call it. They make it very often, although it smells badly, especially in winter, either because they do not know how to prepare it rightly, or do not wish to take the trouble to do so. They make two kinds of it and prepare it very well when they choose. When they use fish the *migan* does not smell badly, but only when it is made with venison. After it is all cooked, they take out the fish, pound it very fine and then put it all together into the pot, not taking the trouble to remove the appendages, scales or inwards, as we do, which generally causes a bad taste. It being thus prepared, they deal out to each one his portion. This *migan* is very thin and without much substance, as may be well supposed. As for drink, there is no need of it, the *migan* being sufficiently thin of itself.

They have another kind of *migan*, namely, they roast new corn before it is ripe, which they preserve and cook whole with fish, or flesh when they have it. Another way is this: They take Indian corn, which is very dry, roast it in the ashes, then bray it and reduce it to meal as in the former case. This they lay up for the journeys which they undertake here and there. The *migan* made in the latter manner is the best according to my taste. In preparing it, they cook a large quantity of fish and meat, which they cut into pieces and put into great kettles, which they fill with water and let it all boil well. When this is done, they gather with a spoon from the surface the fat which comes from the meat and fish. Then they put in the meal of the roasted corn, constantly stirring it until the *migan* is cooked and thick as soup. They give to each one a portion, together with a spoonful of the fat. This dish they are accustomed to prepare for banquets, but they do not generally make it. . . .

They have another way of eating the Indian corn. In preparing it, they take it in the ear and put it in water under the mud, leaving it two or three months in this state until they think it is putrefied. Then they remove it and eat it boiled with meat or fish. They also roast it, and it is better so than boiled. But I assure you that there is nothing that smells so badly as this corn as it comes from the water all muddy. Yet the women and children take it and suck it like sugar cane, nothing seeming to them to taste better, as they show by their manner. In general they have two meals a day. As for ourselves, we fasted all of Lent and longer, in order to influence them by our example. But it was time lost.

They also fatten bears, which they keep two or three years, for the purpose of their bouquets. I observed that if this people had domestic animals they would be interested in them and care for them very well, and I showed them the way to keep them, which would be an easy thing for them, since they have good grazing grounds in their country, and in large quantities, for all kinds of animals, horses, oxen, cows, sheep, swine and other kinds, for lack of which one would consider them badly off, as they seem to be. Yet with all their drawbacks they seem to me to live happily among themselves, since their only ambition is to live and support themselves, and they lead a more settled life than those who wander through the forests like brute beasts. They eat many squashes, which they boil, and roast in the ashes.

In regard to their dress, they have various kinds and styles made of the skins of wild beasts, both those which they capture themselves and others which they get in exchange for their Indian corn, meal, porcelain and fishing nets from the Algonquins, Nipissings and other tribes, which are hunters having no fixed abodes. All their clothes are of one uniform shape, not varied by any new styles. They prepare and fit very well the skins, making their breeches of deerskin rather large, and their stockings of another piece, which extend up to the middle and have many folds. Their shoes are made of the skins of deer, bears and beaver, of which they use great numbers. Besides they have a robe of the same fur, in the form of a cloak, which they wear in the Irish or Egyptian style, with sleeves which are attached with a string behind. This is the way they are dressed in winter . . .

Most of them paint the face black and red. These colors they mix with oil made from the seed of the sunflower, or with bear's fat or that of other animals. They also dye their hair, which some wear long, others short, others on one side only. The women and girls always wear their hair in one uniform style. They are dressed like men, except that they always have their robes girt about them, which extend down to the knee. They are not at all ashamed to expose the body from the middle up and from the knees down, unlike the men, the rest being always covered. They are loaded with quantities of porcelain, in the shape of necklaces and chains, which they arrange in the front of their robes and attach to their waists. They also wear bracelets and earrings. They have their hair carefully combed, dyed and oiled. Thus they go to the dance, with a knot of their hair behind bound up with eelskin, which they use as a cord. Sometimes they put on plates a foot square, covered with porcelain, which hang on the back. Thus gaily dressed and habited, they delight to appear in the dance, to which their fathers and mothers send them, forgetting nothing that they can devise to embellish and set off their daughters. I can testify that I have seen at dances a girl who had more than twelve pounds of porcelain on her person, not including the other bagatelles with which they are loaded and bedecked.

All these people have a very jovial disposition, although there are many of them who have a sad and gloomy look. Their bodies are well proportioned. Some of the men and women are well formed, strong and robust. There is a moderate number of pleasing and pretty girls, in respect to figure, color and expression, all being in harmony. Their blood is but little deteriorated, except when they are old. There are among these tribes powerful women of extraordinary height. These have almost the entire care of the house and work; namely, they till the land, plant the Indian corn, lay up a store of wood for the winter, beat the hemp and spin it, making from the thread fishing nets and other useful things. The women harvest the corn, house it, prepare it for eating and attend to household matters. Moreover, they are expected to attend their husbands from place to place in the fields, filling the office of pack mule in carrying the baggage, and to do a thousand other things. All the men do is to hunt for deer and other animals, fish, make their cabins and go to war. Having done these things, they then go to other tribes with which they are acquainted to traffic and make exchanges. On their return, they give themselves up to festivities and dances, which they give to each other, and when these are over they go to sleep, which they like to do best of all things.

They have some sort of marriage, which is as follows: When a girl has reached the age of eleven, twelve, thirteen, fourteen or fifteen years she has suitors, more or less according to her attractions, who woo her for some time. After this, the consent of their fathers and mothers is asked, to whose will the girls often do not submit, although the most discreet and considerate do so. The lover or suitor presents to the girl some necklaces, chains and bracelets of porcelain. If the girl finds the suitor agreeable, she receives the present. Then the lover comes and remains with her three or four nights, without saying anything to her during the time. They receive thus the fruit of their affections. Whence it happens very often that, after from eight to fifteen days, if they cannot agree, she quits her suitor, who forfeits his necklaces and other presents that he has made, having received in return only a meager satisfaction. Being thus disappointed in his hopes, the man seeks another woman, and the girl another suitor, if it seems to them desirable. Thus they continue to do until a favorable union is formed. It sometimes happens that a girl thus passes her entire youth, having more than twenty mates, which twenty are not alone in the enjoyment of the creature, mated though they are; for when night comes the young women run from one cabin to another, as do also the young men on their part, going where it seems good to them, but always without any violence, referring the whole matter to the pleasure of the woman. Their mates will do account, nor do they incur any reproach or insult, such being the custom of the country.

Now, the time when they do not leave their mates is when they have children. The preceding mate returns to her, renews the affection and friendship which he had borne her in the past, asserting that it is greater than that of any other one, and that the child she has is his and of his begetting. The next says the same to her. In fine, the victory is with the stronger, who takes the woman for his wife. Thus it depends upon the choice of the woman to take and accept him who shall please her best, having meantime in her searching and loves gained much porcelain and, besides, the choice of a husband. The woman remains with him without leaving him; or if she do leave him, for he is on trial, it must be for some good reason other than impotence. But while with this husband, she does not cease to give herself free rein, yet remains always at home, keeping up a good appearance. Thus the children which they have together, born from such a woman, cannot be sure of their legitimacy. Accordingly, in view of this uncertainty, it is their custom that the children never succeed to the property and honors of their fathers, there being doubt, as above indicated, as to their paternity. They make, however, the children of their sisters, from whom they are known to have issued, their successors and heirs.

The following is the way they nourish and bring up their children: They place them during the day on a little wooden board, wrapping them up in furs or skins. To this board they bind them, placing them in an erect position, and leaving a little opening for the child to do its necessities. If it is a girl, they put a leaf of Indian corn between the thighs, which presses against its privates. The extremity of the leaf is carried outside in a turned position, so that the water of the child runs off on it without inconvenience. They put also under the children the down of certain reeds that we call hare's-foot, on which they rest very softly. They also clean them with the same down. As an ornament for the child, they adorn the board with beads, which they also put on its neck, however small it may be. At night they put it to bed, entirely naked, between the father and mother. It may be regarded as a great miracle that God should thus preserve it so that no harm befalls it, as might be expected, from suffocation, while the father and mother are in deep sleep, but that rarely happens. The children have great freedom among these tribes. The fathers and mothers indulge them too much and never punish them. Accordingly they are so bad and of so vicious a nature that they often strike their mothers and others. The most vicious, when they have acquired the strength and power, strike their fathers. They do this whenever the father or mother does anything that does not please them. This is a sort of curse that God inflicts upon them.

In respect to laws, I have not been able to find out that they have any, or anything that approaches them, inasmuch as there is not among them any correction, punishment or censure of evil-doers, except in the way of vengeance when they return evil for evil, not by rule but by passion, which produces among them conflicts and differences, which occur very frequently.

Moreover, they do not recognize any divinity, or worship any God and believe in anything whatever, but live like brute beasts. They have, however, some respect for the devil or something so called, which is a matter of uncertainty, since the word which they use thus has various significations and comprises in itself various things. . . .

Early Americans: A Close-up

PETER KALM

FROM *Travels in North America*

1748–51

To European naturalists, early America afforded a boundless opportunity not only to tramp through virgin forest and discover new specimens but also to tap a rich repository of useful plants and trees. It was for the latter purpose that in 1747 the Swedish Academy of Sciences selected thirty-one-year-old Peter Kalm, professor of natural history and economy at Åbo, to go to America. It made the appointment at the recommendation of none other than the celebrated botanist Linnaeus, whose pupil Kalm had been.

Kalm soon set out on his formidable journey and, after passing six months in England while waiting for a ship, landed in Philadelphia in September 1748. During the next two and a half years he roamed for months on end through Pennsylvania, New York, New Jersey and southern Canada. While he dutifully collected seeds and took notes on plant and animal life, he seems to have been almost equally interested in the products and activities of men—bark boats, asbestos, toothache remedies, church services, building materials, hospitals, Indian dialects, longevity among settlers, tobacco pouches, oil wells, Jesuits and refrigeration. Combining a scientist's curiosity and conscientiousness with a native candor, his opinions of the settlers he met are vigorous and revealing. In the selections below he makes very plain his views on the education of children, the position of servants and Negroes, the women of French Canada, the New York Dutch, a Jew, and Quakers. After his return to Sweden he achieved distinction not only as a botanist but also as a Lutheran clergyman.

CHILDREN, SERVANTS AND NEGROES

THE education of children among the English in this country was well established in many ways. They had separate schools for small boys and girls. When a child was a little over three it was sent to school both morning and afternoon. They probably realized that such little children would not be able to read much, but they would be rid of them at home and thought it would protect them from any misbehavior. Also they would acquire a liking for being with other children. Englishmen used only one kind of letters, i.e., Latin. So the youth could learn them easier than is the case in Sweden, where children have to learn both the Latin and the Swedish alphabet. We ought to do the same in Sweden, because in general the letters are more even and look better. They are also more readable and heavier in type, a great advantage for weak or old eyes. Ordinarily the English write a very clear and readable script. In fact a great number of their women also write very neatly, at least not in such a scrawl as some of our Swedish men and women. It is probably just as easy to learn to write well as carelessly. One reason for the superiority of English penmanship is the character of the children's copybooks, which are made of clean paper, on every leaf of which are letters neatly and legibly engraved in copper. These copybooks are also reasonable in price. We ought to imitate this method more.

Servants. The servants which are employed in the English-American colonies are either free persons or slaves, and the former, again, are of two different classes.

1. Those who are entirely free serve by the year. They are not only allowed to leave their service at the expiration of their year, but may leave it at any time when they do not agree with their masters. However, in that case they are in danger of losing their wages, which are very considerable. A manservant who has some ability gets between sixteen and twenty pounds in Pennsylvania currency, but those in the country do not get so much. A maidservant gets eight or ten pounds a year. These servants have their food besides their wages, but they must buy their own clothes, and whatever they get of these as gifts they must thank their master's generosity for.

2. *Indenture.* The second kind of free servants consists of such persons as annually come from Germany, England and other countries, in order to settle here. These newcomers are very numerous every year: there

are old and young of both sexes. Some of them have fled from oppression under which they have labored. Others have been driven from their country by religious persecution, but most of them are poor and have not money enough to pay their passage, which is between six and eight pounds sterling for each person. Therefore they agree with the captain that they will suffer themselves to be sold for a few years on their arrival. In that case the person who buys them pays the freight for them; but frequently very old people come over who cannot pay their passage; they therefore sell their children for several years, so that they serve both for themselves and for their parents. There are likewise some who pay part of their passage, and they are sold only for a short time.

From these circumstances it appears that the price on the poor for-eigners who come over to North America varies considerably, and that some of them have to serve longer than others. When their time has expired, they get a new suit of clothes from their master and some other things. He is likewise obliged to feed and clothe them during the years of their servitude. Many of the Germans who come hither bring money enough with them to pay their passage, but prefer to be sold, hoping that during their servitude they may get a knowledge of the language and character of the country and the life, that they may the better be able to consider what they shall do when they have gotten their liberty. Such servants are preferable to all others, because they are not so expensive. To buy a Negro or black slave requires too much money at one time; and men or maids who get yearly wages are likewise too costly. But this kind of servant may be gotten for half the money, and even for less; for they commonly pay four-teen pounds, Pennsylvania currency, for a person who is to serve four years, and so on in proportion. . . .

3. The *Negroes* or blacks constitute the third kind. They are in a manner slaves; for when a Negro is once bought, he is the purchaser's servant as long as he lives, unless he gives him to another, or sets him free. However, it is not in the power of the master to kill his Negro for a fault, but he must leave it to the magistrates to proceed according to the laws. Formerly the Negroes were brought over from Africa and bought by almost everyone who could afford it, the Quakers alone being an exception. But these are no longer so particular and now they have as many Negroes as other people. However, many people cannot conquer the idea of its being contrary to the laws of Christianity to keep slaves. There are likewise several free Negroes in town, who have been lucky enough to get a very zealous Quaker for their master, who gave them their liberty after they had faithfully served him for a time.

At present they seldom bring over any Negroes to the English colonies, for those which were formerly brought thither have multiplied rapidly. In regard to their marriage they proceed as follows: In case you have not only male but likewise female Negroes, they may intermarry, and then the children are all your slaves. But if you possess a male Negro only and he has an inclination to marry a female belonging to a different master, you do not hinder your Negro in so delicate a point, but it is of no advantage to you, for the children belong to the master of the female. A man who kills his Negro is, legally, punishable by death, but there is no instance here of a white man ever having been executed for this crime. A few years ago it happened that a master killed his slave. His friends and even the magistrates secretly advised him to make his escape, as otherwise they could not avoid taking him prisoner, and then he would be condemned to die according to the laws of the country, without any hopes of being saved. This leniency was granted toward him, that the Negroes might not have the satisfaction of seeing a master executed for killing his slave. This would lead them to all sorts of dangerous designs against their masters, and to value themselves too much.

The Negroes were formerly brought from Africa, as I mentioned before, but now this seldom happens, for they are bought in the West Indies, or American Islands, whither they were originally brought from their own country. It has been found that in transporting the Negroes from Africa directly to these northern countries, they have not such good health as when they come gradually, by shorter stages, and are first carried from Africa to the West Indies, and thence to North America. It has frequently been found that the Negroes cannot stand the cold here so well as the Europeans or whites; for while the latter are not in the least affected by the cold, the toes and fingers of the former are frequently frozen. . . .

The price of Negroes differs according to their age, health and ability. A full-grown Negro costs from forty to a hundred pounds of Pennsylvania currency. There are even examples that a gentleman has paid a hundred pounds for a black slave at Philadelphia and refused to sell him again for the same money. A Negro boy or girl two or three years old can hardly be got for less than eight or fourteen pounds in Pennsylvania money. Not only the Quakers but also several Christians of other denominations sometimes set their Negroes at liberty. This is done in the following manner: When a gentleman has a faithful Negro who has done him great services, he sometimes declares him independent at his own death. This is, however, very expensive; for they are obliged to make a provision for the Negro thus set at liberty, to afford him subsistence when he is grown old, that he may not be driven by necessity to wicked actions, or that he may not fall a charge to anybody, for these free Negroes become very lazy and indolent afterward. But the children which the free Negro has begot during his servitude are all slaves, though their father be free. On the other hand, those Negro children which are born after the parent was freed are free. The Negroes in the North American colonies are treated more mildly and fed better than those in the West Indies. They have as good food as the rest of the servants, and they possess equal advantages in all things, except their being obliged to serve their whole lifetime and get no other wages than what their master's goodness allows them. They are likewise clad at their master's expense. On the contrary, in the West Indies, and especially in the Spanish Islands, they are treated very cruelly; therefore no threats make more impression upon a Negro here than that of sending him over to the West Indies, in case he will not reform. . . .

The Women of Canada

The ladies in Canada are generally of two kinds: those who come over from France and those who are natives. The former possess the politeness peculiar to the French nation; the latter may be divided into those of Quebec and Montreal. The first of these are equal to the French ladies in good breeding, having the advantage of frequently conversing with the French gentlemen and ladies who come every summer with the King's ships and stay several weeks at Quebec, but seldom go to Montreal. The ladies of this last place are accused by the French of being contaminated by the pride and conceit of the Indians, and of being much wanting in French good breeding. What I have mentioned about their dressing their heads too profusely is the case with all the ladies throughout Canada. Their hair is always curled, even when they are at home in a dirty jacket and a short coarse skirt that does not reach to the middle of their legs. On Sundays and visiting days they dress so gaily that one is almost induced to think their parents in origin and social position to be among the best in the realm. The Frenchmen, who consider things in their true light, complain very much that a great number of the ladies in Canada have got into the pernicious custom of taking too much care of their dress, and squandering all their fortune and more upon it, instead of sparing something for future times. They are no less attentive to having the newest fashion; the best and most expensive dresses are discarded and cut to pieces; and they smile inwardly when their sisters are not dressed according to their fancy. But what they get as new fashions are often old and discarded in France by the time they are adopted in Canada, for the ships come but once every year from abroad, and the people in Canada consider that as the new fashion for the whole year which the people on board brought with them or which they imposed upon them as new.

The ladies in Canada, and especially at Montreal, are very ready to laugh at any blunders strangers make in speaking; but they are very excusable. People laugh at what appears uncommon and ridiculous. In Canada nobody ever hears the French language spoken by anyone but Frenchmen, for strangers seldom come there, and the Indians are naturally too proud to learn French, and compel the French to learn their language. Therefore it naturally follows that the sensitive Canadian ladies cannot hear anything uncommon without laughing at it. One of the first questions they put to a stranger is whether he is married; the next, how he likes the ladies in the country, and whether he thinks them handsomer than those of his own country; and the third, whether he will take one home with him.

There are some differences between the ladies of Quebec and those of Montreal: Those of the latter place seemed to be generally handsomer than those of the former. The women seemed to me to be somewhat too free at Quebec, and of a more becoming modesty at Montreal. The ladies at Quebec, especially the unmarried ones, are not very industrious. A girl of eighteen is reckoned very poorly off if she cannot enumerate at least twenty lovers. These young ladies, especially those of a higher rank, get up at seven and dress till nine, drinking their coffee at the same time. When they are dressed they place themselves near a window that opens into the street, take up some needlework and sew a stitch now and then, but turn their eyes into the street most of the time. When a young fellow comes in, whether they are acquainted with him or not, they immediately lay aside their work, sit down by him, and begin to chat, laugh, joke and invent *double-entendres* and make their tongues go like a lark's wings; this is considered *avoir beaucoup d'esprit*. In this manner they frequently pass the whole day, leaving their mothers to do all the work in the house. In Montreal the girls are not quite so flighty, and more industrious. It is not uncommon to find them with the maid in the kitchen. They are always at their needlework or doing some necessary business in the house. They are likewise cheerful and content; and nobody can say that they lack either wit or charms. Their fault is that they think too well of themselves. However, the daughters of all ranks, without exception, go to market, buy watermelons, pumpkins and other food and carry it home themselves. They rise as soon and go to bed as late as any of the people in the house.

I have been assured that in general their fortunes are not great and are rendered still more scarce by the number of children and the small revenues in a house. The girls at Montreal are very much displeased that those at Quebec get husbands sooner than they. The reason for this is that many young gentlemen who come over from France with the ships are captured by the ladies at Quebec and marry them; but as these gentlemen seldom go up to Montreal, the girls there are not often so happy as those of the former place.

DUTCH CUSTOMS

IN New York I had lodgings with Mrs. van Wagenen, a woman of Dutch extraction whose dwelling was opposite the new Dutch church. She as well as everyone in her house was quite polite and kind. It is true that the Dutch both in speech and in outward manners were not as polite and well-bred as the English, and still less so than the French, but their intentions were good and they showed their kindly spirit in all they did. When a Frenchman talks about a man in his presence and even in his absence he always uses *"monsieur"*—e.g., *"Donnez à Monsieur,* etc." An English-man says, "Give the gentleman, etc.," while the Dutch always said, *"Giw dese man."* The women were treated in the same way without ceremony, and yet the Dutchman always had the same good intentions as he who used more formality. If several persons of Dutch extraction should come into a house at this time of the year, as many as could be accommodated would sit down about the fire. Then if any others should happen in, they pretended not to see them. Even though they saw them and conversed with them, they did not consider it wise to move from the fire and give the others a little room, but they sat there like lifeless statues. The French and English always made room by moving a little. When one spoke of refinement as the word is now used, and in applying it to the French and Dutch, it was just as if the one had lived a long time at the court while the other, a peasant, had scarcely ever visited the city. The difference be-tween the English and the Dutch was like that of a refined merchant in the city and a rather crude farmer in the country. But it is well to remem-ber that there are exceptions to every rule.

I have lived now for almost a week in a house with a good-sized family. There was the same perpetual evening meal of porridge made of corn meal. (The Dutch in Albany as well as those in New York called this porridge *sappaan*.) It was put into a good-sized dish and a large hole made in its center into which the milk was poured, and then one proceeded to help oneself. When the milk was gone, more was added until all the porridge had been consumed. Care was usually taken that there should be no waste, so that when all had eaten, not a bit of porridge should remain. After the porridge one ate bread and butter to hold it down. I had observed from my previous contacts with people of Dutch extraction that their evening meal usually consisted of this *sappaan*. For dinner they rarely had more than one dish, meat with turnips or cabbage; occasionally there were two [dishes]. They never served more than was consumed before they left the table. Nearly all women who had passed their fortieth year smoked tobacco; even those who were considered as belonging to the foremost families. I frequently saw about a dozen old ladies sitting about the fire smoking. Once in a while I discovered newly married wives of twenty and some years sitting there with pipes in their mouths. But nothing amused me more than to observe how occupied they were with the placing of the warming pans beneath their skirts. In a house where there were four women present it was well nigh impossible to glance in the direction of the fire without seeing at least one of them busily engaged in replacing the coals in her warming pan. Even their Negro women had acquired this habit, and if time allowed, they also kept warming pans under their skirts.

A JEW

THE Jew (whom Kalm met on a vessel going from New York to New Brunswick) was a rather good-natured and polite man and it would scarcely have been possible to take him for a Jew from his appearance. During the evening of this day which ushered in his Sabbath he was rather quiet, though he conversed with me about all kinds of things, and he himself often began the discourse. He told me that the Jews never cook any food for themselves on Saturday, but that it is done on the day before. Yet, he said, they keep a fire in their houses on Saturdays during the winter. Furthermore, he said that the majority of the Jews do not eat pork, but that this custom does not trouble the conscience of the young people when on their journeys, for then they eat whatever they can get, and that even together with the Christians.

The Quakers

The Quakers in this town attend meetings three times on Sunday—from ten to twelve in the morning, at two, and finally at six in the evening. Besides, they attend services twice during the week, namely on Tuesdays from ten to twelve and on Thursdays at the same time. Then also a religious service is held in the church the last Friday of each month, not to mention their general gatherings, which I shall discuss presently.

Today we appeared at ten, as the bells of the English church were ringing. We sat down on benches made like those in our academies on which the students sit. The front benches, however, were provided with a long, horizontal pole in the back, against which one could lean for support. Men and women sit apart. (In London they sat together). . . . When a man comes into the meetinghouse he does not remove or raise his hat, but goes and sits down with his hat on. Here we sat and waited very quietly from ten o'clock to a quarter after eleven, during which the people gathered and then waited for inspiration of the spirit to speak. Finally, one of the two old men in the front pew rose, removed his hat, turned hither and yon, and began to speak, but so softly that even in the middle of the church, which was not very large, it was impossible to hear anything except the confused murmur of the words. Later he began to talk a little louder, but so slowly that four or five minutes elapsed between the sentences; then the words came both louder and faster. In their preaching the Quakers have a peculiar mode of expression, which is half singing, with a strange cadence and accent, and ending each cadence, as it were, with a full or partial sob. Each cadence consists of from two to four syllables, but sometimes more, according to the demand of the words and meaning; e.g., "My friends/put in your mind/we can/do nothing/good of ourself/without God's/help and assistance," etc. In the beginning the sobbing is not heard so plainly, but the deeper and further the reader or preacher gets into his sermon the more violent is the sobbing between the cadences. The speaker today had no gestures, but turned in various directions; sometimes he placed a hand on his chin and during most of the sermon kept buttoning and unbuttoning his vest. The gist of his sermon was that we can do nothing of ourselves without the help of our Savior. When he had stood for a while using his singsong method he changed his manner of delivery and spoke in a more natural way, or as ministers do when they read a prayer. Shortly afterward, however, he reverted to his former practice, and at the end, just as he seemed to have attained a certain momentum, he stopped abruptly, sat down and put on his hat. After that we sat quietly for a while looking at each other until one of the old women in the front pew arose, when the whole congregation stood up and the men removed their hats. The woman turned from the people to the wall and began to read extemporaneously a few prayers with a loud but fearfully sobbing voice. When she was through she sat down, and the whole congregation with her, when the clock struck twelve, whereupon after a short pause each one got up and went home. . . .

The meetinghouse was whitewashed inside and had a gallery almost all the way around. The tin candleholders on the pillars supporting the gallery constituted the only ornaments of the church. There was no pulpit, altar, baptismal font or bridal pew, no *prie-dieu* or collection bag, no clergyman, cantor or church beadle, and no announcements were read after the sermon, nor were any prayers said for the sick.——This was the way the service was conducted today.

But otherwise there are often infinite variations. Many times after a long silence a man rises first, and when he gets through a woman rises and preaches; after her comes another man or woman; occasionally only the women speak; then again a woman might start [followed by a man], and so on alternately; sometimes only men rise to talk; now and then either a man or a woman gets up, begins to puff and sigh, and endeavors to speak, but is unable to squeeze out a word and so sits down again. Then it happens also that the whole congregation gathers in the meeting-house and sits there silently for two hours, waiting for someone to preach; but since none has prepared himself or feels moved by the spirit, the whole audience rises again at the end of the period and goes home without the members having accomplished anything in the church except sitting and looking at each other. . . .

I shall now say something about their clothes and manners, insofar as they vary from those of others. The women have no clothing that differs from that of the other English [ladies], except that I do not remember having seen them wear cuffs, and although they censure all adornment I have seen them wear just as gaudy shoes as other Englishwomen. But the men's clothes differ somewhat from those of other gentlemen. For instance, they have no buttons on their hats, and these are neither turned up entirely nor turned down, but just a trifle folded up on the side and covered with black silk, so that they look like the headgear of our Swedish clergymen. They wear no cuffs; they never take off their hats, neither when they meet anyone nor when they enter a stranger's house or receive friends at their own home; they make no bows and hate all courtesies; and the only form of address is "my friend" or "thee" and "thou." A son addresses his mother with "thee." In the plural for "they" one says "I and the Friends," naming them. Although they pretend not to have their clothes made after the latest fashion, or to wear cuffs and be dressed as gaily as others, they strangely enough have their garments made of the finest and costliest material that can be procured. So far as food is concerned, other Englishmen regard the Quakers as semi-Epicureans; for no people want such choice and well-prepared food as the Quakers. The staunchest Quaker families in the city are said to live the best.

Pioneer Life

FRANÇOIS ANDRÉ MICHAUX

FROM *Travels to the West of the Alleghany Mountains into Ohio, Kentucky and Tennessee*

1801–3

The career of François Michaux was strikingly like that of his father, André, a distinguished French botanist. The elder Michaux capped a career that had taken him as far afield as Persia with ten years' study of the botany of America and two books on the subject. He set up a botanic garden on a plantation outside Charleston, and it was there that his son André repeatedly came to pursue his own studies of forestry —studies that eventually led to his classic treatise on trees, The North American Sylva.

In 1801–3 Michaux made a trip into the frontier country beyond the Alleghenies out of which came a journal that gives us some fresh and vivid glimpses of pioneer life and pristine America. In that account Michaux tells how he docked at Charleston in October 1801 only to find the city in the grip of its annual yellow-fever epidemic. After recovering from an attack himself, he visited New York and Philadelphia and then, in June 1802, started westward through Pennsylvania. The first excerpts below present some of his impressions of pioneer settlements.

Log Houses, Inns and Heavy Drinkers

At Philadelphia the houses are built with brick. In the other town and country places that surround them, the half, and even frequently the whole, is built with wood; but at places within seventy or eighty miles of the sea, in the central and southern states, and again more particularly in those situated to the westward of the Alleghany Mountains, one third of the inhabitants reside in log houses. These dwellings are made with the trunks of trees, from twenty to thirty feet in length, about five inches in diameter, placed one upon another, and kept up by notches cut at their extremities. The roof is formed with pieces of similar length to those that compose the body of the house, but not quite so thick, and gradually sloped on each side. Two doors, which often supply the place of windows, are made by sawing away a part of the trunks that form the body of the house; the chimney, always placed at one of the extremities, is likewise made with the trunks of trees of a suitable length; the back of the chimney is made of clay, about six inches thick, which separates the fire from the wooden walls. Notwithstanding this want of precaution, fires very seldom happen in the country places. The space between these trunks of trees is filled up with clay, but so very carelessly that the light may be seen through in every part; in consequence of which these huts are exceedingly cold in winter, notwithstanding the amazing quantity of wood that is burned. The doors move upon wooden hinges, and the greater part of them have no locks. In the night time they only push them to, or fasten them with a wooden peg. Four or five days are sufficient for two men to finish one of these houses, in which not a nail is used. Two great beds receive the whole family. It frequently happens that in summer the children sleep upon the ground, in a kind of rug. The floor is raised from one to two feet above the surface of the ground, and boarded. They generally make use of feather beds, or feathers alone, and not mattresses. Sheep being very scarce, the wool is very dear; at the same time they reserve it to make stockings. The clothes belonging to the family are hung up round the room, or suspended upon a long pole. . . .

Inns are very numerous in the United States, and especially in the little towns; yet almost everywhere, except in the principal towns, they are very bad, notwithstanding rum, brandy, and whiskey are in plenty.

In fact, in houses of the above description all kinds of spirits are considered the most material, as they generally meet with great consumption. Travelers wait in common till the family go to meals. At breakfast they make use of very indifferent tea, and coffee still worse, with small slices of ham fried in the stove, to which they sometimes add eggs and broiled chicken. At dinner they give a piece of salt beef and roasted fowls, and rum and water as a beverage. In the evening, coffee, tea and ham. There are always several beds in the rooms where you sleep; seldom do you meet with clean sheets. Fortunate is the traveler who arrives on the day they happen to be changed, although an American would be quite indifferent about it. . . .

We arrived at Bedford in the dusk of the evening and took lodgings at an inn, the landlord of which was an acquaintance of the American officer with whom I was traveling. His house was commodious, and elevated one story above the ground floor, which is very rare in that part of the country. The day of our arrival was a day of rejoicing for the country people, who had assembled together in this little town to celebrate the suppression of the tax laid upon the whiskey distilleries— rather an arbitrary tax, that had disaffected the inhabitants of the interior against the late President, Mr. Adams. The public houses, inns, and more especially the one where we lodged, were filled with the lower class of people, who made the most dreadful riot and committed such horrible excesses that is almost impossible to form the least idea of. The rooms, stairs and yard were strewed with drunken men; and those who had still the power of speech uttered nothing but the accents of rage and fury. A passion for spirituous liquors is one of the features that characterize the country people belonging to the interior of the United States. This passion is so strong that they desert their homes every now and then to get drunk in public houses; in fact, I do not conceive there are ten out of a hundred who have resolution enough to desist from it a moment provided they had it by them, notwithstanding their usual beverage in summer is nothing but water, or sour milk. They care very little for cider, which they find too weak.

[After passing through Pittsburgh, Michaux and a companion buy a canoe and embark on the Ohio at Wheeling. They sail 350 miles in ten days amidst such scenes as the one described below.]

The Banks of the Ohio

WHAT makes the situation more beautiful is that for four or five miles on this side the Point [Point Pleasant], the Ohio, four hundred fathoms broad, continues the same breadth the whole of that extent and presents on every side the most perfect line. Its borders, sloping, and elevated from twenty-five to forty feet, are, as in the whole of its windings, planted, at their base, with willows from fifteen to eighteen feet in height, the drooping branches and foliage of which form a pleasing contrast to the sugar maples, red maples and ash trees situated immediately above. The latter, in return, are overlooked by palms, poplars, beeches, magnolias of the highest elevation, the enormous branches of which, attracted by a more splendid light and easier expansion, extend toward the borders, over-shadowing the river, at the same time completely covering the trees situated under them. This natural display, which reigns upon the two banks, affords on each side a regular arch, the shadow of which, reflected by the crystal stream, embellishes in an extraordinary degree this magnificent *coup d'oeil*.

[He sums up the pioneer spirit with a classic description of the restless westering that marked the first settlers.]

The Pioneer Spirit

MORE than half of those who inhabit the borders of the Ohio are again the first inhabitants, or, as they are called in the United States, the first settlers, a kind of men who cannot settle upon the soil that they have cleared, and who under pretense of finding a better land, a more whole-some country, a greater abundance of game, push forward, incline per-petually toward the most distant points of the American population, and go and settle in the neighborhood of the savage nations, whom they brave even in their own country. Their ungenerous mode of treating them stirs up frequent broils that bring on bloody wars, in which they generally fall victims, rather on account of their being so few in number than through defect or courage.

Prior to our arrival at Marietta, we met one of those settlers, an inhabitant of the environs of Wheeling, who accompanied us down the Ohio, and with whom we traveled for two days. Alone in a canoe from eighteen to twenty feet long, and from twelve to fifteen inches broad, he was going to survey the borders of the Missouri for a hundred and fifty miles beyond its *embouchure*. The excellent quality of the land, that is reckoned to be more fertile there than that on the borders of the Ohio, and which the Spanish government at that time ordered to be distributed gratis, the quantity of beavers, elks and more especially bisons, were the motives that induced him to emigrate into this remote part of the country, whence, after having determined on a suitable spot to settle there with his family, he was returning to fetch them from the borders of the Ohio, which obliged him to take a journey of fourteen or fifteen hundred miles. His costume, like that of all the American sportsmen, consisted of a waistcoat with sleeves, a pair of pantaloons and a large red-and-yellow worsted sash. A carabine, a tomahawk or little ax, which the Indians make use of to cut wood and to terminate the existence of their enemies, two beaver snares and a large knife suspended at his side constituted his sporting dress. A rug comprised the whole of his luggage. Every evening he encamped on the banks of the river, where, after having made a fire, he passed the night; and whenever he conceived the place favorable for the chase, he remained in the woods for several days together, and with the produce of his sport he gained the means of subsistence, and new ammunition with the skins of the animals that he had killed.

Such were the first inhabitants of Kentucky and Tennessee, of whom there are now remaining but a very few. It was they who began to clear those fertile countries and wrested them from the savages who ferociously disputed their right; it was they, in short, who made themselves masters of the possessions, after five or six years' bloody war; but the long habit of a wandering and idle life has prevented their enjoying the fruit of their labors, and profiting by the very price to which these lands have risen in so short a time. They have emigrated to more remote parts of the country and formed new settlements. It will be the same with most of those who inhabit the borders of the Ohio. The same inclination that led them there will induce them to emigrate from it. To the latter will succeed fresh emigrants, coming also from the Atlantic states, who will desert their possessions to go in quest of a milder climate and a more fertile soil.

The money that they will get for them will suffice to pay for their new acquisitions, the peaceful delight of which is assured by a numerous population. The last comers instead of log houses, with which the present inhabitants are contented, will build wooden ones, clear a greater quantity of land, and be as industrious and persevering in the melioration of their new possessions as the former were indolent in everything, being so fond of hunting. To the culture of Indian corn they will add that of other grain, hemp and tobacco; rich pasturages will nourish innumerable flocks, and an advantageous sale of all the country's produce will be assured them through the channel of the Ohio.

[Passing through Kentucky he comments on the terrain and some of the pursuits for which Kentuckians were already famous, such as breeding horses. In the passage below he describes their attitudes toward strangers and their religious camp meetings.]

KENTUCKIANS

THE inhabitants of Kentucky, as we have before stated, are nearly all natives of Virginia, and particularly the remotest parts of that state; and exclusive of the gentlemen of the law, physicians, and a small number of citizens who have received an education suitable to their professions in the Atlantic states, they have preserved the manners of the Virginians. With them the passion for gaming and spirituous liquors is carried to excess, which frequently terminates in quarrels degrading to human nature. The public houses are always crowded, more especially during the sittings of the courts of justice. Horses and lawsuits comprise the usual topic of their conversation. If a traveler happens to pass by, his horse is appreciated; if he stops, he is presented with a glass of whiskey and then asked a thousand questions, such as, Where do you come from? Where are you going? What is your name? Where do you live? What profession? Were there any fevers in the different parts of the country you came through? These questions, which are frequently repeated in the course of a journey, become tedious, but it is easy to give a check to their inquiries by a little address, their only object being the gratification of that curiosity so natural to people who live isolated in the woods and seldom see a stranger. They are never dictated by mistrust; for from whatever part of the globe a person comes, he may visit all the ports and principal towns of the United States, stay there as long as he pleases and travel in any part of the country without ever being interrogated by a public officer. . . .

Among the various sects that exist in Kentucky, those of the Methodists and Anabaptists are the most numerous. The spirit of religion has acquired a fresh degree of strength within these seven or eight years among the country inhabitants, since, independent of Sundays, which are scrupulously observed, they assemble, during the summer, in the course of the week, to hear sermons. These meetings, which frequently consist of two or three thousand persons who come from all parts of the country within fifteen or twenty miles, take place in the woods and continue for several days. Each brings his provisions and spends the night round a fire. The clergymen are very vehement in their discourses. Often in the midst of the sermons the heads are lifted up, the imaginations exalted, and the inspired fall backward, exclaiming, "Glory! glory!" This species of infatuation happens chiefly among the women, who are carried out of the crowd and put under a tree, where they lie a long time extended, heaving the most lamentable sighs.

There have been instances of two or three hundred of the congregation being thus affected during the performance of divine service; so that one third of the hearers were engaged in recovering the rest. While I was at Lexington I was present at one of these meetings. The better-informed people do not share the opinion of the multitude with regard to this state of ecstasy, and on this account they are branded with the appellation of "bad folks." Except during the continuance of this preaching, religion is very seldom the topic of conversation. Although divided into several sects, they live in the greatest harmony; and whenever there is an alliance between the families, the difference of religion is never considered as an obstacle; the husband and wife pursue whatever kind of worship they like best, and their children, when they grow up, do just the same, without the interference of their parents.

[After reconnoitering Tennessee, Michaux recrossed the Alleghenies and toured Georgia and the Carolinas before returning to Charleston. He sailed for France in March 1803. In later years he retired to a country estate in France and lived on until 1855.]

A Note on the Not So Noble Savage

MERIWETHER LEWIS and WILLIAM CLARK

FROM *The Lewis and Clark Journals*

1804–6

Although the Scottish explorer Sir Alexander Mackenzie had traversed the North American continent in 1793, it was the crossing made by the Lewis and Clark expedition that opened the American West. Sponsored by Thomas Jefferson (whom Lewis had served as secretary), the expedition set out from St. Louis in 1804, ascended the Missouri to its forks and then followed the Jefferson fork to its source in what is today Montana. With the aid of an Indian woman guide, Sacajawea, they crossed the Rockies, embarked on a tributary of the Columbia River and sailed to the Pacific. On the return journey, Lewis led one party down the Marias River while Clark took the main body down the Yellowstone. They were back in St. Louis by September 1806, having covered eight thousand miles, blazed a trail to the Pacific, encountered unknown Indian tribes and collected valuable scientific material. Lewis died mysteriously in 1809, but Clark went on to become a territorial governor and a superintendent of Indian affairs.

The edition of the Journals used here contains contributions not only by Lewis and Clark but by other members of the expedition. The first excerpt describes some curious customs of four Northwest Coast Indian tribes and the second a skirmish between Captain Lewis' party and a band of Minnetarees.

SOME INDIANS OF THE NORTHWEST COAST

T UESDAY, [JANUARY] 21 [1806].—Two of the hunters came back with three elk, which form a timely addition to our stock of provisions. The Indian visitors left us at twelve o'clock.

The Killamucks, Clatsops, Chinnooks, and Cathlamahs, the four neighboring nations with whom we have had most intercourse, preserve a general resemblance in person, dress, and manners. They are commonly of a diminutive stature, badly shaped, and their appearance by no means prepossessing. They have broad thick flat feet, thick ankles, and crooked legs: the last of which deformities is to be ascribed, in part, to the universal practice of squatting, or sitting on the calves of their legs and heels, and also to the tight bandages of beads and strings worn round the ankles, by the women, which prevent the circulation of the blood, and render the legs, of the females particularly, ill shaped and swollen. The complexion is the usual copper-colored brown of the North American tribes, though the complexion is rather lighter than that of the Indians of the Missouri and the frontier of the United States; the mouth is wide and the lips thick; the nose of a moderate size, fleshy, wide at the extremities, with large nostrils, and generally low between the eyes, though there are rare instances of high aquiline noses; the eyes are generally black, though we occasionally see them of a dark yellowish brown, with a black pupil. But the most distinguishing part of their physiognomy is the peculiar flatness and width of their forehead, a peculiarity which they owe to one of these customs by which nature is sacrificed to fantastic ideas of beauty. The custom, indeed, of flattening the head by artificial pressure during infancy prevails among all the nations we have seen west of the Rocky Mountains. To the east of that barrier, the fashion is so perfectly unknown that there the western Indians, with the exception of the Alliatan or Snake nation, are designated by the common name of Flatheads. The singular usage, which nature could scarcely seem to suggest to remote nations, might perhaps incline us to believe in the common and not very ancient origin of all the western nations. Such an opinion might well accommodate itself with the fact, that while on the lower parts of the Columbia both sexes are universally flatheads, the custom diminishes in receding eastward, from the common center of the infection, till among the remoter tribes near the mountains nature recovers her rights, and the wasted folly is confined to a few females. Such opinions, however, are corrected or weakened by considering that the flattening of the head is not, in fact, peculiar to that part of the continent, since it was among the first objects which struck the attention of Columbus.

But wherever it may have begun, the practice is now universal among these nations. Soon after the birth of her child, the mother, anxious to procure for her infant the recommendation of a broad forehead, places it in the compressing machine, where it is kept for ten or twelve months; though the females remain longer than the boys. The operation is so gradual that it is not attended with pain; but the impression is deep and permanent. The heads of the children, when they are released from the bandage, are not more than two inches thick about the upper edge of the forehead, and still thinner above: nor with all its efforts can nature ever restore its shape, the heads of grown persons being often in a straight line from the nose to the top of the forehead.

The hair of both sexes is parted at the top of the head, and thence falls loosely behind the ears, over the back and shoulders. They use combs, of which they are very fond, and indeed, contrive without the aid of them to keep their hair in very good order. The dress of the man consists in a small robe, reaching to the middle of the thigh, tied by a string across the breast, with its corners hanging loosely over their arms. These robes are, in general, composed of the skins of a small animal, which we have supposed to be the brown mungo. They have besides, those of the tiger, cat, deer, panther, bear, and elk, which last is principally used in war parties. Sometimes they have a blanket, woven with the fingers, from the wool of their native sheep; occasionally a mat is thrown over them to keep off rain; but except this robe, they have no other article of clothing during winter or summer, so that every part of the body, but the back and shoulders, is exposed to view. They are very fond of the dress of the whites, whom they call *pashisheooks* or cloth-men; and whenever they can procure any clothes, wear them in our manner: the only article, indeed, which we have not seen among them is the shoe.

The robe of the women is like that worn by the men, except that it does not reach below the waist. Those most esteemed are made of strips of sea-otter skin, which being twisted are interwoven with silk-grass, or the bark of the white cedar, in such a manner that the fur appears equally on both sides, so as to form a soft and warm covering. The skin of the raccoon or beaver are also employed in the same way, though on other occasions these skins are simply dressed in the hair, and worn without further preparation. The garment which covers the body from the waist as low as the knee before and the thigh behind, is the tissue already described, and is made either of the bruised bark of white cedar, the twisted cords of silk-grass, or of flags and rushes. Neither leggings nor moccasins are ever used, the mildness of the climate not requiring them as a security from the weather, and their being so much in the water rendering them an encumbrance. The only covering for the head is a hat made of bear-grass, and the bark of cedar, interwoven in a conic form, with a knob of the same shape at the top. It has no brim, but is held on the head by a string passing under the chin, and tied to a small rim inside of the hat. The colors are generally black and white only, and these are made into squares, triangles, and sometimes rude figures of canoes and seamen harpooning whales. This is all the usual dress of females; but if the weather be unusually severe, they add a vest formed of skins like the robe, tied behind, without any shoulder-straps to keep it up. As this vest covers the body from the armpits to the waist, it conceals the breasts, but on all other occasions they are suffered to remain loose and exposed, and present, in old women especially, a most disgusting appearance.

Sometimes, though not often, they mark their skins by puncturing and introducing some colored matter: this ornament is chiefly confined to the women, who imprint on their legs and arms, circular or parallel dots. On the arm of one of the squaws we read the name of J. Bowman, apparently a trader who visits the mouth of the Columbia. The favorite decoration however of both sexes are the common coarse blue or white beads, which are folded very tightly round their wrists and ankles, to the width of three or four inches, and worn in large loose rolls round the neck, or in the shape of earrings, or hanging from the nose, which last mode is peculiar to the men. There is also a species of wampum very much in use, which seems to be worn in its natural form without any preparation. Its shape is a cone somewhat curved, about the size of a raven's quill at the base, and tapering to a point, its whole length being from one to two and a half inches, and white, smooth, hard and thin. A small thread is passed through it, and the wampum is either suspended from the nose, or passed through the cartilage horizontally, and forms a ring, from which other ornaments hang. This wampum is employed in the same way as the beads, but is the favorite decoration for the noses of the men. The men also use collars made of bears' claws, the women and children those of elks' tusks, and both sexes are adorned with bracelets of copper, iron, or brass, in various forms.

FORWARD FEMALES

YET all these decorations are unavailing to conceal the deformities of nature and the extravagance of fashion; nor have we seen any more disgusting object than a Chinnook or Clatsop beauty in full attire. The broad flat foreheads, their falling breasts, their ill-shaped limbs, the awkwardness of their positions, and the filth which intrudes through their finery: all these render a Chinnook or Clatsop beauty in full attire, one of the most disgusting objects in nature. Fortunately this circumstance conspired with the low diet and laborious exercise of our men, to protect them from the persevering gallantry of the fair sex, whose kindness always exceeded the ordinary courtesies of hospitality. Among these people, as indeed among all Indians, the prostitution of unmarried women is so far from being considered criminal or improper, that the females themselves solicit the favors of the other sex, with the entire approbation of their friends and connections. The person is in fact often the only property of a young female, and is therefore the medium of trade, the return for presents, and the reward for services. In most cases, however, the female is so much at the disposal of her husband or parent, that she is farmed out for hire. The Chinnook woman who brought her six female relations to our camp had regular prices, proportioned to the beauty of each female; and among all the tribes, a man will lend his wife or daughter for a fishhook or a strand of beads. To decline an offer of this sort is indeed to disparage the charms of the lady, and therefore gives such offence that although we had occasionally to treat the Indians with rigor, nothing seemed to irritate both sexes more than our refusal to accept the favors of the females. On one occasion we were amused by a Clatsop, who having been cured of some disorder by our medical skill, brought his sister as a reward for our kindness. The young lady was quite anxious to join in this expression of her brother's gratitude, and mortified that we did not avail ourselves of it; she could not be prevailed on to leave the fort, but remained with Chaboneau's wife, in the next room to ours, for two or three days, declining all the solicitations of the men, till finding, at last, that we did not relent, she went away, regretting that her brother's obligations were unpaid.

The little intercourse which the men have had with these women is, however, sufficient to apprise us of the prevalence of the venereal disease, with which one or two of the party had been so much afflicted, as to render a salivation necessary. The infection in these cases was communicated by the Chinnook women. The others do not appear to be afflicted with it to any extent: indeed, notwithstanding this disorder is certainly known to the Indians on the Columbia, yet the number of infected persons is very inconsiderable. The existence of such a disorder is very easily detected, particularly in the men, in their open style of dress; yet in the whole route down the Columbia, we have not seen more than two or three cases of gonorrhoea, and about double that number of lues venerea. There does not seem to be any simples which are used as specifics in this disorder, nor is any complete cure ever effected. When once a patient is seized, the disorder ends with his life only; though from the simplicity of their diet, and the use of certain vegetables, they support it for many years with but little inconvenience, and even enjoy tolerable health; yet their life is always abridged by decrepitude or premature old age. The Indians who are mostly successful in treating this disorder are the Chippeways. Their specifics are the root of the lobelia and that of a species of sumac, common to the United States, the neighborhood of the Rocky Mountains, and to the countries westward, and which is readily distinguished by being the smallest of its kind, and by its winged rib, or common footstalk, supporting leaves oppositely pinnate. Decoctions of the roots are used very freely, without any limitation, and are said to soften the violence of the lues, and even to be sovereign in the cure of the gonorrhoea.

The Clatsops and other nations at the mouth of the Columbia have visited us with great freedom, and we have endeavored to cultivate their intimacy, as well for the purpose of acquiring information as to leave behind us impressions favorable to our country. In their intercourse with us they are very loquacious and inquisitive. Having acquired much of their language, we are enabled, with the assistance of gestures, to hold conversations with great ease. We find them inquisitive and loquacious, with understandings by no means deficient in acuteness, and with very retentive memories; and though fond of feasts, and generally cheerful, they are never gay. Everything they see excites their attention and inquiries, but having been accustomed to see the whites, nothing appeared to give them more astonishment than the air-gun. To all our inquiries they answer with great intelligence, and the conversation rarely slackens, since there is a constant discussion of the events, and trade, and politics, in the little but active circle of Killamucks, Clatsops, Cathlamahs, Wahkiacums, and Chinnooks. Among themselves, the conversation generally turns on the subjects of trade, or smoking, or eating, or connection with females, before whom this last is spoken of with a familiarity which would be in the highest degree indecent, if custom had not rendered it inoffensive.

THE TREATMENT OF WOMEN

THE treatment of women is often considered as the standard by which the moral qualities of savages are to be estimated. Our own observation, however, induced us to think that the importance of the female in savage life has no necessary relation to the virtues of the men, but is regulated wholly by their capacity to be useful. The Indians whose treatment of the females is mildest, and who pay most deference to their opinions, are by no means the most distinguished for their virtues; nor is this deference attended by any increase of attachment, since they are equally willing with the most brutal husband, to prostitute their wives to strangers. On the other hand, the tribes among whom the women are very much debased possess the loftiest sense of honor, the greatest liberality, and all the good qualities of which their situation demands the exercise. Where the women can aid in procuring subsistence for the tribe, they are treated with more equality, and their importance is proportioned to the share which they take in that labor; while in countries where subsistence is chiefly procured by the exertions of the men, the women are considered and treated as burdens. Thus, among the Clatsops and Chinnooks, who live upon fish and roots, which the women are equally expert with the men in procuring, the former have a rank and influence very rarely found among Indians. The females are permitted to speak freely before the men, to whom indeed they sometimes address themselves in a tone of authority. On many subjects their judgments and opinions are respected, and in matters of trade their advice is generally asked and pursued. The labors of the family, too, are shared almost equally. The men collect wood and make fires, assist in cleansing the fish, make the houses, canoes, and wooden utensils; and whenever strangers are to be entertained, or a great feast prepared, the meats are cooked and served up by the men. The peculiar province of the female is to collect roots and to manufacture the various articles which are formed of rushes, flags, cedar-bark, and bear-grass; but the management of the canoes, and many of the occupations, which elsewhere devolves wholly on the female, are here common to both sexes.

The observation with regard to the importance of females, applies with equal force to the treatment of old men. Among tribes who subsist by hunting, the labors of the chase and the wandering existence to which that occupation condemns them, necessarily throws the burden of procuring provisions on the active young men. As soon, therefore, as a man is unable to pursue the chase, he begins to withdraw something from the precarious supplies of the tribe. Still, however, his counsels may compensate his want of activity; but in the next stage of infirmity, when he can no longer travel from camp to camp, as the tribe roams about for subsistence, he is then found to be a heavy burden. In this situation they are abandoned among the Sioux, Assiniboins, and the hunting tribes on the Missouri. As they are setting out for some new excursion, where the old man is unable to follow, his children, or nearest relations, place before him a piece of meat and some water, and telling him that he has lived long enough, that it is now time for him to go home to his relations, who could take better care of him than his friends on earth, leave him, without remorse, to perish, when his little supply is exhausted. The same custom is said to prevail among the Minnetarees, Ahnahawas, and Ricaras, when they are attended by old men on their hunting excursions. Yet, in their villages, we saw no want of kindness to old men. On the contrary, probably because in villages the means of more abundant subsistence renders such cruelty unnecessary, the old people appeared to be treated with attention, and some of their feasts, particularly the buffalo dances, were intended chiefly as a contribution for the old and infirm.

The dispositions of these people seem mild and inoffensive, and they have uniformly behaved to us with great friendship. They are addicted to begging and pilfering small articles, when it can be done without danger of detection, but do not rob wantonly, nor to any large amount; and some of them having purloined some of our meat, which the hunters had been obliged to leave in the woods, they voluntarily brought some dogs a few days after, by way of compensation. Our force and great superiority in the use of firearms, enable us always to command, and such is the friendly deportment of these people that the men have been accustomed to treat them with the greatest confidence. It is therefore with difficulty that we can impress on our men a conviction of the necessity of being always on our guard, since we are perfectly acquainted with the treacherous character of Indians in general. We are always prepared for an attack, and uniformly exclude all large parties of Indians from the fort. Their large houses usually contain several families, consisting of the parents, their sons and daughters-in-law, and grandchildren, among whom the provisions are common, and whose harmony is scarcely ever interrupted by disputes. Although polygamy is permitted by their customs, very few have more than a single wife, and she is brought immediately after the marriage into the husband's family, where she resides until increasing numbers oblige them to seek another house. In this state the old man is not considered as the head of the family, since the active duties, as well as the responsibility, fall on some of the younger members. As these families gradually expand into bands or tribes or nations, the paternal authority is represented by the chief of each association. This chieftain however is not hereditary; his ability to render service to his neighbors, and the popularity which follows it, is at once the foundation and the measure of his authority, the exercise of which does not extend beyond a reprimand for some improper action.

DRINKING AND GAMBLING

THE harmony of their private life is indeed secured by their ignorance of spirituous liquors, the earliest and most dreadful present which civilization has given to the other natives of the continent. Although they have had so much intercourse with whites, they do not appear to possess any knowledge of those dangerous luxuries; at least they have never inquired after them, which they probably would have done if once they had been introduced among them. Indeed, we have not observed any liquor of an intoxicating quality used among these or any Indians west of the Rocky Mountains, the universal beverage being pure water. They however sometimes almost intoxicate themselves by smoking tobacco of which they are excessively fond, and the pleasures of which they prolong as much as possible, by retaining vast quantities at a time, till after circulating through the lungs and stomach it issues in volumes from the mouth and nostrils. But the natural vice of all these people is an attachment for games of hazard which they pursue with a strange and ruinous avidity. The games are of two kinds. In the first, one of the company assumes the office of banker, and plays against the rest. He takes a small stone, about the size of a bean, which he shifts from one hand to the other with great dexterity, repeating at the same time a song adapted to the game, and which serves to divert the attention of the company, till having agreed on the stake, he holds out his hands, and the antagonist wins or loses as he succeeds or fails at guessing in which hand the stone is. After the banker has lost his money, or whenever he is tired, the stone is transferred to another, who in turn challenges the rest of the company. The other game is something like the play of ninepins; two pins are placed on the floor, about the distance of a foot from each other, and a small hole made behind them. The players then go about ten feet from the hole, into which they try to roll a small piece resembling the men used at draughts; if they succeed in putting it into the hole, they win the stake; if the piece rolls between the pins, but does not go into the hole, nothing is won or lost; but the wager is wholly lost if the checker rolls outside of the pins. Entire days are wasted at these games, which are often continued through the night round the blaze of their fires, till the last article of clothing or even the last blue bead is won from the desperate adventurer.

[As they pass the forks of the Marias River on their return journey, Captain Lewis' party meets a band of Minnetarees whom they know to be hostile.]

A Skirmish with the Minnetarees

... When the two parties came within a hundred yards of each other, all the Indians, except one, halted; Captain Lewis therefore ordered his two men to halt while he advanced, and after shaking hands with the Indian, went on and did the same with the others in the rear, while the Indian himself shook hands with the two men. They all now came up, and after alighting, the Indians asked to smoke with us. Captain Lewis, who was very anxious for Drewyer's safety, told them that the man who had gone down the river had the pipe, and requested that as they had seen him one of them would accompany R. Fields to bring him back. To this they assented, and Fields went with a young man in search of Drewyer. Captain Lewis now asked them by signs if they were the Minnetarees of the north, and was sorry to learn by their answer that his suspicion was too true. He then inquired if there was any chief among them. They pointed out three; but though he did not believe them, yet it was thought best to please them, and he therefore gave to one a flag, to another a medal, and to a third a handkerchief. They appeared to be well satisfied with these presents, and now recovered from the agitation into which our first interview had thrown them, for they were really more alarmed than ourselves at the meeting. In our turn, however, we became equally satisfied on finding that they were not joined by any more of their companions, for we consider ourselves quite a match for eight Indians, particularly as these have but two guns, the rest being armed with only eye-dogs and bows and arrows.

As it was growing late Captain Lewis proposed that they should encamp together near the river; for he was glad to see them and had a great deal to say to them. They assented; and being soon joined by Drewyer, we proceeded towards the river, and after descending a very steep bluff, two hundred and fifty feet high, encamped in a small bottom. Here the Indians formed a large semi-circular tent of dressed buffalo skins, in which the two parties assembled, and by means of Drewyer the evening was spent in conversation with the Indians. They informed us that they were a part of a large band which at present lay encamped on the main branch of Maria's River, near the foot of the Rocky Mountains, and at the distance of a day and a half's journey from this place. Another large band were hunting buffalo near the Broken Mountains, from which they would proceed in a few days to the north of Maria's River. With the first of these there was a white man. They added, that from this place to the establishment on the Saskashawan, at which they trade, is only six days' easy march; that is, such a day's journey as can be made with their women and children, so that we computed the distance at one hundred and fifty miles. There they carry the skins of wolves and some beavers, and exchange them for guns, ammunition, blankets, spirituous liquors, and the other articles of Indian traffic. . . . Finding them very fond of the pipe, Captain Lewis, who was desirous of keeping a constant watch during the night, smoked with them until a late hour, and as soon as they were all asleep, he woke R. Fields, and ordering him to rouse us all in case any Indian left the camp, as they would probably attempt to steal our horses, he lay down by the side of Drewyer in the tent with all the Indians, while the Fields were stretched near the fire at the mouth of it. At sunrise,

SUNDAY, [JULY] 27, [1806] the Indians got up and crowded round the fire near which J. Fields, who was then on watch, had carelessly left his rifle, near the head of his brother, who was still asleep. One of the Indians slipped behind him, and unperceived, took his brother's and his own rifle, while at the same time two others seized those of Drewyer and Captain Lewis. As soon as Fields turned round, he saw the Indian running off with the rifles, and instantly calling his brother, they pursued him for fifty or sixty yards, and just as they overtook him, in the scuffle for the rifles, R. Fields stabbed him through the heart with his knife; the Indian ran about fifteen steps and fell dead. They now ran back with their rifles to the camp. The moment the fellow touched his gun, Drewyer, who was awake, jumped up and wrested her from him. The noise awoke Captain Lewis, who instantly started from the ground and reached to seize his gun, but finding her gone, drew a pistol from his belt and turning about saw the Indian running off with her. He followed him and ordered him to lay her down, which he was doing just as the Fields came up, and were taking aim to shoot him, when Captain Lewis ordered them not to fire, as the Indian did not appear to intend any mischief. He dropped the gun and was going slowly off as Drewyer came out and asked permission to kill him, but this Captain Lewis forbid as he had not yet attempted to shoot us. But finding that the Indians were now endeavoring to drive off all the horses, he ordered three of them to follow the main party who were chasing the horses up the river, and fire instantly upon the thieves; while he, without taking time to run for his shot-pouch, pursued the fellow who had stolen his gun and another Indian, who were driving away the horses on the left of the camp. He pressed them so closely that they left twelve of their horses, but continued to drive off one of our own. At the distance of three hundred paces they entered a steep niche in the river bluffs, when Captain Lewis, being too much out of breath to pursue them any further, called out, as he did several times before, that unless they gave up the horse he would shoot them. As he raised his gun one of the Indians jumped behind a rock and spoke to the other, who stopped at the distance of thirty paces, as Captain Lewis shot him in the belly. He fell on his knees and right elbow, but raising himself a little, fired, and then crawled behind a rock. The shot had nearly been fatal, for Captain Lewis, who was bareheaded, felt the wind of the ball very distinctly. Not having his shot-pouch, he could not reload his rifle, and having only a single load also for his pistol, he thought it most prudent not to attack the Indians, and therefore retired slowly to the camp. He was met by Drewyer, who hearing the report of the guns, had come to his assistance, leaving the Fields to pursue the Indians. Captain Lewis ordered him to call out to them to desist from the pursuit, as we could take the horses of the Indians in place of our own, but they were at too great a distance to hear him. He

ABOVE, Champlain and his men join the Algonquins in a battle against the Iroquois. [See pages 786-796.]

BELOW, a sketch of Flathead Indians showing the effects of their head-flattening practice. Note baby on mother's back, with forehead being flattened. [See pages 815-827.]

America North

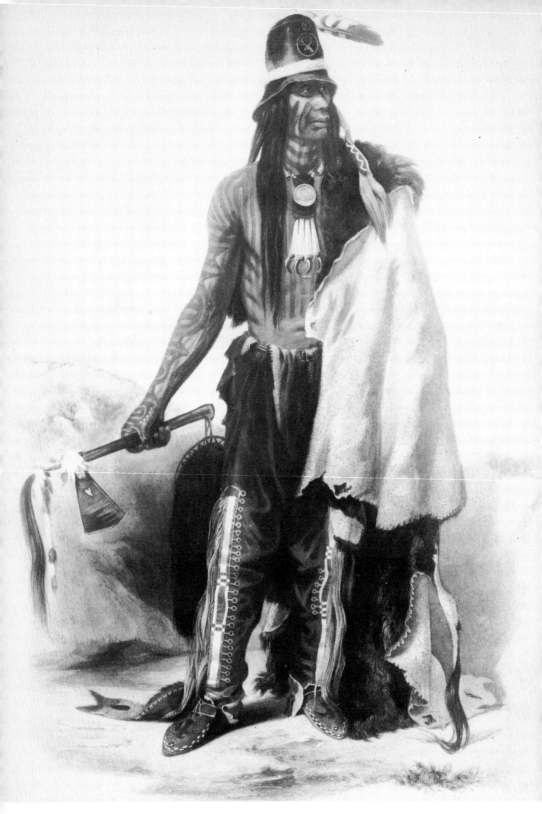

A painting of a Minatarre by Carl Bodmer, made about 25 years after the skirmish with a band of Minatarres described by Lewis and Clark on pages 824-827.

ABOVE, an illustration from Gregg's *Commerce of the Prairies* showing a caravan formation on the Santa Fé Trail. [See pages 828-834.]

BELOW, Mandan braves indulging in a torture orgy to prove their courage. [See pages 835-843.]

ABOVE, a self-portrait of George Catlin painting one of the thousands of Indian pictures for which he became world-famous. [See pages 835-843.]

BELOW, New York's Broadway as seen from Astor House in 1850. J. Clarence Davies Collection, Museum of the City of New York. [See pages 844-852.]

ABOVE, Indians hunting bison, or buffalo, as described by Parkman. [*See pages* 853-862.]

BELOW, J. Goldsborough Bruff, on home-made snowshoes, searches for fuel during an enforced winter stay in the Sierra Nevada. [*See pages* 863-871.]

Winter in S. Nevada
author on Snow-Shoes, seeking fuel

ABOVE LEFT and RIGHT, exterior and interior
views of the crowding on New York street railroad cars in the 1860s. [See pages 872-875.]

RIGHT, a concert on the piazza of a Saratoga
hotel in the 1870s. Courtesy of The New-
York Historical Society. [See pages 887-891.]

ABOVE, lower New York's skyline and river front in 1891. Museum of the City of New York.

BELOW, Harvard Varsity Football Team of 1894, which played in the game described by Paul Bourget. Courtesy of the Harvard A.A. News [See pages 901-907.]

therefore returned to the camp, and whilst he was saddling the horses, the Fields returned with four of our own, having followed the Indians until two of them swam the river, two others ascended the hills, so that the horses became dispersed. We, however, were rather gainers by this contest, for we took four of the Indian horses, and lost only one of our own. Besides which, we found in the camp four shields, two bows with quivers, and one of the guns, which we took with us, and also the flag which we had presented to them, but left the medal round the neck of the dead man, in order that they might be informed who we were. . . .

[Expecting retaliation by a larger band of Indians, they hurry toward a junction with the other detachment of their party.]

. . . HE [Captain Lewis] told them also that it was his determination, in case they were attacked in crossing the plains, to tie the bridles of the horses and stand together till they had either routed their enemies or sold their lives as dearly as possible. To this they all assented, and we therefore continued our route to the eastward, till at the distance of twelve miles we came near the Missouri, when we heard a noise which seemed like the report of a gun. We therefore quickened our pace for eight miles further, and about five miles from the Grog Spring, now heard distinctly the noise of several rifles from the river. We hurried to the bank, and saw with exquisite satisfaction our friends coming down the river. . . .

[Rejoining Captain Clark's detachment, they proceed by canoe down the Missouri and soon reach St. Louis.]

The Santa Fé Trail

JOSIAH GREGG

FROM *Commerce of the Prairies*

1831–40

A studious boy, Josiah Gregg was something of a misfit on the Missouri frontier farm where he spent his childhood. After a few years of teaching school and studying medicine, his health failed, and doctors told him—just as they were to tell young Francis Parkman some fifteen years later—to try the prairie. Taking their advice, in 1831 he joined a merchant caravan bound for New Mexico eight hundred miles away. Life on the Santa Fé Trail worked wonders for his health, and for nine years he traveled back and forth across the southern Great Plains, profitably trading wagonloads of dry goods and hardware for Mexican silver and mules. Hardly a gifted writer (although it may be the rewriting, which he commissioned, that is responsible for the flourishes in his narrative), Gregg was a reliable observer, and his book is packed with information on the Southwest and northern Mexico before they were tamed by farms, fences and roads.

After leaving the trail, Gregg again studied medicine and practiced it for a few years. In 1848 he went west on a botanical field trip and while in a gold-rush town was commissioned to find a direct route across the mountains to the coast. He reached the coast but was killed by a fall in 1850, at the age of forty-four.

In his book, chapters describing his experiences on the trail alternate with others on the natural history, resources, trade and inhabitants of the area. It is from the autobiographical sections that the extracts below are taken.

WAGON TRAINS AND WAGON WHEELS

As the caravan was passing under the northern base of the Round Mound, it presented a very fine and imposing spectacle to those who were upon its summit. The wagons marched slowly in four parallel columns, but in broken lines, often at intervals of many rods between. The unceasing "crack, crack," of the wagoners' whips, resembling the frequent reports of distant guns, almost made one believe that a skirmish was actually taking place between two hostile parties: and a hostile engagement it virtually was to the poor brutes, at least; for the merciless application of the whip would sometimes make the blood spirt from their sides—and that often without any apparent motive of the wanton *carrettieri*, other than to amuse themselves with the flourishing and loud popping of their lashes!

The rear wagons are usually left without a guard; for all the loose horsemen incline to be ahead, where they are to be seen moving in scattered groups, sometimes a mile or more in advance. As our camp was pitched but a mile west of the Round Mound, those who lingered upon its summit could have an interesting view of the evolutions of "forming" the wagons, in which the drivers by this time had become very expert. When marching four abreast, the two exterior lines spread out and then meet at the front angle; while the two inner lines keep close together until they reach the point of the rear angle, when they wheel suddenly out and close with the hinder ends of the other two; thus systematically concluding a right-lined quadrangle, with a gap left at the rear corner for the introduction of the animals.

Our encampment was in a beautiful plain, but without water, of which, however, we had had a good supply at noon. Our cattle, as was the usual custom, after having grazed without for a few hours, were now shut up in the pen of the wagons. Our men were all wrapt in peaceful slumber, except the guard, who kept their silent watch around the encampment; when all of a sudden, about the ominous hour of midnight, a tremendous uproar was heard, which caused every man to start in terror from his blanket couch, with arms in hand. Some animal, it appeared, had taken fright at a dog, and by a sudden start, set all around him in violent motion: the panic spread simultaneously throughout the pen; and a scene of rattle, clash, and "lumbering" ensued, which far surpassed everything we had yet witnessed. A general "stampede" (*estampida*, as the Mexicans say) was the result. Notwithstanding the wagons were tightly bound together, wheel to wheel, with ropes or chains, and several stretched across the gaps at the corners of the *corral*, the oxen soon burst their way out; and though mostly yoked in pairs, they went scampering over the plains, as though Tam O'Shanter's "cutty-sark" Nannie had been at their tails. All attempts to stop them were vain; for it would require "Auld Clootie" himself to check the headway of a drove of oxen, when once thoroughly frightened. Early the following morning we made active exertions to get up a sufficient quantity of teams to start the caravan. At Rock Creek, a distance of six or seven miles, we were joined by those who had gone in pursuit of the stock. All the oxen were found, except some half a dozen, which were never recovered. No mules were lost: a few that had broken loose were speedily retaken. The fact is, that though mules are generally easiest scared, oxen are decidedly the worst when once started. The principal advantage of the latter in this respect is that Indians have but little inducement to steal them, and therefore few attempts would be made upon a caravan of oxen.

We were now entering a region of rough, and in some places, rocky road, as the streams which intervene from this to the mountains are all bordered with fine sandstone. These rugged passes acted very severely upon our wagons, as the wheels were by this time becoming loose and "shackling," from the shrink of the wood, occasioned by the extreme dryness and rarity of this elevated atmosphere. The spokes of some were beginning to reel in the hubs, so that it became necessary to brace them with "false spokes," firmly bound with "buffalo tug." On some occasions, the wagon tires have become so loose upon the felloes as to tumble off while travelling. The most effective mode of tightening slackened tires (at least that most practiced on the plains, as there is rarely a portable forge in company), is by driving strips of hoop-iron around between the tire and felloe—simple wedges of wood are sometimes made to supply the place of iron. During halts I have seen a dozen wheels being repaired at the same time, occasioning such a clitter-clatter of hammers that one would almost fancy himself in a ship yard. . . .

PRAIRIE FIRE AND PAWNEE ATTACK

ON the 25th of February we set out from Santa Fé: but owing to some delays, we did not leave San Miguel till the 1st of March. As the pasturage was yet insufficient for our animals, we here provided ourselves with over six hundred bushels of corn, to feed them on the way. This time our caravan consisted of twenty-eight wagons, two small cannons, and forty-seven men, including sixteen Mexicans and a Comanche Indian who acted in the capacity of guide. Two gentlemen of Baltimore, Messrs. S. Wethered and J. R. Ware, had joined our caravan with one wagon and three men, making up the aggregate above mentioned. We had also a caballada of more than two hundred mules, with nearly three hundred sheep and goats. The sheep were brought along partially to supply us with meat in case of emergency; the surplusage, however, could not fail to command a fair price in the United States.

Instead of following the trail of the year before, I determined to seek a nearer and better route down the south side of the Canadian river, under the guidance of the Comanche; by which movement, we had again to travel a distance of four hundred miles over an entirely new country. We had just passed the Laguna Colorado, where, the following year, a division of Texan volunteers, under General McLeod, surrendered to Col. Archuleta, when our fire was carelessly permitted to communicate with the prairie grass. As there was a head-wind blowing at the time, we very soon got out of reach of the conflagration; but the next day, the wind having changed, the fire was again perceived in our rear approaching us at a very brisk pace. The terror which these prairie conflagrations are calculated to inspire, when the grass is tall and dry, as was the case in the present instance, has often been described, and though the perils of these disasters are not unfrequently exaggerated, they are sometimes sufficient to daunt the stoutest heart. Mr. Kendall relates a frightful incident of this kind which occurred to the Texan Santa Fé Expedition; and all those who have crossed the Prairies have had more or less experience as to the danger which occasionally threatens the caravans from these sweeping visitations. The worst evil to be apprehended with those bound for Santa Fé is from the explosion of gunpowder, as a keg or two of twenty-five pounds each is usually to be found in every wagon. When we saw the fire gaining so rapidly upon us, we had to use the whip very unsparingly; and it was only when the lurid flames were actually rolling upon the heels of our teams that we succeeded in reaching a spot of short-grass prairie, where there was no further danger to be apprehended.

The head way of the conflagration was soon after checked by a small stream which traversed our route; and we had only emerged fairly from its smoke, on the following day (the 9th), when our Comanche guide returned hastily from his accustomed post in advance, and informed us that he had espied three buffaloes, not far off. They were the first we had met with, and, being heartily anxious for a change from the dried beef with which we were provided, I directed the Comanche, who was by far our surest hunter, to prepare at once for the *chasse*. He said he preferred to hunt on horseback and with his bow and arrow; and believing my riding horse the fleetest in company (which, by the by, was but a common pony, and thin in flesh withal), I dismounted and gave him the bridle, with many charges to treat him kindly, as we still had a long journey before us. "Don't attempt to kill but one—that will serve us for the present!" I exclaimed, as he galloped off. The Comanche was among the largest of his tribe—bony and muscular—weighing about two hundred pounds; but once at his favorite sport, he very quickly forgot my injunction, as well as the weakness of my little pony. He soon brought down two of his game—and shyly remarked to those who followed in his wake, that, had he not feared a scolding from me, he would not have permitted the third to escape.

On the evening of the 10th our camp was pitched in the neighborhood of a ravine in the prairie, and as the night was dark and dreary, the watch tried to comfort themselves by building a rousing fire, around which they presently drew, and commenced "spinning long yarns" about Mexican fandangoes and black-eyed damsels. All of a sudden the stillness of the night was interrupted by a loud report of fire-arms, and a shower of bullets came whizzing by the ears of the heedless sentinels. Fortunately, however, no one was injured; which must be looked upon as a very extraordinary circumstance, when we consider what a fair mark our men, thus huddled round a blazing fire, presented to the rifles of the Indians. The savage yells, which resounded from every part of the ravine, bore very satisfactory testimony that this was no false alarm; and the "Pawnee whistle" which was heard in every quarter, at once impressed us with the idea of its being a band of that famous prairie banditti.

Every man sprang from his pallet with rifle in hand; for, upon the Prairies, we always sleep with our arms by our sides or under our heads. Our Comanche seemed at first very much at a loss what to do. At last, thinking it might possibly be a band of his own nation, he began a most boisterous harangue in his vernacular tongue, which he continued for several minutes; when finding that the enemy took no notice of him, and having been convinced also, from an occasional Pawnee word which he was able to make out, that he had been wasting breath with the mortal foes of his race, he suddenly ceased all expostulations, and blazed away with his rifle, with a degree of earnestness which was truly edifying, as if convinced that that was the best he could do for us.

It was now evident that the Indians had taken possession of the entire ravine, the nearest points of which were not fifty yards from our wagons: a warning to prairie travellers to encamp at a greater distance from whatsoever might afford shelter for an enemy. The banks of the gully were low, but still they formed a very good breastwork, behind which the enemy lay ensconced, discharging volleys of balls upon our wagons, among which we were scattered. At one time we thought of making an attempt to rout them from their fortified position; but being ignorant of their number, and unable to distinguish any object through the dismal darkness which hung all around, we had to remain content with firing at random from behind our wagons, aiming at the flash of their guns, or in the direction whence any noise appeared to emanate. Indeed their yelling was almost continuous, breaking out every now and then in the most hideous screams and vociferous chattering, which were calculated to appal such timorous persons as we may have had in our caravan. All their screeching and whooping, however, had no effect—they could not make our animals break from the enclosure of the wagons, in which they were fortunately shut up; which was no doubt their principal object for attacking us.

I cannot forbear recording a most daring feat performed by a Mexican muleteer, named Antonio Chavez, during the hottest of the first onset. Seeing the danger of my two favorite riding-horses, which were tethered outside within a few paces of the savages, he rushed out and brought safely in the most valuable of the two, though fusil-balls were showering around him all the while. The other horse broke his halter and made his escape.

Although sundry scores of shots had been fired at our people, we had only two men wounded. One, a Mexican, was but slightly injured in the hand, but the wound of the other, who was an Italian, bore a more serious aspect, and deserves especial mention. He was a short, corpulent fellow, and had been nicknamed "Dutch"—a loquacious chicken-hearted *fainéant*, and withal in the daily habit of gorging himself to such an enormous extent that every alternate night he was on the sick-list. On this memorable occasion, Dutch had "foundered" again, and the usual prescription of a double dose of Epsom salts had been his supper potion. The skirmish had continued for about an hour, and although a frightful groaning had been heard in Dutch's wagon for some time, no one paid any attention to it, as it was generally supposed to be from the effects of his dose. At length, however, some one cried out, "Dutch is wounded!" I immediately went to see him, and found him writhing and twisting himself as if in great pain, crying all the time that he was shot. "Shot!—

where?" I inquired. "Ah! in the head, sir." "Pshaw! Dutch, none of that; you've only bumped your head in trying to hide yourself." Upon lighting a match, however, I found that a ball had passed through the middle of his hat, and that, to my consternation, the top of his head was bathed in blood. It turned out, upon subsequent examination, that the ball had glanced upon the skull, inflicting a serious-looking wound, and so deep that an inch of sound skin separated the holes at which the bullet had entered and passed out. Notwithstanding I at first apprehended a fracture of the skull, it very soon healed, and Dutch was "up and about" again in the course of a week. . . .

The enemy continued the attack for nearly three hours, when they finally retired, so as to make good their retreat before daylight. As it rained and snowed from that time till nine in the morning, their "sign" was almost entirely obliterated, and we were unable to discover whether they had received any injury or not. It was evidently a foot party, which we looked upon as another proof of their being Pawnees; for these famous marauders are well known to go forth on their expeditions of plunder without horses, although they seldom fail to return well mounted.

Their shot had riddled our wagons considerably: in one we counted no less than eight bullet-holes. We had the gratification to believe, however, that they did not get a single one of our animals: the horse which broke away at the first onset, doubtless made his escape; and a mule which was too badly wounded to travel was dispatched by the muleteers, lest it should fall into the hands of the savages, or into the mouths of the wolves; and they deemed it more humane to leave it to be eaten dead than alive. We also experienced considerable damage in our stock of sheep, a number of them having been devoured by wolves.

Self-Torture and Wild Horses

GEORGE CATLIN

FROM *Letters and Notes on the Manners, Customs, and Condition of the North American Indians*

1832–39

George Catlin was a fashionable New York portrait painter when he suddenly decided in his thirties to paint Indians instead of the social élite. Actually, his interest in frontier and Indian life was not surprising, for his father had served for eight years in the Revolutionary Army and his mother had been carried off by Indians as a child at the famous massacre in Pennsylvania's Wyoming Valley. Inspired by the sight of a delegation of noble-looking Indians, he now determined to put these people on canvas before—as he never wearied of pointing out—they were wiped out forever.

Leaving wife and home in 1832, he roamed western America for eight years, visiting forty-eight tribes and bringing back more than six hundred always painstaking and sometimes dramatic paintings of Indians and their lives, along with the notes for a massive report. Assembling his pictures and taking several Indians with him, he toured Europe and America with what he called "Catlin's Gallery of the North American Indian" (now a part of the Smithsonian Institution in Washington, D.C.).

Between 1852 and 1857 Catlin made a series of journeys that took him to British Guiana, through the Amazon Valley to the Pacific, down to Tierra del Fuego, up the Pacific coast to the Aleutians and Siberia, south to California and the Apache country, along the Rio Grande and across the Gulf of Mexico to Yucatán, with pauses for painting Indians all along the way. Out of these travels came such books as Last Rambles amongst the Indians of the Rocky Mountains and the Andes *and* My Life among the Indians.

When not taken up with glorifying or defending the red man, Catlin's writings could be as graphic and authentic as the best of his paintings. In the first selection below he describes self-torture among the Mandan Indians of the upper Missouri and in the second the taming of wild horses.

Orgy of Self-Torture

. . . Two men having taken their positions near the middle of the lodge for the purpose of inflicting the tortures—the one with the scalping-knife, and the other with the bunch of splints . . . in his hand, one at a time the young fellows, already emaciated with fasting and thirsting and waking for nearly four days and nights, advanced from the side of the lodge and placed himself on his hands and feet, or otherwise, as best suited for the performance of the operation, where he submitted to the cruelties in the following manner: An inch or more of the flesh on each shoulder, or each breast was taken up between the thumb and finger by the man who held the knife in his right hand; and the knife, which had been ground sharp on both edges, and then hacked and notched with the blade of another, to make it produce as much pain as possible, was forced through the flesh below the fingers, and being withdrawn, was followed with a splint or skewer from the other, who held a bunch of such in his left hand, and was ready to force them through the wound. There were then two cords lowered down from the top of the lodge (by men who were placed on the lodge outside for the purpose), which were fastened to these splints or skewers, and they instantly began to haul him up; he was thus raised until his body was just suspended from the ground where he rested, until the knife and a splint were passed through the flesh or integuments in a similar manner on each arm below the shoulder (over the *brachialis externus*), below the elbow (over the *extensor carpi radialis*), on the thighs (over the *vastus externus*), and below the knees (over the *peroneus*).

In some instances they remained in a reclining position on the ground until this painful operation was finished, which was performed, in all instances, exactly on the same parts of the body and limbs; and which, in its progress, occupied some five or six minutes.

Each one was then instantly raised with the cords, until the weight of his body was suspended by them, and then, while the blood was streaming down their limbs, the bystanders hung upon the splints each man's appropriate shield, bow and quiver, etc.; and in many instances, the skull of a buffalo with the horns on it, was attached to each lower arm and each lower leg, for the purpose, probably, of preventing by their great weight, the struggling, which might otherwise take place to their disadvantage whilst they were hung up.

When these things were all adjusted, each one was raised higher by the cords, until these weights all swung clear from the ground, leaving his feet, in most cases, some six or eight feet above the ground. In this plight they at once became appalling and frightful to look at—the flesh, to support the weight of their bodies, with the additional weights which were attached to them, was raised six or eight inches by the skewers; and their heads sunk forward on the breasts, or thrown backwards, in a much more frightful condition, according to the way in which they were hung up.

The unflinching fortitude, with which every one of them bore this part of the torture surpassed credulity; each one as the knife was passed through his flesh sustained an unchangeable countenance; and several of them, seeing me making sketches, beckoned me to look at their faces, which I watched through all this horrid operation, without being able to detect anything but the pleasantest smiles as they looked me in the eye, while I could hear the knife rip through the flesh, and feel enough of it myself to start involuntary and uncontrollable tears over my cheeks.

Surrounded by imps and demons as they appear, a dozen or more, who seem to be concerting and devising means for his exquisite agony, gather around him, when one of the number advances towards him in a sneering manner, and commences turning him around with a pole which he brings in his hand for the purpose. This is done in a gentle manner at first; but gradually increased, when the brave fellow, whose proud spirit can control its agony no longer, burst out in the most lamentable and heart-rending cries that the human voice is capable of producing, crying forth a prayer to the Great Spirit to support and protect him in this dreadful trial; and continually repeating his confidence in his protection. In this condition he is continued to be turned, faster and faster— and there is no hope of escape from it, nor chance for the slightest relief, until by fainting, his voice falters, and his struggling ceases, and he hangs, apparently, a still and lifeless corpse! . . .

When brought to this alarming and most frightful condition, and the turning has gradually ceased, as his voice and his strength have given out, leaving him to hang entirely still, and apparently lifeless; when his tongue is distended from his mouth, and his *medicine-bag*, which he has affectionately and superstitiously clung to with his left hand, has dropped to the ground; the signal is given to the men on top of the lodge, by gently striking the cord with the pole below, when they very gradually and carefully lower him to the ground.

In this helpless condition he lies, like a loathsome corpse to look at, though in the keeping (as they call it) of the Great Spirit, whom he trusts will protect him, and enable him to get up and walk away. As soon as he is lowered to the ground thus, one of the bystanders advances, and pulls out the two splints or pins from the breasts and shoulders, thereby disengaging him from the cords by which he has been hung up; but leaving all the others with their weights, etc. hanging to his flesh.

In this condition he lies for six or eight minutes, until he gets strength to rise and move himself, for no one is allowed to assist or offer him aid, as he is here enjoying the most valued privilege which a Mandan can boast of, that of "trusting his life to the keeping of the Great Spirit," in this time of extreme peril.

As soon as he is seen to get strength enough to rise on his hands and feet, and drag his body around the lodge, he crawls with the weights still hanging to his body, to another part of the lodge, where there is another Indian sitting with a hatchet in his hand, and a dried buffalo skull before him; and here, in the most earnest and humble manner, by holding up the little finger of his left hand to the Great Spirit, he expresses to Him, in a speech of a few words, his willingness to give it as a sacrifice; when he lays it on the dried buffalo skull, where the other chops it off near the hand, with a blow of the hatchet!

Nearly all of the young men whom I saw passing this horrid ordeal, gave in the above manner, the little finger of the left hand; and I saw also several, who immediately afterwards (and apparently with very little concern or emotion), with a similar speech, extended in the same way, the *fore*-finger of the same hand, and that too was struck off; leaving on the left hand only the two middle fingers and the thumb; all which they deem absolutely essential for holding the bow, the only weapon for the left hand.

One would think that this mutilation had thus been carried quite far enough; but I have since examined several of the head chiefs and dignitaries of the tribe, who have also given, in this manner, the little finger of the right hand, which is considered by them to be a much greater sacrifice than both of the others; and I have found also a number of their most famous men, who furnish me incontestable proof, by five or six corresponding scars on each arm, and each breast, and each leg, that they had so many times in their lives submitted to this almost incredible operation, which seems to be optional with them; and the oftener they volunteer to go through it, the more famous they become in the estimation of their tribe.

No bandages are applied to the fingers which have been amputated, nor any arteries taken up; nor is any attention whatever paid to them or the other wounds; but they are left (as they say) "for the Great Spirit to cure, who will surely take good care of them." It is a remarkable fact (which I learned from a close inspection of their wounds from day to day) that the bleeding is but very slight and soon ceases, probably from the fact of their extreme exhaustion and debility, caused by want of sustenance and sleep, which checks the natural circulation, and admirably at the same time prepares them to meet the severity of these tortures without the same degree of sensibility and pain, which, under other circumstances, might result in inflammation and death.

During the whole of the time of this cruel part of these most extraordinary inflictions, the chiefs and dignitaries of the tribe are looking on, to decide who are the hardiest and "stoutest hearted"—who can hang the longest by his flesh before he faints, and who will be soonest up, after he has been down; that they may know whom to appoint to lead a war-party, or place at the most honourable and desperate post. The four old men are incessantly beating upon the sacks of water and singing the whole time, with their voices strained to the highest key, vaunting forth, for the encouragement of the young men, the power and efficacy of the medicine-pipe, which has disarmed the monster O-kee-he-de (or Evil Spirit), and driven him from the village, and will be sure to protect them and watch over them through their present severe trial.

As soon as six or eight had passed the ordeal as above described, they were led out of the lodge, with their weights hanging to their flesh, and dragging on the ground, to undergo another, and still more appalling mode of suffering in the center of the village, and in presence of the whole nation, in the manner as follows:—

The signal for the commencement of this part of the cruelties was given by the old master of ceremonies, who again ran out as in the buffalo-dance, and leaning against the big canoe, with his *medicine-pipe* in his hand, began to cry. This was done several times in the afternoon, as often as there were six or eight who had passed the ordeal just described within the lodge, who were then taken out in the open area, in the presence of the whole village, with the buffalo skulls and other weights attached to their flesh, and dragging on the ground! There were then in readiness, and prepared for the purpose, about twenty young men, selected of equal height and equal age; with their bodies chiefly naked, with beautiful (and similar) head-dresses of war-eagle's quills, on their heads, and a wreath made of willow boughs held in the hands between them, connecting them in a chain or circle in which they ran around the *big canoe*, with all possible speed. . . .

Then were led forward the young men who were further to suffer, and being placed at equal distances apart, and outside of the ring just described, each one was taken in charge of two athletic young men, fresh and strong, who stepped up to him, one on each side, and by wrapping a broad leather strap around his wrists, without tying it, grasped it firm underneath the hand, and stood prepared for what they call *Eh-ke-na-ka-nah-pick*, the last race. . . .

In this condition they stand, pale and ghastly, from abstinence and loss of blood, until all are prepared, and the word is given, when all start and run around, outside of the other ring; and each poor fellow, with his weights dragging on the ground, and his furious conductors by his side, who hurry him forward by the wrists, struggles in the desperate emulation to run longer without "dying" (as they call it) than his comrades, who are fainting around him and sinking down, like himself, where their bodies are dragged with all possible speed, and often with their faces in the dirt. In the commencement of this dance or race they all start at a moderate pace, and their speed being gradually increased, the pain becomes so excruciating that their languid and exhausted frames give out, and they are dragged by their wrists until they are disengaged from the weights that were attached to their flesh, and this must be done by such violent force as to tear the flesh out with the splint, which (as they say) can never be pulled out end-wise, without greatly offending the Great Spirit and defeating the object for which they have thus far suffered. The splints or skewers which are put through the breast and the shoulders, take up a part of the pectoral or trapegius muscle, which is necessary for the support of the great weight of their bodies, and which, as I have before mentioned, are withdrawn as soon as he is lowered down—but all the others, on the legs and arms, seem to be very ingeniously passed through the flesh and integuments without taking up the muscle, and even these, to be broken out, require so strong and so violent a force that most of the poor fellows fainted under the operation, and when they were freed from the last of the buffalo skulls and other weights (which was often done by some of the bystanders throwing the weight of their bodies on to them as they were dragging on the ground), they were in every instance dropped by the persons who dragged them, and their bodies were left, appearing like nothing but a mangled and a loathsome corpse! At this strange and frightful juncture, the two men who had dragged them, fled through the crowd and away upon the prairie, as if they were guilty of some enormous crime, and were fleeing from summary vengeance.

Each poor fellow, having thus patiently and manfully endured the privations and tortures devised for him, and (in this last struggle with the most appalling effort) torn himself loose from them and his tormentors, he lies the second time, in the "keeping (as he terms it) of the Great Spirit," to whom he issued his repeated prayers, and entrusted his life . . .

BREAKING A WILD HORSE

THE usual mode of taking the wild horses is by throwing the *laso*, whilst pursuing them at full speed, and dropping a noose over their necks, by which their speed is soon checked, and they are "choked down." The laso is a thong of raw-hide, some ten or fifteen yards in length, twisted or braided, with a noose fixed at the end of it; which, when the coil of the laso is thrown out, drops with great certainty over the neck of the animal, which is soon conquered.

The Indian, when he starts for a wild horse, mounts one of the fleetest he can get, and coiling his laso on his arm, starts off under the "full whip," till he can enter the band, when he soon gets it over the neck of one of the number; when he instantly dismounts, leaving his own horse, and runs as fast as he can, letting the laso pass out gradually and carefully through his hands, until the horse falls for want of breath, and lies helpless on the ground, at which time the Indian advances slowly towards the horse's head, keeping his laso tight upon its neck, until he fastens a pair of hobbles on the animal's two forefeet, and also loosens the laso (giving the horse chance to breathe), and gives it a noose around the under jaw, by which he gets great power over the affrighted animal, which is rearing and plunging when it gets breath; and by which, as he advances, hand over hand, towards the horse's nose, he is able to hold it down and prevent it from throwing itself over on its back, at the hazard of its limbs. By this means he gradually advances, until he is able to place his hand on the animal's nose and over its eyes; and at length to breathe in its nostrils, when it soon becomes docile and conquered; so that he has little else to do than to remove the hobbles from its feet, and lead or ride it into camp.

This "breaking down" or taming, however, is not without the most desperate trial on the part of the horse, which rears and plunges in every possible way to effect its escape, until its power is exhausted, and it becomes covered with foam; and at last yields to the power of man, and becomes his willing slave for the rest of its life. By this very rigid treatment, the poor animal seems to be so completely conquered, that it makes no further struggle for its freedom; but submits quietly ever after, and is led or rode away with very little difficulty. Great care is taken, however, in this and in subsequent treatment, not to subdue the spirit of the animal, which is carefully preserved and kept up, although they use them with great severity; being, generally speaking, cruel masters.

The wild horse of these regions is a small, but very powerful animal; with an exceedingly prominent eye, sharp nose, high nostril, small feet and delicate leg; and undoubtedly have sprung from a stock introduced by the Spaniards, at the time of the invasion of Mexico; which having strayed off upon the prairies, have run wild, and stocked the plains from this to Lake Winnepeg, two or three thousand miles to the North.

This useful animal has been of great service to the Indians living on these vast plains, enabling them to take their game more easily, to carry their burthens, etc.; and no doubt render them better and handier service than if they were of a larger and heavier breed. Vast numbers of them are also killed for food by the Indians, at seasons when buffaloes and other game are scarce. They subsist themselves both in winter and summer by biting at the grass, which they can always get in sufficient quantities for their food.

Whilst on our march we met with many droves of these beautiful animals, and several times had the opportunity of seeing the Indians pursue them, and take them with the laso. The first successful instance of the kind was effected by one of our guides and hunters, by the name of Beatte, a Frenchman, whose parents had lived nearly their whole lives in the Osage village; and who, himself, had been reared from infancy amongst them; and in a continual life of Indian modes and amusements, had acquired all the skill and tact of his Indian teachers, and probably a little more; for he is reputed, without exception, the best hunter in these Western regions.

This instance took place one day whilst the regiment was at its usual halt of an hour, in the middle of the day.

When the bugle sounded for a halt, and all were dismounted, Beatte and several others of the hunters asked permission of Col. Dodge to pursue a drove of horses which were then in sight, at a distance of a mile or more from us. The permission was given, and they started off, and by following a ravine, approached near to the unsuspecting animals, when they broke upon them and pursued them for several miles in full view of the regiment. Several of us had good glasses, with which we could plainly see every movement and every manoeuvre. After a race of two or three miles, Beatte was seen with his wild horse down, and the band and the other hunters rapidly leaving him.

Seeing him in this condition, I galloped off to him as rapidly as possible, and had the satisfaction of seeing the whole operation of "breaking down," and bringing in the wild animal . . . When he had conquered the horse in this way, his brother, who was one of the unsuccessful ones in the chase, came riding back, and leading up the horse of Beatte which he had left behind, and after staying with us a few minutes, assisted Beatte in leading his conquered wild horse towards the regiment, where it was satisfactorily examined and commented upon, as it was trembling and covered with white foam, until the bugle sounded the signal for marching, when all mounted; and with the rest, Beatte, astride of his wild horse, which had a buffalo skin girted on its back, and a halter, with a cruel noose around under the under jaw. In this manner the command resumed its march, and Beatte astride of his wild horse, on which he rode quietly and without difficulty, until night; the whole thing, the capture, and breaking, all having been accomplished within the space of one hour, our usual and daily halt at midday.

Broadway, Slums, and a Steamboat on the Ohio

CHARLES DICKENS

FROM *American Notes*

1842

With its lurid impressions of America and its violent opinions—especially on the evils of slavery—it is easy to see why the book Dickens wrote about his visit to America in 1842 should have aroused so much resentment. Thirty years old and already a famous novelist, Dickens was welcomed royally, but this failed to assuage his resentment against American publishers who did not honor his copyright or pay him royalties. As he made his hasty five-month swing from Boston south to Baltimore, west to St. Louis (including a jaunt onto the open prairie), thence to Niagara Falls and lower Canada, and finally back again to New York, he became increasingly critical. Like such earlier British travelers as Mrs. Trollope and Frederick Marryat, he described Americans as distrustful, prone to "smart dealing," humorless and coarse. But whereas in Mrs. Trollope there is little else to say, in Dickens there is some awareness that much of what he saw was the rawness and ferment of a people building a civilization in a wilderness. As in his novels (including Martin Chuzzlewit, in which he used much of his American experience), there is in American Notes the wonderful vitality and fervor, the passionate convictions, the genius for farce and pathos. There is also, by the same token, emotional excess and caricature.

In 1867–68 he returned to America on an immensely successful lecture *tour, and declared that the twenty-five years since his first visit had seen such great changes in America—not the least being the emancipation of the slaves—that few or none of his criticisms still applied.*

[Dickens and his wife arrive in Boston in January 1842, after an eighteen-day run from Liverpool. Because his novels have exposed the sorry conditions in certain English schools and almshouses, he is taken to see all kinds of public institutions and devotes his Boston chapter to a home for the blind, an insane asylum, a prison, and so forth. He seems somewhat surprised to find most of these praiseworthy; indeed, his admiration of the edifying activities of working girls under the Lowell factory system is almost condescending. In New York he again visits various public institutions but concentrates on the city's slums.]

BROADWAY

THE beautiful metropolis of America is by no means so clean a city as Boston, but many of its streets have the same characteristics; except that the houses are not quite so fresh-coloured, the signboards are not quite so gaudy, the gilded letters not quite so golden, the bricks not quite so red, the stone not quite so white, the blinds and area railings not quite so green, the knobs and plates upon the street doors not quite so bright and twinkling. There are many by-streets, almost as neutral in clean colours, and positive in dirty ones, as by-streets in London; and there is one quarter, commonly called the Five Points, which, in respect of filth and wretchedness, may be safely backed against Seven Dials, or any other part of famed St. Giles.

The great promenade and thoroughfare, as most people know, is Broadway; a wide and bustling street, which, from the Battery Gardens to its opposite termination in a country road, may be four miles long. Shall we sit down in an upper floor of the Carlton House Hotel (situated in the best part of this main artery of New York), and when we are tired of looking down upon the life below, sally forth arm-in-arm, and mingle with the stream?

Warm weather! The sun strikes upon our heads at this open window, as though its rays were concentrated through a burning-glass; but the day is in its zenith, and the season an unusual one. Was there ever such a sunny street as this Broadway! The pavement-stones are polished with the tread of feet until they shine again; the red bricks of the houses might be yet in the dry, hot kilns; and the roofs of those omnibusses look as though, if water were poured on them, they would hiss and smoke, and smell like half-quenched fires. No stint of omnibusses here! Half-a-dozen have gone by within as many minutes. Plenty of Hackney cabs and coaches too; gigs, phaetons, large-wheeled tilburies, and private carriages— rather of a clumsy make, and not very different from the public vehicles, but built for the heavy roads beyond the city pavement. Negro coachmen and white; in straw hats, black hats, white hats, glazed caps, fur caps; in coats of drab, black, brown, green, blue, nankeen, striped jean and linen; and there, in that one instance (look while it passes, or it will be too late), in suits of livery. Some southern republican that, who puts his blacks in uniform, and swells with Sultan pomp and power. Yonder, where that phaeton with the well-clipped pair of greys has stopped— standing at their heads now—is a Yorkshire groom, who has not been very long in these parts, and looks sorrowfully round for a companion pair of top-boots, which he may traverse the city half a year without meeting. Heaven save the ladies, how they dress! We have seen more colours in these ten minutes, than we should have seen elsewhere, in as many days. What various parasols! what rainbow silks and satins! what pinking of thin stockings, and pinching of thin shoes, and fluttering of ribbons and silk tassels, and display of rich cloaks with gaudy hoods and linings! The young gentlemen are fond, you see, of turning down their shirt-collars and cultivating their whiskers, especially under the chin; but they cannot approach the ladies in their dress or bearing, being, to say the truth, humanity of quite another sort.

THE SLUMS

MOUNT up these other stairs with no less caution (there are traps and pitfalls here, for those who are not so well escorted as ourselves) into the housetop; where the bare beams and rafters meet overhead, and calm night looks down through the crevices in the roof. Open the door of one

of these cramped hutches full of sleeping Negroes. Pah! They have a
charcoal fire within; there is a smell of singeing clothes, or flesh, so close
they gather round the brazier; and vapours issue forth that blind and
suffocate. From every corner, as you glance about you in these dark
retreats, some figure crawls half-awakened, as if the Judgement-hour were
near at hand, and every obscene grave were giving up its dead. Where
dogs would howl to lie, women, and men, and boys slink off to sleep,
forcing the dislodged rats to move away in quest of better lodgings.

Here too are lanes and alleys, paved with mud knee-deep: underground
chambers, where they dance and game; the walls bedecked with rough
designs of ships, and forts, and flags, and American Eagles out of number:
ruined houses, open to the street, whence through wide gaps in the walls,
other ruins loom upon the eye, as though the world of vice and misery
had nothing else to show: hideous tenements which take their name from
robbery and murder: all that is loathsome, drooping, and decayed is here.

> [He visits Philadelphia, Washington (where his description
> of corrupt and degraded legislators is nothing less than fero-
> cious) and Richmond. Turning westward, he crosses the
> Alleghenies to Pittsburgh and then takes a steamboat on
> the Ohio.]

STEAMBOAT ON THE OHIO

THE *Messenger* was one among a crowd of high-pressure steamboats,
clustered together by the wharf-side, which, looked down upon from the
rising ground that forms the landing-place, and backed by the lofty bank
on the opposite side of the river, appeared no larger than so many
floating models. She had some forty passengers on board, exclusive of the
poorer persons on the lower deck; and in half an hour, or less, proceeded
on her way.

We had, for ourselves, a tiny state-room with two berths in it, opening
out of the ladies' cabin. There was undoubtedly something satisfactory
in this "location," inasmuch as it was in the stern, and we had been a
great many times gravely recommended to keep as far aft as possible,
"because the steamboats generally blew up forward." Nor was this an

unnecessary caution, as the occurrence and circumstances of more than one such fatality during our stay sufficiently testified. Apart from this source of self-congratulations, it was an unspeakable relief to have any place, no matter how confined, where one could be alone . . .

If the native packets I have already described be unlike anything we are in the habit of seeing on water, these Western vessels are still more foreign to all the ideas we are accustomed to entertain of boats. I hardly know what to liken them to, or how to describe them.

In the first place, they have no mast, cordage, tackle, rigging, or other such boat-like gear; nor have they anything in their shape at all calculated to remind one of a boat's head, stern, sides, or keel. Except that they are in the water, and display a couple of paddle-boxes, they might be intended, for anything that appears to the contrary, to perform some unknown service, high and dry, upon a mountain-top. There is no visible deck, even: nothing but a long, black, ugly roof, covered with burnt-out feathery sparks; above which tower two iron chimneys, and a hoarse escape-valve, and a glass steerage-house. Then, in order as the eye descends towards the water, are the sides, and doors, and windows of the staterooms, jumbled as oddly together as though they formed a small street, built by the varying tastes of a dozen men: the whole is supported on beams and pillars resting on a dirty barge, but a few inches above the water's edge: and in the narrow space between this upper structure and this barge's deck, are the furnace fires and machinery, open at the sides to every wind that blows, and every storm of rain it drives along its path.

Passing one of these boats at night, and seeing the great body of fire, exposed as I have just described, that rages and roars beneath the frail pile of painted wood: the machinery, not warded off or guarded in any way, but doing its work in the midst of the crowd of idlers and emigrants and children, who throng the lower deck; under the management, too, of reckless men whose acquaintance with its mysteries may have been of six months' standing: one feels directly that the wonder is, not that there should be so many fatal accidents, but that any journey should be safely made.

Within, there is one long narrow cabin, the whole length of the boat; from which the staterooms open, on both sides. A small portion of it at the stern is partitioned off for the ladies; and the bar is at the opposite extreme. There is a long table down the centre, and at either end a stove. The washing apparatus is forward, on the deck. It is a little better than on board the canal-boat, but not much. In all modes of travelling, the American customs, with reference to the means of personal cleanliness and wholesome ablution, are extremely negligent and filthy; and I strongly incline to the belief that a considerable amount of illness is referable to this cause.

We are to be on board the *Messenger* three days: arriving at Cincinnati (barring accidents) on Monday morning. There are three meals a day. Breakfast at seven, dinner at half-past twelve, supper about six. At each, there are a great many small dishes and plates upon the table, with very little in them; so that although there is every appearance of a mighty "spread," there is seldom really more than a joint: except for those who fancy slices of beetroot, shreds of dried beef, complicated entanglements of yellow pickle; maize, Indian corn, apple-sauce, and pumpkin.

Some people fancy all these little dainties together (and sweet preserves besides), by way of relish to their roast pig. They are generally those dyspeptic ladies and gentlemen who eat unheard-of quantities of hot corn-bread (almost as good for the digestion as a kneaded pincushion), for breakfast, and for supper. Those who do not observe this custom, and who help themselves several times instead, usually suck their knives and forks meditatively, until they have decided what to take next: then pull them out of their mouths; put them in the dish; help themselves; and fall to work again. At dinner, there is nothing to drink upon the table, but great jugs full of cold water. Nobody says anything, at any meal, to anybody. All the passengers are very dismal, and seem to have tremendous secrets weighing on their minds. There is no conversation, no laughter, no cheerfulness, no sociality, except in spitting; and that is done in silent fellowship round the stove, when the meal is over. Every man sits down, dull and languid; swallows his fare as if breakfasts, dinners and suppers were necessities of nature never to be coupled with recreation or enjoyment; and having bolted his food in a gloomy silence, bolts himself, in the same state. But for these animal observances, you might suppose the whole male portion of the company to be the melancholy ghosts of departed book-keepers, who had fallen dead at the desk: such is their weary air of business and calculation. Undertakers on duty would be sprightly beside them; and a collation of funeral baked-meats, in comparison with these meals, would be a sparkling festivity.

The people are all alike, too. There is no diversity of character. They travel about on the same errands, say and do the same things in exactly the same manner, and follow in the same dull cheerless round. All down the long table, there is scarcely a man who is in anything different from his neighbour. It is quite a relief to have, sitting opposite, that little girl of fifteen with the loquacious chin: who, to do her justice, acts up to it, and fully identifies Nature's handwriting, for of all the small chatterboxes that ever invaded the repose of a drowsy ladies' cabin, she is the first and foremost. The beautiful girl, who sits a little beyond her—further down the table there—married the young man with the dark whiskers, who sits beyond *her*, only last month. They are going to settle in the very Far West, where he has lived four years, but where she has never been. They were both overturned in a stage-coach the other day (a bad omen any-where else, where overturns are not so common), and his head, which bears the marks of a recent wound, is bound up still. She was hurt too, at the same time, and lay insensible for some days; bright as her eyes are, now.

Further down still, sits a man who is going some miles beyond their place of destination, to "improve" a newly-discovered copper mine. He carries the village—that is to be—with him: a few frame cottages, and an apparatus for smelting the copper. He carries its people too. They are partly American and partly Irish, and herd together on the lower deck; where they amused themselves last evening till the night was pretty far advanced, by alternately firing off pistols and singing hymns.

They, and the very few who have been left at table twenty minutes, rise, and go away. We do so too; and passing through our little state-rooms, resume our seats in the quiet gallery without.

A fine broad river always, but in some parts much wider than in others: and then there is usually a green island, covered with trees, dividing it into two streams. Occasionally, we stop for a few minutes, maybe to take in wood, maybe for passengers, at some small town or village (I ought to say city, every place is a city here); but the banks are for the most part deep solitudes, overgrown with trees, which, hereabouts, are already in leaf and very green. For miles, and miles, and miles, these solitudes are unbroken by any sign of human life or trace of human footstep; nor is anything seen to move about them but the blue jay, whose colour is so bright, and yet so delicate, that it looks like a flying flower. At lengthened intervals a log cabin, with its little space of cleared land about it, nestles under a rising ground, and sends its thread of blue smoke curling up into the sky. It stands in the corner of the poor field of wheat, which is full of great unsightly stumps, like earthy butchers'-blocks. Sometimes the ground is only just now cleared: the felled trees lying yet upon the soil: and the log-house only this morning begun. As we pass this clearing, the settler leans upon his axe or hammer, and looks wistfully at the people from the world. The children creep out of the temporary hut, which is like a gipsy tent upon the ground, and clap their hands and shout. The dog only glances round at us; and then looks up into his master's face again, as if he were rendered uneasy by any suspension of the common business, and had nothing more to do with pleasurers. And still there is the same, eternal foreground. The river has washed away its banks, and stately trees have fallen down into the stream. Some have been there so long, that they are mere dry grizzly skeletons. Some have just toppled over, and having earth yet about their roots, are bathing their green heads in the river, and putting forth new shoots and branches. Some are almost sliding down, as you look at them. And some were drowned so long ago, that their bleached arms start out from the middle of the current, and seem to try to grasp the boat, and drag it under water.

Through such a scene as this, the unwieldy machine takes its hoarse sullen way: venting, at every revolution of the paddles, a loud high-pressure blast; enough, one would think, to waken up the host of Indians who lie buried in a great mound yonder: so old, that mighty oaks and other forest trees have struck their roots into its earth; and so high, that it is a hill, even among the hills that Nature planted round it. The very river, as though it shared one's feelings of compassion for the extinct tribes who lived so pleasantly here, in their blessed ignorance of white existence, hundreds of years ago, steals out of its way to ripple near this mount: and there are few places where the Ohio sparkles more brightly than in Big Grave Creek.

All this I see, as I sit in the little stern-gallery mentioned just now. Evening slowly steals upon the landscape, and changes it before me, when we stop to see some emigrants ashore.

Five men, as many women, and a little girl. All their worldly goods are a bag, a large chest, and an old chair: one, old, high-backed, rush-buttomed chair: a solitary settler in itself. They are rowed ashore in the boat, while the vessel stands a little off awaiting its return, the water being shallow. They are landed at the foot of a high bank, on the summit of which are a few log cabins, attainable only by a long winding path. It is growing dusk; but the sun is very red, and shines in the water and on some of the tree-tops, like fire.

The men get out of the boat first; help out the women; take out the bag, the chest, the chair; bid the rowers "good-bye"; and shove the boat off for them. At the first plash of the oars in the water, the oldest woman of the party sits down in the old chair, close to the water's edge, without speaking a word. None of the others sit down, though the chest is large enough for many seats. They all stand where they landed, as if stricken into stone; and look after the boat. So they remain, quite still and silent:

the old woman and her old chair, in the centre; the bag and chest upon the shore, without anybody heeding them: all eyes fixed upon the boat. It comes alongside, is made fast, the men jump on board, the engine is put in motion, and we go hoarsely on again. There they stand yet, without the motion of a hand. I can see them through my glass, when, in the distance and increasing darkness, they are mere specks to the eye: lingering there still: the old woman in the old chair, and all the rest about her: not stirring in the least degree. And thus I slowly lose them.

[He goes far enough beyond St. Louis to get a taste of the prairie and then turns eastward again. He makes a pilgrimage to Niagara Falls, which he finds as stunning as other travelers had said it was, and after a brief visit to Canada returns to New York to board ship for London.]

Boston Brahmin at a Buffalo Hunt

FRANCIS PARKMAN

FROM *The Oregon Trail*

1846

Destined to become one of America's great historians, Francis Parkman was only twenty-three and fresh out of Harvard when he set forth to see the American West. He undertook the trip partly for his health (illness was in some later periods to cripple him) and partly to study the Indians. His experiences in his five months on the trail from St. Louis to Fort Laramie in Wyoming were to stand him in good stead when he came to write his formidable history of the French and Indian War. Meanwhile, he wrote a series of magazine articles (later made into The Oregon Trail) *about his experiences with mountain men, hunter guides, half-breeds, emigrants, and especially Indians, describing them with an intimacy and freshness that make his book a classic of its kind. Although hardly aware of the full implications of what he saw, Parkman gives us some unforgettable scenes from the life of the Plains Indians just before the tide of white civilization engulfed them forever. One of the most memorable is that of the buffalo-hunting camp described in the passage below.*

L ONG before daybreak the Indians broke up their camp. The women of Mene-Seela's lodge were as usual among the first that were ready for departure, and I found the old man himself sitting by the embers of the decayed fire, over which he was warming his withered fingers, as the morning was very chill and damp. The preparations for moving were even more confused and disorderly than usual. While some families were leaving the ground, the lodges of others were still standing untouched. At this old Mene-Seela grew impatient, and walking out to the middle of the village, he stood with his robe wrapped close around him, and harangued the people in a loud, sharp voice. Now, he said, when they were on an enemy's hunting-grounds, was not the time to behave like children; they ought to be more active and united than ever. His speech had some effect. The delinquents took down their lodges and loaded their pack-horses; and when the sun rose, the last of the men, women, and children had left the deserted camp.

The movement was made merely for the purpose of finding a better and safer position. So we advanced only three or four miles up the little stream, when each family assumed its relative place in the great ring of the village, and the squaws set actively at work in preparing the camp. But not a single warrior dismounted from his horse. All the men that morning were mounted on inferior animals, leading their best horses by a cord, or confiding them to the care of boys. In small parties they began to leave the ground and ride rapidly away over the plains to the westward. I had taken no food, and not being at all ambitious of farther abstinence, I went into my host's lodge, which his squaws had set up with wonderful despatch, and sat down in the center, as a gentle hint that I was hungry. A wooden bowl was soon set before me, filled with the nutritious preparation of dried meat, called *pemmican* by the northern voyagers, and *wasna* by the Dahcotah. Taking a handful to break my fast upon, I left the lodge just in time to see the last band of hunters disappear over the ridge of the neighboring hill. I mounted Pauline and galloped in pursuit, riding rather by the balance than by any muscular strength that remained to me. From the top of the hill I could overlook a wide extent of desolate prairie, over which, far and near, little parties of naked horsemen were rapidly passing. I soon came up to the nearest, and we had not ridden a mile before all were united into one large and compact body. All was haste and eagerness. Each hunter whipped on his horse, as if anxious to be the first to reach the game. In such movements among the Indians this is always more or less the case; but it was especially so in the present instance, because the head chief of the village was absent, and there were but few "soldiers," a sort of Indian police, who among their other functions usually assume the direction of a buffalo hunt. No man turned to the right hand or to the left. We rode at a swift canter straight forward, up hill and down hill, and through the stiff, obstinate growth of the endless wild-sage bushes. For an hour and a half the same red shoulders, the same long black hair, rose and fell with the motion of the horses before me. Very little was said, though once I observed an old man severely reproving Raymond for having left his rifle behind him, when there was some probability of encountering an enemy before the day was over. As we galloped across a plain thickly set with sage-bushes, the foremost riders vanished suddenly from sight, as if diving into the earth. The arid soil was cracked into a deep ravine. Down we all went in succession and galloped in a line along the bottom, until we found a point where, one by one, the horses could scramble out. Soon after, we came upon a wide shallow stream, and as we rode swiftly over the hard sand-beds and through the thin sheets of rippling water, many of the savage horsemen threw themselves to the ground, knelt on the sand, snatched a hasty draught, and leaping back again to their seats, galloped on as before.

Meanwhile scouts kept in advance of the party; and now we began to see them on the ridges of the hills, waving their robes in token that buffalo were visible. These, however, proved to be nothing more than old straggling bulls, feeding upon the neighboring plains, who would stare for a moment at the hostile array and then gallop clumsily off. At length we could discern several of these scouts making their signals to us at once; no longer waving their robes boldly from the top of the hill, but standing lower down, so that they could not be seen from the plains beyond. Game worth pursuing had evidently been discovered. The excited Indians now urged forward their tired horses even more rapidly than before. Pauline, who was still sick and jaded, began to groan heavily; and her yellow sides were darkened with sweat. As we were crowding together over a lower intervening hill, I heard Reynal and Raymond shouting to me from the left; and, looking in that direction, I saw them riding away behind a party of about twenty mean-looking Indians. These were the relatives of Reynal's squaw, Margot, who, not wishing to take part in the general hunt, were riding towards a distant hollow, where they saw a small band of buffalo which they meant to appropriate to themselves. I answered to the call by ordering Raymond to turn back and follow me. He reluctantly obeyed, though Reynal, who had relied on his assistance in skinning, cutting up, and carrying to camp the buffalo that he and his party should kill, loudly protested, and declared that we should see no sport if we went with the rest of the Indians. Followed by Raymond, I pursued the main body of hunters, while Reynal, in a great rage, whipped his horse over the hill after his ragamuffin relatives. The Indians, still about a hundred in number, galloped in a dense body at some distance in advance, a cloud of dust flying in the wind behind them. I could not overtake them until they had stopped on the side of the hill where the scouts were standing. Here each hunter sprang in haste from the tired animal he had ridden, and leaped upon the fresh horse he had brought with him. There was not a saddle or a bridle in the whole party. A piece of buffalo-robe, girthed over the horse's back, served in the place of the one, and a cord of twisted hair, lashed round his lower jaw, answered for the other. Eagle feathers dangled from every mane and tail, as marks of courage and speed. As for the rider, he wore no other clothing than a light cincture at his waist, and a pair of moccasins. He had a heavy whip, with a handle of solid elk-horn, and a lash of knotted bull-hide, fastened to his wrist by a band. His bow was in his hand, and his quiver of otter or panther skin hung at his shoulder. Thus equipped, some thirty of the hunters galloped away towards the left, in order to make a circuit under cover of the hills, that the buffalo might be assailed on both sides at once. The rest impatiently waited until time enough had elapsed for their companions to reach the required position. Then riding upward in a body, we gained the ridge of the hill, and for the first time came in sight of the buffalo on the plain beyond.

They were a band of cows, four or five hundred in number, crowded together near the bank of a wide stream that was soaking across the sand-beds of the valley. This valley was a large circular basin, sun-scorched and broken, scantily covered with herbage, and surrounded with high barren hills, from an opening in which we could see our allies galloping out upon the plain. The wind blew from that direction. The buffalo, aware of their approach, had begun to move, though very slowly and in a compact mass. I have no farther recollection of seeing the game until we were in the midst of them, for as we rode down the hill other objects engrossed my attention. Numerous old bulls were scattered over the plain, and, ungallantly deserting their charge at our approach, began to wade and plunge through the quicksands of the stream, and gallop away towards the hills. One old veteran was straggling behind the rest, with one of his fore-legs, which had been broken by some accident, dangling about use-lessly. His appearance, as he went shambling along on three legs, was so ludicrous that I could not help pausing for a moment to look at him. As I came near, he would try to rush upon me, nearly throwing himself down at every awkward attempt. Looking up, I saw the whole body of Indians full an hundred yards in advance. I lashed Pauline in pursuit and reached them just in time; for, at that moment, each hunter, as if by a common impulse, violently struck his horse, each horse sprang forward, and, scattering in the charge in order to assail the entire herd at once, we all rushed headlong upon the buffalo. We were among them in an instant. Amid the trampling and the yells I could see their dark figures running hither and thither through clouds of dust, and the horsemen darting in pursuit. While we were charging on one side, our companions attacked the bewildered and panic-stricken herd on the other. The uproar and confusion lasted but a moment. The dust cleared away, and the buffalo could be seen scattering as from a common center, flying over the plain singly, or in long files and small compact bodies, while behind them followed the Indians, riding at furious speed, and yelling as they launched arrow after arrow into their sides. The carcasses were strewn thickly over the ground. Here and there stood wounded buffalo, their bleeding sides feathered with arrows; and as I rode by them their eyes would glare, they would bristle like gigantic cats, and feebly attempt to rush up and gore my horse.

I left camp that morning with a philosophic resolution. Neither I nor my horse were at that time fit for such sport, and I had determined to remain a quiet spectator; but amid the rush of horses and buffalo, the uproar and the dust, I found it impossible to sit still; and as four or five buffalo ran past me in a line, I lashed Pauline in pursuit. We went plunging through the water and the quicksands, and clambering the bank, chased them through the wild-sage bushes that covered the rising ground beyond. But neither her native spirit nor the blows of the knotted bull-hide could supply the place of poor Pauline's exhausted strength. We could not gain an inch upon the fugitives. At last, however, they came full upon a ravine too wide to leap over; and as this compelled them to turn abruptly to the left, I contrived to get within ten or twelve yards of the hindmost. At this she faced about, bristled angrily, and made a show of charging. I shot at her, and hit her somewhere in the neck. Down she tumbled into the ravine, whither her companions had descended before her. I saw their dark backs appearing and disappearing as they galloped along the bottom; then, one by one, they scrambled out on the other side, and ran off as before, the wounded animal following with the rest.

Turning back, I saw Raymond coming on his black mule to meet me; and as we rode over the field together, we counted scores of carcasses lying on the plain, in the ravines, and on the sandy bed of the stream. Far away in the distance, horsemen and buffalo were still scouring along, with clouds of dust rising behind them; and over the sides of the hills long files of the frightened animals were rapidly ascending. The hunters began to return. The boys, who had held the horses behind the hill, made their appearance, and the work of flaying and cutting up began in earnest all over the field. I noticed my host Kongra-Tonga beyond the stream, just alighting by the side of a cow which he had killed. Riding up to him, I found him in the act of drawing out an arrow, which, with the exception of the notch at the end, had entirely disappeared in the animal. I asked him to give it to me, and I still retain it as a proof, though by no means the most striking one that could be offered, of the force and dexterity with which the Indians discharge their arrows.

The hides and meat were piled upon the horses, and the hunters began to leave the ground. Raymond and I, too, getting tired of the scene, set out for the village, riding straight across the intervening desert. There was no path, and as far as I could see, no landmarks sufficient to guide us; but Raymond seemed to have an instinctive perception of the point on the horizon towards which we ought to direct our course. Antelope were bounding on all sides, and as is always the case in the presence of buffalo, they seemed to have lost their natural shyness. Bands of them would run lightly up the rocky declivities, and stand gazing down upon us from the summit. At length we could distinguish the tall white rocks and the old pine-trees that, as we well remembered, were just above the site of the encampment. Still we could see nothing of the camp itself, until, mounting a grassy hill, we saw the circle of lodges, dingy with storms and smoke, standing on the plain at our feet.

I entered the lodge of my host. His squaw instantly brought me food and water, and spread a buffalo-robe for me to lie upon; and being much fatigued, I lay down and fell asleep. In about an hour, the entrance of Kongra-Tonga, with his arms smeared with blood to the elbows, awoke me; he sat down in his usual seat, on the left side of the lodge. His squaw gave him a vessel of water for washing, set before him a bowl of boiled meat, and, as he was eating, pulled off his bloody moccasins and placed fresh ones on his feet; then outstretching his limbs, my host composed himself to sleep.

And now the hunters, two or three at a time, came rapidly in, and each consigning his horses to the squaws, entered his lodge with the air of a man whose day's work was done. The squaws flung down the load from the burdened horses, and vast piles of meat and hides were soon gathered before every lodge. By this time it was darkening fast, and the whole village was illuminated by the glares of fires. All the squaws and children were gathered about the piles of meat, exploring them in search of the daintiest portions. Some of these they roasted on sticks before the fires, but often they dispensed with this superfluous operation. Late into the night the fires were still glowing upon the groups of feasters engaged in this savage banquet around them.

Several hunters sat down by the fire in Kongra-Tonga's lodge to talk over the day's exploits. Among the rest, Mene-Seela came in. Though he must have seen full eighty winters, he had taken an active share in the day's sport. He boasted that he had killed two cows that morning, and would have killed a third if the dust had not blinded him so that he had to drop his bow and arrows and press both hands against his eyes to stop the pain. The fire-light fell upon his wrinkled face and shrivelled figure as he sat telling his story with such inimitable gesticulation that every man in the lodge broke into a laugh.

Old Mene-Seela was one of the few Indians in the village with whom I would have trusted myself alone without suspicion, and the only one from whom I should have received a gift or a service without the certainty that it proceeded from an interested motive. He was a great friend to the whites. He liked to be in their society, and was very vain of the favors he had received from them. . . .

We remained encamped on this spot five days, during three of which the hunters were at work incessantly, and immense quantities of meat and hides were brought in. Great alarm, however, prevailed in the village. All were on the alert. The young men ranged the country as scouts, and the old men paid careful attention to omens and prodigies, and especially to their dreams. In order to convey to the enemy (who, if they were in the neighborhood, must inevitably have known of our presence) the impression that we were constantly on the watch, piles of sticks and stones were erected on all the surrounding hills, in such a manner as to appear at a distance like sentinels. Often, even to this hour, that scene will rise before my mind like a visible reality: the tall white rocks; the old pine-trees on their summits; the sandy stream that ran along their bases and half encircled the village; and the wild-sage bushes, with their dull green hue and their medicinal odor, that covered all the neighboring declivities. Hour after hour the squaws would pass and repass with their vessels of water between the stream and the lodges. For the most part, no one was to be seen in the camp but women and children, two or three superannuated old men, and a few lazy and worthless young ones. These, together with the dogs, now grown fat and good-natured with the abundance in the camp, were its only tenants. Still it presented a busy and bustling scene. In all quarters the meat, hung on cords of hide, was drying in the sun, and around the lodges, the squaws, young and old, were laboring on the fresh hides stretched upon the ground, scraping the hair from one side and the still adhering flesh from the other, and rubbing into them the brains of the buffalo, in order to render them soft and pliant.

In mercy to myself and my horse, I did not go out with the hunters after the first day. Of late, however, I had been gaining strength rapidly, as was always the case upon every respite of my disorder. I was soon able to walk with ease. Raymond and I would go out upon the neighboring prairies to shoot antelope, or sometimes to assail straggling buffalo, on foot; an attempt in which we met with rather indifferent success. As I came out of Kongra-Tonga's lodge one morning, Reynal called to me from the opposite side of the village, and asked me over to breakfast. The breakfast was a substantial one. It consisted of the rich, juicy hump-ribs of a fat cow; a repast absolutely unrivalled in its way. It was roasting before the fire, impaled upon a stout stick, which Reynal took up and planted in the ground before his lodge; when he, with Raymond and myself, taking our seats around it, unsheathed our knives and assailed it with good will. In spite of all medical experience, this solid fare, without bread or salt, seemed to agree with me admirably.

. . . For the rest of that day we lay smoking and talking in Reynal's lodge. This indeed was no better than a hut, made of hides stretched on poles, and entirely open in front. It was well carpeted with soft buffalo-robes, and here we remained, sheltered from the sun, surrounded by the domestic utensils of Madame Margot's household. All was quiet in the village. Though the hunters had not gone out that day, they lay sleeping in their lodges, and most of the women were silently engaged in their heavy tasks. A few young men were playing at a lazy game of ball in the area of the village; and when they became tired, some girls supplied their place with a more boisterous sport. At a little distance, among the lodges, some children and half-grown squaws were playfully tossing one of their number in a buffalo-robe—an exact counterpart of the ancient pastime from which Sancho Panza suffered so much. Farther out on the prairie, a host of little naked boys were roaming about, engaged in various rough games, or pursuing birds and ground-squirrels with their bows and arrows; and woe to the unhappy little animals that fell into their merciless, torture-loving hands. A squaw from the next lodge, a notable housewife, named Weah Washtay, or the Good Woman, brought us a large bowl of *wasna*, and went into an ecstasy of delight when I presented her with a green glass ring, such as I usually wore with a view to similar occasions.

The sun went down, and half the sky was glowing fiery red, reflected on the little stream as it wound away among the sage-bushes. Some young men left the village, and soon returned, driving in before them all the horses, hundreds in number, and of every size, age, and color. The hunters came out, and each securing those that belonged to him, examined their condition, and tied them fast by long cords to stakes driven in front of his lodge. It was half an hour before the bustle subsided and tranquillity was restored again. By this time it was nearly dark. Kettles were hung over the fires, around which the squaws were gathered with their children, laughing and talking merrily. A circle of a different kind was formed in the center of the village. This was composed of the old men and warriors of repute, who sat together with their white buffalo-robes drawn close around their shoulders; and as the pipe passed from hand to hand, their conversation had not a particle of the gravity and reserve usually ascribed to Indians. . . .

As it grew late, I walked across the village to the lodge of my host, Kongra-Tonga. As I entered I saw him, by the blaze of the fire in the middle, reclining half asleep in his usual place. The couch was by no means an uncomfortable one. It consisted of buffalo-robes, laid together on the ground, and a pillow made of whitened deer-skin, stuffed with feathers and ornamented with beads. At his back was a light framework of poles and slender reeds, against which he could lean with ease when in a sitting posture; and at the top of it, just above his head, hung his bow and quiver. His squaw, a laughing, broad-faced woman, apparently had not yet completed her domestic arrangements, for she was bustling about the lodge, pulling over the utensils and the bales of dried meat that were ranged carefully about it. Unhappily, she and her partner were not the only tenants of the dwelling; for half a dozen children were scattered about, sleeping in every imaginable posture. My saddle was in its place at the head of the lodge, and a buffalo-robe was spread on the ground before it. Wrapping myself in my blanket, I lay down; but had I not been extremely fatigued, the noise in the next lodge would have prevented my sleeping. There was the monotonous thumping of the Indian drum, mixed with occasional sharp yells, and a chorus chanted by twenty voices. A grand scene of gambling was going forward with all the appropriate formalities. The players were staking on the chances of the game their ornaments, their horses, and as the excitement rose, their garments, and even their weapons; for desperate gambling is not confined to the hells of Paris. The men of the plains and forests no less resort to it as a relief to the tedious monotony of their lives, which alternate between fierce excitement and listless inaction. I fell asleep with the dull notes of the drum still sounding on my ear; but these orgies lasted without intermission till daylight. I was soon awakened by one of the children crawling over me, while another larger one was tugging at my blanket and nestling himself in a very disagreeable proximity. I immediately repelled these advances by punching the heads of these miniature savages with a short stick which I always kept by me for the purpose; and as sleeping half the day and eating much more than is good for them makes them extremely restless, this operation usually had to be repeated four or five times in the course of the night. My host himself was the author of another formidable annoyance. All these Indians, and he among the rest, think themselves bound to the constant performance of certain acts as the condition on which their success in life depends, whether in war, love, hunting, or any other employment. These "medicines," as they are called, which are usually communicated in dreams, are often absurd enough. Some Indians will strike the butt of the pipe against the ground every time they smoke; others will insist that everything they say shall be interpreted by contraries; and Shaw once met an old man who conceived that all would be lost unless he compelled every white man he met to drink a bowl of cold water. My host was particularly unfortunate in his allotment. The spirits had told him in a dream that he must sing a certain song in the middle of every night; and regularly at about twelve o'clock his dismal monotonous chanting would awaken me, and I would see him seated bolt upright on his couch, going through his dolorous performance with a most business-like air. There were other voices of the night, still more inharmonious. Twice or thrice, between sunset and dawn, all the dogs in the village, and there were hundreds of them, would bay and yelp in chorus; a horrible clamor, resembling no sound that I have ever heard, except perhaps the frightful howling of wolves that we used sometimes to hear, long afterwards, when descending the Arkansas on the trail of General Kearney's army. This canine uproar is, if possible, more discordant than that of the wolves. Heard at a distance slowly rising on the night, it has a strange unearthly effect, and would fearfully haunt the dreams of a nervous man; but when you are sleeping in the midst of it, the din is outrageous. One long, loud howl begins it, and voice after voice takes up the sound, till it passes around the whole circumference of the village, and the air is filled with confused and discordant cries, at once fierce and mournful. It lasts a few moments, and then dies away into silence.

Gold-Rush Fever

J. GOLDSBOROUGH BRUFF

FROM *Gold Rush*

1849–51

After a youthful Wanderjahr *of three or four years as a seaman, J. Goldsborough Bruff settled down in 1827 in his native Washington, D.C. For sixty years he led a quiet, conscientious life as a government draftsman and pillar of the community—except for one interlude of high adventure. That interlude was the twenty-seven months he spent on the Oregon-California trail and in the mining camps and boom cities of the West. It is a measure of the strength of the westering urge and the gold-rush fever that it struck a solidly rooted family man at the age of forty-five with such force.*

Bruff helped to organize a semimilitary mining company composed of sixty-six Washingtonians and was chosen to be its captain in a hunt for gold. He led them across the two thousand miles of prairie, desert and mountains from the Missouri frontier to the western slope of the Sierra Nevada and, despite the perils of scurvy, cholera, dysentery, Indians and starvation, brought them through with only one death. Then, thirty-five miles from the "Settlements," he decided to let the others make the last hard lap while he guarded the company's goods until help could be sent to him. When no one returned for him, he passed a long winter of extreme privation and finally staggered down into the Settlements in April 1850, more than a year after leaving Washington. He found no gold in the year he spent on the Coast, and in the summer of 1851 he returned home by way of the Isthmus of Panama.

Bruff's journals and drawings are rough in form, but they constitute one of the most graphic and circumstantial day-by-day records of the greatest wave of American westward emigration—the California gold rush.

[The members of the Washington City Mining Company assemble in April 1849 at St. Joseph, Missouri, but, finding tens of thousands of emigrants waiting to be ferried across the Missouri, go farther up the river in order to get across. At first the trail follows a natural route up the Platte River, but after Fort Laramie the way to Fort Hall and into California bears ever increasing testimony to the hardships of the journey—dead oxen, abandoned wagons, sick emigrants, and grave markers like milestones. Bruff makes the following typical entry on the latter part of the journey, as he passes over the summit of the Sierra Nevada.]

[O]CTOBER] 3 [1849].—Commences clear; light breeze from the N. Temp. 26°. Much frost and ice.

Found here, last night, a mule wagon belonging to two brothers Beans, of Maryland, one of them ill with the scurvy. Mr. B. very kindly gave me a piece of bacon for my own use: ours long since out.

We moved up very early to ascend the Pass—up a steep, hard, sandy, and winding road. The first ascent of about ¼ mile was gentle enough, and brought us to a sort of valley with a spring and rill in it and some bunch grass. Here was a grave, thus enscribed:—

JNO. A. DAWSON,
ST. LOUIS, MO.
DIED OCT. 1st 1849,
FROM EATING A POISONOUS
ROOT AT THE SPRING

The spring just below. In this first valley, or platform, above the base, saw numerous ox-camps breaking up and moving forward. Some had a team of ten yoke of oxen.

. . . In the second valley, or rise, more ox trains moving ahead. Reached the foot of the big hill, a long and smooth sand drag, pretty steep ascent. Ten dead oxen marked the trail. Across the road, about midway up this hill, lay an ox on his knees, dying, and covered with an old gum coat by his compassionate owner; but it was unavailing—the dust was suffocating, and the animals and wheels went over him in the haste and trouble of the steep ascent. The first wagon of my train which reached the top of the Pass displayed the stars-and-stripes to encourage those in the rear. Found many ox-wagons on the flat top of the Pass. Temp. on top the Pass at 8 A.M. 44°.

The Western descent was long and smooth, about 1 mile and continued on the inclined plain below to a small rill of very cold and clear water, and fine grass. This is one of the fountain sources of Pitt River—head of the Sacramento. The hills around are thickly timbered with firs and other kinds of tall pine trees.

While on top of the Pass, looking down the Eastern side at the bustle, and directing the ascent, I was amused. I thought the infirm ox in the road below occupied rather an unenviable position. In the centre of a very broad, sandy, and dusty road, men urging their heavy ox-trains up the steep hill, with lashes, imprecations, and shouts, some riding up on horses and mules, and clouds of blinding dust and sand flying. There rode up an old man on a jaded horse; a mattress covered the horse, the sick man astride and laying over on his breast, with a coverlid thrown over him and a corner trailing in the dust. He looked pale and haggard; had his arms around the neck of the old horse. He was afflicted with the flux and scurvy. Another unfortunate followed him on a mule, enveloped in a blue blanket and barely able to retain his seat; he had the fever and ague. Some small boys, not over ten years of age, were leading jaded animals up. Women were seen with the trains, occupied at chocking the wheels, while the oxen were allowed to blow, on the ascent. A man had a baby in his arms, and in midst of the thick dust was urging up his team. Some wagons had as many as twelve yoke of oxen in them. One wagon, with women and children in it, when near the summit, became uncoupled and down hill it ran—*stern foremost*, with great rapidity. The women and children screamed, men shouted, and with all the rest of the fuss, there was a great clamor. A dead ox, a short distance in front of a heavy team, and men by them, brought up the backing-out vehicle, most luckily without damage to any one.

[Three weeks later, on the western slope of the mountains, Bruff sends his men the thirty-odd miles into the Settlements and stays behind to guard company property. When no one returns to help him, he and two chance acquaintances, William Poyle and an old hunter named Clough, undergo a winter in the hills. In addition to their other burdens, Bruff has agreed to take care of a little boy abandoned by an irresponsible adventurer named Lambkin.]

[DECEMBER] 31ST.—Commences hazy; moderate wind S.E. Temp. 35°. Meridian ditto. Temp. 53°.

Clough soon constructed a hand-sled. We stowed everything compact in the lodge; then put on the sled a small tent, bedding, camp utensils, arms, ammunition, etc. and the boy on top, wrapped up in a blanket. I had a large knapsack filled with note books, drawings, etc., a haversack with various articles in it, a small camp kettle, lantern, double-gun, and my pockets full of small articles. Poyle and Clough fixed trace ropes to the sled with loops, which they threw over their shoulders, and at 3 P.M. we moved away from the scene of pleasure and suffering. The sled was a heavy drag, and I heartily pitied poor Poyle. I could not assist them, for I had as much as I could stagger under. Ascending a hill was done by jerking the sled a few yards at a time, and we were compelled to lighten our load by dropping, ¾ miles from the cabin, coffee, salt, camp utensils, etc. We did not reach the cabin till 7 at night, and I fainted at the door.

Roberts' folks apprehend another storm; they have but two pieces of dried venison on hand. I proposed to these folks that if they would furnish us flour for supper, and rations sufficient to carry my friends Poyle and Clough in, that they would go to the settlements and bring out a supply, and I would return the amount with interest. So they measured 7 tin-cup-fulls (about a pint each) of sour flour, a few slices of venison to broil, and a rib-piece to boil. Poyle with his usual alacrity and skill soon baked four thin pancakes, and broiled the slices of meat in the embers while the ribs were boiling. This with coffee afforded us another fine meal—delicious! We are exceedingly fagged down. Roberts had a tent standing near the cabin, and we threw our bedding in it and put the child in. Poyle engaged after supper in baking rolls for the tramp to settlements. Good souls! He and Clough, compassionating my situation, are resolved to go off tonight!

I wrote a note to Col. Davis, and another to Mr. Myers for succor.

Sunset came as commencement. Temp. 40°. The poor German is here. Has been taken ill, and Roberts made him a comfortable pallet before the fire. Child and myself ill all night.

JANUARY 1ST, 1850. Commences with snow storm; moderate S.E. wind. Temp. 40°. My head violently affected; the younger Roberts yesterday, his father and myself, and the child, ill all last night, with violent pains and heat in the stomach and intestines. I obtained some relief from camphor. Roberts and sons took opiates. Our being simultaneously attacked with these violent symptoms caused me to apprehend that we had been poisoned; and at first I attributed it to the bad flour but recollected that I heard Mrs. Roberts say that the substance she put in the bread, to lighten it, she *thought* was Sal Eratus; and I asked if it might not be something else—of a poisonous nature. She submitted it to my examination, and from its character and the effects of the bread on us, was convinced that the substance was *caustic soda!*—and threw it away.

Poyle and Clough started at midnight last night, assuring me of succor in four days; we shook hands, and I bade them Godspeed. Poyle insisted on my taking four rolls of bread last night, and I ate two, reserving the other for the boy. We—the males here—are very sick today, the old man worst.

Meridian: snow and drizzle, moderate wind S.E., Temp. 46°. Sunset cloudy, wind same. Temp. 42°.

Child's illness increasing, I endeavoured to feed him with a little broth Mrs. Roberts had kindly made for him. We did all we could for the poor little sufferer, but by 11 A.M. he was extricated from all the hardships of this life.

The German went in. I gave him a note to hand to Poyle. We feel a little better this afternoon.

The extraordinary effects of the bread on us has caused great anxiety about our good friends on their way down the mountains. I am very weak and stiff in calves of legs and loins. I endeavoured to go back ¾ miles for some effects we had to throw out when hauling our sled here—but too weak, and staggered about over stones and snow in vain, and returned exhausted. Great headache at night, took camphor. I procured a piece of white cotton, stripped the boy, washed him with snow, tied him up in the cloth, and secured the tent to prevent the wolves carrying him off. Great burning in my stomach and bowels, swelled body, acrid taste, and violent headache. Laid on Roberts' floor in misery till near day, when I obtained a nap. The three Roberts also ill all night, with similar symptoms. A clear night.

[JANUARY] 2ND.—Commences with very light snow, light wind from the S.E. Temp. 34°.

Boarding with Roberts. To return the amount of provisions in kind, on the return of my friends. We had a hearty breakfast of pancakes, venison stew, and coffee. Occasional light snow and drizzle all the forenoon.

Meridian: drizzly, light wind from S.E. Temp. 36°.

At 10 A.M. I cleared away the fire in front of my tent, within five feet of it, and assisted by young Roberts dug a grave on the spot and buried the boy. I then piled stones on the grave, procured a small piece of plank, made a headboard, and set it up, with this inscription:—

WILLIAM,

INFANT SON OF

LAMBKIN,

AN UNNATURAL

FATHER,

DIED, JAN. 1, 1850

[Exhausted by hunger and exposure, Bruff makes a desperate effort to reach the Settlements.]

[APRIL] 6TH [1850].—Showers and mists. Strong S.S.E. wind. Temp. 50°. After great difficulty, on account of damp and weakness, this morning I made a fire. Hunted over the old camping-place and procured about 2 oz. of the minute sprouts of lettuce, etc., made coffee, drank it. Ate the grounds and the salad. Was wet and cold, took a couple of wagon-wheels and laid them on my fire which, after a while, burnt well, and I dried and warmed myself. Boiled some bits of hide in my coffee-pot, and gave it to my pup for her breakfast, poor thing. She is a mere skeleton, but as watchful as ever. While strapping on my pack, to pursue my arduous journey, a large yellow wolf came in sight and howled, when Nevada jumped up, ran towards the wolf some distance, and barked vehemently. About 10 A.M. when I moved off, I called my dog, and left the wolf on the side of a hill looking at us. I was lame with the pains in my legs, and needless to say, excessively weak. Shoulders much chafed with knapsack straps. I proceeded but a short distance and reached a cartbody on left of the road, when the hill descended rapidly to a deep brushy bottom with a rill in it. The wind blew strong and cold and I managed, somehow, for I do not know what gave me the strength, to turn the cartbed on its side, against a large granite rock, to break off the uncharitable wind. I sat my gun against the rock, dropped my knapsack, etc., and in this shelter was compelled to rest. I ate a piece of candle, endeavoured to fix my straps so as not to gall my shoulders, and staggered on again. Meridian: flying clouds, and fresh gales from the S.S.E. Temp. 62°.

Thus I proceeded perhaps 1½ miles more, halting at every stone and stump where I could sit and support my knapsack: every 20 or 30 paces at the most. Oak trees scattered about looking much like an old apple-orchard. This was a sort of valley table-land. On the right, about ¼ mile, the hill abruptly descended to a brook. I saw no place to shelter myself for the night, and it was drizzling, and threatening to rain heavy. Travellers had consumed all the ready fuel, and in my weak state, to be exposed all night to wet and cold, would assuredly incapacitate me from walking tomorrow. I crossed over to the left of the road, intending to cut out a niche in a large bush I saw, to get in for the night. As for sleep, I need not expect it, except that repose which is not disturbed by dreams. I threw down my packs, was about to draw my bowie-knife, when something caused me to look ahead, and on the left of the road, under a tree, I perceived a group of men, one in the act of charging a gun. I at first thought them Indians, and resolved to visit them and obtain food or die. I cocked my gun, and walked with considerable energy some 300 yards and reached the spot; found they were white men. I saluted them, staggered, fell, and asked in the name of God for something to eat, that I was starving! One of them said he believed they had a piece of cold bread, and handed it to me, with a little salt pork grease. It soon disappeared. I now ascertained that this was a *prospecting* party, from the neighborhood of Lassen's, bound to the vicinity of the Cabin. They were Messrs. Barton, Collier, Darrow, Warren, Boston, O'Neil, and Bateman. It was about 3:30 P.M. and they informed me that this spot is about 16 miles from Davis' rancho. So then I [have] travelled 14 miles:—seven to "Steep Hollow," and seven this side of it. Surely my mind has dragged my feeble body on; physically alone, it were impossible!

Sunset cloudy, fresh breeze S.E. Temp. 60°. At dusk I had the luxury of a pipe, but it rendered me so nervous, I dare not repeat it. Two of this party had known me, and also knew before meeting me that I was in the hills. They huddled together under the shelter, from the rain, and invited me to do so, but there was no room, and I was satisfied to rest my weary head and shelter my shoulders only between their legs. I gave my dog a pork bone.

Observed on the right of the road, a grave:—

C. FORMAN,
DIED SEP: 25.—1849,
AGED 21 YEARS.

APRIL 7TH.—Commences drizzly, moderate S.E. wind. Temp. 50°. The party dried their blankets, cooked breakfast of flour cakes, fried pork, and coffee, inviting me to partake. I needed no pressing to do so. They cut up and equally divided the cakes, handing each his share. They, no doubt, ate a hearty breakfast, but it seemed to me to be only a mouthful. I briefly related my recent sufferings and that I feared much I had not sufficient strength to carry me in, *having nothing to eat*, and was growing weaker every hour. "Oh! Captain!" said one, "you can soon get in now; you needn't be alarmed." And they shouldered their blankets and *sacks of flour* and said "good-bye Captain," and resumed their journey! It was about 10 A.M. when my *charitable* friends left me. I say charitable, for unless I had just then obtained such succour, I never could have survived the night. Nature had done wonders but she was exhausted. I rested some time after they left and warmed myself. I thought how differently I would have acted towards one of them, had our positions been reversed. They saw my pale and haggard face, and my weakness; yet not one said, "Here's a handful of flour to go in upon." They, hearty and robust, with eight or ten days' full rations, and I, an emaciated starveling! Such is human nature!

[Bruff spends the remainder of 1850 at Lassen's Rancho, taking part in a fruitless hunt for a "Gold Lake." He goes on into Sacramento just in time to be caught up in another futile "rush," this time to find gold in bluffs along the coast. Moving on to San Francisco, he reports the following characteristic incident there.]

JUNE 11TH, 1851.—At 2 A.M. the notorious Jenkins—burglar, murderer, and robber—paid the penalty of his rascalities, being hung by the populace to the gable end of the old adobe in the plaza, *"till dead,* dead, dead." A pleasant morning. The body of the hanged was laid out in the Engine House, close by, and afterwards removed to the Police Office, a considerable crowd lingering about the plaza all day. At 4 P.M. another crowd assembled in the plaza, which were addressed by some young lawyer. I was told that Jenkins had been transported for life to New South Wales some fourteen years since from England; and escaped from there, and arrived in this country about two years ago; since which he has led an industrious life of villainy, till it was terminated, as it should have been long ago. They say that he smoked a cigar on the way to the plaza; and when a minister of the gospel offered him spiritual consolation while the rope was around his neck, he repulsed him in the most rude and insolent manner. On searching his pockets, preparatory to running him up, they found 200 dollars in gold, and enquired if he had any friends to whom it might be given? He answered negatively, and told them to scatter it among the mob. After death, they found that his ankles were calloused, and marked by the long wear of shackles. While the culprit was hanging, a fellow in the crowd sang out, "Sarved him right, by G—d!" and he was instantly floored by a Sydney convict standing near; when the last-named chap was as promptly seized by the mob, decorated by the shackles which had just before graced Jenkins, and hurried off to the Police Office. A man who had hold of the rope running Jenkins up to the beam had his pocket picked of a small amount of gold while thus engaged.

[Bruff leaves for Panama by steamer on June 14, crosses the Isthmus on muleback and takes a boat up the Atlantic coast to New York, arriving home in Washington on July 20, 1851.]

New York Streetcars and Western Manners

ANTHONY TROLLOPE

FROM *North America*

1861–62

As we have seen in the Africa section (*page 355*), Anthony
Trollope was already a seasoned traveler when he touched at New York
on his way home to England from a Post Office assignment in the West
Indies. The brief visit whetted his interest, and in 1861 he took leave from
his government post—he was by then an established novelist—and spent
seven months on the Eastern Seaboard, in Canada, and as far west as Iowa.

Although the Civil War did not interfere with his observations, he was
disturbed by it and devoted much of his long book about North America
to the arguments and prospects of both sides. This preoccupation, and a
lack of individual characterization, makes part of the book now seem
tedious. Only occasionally, as in the passages below, are we reminded
that he was a master of his profession—especially in the observation of the
routine things of life—and second only to Dickens and Thackeray in his
time.

Trollope made many criticisms of American character and habits but
he never matched the disdain displayed thirty years earlier by his mother,
Frances Trollope, in her Domestic Manners of the Americans. The best
known of her 114 books, it was the product of her attempt to recoup the
family fortunes by going to America and setting up an "Oriental bazaar"

in Cincinnati. *This fantastic venture was a fiasco, but the book—despite its bitter views and grotesque distortions—was a great success.*

In the remaining twenty years of his life, Trollope made three other visits to America, two to Australia and one to South Africa.

[Landing in Boston in September 1861, Trollope and his wife make a preliminary tour of New England, Canada and several Midwestern states and then return to New York. He admires certain qualities in New Yorkers but, in what had become a settled tradition among British travelers, makes much of the crassness and bad manners of some of New York's citizens.]

STREETCARS AND GRACELESS WOMEN

THE street cars are manned with conductors, and therefore are free from many of the perils of the omnibus, but they have perils of their own. They are always quite full. By that I mean that every seat is crowded, that there is a double row of men and women standing down the centre, and that the driver's platform in front is full, and also the conductor's platform behind. That is the normal condition of a street car in the Third Avenue. You, as a stranger in the middle of the car, wish to be put down at, let us say, 89th Street. In the map of New York now before me the cross streets running from east to west are numbered up northwards as far as 154th Street. It is quite useless for you to give the number as you enter. Even an American conductor, with brains all over him, and an anxious desire to accommodate, as is the case with all these men, cannot remember. You are left therefore in misery to calculate the number of the street as you move along, vainly endeavouring through the misty glass to decipher the small numbers which after a day or two you perceive to be written on the lamp posts.

But I soon gave up all attempts at keeping a seat in one of these cars. It became my practise to sit down on the outside iron rail behind, and as the conductor generally sat in my lap I was in a measure protected. As for the inside of these vehicles, the women of New York were, I must confess, too much for me. I would no sooner place myself on a seat, than I would be called on by a mute, unexpressive, but still impressive stare into my face, to surrender my place. From cowardice if not from gallantry I would always obey; and as this led to discomfort and an irritated spirit, I preferred nursing the conductor on the hard bar in the rear.

And here if I seem to say a word against women in America, I beg that it may be understood that I say that word only against a certain class; and even as to that class I admit that they are respectable, intelligent, and, as I believe, industrious. Their manners, however, are to me more odious than those of any other human being that I ever met elsewhere. Nor can I go on with that which I have to say without carrying my apology further, lest perchance I should be misunderstood by some American women whom I would not only exclude from my censure, but would include in the very warmest eulogium which words of mine could express as to those of the female sex whom I love and admire the most. I have known, do know, and mean to continue to know as far as in me may lie, American ladies as bright, as beautiful, as graceful, as sweet, as mortal limits for brightness, beauty, grace and sweetness will permit. They belong to the aristocracy of the land, by whatever means they may have become aristocrats. In America one does not enquire as to their birth, their training, or their old names. The fact of their aristocratic power comes out in every word and look. It is not only so with those who have travelled or with those who are rich. I have found female aristocrats with families and slender means, who have as yet made no grand tour across the ocean. These women are charming beyond expression. It is not only their beauty. Had he been speaking of such, Wendell Phillips would have been right in saying that they have brains all over them. So much for those who are bright and beautiful; who are graceful and sweet! And now a word as to those who to me are neither bright nor beautiful; and who can be to none either graceful or sweet. . . .

I have spoken of this with reference to street cars, because in no position of life does an unfortunate man become more liable to these anti-feminine atrocities than in the centre of one of these vehicles. The woman, as she enters, drags after her a misshapen, dirty mass of battered wirework, which she calls her crinoline, and which adds as much to her grace and comfort as a log of wood does to a donkey when tied to the animal's leg in a paddock. Of this she takes much heed, not managing it so that it may be conveyed up the carriage with some decency, but striking it about against men's legs, and heaving it with violence over people's knees. The touch of a real woman's dress is in itself delicate; but these blows from a harpy's fins are loathsome. If there be two of them they talk loudly together, having a theory that modesty has been put out of court by women's rights. But, though not modest, the woman I describe is ferocious in her propriety. She ignores the whole world around her, and as she sits with raised chin and face flattened by affection, she pretends to declare aloud that she is positively not aware that any man is even near her. She speaks as though to her, in her womanhood, the neighbourhood of men was the same as that of dogs or cats. . . .

> [Aware that Boston had once been the stronghold of Puritanism, Trollope is impressed by its gracious social life as well as its intellectual eminence.]

GOOD LIVING IN BOSTON

I SHALL always look back to social life in Boston with great pleasure. I met there many men and women whom to know is a distinction, and with whom to be intimate is a great delight. It was a Puritan city, in which strict old Roundhead sentiments and laws used to prevail; but now-a-days ginger is hot in the mouth there, and in spite of the war there were cakes and ale. There was a law passed in Massachusetts in the old days that any girl should be fined and imprisoned who allowed a young man to kiss her. That law has now, I think, fallen into abeyance, and such matters are regulated in Boston much as they are in other large towns further eastward. It still, I conceive, calls itself a Puritan city, but it has divested its Puritanism of austerity, and clings rather to the politics and public bearing of its old fathers than to their social manners and pristine severity of intercourse. The young girls are, no doubt, much more comfortable under the new dispensation—and the elderly men also, as I fancy. Sunday, as regards the outer streets, is sabbatical. But Sunday evenings within doors I always found to be what my friends in that country call "quite a good time." It is not the thing in Boston to smoke in the streets during the day; but the wisest, the sagest, and the most holy—even those holy men whom the lecturer saw around him—seldom refuse a cigar in the dining-room as soon as the ladies have gone. Perhaps even the wicked weed would make its appearance before that sad eclipse, thereby postponing, or perhaps absolutely annihilating, the melancholy period of widowhood to both parties, and would light itself under the very eyes of those who in sterner cities will lend no countenance to such lightings. Ah me, it was very pleasant! I confess I like this abandonment of the stricter rules of the more decorous world. I fear that there is within me an aptitude to the milder debaucheries which makes such deviations pleasant. I like to drink and I like to smoke, but I do not like to turn women out of the room. Then comes the question whether one can have all that one likes together. In some small circles in New England I found people simple enough to fancy that they could. In Massachusetts the Maine Liquor Law is still the law of the land, but, like that other law to which I have alluded, it has fallen very much out of use. At any rate it had not reached the houses of the gentlemen with whom I had the pleasure of making acquaintance. But here I must guard myself from being misunderstood. I saw but one drunken man through all New England, and he was very respectable. He was, however, so uncommonly drunk that he might be allowed to count for two or three. The Puritans of Boston are, of course, simple in their habits and simple in their expenses. Champagne and canvas-back ducks I found to be the provisions most in vogue among those who desired to adhere closely to the manners of their forefathers. Upon the whole I found the ways of life which had been brought over in the *Mayflower* from the stern sects of England, and preserved through the revolutionary war for liberty, to be very pleasant ways, and I made up my mind that a Yankee Puritan can be an uncommonly pleasant fellow. I wish that some of them did not dine so early; for when a man sits down at half-past two, that keeping up of the after-dinner recreations till bedtime becomes hard work.

In Boston the houses are very spacious and excellent, and they are always furnished with those luxuries which it is so difficult to introduce into an old house. They have hot and cold water pipes into every room, and baths attached to the bed-chambers. It is not only that comfort is increased by such arrangements, but that much labour is saved. In an old English house it will occupy a servant the best part of the day to carry water up and down for a large family. Everything also is spacious, commodious, and well lighted. I certainly think that in house-building the Americans have gone beyond us, for even our new houses are not commodious as are theirs.

[He spends a winter month in Washington, where his chief impression is of mud and unfinished public buildings. Early in 1862 he makes another trip west and gathers the impressions summarized below.]

MEN AND MANNERS BEYOND THE MISSISSIPPI

IN the West I found the men gloomy and silent—I might almost say sullen. A dozen of them will sit for hours round a stove, speechless. They chew tobacco and ruminate. They are not offended if you speak to them, but they are not pleased. They answer with monosyllables, or, if it be practicable, with a gesture of the head. They care nothing for the graces—or shall I say, for the decencies of life? They are essentially a dirty people. Dirt, untidiness, and noise seem in nowise to afflict them. Things are constantly done before your eyes, which should be done and might be done behind your back. No doubt we daily come into the closest contact with matters which, if we saw all that appertains to them, would cause us to shake and shudder. In other countries we do not see all this, but in the western States we do. I have eaten in Bedouin tents, and have been ministered to by Turks and Arabs. I have sojourned in the hotels of old Spain and of Spanish America. I have lived in Connaught, and have taken up my quarters with monks of different nations. I have, as it were, been educated to dirt, and taken out my degree in outward abominations. But my education had not reached a point which would enable me to live at my ease in the western States. A man or woman who can do that may be said to have graduated in the highest honours, and to have become absolutely invulnerable, either through the sense of touch, or by the eye, or by the nose. Indifference to appearances is there a matter of pride. A foul shirt is a flag of triumph. A craving for soap and water is as the wail of the weak and the confession of cowardice.

This indifference is carried into all their affairs, or rather this manifestation of indifference. A few pages back, I spoke of a man whose furniture had been sold to pay a heavy tax raised on him specially as a secessionist; the same man had also been refused the payment of rent due to him by the Government, unless he would take a false oath. I may presume that he was ruined in his circumstances by the strong hand of the Northern army. But he seemed in nowise to be unhappy about his ruin. He spoke with some scorn of the martial law of Missouri, but I felt that it was esteemed a small matter by him that his furniture was seized and sold. No men love money with more eager love than these western men, but they bear the loss of it as an Indian bears his torture at the stake. They are energetic in trade, speculating deeply whenever speculation is possible; but nevertheless they are slow in motion, loving to loaf about. They are slow in speech, preferring to sit in silence, with the tobacco between their teeth. They drink, but are seldom drunk to the eye; they begin it early in the morning, and take it in a solemn, sullen, ugly manner, standing always at a bar; swallowing their spirits, and saying nothing as they swallow it. They drink often, and to great excess; but they carry it off without noise, sitting down and ruminating over it with the everlasting cud within their jaws. I believe that a stranger might go into the West, and passing from hotel to hotel through a dozen of them, might sit for hours at each in the large everlasting public hall, and never have a word addressed to him. . . .

I cannot part with the West without saying in its favour that there is a certain manliness about its men, which gives them a dignity of their own. It is shown in that very indifference of which I have spoken. Whatever turns up the man is still there—still unsophisticated and still unbroken. It has seemed to me that no race of men requires less outward assistance than these pioneers of civilization. They rarely amuse themselves. Food, newspapers, and brandy-smashes suffice for life; and while these last, whatever may occur, the man is still there in his manhood. The fury of the mob does not shake him, nor the stern countenance of his present martial tyrant. Alas! I cannot stick to my text by calling him a just man. Intelligence, energy, and endurance are his virtues. Dirt, dishonesty, and morning drinks are his vices.

All native American women are intelligent. It seems to be their birthright. In the eastern cities they have, in their upper classes, superadded womanly grace to this intelligence, and consequently they are charming as companions. They are beautiful also, and, as I believe, lack nothing that a lover can desire in his love. But I cannot fancy myself much in love with a western lady, or rather with a lady in the West. They are as sharp as nails, but then they are also as hard. They know, doubtless, all that they ought to know, but then they know so much more than they ought to know. They are tyrants to their parents, and never practise the virtue of obedience till they have half-grown-up daughters of their own. They have faith in the destiny of their country, if in nothing else; but they believe that [that] destiny is to be worked out by the spirit and talent of the young women. I confess that for me Eve would have had no charms had she not recognised Adam as her lord. I can forgive her in that she tempted him to eat the apple. Had she come from the West country she would have ordered him to make his meal, and then I could not have forgiven her. . . .

A PREFERENCE FOR THE EAST

As the general result of my sojourn in the country, I must declare that I was always happy and comfortable in the eastern cities, and generally unhappy and uncomfortable in the West. I had previously been inclined to think that I should like the roughness of the West, and that in the East I should encounter an arrogance which would have kept me always on the verge of hot water; but in both these surmises I found myself to have been wrong. And I think that most English travellers would come to the same conclusion. The western people do not mean to be harsh or uncivil, but they do not make themselves pleasant. In all the eastern cities—I speak of the eastern cities north of Washington—a society may be found which must be esteemed as agreeable by Englishmen who like clever genial men, and who love clever pretty women.

A Stagecoach on the Prairie and the Camel That Ate an Overcoat

MARK TWAIN

FROM *Roughing It*

1861–65

Beguiled by Tom Sawyer and Huck Finn, we are likely to forget that Mark Twain first achieved fame as a writer on travel (see pages 619–27). Except for the reprinting of his "Jumping Frog" story, he was an unknown California newspaperman of thirty-one when he came back from Hawaii to write the series of travel articles—and develop the lecture —that made him famous.

Circumstances had made Samuel Clemens a wanderer. From his thirteenth year to his twenty-second he was first an apprentice printer and then a journeyman in cities from St. Louis to New York. After that he piloted a steamboat on the Mississippi. Then, in 1861, he went west and roved for almost seven years from the mining camps and boom towns of Nevada to the newspaper offices of San Francisco.

Having tasted fame with his Sandwich Island pieces, he took a cruise to the Holy Land and described the journey in The Innocents Abroad. The immense success of that book led him to follow it up with A Tramp Abroad (1880) and Following the Equator (1897). It also led him to exploit his wanderings in the Far West, and in 1872 he published Roughing It. Although less a record of travel than of picaresque adventure, it captures more of the spirit of western life than many a more serious book.

Even more than his other travel books, it uses every device of American frontier humor: grotesque exaggeration, the piling of digression on *digression, the abrupt plunge from the solemn to the ridiculous, from refined sentiment to crude joke. Of the essence too is irreverence, a readiness to mock the pompous, the hoary or just the unfamiliar. To all this, however, Twain added great gifts of his own: mother wit, superb timing, social conscience and a novelist's sense of character. It is because of these that although the frontier is long gone and some of Twain's humor is dated, the best of such a book as* Roughing It *seems as shrewd and funny as ever.*

[Mark Twain was twenty-six, with his experiences as a journeyman printer and steamboat pilot behind him, when his brother Orion was appointed Secretary of Nevada Territory and offered to take Sam along with him. Sam jumped at the chance. They started from the Missouri frontier, taking a steamboat up the Missouri River to St. Joseph and there buying passage on the overland stage, destination Carson City. The passage below describes the second day out.]

Aʙᴏᴜᴛ an hour and a half before daylight we were bowling along smoothly over the road—so smoothly that our cradle only rocked in a gentle, lulling way, that was gradually soothing us to sleep, and dulling our consciousness—when something gave away under us! We were dimly aware of it, but indifferent to it. The coach stopped. We heard the driver and conductor talking together outside, and rummaging for a lantern, and swearing because they could not find it—but we had no interest in whatever had happened, and it only added to our comfort to think of those people out there at work in the murky night, and we snug in our nest with the curtains drawn. But presently, by the sounds, there seemed to be an examination going on, and then the driver's voice said:

"By George, the thoroughbrace is broke!"

This startled me broad awake—as an undefined sense of calamity is always apt to do. I said to myself: "Now, a thoroughbrace is probably part of a horse; and doubtless a vital part, too, from the dismay in the driver's voice. Leg, maybe—and yet how could he break his leg waltzing along such a road as this? No, it can't be his leg. That is impossible, unless he was reaching for the driver. Now, what can be the thoroughbrace of a horse, I wonder? Well, whatever comes, I shall not air my ignorance in this crowd, anyway."

Just then the conductor's face appeared at a lifted curtain, and his lantern glared in on us and our wall of mail matter. He said:

"Gents, you'll have to turn out a spell. Thoroughbrace is broke."

We climbed out into a chill drizzle, and felt ever so homeless and dreary. When I found that the thing they called a "thoroughbrace" was the massive combination of belts and springs which the coach rocks itself in, I said to the driver:

"I never saw a thoroughbrace used up like that, before, that I can remember. How did it happen?"

"Why, it happened by trying to make one coach carry three days' mail —that's how it happened," said he. "And right here is the very direction which is wrote on all the newspaper-bags which was to be put out for the Injuns for to keep 'em quiet. It's most uncommon lucky, becuz it's so nation dark I should 'a' gone by unbeknowns if that air thoroughbrace hadn't broke."

I knew that he was in labor with another of those winks of his, though I could not see his face, because he was bent down at work; and wishing him a safe delivery, I turned to and helped the rest get out the mail-sacks. It made a great pyramid by the roadside when it was all out. When they had mended the thoroughbrace we filled the two boots again, but put no mail on top, and only half as much inside as there was before. The conductor bent all the seat-backs down, and then filled the coach just half full of mail-bags from end to end. We objected loudly to this, for it left us no seats. But the conductor was wiser than we, and said a bed was better than seats, and, moreover, this plan would protect his thoroughbraces. We never wanted any seats after that. The lazy bed was infinitely preferable. I had many an exciting day, subsequently, lying on it reading the statutes and the dictionary, and wondering how the characters would turn out.

The conductor said he would send back a guard from the next station to take charge of the abandoned mail-bags, and we drove on.

It was now just dawn; and as we stretched our cramped legs full length on the mail-sacks, and gazed out through the windows across the wide wastes of greensward clad in cool, powdery mist, to where there was an expectant look in the eastern horizon, our perfect enjoyment took the form of a tranquil and contented ecstasy. The stage whirled along at a spanking gait, the breeze flapping curtains and suspended coats in a most exhilarating way; the cradle swayed and swung luxuriously, the pattering of the horses' hoofs, the cracking of the driver's whip, and his "Hi-yi! g'lang!" were music; the spinning ground and the waltzing trees appeared to give us a mute hurrah as we went by, and then slack up and look after us with interest, or envy, or something; and as we lay and smoked the pipe of peace and compared all this luxury with the years of tiresome city life that had gone before it, we felt that there was only one complete and satisfying happiness in the world, and we had found it.

After breakfast, at some station whose name I have forgotten, we three climbed up on the seat behind the driver, and let the conductor have our bed for a nap. And by and by, when the sun made me drowsy, I lay down on my face on top of the coach, grasping the slender iron railing, and slept for an hour more. That will give one an appreciable idea of those matchless roads. Instinct will make a sleeping man grip a fast hold of the railing when the stage jolts, but when it only swings and sways, no grip is necessary. Overland drivers and conductors used to sit in their places and sleep thirty or forty minutes at a time, on good roads, while spinning along at the rate of eight or ten miles an hour. I saw them do it, often. There was no danger about it; a sleeping man *will* seize the irons in time when the coach jolts. These men were hard worked, and it was not possible for them to stay awake all the time.

By and by we passed through Marysville, and over the Big Blue and Little Sandy; thence about a mile, and entered Nebraska. About a mile further on, we came to the Big Sandy—one hundred and eighty miles from St. Joseph.

As the sun was going down, we saw the first specimen of an animal known familiarly over two thousand miles of mountain and desert—from Kansas clear to the Pacific Ocean—as the "jackass rabbit." He is well named. He is just like any other rabbit, except that he is from one-third to twice as large, has longer legs in proportion to his size, and has the most preposterous ears that ever were mounted on any creature but a jackass. When he is sitting quiet, thinking about his sins, or is absent-minded or unapprehensive of danger, his majestic ears project about him conspicuously; but the breaking of a twig will scare him nearly to death, and then he tilts his ears back gently and starts for home. All you can see, then, for the next minute, is his long gray form stretched out straight and "streaking it" through the low sage-brush, head erect, eyes right, and ears just canted a little to the rear, but showing you where the animal is, all the time, the same as if he carried a jib. Now and then he makes a marvelous spring with his long legs, high over the stunted sage-brush, and scores a leap that would make a horse envious. Presently, he comes down to a long, graceful "lope," and shortly he mysteriously disappears. He has crouched behind a sage-bush, and will sit there and listen and tremble until you get within six feet of him, when he will get under way again. But one must shoot at this creature once, if he wishes to see him throw his heart into his heels, and do the best he knows how. He is frightened clear through.

now, and he lays his long ears down on his back, straightens himself out like a yardstick every spring he makes, and scatters miles behind him with an easy indifference that is enchanting.

Our party made this specimen "hump himself," as the conductor said. The Secretary started him with a shot from the Colt; I commenced spitting at him with my weapon; and all in the same instant the old "Allen's" whole broadside let go with a rattling crash, and it is not putting it too strong to say that the rabbit was frantic! He dropped his ears, set up his tail, and left for San Francisco at a speed which can only be described as a flash and a vanish! Long after he was out of sight we could hear him whiz.

I do not remember where we first came across "sage-brush," but as I have been speaking of it I may as well describe it. This is easily done, for if the reader can imagine a gnarled and venerable live-oak tree reduced to a little shrub two feet high, with its rough bark, its foliage, its twisted boughs, all complete, he can picture the sage-brush exactly. Often, on lazy afternoons in the mountains I have lain on the ground with my face under a sage-bush, and entertained myself with fancying that the gnats among its foliage were lilliputian birds, and that the ants marching and counter-marching about its base were lilliputian flocks and herds, and myself some vast loafer from Brobdingnag waiting to catch a little citizen and eat him.

It is an imposing monarch of the forest in exquisite miniature, is the sage-brush. Its foliage is a grayish green, and gives that tint to desert and mountain. It smells like our domestic sage, and "sage-tea" made from it tastes like the sage-tea which all boys are so well acquainted with. The sage-brush is a singularly hardy plant, and grows right in the midst of deep sand, and among barren rocks where nothing else in the vegetable world would try to grow, except "bunch-grass." The sage-bushes grow from three to six or seven feet apart, all over the mountains and deserts of the Far West, clear to the borders of California. There is not a tree of any kind in the deserts, for hundreds of miles—there is no vegetation at all in a regular desert, except the sage-brush and its cousin the "greasewood," which is so much like the sage-brush that the difference amounts to little. Camp-fires and hot suppers in the deserts would be impossible but for the friendly sage-brush. Its trunk is as large as a boy's wrist (and from that up to a man's arm), and its crooked branches are half as large as its trunk—all good, sound, hard wood, very like oak.

When a party camps, the first thing to be done is to cut sage-brush; and in a few minutes there is an opulent pile of it ready for use. A hole a foot wide, two feet deep, and two feet long, is dug, and sage-brush chopped up and burned in it till it is full to the brim with glowing coals; then the cooking begins, and there is no smoke, and consequently no swearing. Such a fire will keep all night, with very little replenishing; and it makes a very sociable camp-fire, and one around which the most impossible reminiscences sound plausible, instructive, and profoundly entertaining.

Sage-brush is very fair fuel, but as a vegetable it is a distinguished failure. Nothing can abide the taste of it but the jackass and his illegitimate child, the mule. But their testimony to its nutritiousness is worth nothing, for they will eat pine-knots, or anthracite coal, or brass filings, or lead pipe, or old bottles, or anything that comes handy, and then go off looking as grateful as if they had had oysters for dinner. Mules and donkeys and camels have appetites that anything will relieve temporarily, but nothing satisfy. In Syria, once, at the headwaters of the Jordan, a camel took charge of my overcoat while the tents were being pitched, and examined it with a critical eye, all over, with as much interest as if he had an idea of getting one made like it; and then, after he was done figuring on it as an article of apparel, he began to contemplate it as an article of diet. He put his foot on it, and lifted one of the sleeves out with his teeth, and chewed and chewed at it, gradually taking it in, and all the while opening and closing his eyes in a kind of religious ecstasy, as if he had never tasted anything as good as an overcoat before in his life. Then he smacked his lips once or twice, and reached after the other sleeve. Next he tried the velvet collar, and smiled a smile of such contentment that it was plain to see that he regarded that as the daintiest thing about an overcoat. The tails went next, along with some percussion-caps and cough-candy, and some fig-paste from Constantinople. And then my newspaper correspondence dropped out, and he took a chance in that—manuscript letters written for the home papers. But he was treading on dangerous ground, now. He began to come across solid wisdom in those documents that was rather weighty on his stomach; and occasionally he would take a joke that would shake him up till it loosened his teeth; it was getting to be perilous times with him, but he held his grip with good courage and hopefully, till at last he began to stumble on statements that not even a camel could swallow with impunity. He began to gag and gasp, and his eyes to stand out, and his forelegs to spread, and in about a quarter of a minute he fell over as stiff as a carpenter's work-bench, and died a death of indescribable agony. I went and pulled the manuscript out of his mouth, and found that the sensitive creature had choked to death on one of the mildest and gentlest statements of fact that I ever laid before a trusting public.

I was about to say, when diverted from my subject, that occasionally one finds sage-bushes five or six feet high, and with a spread of branch and foliage in proportion, but two or two and a half feet is the usual height.

[Twain then describes the long journey across the plains, including pony riders, mountain desperadoes, the Great Salt Lake, Mormons, and finally the arrival in Carson City. After an idyllic camping trip to magnificent Lake Tahoe he is smitten with the silver fever; he tells of wild prospecting sorties, booming shares, fortunes won and lost overnight. Eventually he joins the staff of the *Territorial Enterprise* and later of newspapers in San Francisco. In the closing pages he is on the tour of Hawaii which led to the series of articles that made him famous.]

Saratoga: "The Democratization of Elegance"

HENRY JAMES

FROM *Portraits of Places*

1870–82

In the travel sketches of Henry James, as in his novels, there is a polarization of feeling between Europe and America, with the current running, so to speak, toward the Old World. In such cities as Venice (see pages 606–11) and London he found a rich accumulation of history, culture and tradition, a sense of order and permanence, that he missed in the United States. Even those places in America that had meaning for him—such as Newport, Boston and a few neighborhoods in New York— aroused mainly a kind of nostalgia in him.

But the very contrast between the two worlds also fascinated him. So he came back to the American theme again and again, and The American Scene *(1907), sketches he collected on his return to America after an absence of twenty-one years, is perhaps the most impressive of his travel books. It exhibits to the full the extraordinary discrimination and sensitivity that are his special stamp.*

[The following passages are from one of James's earliest travel sketches, "Saratoga," which first appeared in *The Nation* in August 1870.]

T HE piazzas of these great hotels may very well be the biggest of all piazzas. They have not architectural beauty; but they doubtless serve their purpose—that of affording sitting-space in the open air to an immense number of persons. They are, of course, quite the best places to observe the Saratoga world. In the evening, when the "boarders" have all come forth and seated themselves in groups, or have begun to stroll in (not always, I regret to say, to the sad detriment of the dramatic interest, bisexual) couples, the big heterogeneous scene affords a great deal of entertainment. Seeing it for the first time, the observer is likely to assure himself that he has neglected an important item in the sum of American manners. The rough brick wall of the house, illumined by a line of flaring gas-lights, forms a natural background to the crude, impermanent, discordant tone of the assembly. In the larger of the two hotels, a series of long windows open into an immense parlor—the largest, I suppose, in the world, and the most scantily furnished in proportion to its size. A few dozen rocking-chairs, an equal number of small tables, tripods to the eternal ice-pitcher, serve chiefly to emphasize the vacuous grandeur of the spot. On the piazza, in the outer multitude, ladies largely prevail, both by numbers and (you are not slow to perceive) by distinction of appearance. The good old times of Saratoga, I believe, as of the world in general, are rapidly passing away. The time was when it was the chosen resort of none but "nice people." At the present day, I hear it constantly affirmed, "the company is dreadfully mixed." What society may have been at Saratoga when its elements were thus simple and severe, I can only vaguely and mournfully conjecture. I confine myself to the dense, democratic, vulgar Saratoga of the current year. You are struck, to begin with, at the hotels, by the numerical superiority of the women; then, I think, by their personal superiority. It is incontestably the case that in appearance, in manner, in grace and completeness of aspect, American women surpass their husbands and brothers; the relation being reversed among some of the nations of Europe. Attached to the main entrance of the Union Hotel, and adjoining the ascent from the street to the piazza, is a "stoop" of mighty area, which, at most hours of the day and evening, is a favored lounging-place of men. I should add, after the remark I have just made, that even in the appearance of the usual American male there seems to me to be a certain plastic intention. It is true that the lean, sallow, angular Yankee of tradition is dignified mainly by a look of decision, a hint of unimpassioned volition, the air of "smartness." This in some degree redeems him, but it fails to make him handsome. But in the average American of the present time, the typical leanness and sallowness are less than in his fathers, and the individual acuteness is at once equally marked and more frequently united with merit of form. Casting your eye over a group of your fellow-citizens in the portico of the Union Hotel, you will be inclined to admit that, taking the good with the bad, they are worthy sons of the great Republic. I have found, at any rate, a great deal of entertainment in watching them. They suggest to my fancy the swarming vastness—the multifarious possibilities and activities—of our young civilisation. They come from the uttermost ends of the Union—from San Francisco, from New Orleans, from Alaska. As they sit with their white hats tilted forward, and their chairs tilted back, and their feet tilted up, and their cigars and toothpicks forming various angles with these various lines, I seem to see in their faces a tacit reference to the affairs of a continent. They are obviously persons of experience— of a somewhat narrow and monotonous experience certainly; an experience of which the diamonds and laces which their wives are exhibiting hard by are, perhaps, the most substantial and beautiful result; but, at any rate, they have *lived* in every fibre of the will. For the time, they are lounging with the Negro waiters, and the boot-blacks, and the news-vendors; but it was not in lounging that they gained their hard wrinkles and the level impartial regard which they direct from beneath their hat-rims. They are not the mellow fruit of a society which has walked hand-in-hand with tradition and culture; they are hard nuts, which have grown and ripened as they could. When they talk among themselves, I seem to hear the cracking of the shells.

If the men are remarkable, the ladies are wonderful. Saratoga is famous, I believe, as the place of all places in America where women adorn themselves most, or as the place, at least, where the greatest amount of dressing may be seen by the greatest number of people. Your first impression is therefore of the—what shall I call it?—of the abundance of petticoats. Every woman you meet, young or old, is attired with a certain amount of richness, and with whatever good taste may be compatible with such a mode of life. You behold an interesting, indeed a quite momentous spectacle: the democratization of elegance. If I am to believe what I hear —in fact, I may say what I overhear—many of these sumptuous persons have enjoyed neither the advantages of a careful education nor the privileges of an introduction to society. She walks more or less of a queen, however, each uninitiated nobody. She often has, in dress, an admirable instinct of elegance and even of what the French call "chic." This instinct occasionally amounts to a sort of passion; the result then is wonderful. You look at the coarse brick walls, the rusty iron posts of the piazza, at the shuffling Negro waiters, the great tawdry steamboat-cabin of a drawing-room—you see the tilted ill-dressed loungers on the steps—and you finally regret that a figure so exquisite should have so vulgar a setting. Your resentment, however, is speedily tempered by reflection. You feel the impertinence of your old reminiscences of English and French novels, and of the dreary social order in which privacy was the presiding genius and women arrayed themselves for the appreciation of the few. The crowd, the tavern-loungers, the surrounding ugliness and tumult and license, constitute the social medium of the young lady you are so inconsistent as to admire; she is dressed for publicity. The thought fills you with a kind of awe. The social order of tradition is far way indeed, and as for the trans-atlantic novels, you begin to doubt whether she is so amiably curious as to read even the silliest of them. To be dressed up to the eyes is obviously to give pledges to idleness. I have been forcibly struck with the apparent absence of any warmth and richness of detail in the lives of these wonderful ladies of the piazzas. We are freely accused of being an eminently wasteful people; and I know of few things which so largely warrant the accusation as the fact that these conspicuous *élégantes* adorn themselves, socially speaking, to so little purpose. To dress for every one is, practically to dress for no one. There are few prettier sights than a charmingly-dressed woman, gracefully established in some shady spot, with a piece of needle-work or embroidery, or a book. Nothing very serious is accomplished, probably, but an aesthetic principle is recognized. The embroidery and the book are a tribute to culture, and I suppose they really figure somewhere out of the opening scenes of French comedies. But here at Saratoga, at any hour of morning or evening, you may see a hundred rustling beauties whose rustle is their sole occupation. . . .

I have indeed observed cases of a sort of splendid social isolation here, which are not without a certain amount of pathos—people who know no one, who have money and finery and possessions, only no friends. Such at least is my inference, from the lonely grandeur with which I see them invested. Women, of course, are the most helpless victims of this cruel situation, although it must be said that they befriend each other with a generosity for which we hardly give them credit. I have seen women, for instance, at various "hops," approach their lonely sisters and invite them to waltz, and I have seen the fair invited surrender themselves eagerly to this humiliating embrace. Gentlemen at Saratoga are at a much higher premium than at European watering-places. It is an old story that in this country we have no "leisure-class"—the class from which the Saratogas of Europe recruit a large number of their male frequenters. A few months ago, I paid a visit to an English "bath," commemorated in various works of fiction, where, among many visible points of difference from American resorts, the most striking was the multitude of young men who had the whole day on their hands. While their sweethearts and sisters are waltzing together, our own young men are rolling up greenbacks in counting-houses and stores. . . .

Lady in the Wild West

ISABELLA BIRD BISHOP

FROM A *Lady's Life in the Rocky Mountains*

1873

As described on page 110, Isabella Bird (later Mrs. John Bishop), daughter of an English clergyman, first went abroad at twenty-one. During the next fifty years she became one of the outstanding travelers of her time and author of almost a dozen of the most interesting books of their kind. Beginning in 1854 with a trip to America for her health, she circled the earth three times—almost always traveling alone—and sojourned in such places as the upper Yangtze, the Malay jungle, Tibet, Persia, Japan, Hawaii, Canada, New Zealand, Korea and Morocco. Small, soft-spoken, unassuming, and of deep religious convictions, she was none-theless an extraordinarily persevering traveler, a mettlesome horsewoman and a stoic in the face of hardships. Her books are a spirited and occasionally brilliant record of her love of wild places and her interest in strange peoples. Such was her accomplishment that she was the first woman elected to the Royal Geographical Society.

After several visits to America she went to Australia and New Zealand in 1872 and spent seven months in Hawaii, a stay she vividly described in Six Months in the Sandwich Islands. *She sailed from there to America and rested for many months in a Western sanatorium. In the autumn of 1873 she went by train from San Francisco into the Sierra Nevada and then set out on a four-month, 800-mile trip through the Rockies. From the letters she wrote her sister (later collected in book form) we get some unforgettable glimpses of settler life, frontier towns, a roundup and a notorious desperado, "Mountain Jim" Nugent, whose confidence she won with her understanding and sympathy.*

[From Truckee, Nevada, she passes through Wyoming and
Utah and into Colorado. At one point she stays for a time
with a poor settler family near Fort Collins, Colorado.]

MOUNTAIN SETTLERS

My life has grown less dull from their having become more interesting
to me, and as I have "made myself agreeable," we are on fairly friendly
terms. My first move in the direction of fraternizing was, however, snubbed.
A few days ago, having finished my own work, I offered to wash up
the plates, but Mrs. C., with a look which conveyed more than words, a
curl of her nose, and a sneer in her twang, said, "Guess you'll make more
work nor you'll do. Those hands of yours" (very brown and coarse they
were) "ain't no good; never done nothing, I guess." Then to her awkward
daughter: "This woman says she'll wash up! Ha! ha! look at her arms
and hands!" This was the nearest approach to a laugh I have heard, and
have never seen even a tendency towards a smile. Since then I have risen
in their estimation by improvising a lamp—Hawaiian fashion—by putting a
wisp of rag into a tin of fat. They have actually condescended to sit up till
the stars come out since. . . .

Chalmers came from Illinois nine years ago, pronounced by the doctors
to be far gone in consumption, and in two years he was strong. They are a
queer family; somewhere in the remote Highlands I have seen such
another. Its head is tall, gaunt, lean, and ragged, and has lost one eye.
On an English road one would think him a starving or a dangerous beggar.
He is slightly intelligent, very opinionated, and wishes to be thought well-
informed, which he is not. He belongs to the straitest sect of Reformed
Presbyterians ("Psalm-singers"), but exaggerates anything of bigotry and
intolerance which may characterize them, and rejoices in truly merciless
fashion over the excision of the philanthropic Mr. Stuart, of Philadelphia,
for worshipping with congregations which sing hymns. His great boast is
that his ancestors were Scottish Covenanters. He considers himself a profound theologian, and by the pine logs at night discourses to me on the
mysteries of the eternal counsels and the divine decrees. Colorado, with
its progress and its future, is also a constant theme. He hates England
with a bitter, personal hatred, and regards any allusions which I make to

the progress of Victoria as a personal insult. He trusts to live to see the downfall of the British monarchy and the disintegration of the empire. . . .

They have one hundred and sixty acres of land, a "squatter's claim," and an invaluable water-power. He is a lumberer, and has a saw-mill of a very primitive kind. I notice that every day something goes wrong with it, and this is the case throughout. If he wants to haul timber down, one or other of the oxen cannot be found; or if the timber is actually under way, a wheel or a part of the harness gives way, and the whole affair is at a standstill for days. The cabin is hardly a shelter, but is allowed to remain in ruins because the foundation of a frame-house was once dug. A horse is always sure to be lame for want of a shoe-nail, or a saddle to be useless from a broken buckle, and the wagon and harness are a marvel of temporary shifts, patchings, and insecure linkings with strands of rope. Nothing is ever ready or whole when it is wanted. Yet Chalmers is a frugal, sober, hard-working man, and he, his eldest son, and a "hired man" "rise early," "going forth to their work and labour till the evening;" and if they do not "late take rest," they truly "eat the bread of carefulness." It is hardly surprising that nine years of persevering shiftlessness should have resulted in nothing but the ability to procure the bare necessaries of life.

Of Mrs. C. I can say less. She looks like one of the English poor women of our childhood—lean, clean, toothless—and speaks, like some of them, in a piping, discontented voice, which seems to convey a personal reproach. All her waking hours are spent in a large sun-bonnet. She is never idle for one minute, is severe and hard, and despises everything but work. I think she suffers from her husband's shiftlessness. She always speaks of me as "this" or "that woman." The family consists of a grown-up son, a shiftless, melancholy-looking youth, who possibly pines for a wider life; a girl of sixteen, a sour, repellent-looking creature, with as much manners as a pig; and three hard, unchildlike younger children. By the whole family all courtesy and gentleness of act or speech seem regarded as "works of the flesh," if not of "the devil." They knock over all one's things without apologizing or picking them up, and when I thank them for anything they look grimly amazed. I feel that they think it sinful that I do not work as hard as they do. I wish I could show them "a more excellent way." This hard greed, and the exclusive pursuit of gain, with the indifference to all which does not aid in its acquisition, are eating up family love and life throughout the West. I write this reluctantly, and after a total experience of nearly two years in the United States. They seem to have no "Sunday clothes," and few of any kind. The sewing-machine, like most other things, is out of order. One comb serves the whole family. Mrs. C. is cleanly in her person and dress, and the food, though poor, is clean. . . .

Sunday was a dreadful day. The family kept the Commandment literally, and did no work. Worship was conducted twice, and was rather longer than usual. . . .

The cabin, with its mud roof under the shade of the trees, gave a little shelter, but it was occupied by the family, and I longed for solitude. I took the *Imitation of Christ,* and strolled up the canyon among the withered, crackling leaves, in much dread of snakes, and lay down on a rough table which some passing emigrant had left, and soon fell asleep. When I awoke it was only noon. The sun looked wicked as it blazed like a white magnesium light. A large tree-snake (quite harmless) hung from the pine under which I had taken shelter, and looked as if it were going to drop upon me. I was covered with black flies. The air was full of a busy, noisy din of insects, and snakes, locusts, wasps, flies, and grasshoppers were all rioting in the torrid heat. Would the sublime philosophy of Thomas a Kempis, I wondered, have given way under this? All day I seemed to hear in mockery the clear laugh of the Hilo streams, and the drip of Kona showers, and to see as in a mirage the perpetual green of windward Hawaii. I was driven back to the cabin in the late afternoon, and in the evening listened for two hours to abuse of my own country, and to sweeping condemnations of all religionists outside of the brotherhood of "Psalm-singers." . . .

[She makes her headquarters in a cabin on a rude ranch run by two Welsh families at Estes Park, Colorado, in a magnificent setting in the mountains near Longs Peak. For eight dollars a week she gets food, the unlimited use of a horse, and such exciting activities as the one described below.]

THE LADY RIDES IN A ROUNDUP

SHALL I ever get away? We were to have had a grand cattle-hunt yesterday, beginning at 6:30, but the horses were all lost. Often out of fifty horses all that are worth anything are marauding, and a day is lost in hunting for them in the canyons. However, before daylight this morning

Evans called through my door, "Miss Bird, I say we've got to drive cattle fifteen miles, I wish you'd lend a hand; there's not enough of us; I'll give you a good horse."

The scene of the drive is at a height of 7,500 feet, watered by two rapid rivers. On all sides mountains rise to an altitude of from 11,000 to 15,000 feet, their skirts shaggy with pitch-pine forests, and scarred by deep canyons, wooded and boulder-strewn, opening upon the mountain pasture previously mentioned. Two thousand head of half-wild Texan cattle are scattered in herds throughout the canyons, living on more or less suspicious terms with grizzly and brown bears, mountain lions, elk, mountain sheep, spotted deer, wolves, lynxes, wild cats, beavers, minks, skunks, chipmunks, eagles, rattlesnakes, and all the other two legged, four-legged, vertebrate and invertebrate inhabitants of this lonely and romantic region. On the whole, they show a tendency rather to the habits of wild than of domestic cattle. They march to water in Indian file, with the bulls leading, and when threatened, take strategic advantage of ridgy ground, slinking warily along in the hollows, the bulls acting as sentinels, and bringing up the rear in case of an attack from dogs. Cows have to be regularly broken in for milking, being as wild as buffaloes in their unbroken state; but, owing to the comparative dryness of the grasses, and the system of allowing the calf to have the milk during the daytime, a dairy of 200 cows does not produce as much butter as a Devonshire dairy of fifty. Some "necessary" cruelty is involved in the stockman's business, however humane he may be. The system is one of terrorism, and from the time that the calf is bullied into the branding pen, and the hot iron burns into his shrinking flesh, to the day when the fatted ox is driven down from his boundless pastures to be slaughtered in Chicago, "the fear and dread of man" are upon him.

The herds are apt to penetrate the savage canyons which come down from the Snowy Range, when they incur a risk of being snowed up and starved, and it is necessary now and then to hunt them out and drive them down to the "park." On this occasion, the whole were driven down for a muster, and for the purpose of branding the calves.

After a 6:30 breakfast this morning, we started, the party being composed of my host, a hunter from the Snowy Range, two stockmen from the Plains, one of whom rode a violent buck-jumper and was said by his comrade to be the "best rider in North Americay," and myself. We were all mounted on Mexican saddles, rode, as the custom is, with light snaffle bridles, leather guards over our feet, and broad wooden stirrups, and each carried his lunch in a pouch slung on the lassoing horn of his saddle. Four big, badly-trained dogs accompanied us. It was a ride of nearly thirty miles, and of many hours, one of the most splendid I ever took.

We never got off our horses except to tighten the girths, we ate our lunch with our bridles knotted over our saddle-horns, started over the level at full gallop, leapt over trunks of trees, dashed madly down hillsides rugged with rocks or strewn with great stones, forded deep, rapid streams, saw lovely lakes and views of surpassing magnificence, startled a herd of elk with uncouth heads and monstrous antlers, and in the chase, which for some time was unsuccessful, rode to the very base of Long's Peak, over 14,000 feet high . . .

Emerging from this, we caught sight of a thousand Texan cattle feeding in a valley below. The leaders scented us, and, taking fright, began to move off in the direction of the open "park," while we were about a mile from and above them. "Head them off, boys!" our leader shouted; "all aboard; hark away!" and with something of the "High, tally-ho in the morning!" away we all went at a hand-gallop down-hill. I could not hold my excited animal; down-hill, up-hill, leaping over rocks and timber, faster every moment the pace grew, and still the leader shouted, "Go it, boys!" and the horses dashed on at racing speed, passing and repassing each other, till my small but beautiful bay was keeping pace with the immense strides of the great buck-jumper ridden by "the finest rider in North Americay," and I was dizzied and breathless by the pace at which we were going. A shorter time than it takes to tell it brought us close to and abreast of the surge of cattle. The bovine waves were a grand sight: huge bulls, shaped like buffaloes, bellowed and roared, and with great oxen and cows with yearling calves, galloped like racers, and we galloped alongside of them, and shortly headed them, and in no time were placed as sentinels across the mouth of the valley. It seemed like infantry awaiting the shock of cavalry as we stood as still as our excited horses would allow. I almost quailed as the surge came on, but when it got close to us my comrades hooted fearfully, and we dashed forward with the dogs, and, with bellowing, roaring, and thunder of hoofs, the wave receded as it came. I rode up to our leader, who received me with much laughter. He said I was "a good cattleman," and that he had forgotten that a lady was of the party till he saw me "come leaping over the timber, and driving with the others."

It was not for two hours after this that the real business of driving began, and I was obliged to change my thoroughbred for a well-trained cattle-horse—a *broncho*, which could double like a hare, and go over any ground. I had not expected to work like a *vachero*, but so it was, and my Hawaiian experience was very useful. We hunted the various canyons and known "camps," driving the herds out of them; and, until we had secured 850 head in the *corral* some hours afterwards, we scarcely saw each other to speak to. . . .

It was getting late in the day, and a snowstorm was impending, before I was joined by the other drivers and herds, and as the former had diminished to three, with only three dogs, it was very difficult to keep the cattle together. You drive them as gently as possible, so as not to frighten or excite them, riding first on one side, then on the other, to guide them; and if they deliberately go in a wrong direction, you gallop in front and head them off. The great excitement is when one breaks away from the herd and gallops madly up and down hill, and you gallop after him anywhere, over and among rocks and trees, doubling when he doubles, and heading him till you get him back again. . . .

Just at dusk we reached the corral—an acre of grass enclosed by stout post-and-rail fences seven feet high, and by much patience and some subtlety lodged the whole herd within its shelter, without a blow, a shout, or even a crack of a whip, wild as the cattle were. It was fearfully cold. We galloped the last mile and a half in four and a half minutes, reached the cabin just as snow began to fall, and found strong, hot tea ready. . . .

Evans offers me six dollars a week if I will stay into the winter and do the cooking after Mrs. Edwards leaves! I think I should like playing at being a "hired girl" if it were not for the bread-making! But it would suit me better to ride after cattle. The men don't like "baching," as it is called in the wilds—i.e., "doing for themselves." . . .

[She visits Denver and crosses the Tarryall Peak into the South Park area. When she returns to the Estes Park ranch she finds that the two Welsh families have dismantled the cabin and left for the winter, and that two men, a Mr. Kavan and a Mr. Buchan, are "baching" it there to look after the stock until the Evans family returns. At first the young men are embarrassed by her coming, but she soon makes herself so useful that all three stay on for a month.]

HIBERNATING IN THE HIGH ROCKIES

WE have lost count of time, and can only agree on the fact that the date is somewhere near the end of November. Our life has settled down into serenity, and our singular and enforced partnership is very pleasant. We might be three men living together, but for the unvarying courtesy and consideration which they show to me. Our work goes on like clockwork; the only difficulty which ever arises is that the men do not like me to do anything that they think hard or unsuitable, such as saddling a horse or bringing in water. The days go very fast; it was 3:30 today before I knew that it was 1:00. It is a calm life without worries. The men are so easy to live with; they never fuss, or grumble, or sigh, or make a trouble of anything. It would amuse you to come into our wretched little kitchen before our disgracefully late breakfast, and find Mr. Kavan busy at the stove frying venison, myself washing the supper-dishes, and Mr. Buchan drying them, or both the men busy at the stove while I sweep the floor. Our food is a great object of interest to us, and we are ravenously hungry now that we have only two meals a day. About sundown each goes forth to his "chores"—Mr. K. to chop wood, Mr. B. to haul water, I to wash the milk-pans and water the horses. . . .

Thanksgiving Day. The thing dreaded has come at last, the snow-storm, with a north-east wind. It ceased about midnight, but not till it had covered my bed. Then the mercury fell below zero, and everything froze. I melted a tin of water for washing by the fire, but it was hard frozen before I could use it. My hair, which was thoroughly wet with the thawed snow of yesterday, is hard frozen in plaits. The milk and treacle are like rock, the eggs have to be kept on the coolest part of the stove to keep them fluid. Two calves in the shed were frozen to death. Half our floor is deep in snow, and it is so cold that we cannot open the door to shovel it out. The snow began again at eight this morning, very fine and hard. It blows in through the chinks and dusts this letter while I write. Mr. Kavan keeps my ink-bottle close to the fire, and hands it to me every time that I need to dip my pen. We have a huge fire, but cannot raise the temperature above 20°. Ever since I returned the lake has been hard enough to bear a wagon, but today it is difficult to keep the waterhole open by the constant use of the axe. The snow may either melt or block us in. Our only anxiety is about the supplies. We have tea and coffee enough to last over to-morrow, the sugar is just done, and the flour is getting low. It is really serious that we have "another mouth to feed," and the new-comer [a young traveler, a theological student, who has decided to stay with them] is a ravenous creature, eating more than the three of us. It dismays me to see his hungry eyes gauging the supply at breakfast, and to see the loaf disappear. He told me this morning that he could eat the whole of what was on the table. He is mad after food, and I see that Mr. K. is starving himself to make it hold out. Mr. Buchan is very far from well, and dreads the prospect of "half rations." All this sounds laughable, but we shall not laugh if we have to look hunger in the face! Now in the evening the snow clouds, which have blotted out all things, are lifting, and the winter scene is wonderful. The mercury is 5° below zero, and the aurora is glorious. In my unchinked room the mercury is 1° below zero. Mr. Buchan can hardly get his breath; the dryness is intense. We spent the afternoon cooking the Thanksgiving dinner. I made a wonderful pudding, for which I had saved eggs and cream for days, and dried and stoned cherries supplied the place of currants. I made a bowl of custard for sauce, which the men said was "splendid;" also a rolled pudding, with molasses; and we had venison steaks and potatoes, but for tea we were obliged to use the tea-leaves of the morning again. I should think that few people in America have enjoyed their Thanksgiving dinner more. We had urged Mr. Nugent to join us, but he refused, almost savagely, which we regretted. My four-pound cake made yesterday is all gone! This wretched boy confesses that he was so hungry in the night that he got up and ate nearly half of it. He is trying to cajole me into making another.

Skyscrapers, Stockyards and a Football Game at Harvard

PAUL BOURGET

FROM *Outre-Mer: Impressions of America*

1893–94

Charles Joseph Paul Bourget was already a well-known French novelist and poet as well as a veteran traveler when he decided to add the New World to the places he had visited. He arrived in August 1893, and spent almost ten months in the East, the Middle West and the South. His impressions appeared first in a series of articles in James Gordon Bennett's New York Herald and then in a book called Outre-Mer (Beyond the Sea).

The United States that awaited Bourget was no longer the Europe-oriented strip of seaboard cities raveling out into frontier settlements that confronted such visitors as Kalm, Michaux, Dickens and the Trollopes; it was a young colossus with industrial centers from coast to coast and a way of life completely its own. Bourget, a sensitive, thoughtful man with an aesthetic bent, reacted to America with that combination of wonder and distaste, hope and distrust with which a European humanist was likely to view so much material wealth and mechanization and such an aggressive spirit. His book is made up chiefly of essays and psychological analyses; occasionally, however, he illustrates these with a striking description such as that of the Chicago stockyards or with a quaint report such as his account of that monstrous spectacle, a college football game.

SKYLINE AND SKYSCRAPER

L EANING over the ship's rail on the side toward New York, I succeed in distinguishing a mass of diminutive houses, an ocean of low buildings, from the midst of which uprise, like cliffbound islets, brick buildings so daringly colossal that, even at this distance, their height overpowers my vision. I count the stories above the level of the roofs; one has ten, another twelve. Another, not yet finished, has a vast iron framework, outlining upon the sky the plan of six more stories above the eight already built. Gigantic, colossal, enormous, daring, there are no words—words are inadequate to this apparition, this landscape, in which the vast outlet of the river serves as a frame for the display of still vaster human energy. Reaching such a pitch of collective effort, this energy has become an element of nature itself. . . .

These various pictures and reflections followed me as I crossed the threshold of certain New York hotels which had been pointed out to me as most recently built. They are all edifices of the kind which, in Chicago, they call "sky scrapers" and "cloud pressers." One is ten stories high, another twelve, another fourteen. The last and newest has seventeen.

CHICAGO SLAUGHTERHOUSE

THE carriage stops before a building which, in its massiveness and want of character, is like all other manufactories. My companions and I enter a court, a sort of alley, crowded with packing boxes, carts, and people. A miniature railway passes along it, carrying packing boxes to a waiting train, entirely composed of refrigerator cars, such as I saw so many of as I came to Chicago. Laborers were unloading these packing boxes; others were coming and going, evidently intent upon their respective duties. There was no sign of administrative order, as we conceive it, in this establishment, which was yet so well ordered. But already one of the engineers had led us up a staircase, and we enter an immense hall, reeking with heavy moisture saturated with a strong acrid odor, which seems to seize you by the throat. We are in the department where the hogs are cut up. There are hundreds of men hard at work, whom we have not time so much as to look at. Our guide warns us to stand aside, and before us glides a file of porkers, disemboweled and hung by their hind feet from a rod, along which they slip toward a vaulted opening, where innumerable other such files await them. The rosy flesh, still ruddy with the life that but now animated them, gleams under the electric light that illuminates those depths. We go on, avoiding these strange encounters as best we may, and reach at last, with feet smeared in a sort of bloody mud, a platform whence we can see the initial act of all this labor, which now seems so confused but which we shall shortly find so simple and easy to understand. There are the pigs, in a sort of pit, alive, grunting and screaming, as if they had a vision of the approach of the horrible machine, from which they can no more escape than a doomed man whose head lies on the guillotine. It is a sort of movable hook, which, being lowered by a man, seizes one of the creatures by the cord which ties its hind legs together. The animal gives a screech, as he hangs, head downward, with quivering snout and a spasmodic agitation of his short forelegs. But already the hook has slid along the iron bar, carrying the hapless victim to a neighboring recess where, as it slips by, a man armed with a long knife cuts its throat, with a slash so well aimed and effective that there is no need to repeat it. The creature utters a more terrific screech, a stream of blood spurts out, jet-black and as thick as your arm. The snout quivers more pitifully, the short legs are agitated more frantically, but the death struggle only quickens the motion of the hook, which glides on to a third attendant.

The latter, with a quick movement, cuts down the animal. The hook slides back, and the carcass falls into a sort of canal tank filled with boiling water, in which an automatic rake works with a quick vibratory motion. In a few seconds it has caught the creature, turned it over and over, caught it again, and thrown the scalded carcass to another machine, which in a few more seconds has shaved it from head to tail. In another second, another hook has descended, and another bar carries that which, four minutes ago, was a living, suffering creature, toward that arched opening where, on coming in, I had seen so many similar relics. It is already the turn of another to be killed, shaved, and finished off. The operation is of such lightning quickness that you have no time to realize its atrocity. You have no time to pity the poor things, no time to marvel at the cheerfulness with which the butcher—a redheaded giant, with shoulders broad enough to carry an ox—goes on with his horrible work.

And yet, even in its lower forms, life is something so mysterious, the death and sufferings, even of a creature of the humblest order, are something so tragic when, instead of carelessly picturing them, you look them thus full in the face, that all spectators, and they are many, cease to laugh and joke. For my part, before this coarse slaughterhouse scene I felt myself seized with an unreasoning sadness, very short but very intense, as if, for a few minutes, the spirit of Thomas Graindorge had passed before me,

—the philosophic dealer in salt pork and oil, so dear to my master, Taine [Hippolyte Taine—see pages 590–96]. It suddenly seemed as if I saw before me existence itself, and all the work of nature, incarnated in a pitiable symbol. . . .

We went into the department reserved for the cattle. Here the death struggle is different. No outcry, almost no blood; no terrified expectation on the creature's part. And the scene is all the more tragic. The animals are penned by twos, in stalls like those of a stable, though without the manger. You see them trying, with their intelligence and their gentleness, to accommodate themselves to the narrow space. They gaze with their large, soft eyes—upon whom? The butcher, standing in a passageway a little above them. This man holds in his hand a slender bludgeon of steel. He is waiting until the ox is in the right position. You see him gently, caressingly, guiding the animal with the tip of his bludgeon. Suddenly he uplifts it. It falls upon the creature's forehead, and it sinks down in a lifeless heap.

In an instant a hook has lifted it up, blood pouring from the mouth and nostrils, its large glassy eyes overshadowed with a growing darkness, and within another minute another man has stripped the skin from the breast, letting it hang down like an apron, has cut open the carcass, and sent it by the expeditious method of the sliding bar, to take its place in the refrigerating-room. Thousands of them await here the time for being carried and hung up in other rooms, also of ice, but on wheels, ready to be despatched. I see the closing of the last car of a train on the point of departure. The locomotive whistles and puffs; the bell rings. On what table of New York or Boston, Philadelphia or Savannah, will at last appear this meat, fattened on the prairie pasture-lands of some district in some Western State, and here prepared in such a way that the butcher will have merely to cut it into pieces? It will arrive as fresh, as intact, as if there had not been thousands and thousands of miles between the birth, death, and dismemberment of the enigmatical and peaceable creature.

A Football Game

HAVING exaggerated his nervous and voluntary tension to the pitch of abuse, almost to vice, it is impossible that the American should amuse himself as we Latins do, who hardly conceive of pleasure without a certain relaxation of the senses, mingled with softness and luxury. . . .

Their pleasures seem, in fact, to imply, like their ideas and their labors, something unrestrained and immoderate, a very vigorous excitement, always bordering on violence, or, rather, on roughness and restlessness. Even in his diversions the American is too active and too self-willed. . . .

The most vehement of those pleasures and the most deeply national are those of sport. Interpret the word in its true sense, and you will find in it nothing of the meaning which we French attach to it, who have softened the term in adopting it, and who make it consist above all of elegance and dexterity. For the American, "sport" has ever in it some danger, for it does not exist without the conception of contest and daring. . . .

Among the distractions of sport, none has been more fashionable for several years past than football. I was present last autumn, in the peaceful and quiet city of Cambridge, at a game between the champions of Harvard College—the "team," as they say here—and the champions of the University of Pennsylvania. I must go back in thought to my journey in Spain to recall a popular fever equal to that which throbbed along the road between Boston and the arena where the match was to take place. The electric cars followed one another at intervals of a minute, filled with passengers, who, seated or standing, or hanging on the steps, crowded, pushed, crushed one another. Although the days of November are cruelly cold under a Massachusetts sky, the place of contest, as at Rome for the gladiatorial combats, was in a sort of open-air enclosure. A stone's throw away from Memorial Hall and the other buildings of the university, wooden stands were erected. On these stands were perhaps fifteen thousand spectators, and in the immense quadrilateral hemmed in by the stands were two teams composed of eleven youths each waiting for the signal to begin.

What a tremor in that crowd, composed not of the lower classes, but of well-to-do people, and how the excitement increased as time went on! All held in their hands small red flags and wore tufts of red flowers. Crimson is the color of the Harvard boys. Although a movement of feverish excitement ran through this crowd, it was not enough for the enthusiasts of the game. Propagators of enthusiasm, students with unbearded, deeply lined faces, passed between the benches and still further increased the ardor of the public by uttering the war cry of the university, the "Rah! rah! rah!" thrice repeated, which terminates in the frenzied call, "Haaar-vard." The partisans of the "Pennsies" replied by a similar cry, and in the distance, above the palings of the enclosure, we could see clusters of other spectators, too poor to pay the entrance fee, who had climbed into the branches of the leafless trees, their faces outlined against the autumn sky with the daintiness of the pale heads in Japanese painted fans.

The signal is given and the play begins. It is a fearful game, which by itself would suffice to indicate the differences between the Anglo-Saxon and the Latin world—a game of young bulldogs brought up to bite, to rush upon the quarry; the game of a race made for wild attack, for violent defense, for implacable conquests and desperate struggles. With their leather vests, with the Harvard sleeves of red cloth, and the Pennsylvania blue-and-white vests and sleeves, so soon to be torn—with the leather gaiters to protect their shins, with their great shoes and their long hair floating around their pale and flushed faces, these scholarly athletes are at once admirable and frightful to see when once the demon of contest has entered into them. At each extremity of the field is a goal, representing, at the right end, one of the teams, at the left the other. The entire object is to throw an enormous leather ball, which the champion of one or the other side holds in turn. It is in waiting for this throw that all the excitement of this almost ferocious amusement is concentrated. He who holds the ball is there, bent forward, his companions and his adversaries likewise bent down around him in the attitude of beasts of prey about to spring. All of a sudden he runs to throw the ball, or else with a wildly rapid movement he hands it to another, who rushes off with it. All depends on stopping him.

The roughness with which they seize the bearer of the ball is impossible to imagine without having witnessed it. He is grasped by the middle of the body, by the head, by the legs, by the feet. He rolls over and his assailants with him, and as they fight for the ball and the two sides come to the rescue, it becomes a heap of twenty-two bodies tumbling on top of one another, like an inextricable knot of serpents with human heads. This heap writhes on the ground and tugs at itself. One sees faces, hair, backs, or legs appearing in a monstrous and agitated melee. Then this murderous knot unravels itself, and the ball, thrown by the most agile, bounds away and is again followed with the same fury. It continually happens that, after one of those frenzied entanglements, one of the combatants remains on the field motionless, incapable of rising, so much has he been hit, pressed, crushed, thumped.

A doctor whose duty it is to look after the wounded arrives and examines him. You see those skilled hands shaking a foot, a leg, rubbing the sides, washing a face, sponging the blood which streams from the forehead, the eyes, the nose, the mouth. A compassionate comrade assists in the business and takes the head of the fainting champion on his knee. Sometimes the unlucky player must be carried away. More frequently, however, he recovers his senses, stretches himself, rouses up, and ends by scrambling to his feet. He makes a few steps, leaning on the friendly shoulder, and no sooner is he able to walk than the game begins afresh, and he joins in again with a rage doubled by pain and humiliation.

If the roughness of this terrible sport was for the spectators only the occasion of a nervous excitement of a few hours, the young athletes would not give themselves up to it with this enthusiasm which makes them accept the most painful, sometimes the most dangerous of trainings. . . .

No sooner are such matches as these in preparation than the portraits of the various players are in all the papers. The incidents of the game are described in detail with graphic pictures, in order that the comings and goings of the ball may be better followed. Conquerors and conquered are alike interviewed. From a celebrated periodical the other day I cut out an article signed "A Football Scientist," wherein the author sought to show that the right tactics to follow in this game were the same as those used by Napoleon.

Florida

ALISTAIR COOKE

FROM *One Man's America*

1946–52

Since America's colonial days it has been fashionable for British visitors (except for the occasional unfashionable scholar) to mock American ways and manners. From Dickens to such twentieth-century writers as Evelyn Waugh, J. B. Priestley and Geoffrey Gorer, they have had a field day with the more vulgar and blatant aspects of America. But such an attitude, based in part on the assumption that the critic comes from a superior society, grows tiresome. It is thus a relief to come upon the reports of Alistair Cooke—not because he is uncritical or lacks sting, but because he is witty without being venomous, is critical without being peevish, knows the country better than do most natives, and stayed long enough to want to remain permanently.

Cooke came to the United States for graduate study in 1932, returned a few years later as a commentator for BBC and since 1948 has been chief American correspondent for the Manchester Guardian and a familiar figure on American television. Out of some of the BBC weekly radio talks he gave between 1946 and 1952 he put together a book of twenty-nine essays called One Man's America. Informal, urbane, full of shrewd insights and characterizations, these reports on an extraordinary variety of American types and customs are among the most perceptive of their kind. One of the best, reprinted below, is that on Florida.

Ponce de Leon, the first white man to touch the Florida coast, in 1513, thought he would find there the fountain of youth. And De Soto, twenty-six years later, went looking for gold. Four hundred years later, in a nation which clings to its youth more than any other nation, the daydream of the winter visitor is much the same. And the centuries shake hands in the spectacle of an aging Midwestern farmer and his wife driving southeast in a De Soto car, or a show-girl off on the night train for Miami and a little private project of her own, from which digging for gold is not excluded.

It would depress a Floridian to hear me approach his state in this, the condescending Northern, way. For to most Americans Florida is not a state but a state of mind, not a place to live at all but a place to work off a year's inhibitions in a few determined weeks of pleasure. But Florida itself is a little to blame for this reputation. Though it has a great trade in citrus fruit, and a developing cattle-market, a cigar industry, and a wealth of what Americans call folkways, it boasts that its most marketable commodity is its climate. And it spends millions of dollars a year describing that climate in print in the hope of attracting, and attracting back, into the state several score million dollars' worth of winter tourists. As early as 1910 a newspaper in St. Petersburg, on the west coast of the peninsula, offered to give away its whole daily edition any time in the year when the sun failed to shine before three in the afternoon. They have had to pay the forfeit no more than four or five times a year.

Before going into the life of a state that has been called the last economic frontier, and which I should call the Unknown State, it might be as well to picture where it is and what it looks like.

It hangs down from the extreme eastern corner of the United States like a pistol held at the head of the Caribbean. The handle touches Alabama. The chamber forms the coast that faces on the Gulf of Mexico. The long barrel pointing south and west forms the peninsula, four hundred miles long, and it is this that means Florida to Americans. What they *think* of, however, as Florida is the shining rim of the pistol's foresight— the linked strands of beaches where in the past twenty years towering hotels, shops in rainbow colors, yacht harbors, trailer camps, and a whole market-place of pleasure has been built on a long strip of coastline literally dredged up from the ocean. There was a time only a generation ago when no one probed this ocean except Greek sponge-fishers, who have now settled westward along the Gulf Coast. But today the ocean dashes gently against the most expensive bodies, the best-fed stomachs, and some of the sharpest heads in America. Today the offshore waters flash with dinghies and yachts from which, as Westbrook Pegler says, "fishermen use little fish the size of billygoats as bait for fish the size of cows."

Like many another American institution, then, Florida is the victim of its advertising. Of course, the curse of bad advertising is that it creates a false issue which the wise as well as the stupid come to think is the essential thing to talk about; so that even people who repudiate the advertising don't know anything else to look for. If they don't like salt water or find the beach-life vacuous, then that is all there is to Florida, and it's a miserable thing.

The physical approach to the pleasure domes of Miami and Miami Beach contributes to this deception. For it is not what the travel-folders illustrate. You cross the Georgia border and streak monotonously over bare, cut-over pine-land. You may just glimpse a few Negroes chipping the pine trees for gum, which is then distilled into turpentine. But mostly you will see nothing but sandy wastes, decorated at times by piles of lumber. A few cattle, and pigs snuffling in cypress swamps. You race through run-down shrimp ports. Slowly the vegetation, such as there is of it, gets more tropical, but never lush. Cabbage palms blob by, and at the water's edge you see cormorants trundling, like model planes in trouble. The last hundred miles are an assault and battery by advertising. Haphazard battalions of billboards go by, advertising miraculously profitable orange groves, night-clubs, trailer camps, ice cream, real estate ("This is God's country—you'd be at home in Heaven"). Your mileage is calculated for you by roadside signs screaming "Only ten miles to tupelo honey," or two miles to an alligator farm, or "Twelve miles to Sandy's super-duper jumbo hamburgers." Occasionally there is a crude sign painted by some wandering evangelist and striking a chillier note: "Prepare to Meet Thy God."

You might remember that sign when you come to open the state guidebook and find on an early page this warning: "Caution to Tourists: do not enter bushes at the sides of highway; snakes and redbugs usually infest such places." That may be a shock to the tourist, but if he followed it up he might go on to learn something of the state as it is only ten miles inland from Miami's garish suburbs, and there meet a Florida that is much as it was a thousand years ago. In none of the forty-eight states does life leap so suddenly, in an hour's motor drive, from the suburban snooze to the primeval ooze. Only a thin strip of pine and palmetto woods stands guardian between what we laughingly call "civilization as we know it" and the seething cypress swamp known as the Everglades; where four hundred species and sub-species of birds carol and whine over a slimy wilderness dignified by the white plumes of the egret; where orchid trees of a thousand blooms rise out of the pure muck that seems to have inundated the whole visible earth. It is at night that this contrast is most compelling. And you feel it most dramatically going west from Miami. Go by plane and in a minute or two Miami is a scum of bright bubbles on the edge of a stagnant pond. Or drive out at twilight, as the floodlights are switched on to the vertical hotels, and the bartenders begin to rattle their ice, and blondes with coal-black tans appear in their backless finery. Within a half-hour Miami is a memory of a Hollywood musical to a man stranded on the Amazon. An eagle circles against a purple sky. A buzzard flaps away from some dark carrion on the road ahead. You stop your motor and see no living thing. But the loneliness, and the awe of living close to a jungle before it was ever tamed into lumber or tailored into farms or gardens, is intensified by the insane symphony of sound that strikes your ear. Over a bubbling, rumbling percussion of bullfrogs, you will hear the chuck-chuck of tropical woodpeckers, the wheezy sigh of bull-rats, a low slush of alligator. If you are lucky you may see the scarlet glowing wing of a flamingo. The din lets up for a moment, and then you are terrified into alertness again by a thin wailing sound, like that of a lost man gone crazed. It is the everyday song of a water-bird that hobbles as it walks and is known as the limpkin.

Yet inside this dense inland swamp there are living humans who seldom come out. They are the Seminole Indians, who have mingled with the white man possibly less than any other tribe in the United States. They have a long and resentful history of relations with him and there is no certainty that they yet regard themselves as being at peace with the United States Government. A final treaty of peace between the Seminoles and the Government was signed in 1934, and another "final" treaty in 1937. They live entirely by hunting and they hunt well. Because most of the land is under water, they live on encampments built of dried tree-trunks fastened together like the spokes of a wheel. The family pots and pans are anchored nearby on rafts. When it's wet they sleep on platforms made of saplings above the swamp and covered with a roof of palm leaves. Here, an hour from Miami, they worship their god Yo-He-Wah, who is the symbol of all virtue and purity and love, and whose name may never be mentioned except at a religious festival. They disapprove of capital punishment, they rule themselves with a council of medicine men, and they have rather curious beliefs about marriage. Being so near and yet so far from the civilized whites of Miami and Palm Beach, they look on marriage as a sacred and serious undertaking which may only be severed —indeed must be severed—for a single reason. The reason is "incompatibility." There are no other grounds for divorce, because in their primitive way they think it is a crime to stay married to someone you no longer love.

This contrast between the pleasure industry of Miami and the timeless life of the Seminoles, between a façade of civilization and the primitive culture that lies behind it, is not unique in the United States. You might recall the community of Salt Lake City and the almost unexplored Robber's Roost country that lies not far away. The luxury hotels and saloons of Las Vegas, Nevada, lie on the very edge of the fearful Mojave Desert. You might even discover that only ninety miles from New York is the fashionable resort of Southampton and scratching its handsome back is the scrubby reservation of the Shinnecock Indians. But nowhere is the contrast so extreme as it is in Florida. It is so vivid to the tourist that he comes into Florida and goes out of it under the impression that the state has nothing behind the night-clubs, the beaches, and the race-track but a mess of swamp. However, when the tourists depart in the late winter, they leave behind one-half the winter population. These are the two million Floridians who live neither on the east coast nor in the swamp. They have a life of their own, and it is time to talk about them, who inhabit the other three-quarters of the Unknown State.

Running down the center of the peninsula and across to its west coast is a lakeland district which is busy harvesting Florida's second money crop —the first being, of course, the tourists. These people, too, sell the climate, in the shape of oranges and grapefruit and, since the war, in the shape of little cans containing their concentrated juices. The Government set up a laboratory early in the war to make citrus concentrate under the Lend-Lease program. It was a brilliant reply to the challenge of the Nazi submarines, which just then were sinking Allied tankers and freighters every night from the Jersey coast to the Florida keys. One shipload of concentrate could be converted when it was safe in port into as much orange-juice as it would otherwise take five ships to carry. The conversion process is very simple. It requires one housewife and running water. Each can of concentrate can be watered down to make whole orange-juice of five times the volume of the original. Like other expedients thought up in wartime, this experiment done in the name of the Allies is now paying off handsomely for the natives. For the Government, in its little laboratory at Dundein, incidentally disposed of a prejudice that is common not only to you and me but to the Florida orange-growers. It is the idea that oranges are something to get juice out of. The firm that took over and expanded the government laboratory when the war was over is now a very profitable commercial enterprise canning a fortune in concentrated orange-juice and boasting that orange-juice is a by-product. Once the juice is out, they are left with what used to be thrown away: with the pulp, the peel, the seeds. Now they extract from the seeds oleomargarine, vegetable fats for cooking, and a dye that will fix any known color in artificial silk. From the colored layer of the peel they extract terpenes for battleship paint, and carotene, which provides trillions of units a year of vitamin A. From the white pulp they get pectin, a superlative jelling agent and a medical godsend for the early treatment of deep wounds. That still leaves cellulose and sugar, from which they take ethyl alcohol for gun cotton, the vitamin B complex, and feed yeast for cattle. So the orange grove has turned into a chemical industry.

They joke in Florida about how, at the end of the winter, a trainload of millionaires going home will be shunted on to a siding to let a trainload of cabbages go through. If you are a Florida truck-farmer this is no joke. Most of the land of Florida is poor land, and of its thirty-five million acres only five million are in crops. The climate of the central region and the Gulf Coast is not much more genial than the climate of Georgia and South Carolina to the north. So in late winter there's always a race on to ship north the vegetables which in a few weeks will be ready for delivery from Georgia and the Carolinas. They will be harvesting them up there in the early spring, and once they start, that is the end of the Florida crop. Hence when a train of cabbages starts north, the signals go down all the way and there's nobody important enough to slow it, especially if the weather in the Carolinas has taken a turn for the better.

Floridians have always regretted having to wince when anybody mentions beef or praises the cattle bred in Texas and fattened in Kansas and Iowa. Florida has been trying for a hundred years to build up a cattle-bowl to compete with Texas. But scrub pineland is not the best pasture. And Florida was pestered for decades by a tick which other states killed off through compulsory cattle-dipping laws. The Florida cattlemen would not dip their cattle, and when the state tried to make them they dynamited the vats. They were rebellious because they knew that the Florida tick is a special bug that thrives not only on cattle but on deer and dogs and horses. You can imagine the feelings of the race-track owners when a quarantine was extended to race-horses. But there was no hope for a cattle industry until the cattlemen gave in. Just before the war they did and today you will see forest fires everywhere—the favorite method, and in this poor land the compulsory method, of burning the range for better pasture. The result, I am staggered to confess, is the best beef I have tasted anywhere.

You may have been trying to picture the people of Florida. It is quite a strain. For Florida is in the South but not of it. Two-party politics rears its hydra head again. Most of the native Southerners are in the north of the state; the southern part is ninety per cent Northern, people who came here in the last forty years to retire, to run a small orange farm, to sell real estate, to mock at their families stuck in the Northern winters. But there are two industries run by what you can be bold enough to call traditional Floridians, by people who are not seen on beaches, who seldom pitch horseshoes and never lunch at tables carrying a vase of camellias.

They are the cigar industry and the turpentine industry. The cigar industry offers an ironic little essay in labor relations. Eighty years ago some Cuban cigar-makers came up to Key West to avoid the import duty on Cuban cigars and to free themselves from the pressure of a growing Cuban labor union. But the cigar-workers promptly started their unions in Key West. Mr. Ybor, the leading manufacturer, who must have heard about the boundless possibilities of self-expression in God's country, decided to move his pitch. He moved his factories once more. But the unions didn't have to move. They just growed wherever the manufacturer moved his tent. Mr. Ybor eventually landed up in Tampa. There were only a few hundred people there in 1880. Today the population includes about twenty thousand Cubans and ten thousand Italians. Every kind of "discipline" was exercised to suppress the growing unions and in the 1920's there was a militant parade of the Ku Klux Klan. But, one cigar-worker recalled, "We just sat on our porches with our guns across our laps and watched the parade. It sure was a quiet parade." The strike that brought on this visitation of the familiar hooded men lasted ten months and the Florida cigar-trade has barely regained what it lost to its competitors. In 1935 the older cigar-workers sent a petition to the Cuban Government asking to be taken back and pensioned off. Nothing came of it. The travel literature tells you of the glow and charm of the Latin life of the cigar-workers. Perhaps they are thinking of a colored witch-doctor, just out of jail for practicing voodoo, who sneaks from shack to wretched shack in Tampa selling charms to wear around the neck, a particular high-priced charm guaranteed "to ward off unemployment."

The turpentine industry, the chipping of pine trees for the resinous gum, which is then distilled to get turpentine and rosin, is an American industry more than three hundred years old. Its enforced wanderings are typical of the American appetite for raping the timber and the soil of one region and then moving on with a smack of the lips to the next virgin territory. It started in northern New England in the seventeenth century, and when the forests of New Hampshire and Massachusetts and Connecticut were tapped dry it moved down to the Carolinas and by the same ruinous process south into Georgia. When the Georgia trees were giving out, down into Florida. "A turpentine nigger" is in Florida a term of contempt. It is also the name of a mystery not one Floridian in a thousand has ever seen.

In the swampy interior the turpentine Negroes live in camps and are supervised by a "rider," a foreman on horseback, employed by the turpentine corporation. They seldom if ever come out of the jungle. They tap away for a few dollars a day, they produce children, often they are married, their women work with them. America to them is a small clearing for work, a fringe of dark pine, a two-room cabin in which they breed and die. Their life on this earth is at the disposal of the rider. He is the law, the good or bad provider, the judge of all their ways. They call him the Captain. Their drabness, their suppressed hopes, their sense of lowliness and sin are thoroughly purged once a week at what they call a jook party or tonk. These parties are the dim and little-known origin of the honky-tonk and the juke box. A Saturday night jook is a simple uninhibited orgy of drinking, dancing, singing, gambling, love-play, and occasionally knife-play, in the pines outside. If you could have got into one of these jungles in the 1930's* you would have heard all that is most melancholy and desperate in the only indigenous American music—the blues. They cover every topic these people have heard of and all the work they or their kind have done. Blues about the pine tree that flowed gum till Judgment Day; about the lightning that struck the Captain down and freed them from the jungle; about John Henry, who in this version ran away to the Gulf Coast and made a kingly fortune plucking sponges from the ocean bed with his naked hands. And when their special grievances are exhausted, they revert as country Negroes do everywhere in the South to the perpetual themes captured and taunted for all time in one tune, three lines of lyric, twelve bars of music: the song of people to whom life consists of a few riotous or appalling propositions—the need of a woman, the misery of a lover gone, the hope of a train to take you away from unhappiness, a train to bring you back to what is familiar and warm.

---

* They are now all but abandoned. A new process has transferred the work to large steam distilleries, which produce less folk-song but less misery.

When you see me comin', raise your window high,
When you see me comin', raise your window high,
But if you see me goin', hang yo' head and cry.

And far from these jungles, wherever you go in inland Florida, you will hear against the weird sky the songs of Negroes. In the orange fields, pulling a sack from tree to tree, a fat girl shouts up to the bristling sun: "Go down, Ol' Hannah, don't you rise no mo'." By a railroad branch line near enough to the sea to taste a salt breeze, three Negroes squatting near the track hunched their shoulders and slapped their feet and sang:

God rode out the ocean,
Chained the lightnin' to his wheel;
Stepped on land at West Palm Beach,
And the wicked hearts did yield.

If you roam long and far enough you will begin to compose a picture of Florida whose symbol is no girl in an evening gown and golden tan. You will come away from it with a memory of an old crone, around her neck the diamond necklace of Miami Beach, and for the rest a woman part Indian, part Negro, part Spanish, mostly Southern mountaineer; who grows oranges and smells of turpentine; who practices voodoo and smokes cigars; who counts cheap beads with her hands and keeps a union card in her pocket.

Polar Places

Eskimo Interlude

WILLIAM EDWARD PARRY

FROM *Three Voyages for the Discovery of a North-west Passage* AND *Narrative of an Attempt to Reach the North Pole*

1819–27

Men had been seeking a Northwest Passage to the Indies for at least 250 years when Edward Parry began his quest in 1819. He never reached the Pacific, but his three voyages—as well as his later attempt to reach the North Pole—marked such advances in Arctic travel that he ranks second only to Peary as a Polar explorer.

Parry began his career young: he joined the British Navy when he was thirteen and by the age of twenty-one was a lieutenant on duty protecting whalers off Spitsbergen. He was second in command on John Ross's Arctic expedition in 1818 and the following year was chosen to lead an expedition of his own in search of the Northwest Passage. He took his two ships as far west as longitude 110° and then, blocked by ice, wintered for ten months on Melville Island. The following summer he reached 114° W. before ice turned him back. On a second voyage (1821–23) and a third (1824–25) he was again balked by the early closing in of winter. Although he never succeeded in finding a passage, and on the last attempt saw one of his ships trapped and crushed by the ice, he reduced hardship and illness to a minimum and made important observations of ice, climate, channels, currents and geographic features.

For his dash toward the Pole in 1827 Parry sailed to Spitsbergen and then as far north as possible before taking to specially constructed steel boats equipped with iron runners so that they could be used as sledges.

With these novel amphibious vehicles he managed to get to 82° 14′ N. or only 445 miles from the Pole, before being driven back by the backward drift of the ice, lakes of water on the ice, and rain.

The arrangements Parry made for keeping his men content during the almost year-long winterings reveal a thoughtful leader, as does his sympathetic interest in the Melville Island Eskimos whom he describes in the passages below. After his polar dash he was knighted and in 1852 was made an admiral.

[On his second voyage Parry sails through Hudson Strait. After exploring about six hundred miles of the north coast of the North American continent he is compelled to pass the winter at Winter Island. There he and his men become friendly with a group of some two hundred Eskimos of the area.]

The Melville Eskimos and a Portrait of a Woman

[APRIL 1822] Having distributed some bread-dust among the women, we told old Illumea and her daughter Togolat that we proposed taking up our lodging in their hut for the night. It is a remarkable trait in the character of these people that they always thank you heartily for this, as well as for eating any of their meat; but board and lodging may be given to *them* without receiving the slightest acknowledgment either in word or deed. As it was late before the men returned, I asked Togolat to get the rest of the women to perform some of their games, with the hope of seeing something that was new. I had scarcely time to make the proposal when she darted out of the hut, and quickly brought every female that was left at the village, not excepting even the oldest of them, who joined in the performance with the same alacrity as the rest. I could, however, only persuade them to go through a tedious song we often before heard, which was now, indeed, somewhat modified by their insisting on our taking our turns in the performance, all which did not fail to create among them never-ceasing merriment and laughter. Neither their want of food and fuel, nor the uncertain prospect of obtaining any that night, was sufficient to deprive these poor creatures of that cheerfulness and good-humour which it seems at all times their peculiar happiness to enjoy.

The night proved very thick, with small snow, and as disagreeable and dangerous for people adrift upon floating ice as can well be imagined. If the women, however, gave their husbands a thought, or spoke of them to us, it was only to express a very sincere hope that some good news might shortly arrive of their success. Our singing party had not long been broken up, when it was suddenly announced by one of the children, the usual heralds on such occasions, that the men had killed something on the ice. The only two men who were at home instantly scrambled on their outer jackets, harnessed their dogs, and set off to assist their companions in bringing home the game, while the women remained for an hour in anxious suspense as to the extent of their husbands' success. At length one of the men arrived with the positive intelligence of two walruses having been taken, and brought with him a portion of these animals as large as he could drag over the snow. If the women were only cheerful before, they were now absolutely frantic. A general shout of joy instantly re-echoed through the village; they ran into each other's huts to communicate the welcome intelligence, and actually hugged one another in an ecstasy of delight by way of congratulation. One of them, Arnalooa, a pretty young woman of nineteen or twenty, knowing that a dog belonging to her husband was still at the huts, and that there was no man to take him down on the ice, ran out instantly to perform that office; and with a hardihood not to be surpassed by any of the men, returned, after two hours' absence, with her load of walrus flesh, and without even the hood thrown over her head to shelter her from the inclemency of the weather.

When the first burst of joy had at length subsided, the women crept, one by one, into the apartment where the first portion of the seahorses had been conveyed, which is always that of one of the men immediately concerned in the killing of them. Here they obtained blubber enough to set all their lamps alight, besides a few scraps of meat for their children and themselves. From this time, which was nine o'clock, till past midnight, fresh cargoes were continually arriving; the principal part being brought in by the dogs, and the rest by the men, who, tying the thong which held it round their waist, dragged in each his separate portion. Before the whole was brought in, however, some of them went out three times to the scene of action, though the distance was a mile and a half.

Every lamp now swimming with oil, the huts exhibited a blaze of light, and never was there a scene of more joyous festivity than while the operation of cutting up the walruses continued. I took the opportunity, which their present good-humour afforded, to obtain a perfect head and tusks of one of these animals, which we had not been able to do before; and, indeed, so much were their hearts opened by the scene of abundance before them that I believe they would have given us anything we asked for. This disposition was considerably increased also by their taking into their heads that their success was in some way or other connected with, or even owing to, our having taken up our night's lodging at the huts.

After viewing all this festivity for some time, I felt disposed to rest; and, wrapping myself up in my fur coat, lay down on one of the beds which Illumea had given up for our accommodation, as well as her *keipik*, or large deerskin blanket, which she rolled up for my pillow. The poor old woman herself sat up by her lamp, and in that posture seemed perfectly well satisfied to doze away the night. The singularity of my night's lodging made me awake several times, when I always found some of the Eskimos eating, though, after we lay down, they kept quite quiet for fear of disturbing us. Mr. Halse, who was still more wakeful, told me that some of them were incessantly employed in this manner for more than three hours. Indeed, the quantity of meat that thus they contrive to get rid of is almost beyond belief.

Having at length enjoyed a sound nap, I found on waking, about five o'clock, that the men were already up, and had gone out to renew their labours on the ice, so that several of them could not have rested more than two or three hours. This circumstance served to correct a notion we had entertained, that, when once abundantly supplied with food, they took no pains to obtain more till want began again to stare them in the face. It was now more pleasing to be assured that, even in the midst of plenty, they did not indolently give themselves up to repose, but were willing to take advantage of every favourable opportunity to increase their store. It is certain, indeed, that, were these people more provident (or, in other words, less gluttonous, for they do not waste much), they might never know what it is to want provisions, even during the most inclement part of the year. The state of the ice was today very unfavourable for their purpose, being broken into pieces so small that they could scarcely venture to walk upon it.

The morning of the 5th proved favourable for a journey I had in contemplation to the distant huts, to which Iligliuk [an Eskimo woman], who had come to Winter Island the day before, promised to be my guide. At six o'clock I set out, accompanied by Mr. Bushnan and two of the men, carrying with us a supply of bread-dust, besides our own provisions and blankets. As the distance was too great for her son Sioutkuk to walk, we were uncertain, till the moment of setting out, how this was to be managed, there being no sledge at hand for the purpose. We found, however, that a man, whom we had observed for some time at work among the hummocks of ice upon the beach, had been employed in cutting out of that abundant material a neat and serviceable little sledge, hollowed like a bowl or tray, out of a solid block, and smoothly rounded at the bottom. The thong to which the dogs were attached was secured to a groove cut round its upper edge; and the young seal-catcher, seated in this simple vehicle, was dragged along with great convenience and comfort.

The ice over which we travelled was a level flow that had never suffered disturbance since its first formation in the autumn, and with not more than an inch and a half of snow upon it. The path being distinctly marked out by the people, sledges, and dogs that had before travelled upon it, one might, without any great stretch of the imagination, have almost fancied it a road leading over a level and extensive heath towards a more civilized and substantial village than that which we were now approaching. Iligliuk walked as nimbly as the best of us: and, after two hours' and a half brisk travelling, we arrived at the huts, and were received by the women (for all the men were absent) with every expression of kindness and welcome. . . .

These huts, four in number, were, in the mode of their construction, exact counterparts of those at Winter Island on our first visit, but, being new and clean, presented a striking contrast with the latter, in their present disordered and filthy state. What gave a peculiarity, as well as beauty also, to the interior appearance of these habitations was their being situated on the ice, which, being cleared of the snow, presented a flooring of that splendid blue which is, perhaps, one of the richest colours that nature affords. A seal or two having been lately procured, every lamp was now blazing, and every *ootkoseek* smoking with a hot mess, which, together with the friendly reception we experienced, and a little warmth and fatigue from travelling, combined in conveying to our minds an idea of comfort which we could scarcely believe an Eskimo hut capable of exciting.

On the arrival of the men, who came in towards evening with two seals as the reward of their labour, we were once more greeted and welcomed. Arnaneelia, in particular, who was a quiet, obliging, and even amiable man, was delighted to find my quarters were to be in his apartment, where Aneetka, his wife, a young woman of about twenty-three, had already arranged everything for my accommodation; and both these poor people now vied with each other in their attention to my comfort. . . .

Toolooak having been concerned in killing one of the seals just brought in, it fell to his mother's lot to dissect it, the *neitiek* being the only animal which the women are permitted to cut up. We had therefore an opportunity of seeing this filthy operation once more performed, and entirely by the old lady herself, who was soon up to her elbows in blood and oil. Before a knife is put into the animal, as it lies on its back, they pour a little water into its mouth, and touch each flipper and the middle of the belly with a little lamp-black and oil taken from the under part of the lamp. What benefit was expected from this preparatory ceremony we could not learn, but it was done with a degree of superstitious care and seriousness that bespoke its indispensable importance. The boys came eagerly into the hut as usual, and held out their foreheads for the old woman to stick the charms upon them; and it was not till now that we learned from Iligliuk the efficacy of this very useful custom. As soon as this dirty operation was at an end, during which the numerous by-standers amused themselves in chewing the intestines of the seal, the strangers retired to their own huts, each bearing a small portion of the flesh and blubber, while our hosts enjoyed a hearty meal of boiled meat and hot gravy soup. Young Sioutkuk ate at least three pounds of solid meat in the first three hours after our arrival at the huts, besides a tolerable proportion of soup, all which his mother gave him whenever he asked it, without the smallest remark of any kind. We now found that they depended on catching seals alone for their subsistence, there being no walruses in this neighbourhood. As they were several miles from any open water, their mode of killing them was entirely confined to watching for the animals coming up in the holes they make through the ice.

In the course of the evening our conversation happened to turn on the Indians, a people whom none of these Eskimos had ever seen; but with whose ferocity and decided hostility to their own nation they seemed to be well acquainted. They described, also, their peculiar manner of paddling their canoes, and were aware that they made use of the kind of snow-shoes which we showed them. When I related to them, as well as I was able, the massacre of the Eskimos recorded by Hearne [explorer of arctic Canada in the 1770s], and gave them to understand that the Indians spared neither age nor sex, it seemed to chill them with horror, and I was almost sorry that I had told them the story.

APRIL 11.—We were now glad to begin making some show of re-equipping the ships for sea; for though this was a business that might, if necessary, have been very well accomplished in two or three weeks, it was better to employ the men in occupations having an evident and determinate object, than in those less obviously useful ones to which it was necessary to resort during the winter. We therefore brought down some of the boats to the ships to repair, put up the forge on the ice, and built a snow house over it, and set about various other jobs, which made the neighbourhood of the ships assume a busy and bustling appearance.

I had today a visit from Okotook and Iligliuk, who, with their son, came in upon their sledge from the distant huts. Being desirous of entertaining them well, in return for their late hospitality, we provided abundance to eat, and showed them everything about the ship that we thought likely to amuse them. Of all the wonders they had ever seen on board, there was nothing which seemed to impress them so strongly with a sense of our superiority as the forge, and the work which the armourer performed with it. The welding of two pieces of iron especially excited their admiration, and I never saw Iligliuk express so much astonishment at anything before. Even in this her superior good sense was observable, for it was evident that the utility of what she saw going on was what forced itself upon her mind; and she watched every stroke of the hammer and each blast of the bellows with extreme eagerness, while numbers of the other Eskimos looked stupidly on, without expressing the smallest curiosity or interest in the operation, except by desiring to have some spear-heads fashioned out by this means. Iligliuk was always very much entertained also by pictures having any relation to the Eskimos in other parts, and derived great entertainment from a description of any difference in their clothes, utensils, or weapons. Of these the sail in an Eskimo boat seemed particularly to attract her notice; but, in general, she had no inclination to admit the inferiority of her own tribe to any other. She was always extremely inquisitive about her own sex, whether *Innuees* [Eskimos] or *Kabloonas* [Europeans], listening with eager attention to any account of their dress or occupations, and in common, I believe, with all the rest of the Eskimos, wondered how we came to travel to their country without our wives. . . .

A number of Eskimos came to the ships on the 25th, notwithstanding a strong breeze from the S.W.b.W., with a considerable snowdrift. From these people we learned that Okotook's complaint had increased since Mr. Skeoch's visit, and that he was now extremely ill. . . . Mr. Bushnan, therefore, without waiting for the return of the sledges, set out for the village at an early hour in the forenoon, accompanied by the sergeant of marines. At eleven at night our party returned on board, bringing on a sledge Okotook, Iligliuk, and their son. That Iligliuk would accompany her husband, I, of course, took for granted and wished; but as the boy could do us no good, and was, moreover, a desperate eater, I had desired Mr. Bushnan to try whether a slight objection to his being of the party would induce Okotook to leave him with his other relations. This he had cautiously done; but, the instant the proposal was made, Okotook, without any remark, began to take off the clothes he had himself just dressed in to set out. No farther objection being made, however, he again prepared for the journey, Iligliuk assisting him with the most attentive solicitude. Before the invalid was suffered to leave his apartment, some of the bystanders sent for Ewerat, now better known to our people by the undignified appellation of the "conjuror." Ewerat, on this occasion, maintained a degree of gravity and reserve calculated to inspire somewhat more respect than we had hitherto been disposed to entertain for him in that capacity. Placing himself at the door of the apartment opposite Okotook, who was still seated on the bed, he held both his thumbs in his mouth, keeping up a silent but solemn converse with his *toorngow* [familiar spirit], the object of which was, as Mr. Bushnan presently afterwards found, to inquire into the efficacy and propriety of the sick man's removal. Presently he began to utter a variety of confused and inarticulate sounds; and it being at length understood that a favourable answer had been given, Okotook was carried out and placed on the sledge, Ewerat still mumbling his thumbs and muttering his incantations as before. . . .

Okotook was extremely ill on his arrival, having been three hours on the sledge, and Iligliuk, who, as Mr. Bushnan told me, had scarcely taken her eyes off her husband's face the whole time, seemed almost worn out with fatigue and anxiety. . . .

On the 26 . . . our patient felt much the better for a comfortable night's lodging, and now submitted with great patience to the application of a blister, though I believe his confidence in our mode of cure was afterwards shaken for a time by the pain which it occasioned. Both he and Iligliuk, however, seemed very sensibly to feel the comforts and advantages of their present quarters; and a *"coyenna"* (thanks) now and then fell from their lips. . . .

One of Okotook's brothers had arrived from the huts, bringing with him some walrus-flesh to tempt the appetite of the invalid, whose stomach, however, very fortunately for his complaint, was not disposed to this kind of delicacy. When his brother was about to return, Okotook took it into his head to send his son away with him, probably because he heard they had the day before killed two seals, which afforded better feeding than we had to give him; be this as it may, we were not sorry that he went, and the boy himself seemed no less pleased; for, without playfellows or amusement of any kind, his time hung very heavily on his hands while he remained on board. It was amusing to see Okotook take a dose of physic for the first time in his life today. He knew its taste was not pleasant, but this was certainly not all that he dreaded; for, before he put the cup to his lips with one hand, he held on to his wife with the other, and she held him with both hers, as though they expected an explosion, or some such catastrophe, as the immediate effect of the potion; nor did he venture to relinquish his hold till the taste began to leave his mouth. The quantity of water which he drank in the course of the four-and-twenty hours is beyond conception; and the cabin fire could scarcely, by the melting of snow, furnish enough for their consumption. These people are extremely particular as to the purity of the water they drink. Some that had been melted in our steamer, and which I thought very good, neither of them would touch, or, at least, always spat out again. If the water was much above the temperature of 32°, they also disliked it, and immediately put snow into it to cool it down. Iligliuk, who came on board with one side of her hair loose, loosened the other also today, in consequence of her fancying Okotook worse, though it was only the annoyance of the blister that made him uneasy; for even in this sequestered corner of the globe dishevelled locks bespeak mourning. It was not, however, with her the mere semblance of grief, for she was really much distressed throughout the day, all our endeavours not availing to make her understand how one pain was to be removed by inflicting another.

Captain Lyon being desirous of having some little clothes made as models of the Eskimos' costume, and thinking Iligliuk's present leisure afforded her a good opportunity of making them, had yesterday obtained her promise that she would do so. Okotook being now very much better, and she having herself resumed her usual gayety in consequence, I pressed her to commence her work, and placed the skins before her, when she said that she could not do them here, as she had no needles. These being supplied her, she now complained of having no tooktoo-e-walloo [reindeer sinew], their usual thread. This difficulty, unfortunately for Iligliuk's credit, was as easily overcome as the other; and when scissors, pattern clothes, and all the other requisites were laid before her, she was at length driven to the excuse that Okotook's illness would not permit her to do it. Seeing us half laughing at the absurdity of these excuses, and half angry at the selfish indolence which prompted them, she at last flatly asserted that Okotook desired her not to work, which, though we knew it to be a falsehood, the latter did not deny. We then supposed that some superstition might be at the bottom of this; but having, a little while after, by way of experiment, thrown Iligliuk some loose beads upon the table, she eagerly employed herself for half an hour in stringing them that not one might be lost; which proved that, where her own gratification or interest were concerned, Okotook's illness was not suffered to interfere. This anecdote shows, in a strong light, that deep-rooted selfishness, which, in numberless instances, notwithstanding the superiority of Iligliuk's understanding, detracted from the amiability of her disposition. The fact was that she did not feel inclined so far to exert herself as to comply with Captain Lyon's request; and the slight degree of gratitude and proper feeling which was requisite to overcome that disinclination was altogether wanting.

I have related this anecdote just as it occurred, with the hope of showing the true disposition of these people, and not with a view of unduly depreciating the character of our friend Iligliuk. I am, however, compelled to acknowledge that, in proportion as the superior understanding of this extraordinary woman became more and more developed, her head (for what female head is indifferent to praise?) began to be turned with the general attention and numberless presents she received. The superior decency and even modesty of her behaviour had combined, with her intellectual qualities, to raise her, in our estimation, far above her companions; and I often heard others express what I could not but agree in, that for Iligliuk alone, of all the Eskimo women, that kind of respect could be entertained which modesty in a female never fails to command in our sex. Thus regarded, she had always been freely admitted into the ships, the quartermasters at the gangway never thinking of refusing entrance to the "wise woman," as they called her. Whenever any explanation was necessary between the Eskimos and us, Iligliuk was sent for as an interpreter; information was chiefly obtained through her, and she thus found herself rising into a degree of consequence to which, but for us, she could never have attained. Notwithstanding a more than ordinary share of good sense on her part, it will not, therefore, be wondered at if she became giddy with her exaltation, assuming certain airs which, though infinitely diversified in their operation according to circumstances, perhaps universally attend a too sudden accession of good fortune in every child of Adam from the equator to the poles. The consequence was that Iligliuk was soon spoiled; considered her admission into the ships and most of the cabins no longer as an indulgence, but a right; ceased to return the slightest acknowledgment for any kindness or presents; became listless and inattentive in unravelling the meaning of our questions, and careless whether her answers conveyed the information we desired. In short, Iligliuk in February and Iligliuk in April were confessedly very different persons; and it was at last amusing to recollect, though not very easy to persuade one's self, that the woman who now sat demurely in a chair, so confidently expecting the notice of those around her, and she who had at first, with eager and wild delight, assisted in cutting snow for the building of a hut, and with the hope of obtaining a single needle, were actually one and the same individual.

[They spend a second brief summer probing for a westward passage, but are again forced into winter quarters in the Melville Island area. Impatient at the failure of the ice to break up even during early summer, they cut their way out in August and sail for England.]

North of Siberia

NILS ADOLF ERIK NORDENSKIÖLD

FROM *The Voyage of the Vega round Asia and Europe*

1878–79

> It was a Finnish-born mineralogist and geographer, Nils Adolf Erik Nordenskiöld, who completed the first Northeast Passage—a voyage eastward from the Atlantic to the Pacific along the northern coast of Europe and Asia—after more than 300 years of unsuccessful efforts by others.
>
> Nordenskiöld had already made voyages to Spitsbergen, Greenland and across the Kara Sea when he set out from his adopted homeland, Sweden, in June 1878, in the specially equipped steamer Vega. The expedition doubled Norway's North Cape, crossed the Kara Sea, rounded Cape Chelyuskin, the northernmost promontory of the Old World, and pushed eastward. It was within a few miles of the open waters of Bering Strait when, late in September, it was trapped by winter ice.
>
> Just as other parts of Nordenskiöld's book are enriched with a history of Arctic exploration and with observations of animal life, weather, ice and the remains of mammoths, so this part includes an expert account (see the excerpt below) of the travelers' winter-long contact with the rarely described primitive peoples of northernmost Siberia, the coast Chukchis and the reindeer Chukchis.
>
> Once released from the ice, the Vega sailed into Bering Strait and down the coast of Asia to Japan (see pages 124–33 in the section on the Orient). Having completed the first Northeast Passage, it then went on to complete the first circumnavigation of Eurasia.

THE COAST CHUKCHIS

Now, however, a pleasant change began, as we at last came in contact
with natives. In the whole stretch from Yugor Schar to Cape Shelagski we
had seen neither men nor human habitations, if I except the old uninhabited hut between Cape Chelyuskin and the Khatanga. But on September 6, when we were a little way off Cape Shelagski, two boats were sighted.
Every man, with the exception of the cook—who could be induced by no
catastrophe to leave his pots and pans, and who had circumnavigated Asia
and Europe perhaps without having been once on land—rushed on deck.
The boats were of skin, built in the same way as the umiaks or women's
boats of the Eskimo. They were fully laden with laughing and chattering
natives, men, women, and children, who indicated by cries and gesticulations that they wished to come on board. The engine was stopped, the
boats lay to, and a large number of skin-clad, bareheaded beings climbed up
over the gunwale in a way that clearly indicated that they had seen vessels
before. A lively talk began, but we soon became aware that none of the
crew of the boats or the vessel knew any language common to both. It was
an unfortunate circumstance, but signs were employed as far as possible.
This did not prevent the chatter from going on, and great gladness soon
prevailed, especially when some presents, mainly consisting of tobacco and
Dutch clay pipes, began to be distributed. It was remarkable that none
of them could speak a single word of Russian, while a boy could count
tolerably well up to ten in English, which shows that the natives here
come into closer contact with American whalers than with Russian traders.
They acknowledged the name Chukch or *Chautchu*.

Many of them were tall, well-grown men. They were clothed in close-
fitting skin trousers and *pesks* of reindeer skin. The head was bare, the hair
always clipped short, with the exception of a small fringe in front, where
the hair had a length of four centimeters and was combed down over the
brow. Some had a cap, of a sort used by the Russians at Chabarova, stuck
into the belt behind, but they appeared to consider the weather still too
warm for the use of this head covering. The hair of most of them was
bluish black and exceedingly thick. The women were tattooed with black
or bluish-black lines on the brow and nose, a number of similar lines on
the chin and finally some embellishments on the cheeks. The type of face
did not strike one as so unpleasant as that of the Samoyeds or the Eskimos.
Some of the young girls were even not absolutely ugly. In comparison with
the Samoyeds they were even rather cleanly, and had a beautiful, almost

reddish-white complexion. Two of the men were quite fair. Probably they were descendants of Russians who, for some reason or other, as prisoners of war or fugitives, had come to live among the chukchis and had been nationalized by them.

In a little while we continued our voyage, after the Chukchis had returned to their boats, evidently well pleased with the gifts they had received and the leaf tobacco I had dealt out in bundles—along with the clay pipes, of which everyone got as many as he could carry between his fingers—with the finery and old clothes which my comrades and the crew strewed around them with generous hand. . . .

Trapped by the Ice

. . . I was wandering about along with my comrades on the slopes near the beach in order, so far as the falling darkness permitted, to examine its natural conditions, when Johnsen came down; he informed us that from the top of the height one could hear bustle and noise and see fires at an encampment on the other side of the headland. He supposed that the natives were celebrating some festival. I had a strong inclination to go thither in order, as I thought, to take farewell of the Chukchis, for I was quite certain that on some of the following days we should sail into the Pacific. But it was already late in the evening and dark, and we were not yet sufficiently acquainted with the disposition of the Chukchis to go by night, without any serious occasion, in small numbers and provided only with the weapons of the chase, to an encampment with which we were not acquainted. It was not until afterward that we learned that such a visit was not attended with any danger. Instead of going to the encampment, as the vessel in any case could not weigh anchor this evening, we remained some hours longer on the beach and lighted there an immense log fire of driftwood, round which we were soon all collected, chatting merrily about the remaining part of the voyage in seas where not cold but heat would trouble us, and where our progress at least would not be obstructed by ice, continual fog and unknown shallows. None of us then had any idea that, instead of the heat of the tropics, we would for the next ten months be experiencing a winter at the pole of cold, frozen in on an unprotected road, under almost continual snowstorms, and with a temperature which often sank below the freezing point of mercury.

The evening was glorious, the sky clear, and the air so calm that the flames and smoke of the log fire rose high against the sky. The dark surface of the water, covered as it was with a thin film of ice, reflected its light as a fire way straight as a line, bounded far away at the horizon by a belt of ice, whose inequalities appeared in the darkness as the summits of a distant high mountain chain. The temperature in the quite draft-free air was felt to be mild, and the thermometer showed only two degrees under the freezing point. This slight degree of cold was, however, sufficient to cover the sea in the course of the night with a sheet of newly frozen ice, which, as the following days' experience showed, at the more open places could indeed only delay, not obstruct, the advance of the *Vega*, but which, however, bound together the fields of drift ice collected off the coast so firmly that a vessel, even with the help of steam, could with difficulty force her way through.

When on the following day, September 28, we had sailed past the headland which bounds Kolyuchin Bay on the east, the channel next the coast, clear of drift ice, but covered with newly formed ice, became suddenly shallow. The depth was too small for the *Vega*, for which we had now to seek a course among the blocks of ground ice and fields of drift ice in the offing. The night's frost had bound these so firmly together that the attempt failed. We were thus compelled to lie to at a ground ice so much the more certain of getting off with the first shift of the wind, and of being able to traverse the few miles that separated us from the open water at Bering Strait, as whalers on several occasions had not left this region until the middle of October. . . .

The ground ice to which the *Vega* was moored on September 29, and under which she lay during the course of the winter, was about forty meters long and twenty-five meters broad; its highest point lay six meters above the surface of the water. It was thus not very large, but gave the vessel good shelter. This ground ice, along with the vessel and the newly formed ice field lying between it and the shore, was indeed moved considerably nearer land during the violent autumn storms. A groan or two and a knocking sound in the hull of the vessel indicated that it did not escape very severe pressure; but the *Vega* did not during the course of the winter suffer any damage, either from this or from the severe cold, during which sharp reports often indicated that some crack in the woodwork had widened through the freezing of the water that had made its way into the vessel. "Cold so that the walls crack" is a well-known expression, with which we inhabitants of the north often connect memories from some stormy winter evening passed by the home hearth; but here these reports heard in our cabins, especially at night, were unpleasant enough, giving rise to fears that the newly formed or widened cracks would cause dangerous leaks in the vessel's hull. In consequence of iron contracting more than wood under the influence of cold, the heads of the iron bolts with which the ship's timbers were fastened together sank deep into the outside planking in the course of the winter. But no serious leak arose in this way, perhaps because the cold only acted on that part of the vessel which lay above the surface of the water. . . .

[They remain icebound from the end of September to the middle of the following July.]

RELEASED BY THE ICE

IN summer there must be found here green meadows covered with pretty tall grass, but at the time of our departure vegetation had not attained any great development, and the flowers that could be discovered were few. I presume, however, that a beautiful arctic flower world grows up here, although, in consequence of the exposure of the coast country to the north winds, poor in comparison with the vegetation in sheltered valleys in the interior of the country. There are found there too pretty high bushes, but, on the other hand, trees are represented at Pitlekaj only by a low species of willow which creeps along the ground.

We did not, however, see even this "wood" in full leaf. For in order that full summer heat may begin it is necessary, even here, that the ice break up, and this longed-for moment appeared to be yet far distant. The ice indeed became clear of snow in the beginning of July, and thus the slush and the flood water were lessened, which during the preceding weeks had collected on its surface and made it very difficult to walk from the vessel to land. Now, again pretty dry-shod and on a hard blue ice surface, we could make excursions in the neighborhood of the vessel. We had to be cautious, however. The former cracks had in many places been widened to greater or smaller openings by the flood water running down, and where a thin black object—a little gravel, a piece of tin from the preserved provision cases, etc.—had lain on the ice there were formed round holes, resembling the seal holes which I saw in spring laid bare after the melting of the snow on the ice in the fjords of Spitsbergen. The strength of the ice besides was nearly unaltered, and on July 16 a heavily loaded double sledge could still be driven from the vessel to the shore.

On the seventeenth the "year's ice" next the land at last broke up, so that an extensive land clearing arose. But the ground ices were still undisturbed, and between these the "year's ice" even lay so fast that all were agreed that at least fourteen days must still pass before there was any prospect of getting free.

When on the sixteenth, the reindeer-Chukchi Yettugin came on board and, talking of the collection of whalebones in which we had been engaged some days before, informed us that there was a mammoth bone at his tent, and that a mammoth tusk stuck out at a place where the spring floods had cut into the bank of a river which flows from Table Mount to Riraitinop, I therefore did not hesitate to undertake an excursion to the place. Our absence from the vessel was reckoned at five or six days. It was my intention to go up the river in a skin boat belonging to Notti to the place where the mammoth tusk was, and thence to proceed on foot to Yettugin's tent. Yettugin assured us that the river was sufficienly deep for the flat-bottomed boat. But when we had traveled a little way into the country it appeared that the river had fallen considerably during the day that Yettugin passed on the vessel. So certain was I, however, that the ice barrier would not yet for a long time be broken up, that I immediately after my return from the excursion, which had thus been rendered unsuccessful, made arrangements for a new journey in order with other means of transport to reach the goal.

While we were thus employed the forenoon of the eighteenth passed. We sat down to dinner at the usual time, without any suspicion that the time of our release was now at hand. During dinner it was suddenly observed that the vessel was moving slightly. Polander rushed on deck, saw that the ice was in motion, ordered the boiler fires to be lighted, the engine having long ago been put in order in expectation of this moment, and in two hours, by 3:30 P.M. on July 18, the *Vega*, decked with flags, was under steam and sail again on the way to her destination. . . .

Now for the first time, after 336 years of previous attempts, and when most men experienced in sea matters had declared the undertaking impossible, the Northeast passage had at last been achieved.

[In retrospect he describes some interesting Chukchi customs.]

Chukchi Dogs

. . . The number of dogs that are harnessed to each sledge is variable. I have seen a Chukchi riding behind two small lean dogs, who, however, appeared to draw their heavy load over even hard snow without any extraordinary exertion. At other sledges I have seen ten or twelve dogs, and a sledge laden with goods was drawn by a team of twenty-eight. The dogs are generally harnessed one pair before another to a long line common to all, sometimes in the case of short excursions more than two abreast, or so irregularly that their position in relation to the sledge appears to have depended merely on the accidental length of the draft line and the caprice of the driver. The dogs are guided not by reins but by continual crying and shouting, accompanied by lashes from a long whip. There is, besides, in every properly equipped sledge a short and thick staff mounted with iron, with a number of iron rings attached to the upper end. When nothing else will do, this staff is thrown at the offending animal. The staff is so heavy that the animal may readily get its death by such a throw. The dogs know this, and in consequence are so afraid of this grim implement that the rattling of the rings is sufficient to induce them to put forth extreme efforts. During rests the team is tied to the staff, which is driven into the snow.

The dog harness is made of inch-wide straps of skin, forming a neck or shoulder band, united on both sides by a strap to a girth, to one side of which the draft strap is fastened. Thanks to the excellent protection against the harness galling which the bushy coat of the dogs affords, little attention is needed for the harness, and I have never seen a single dog that was idle in consequence of sores from the harness. On the other hand, their feet are often hurt by the sharp snow. On this account the equipment of every sledge embraces a number of dog shoes. They are used only in case of need.

The Chukchi dogs are the same breed as, but smaller than, the Eskimo dogs in Danish Greenland. They resemble wolves, are long-legged, long-haired, and shaggy. The ears are short, commonly upright; their color very variable, from black or white, and black or white spotted, to gray or yellowish brown. For innumerable generations they have been used as draft animals, while as watchdogs they have not been required in a country where theft or robbery appears never to take place. The power of barking they have therefore completely lost, or perhaps they never possessed it. Even a European may come into the outer tent without any of the dogs there informing their owners sleeping in the inner tent by a sound of the foreigner's arrival.

On the other hand, they are good, though slow, draft animals, being capable of long-continued exertion. They are as dirty and as peaceable as their owners. There are no fights made between dog teams belonging to different tents, and they are rare between the dogs of an encampment and those of strangers. In Europe dogs are the friends of their masters and the enemies of each other; here they are the friends of each other and the slaves of their masters. In winter they appear in case of necessity to get along with very little food; they are then exceedingly lean, and for the most part lie motionless in some snowdrift. They seldom leave the neighborhood of the tent alone, not even to search for food or hunt at their own hand and for their own account. This appears to me so much the more remarkable, as they are often several days, I am inclined to say weeks, in succession without getting any food from their masters. A piece of a whale, with the skin and part of the flesh adhering, washed out of frozen sandy strata thus lay untouched some thousand paces from Pitlekaj; and the neighborhood of the tents, where the hungry dogs were constantly wandering about, formed, as has been already stated, a favorite haunt for ptarmigan and hares during winter. Young dogs some months old are already harnessed along with the team in order that they may in time become accustomed to the draft tackle. During the cold season the dogs are permitted to live in the outer tent, the females with their young even in the inner. We had two Scotch collies with us on the *Vega*. They at first frightened the natives very much with their bark. To the dogs of Chukchis they soon took the same superior standing as the European claims for himself in relation to the savage. The dog was distinctly preferred by the female Chukchi canine population, and that too without the fights to which such favor on the part of the fair commonly gives rise. A numerous canine progeny of mixed Scotch-Chukchi breed has thus arisen in Pitlekaj. The young dogs had a complete resemblance to their father, and the natives were quite charmed with them.

When a dog is to be killed the Chukchi stabs it with his spear, and then lets it bleed to death. Even when the scarcity was so great that the natives at Pitlekaj and Yinretlen lived mainly on the food we gave them, they did not eat the dogs they killed.

Liquor among the Chukchis

Spirits, to which they are exceedingly addicted, they call, as has been already stated, in conversation with Europeans, "ram," the pronouncing of the word being often accompanied by a hawking noise, a happy expression, and a distinctive gesture, which consisted in carrying the open right hand from the mouth to the waist, or in counterfeiting the unintelligible talk of a drunken man. Among themselves they call it fire water—*akmimil*. The promise of it was the most efficient means of getting an obstinate Chukchi to comply with one's wishes. In case they undertook to drive us with their dog teams, they were never desirous of finding out whether any stock of provisions was taken along, but warned by our parsimony in dealing out spirituous liquor, they were unwilling to start until they had examined the stock of "ram." That drunkenness, not the satisfying of the taste, was in this case the main object, is shown by the circumstance that they often fixed as price for the articles they saw we were anxious to have such a quantity of brandy as would make them completely intoxicated. When on one occasion I appeared very desirous of purchasing a fire drill, which was found in a tent inhabited by a newly wedded pair, the young and very pretty housewife undertook the negotiation and immediately began by declaring that her husband could not part with the fire-producing implement unless I gave him the means of getting quite drunk, for which, according to her statement, which was illustrated by lively gesticulations representing the different degrees of intoxication, eight glasses were required. Not until the man had got so many would he be content—that is, dead drunk. I have myself observed, however, on several occasions that two small glasses are sufficient to make them unsteady on the legs. Under the influence of liquor they are cheerful, merry and friendly, but troublesome by their excessive caressing. When in the company of intoxicated natives, one must take good care that he does not unexpectedly get a kiss from some old greasy seal hunter. Even the women readily took a glass, though evidently less addicted to intoxicants than the men. They, however, got their share, as did even the youngest of the children. When, as happened twice in the course of the winter, an encampment was fortunate enough to get a large stock of brandy sent it from Bering Strait, the intoxication was general, and, as I have already stated, the bluish-yellow eyes the next day showed that quarrelsomeness had been called forth even among this peace-loving people by their dear *akmimil*. During our stay at the villages nearer Bering Strait two murders even took place, of which one at least was committed by an intoxicated man.

However slight the contact the Chukchis have with the world that has reached the standpoint of the brandy industry, this means of enjoyment, however, appears to be the object of regular barter. Many of the Chukchis who traveled past us were intoxicated and shook with pride a not quite empty keg or sealskin sack, to let us hear by the dashing that it contained liquid. One of the crew, whom I asked to ascertain what sort of spirit it was, made friends with the owner and induced him at last to part with about a thimbleful of it; more could not be given. According to the sailor's statement it was without color and flavor, clear as crystal, but weak. It was thus probably Russian corn brandy, not gin. . . .

Polar Places

ABOVE, the crews of two of William Edward Parry's ships cutting through the ice into Winter Harbor in September 1819. BELOW, a Winter Island Eskimo and his wife. [See pages 919-929.]

ABOVE, Chukchi girls dancing at Indian Point, Siberia. BELOW, a Chukchi winter house at Moriinsky Post, Siberia. Both photographs courtesy of the American Museum of Natural History. [See pages 930-938.]

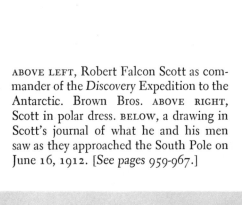

ABOVE LEFT, Robert Falcon Scott as commander of the *Discovery* Expedition to the Antarctic. Brown Bros. ABOVE RIGHT, Scott in polar dress. BELOW, a drawing in Scott's journal of what he and his men saw as they approached the South Pole on June 16, 1912. [See pages 959-967.]

Jan. 16. 1912.

ABOVE, Peter Freuchen with his Eskimo wife and children on a visit to Denmark.

RIGHT, a later portrait of Freuchen. Courtesy of Julian Messner, Inc. [See pages 939-945.]

BELOW, a newly built igloo being finished off. Three Lions, Inc. [See pages 968-975.]

Wanderer in Greenland

PETER FREUCHEN

FROM *Arctic Adventure: My Life in the Frozen North*

1907–34

Peter Freuchen was studying at the university in Copenhagen when he was possessed by the idea of exploring northern Greenland. He gave up his aim of becoming a physician and served as a stoker on a ship to Greenland in order to secure a place on the Erichsen polar expedition of 1907–8. Once on the expedition, he volunteered to spend a winter alone observing the weather. Not long afterward he met Greenland-born Knud Rasmussen, later to become a noted Arctic explorer; together they started a trading post on the west Greenland coast and founded the Eskimo settlement that Freuchen named Thule. In time Freuchen married an Eskimo woman, and for more than fifteen years he lived as an Eskimo, not only because he believed it was the best way to live in such an environment but also because he loved it. A huge, tremendously energetic man, he was descended on his mother's side from a line of seafarers, and seemed made for the primitive, physical life of the north. His feats of endurance and courage made him a Greenland legend.

Professionally he was a journalist and the author of many popular autobiographical and fictional books about Eskimos and the Far North. In the late 1930s his island off the Danish coast became a haven for refugees from Nazism (besides his national sympathies, he was of Jewish descent), and during the German occupation he served in the resistance and was repeatedly imprisoned. Although he never stopped traveling (one of his more unusual journeys was a nine-month tour of Soviet Siberia in 1937), he spent most of his later years in the United States, where he died in 1959.

Arctic Adventure, from which the passages below are taken, is an exuberant and sometimes boisterous account of the years when he lived with the Eskimos and roamed the Greenland coast.

[In January 1923, on the way back to Greenland from an expedition to the Canadian Arctic, Freuchen has occasion to make a day's journey by himself and is caught in a bad storm.]

THE TRAP

I MADE the trip well enough and loaded the boxes on the sledge, but shortly after I had turned about, the wind started to blow harder, howling like a fiend. The drifts were alive under my feet, and it was impossible for me to follow the tracks. The wind turned into a storm, the storm into a gale.

I was lost. It was impossible to determine directions, as I could not see the hills. Fortunately it was not a mountainous country, so the danger of falling into ravines was eliminated. Also the direction of the wind was more or less constant, and I could be guided to a certain extent by that.

The storm was blinding, and I stopped several times to examine the snow with the thought of building myself an igloo and holing up until the gale abated, but the snow was packed too solid. Whenever I halted I had difficulty in getting the tired dogs on their feet again.

Still I kept fighting forward. I was growing more tired by the minute, but the dogs understood me now. I dropped my load again, keeping nothing but my sleeping bag with the extra kamiks and a small square of bearskin. I walked ahead of the dogs and they followed along after me. With no load I ought to be able to get back to camp.

I had to stop now and then to turn my back to the wind and catch my breath. It was so bad that I could scarcely stand upright, and finally had to go back to the sledge and hang on to the upstanders. I could not swing my whip against the gale, and the dogs refused to go ahead.

By this time I could not be far from the others, and I decided that it would be better for me to stop than to run the risk of passing them. I was hungry, too, and when I reached a large rock behind which the wind had hollowed out a depression, I stopped. The dogs scuttled into the hole, curled up together, and in no time were covered by the snow.

I tried to slice snow blocks with my knife, but the snow was packed almost as solid as ice, and was as hard to penetrate as wood or soil. There was no possibility of making an igloo, so I gave up and sat down. But it was too uncomfortable to sit still for long, and I soon got up. Then I tried the old game of closing my eyes, walking twenty paces forward, turning to the right and walking twenty paces, repeating it twice more and then looking about to discover how far I was from my starting point. I did that for hours, checking on the effect of the wind on my walking, but I soon became too exhausted to stand upright.

Then a craving for sleep gripped me. I felt almost nauseated, and thought that if I could dig a sort of grave under my sledge I might be protected from the gale. I moved the sledge and gouged out a hole where it had been, took the piece of bearskin and laid it in the hole for a pillow; then I shoved the sledge over the little grave and crawled in at one end, hauling the bag with my kamiks in after me to serve as a door.

The space was just large enough for me to lie flat, and I immediately went to sleep. It was comforting to be out of the wind and the drifting snow, but I awakened after a time and realized that something was wrong. For a moment I could not tell what it was, but then it came over me that there was no feeling in my left foot.

That is bad. So long as a frozen limb is painful, it is comparatively harmless, but when there is no sensitivity left, look out!

My first thought was to crawl out and run about to get circulation started again. I tried to move the bag at my feet but so much snow had piled up outside that I could not budge it. That frightened me, and I threshed about until I felt a little warmer and more comfortable. Considering my situation a bit more calmly, I decided that nothing could be gained by wasting my strength in this hysterical fashion. In order to get out of my grave I would have to tear down the entire shelter. And I went to sleep again.

When I wakened the second time I was more than ever conscious of the cold. I would have to get out or freeze stiff as a poker. It was still impossible to kick the bag away, and the space was too narrow to permit my bending down and pulling it up. Then I attempted to turn over, lifting the sledge above me, but it was evidently weighted down by a heavy drift. I was buried alive.

Completely up against it, my mind turned to any possible solution. Slowly the desperateness of my situation dawned upon me. The snow was hard and could not be dug away with hands hampered by mittens. I opened one of my watches (I had two in the pockets of my underwear) and felt the time. It was the middle of the day, yet I was in total darkness.

I decided to sacrifice one of my hands, let it freeze and use it as a spade to dig my way out. I pitied myself, as I had plenty of uses for both hands. But even this was a flop. I satisfied myself that my hands, even if frozen, could not be used for tools. They cannot be kept stiff, and break easily. I had to give up the idea and held the frozen hand against my body to thaw it out.

Then I resorted to using my head. One thought that came to me was to try to move my bowels and form a chisel of the excrement, which would immediately freeze, to dig the hard snow. But first I decided to take the piece of bearskin under my head and scrape with it.

I chewed on the edge of the skin and it froze hard as glass instantly. With this it was possible to dig. I remember that time after time I put it back into my mouth to moisten it and let it freeze again. I lay there with my eyes closed and scraped away. When a man is in the dark it is some comfort for him to keep his eyes shut—at least then he cannot see even if it is daylight. I made progress, but what slow progress!

My clothes were the same as the natives'—two layers of skin, the inner one with the fur turned in, and the outer with the fur turned out. I wore no belt and the garments hung loose about me so that I would not sweat. The idea is always to remain a little cool, but dry—it not only makes clothes last longer but prevents rheumatism when a man grows older.

Now, however, my movements in the grave pulled the coats up so that the loose snow I scraped away worked its way up against my bare stomach. Still I kept at it, and after a while had a hole leading into the open.

With success in sight I grew impatient. I could not forget that my foot was frozen, and as the hole grew a little larger it looked so tempting that I tried to work my way out through it. I had to bend in a snakelike coil to get my head down to the opening, but I did it and pushed onward. But the hole was still too small, and I stuck fast with only half my face out.

Unfortunately my whiskers were directly beneath the broad frozen mud runner and, as there is always moisture about the mouth, they froze fast to the runner and I could not move either forward or backward. I was so doubled up in my grave that I had no strength to do a thing. Outside I saw the heavens and felt the snow, but I was caught like a fox in a trap, and I felt sure that this was the end.

How long I lay in that cramped position I do not know. Perhaps I fainted. The snow had covered the upper part of my face, filled my eyes and nose so that I could scarcely breathe. The air was a vicious mixture of flying snow and, as I inhaled it, I knew that I could not last for long. My thoughts turned to my home in Denmark, to my mother, and to my good friend Magdalene who had not written to me. I decided that I would have to write her. At the same moment I realized how ridiculous it was to plan anything in my situation.

I was suddenly so angry that I made a last effort and jerked my head back into the hole.

The relief was heavenly. The grave felt cozy again. I wiped my eyes free of snow and rubbed my face, which, I could tell, was badly frozen. Then I felt something warm and sticky coursing down my neck. It was blood. I had yanked part of my beard away and the skin with it. I ran my hand along the sledge runner above and felt the hair frozen to it. Then I became aware of the stinging of my face. Since then I have never had quite so much beard around my mouth.

But I had no time to lie idle. I was growing more ravenous by the minute, and once more it was dark outside, so I went back to the job of digging myself out with the frozen bearskin.

Working in spurts of nervous energy I soon had scraped a hole which I was sure would be large enough to let me through. I was as excited as a young actress making her debut—this was my chance for life and I crammed my head through the opening. The drift filled my eyes immediately, and I was caught once more at the shoulders.

I had heard that a dying man is able to make a last superhuman effort to save himself. I exhaled, and jammed myself a little farther into the opening. Then, the craving for air being overwhelming, I sucked my lungs full, expanding my chest to its utmost. It was painful, but I felt the sledge give slightly above me, and I inched forward, repeated the process and this time the sledge moved perceptibly.

Inch by inch I pushed ahead until I found myself with my right arm free. I gave one last lunge and was out!

There standing upright on the sledge, weighted down with snow, was my snow knife. If I had only been wise enough to take it inside with me, none of this would have happened.

I got to my feet, and immediately tumbled over. I thought nothing of it and got up again, only to fall once more. Then I realized that something was seriously wrong with my left foot—there was no feeling in it whatever. I beat it with my knife, and felt nothing. Then I examined it closer and found not only the foot but the leg frozen. It was impossible to bend the joints and impossible to stand upright, so I crawled.

I first looked for the dogs. They were still asleep and buried in the snow, so I did not disturb them. In two hours and a half of crawling I was close to our camp. Suddenly I saw a dog standing just ahead of me. He became frightened, turned about and ran. I followed the dog's tracks and reached the igloo.

My friends cut off my kamik and found that the foot was as bad as I had anticipated. There was but one consolation: it did not hurt so long as it was frozen. I ate enough food to satisfy me, and then went to sleep. When the leg thawed out it would be impossible to rest.

A throbbing pain wakened me before long and we decided to take a look at the foot. Never would I have believed that such a change could occur in so short a time. My foot was puffed up like a football, and Bangsted's false optimism sickened me almost as much as did the injured limb.

Next day it was plain to see that the foot would only handicap me in walking, so we resolved to return to our base at once. All of us were in a bad mood. I cursed my luck, but that did not help us now.

We left most of our outfit—Dr. Mathiassen would pass here later on his trip to Ponds Inlet and pick it up—and with light sledges we set out. I rode on Akrioq's sledge, and made a point of keeping the foot frozen. It did not hurt me then. But it was a bad week.

When we passed Awa's house we discovered a native woman doctor who said she specialized in healing frozen limbs. She volunteered to accompany me to Danish Island, and I accepted her offer.

Thus I returned only to lie flat on my back and watch the others busy as bees completing their three years' researches and investigations.

Gangrene, as it develops in a frozen limb, is not so painful as it is odorous. It stinks to heaven, and one cannot get away from it. The nurse had a special cure. She captured small lemmings, the Arctic mice which multiply faster than guinea pigs, killed them beside me and laid the warm skins on the open wounds, bloody side down. After some hours, during which she caught more, she peeled off the skins, the decayed flesh adhering to them, and replaced them with new ones. She also muttered magic formulas over the foot and sang pain-killing songs.

Nevertheless, the flesh fell away until the bones protruded. I could endure no blankets touching it, and the sight of it sent my nerves jangling. If the room was warm, the stench was unendurable; if it was cold, I froze. I went through a living hell, and each night felt that the old man with the scythe was close after me.

When a man is sick and cold and lonely he gets strange ideas, and one day I told the nurse that I wanted to have those toes off. She thought that might be the best thing to do, and she knew just how to do it: bite them off at the joints and prevent the ghosts from occupying my body—her mouth would close the wounds immediately. I thanked her very much, but took no stock in her method; fitted a nail puller over each toe and banged it off with a hammer.

I cannot attempt to describe the physical pain—but there was a spiritual pain, too, in discarding a portion of my own body, even a part that would never be of any use to me again.

[Eventually the leg had to be amputated and replaced by a wooden one, but this seems to have done little to diminish Freuchen's love of travel in its most exciting forms.]

Doing as the Eskimos Do

VILHJALMUR STEFANSSON

FROM *My Life with the Eskimo*

1908–12

One of Vilhjalmur Stefansson's chief distinctions as an explorer is the success with which he applied his theory that the way to meet
the challenge of the Arctic is to live in it as the natives do. Clothing and
sheltering himself and getting food much as the Eskimo does, he made long
treks across the Far North as far back as 1906, apparently with no more
hardship than if he were camping in the Maine woods.

Born in 1879 of Icelandic parents pioneering in Manitoba but later
forced by famine and flood to move to North Dakota, he attended colleges in the United States and then went on to Harvard Divinity School.
After a period of graduate study in anthropology, he did archaeological
work in Iceland in 1904 and again in 1905. His first taste of Eskimo life
came in 1906 when a polar expedition failed to meet him on the Arctic
Ocean, and he happily spent the winter alone with the Mackenzie Eskimos,
learning their language and how to survive as they did. Backed by the
American Museum of Natural History and the Geological Survey of
Canada, he then undertook an expedition, which lasted more than four
years, among the Eskimos on the northern coast of North America. His
account of this sojourn, My Life with the Eskimo, tells how he traveled for
the most part with only two or three Eskimo companions, visited natives
who had never seen a white man before (see the excerpt below), and found
others who became known, from his descriptions, as the "Blond Eskimo."
From 1913 to 1918 he led an Arctic expedition which mapped more than
100,000 square miles of uncharted territory and made several notable dis-

coveries of rivers and land areas, including one in which Stefansson and two companions crossed a part of Beaufort Sea on moving ice.

Besides being an explorer, Stefansson is an expert ethnologist and an authority on the history of exploration. He is also the author of many books on his own and others' Arctic travels, and has collected at Dartmouth College one of the greatest libraries on the Arctic.

[Stefansson and a companion, Dr. Rudolph Anderson, a naturalist, leave Edmonton, Canada, in May 1908. Traveling northward mostly by the freight scows of the Hudson's Bay Company, they reach the Arctic Ocean late in July. After spending a year and a half among the semicivilized Eskimos between Point Barrow, Alaska, and Cape Parry, Canada, Stefansson decides to move eastward to the Coronation Gulf area, a region thought to be uninhabited.]

THE DISCOVERY OF A STONE-AGE PEOPLE

ALTHOUGH minutes are seldom of enough value with us in the North to waste ink in recording them, I have set down the fact that it was 1:45 on the afternoon of April 21st, 1910, that we finally made our long-planned start from Langton Bay on our trip toward Coronation Gulf.

We were now fairly started for the unknown, but no one but myself was very enthusiastic over the enterprise. The reluctance of my people was due in part only (and in less part) to their fear of finding the unknown country gameless—they feared to find it inhabited by a barbarous and bloodthirsty race of which the Baillie Islands Eskimo had been telling us grotesque tales whenever our party and they came together. These dreaded people were the Nagyuktogmiut, the people of the caribou antler, who lived far to the east, and who used to come in semi-hostile contact with their ancestors long ago.

"These people bear the name of the caribou antler," they had told us, "because of a peculiar custom they have. When a woman becomes of marriageable age her coming-out is announced several days in advance. At the appointed time she is made to take her place in an open space out-of-doors, and all the men who want wives form around her in a circle, each armed with the antler of a large bull caribou. The word is given, and they all rush at her, each trying to hook her toward him with the antler. Often the woman is killed in the scrimmage, but if some one succeeds in getting her alive from the others he takes her for a wife. As strength and the skill which experience gives are the main requirements for success, some of the Nogyuktogmiut have a great many wives, while most of them have none. Because so many women are killed in this way there are twice as many men as women among them. We know many stories, of which this is one, to show what queer people these Easterners are. They also kill all strangers." That was the way all stories of the Easterners ended. Like Cato's *Delenda est Carthago*, "they kill all strangers" were the unvarying words that finished every discussion of the Nagyuktogmiut by the Baillie Islanders.

No matter how fabulous a story sounds, there is usually a basis of fact; when we at last got to these Easterners we found that the kernel of truth consisted in the fewness of women as compared with men, but the reason for this fact had nothing to do with caribou antlers, but was instead connected with the fact that they practice the Spartan custom of exposing new-born children, and especially female children, with the result that women among them are much fewer than men.

When we finally made our start for the east we were in many respects poorly equipped for spending a year away from any possible source of supplies other than those which the Arctic lands themselves can furnish. When I had planned this undertaking in New York, I had counted on having good dogs, but the good dogs were now dead. I had counted on Dr. Anderson's company and cooperation, but necessity (chiefly the lack of ammunition for our rifles for the coming year) had dictated that he should go west for supplies, and that I should depend on Eskimo companions alone. I had counted on having a silk tent and other light equipment for summer use, and the lightest and most powerful rifles and high-power ammunition, but during one of our winter periods of shortage of food I had been compelled to abandon many of these things at a distance from which they could not now be got. Instead of the ten-pound silk tent, I therefore had to take a forty-pound canvas one, old and full of holes; I had only two hundred rounds for my Mannlicher-Schoenauer 6.5 mm. rifle, and had to piece out with far heavier and less powerful black-powder rifles and ammunition. In all we had four rifles of three different calibers, and a total of nine hundred and sixty rounds of three kinds of ammunition, when the right thing obviously is to have but one kind of rifle and ammunition. Had one of our rifles broken we should have had to throw away the ammunition suited to that gun. . . .

We had with us on starting from Langton Bay about two weeks' supplies. These were neither here nor there as provisions for a year's exploration

—we would have been quite as well off had we started with only two days' supplies. From the outset, therefore, we tried to provide each day food for that day from the animals of the land. In carrying out such a programme for a party of four each had to do his share. My main reliance was the Alaskan man Natkusiak, and the woman Pannigabluk; the Mackenzie River boy Tannaumirk, a boy in character, though perhaps twenty-five in years, was a cheerful and companionable sort of fellow, but without initiative and (like many of his countrymen nowadays) not in the best of health. Our general plan was that the three Eskimo took care of the sled, one, usually the woman, walking ahead to pick out a trail through the rough sea ice, and the other two steadying the sled from upsetting too often, and pulling in harness at the same time to help the dogs. If they saw a seal or a bear, one of them would go after him while the other two waited at the sled, cooked a lunch if it was near midday, or made camp if night was approaching. If by camp-time no game had yet been seen, the woman Pannigabluk would stay by the camp to cook supper, while the two men went off in different directions to hunt. That the two should go in different directions was wise, for it doubled the chances of seeing game, but it at times caused unnecessary waste of ammunition and the killing of more meat than was needed. The very first time that both men went out to hunt in this manner, for instance, Natkusiak killed two seven- or eight-hundred-pound bearded seals in one shot, and Tannaumirk a big, fat grizzly bear in four shots. This was meat enough for several weeks if we had (Eskimo fashion) stayed there to eat it up; traveling as we were, heavily loaded through rough ice, we could not take along more than a hundred pounds of meat.

Although the Eskimo frequently killed an animal or two if they happened on them along the line of march, their chief business was getting the sled load as many miles ahead as convenient during the day, which was seldom over fifteen miles in a working day averaging perhaps eight hours. We were in no hurry, for we had no particular distance to go and no reason to hasten back, but expected to spend the summer wherever it overtook us, and the winter similarly in its turn.

My companions traveled along the coast, made camp, and cooked, while I took upon myself the main burden of the food-providing. With this in view I used to strike inland about five miles in the morning, starting often a good while before the Eskimo broke camp, and then walking rapidly eastward parallel to the coast. With my snow-shoes I made easy and rapid progress compared to that of the sled along the coast, unless I happened on caribou. . . .

Generally it is only in times of extreme need that one hunts caribou in a blizzard—not that nine tenths of the blizzards in the Arctic need keep a healthy man indoors; it is merely that the drifting snow (even when you can see as far as two hundred yards) diminishes many times over the chance you have of finding game. If you do find caribou, however, the stronger the gale the better your chance of close approach without being seen, for these animals, though they double their watchfulness in foggy weather, seem to relax it in a blizzard. In the present instance my reason for looking for caribou was that I wanted to kill a few for the moral effect it would have on my party; for in the midst of abundance they would be forced to fall back on their fear of the Nagyuktogmiut as the only argument for retreat, and this they were a bit ashamed of doing, even among themselves. It was therefore great luck for us, although we were in no immediate need of meat, that after a short hunt through the storm I ran into a band of seven cows and young bulls about five miles inland, southwest from Point Pierce. I came upon them quite without cover, but saw them through the drifting snow at three hundred yards before they saw me—the human eye is a great deal keener than that of the caribou, wolf, or any other animal with which I have had experience. By stepping back a few paces till the drifting snow had hidden the caribou again, and then guardedly circling them to leeward, I found a slight ridge which allowed safe approach to within about two hundred yards of where they had been. The main thing in stalking caribou that are not moving is the ability to keep in mind their location accurately while you are circling and winding about so as to approach them from a new direction behind cover of irregular hills and ridges that are of course unfamiliar to you. In this case my plans came suddenly to naught through the caribou appearing on the skyline two hundred yards off. I shot three of them, though we could not possibly use more than the meat of one. The moral effect on my Eskimo of having food to throw away would, I knew, be invaluable to me. Had I killed only one, they would not have believed it to be for any reason other than that I was unable to kill more. This was the only time in a period of fourteen months of continuous "living on the country" that I shot more animals than I thought we should need, although I often had to kill a single large animal, such as a polar bear or bearded seal, when I knew we should be unable to haul with us more than a small part of its meat.

We proceeded eastward along the deserted coast without adventure. "Blessed is that country whose history is uninteresting" applies to Arctic expeditions as well. Having an adventure is a sign that something unexpected, something unprovided against, has happened; it shows that some one is incompetent, that something has gone wrong. For that reason we pride ourselves on the fewness of our adventures; for the same reason we are a bit ashamed of the few we did have. An adventure is interesting enough in retrospect, especially to the person who didn't have it; at the time it happens it usually constitutes an exceedingly disagreeable experience. On May 2d, near Point Dease Thompson, through incompetence of my own, I came near having a serious one; that I did not actually have it was due to the incompetence of a polar bear. After completely outmaneuvering me at the start, he allowed a fondness for grandstand play to lose him the game at the critical moment.

The thing happened in the afternoon. As usual, I was hunting caribou eastward along the sea-front of the Melville Mountains that lie parallel to the coast a few miles inland. The sled and the Eskimo were traveling more slowly along the coast and were several miles behind—for one thing the sled was heavy and the ice rough; for another, they used to stop an hour or so each day to cook a lunch at which I was seldom able to join them. I had seen no caribou all day nor the day before, and our meat was low; therefore I stopped whenever I came to the top of a commanding hill to sweep the country carefully with my binoculars. The land showed nothing but a white wolf or arctic fox now and then; ptarmigan there were, but they are too small game for a party of four that is going to go a year on nine hundred and sixty rounds of ammunition; the foxes, too, were beneath our notice, though their meat is excellent; but a wolf that came within two hundred yards seldom got by me, for a fat one weighs a hundred pounds, and all of us preferred them at this season to caribou, except Pannigabluk, who would not taste the meat because it is taboo to her people.

This day the wolves did not come near, and the first hopeful thing I saw was a yellow spot on the sea ice about three miles off. After watching it for five minutes or so I was still unable to determine whether or not the spot was yellow ice or something else than ice; had my party been abreast of me or ahead I should have given up and moved on, but as they were several miles behind I put in a half-hour watching this thing that was a bit yellower than ice should be; now and then I looked elsewhere, for a caribou or grizzly may at any time come out from behind a hill, a polar bear from behind a cake of ice, or a seal out of his hole. After sweeping the entire circle of the horizon perhaps for the sixth time I noted that the yellow spot had disappeared—it was, therefore, a polar bear that had been lying down; after sleeping too long in one position he had stood up and lain down again behind an ice cake.

A moment after noting this I was running as hard as I could in the direction of the bear, for there was no telling how soon he would start traveling or how fast he would go. I had, as soon as I began to suspect the yellow spot might be a bear, taken careful note of the topography behind me with relation to the spot's position out on the rough sea ice, for it is as difficult to keep a straight line toward an invisible object among the ice cakes and pressure ridges as it is in a forest. The mountains behind, however, could always be seen, and by their configuration I tried to guide myself straight toward the bear. Every three or four hundred yards I would climb a high pressure ridge and have a look around with the glasses, but nothing was to be seen. I did not, in fact, expect to see anything unless the bear had commenced traveling, in which case he would perhaps expose himself by crossing a high ridge. When at last I got to the neighborhood of the animal, according to my calculations, I climbed an especially high ridge and spent a longer time than usual sweeping the surroundings with the glasses and studying individual ice cakes and ridges, with the hope of recognizing some of those I had seen from the mountains to be in the neighborhood of my bear; but everything looked different on near approach, and I failed to locate myself to my own satisfaction. I had decided to go a quarter of a mile or so further before beginning to circle in quest of the bear's tracks. My rifle was buckled in its case slung across my back, and I was slowly and cautiously clambering down the far side of a pressure ridge, when I heard behind me a noise like the spitting of a cat or the hiss of a goose. I looked back and saw, about twenty feet away and almost above me, a polar bear.

Had he come the remaining twenty feet as quietly and quickly as a bear can, the literary value of the incident would have been lost forever; for, as the Greek fable points out, a lion does not write a book. From his eye and attitude, as well as the story his trail told afterward, there was no doubting his intentions: the hiss was merely his way of saying, "Watch me do it!" Or at least that is how I interpreted it; possibly the motive was chivalry, and the hiss was his way of saying "*Garde!*" Whichever it was, it was the fatal mistake of a game played well to that point; for no animal on earth can afford to give warning to a man with a rifle. And why should he? Has a hunter ever played fair with one of them?

Afterward the snow told plainly the short—and, for one of the participants, tragic story. I had underestimated the bear's distance from shore, and had passed the spot where he lay, going a hundred yards or two to windward; on scenting me he had come up the wind to my trail, and had then followed it, walking about ten paces to leeward of it, apparently following my tracks by smelling them from a distance. The reason I had not seen his approach was that it had not occurred to me to look back over my own trail; I was so used to hunting bears that the possibility of one of them assuming my own role and hunting me had been left out of consideration. A good hunter, like a good detective, should leave nothing out of consideration.

On May 9th, nineteen days out from Langton Bay, we came upon signs that made our hearts beat faster. It was at Point Wise, where the open sea begins to be narrowed into Dolphin and Union straits by the near approach to the mainland of the mountainous shores of Victoria Island. The beach was strewn with pieces of driftwood, and on one of them we found the marks of recent choppings with a dull adze. A search of the beach for half a mile each way revealed numerous similar choppings. Evidently the men who had made them had been testing the pieces of wood to see if they were sound enough to become the materials for sleds or other things they had wished to make. Those pieces which had but one or two adze marks had been found unsound; in a few places piles of chips showed that a sound piece had been found there and had been roughed down for transportation purposes on the spot. Prepossessed by the idea that Victoria Island was probably inhabited because Rae had seen people on its southwest coast in 1851, and the mainland probably uninhabited because Richardson had failed to find any people on it in 1826 and again in 1848, I decided that the men whose traces we saw were probably Victoria Islanders who had with sleds crossed the frozen straits from the land whose mountains we could faintly see to the north, and had returned to its woodless shores with the driftwood they had picked up here. We learned later that this supposition was wrong; the people whose traces we found were mainland dwellers whose ancestors must have been hunting inland to the south when Richardson twice passed without seeing them.

The night after this discovery we did not sleep much. The Eskimo were more excited than I was, apparently, and far into the morning they talked and speculated on the meaning of the signs. Had we come upon traces of the Nagyuktogmiut "who kill all strangers"? Fortunately enough, my long-entertained fear that traces of people would cause a panic in my party was not realized. In spite of all their talk, and in spite of the fact that they were seriously afraid, the curiosity as to what these strange people would prove to be like—in fine, the spirit of adventure, which seldom crops out in an Eskimo—was far stronger than their fears. We were therefore up early the next morning, and soon out on the road.

All that day we found along the beach comparatively fresh traces of people, chiefly shavings and chips where the hewing and shaping of wood had taken place. None seen that day were of the present winter, though some seemed to be of the previous summer; but the next morning, just east of Point Young, we found at last human footprints in the crusted snow and sled tracks that were not over three months old. That day at Cape Bexley we came upon a deserted village of over fifty snow houses; their inhabitants had apparently left them about midwinter, and it was now the 12th of May.

The size of the deserted village took our breath away. Tannaumirk, the young man from the Mackenzie River, had never seen an inhabited village among his people of more than twelve or fifteen houses. All his old fears of the Nagyuktogmiut "who kill all strangers" now came to the surface afresh; all the stories that he knew of their peculiar ways and atrocious deeds were retold by him that evening for our common benefit.

A broad but three months' untraveled trail led north from this village site across the ice toward Victoria Island. My intentions were to continue east along the mainland into Coronation Gulf, but I decided nevertheless to stop here long enough to make an attempt to find the people at whose village we had camped. We would leave most of our gear on shore, with Pannigabluk to take care of it, while the two men and myself took the trail across the ice. This was according to Eskimo etiquette—on approach to the country of strange or distrusted people non-combatants are left behind, and only the able men of the party advance to a cautious parley. In this case the Mackenzie River man, Tannaumirk, was frightened enough to let his pride go by the board and to ask that he, too, might stay on shore at the camp. I told him he might, and Natkusiak and I prepared to start alone with a light sled, but at the last moment Tannaumirk decided he preferred to go with us, as the Nagyuktogmiut were likely in our absence to discover our camp, to surprise it by night, and to kill him while he slept. It would be safer, he thought, to go with us. Pannigabluk was much the coolest of the three Eskimo; if she was afraid to be left alone on shore she did not show it; she merely said that she might get lonesome if we were gone more than three or four days. We left her cheerfully engaged in the mending of our worn footgear, and at 2:30 P.M., May 13th, 1910, we took the old but nevertheless plain trail northward into the rough sea ice.

It was only near shore that the ice was rough, and with our light sled we made good progress; it was the first time on the trip that we did not have to pull in harness ourselves; instead we took turns in riding, two sitting on the sled at the same time and one running ahead to cheer the dogs on. We made about six miles per hour, and inside of two hours we arrived at another deserted village, about a month more recent than the one found at Cape Bexley. We were, therefore, on the trail not of a traveling party but of a migratory community.

As we understood dimly then and know definitely now, each village on such a trail should be about ten miles from the next preceding, and should be about a month more recent. The explanation of this is simple. The village of a people who hunt seal on level "bay" ice must not be on shore, for it is not convenient for a hunter to go more than five miles at the most from camp to look for the seal-holes, and naturally there are no seal-holes on land; the inhabitants of a sea village can hunt through an entire circle whose radius is about five miles; the inhabitants of a shore village can hunt through only half a circle of the same radius, for the other half of it will be on land. When the frost overtakes the seals in the fall, each of them, wherever he happens to be, gnaws several holes in the thin ice and rises to these whenever he needs to breathe. As the ice thickens he keeps them open by continuous gnawing, and for the whole of the winter that follows he is kept a prisoner in their neighborhood because of the fact that if he ever went to a considerable distance he would be unable to find a place to reach the air, and would therefore die of suffocation. By the aid of their dogs the Eskimo find these breathing-holes of the seals underneath the snow that hides them in winter, and spear the animals as they rise for air. In a month or so the hunters of a single village will have killed all the seals within a radius of about five miles; they must then move camp about ten miles, so that a five-mile circle around their next camp shall be tangent to the five-mile circle about their last one; for if the circles overlapped there would be that much waste territory within the new circle of activities. If, then, you are following such a trail and come to a village about four months old, you will expect to find the people who made it not more than forty miles off.

In the present case our task was simplified by the fact that the group we were following had not moved straight ahead north, but had made their fourth camp west of the second. Standing on the roofs of the houses of the second camp, we could see three seal-hunters a few miles to the west, each sitting on his block of snow by a seal-hole waiting for the animal to rise.

The seal-hunters and their camp were up the wind, and our dogs scented them. As we bore swiftly down upon the nearest of the sealers the dogs showed enthusiasm and anticipation as keen as mine, keener by a great deal than did my Eskimo. As the hunter was separated from each of his fellow huntsmen by a full half-mile, I thought he would probably be frightened if all of us were to rush up to him at the top speed of our dogs. We therefore stopped our sled several hundred yards away. Tannaumirk had become braver now, for the lone stranger did not look formidable, sitting stooped forward as he was on his block of snow beside the seal-hole; he accordingly volunteered to act as our ambassador, saying that the Mackenzie dialect (his own) was probably nearer the stranger's tongue than Natkusiak's. This seemed likely, so I told him to go ahead. The sealer sat motionless as Tannaumirk approached him; I watched him through my glasses and saw that he held his face steadily as if watching the seal-hole, but that he raised his eyes every second or two to the (to him) strange figure of the man approaching. He was evidently tensely ready for action. Tannaumirk by now was thoroughly over his fears, and would have walked right up to the sealer, but when no more than five paces or so intervened between them the sealer suddenly jumped up, grasping a long knife that had lain on the snow beside him, and poising himself as if to receive an attack or to be ready to leap forward suddenly. This scared our man, who stopped abruptly and began excitedly and volubly to assure the sealer that he and all of us were friendly and harmless, men of excellent character and intentions.

I was, of course, too far away to hear, but Tannaumirk told me afterward that on the instant of jumping up the sealer began a monotonous noise which is not a chant nor is it words—it is merely an effort to ward off dumbness, for if a man who is in the presence of a spirit does not make at least one sound each time he draws his breath, he will be stricken permanently dumb. This is a belief common to the Alaska and Coronation Gulf Eskimo. For several minutes Tannaumirk talked excitedly, and the sealer kept up the moaning noise, quite unable to realize, apparently, that he was being spoken to in human speech. It did not occur to him for a long time, he told us afterward, that we might be something other than spirits, for our dogs and dog harness, our sleds and clothes, were such as he had never seen in all his wanderings; besides, we had not, on approaching, used the peace sign of his people, which is holding the hands out to show that one does not carry a knife.

After what may have been anything from five to fifteen minutes of talking and expostulation by Tannaumirk, the man finally began to listen and then to answer. The dialects proved to differ about as much as Norwegian does from Swedish, or Spanish from Portuguese. After Tannaumirk had made him understand the assurance that we were of good intent and character, and had showed by lifting his own coat that he had no knife, the sealer approached him cautiously and felt of him, partly (as he told us later) to assure himself that he was not a spirit, and partly to see if there were not a knife hidden somewhere under his clothes. After a careful examination and some further parley, he told Tannaumirk to tell us that they two would proceed home to the village, and Natkusiak and I might follow as far behind as we were now; when they got to the village we were to remain outside it till the people could be informed that we were visitors with friendly intentions.

As we proceeded toward the village other seal-hunters gradually converged toward us from all over the neighboring four or five square miles of ice and joined Tannaumirk and his companion, who walked about two hundred yards ahead. As each of these was armed with a long knife and a seal-spear, it may be imagined that the never very brave Tannaumirk was pretty thoroughly frightened—to which he owned up freely that night and the few days next following, though he had forgotten the circumstance completely by next year, when we returned to his own people in the Mackenzie district, where he is now a drawing-room lion on the strength of his adventures in the far east. When we approached the village every man, woman, and child was outdoors, waiting for us excitedly, for they could tell from afar that we were no ordinary visitors. The man whom we had first approached—who that day acquired a local prominence which still distinguishes him above his fellows—explained to an eagerly silent crowd that we were friends from a distance who had come without evil intent, and immediately the whole crowd (about forty) came running toward us. As each came up he would say: "I am So-and-so. I am well disposed. I have no knife. Who are you?" After being told our names in return, and being assured that we were friendly, and that our knives were packed away in the sled and not hidden under our clothing, each would express his satisfaction and stand aside for the next to present himself. Sometimes a man would present his wife, or a woman her husband, according to which came up first. The women were in more hurry to be presented than were the men, for they must, they said, go right back to their houses to cook us something to eat.

After the women were gone the men asked us whether we preferred to have our camp right in the village or a little outside it. On talking it over we agreed it would be better to camp about two hundred yards from the other houses, so as to keep our dogs from fighting with theirs. When this was decided, half a dozen small boys were sent home to as many houses to get their fathers' snow-knives and house-building mittens. We were not allowed to touch a hand to anything in camp-making, but stood idly by, surrounded continually by a crowd who used every means to show how friendly they felt and how welcome we were, while a few of the best house-builders set about erecting for us the house in which we were to live as long as we cared to stay with them. When it had been finished and furnished with the skins, lamp, and the other things that go to make a snow house the coziest and most comfortable of camps, they told us they hoped we would occupy it at least till the last piece of meat in their storehouses had been eaten, and that so long as we stayed in the village no man would hunt seals or do any work until his children began to complain of hunger. It was to be a holiday, they said, for this was the first time their people had been visited by strangers from so great a distance that they knew nothing of the land from which they came.

These simple, well-bred, and hospitable people were the savages whom we had come so far to see. That evening they saw for the first time the lighting of a sulphur match; the next day I showed them the greater marvels of my rifle; it was a day later still that they first understood that I was one of the white men of whom they had heard from other tribes, under the name *kablunat*.

I asked them: "Couldn't you tell by my blue eyes and the color of my beard?"

"But we didn't know," they answered, "what sort of complexions the *kablunat* have. Besides, our next neighbors north have eyes and beards like yours." That was how they first told us of the people whose discovery has brought up such important biological and historical problems, the people who have since become known to newspaper readers as the "Blond Eskimo."

> [Later that month he discovers the Blond Eskimos, a light-haired people thought to be of Norse-Greenlandic origin. He then spends a summer among the Copper Eskimos and treks back and forth across the Barren Ground to Great Bear Lake. After further archaeological work in the Langton Bay and Point Barrow areas he returns to Nome in the summer of 1912.]

Fortitude

ROBERT FALCON SCOTT

FROM *Scott's Last Expedition*

1910–12

The history of Antarctic exploration has in it many illustrious names, but none more radiant than that of Robert Falcon Scott. Perhaps the reason for this is that although he used the most modern techniques to further his ends, he placed his greatest faith in man's own fortitude and strength of purpose. In this respect he was above all a product of his training, for he entered England's Royal Navy in 1882, and was thus submitted at the age of fourteen to a tradition that had long idolized manliness, pluck and discipline.

It was these qualities that marked Scott's expeditions, enabling the first (in 1901–4) to push much closer to the South Pole than any before it and the second to make the longest sledge journey on record—almost 1,900 miles—and reach the South Pole despite the failure of all its means of transportation.

Scott was a commander in the Navy when he was chosen to lead what later came to be known as the "Discovery" Expedition. Remarkably well equipped, it distinguished itself by extraordinary sledge journeys and the discovery of the great polar ice cap. After Shackleton (who had been with Scott but was incapacitated by scurvy) had led his own expedition even closer to the Pole in 1909, Scott launched another major expedition in 1910. It met with terrible weather and after the failure of its motorized sledges, ponies and dogs (which, it is said, the English did not really know how to feed or drive), the five-man party that made the final thrust had to haul their loads themselves. What they found, to their unutterable disap-

pointment, when they reached the Pole on January 17, 1912, is described in the first passage below, and what they went through when they turned back is recorded in the second excerpt.

The description of their last days, written in a tent as Scott and his two remaining companions perished slowly of cold and hunger, is unequaled for the sense it conveys of noble courage and dignity in the face of death.

[The expedition sails from New Zealand late in November 1910, runs into stubborn pack ice, but finally sights land on December 31 and establishes a winter station and food depots on the Barrier. A sledge party brings back news that a Norwegian expedition under Amundsen has arrived in the Bay of Whales, but Scott refuses to let this affect his plans. During the continuous winter night from April to September the men keep busy with scientific observation, caring for the animals, lectures, and so forth. They start south on November 1, 1911, but find the snow plains of the Barrier agonizingly slow going. Within a few days the motorized sledges break down, then the ponies have to be killed, and by December 12 the dogs must be sent back. Hauling their own loads, Scott and four others start on January 4, 1912, on the last push toward the Pole over the sandy, gritty snow of the summit plateau.]

THE POLE: TRIUMPH AND DISAPPOINTMENT

TUESDAY, JANUARY 16 [1912].—Camp 68. Height 9,760. T. −23.5°
The worst has happened, or nearly the worst. We marched well in the morning and covered 7½ miles. Noon sight showed us in Lat. 89° 42′ S., and we started off in high spirits in the afternoon, feeling that to-morrow would see us at our destination. About the second hour of the march Bowers' sharp eyes detected what he thought was a cairn; he was uneasy about it, but argued that it must be a sastrugus. Half an hour later he detected a black speck ahead. Soon we knew that this could not be a natural snow feature. We marched on, found that it was a black flag tied to a sledge bearer; near by the remains of a camp; sledge tracks and ski tracks going and coming and the clear trace of dogs' paws—many dogs. This told us the whole story. The Norwegians have forestalled us and are

first at the Pole. It is a terrible disappointment, and I am very sorry for my loyal companions. Many thoughts come and much discussion have we had. To-morrow we must march on to the Pole and then hasten home with all the speed we can compass. All the day dreams must go; it will be a wearisome return. Certainly we are descending in altitude— certainly also the Norwegians found an easy way up.

WEDNESDAY, JANUARY 17.—Camp 69. T. −22° at start. Night −21°. The Pole. Yes, but under very different circumstances from those expected. We have had a horrible day—add to our disappointment a head wind 4 to 5, with a temperature −22°, and companions labouring on with cold feet and hands.

We started at 7:30, none of us having slept much after the shock of our discovery. We followed the Norwegian sledge tracks for some way; as far as we make out there are only two men. In about three miles we passed two small cairns. Then the weather overcast, and the tracks being increasingly drifted up and obviously going too far to the west, we decided to make straight for the Pole according to our calculations. At 12:30 Evans had such cold hands we camped for lunch—an excellent "week-end one." We had marched 7.4 miles. Lat. sight gave 89° 53' 37". We started out and did 6½ miles due south. To-night little Bowers is laying himself out to get sights in terrible difficult circumstances; the wind is blowing hard, T. −21°, and there is that curious damp, cold feeling in the air which chills one to the bone in no time. We have been descending again, I think, and there looks to be a rise ahead; otherwise there is very little that is different from the awful monotony of past days. Great God! this is an awful place and terrible enough for us to have laboured to it without the reward of priority. . . .

[After two days they start back, fighting blizzards, frostbite, and ever increasing hunger. In the following excerpt they have reached Return Camp 33. Here Evans has a bad fall and dies soon afterward.]

THE LAST MARCH

MONDAY, FEBRUARY 19.— . . . R.33. Temp. −17°. We have struggled out 4.6 miles in a short day over a really terrible surface—it has been like pulling over desert sand, not the least glide in the world. If this goes on we shall have a bad time, but I sincerely trust it is only the result of this windless area close to the coast and that, as we are making steadily outwards, we shall shortly escape it. It is perhaps premature to be anxious about covering distance. In all other respects things are improving. We have our sleeping-bags spread on the sledge and they are drying, but, above all, we have our full measure of food again. To-night we had a sort of stew fry of pemmican and horseflesh, and voted it the best hoosh we had ever had on a sledge journey. The absence of poor Evans is a help to the commissariat, but if he had been here in a fit state we might have got along faster. I wonder what is in store for us, with some little alarm at the lateness of the season.

MONDAY, FEBRUARY 20.—R.34. Lunch Temp. −13°; Supper Temp. −15°. Same terrible surface; four hours' hard plodding in morning brought us to our Desolation Camp, where we had the four-day blizzard. We looked for more pony meat, but found none. After lunch we took to ski with some improvement of comfort. Total mileage for day 7—the ski tracks pretty plain and easily followed this afternoon. We have left another cairn behind. Terribly slow progress, but we hope for better things as we clear the land. There is a tendency to cloud over in the S.E. to-night, which may turn to our advantage. At present our sledge and ski leave deeply ploughed tracks which can be seen winding for miles behind. It is distressing, but as usual trials are forgotten when we camp, and good food is our lot. Pray God we get better travelling as we are not so fit as we were, and the season is advancing apace. . . .

WEDNESDAY, FEBRUARY 22.—R.36. Supper Temp. −2°. There is little doubt we are in for a rotten critical time going home, and the lateness of the season may make it really serious. . . .

FRIDAY, FEBRUARY 24.—Lunch. Beautiful day—too beautiful—an hour after starting, loose ice crystals spoiling surface. Saw depot and reached it middle forenoon. Found store in order except shortage oil—shall have to be *very* saving with fuel—otherwise have ten full days' provision from to-night and shall have less than 70 miles to go. . . . Poor Wilson has a fearful attack snow-blindness consequent on yesterday's efforts. Wish we had more fuel.

Night camp R.38. Temp. −17°. A little despondent again. We had a really terrible surface this afternoon and only covered 4 miles. We are on the track just beyond a lunch cairn. It really will be a bad business if we are to have this pulling all through. I don't know what to think, but the rapid closing of the season is ominous. It is great luck having the horsemeat to add to our ration. . . .

MONDAY, FEBRUARY 27.—Desperately cold last night: −33° when we got up, with −37° minimum. Some suffering from cold feet, but all got good rest. We *must* open out on food soon. But we have done 7 miles this morning and hope for some 5 this afternoon. Overcast sky and good surface till now, when sun shows again. It is good to be marching the cairns up, but there is still much to be anxious about. We talk of little but food, except after meals. . . .

FRIDAY, MARCH 2.—Lunch. Misfortunes rarely come singly. We marched to the [Middle Barrier] depot fairly easily yesterday afternoon, and since that have suffered three distinct blows which have placed us in a bad position. First we found a shortage of oil; with most rigid economy it can scarce carry us to the next depot on this surface [71 miles away]. Second, Titus Oates disclosed his feet, the toes showing very bad indeed, evidently bitten by the late temperatures. The third blow came in the night, when the wind, which we had hailed with some joy, brought dark overcast weather. It fell below −40° in the night, and this morning it took 1½ hours to get our foot gear on, but we got away before eight. We lost cairn and tracks together and made as steady as we could N. by W., but have seen nothing. Worse was to come—the surface is simply awful. In spite of strong wind and full sail we have only done 5½ miles. We are in a *very* queer street since there is no doubt we cannot do the extra marches and feel the cold horribly. . . .

MONDAY, MARCH 5.—Lunch. Regret to say going from bad to worse. We got a slant of wind yesterday afternoon, and going on 5 hours we converted our wretched morning run of 3½ miles into something over 9. We went to bed on a cup of cocoa and pemmican solid with the chill off. (R.47.) The result is telling on all, but mainly on Oates, whose feet are in a wretched condition. One swelled up tremendously last night and he is very lame this morning. We started march on tea and pemmican as last night—we pretend to prefer the pemmican this way. Marched for 5 hours this morning over a slightly better surface covered with high moundy sastrugi. Sledge capsized twice; we pulled on foot, covering about 5½ miles. We are two pony marches and 4 miles about from our depot. Our fuel dreadfully low and the poor Soldier nearly done. It is pathetic enough because we can do nothing for him; more hot food might do a little, but only a little, I fear. We none of us expected these terribly low temperatures, and of the rest of us Wilson is feeling them most; mainly, I fear, from his self-sacrificing devotion to doctoring Oates' feet. We cannot help each other, each has enough to do to take care of himself. We get cold on the march when the trudging is heavy, and the wind pierces our warm garments. The others, all of them, are unendingly cheerful when in the tent. We mean to see the game through with a proper spirit, but it's tough work to be pulling harder than we ever pulled in our lives for long hours, and to feel that the progress is so slow. One can only say "God help us!" and plod on our weary way, cold and very miserable, though outwardly cheerful. We talk of all sorts of subjects in the tent, not much of food now, since we decided to take the risk of running a full ration. We simply couldn't go hungry at this time. . . .

TUESDAY, MARCH 6.— . . . Poor Oates is unable to pull, sits on the sledge when we are track-searching—he is wonderfully plucky, as his feet must be giving him great pain. He makes no complaint, but his spirits only come up in spurts now, and he grows more silent in the tent. We are making a spirit lamp to try and replace the primus when our oil is exhausted. . . .

THURSDAY, MARCH 8.—Lunch. Worse and worse in morning; poor Oates' left foot can never last out, and time over foot gear something awful. Have to wait in night foot gear for nearly an hour before I start changing, and then am generally first to be ready. Wilson's feet giving trouble now, but this mainly because he gives so much help to others. We did 4½ miles this morning and are now 8½ miles from the depot—a ridiculously small distance to feel in difficulties, yet on this surface we know we cannot equal half our old marches, and that for that effort we expend nearly double the energy. The great question is, What shall we find at the depot? If the dogs have visited it we may get along a good distance, but if there is another short allowance of fuel, God help us indeed. We are in a very bad way, I fear, in any case.

SATURDAY, MARCH 10.—Things steadily downhill. Oates' foot worse. He has rare pluck and must know that he can never get through. He asked Wilson if he had a chance this morning, and of course Bill had to say he didn't know. In point of fact he has none. Apart from him, if he went under now, I doubt whether we could get through. With great care we might have a dog's chance, but no more. The weather conditions are awful, and our gear gets steadily more icy and difficult to manage. At the same time of course poor Titus is the greatest handicap. He keeps us waiting in the morning until we have partly lost the warming effect of our good breakfast, when the only wise policy is to be up and away at once; again at lunch. Poor chap! it is too pathetic to watch him: one cannot but try to cheer him up.

Yesterday we marched up the depot, Mt. Hooper. Cold comfort. Shortage on our allowance all round. I don't know that anyone is to blame. The dogs which would have been our salvation have evidently failed. Meares had a bad trip home I suppose.

This morning it was calm when we breakfasted, but the wind came from the W.N.W. as we broke camp. It rapidly grew in strength. After travelling for half an hour I saw that none of us could go on facing such conditions. We were forced to camp and are spending the rest of the day in a comfortless blizzard camp, wind quite foul. [R.52]

SUNDAY, MARCH 11.—Titus Oates is very near the end, one feels. What we or he will do, God only knows. We discussed the matter after breakfast; he is a brave fine fellow and understands the situation, but he practically asked for advice. Nothing could be said but to urge him to march as long as he could. One satisfactory result to the discussion; I practically ordered Wilson to hand over the means of ending our troubles to us, so that any one of us may know how to do so. Wilson had no choice between doing so and our ransacking the medicine case. We have 30 opium tabloids apiece and he is left with a tube of morphine. So far the tragical side of our story. [R.53.] . . .

FRIDAY, MARCH 16 or SATURDAY 17.—Lost track of dates, but think the last correct. Tragedy all along the line. At lunch, the day before yesterday, poor Titus Oates said he couldn't go on; he proposed we should leave him in his sleeping-bag. That we could not do, and we induced him to come on, on the afternoon march. In spite of its awful nature for him he struggled on and we made a few miles. At night he was worse and we knew the end had come.

Should this be found I want these facts recorded. Oates' last thoughts were of his Mother, but immediately before he took pride in thinking that his regiment would be pleased with the bold way in which he met his death. We can testify to his bravery. He has borne intense suffering for weeks without complaint, and to the very last was able and willing to discuss outside subjects. He did not—would not—give up hope till the very end. He was a brave soul. This was the end. He slept through the night before last, hoping not to wake; but he woke in the morning—yesterday. It was blowing a blizzard. He said, "I am just going outside and may be some time." He went out into the blizzard and we have not seen him since.

I take this opportunity of saying that we have stuck to our sick companions to the last. In case of Edgar Evans, when absolutely out of food and he lay insensible, the safety of the remainder seemed to demand his abandonment, but Providence mercifully removed him at this critical moment. He died a natural death, and we did not leave him till two hours after his death. We knew that poor Oates was walking to his death but though we tried to dissuade him, we knew it was the act of a brave man and an English gentleman. We all hope to meet the end with a similar spirit, and assuredly the end is not far.

I can only write at lunch and then only occasionally. The cold is intense, −40° at midday. My companions are unendingly cheerful, but we are all on the verge of serious frostbites, and though we constantly talk of fetching through I don't think any one of us believes it in his heart.

We are cold on the march now, and at all times except meals. Yesterday we had to lay up for a blizzard and to-day we move dreadfully slowly. We are at No. 14 pony camp, only two pony marches from One Ton Depot. We leave here our theodolite, a camera, and Oates' sleeping-bags. Diaries, &c., and geological specimens carried at Wilson's special request, will be found with us or on our sledge.

SUNDAY, MARCH 18.—To-day, lunch, we are 21 miles from the depot. Ill fortune presses, but better may come. We have had more wind and drift from ahead yesterday; had to stop marching; wind N.W., force 4, temp. −35°. No human being could face it, and we are worn out *nearly*.

My right foot has gone, nearly all the toes—two days ago I was proud possessor of best feet. These are the steps of my downfall. Like an ass I mixed a small spoonful of curry powder with my melted pemmican—it gave me violent indigestion. I lay awake and in pain all night; woke and felt done on the march; foot went and I didn't know it. A very small measure of neglect and have a foot which is not pleasant to contemplate. Bowers takes first place in condition, but there is not much to choose after all. The others are still confident of getting through—or pretend to be—I don't know! We have the last *half* fill of oil in our primus and a very small quantity of spirit—this alone between us and thirst. The wind is fair for the moment, and that is perhaps a fact to help. The mileage would have seemed ridiculously small on our outward journey.

MONDAY, MARCH 19.—Lunch. We camped with difficulty last night, and were dreadfully cold till after our supper of cold pemmican and biscuit and a half a pannikin of cocoa cooked over the spirit. Then, contrary to expectation, we got warm and all slept well. To-day we started in the usual dragging manner. Sledge dreadfully heavy. We are 15½ miles from the depot and ought to get there in three days. What progress! We have two days' food but barely a day's fuel. All our feet are getting bad—Wilson's best, my right foot worst, left all right. There is no chance to nurse one's feet till we can get hot food into us. Amputation is the least I can hope for now, but will the trouble spread? That is the serious question. The weather doesn't give us a chance—the wind from N. to N.W. and −40° temp. to-day.

WEDNESDAY, MARCH 21.—Got within 11 miles of depot Monday night; had to lay up all yesterday in severe blizzard. To-day forlorn hope, Wilson and Bowers going to depot for fuel.

THURSDAY, MARCH 22 and 23.—Blizzard bad as ever—Wilson and Bowers unable to start—to-morrow last chance—no fuel and only one or two of food left—must be near the end. Have decided it shall be natural— we shall march for the depot with or without our effects and die in our tracks.

THURSDAY, MARCH 29.—Since the 21st we have had a continuous gale from W.S.W. and S.W. We had fuel to make two cups of tea apiece and bare food for two days on the 20th. Every day we have been ready to start for our depot 11 *miles* away, but outside the door of the tent it remains a scene of whirling drift. I do not think we can hope for any better things now. We shall stick it out to the end, but we are getting weaker, of course, and the end cannot be far.

It seems a pity, but I do not think I can write more.

R. SCOTT

Last entry.

For God's sake look after our people.

[Eight months later the bodies of Captain Scott, Dr. Wilson and Lieutenant Bowers were found in their tent by a search party. The three lay in their sleeping bags, with the evidence indicating that Scott had briefly survived his two companions.]

Life in an Igloo

ROGER P. BULIARD

FROM *Inuk*

1934-49

While a student in his native Burgundy, Roger Buliard was inspired by a report of church missionaries and martyrs who had carried the message of the Catholic Church to the Far North. In time he joined the Oblate Fathers, those "specialists in difficult missions," and after his period of training and a year with the Chasseurs Alpins, he sailed for northern Canada in 1934. For three years he served among the Eskimos at Coppermine, and then he was chosen to found a mission at Minto, five hundred miles north of Coppermine, among the northernmost Eskimos of all. He started the mission in a tent-sized cabin and continued it without interruption for twelve years, living much like the Eskimos (there were only 150 altogether) around him.

Father Buliard came to know the Eskimos thoroughly, and his book Inuk *is a fascinating document, describing in sympathetic but unromantic terms their outlook, temperament, pleasures, pursuits—especially hunting —and daily life in the vast Barren Grounds. In the passage below he paints an intimate picture of igloo life in wintertime.*

T HE Eskimo camp, in winter, is a busy place, a regular miniature city. . . .

Around the white cupolas of the igloos you see a powdering of black dots—the sledges perched out of reach on snowbanks so the dogs can't reach them and chew up the thongs. Rifles and harpoons are planted at the entrances to the igloos, ready for use. Sealskins, drying and bleaching, wave in the icy breeze like stiffened flags. The dogs are rolled up in the snow, heads and feet carefully tucked in, serving each as his own blanket. Nothing moves. It looks for a moment as though the dry cold had surprised the camp, freezing everything—men, objects, beasts—in permanent, still attitudes, like the attitudes of the people of Pompeii after the eruption of Vesuvius. It is as still as death.

But no! The traveler comes closer and sees over each igloo a scarf of faint, whitish vapor that floats lazily, as though benumbed by the frigid air. It is a kind of light reek flowing from the igloos' ventilating holes, like the aftermath of smoke that emerges from a chimney after the fire has gone out. It is all that moves. But it means there is life in those snow mounds, warmth.

Then, all at once, pandemonium breaks loose. Fifty dogs pull at their shackles, growling, howling, barking at the intruder. From the dead-still igloos men and women, roused by the clamor of the agitated dogs, begin to emerge, crouched low. From every mouth comes a joyous exclamation: "*Aodlan!* Travelers!"

"*Kinakia?*" someone says. "Who can it be?"

Then someone else's eyes will recognize the dogs. "*Falla-oyok!*" the shout goes up. "It is the Father!"

They are as happy as children. And whoever you are, they will make you welcome, make you feel as if no other arrival could have pleased them more than yours. Each will come separately toward you and touch your hand. The men come first, forthrightly, then the women, shyly, tentatively, offering only the tips of their fingers. Hiding behind their mothers, the little children steal glances at the Big Eyebrow. Decidedly, you are an event. Your coming brings something new to the camp. You are a diversion.

While you drink your cup of scalding tea, everyone will be asking himself, "Which igloo will he choose to stay in? Who will be honored?" For they all want you, everyone, and whichever snowhouse you choose will become the headquarters and gathering place that night. Until very late a crowd will be massed in your host's igloo, listening to you. You are a guest, a traveler, an event. They sit in a circle around you, their tense faces reacting to your words, eager and solemn under the wan glimmer of the stone lamps. . . .

Igloo!

The word itself has an icy sound and makes the newcomer shiver with cold. Nevertheless, when the trailsman is hungry, exhausted and frozen, the snowhouse makes a comfortable shelter. Inhabited or not, it is a boon to the Arctic traveler. If someone is there, it means a hearty welcome and hot tea, a chance to warm oneself. If it has been abandoned, it means at least ready shelter and that much labor saved. The igloo is the Eskimo's architectural masterpiece, his greatest achievement, the supreme example of his triumph in the fight to adapt his way of life to the demands of this grim country.

To watch an Eskimo build an igloo is a lesson in man's ability to master his environment. With his sharp, saberlike knife or fine snow tester made of caribou antler, the Inuk first determines the thickness of the snow and makes sure it is of the right consistency—not hard, not too soft. Then, at a glance, he visualizes the circuit of his project—a perfect circle, always. In the first half-moon he begins to quarry his snow blocks—rectangles about thirty inches long, twenty inches high, eight inches wide—which he cuts instinctively, adding an almost imperceptible curve to the outer side of each block. His sureness of cut is extraordinary. He works like a skilled sculptor, seeming to give his work only casual attention. He cleaves here, lops off a bit there, and it all looks simple. But every stroke counts, as the snow flies and the Eskimo's fur hood disappears in a cloud of white powder. He does this as simply, as instinctively, as you or I would write a simple word in longhand or tie a bowknot in our shoelace. It is something he has done all his life.

The first tier of snow blocks form a circle around the hole that has been quarried, the blocks leaning toward the inside of the circle, and interlocked, so that the frost may complete the job and cement them. Before he begins the second tier, the Inuk makes a diagonal cut on the top of the first, slanting inward. Now the wall rises quickly, leaning inward, forming a dome. A keystone block is placed at the top of the dome, and crevices are chinked with soft snow.

"*Taimak!*" the Eskimo grunts, looking at his handiwork. "Finished!"

You can climb on the top, walk around, as if it were made of granite and mortar. It is absolutely rigid.

Into the bottom tier a round hole, like the door of an oven, is cut out, just large enough to admit people crawling on all fours. Sometimes a window is added to admit light—a section of clear, fresh-water ice or of parchment made from the intestines of the squareflipper, the bearded seal.

Inside the igloo, toward the rear, a bed platform is built of snow, and a layer of bearskin, fur side down, is spread upon it. Over this a second layer is placed, fur side up. Then the bedding is arranged according to taste, except that the foot of the bed is always against the wall, the head turning in toward the center of the igloo. Facing the bed a snow platform is built to hold the stone lamp, which is soon lighted, offering a cheery glow to the snow interior. Near the lamp a crude arrangement of sticks is jabbed into the wall, and on this you hang whatever you want to dry or thaw out—mitts, boots, frozen fish, and so on. The remainder of the Eskimo's belongings are tossed on the floor. Now he is at home.

The temperature of an igloo is kept near the freezing point, for if it rises above that point the walls begin to thaw and drip unpleasantly, and once thawed they would freeze again, into ice, making the house uncomfortable or even uninhabitable. If the temperature inside becomes too high, or the air stale, the Eskimo householder simply thrusts his snow knife through the roof and the air escapes with a hiss like that of a steam boiler venting itself through the safety valve. Sometimes a small hole is made in the roof to provide ventilation. It is called *krignak*—the nostril.

In more or less permanent camps, the igloo may be ten feet high and large enough to house ten people. These large igloos are always provided with a long covered porch, and often the various snowhouses in a camp are interlinked by a system of snow tunnels. Sometimes one of these snow corridors ends in an empty, uninhabited igloo, a kind of foyer or vestibule, with doors leading from it into three or four occupied igloos. These snow passages connecting the various houses are made in early winter; soon real winter sets in, and the whole settlement is half buried in the snow, so that the Eskimo camp is an icy catacomb.

What of the life in these strange dwellings? Of course, I am used to it now, and I can build a snowhouse with the best of them. But I still remember my first impressions.

Not long after I arrived in the country, Ayallik asked me to visit his camp, out on the ice. It was a lovely December afternoon, cold, with gray mist hanging low above the islands. We had almost reached the village before I saw it—a cluster of igloos nearly buried in the snow. The dogs announced our arrival, and the Inuit emerged. After the usual greetings, Ayallik made it clear that I was to be his guest, and I followed him to his igloo, plunging after him into a dark hole that opened in the clear white snowbank. As I slipped along the passage leading to the house I stumbled over a dog, and he snapped at my calf. Ayallik dived through a second hole and I followed him, on all fours, making my first entrance into an igloo.

A sour smell of rancid grease, wet fur and burrow musk almost knocked me over, but the general aspect was bright, pleasant, homey. A soft reddish light was given off by two stone lamps, one placed on either side of the door, and this soft illumination was reflected from the walls, giving the whole interior a strange but pleasant vaultlike appearance.

I shook hands with an ancient grandmother whose wrinkled, tattooed face wore a smile of welcome. Two girls claimed my outer garments, shaking them free of snow and folding them carefully. A pair of small children drew back into the shadows of the igloo, trying to hide from the Great Eyebrow. I was given a seat on the skin bed, and Ayallik's wife trimmed the lamp wicks and blew up the lazy flame, preparing tea.

I felt that it was my turn to say something. "*Igloo tamna nakoyok*, eh? This is a good snowhouse, eh?"

But Ayallik laughed scornfully, belittling his handiwork in true Eskimo style. Of course, he implied, I should have known that he could really do much better than this. "It is old and dirty," he said. "And built too quickly, with bad snow."

There was an awkward silence, during which they all looked at me quite boldly and exchanged opinions. My Eskimo was not fluent then, nor did I understand too much. "Not smart, these Eyebrows," they were saying, "Ignoramuses, really." But the boiling water on the stone lamp distracted their attention and they left off their analysis of the stupid *krabloonak* to busy themselves with a more important matter—tea.

"But first let us eat some frozen fish," Ayallik's wife, Ongirlak, said. "The Falla must be hungry."

There was a basin full of frozen fish on the floor and a woman took a piece with her greasy fingers, innocently offering it to the Long Robe. There was a hint of a smile at the corners of her mouth, and I understood that it was a kind of test.

The joke was on them. I knew all about frozen fish, and how to eat it. In fact, I already rather liked it, and began to eat like an expert. They watched me for a few minutes, then everyone began to eat. I had passed the test with flying colors.

"You eat like a real Inuk," someone said. "Frozen too, eh."

When the meal was over, Ongirlak, as mistress of the igloo, handed me a piece of ptarmigan skin that had once been white. I was the last to use this community serviette. Before it was handed to me they had all wiped their noses, fingers and lips on it. Well, I thought, "when in Rome . . ."

That night all the camp crowded into Ayallik's igloo, eager to give me the once-over. Many of them had never seen a Catholic priest—a Long Robe—and a number had hardly talked with any white man. My fledgling

Eskimo got a good workout as they plied me with questions about every subject that came within their ken. After that there was singing and the almost ritualistic telling of stories. It was late. At last Ayallik stood up and said, rather brusquely, "Surely the *Krabloonak* would like to sleep."

As if dispersed by a gunshot, the visitors fell to their knees and dived out into the night. When they were gone there was a brief consultation, after which Ayallik decided that I would sleep between the eldest boy and the grandmother.

I slipped into my fur bag. The kids squeezed themselves under the skins, and the wrinkled granny, grumbling and complaining like any old lady, squatted on her heels and stripped off all her clothes. She got into bed, muttering to herself and grunting, tossing about for a while before she fell asleep. Ayallik, meanwhile, had stripped to the nude. With a cheerful "*Alapa!* Cold!" he vanished under his covers. Ongirlak was the last to bed. She plugged the door hole with a snow block and fixed her lamps for the night, beating out all of the flame except for a tiny glow in the corner, a night light. Then she distributed small empty tins, improvised chamber pots, placing one at each of our heads. During the night I was awakened several times as someone noisily relieved himself.

At last Ongirlak was finished with her long day's work. She peeled off her fur clothes, displaying her huge breasts for an instant, then disappeared under the skins. Like most Eskimos, she was asleep the moment she was in bed. They seldom are troubled with insomnia. For one thing, they are too tired, and for another their lives are too simple to build up worry.

As for me, the alien *Krabloonak*, I lay there for a long time, wide awake, gazing around me in the half-light rendered by the two trimmed lamps, listening to the *floc-floc* of water dripping from the walls, though this stopped as the temperature in the igloo dropped and the walls froze. The sleepers' breaths whistled and rose into the cold air, particles of moisture freezing and clinging to their faces, so that soon all were covered with a light frost. The old lady grunted in sleep, still complaining, I guess, and after an hour or so one of the children woke up and groped in the dusk for his tin privy. The tiny flames in the sentinel lamps flickered and threatened to go out, but always rallied just before they seemed ready to die, shooting up sudden, brighter light, illuminating the walls of the now frigid igloo. It was like being in an ice prison, or a burial vault built of snow.

I must finally have fallen asleep, for at dawn I felt them shake me, and came awake. A shy, pale light filtered through the ice window and displayed Ongirlak putting on her parka. Soon she was up, leaning over the lamps, straightening the wicks and blowing up the flames, so that in a few moments the whole igloo was brightly lighted. Last night the walls had been gray-blue; this morning they were totally white, covered with fine frost. I turned in my fur bed and a shower of ice particles, a kind of frigid rain, completed my awakening.

Ayallik and the children remained abed. No one moved but the old lady, who crawled out of her skins, growling like an ancient, disturbed bear, blowing up the second lamp, warming her old hands, then assisting her daughter in the preparation of tea. Soon the hum of boiling water and the tantalizing smell of brewing tea had everyone stirring. While I dressed, Ayallik looked at me in surprise, and remained crouched under the skin until the women served him his mug of tea and slab of frozen fish. He remained in bed for half an hour after this strange breakfast, giving me a rambling account of last night's dreams. At last his wife said, "The weather is nice. Not too cold. Clear, without a breath of wind, either."

This brought Ayallak to life.

"*Kamiksamnik!* My boots!" he commanded. His brow was furrowed by weighty thoughts. What should he do today? Look to his traps? Go fishing? Hunt seals? Finally he decided.

"I shall go to the river and come back tonight. With fish, eh?"

Dressed at last, Ayallik took a little pot of water with him and went outside to ice his sled. I followed, watching him take a mouthful of water, spit it onto a piece of bearskin, and use this to fix a high glaze on the sled's wooden runners. Meanwhile his wife harnessed the dogs, the children tagging at her heels. Finally Ayallik was ready, and the fierce dogs pulled at the traces, themselves eager to be off for a run in the brisk, clear air. Ayallik seated himself on the sled, pulled up the anchor and growled an order. The dogs bolted and streaked off like a flash, the sled bounding wildly from snowbank to snowbank. They had raced perhaps five hundred yards when Ayallik's leader swerved, and sled, man and dogs piled up. The sound of Ayallik's choicest cursing violated the morning air.

Ongirlak, watching from the door of the igloo, laughed quietly to herself, but realized that it wasn't the time to be around and ducked back into the snowhouse. She had work of her own, first folding the bedding, then strewing the floor with fresh clean snow, then taking up the interminable sewing of skins with which the Eskimo woman passes so much of her time. Sitting in the classical tailor's position, elbows resting on her knees, she leaned forward toward the stone lamp so as not to lose any of the light. Methodically, she examined each of the family's garments—parkas, pants, boots, mittens—stretching the tough skin with her teeth, making a patch here or there or closing up a rent seam. This occupied all of her morning. She paused only to feed the children, trim the lamp wicks and make tea for me.

The old granny dreamed aloud, humming to herself some forgotten tune, some ballad she had learned as a girl, too old for the others to remember. She was beyond any useful work. She showed me her fingers, all crooked, like claws, stiff and useless, and told me with a wordless gesture that she was past any kind of service. In the old days they would have taken her out to some deserted igloo and left her there to die. Perhaps, if the chance appeared, someone would help her on her way to her reward. In the meantime, she sat, half dozing, her teeth worn to the gums, her eyes milky and without luster, from too many years passed straining them in the semidarkness of a thousand igloos.

While Ongirlak sewed and the grandmother dreamed, the children came and went at will, teasing the dogs, trying out their little bows and their miniature sleds. The girls ministered tenderly to their hideous, tiny dolls.

All that day I lived in a world of women and children, for all the men of the camp were out—off to the hunting field, or the river, for fish, or on the trail of Nanuk, perhaps, the great waddling polar bear. From time to time a neighbor woman dropped in on Ongirlak to pass the time of day, render a few compliments and drink tea. But the women all seemed bored and listless. They were waiting for the men, waiting to see what the day's hunting had produced. Not until nightfall, when the hunters returned, would the Eskimo camp come really to life. . . .

Bibliography of Sources

THE ORIENT

Marco Polo. *The Book of Ser Marco Polo*, translated by Sir Henry Yule. London, 1870.

Friar Odoric. In *The Principal Navigations, Voyages, Traffiques and Discoveries of the English Nation*, Vol. IV, by Richard Hakluyt. Glasgow, 1903–1905.

Ibn Battuta. *Travels in Asia and Africa, 1325–1354*, translated by H. A. R. Gibb. London, 1929.

Ludovico di Varthema. *The Travels of Ludovico di Varthema*, translated from the Italian by J. W. Jones and edited by G. P. Badger. London, The Hakluyt Society, 1863.

Anthony Jenkinson. In *The Principal Navigations, Voyages, Traffiques and Discoveries of the English Nation*, Vol. II, by Richard Hakluyt. Glasgow, 1903–1905.

Pietro della Valle. *The Travels of Pietro della Valle*, edited by Edward Grey from a translation made in 1664 by G. Havers. London, The Hakluyt Society, 1892.

Évariste Régis Huc. *Travels in Tartary, Thibet, and China*, translated by William Hazlitt. London, 1852.

Robert Fortune. *A Journey to the Tea Countries of China*. London, 1852.

Anna H. Leonowens. *The Romance of the Harem*. Boston, 1873.

George Kennan. *Tent Life in Siberia*. New York, 1874.

J. A. MacGahan. *Campaigning on the Oxus, and the Fall of Khiva*. New York, 1874.

Isabella Bird Bishop. *The Golden Chersonese and the Way Thither*. New York, 1883.

———— *The Yangtze Valley and Beyond*. London, 1900.

N. A. E. Nordenskiöld. *The Voyage of the Vega round Asia and Europe*, translated from the Swedish. New York, 1882.

Sven Hedin. *Through Asia*. New York, 1899.

———— *Trans-Himalaya: Discoveries and Adventures in Tibet*. New York, 1909–1913.

Heinrich Harrer. *Seven Years in Tibet*, translated by Richard Graves. New York, 1954.

THE LEVANT

Benjamin of Tudela. "The Travels of Rabbi Benjamin of Tudela" in *Early Travels in Palestine*, edited by Thomas Wright. London, 1848.

Geofrey Ducket. In *The Principal Navigations, Voyages, Traffiques and Discoveries of the English Nation*, Vol. III, by Richard Hakluyt. Glasgow, 1903–1905.

Thomas Dallam. "The Diary of Thomas Dallam" in *Early Voyages and Travels in the Levant*, edited by J. T.

Bent. London, The Hakluyt Society, 1893.

Lady Mary Wortley Montagu. *The Letters and Works*, edited by Lord Wharncliffe. London, 1861. Revised by W. Moy Thomas, 1898.

John Lloyd Stephens. *Incidents of Travel in Egypt, Arabia Petraea and the Holy Land*. New York, 1837.

Austen Henry Layard. *Early Adven-* tures in Persia, Susiana, and Babylonia. London, 1894.

Richard Burton. *Personal Narrative of a Pilgrimage to Al-Madinah and Meccah*. London, 1855.

Charles Montagu Doughty. *Travels in Arabia Deserta*. London, 1888.

Freya Stark. *The Valleys of the Assassins*. London, 1934.

Lawrence Durrell. *Bitter Lemons*. London, 1957.

AFRICA

Herodotus of Halicarnassus. *History*, translated by George Rawlinson. London, 1860.

William Bosman. *A New and Accurate Description of the Coast of Guinea*, translated from the Dutch. London, 1705.

Mungo Park. *Travels in the Interior Districts of Africa in 1795, 1796, 1797, with an account of a subsequent mission in 1805*. London, 1816.

Richard Lander. *Records of Captain Clapperton's Last Expedition to Africa, with subsequent adventures of the author*. London, 1830.

Paul Du Chaillu. *Explorations and Adventures in Equatorial Africa*. New York, 1861.

John Hanning Speke. *Journal of the Discovery of the Source of the Nile*. New York, 1864.

Samuel White Baker. *The Nile Tribu-* taries of Abyssinia, and the Sword Hunters of the Hamran Arabs. London, 1867.

————— *The Albert N'yanza Great Basin of the Nile*. London, 1866.

David Livingstone. *The Last Journals*, edited posthumously by Horace Waller. London, 1874.

Henry Morton Stanley. *How I Found Livingstone: Travels, Adventures and Discoveries in Central Africa*. New York, 1874.

————— *In Darkest Africa*. New York, 1891.

Anthony Trollope. *South Africa*. London, 1878.

Mary H. Kingsley. *Travels in West Africa*. London, 1897.

R. V. C. Bodley. *Wind in the Sahara*. New York, 1944.

Elizabeth Marshall Thomas. *The Harmless People*. New York, 1959.

THE SOUTH SEAS

Ferdinand Magellan. *Voyage round the world*, by Antonio Pigafetta. From a translation in *A General Collection of Voyages and Travels*, Vol. II, by John Pinkerton. London, 1812.

George Robertson. *The Discovery of Tahiti: A Journal of the Second Voyage* of the H.M.S. Dolphin round the World, edited by Hugh Carrington. London, The Hakluyt Society, 1948.

James Cook. *The Journals of Captain James Cook*, Vol. I, edited by J. C. Beaglehole. Cambridge, The Hakluyt Society, 1955.

—— *The Voyages of Captain James Cook,* selected and edited by Christopher Lloyd. London, 1949.

William Bligh. "Narrative of the Mutiny on the *Bounty,*" in *Standard Library Collection of Voyages and Travels.* London, 1840.

William Lockerby. *The Journal of William Lockerby,* edited by E. G. Thurn and L. C. Wharton. London, The Hakluyt Society, 1925.

Herman Melville. *Typee.* London, 1846.

Charles Sturt. *Narrative of an Expedition into Central Australia during 1844, 5 and 6.* London, 1849.

Robert Louis Stevenson. *In the South Seas, 1888–1890.* New York, 1892.

Thor Heyerdahl. *Aku-Aku.* New York, Chicago, San Francisco, 1958.

A CIRCUIT OF EUROPE

Thomas Coryat. *Coryat's Crudities.* University of Glasgow, 1905.

Hester Lynch Thrale Piozzi. *Observations and Reflections Made in the Course of a Journey through France, Italy, and Germany.* Dublin, 1789.

Arthur Young. *Travels in France and Italy,* edited by M. Betham-Edwards. London, 1892.

William Beckford. *Italy, Spain and Portugal, with an Excursion to the Monasteries of Alcobaça and Batalha.* New York, 1845.

—— *The Journal of William Beckford in Portugal and Spain,* edited by Boyd Alexander. London, 1954.

Abu Taleb. *The Travels of Mirza Abu Taleb Khan in Asia, Africa and Europe,* translated from the Persian by Charles Stewart. London, 1810.

Louis Simond. *Journal of a Tour and Residence in Great Britain during 1810 and 1811.* New York, 1815.

Hermann Pückler-Muskau. *Tour of England, Ireland and France.* Philadelphia, 1833.

Alexandre Dumas. *Travels in Switzerland,* translated by R. W. Plummer and A. Craig Bell and edited by A. Craig Bell. London, 1958.

Théophile Gautier. *Travels in Spain* and *Travels in Russia* in *The Works of*

Théophile Gautier, translated and edited by F. C. De Sumachrist. Boston and New York, 1901.

Charles Dickens. *Pictures from Italy.* London, 1846.

George Borrow. *Wild Wales.* London, 1862.

Hippolyte Taine. *Notes on England,* translated from the French. New York, 1872.

William Dean Howells. *Venetian Life.* Boston, 1866.

Henry James. *Portraits of Places.* Boston, 1884.

Paul Du Chaillu. *The Land of the Midnight Sun.* New York, 1882.

Mark Twain. *A Tramp Abroad.* Hartford, Conn., 1879.

George Augustus Sala. *Paris Herself Again.* London, 1880.

D. H. Lawrence. *Twilight in Italy.* New York, 1916.

Edmund Wilson. *Red, Black, Blond and Olive. Studies in Four Civilizations: Zuñi, Haiti, Soviet Russia, Israel.* New York, 1956.

Rebecca West. *Black Lamb and Grey Falcon.* New York, 1941.

Herbert Kubly. *Easter in Sicily.* New York, 1956.

Santha Rama Rau. *My Russian Journey.* New York, 1959.

AMERICA SOUTH

Christopher Columbus. *The Journal of His First Voyage*, translated from the abstract by Bartolomé de Las Casas and edited by Clements Markham. London, The Hakluyt Society, 1893.

Bernal Díaz del Castillo. *The True History of the Conquest of New Spain*, translated and edited by A. P. Maudslay. London, The Hakluyt Society, 1908–1916.

Francisco Pizarro. "Narrative of the Conquest of Peru by Francisco de Xeres," in *Reports on the Discovery of Peru*, edited by Clements Markham. London, The Hakluyt Society, 1872.

Francisco de Orellana. "Account by Friar Gaspar de Carvajal of the Voyage down the River that Francisco de Orellana Discovered," translated by B. T. Lea and edited by H. C. Eaton, in *The Discovery of the Amazon*, by J. T. Medina. New York, 1934.

Miles Philips. In *The Principal Navigations, Voyages, Traffiques and Discoveries of the English Nation*, Vol. IX, by Richard Hakluyt. Glasgow, 1903–1905.

Johann Jakob von Tschudi. *Travels in Peru*, translated from the German. New York, 1847.

John Lloyd Stephens. *Incidents of Travel in Central America, Chiapas, and Yucatan*. New York, 1841.

Frances Calderón de la Barca. *Life in Mexico during a Residence of Two Years*. New York, 1843.

William Lewis Herndon. *Exploration of the Valley of the Amazon*. Washington, D. C., 1854.

Alain Gheerbrant. *Journey to the Far Amazon*, translated from the French by Edward Fitzgerald. New York, 1954.

AMERICA NORTH

Philip Amadas and Arthur Barlow. In *Principal Navigations, Voyages, Traffiques and Discoveries of the English Nation*, Vol. VIII, by Richard Hakluyt. Glasgow, 1903–1905.

Samuel de Champlain. *Voyages of Samuel de Champlain, 1604–1618*. New York, 1907.

Peter Kalm. *Travels in North America*. The English version of 1770 revised from the original Swedish by Adolph B. Benson, with new material from Kalm's diary notes. New York, 1937.

François André Michaux. *Travels to the West of the Alleghany Mountains in Ohio, Kentucky, and Tennessea [sic], and back to Charleston by the Upper Carolinas*. London, 1805.

Meriwether Lewis and William Clark. *The Journals of Lewis and Clark*. A history of the expedition during the years 1804, 1805 and 1806. New York, 1904.

Josiah Gregg. *Commerce of the Prairies, or the Journal of a Santa Fé Trader*. New York, 1844.

George Catlin. *Letters and Notes on the Manners, Customs and Condition of the North American Indians*. London, 1841.

Charles Dickens. *American Notes*. London, 1842.

Francis Parkman. *The Oregon Trail*. Boston, 1872.

J. Goldsborough Bruff. *Gold Rush: The Journals, Drawings, and Other Papers of J. Goldsborough Bruff*, edited by Georgia Willis Read and Ruth Gaines. New York, 1944.

Anthony Trollope. *North America*. New York, 1862.

Mark Twain. *Roughing It.* Hartford, Conn., 1871.

Henry James. *Portraits of Places.* Boston, 1884.

Paul Bourget. *Outre-Mer: Impressions of America.* New York, 1895.

Isabella Bird Bishop. *A Lady's Life in the Rocky Mountains.* New York, 1879–80.

Alistair Cooke. *One Man's America.* New York, 1952.

POLAR PLACES

William Edward Parry. *Three Voyages for the Discovery of a Northwest Passage* and *Narrative of an Attempt to Reach the North Pole.* New York, 1840.

N. A. E. Nordenskiöld. *The Voyage of the* Vega *round Asia and Europe,* translated from the Swedish. New York, 1882.

Peter Freuchen. *Arctic Adventure: My Life in the Frozen North.* New York, 1935.

Vilhjalmur Stefansson. *My Life with the Eskimo.* New York, 1913.

Robert Falcon Scott. *Scott's Last Expedition: The Personal Journals of Captain R. F. Scott.* London, 1913.

Roger P. Buliard. *Inuk.* New York, 1951.

Index of Travelers

About the Editor

While acquiring various degrees, including a doctorate, at Columbia University in the 1930s, Milton Rugoff taught at several metropolitan colleges. He then turned to the field of publishing and was an editor successively with Alfred A. Knopf, a literary magazine, and a book club. Since 1948 he has been editor of the distinguished books produced by Chanticleer Press. He has edited another anthology, *A Harvest of World Folk Tales*, and has been a book reviewer for many years.

Mr. Rugoff spent two years in Europe during World War II and has since made a number of trips abroad, but his particular boast is that, beginning with a reading of Marco Polo at a very tender age, he has been one of the most tireless, bold and adventuresome of armchair travelers. This book is a selection of the most memorable things he has come across in his literary travels.